WHOSE TRADE ORGANIZATION?

WHOSE TRADE ORGANIZATION?

A Comprehensive Guide to the WTO

———————◆———————

LORI WALLACH AND PATRICK WOODALL, PUBLIC CITIZEN

THE NEW PRESS

NEW YORK
LONDON

Cartoon on page xii by Bülbül www.bulbul.com. Reprinted with permission.

Cartoon on page 283 by Mark Alan Stamaty
© 1991, The Washington Post Writers Group. Reprinted with permission.

Published in the United States by The New Press, New York, 2004
A different book with a similar title was published by Public Citizen, Washington, D.C., 1999.
Distributed by W. W. Norton & Company, Inc., New York

ISBN 1-56584-841-1 (pbk.)
CIP data available

The New Press was established in 1990 as a not-for-profit alternative to the large, commercial
publishing houses currently dominating the book publishing industry. The New Press operates in
the public interest rather than for private gain, and is committed to publishing, in innovative
ways, works of educational, cultural, and community value that are often deemed insufficiently
profitable.

The New Press
38 Greene Street, 4th floor
New York, NY 10013
www.thenewpress.com

In the United Kingdom:
6 Salem Road
London W2 4BU

Composition by Westchester Book Composition

Printed in Canada

2 4 6 8 10 9 7 5 3

To Senator Paul Wellstone (1944–2002), who reminded us that "Politics is what we create by what we do, what we hope for and what we hope to imagine."

CONTENTS

ACKNOWLEDGMENTS

Thanks go to:

Mary Bottari, Timi Gerson, Runako Kumbula, Darshana Patel, and Ron Zucker for help with research and writing. Michelle Sforza contributed much of the early research and writing from our previous edition.

Margrete Strand Ranges for managing much of the circus and GTW staff Kristina Berry, Sara Johnson, Chris Slevin, and Steffan Spencer as well as Jill-Morgan Aubert and Amanda Ballantyne, the footnote dominatrixes. GTW interns Ethan Arpi, Daniel Cloud, Ramy El Dorry, Katherine Lira, Arathi Ravichandran, Emily Sachs, Katherine Sales, and Mackenzie Steinkamp.

Colleagues who provided invaluable guidance and comments and/or contributed text, including Agnes Bertrand, Roberto Bissio, Tony Clarke, Patricia Lovera, Martin Khor, Alan Morrison, Sophia Murphy, Scott Nova, Steve Porter, Pablo Solon, Vandana Shiva, Tyson Slocum, Ashwini Sukthankar, Mark Weisbrot, Rob Weissman, and Vice Yu.

The foundations and individuals, including the Nathan Cummings Foundation, The Rachel E. Golden Foundation, The Lawson Valentine Foundation, Fran and David Korten and Sara Nichols and Bill Magavern, whose special support for this book project were the essential supplement to Global Trade Watch's much-appreciated general support funders. Together, your contributions make this book and all of Global Trade Watch's work possible.

The authors also wish to thank our editor at The New Press, Andrew Hsiao, whose combination of sweet personality, smarts and sharp pen improved our work greatly. Friends and family who helped all of us get through the rigors of writing this book, with special thanks to TJ and Jon.

WHOSE TRADE ORGANIZATION?

"Disregard national boundaries and sovereignty...we're dividing it up into marketing chunks."

Introduction

IT'S NOT ABOUT TRADE

Lori Wallach

Many people are surprised when they first learn that trade is only a small element of the WTO.

But the World Trade Organization—and the sprawling rules that it enforces— actually covers a huge array of subjects not included in past trade agreements that extend far beyond trade matters. The new agreements that were established with the WTO nine years ago included 800-plus pages of one-size-fits-all rules. Those new agreements set constraints on signatory countries' *domestic* food safety standards, environmental and product safety rules, service-sector regulation, investment and development policy, intellectual property standards, government procurement rules, and more.

The establishment of the WTO transformed the nature of global "trade" agreements. The General Agreement on Tariffs and Trade (GATT), a 1947 pact that had governed tariffs and quotas on trade in goods, had included some simple—and objective—principles, like requiring countries to apply the same regulations to foreign and domestic goods. But the new WTO rules are subjective—constraining the *level* of food safety or environmental protection a country can provide or the priorities a country can choose—even if these policies treat domestic and foreign goods equally. Some of the new WTO agreements also force countries to implement specific policies in their domestic laws. For instance, all countries are required to implement certain intellectual property rules, including giving patent owners decades of monopoly control over a vast array of items including plant varieties, seeds, and other things we do not ordinarily think of as private property. Instead of setting terms for *inter*national trade—exchange between different nations—these rules are aimed at eliminating the diversity of national policies, priorities, and cultures to create the uniform world market sought by large multinational corporations.

A key WTO provision specifically requires each signatory to ensure the conformity of its laws, regulations and administrative procedures[1] to the WTO agreements' terms. WTO member nations can challenge as an "illegal trade barrier" any national or local policy of another WTO country, bringing charges before a WTO tribunal comprised of three trade officials who meet behind closed doors. Nations whose policies are judged not to conform with WTO rules are ordered to elimi-nate them or face permanent trade sanctions.

Taken as a whole, the WTO and its agreements are a powerful mechanism for spreading and locking in corporate-led globalization. The WTO is a mechanism to bring every country in the world—ready or not—into an existing global mar-ket designed by corporations, and to take the practices those corporations invented willy-nilly—which, of course, suit their needs—and set them in stone as "WTO rules."

Because its terms are so broad, the WTO has managed to intervene in domestic policies all over the planet. India, like many countries, once had a ban on the patent-ing of seeds and medicines, to make them broadly accessible. A WTO challenge claiming India had failed to implement the required twenty-year patenting system resulted in India reversing its ban—threatening to deprive millions of people of life-giving resources. In Guatemala, implementation of the UNICEF–World Health Organization Code on the labeling of infant formula was gutted after a WTO threat. Consumers and producers in Europe face costly trade sanctions because the European Union (EU) has not implemented a WTO order to import beef containing artificial hormones—the WTO ruled that Europe's standards pro-vided too much consumer protection after a U.S. WTO attack. Meanwhile, a U.S. WTO case forced the EU to eliminate a program that had set aside a small market share for bananas from former Caribbean colonies, leading to the ruin of thou-sands of small family farms in several island nations. Policies aimed at ensuring the continued existence of some Canadian news magazines in the face of massive U.S. magazine imports were abolished after a successful U.S. WTO case. On the other hand, the U.S. saw its gasoline cleanliness standards weakened after a WTO assault on Clean Air Act regulations by several countries. Even though the U.S. signed a global environmental treaty called the Convention on International Trade in Endangered Species, American rules requiring shrimp fishers not to kill sea turtles were diluted after a WTO challenge to U.S. Endangered Species Act reg-ulations enforcing the treaty. Meanwhile, the U.S. State Department, lobbying about how a state law might violate WTO, pressured Maryland legislators to drop a procurement policy aimed at promoting human rights in Nigeria. These are only a few of the negative results of nine years of WTO implementation.

Proponents of this system have called it "free trade" and attack all who criticize it as "protectionist" or "isolationist"—a great irony given the international nature of the opposition. Yet, the WTO's rules have little to do with trade and even less to do with the nineteenth-century free trade philosophies of Adam Smith or David Ricardo.

Indeed, some of the topics covered by the WTO have so little to do with trade that naming these agreements required explanation. Thus, WTO includes an Agreement on Trade Related Intellectual Property and an Agreement on Trade Related Investment. One longtime WTO observer often quips that you can iden-tify which WTO agreements have the least connection to trade by which have the "Trade Related" label slapped on them.

If such an autocratic, antidemocratic system had been imposed on elected governments around the world by force, human rights monitors and UN inspectors would have been dispatched. Instead, the WTO's silent coup d'état will only be reversed by citizen activism and campaigning. A first step for many people is realizing that "trade" is the least of what is covered by the WTO's rules, and then realizing what that means for their daily lives.

THE SECRET HISTORY OF THE WTO

Before November 30, 1999—the day massive anti-WTO protests began in Seattle, Washington—few Americans knew much—if anything—about the mysterious global bureaucracy called the World Trade Organization. But though Seattle was the first time many Americans realized corporate globalization's broad implications for their lives, Public Citizen had made the discovery a decade earlier.

I was working as a lobbyist for Public Citizen's Congress Watch in 1990 on issues such as pesticide regulation and food labeling. During debates over pending legislation, I noticed two very odd things. One, the industry was not fighting us hard enough over things that should have been really disturbing to them. And second, in unguarded moments industry representatives would say things like, "If you strengthen that pesticide law, the U.S. will have problems with the Codex Alimentarius under the new GATT," or, "What do you mean, you want more meat inspection?—that could be a trade barrier."

From school, I understood that GATT was just about cutting tariffs and quotas. But having also done stints on Capitol Hill and in political campaigns, I had developed some radar for incoming sneak attacks. So, I began to get a bad feeling that we were missing something—something really big.

Indeed we were, and so was virtually everyone else in the public-interest community. The more we dug into what was being called a "trade" agreement, the more we realized that the public-interest agenda was facing a massive attack from previously unknown quarters. At stake was the agenda of economic justice and equality, environmental and consumer protection, food safety, and more.

As the public-interest movement and labor unions had been making headway on these struggles through federal legislation, our opponents shifted to a different realm—one where decisions would be made in distant, secretive, unaccountable venues insulated from popular democracy. The same neoliberal forces behind the Reagan and Thatcher "revolutions" opened a new front in their campaign to create a world in which government would be shrunk and human rights and needs would be left to markets and corporations. The plan was to turn the obscure and largely uncontroversial GATT into a Trojan Horse holding an expansive non-trade agenda. So, in 1986, without fanfare, at a GATT summit in Uruguay, new "trade" negotiations had been launched.

Proponents of the Uruguay Round GATT negotiations and the WTO that emerged from them promised that the new system would pose no threat to domestic sovereignty, public-interest policies, or democracy. They also promised enormous economic gains worldwide if the Uruguay Round was implemented: The U.S. trade deficit would decrease by $60 billion in ten years. Latin American countries would boom, and Asian growth would keep pace. Then–U.S. Treasury Secretary Lloyd Bentsen even predicted that passage of the Uruguay Round would result in an additional $1,700 in annual income per U.S. family.

But the more we dug into the negotiations, the more alarmed we got. Public Citizen was not getting into a new issue called "trade," rather the good name of trade was being hijacked to launch an offensive on democratic, accountable governance and decades of public-interest gains won by consumer, environmental, labor, and other citizens' movements worldwide.

In 1991, when we were leaked a copy of the secret draft text, the fight began in earnest. The new rules were being written surreptitiously, and under the influence of the world's largest multinational corporations, with five hundred U.S. corporations officially designated as formal U.S. government advisers. Agreements were written in "GATTese," a language understood mainly by trade lawyers. Secrecy of all WTO documents, sessions, and enforcement tribunals is one of few procedural rules mandated in the WTO text.

There are few people in the world who have actually read the whole text, which establishes the WTO and the 18 major agreements setting rules to which every signatory nation must conform their domestic policies—which WTO enforces. A useful way to understand what the WTO's terms are really about is to focus on the themes that run through all of the WTO's agreements. These include:

- *privatize and commodify* all elements of the economy and society by pushing countries to treat everything from bulk water and public services to genetic materials and food as commodities to be made accessible as new for-profit tradeable units;
- *deregulate* by constraining the role of all levels of government and designating some domestic environmental, food safety and other regulations as trade barriers that must be eliminated;
- *harmonize* by pressuring countries to replace national and local policies with uniform global standards that are presumed to be WTO compliant while national standards providing a greater level of consumer protection in pesticide and meat inspection standards, environmental policies, accounting rules and more are exposed to WTO challenge;
- *"liberalize" investment* by requiring governments to eliminate policies regulating who can own what, including essential services, and to eliminate conditions on investors, such as requiring certain labor standards or environmental protections;
- *"liberalize" finance* by requiring countries to eliminate policies regulating banks, currency trading, derivatives, and stock markets;
- *manage trade* according to WTO rules. In contrast to "free trade," this is a "corporate-managed trade" system because of the special protections it provides for certain interests. For instance the WTO protects subsidies given to agribusiness to export commodities (thus allowing them to be dumped on markets at prices below the cost of production) while certain domestic subsidies to support small farms are characterized as illegal trade distortions;

- *create new property protections,* for instance requiring nations to adopt twenty-year monopoly patents on a wide array of items and giving foreign investors special rights not enjoyed by local businesses or citizens; and
- *homogenize culture and consumer demands* by treating culture as another commodity and eliminating government policies aimed at maintaining diverse media content.

As awareness grew in the U.S. and around the world about what the Uruguay Round "trade" talks were really about, environmental, labor, consumer, and other public-interest groups started raising an alarm. In many nations, especially in the developing world, the establishment of this powerful global commerce agency was incredibly controversial and caused massive protests. In several countries, opposition was so strong that the WTO was only "approved" after extraordinarily antidemocratic maneuvers—including the failure to translate the text so elected officials in many nations literally had no idea what they were approving, and short-notice late-night parliamentary votes in several nations. But in the U.S., most people—including many people in Congress—had no idea what was really at stake. In late 1994, Congress approved the agreement and passed the Uruguay Round Implementing Act. This legislation included hundreds of pages of changes to U.S. law to make existing policy conform to the WTO's rules. The WTO then went into effect worldwide on January 1, 1995.

SEATTLE

In December 1999, what had been a long-growing struggle against corporate globalization and the WTO suddenly burst onto center stage. It took this relatively superficial fight on the streets of Seattle to lure the world's major media to pay attention to the WTO and the existential struggle being fought worldwide against it. Only the threat of broken windows in Seattle prompted the media to begin to expose the WTO's global threat to democracy and the worldwide damage it had already caused.

During those battle-of-Seattle days, 3,000 delegates to the WTO's fourth Ministerial-level summit were gathered inside the Seattle Convention Center. In closed-door "green room" sessions, top-level trade officials from the U.S., Europe, Japan, and a few other nations were huddled with the WTO Secretariat's staff, struggling desperately to hammer out an agreement to launch a new "Millennium" Round of trade talks—designed to expand the WTO's power and scope.

Often vital WTO sessions and decisions are conducted in "green room" sessions where even the majority of WTO country representatives are excluded. The WTO Secretariat, which is supposed to act as a neutral facilitator for all WTO member nations, often works in conjunction with a shortlist of the wealthiest nations and their handpicked allies. No tactic is too shameful. The WTO Secretariat consults with the U.S. and the European Union and then often appoints representatives of the few developing countries known to support their agenda to chair negotiating groups. This gives the appearance of diversity while ensuring the outcomes will not represent the interests of the majority of WTO member countries—which are mostly developing countries.

The tension outside—where phalanxes of police and the National Guard had blocked avenues and intersections and tear gas choked throngs of protesters—was almost equaled in the suites, as pro–WTO-expansion trade officials verbally pummeled ambassadors from the growing number of countries skeptical about WTO expansion. The real-life record of the WTO—and decades of wreckage resulting from similar policies promulgated by the International Monetary Fund (IMF) and World Bank—also meant that in countries around the world, popular movements opposing the WTO had been growing. Indeed, the movement against corporate-led globalization and the WTO began in the developing world where people had already been suffering the results of this model.

Suddenly, the developing world came to learn that plenty of folks in the U.S. were united with them against the WTO and against the sort of world that its rules promote. U.S. officials triumphantly demanded the rest of the world organize itself like privatized, deregulated, Enronified America and berated other nations' officials for being "backwards" if they opposed WTO expansion. But then the whole world got to see for itself that right in the belly of the beast, tens of thousands of U.S. residents were moved to take to the streets against the very model that the U.S. government was trying to impose worldwide.

The protests in Seattle were the icing on a cake that had taken years to stir together and bake. Since the WTO expansion proposal had first been unveiled nearly two years earlier, citizen activists in scores of nations had been campaigning under the slogan "WTO: No New Round, Turnaround!" Campaign strategy had been shaped month by month by the Our World Is Not For Sale Network, a network of social movements and civil-society campaign groups from around the world that had emerged from the successful grassroots battle against a proposed Multilateral Agreement on Investment (MAI).

Thriving grassroots, country-based campaigns forced delegations at the Seattle Ministerial to consider the implications of their actions at home. India and other developing-nation governments faced massive domestic pressure to oppose WTO expansion. The usual WTO ploy of forcing "agreement" on a Ministerial Declaration before the actual ministerial negotiations had failed.

And, in Seattle, when word leaked out that the European Union's trade minister, Pascal Lamy, was poised to give in to U.S. wishes regarding genetically modified organisms, European activists foiled his move by contacting prime ministers, environmental ministers and legislators from nations he was supposed to be representing. Lamy was "reminded" to withhold "European" consent for this key U.S. demand.

The unexpectedly large protests played an enzymatic role in creating a full-blown WTO deadlock, and the summit had to be extended by a day. The major players holed up in closed-door sessions to develop a "take-it-or-leave-it" proposal to present to the rest of the WTO member countries—who were excluded from those sessions.

Anger increased hourly as the many excluded trade ministers met amongst themselves—with CNN's live coverage of the protests buzzing in the background.

Midday on December 3, 1999, blocs of African, Latin American, and Caribbean countries issued public statements, aligning themselves with longtime opponents of WTO expansion like India and Malaysia.

Public Citizen activists and the staff of Public Citizen's Global Trade Watch were scattered across the city that day, linked by walkie-talkies and cell phones. A year earlier, despite our tiny staff and pinched budget, we had sent a senior organizer to Seattle and opened a WTO campaign office. Some folks thought we'd lost our minds, but we had sensed what Public Citizen's founder, Ralph Nader, calls a "trimtab" moment. The trimtab is the small rudder that turns the massive rudder on ocean liners.

The news seemed almost unbelievable when an official from a developing country passed the word. My voice was trembling over the crackling static of the walkie-talkies: "The WTO expansion is stopped! The people have won—there will be no new WTO round!"

A Global Trade Watch staffer who had spent most of the past year in Seattle stood on the corner of Pine Street amid a sea of 30,000 people. He grabbed a megaphone and shouted out the spine-tingling news. The crowd—youth and environmental activists, members of the Steelworkers and Teamsters unions whose early commitment to the WTO fight showed in their numbers that day, and newly activated Seattle residents—roared back. Inside the convention center, I held up my walkie-talkie so the jubilant activists inside could hear the celebration in the street. Friends and allies from India, Canada, Malaysia, the Philippines, Ghana, Chile, and other nations piled into a tearful and smiling global hug in the Convention Center lobby. The Global Trade Watch staffer who had helped coordinate the international WTO campaigning linked arms with her counterparts from Africa, Europe, Latin America, and Asia in a spontaneous jig as a bemused press corps began to gather.

The allegedly unstoppable force of corporate-led globalization had hit the truly immovable mass of grassroots democracy.

The notion that WTO talks could be subjected to democratic accountability was so unimaginable to the U.S., European, and WTO officials pushing expansion that they had not even developed a fallback plan. The Seattle WTO Ministerial staggered to a close with an ad hoc news conference announcing that discussions would continue at the WTO's Geneva headquarters. But back in Geneva in the coming weeks, the topic of discussion was not how to revive WTO expansion, but how to repair the severe damage to the WTO's public legitimacy. A PR campaign—not policy change—was the approach and thus, predictably, four more years of the WTO's damage led to "Seattle-on-the-Sand"—the implosion of the WTO's 2003 Ministerial— as the WTO's growing crisis of legitimacy burst into public view again.

THE WTO'S RECORD: RESULTS ARE IN

Now, nearly nine years since the founding of the WTO, it is clear that the promised economic gains have not materialized. Worse, the WTO fails to meet the most conservative of tests: do no further harm. This book seeks to demystify the WTO and make its track record of diverse damage accessible to those of us living with the results.

We have called on some of the leading WTO experts around the world to help with this book, to enable us to provide comprehensive information on the full array of issues that the WTO implicates. This book examines the WTO's impacts on environmental protection and conservation; food and product safety; access to essential public services; food security and agriculture; public health, worker safety, and access to medicines; jobs, livelihoods, economic development, and standards of living in both rich and poor countries; human and labor rights; and how the WTO and its powerful dispute-resolution enforcement system operate. It also includes a chapter co-authored with allies from Latin America about how the revived push to expand the WTO is linked to a regional push to expand the North American Free Trade Agreement (NAFTA) to thirty-one additional countries through the proposed Free Trade Area of the Americas (FTAA).

This book contains many specific examples and footnotes because it aims to arm people with the strongest case against the WTO: the facts about the WTO's outcomes. Animating many facets of our work is the concept of the "public citizen"—a person who, once empowered with information and tools to effect change, makes being a participant in civic life part of his or her daily routine. Thus, a key goal of Global Trade Watch is to clarify for people that the current globalization model is neither inevitable nor representative of "free trade," a concept that people generally support. All of our work seeks to make the measurable outcomes of this model accessible, while reiterating that if the results are not acceptable, then the model can and must be changed. We work to demonstrate that one *can* be pro-trade and internationalist and still demand transformative change to the current terms of globalization.

Fundamentally, what is really at stake is democratic, accountable governance. Taken as a whole, the review of the WTO's operations documents an insidious shift in decision making on an array of domestic issues away from accountable, inclusive, and democratic fora to distant, secretive, and unaccountable WTO venues.

Much of the information presented here about the disputes adjudicated by the WTO and about corporate and government threats of WTO action has not been publicized previously and was obtained only after extensive investigation. The trend that emerges is of the WTO silently eroding the hard-won balance between public interests in economic equity, environmental protection, health, and safety on one hand, and short-term corporate interests in market control and profitability on the other.

Some of the Findings of Our Review of the WTO's Eight Years in Operation Include

Promised Economic Gains Fail to Materialize

We must await full implementation of the Uruguay Round Agreements before we can fully assess their long-term economic impacts. But the economic trends that have emerged so far indicate serious problems. These trends would have to abruptly reverse course to merely return the developing world to better, pre–Uruguay Round conditions, much less to fulfill many of the outlandish predictions of broad benefits served up by Uruguay Round boosters.

Unbelievably, WTO boosters still argue that the answer to this grinding poverty is more of the same, faster—including a new proposed WTO expansion—and that poverty is being caused by governments not adhering quickly or completely enough to the WTO formula.

Thankfully, the ironclad consensus among economists and policy elites around the world in favor of the model promoted by the WTO rules has loosened dramatically. For some, theory and ideology have been overcome by the facts: the number of people living on less than $1 a day (the World Bank's definition of extreme poverty) has risen since the WTO went into effect and, in many parts of the world, the percentage of people living is such that extreme poverty also has risen.

What we also know today and what has contributed greatly to the shift among elites is that the world has been buffeted by unprecedented financial instability as more countries have adopted the package of policies in the WTO. Economic growth in the developing world has slowed. Income inequality is rising rapidly between and within countries. A report by the United Nations Conference on Trade and Development (UNCTAD) found that, "In almost all developing countries that have undertaken rapid trade liberalization, wage inequality has increased, most often in the context of declining industrial employment of unskilled workers and large absolute falls in their real wages, on the order of 20–30% in Latin American countries."

Despite productivity gains, wages in many countries have failed to rise. Commodity prices are at all-time lows, causing the standard of living for many people to slide, particularly in Asia, Latin America, and Africa. Indeed, in most countries the period under the Uruguay Round has brought dramatic reversals in fortune— and not for the better.

Latin America is foundering, mired in its deepest economic slump since the debt crisis of the 1980s. The corporate economic globalization model with its hallmark of "free" trade, export-oriented development, privatization, and investment liberalization was imposed on Argentina by multilateral institutions such as the IMF, the World Bank, and the WTO. Argentina reorganized its entire political and economic structure to comply with this model, and it was highlighted as a "poster child" for the new global economy—until it imploded with desperate and violent consequences.

East Asia lost decades of economic progress in a crisis caused in part by the very investment and financial service-sector deregulation that WTO rules intensify and spread to other nations. When the U.S. media announced that the crisis was over in 1999, people living in Asia knew better. For instance, in Korea the crisis had quadrupled unemployment and precipitated a 200% increase in absolute poverty.

Global economic indicators generally paint a tragic picture: The median income of the tenth of the world's people living in the richest countries was 77 times greater than the tenth in the poorest in 1980, but by 1999, the richest earned 122 times the poorest countries. Entire regions of the developing world are falling alarmingly behind the wealthiest countries that compose the Organization for Economic Cooperation and Development (OECD). Sub-Saharan Africa's per capita income was one sixth of OECD countries in 1975, but fell to one fourteenth of OECD per capita income in 2000. Over the same period, Latin America and the Caribbean per capita income fell from less than half that of OECD countries to less than a third, and Arab countries' per capita income fell from one quarter of that of OECD countries to one fifth.

In the U.S., the trade deficit is at an all-time high, $435 billion in 2002 and climbing, having ballooned—not declined as promised—from $98 billion before WTO in 1994. The median family income has not risen by $1,700 per year during *any* of the past nine years as promised, despite the fact that the U.S. had a period of unprecedented economic growth. Since the WTO went into effect, the U.S. has seen its industrial base hollowed out with the loss of 2 million manufacturing jobs. Now the service sector and high-tech jobs that we were told by the WTO's supporters would be our employment future are beginning to follow the manufacturing jobs to low-wage countries, with more than 3 million U.S. jobs expected to be shifted to China and other nations by 2015, according to Forrester Research.

Meanwhile, analysis of promised future gains of greater trade liberalization shows that net losses—not gains—would result for most people from further liberalization.

While the economic data demonstrate the absolute failure of the WTO model, they are but one part of the story. Of equal importance, but less well known, is the WTO's consistent record of eroding public-interest policies designed to safeguard the environment, our families' health and safety, human rights, and democracy.

WTO Challenges and Threats Undermine the Public Interest

Since it was created in 1995, the WTO has ruled that every environmental, health or safety policy it has reviewed but one is an illegal trade barrier that must be eliminated or changed. With few exceptions, nations whose laws were declared trade barriers by the WTO—or that were merely threatened with prospective WTO action—have eliminated or watered down their policies to meet WTO requirements. In addition to undermining existing public-interest safeguards, this trend has a chilling effect on countries' inclinations to pass new environmental, human rights, or safety laws.

The WTO's tribunals systematically rule against domestic laws challenged as violating WTO rules. As of January 2003, defending countries have won just 13 out of 88 completed WTO cases—or only 14.8%. (The United States lost two of those three anomalous cases.) Developing countries are among the biggest losers in this system. They generally do not have the money and expertise to either bring cases to the WTO or defend themselves before the WTO. Many simply amend their laws as soon as a WTO threat is issued. As a result, the WTO's full damage to domestic policy is much greater than the WTO's official case record shows. With few exceptions, no one knows about those instances when domestic policies are changed before formal WTO cases are initiated.

Because the WTO is still young, the cases described in this book are merely the beginning, offering a frightening glimpse of what is still to come unless significant changes are made.

Consider what happened to the United States' attempt to reduce emissions from automobiles. The U.S. relaxed its standards designed to limit gasoline contaminants after Venezuela won a WTO challenge against Clean Air Act regulations that it claimed unfairly affected its gasoline industry. In a classic example of WTO double-talk, the panel in this case ruled that a country was free to choose any environmental policy it desired, but could only implement policies that were consistent with WTO rules. The Clinton administration implemented new regulations that it had previously rejected as being effectively unenforceable in order to comply with the WTO order.

Further, WTO rules prohibit countries from treating physically similar products differently based on how they are made or harvested, putting in limbo many laws, like those banning drift-net fishing or requiring less polluting manufacturing processes; as well as laws banning goods made with child labor. For instance, in the eyes of the WTO, tuna caught in dolphin-safe nets should be treated no differently than tuna caught in nets that ensnare dolphins. After Mexico threatened to go to the WTO to enforce a GATT ruling against a U.S. law designed to prevent dolphins from being killed in tuna nets, the Clinton administration worked with some of Congress's leading antienvironmental members to water down the popular U.S. policy. Now, after renewed threats of WTO action, the Bush administration is trying to change the definition of "dolphin safe" on tuna can labels to allow its use on tuna caught with deadly encirclement nets. Only an emergency injunction issued in an ongoing court case has temporarily halted the new policy.

WTO rules launch a race to the bottom by setting a ceiling but no floor on environmental protection and public health and safety. Domestic standards on health, the environment and public safety that are higher than international ones must pass a set of stringent tests in order not to be considered trade barriers. There is no requirement that international standards be met, only that they cannot be exceeded.

A WTO ruling against Europe's ban on beef grown using artificial hormones is a vivid and alarming illustration of the WTO's unacceptable approach to human health and safety. The WTO declared that Europe's ban on meat tainted with artificial growth hormones had to go because the WTO-recognized food standards—from a corporate-influenced body called the Codex Alimentarius—considered such artificial hormones safe. The WTO also said that the ban was WTO-illegal because the Europeans had not scientifically demonstrated that the artificial hormone residues in meat pose an explicit threat to human health, although it is known that the hormones themselves do. The EU refused to cave in to U.S. pressure to accept the beef its consumers do not want. As a result it was hit with $116.8 million per year in WTO-authorized trade sanctions which remain in place.

The WTO system effectively turns the very premise by which most progressive governments have handled food safety and other human health-related policies on its head. Generally, manufacturers are required to prove that a product is safe before it can be sold, and countries ban the product until the company has submitted the proof. Under WTO rules, governments must prove that a product is unsafe before they can ban it.

Another alarming aspect of the WTO system is how nations are effectively used by corporations to challenge policies in other countries. The U.S. was going to bat for Chiquita, the banana giant, when it successfully attacked Europe's preferential treatment of bananas from former EU colonies in the WTO case mentioned above. The U.S. does not produce bananas for export, and most of Chiquita's employees are underpaid farm workers laboring on its vast Central American plantations. The EU rescinded its preferential treatment, devastating many small, independent Caribbean banana farmers. The ultimate result could be destabilization of the very economic foundations of the Caribbean's numerous small democratic nations, meaning U.S. national interest in the region—in drug interdiction, political stability, trade and tourism—could be undermined by the WTO action taken on behalf of Chiquita.[2]

But a country need not always actually challenge another country's laws to change them. Often, the mere threat of a challenge suffices. Most of these cases remain undocumented. However, one known example is the U.S. threat against Guatemala's implementation of the so-called Nestle's Code. Decades of promotion by infant formula corporations resulted in a plague of needless infant deaths that occurred when mothers in developing countries mixed formula with unsanitary water. Reacting to this public health crisis and a global campaign, UNICEF and the World Health Organization created a global code on infant formula marketing which one hundred–plus countries implemented. Sometimes known as the "Nestle's Code," it banned infant formula packaging that depicted healthy, fat babies to ensure that women, particularly illiterate ones, wouldn't associate baby formula with healthy infants and be discouraged from breast-feeding. Gerber Foods, the company whose trademarked logo includes a pudgy, happy infant, took exception to Guatemala's implementation of the Code.[3]

When Guatemala insisted that Gerber remove the baby image from the packaging of products distributed in Guatemala, the company refused, arguing that under the WTO's intellectual property rules, its trademark baby face trumped the health treaty. The U.S. State Department sent a letter to the president of Guatemala threatening a trade case. Defending a case at the WTO can cost hundreds of thousands of dollars. In Guatemala's case, it was a choice between using that money for other public health initiatives, or gambling it on an uncertain outcome before a WTO tribunal. The government decided to weaken the law—by exempting imported breast-milk substitutes—rather than risk the expense for what might be a losing defense. Prior to this, Guatemala had been promoted by UNICEF as a country whose successful implementation of the Code had cut infant mortality.

And while many Americans saw news coverage of Vice President Al Gore's campaign events being protested by AIDS activists, few realized that a WTO threat was underlying this brouhaha. South Africa's efforts to make AIDS treatment more accessible to its population was attacked by international pharmaceutical companies and the Clinton administration as violating patent rights required by the WTO. Global campaigning and pressure ultimately forced a declaration to be issued at the 2001 WTO Doha Ministerial recognizing that the WTO rules in fact do not bar practices such as compulsory licensing for generic production of medicine. However, prior to that, the U.S. filed a formal WTO challenge against Brazilian pharmaceutical policy. Brazil is recognized worldwide as having the most effective public health approach to HIV/AIDS, and its policy of making anti-retroviral drugs available to every infected citizen has saved the lives of millions. The U.S. ultimately withdrew its WTO challenge against Brazil as public pressure on the issue grew. However, in recent WTO talks, the Bush administration single-handedly blocked a WTO agreement which would have clarified that WTO rules allow poor nations to import affordable drugs that have been produced in other countries under compulsory licenses—a practice necessary for the many nations without manufacturing capacity.

WTO Trend: Commerce Always Takes Precedence

Beyond these cases, which are sufficiently disturbing in and of themselves, lies an unnerving theme: In the WTO forum, global commerce takes precedence over everything—democracy, public health, equity, access to essential services, the environment, food safety and more.

Indeed, under WTO rules, global commerce takes precedence over even small business. The Uruguay Round Agreements provide foreign corporations new rights and much greater ease in establishing themselves in every WTO member country. Obviously, small enterprises cannot take advantage of new rights to acquire the telecommunication system of a country, set up a branch abroad or relocate production to another country to avoid the U.S. minimum wage or the costs of environmental or workplace safety requirements. What is worse, however, is that WTO rules forbid some small business promotion policies that could have the effect of discriminating against large foreign businesses—the only businesses likely to enter another country's market.

In recent years, foreign direct investment has shifted dramatically away from the establishment of new enterprises and toward global consolidation through mergers and acquisitions between existing entities. As documented in the following pages, this trend has been most intense in the economic sectors in which WTO agreements have been completed—financial services and telecommunications. This global merger mania is leading to problems with market concentration and, absent some countering force, will increasingly affect consumer prices and access to services. Not only has this trend led to the absorption of small enterprises into global giants, but under WTO rules developing countries have lost many of the safeguards for their infant industries that, for instance, the U.S. enjoyed in its economic development.

In addition, WTO rules seek to commodify everything—to turn everything into a form of property—so that it can be traded. Food is a prime example. Despite enormous growth in food trade, only 15% of the world food supply is traded. A large share of the world's population relies on subsistence farming for its food supply. Subsistence farmers are able to grow crops each year by saving seeds from the previous year. However, under the WTO's new intellectual property guarantees, a company can obtain ownership rights—literally a patent—over the knowledge and effort of the local farmers who bred the perfectly adapted seed over generations. Once a company holds the patent for a particular seed variety, it can force cashless farmers either to pay an annual royalty to use the seed variety, buy new seeds each year or no longer use the variety, which may be the only one available or effective in that region. The expropriation of seed varieties that had been commonly shared resources into private property effectively gives companies license to rob subsistence farmers of their ability to feed themselves and their families.

Regarding services (for example, health care, education, utilities and transportation), the rules encourage privatization and deregulation—essentially promoting the transformation of these public needs into commodities to be sold for profit to those who can afford them. And the WTO constrains government regulation of such private-sector services, meaning globalization of the process that Americans saw unfold in California under the Enron energy deregulation scandal.

Another overarching WTO characteristic is the push for "harmonization." Harmonization is the word industry has given to the replacement of the varied domestic standards of many nations with uniform global standards to allow companies to produce goods and services for a single global market. Harmonization gained a significant boost with the establishment of the WTO, which requires or encourages national governments to harmonize standards on issues such as food and worker safety, pharmaceutical patents, environmental rules and informational labeling of products or to accept different, often less stringent standards as "equivalent" to their own. The U.S. Department of Agriculture (USDA) has declared the meat inspection systems of 32 countries to be equivalent to the U.S. system. Meat from some of these countries comes into the U.S., where it is given a USDA grading label, such as "USDA Choice." USDA has battled against the attempts of consumer groups to obtain the documents under which these equivalence determinations were made. However, we know that in some of the countries declared equivalent, meat inspectors are paid by companies rather than by the government as required under U.S. law.

The premise underlying harmonization is that the world is one huge market. Differences in standards, even if they express differences in cultures and values, are deemed inherently undesirable because they fragment the global market. But this core premise is false. When a single standard is forced on the world, it is impossible to respect the various choices that people in societies throughout the world make about the standards by which they want to live. Consumer groups are skeptical about harmonization because it creates an inherent conflict between industry's goal of unified global markets, and consumer power and democratic government.

Accountable, Democratic Governance Undermined

The very mechanics of the WTO, which are designed to insulate against democratic accountability, preordain this negative outcome. As one WTO staffer admitted to the *Financial Times* in a moment of unguarded candor, the WTO "is the place where governments collude in private against their domestic pressure groups."[4]

Legislators and the public in every country have heard the same refrain, often stated by government officials claiming to hear our pain amidst alligator tears: this country's government would *never* implement such an environment/development/food safety/livelihood–destroying policy . . . but the WTO makes us do it.

The WTO's secretive, unbalanced operations provide the perfect venue for such maneuvers. WTO business is conducted by committees and panels that meet behind closed doors in Geneva, Switzerland. Major decisions are supposed to be taken by consensus, but in reality a handful of major countries often develop take-it-or-leave-it proposals they try to foist on the rest of the countries. Even in the powerful countries calling the shots at the WTO, the environmental, health, education, and other affected ministries are cut out of the process, often learning in the press post-facto that some new WTO decision will require changes in their area of domestic jurisdiction. State and local elected officials are totally cut out—the WTO only recognizes national government signatories, meaning that when state or local laws are challenged at the WTO, state and local officials are excluded unless invited by federal government officials to participate.

Meanwhile, public-interest organizations, the public and the press are put through the WTO hokey-pokey. Speak to the WTO staff about an issue and you're told that the WTO is merely a forum to facilitate intergovernmental cooperation, so go see your country's WTO representative. WTO representatives in Geneva tell you to talk to officials in your national capital, but those officials dolefully claim that there is nothing they can do: the WTO makes them do X, Y or Z unacceptable thing, but, they suggest, maybe it would be worth a visit to the WTO staff.

In sharp contrast to domestic courts and even other international agreements, at the WTO there is a startling lack of transparency, public disclosure or accountability. This leads to overwhelming industry influence, especially by the largest multinational corporations based in the most powerful countries. Even the dispute resolution tribunals meet in secret. The panels rely on documents never made public and on anonymous "experts" to make decisions and issue reports that cannot be accessed by the public until the hearings are over and a binding judgment is issued. WTO panelists are selected for their trade credentials, not their knowledge of an issue in dispute, such as public health, environmental protection or development policy. Most disturbing is the fact that many of these decision makers have a philosophical or commercial stake in the WTO's preeminence—they are not unbiased judges. Basic due process guarantees, such as strict conflict-of-interest rules for judges, the right for meaningful appeals, and openness to the press and public are all missing at the WTO.

In a rich irony, WTO boosters have charged that it is the WTO critics, not the WTO, that are undemocratic. Whom do those civil-society organizations represent, anyway, they scoff, instead of trying to address the systemic secrecy and imbalances in the WTO. The crux of their argument is that the WTO and its rules were agreed upon by the signatory countries and that the WTO is comprised of government representatives who are appointed by elected officials in democratic countries.

First, in many countries WTO "approval" was itself a travesty of democracy. At a minimum, few parliamentarians were informed by trade officials about the nature of what they were approving. In many countries, if votes on WTO membership were to be held now, on a more informed basis, it is likely passage would fail. Second, the WTO boosters are seeking to distract from the main point: the WTO is intentionally designed to insulate against democratic pressure for change. If you do not like a domestic policy, you lobby and organize pressure to change it or you change the elected officials making policy. This is the crux of democracy: the people who will live with the result decide. By removing policy making to a distant venue and in secret and by officials appointed by officials who are appointed by a president or prime minister who was elected and does not stand election again for years, even the worst policies are insulated from change. Third, the fact that countries initially approved the Uruguay Round Agreements does not excuse the secretive, exclusive, unbalanced manner in which the WTO's operations are conducted day to day. The fact that countries agreed to a WTO does not mean that WTO policies forbidding press or public oversight are democratic.

THE CHOICE IS OURS: THE CANCÚN WTO MINISTERIAL MEETING AND BEYOND

The full magnitude of this new global governance system has yet to be seen because some WTO rules have not taken full effect. But it is now time to ask: Whose trade organization is it? It does not appear to belong to or benefit the majority of the world's citizens.

This still-emerging system is not a foregone conclusion. Despite the public-relations efforts of those who benefit from this arrangement to convince us otherwise, the WTO setup is merely one design; it is not inevitable. Putting into place the WTO and the corporate-led globalization it implements required its proponents to undertake an enormous amount of planning, public relations, and political work. If we do not like the outcomes of this design, then we must undertake similar efforts to change it.

Indeed, the fragility of the current system increases with each year its operation brings damaging results. This growing crisis of legitimacy was thrust onto the public stage at the 1999 Seattle WTO Ministerial. Corporate and government defenders of the WTO sought to dismiss the Seattle meltdown as a fluke and exploited the shaky global political atmosphere post–9/11 to force an agreement at the 2001 Doha Ministerial, which temporarily papered over enormous divisions. The September 2003 Cancún WTO Ministerial brought the reality of the WTO's vulnerable state back to center stage. Most corporate interests viewed the Cancún Ministerial as a venue to launch a major expansion of WTO rules.

The full scope of this proposed expansion, which was opposed by the majority of the WTO's signatories that are developing nations, is described in Chapter 6 and in the conclusion of this book. Among the most threatening proposals was a plan to launch new negotiations to establish an additional WTO investment agreement that would cover issues excluded from existing WTO investment rules, such as governments' rights to refuse certain foreign investments, and to determine who can purchase or control natural resources and how currency can be regulated. The goal is to revive the outrageous Multilateral Agreement on Investment, which was killed by global citizen campaigning, by expanding greatly what sorts of investments WTO rules cover, and then to create new rights for foreign investors to operate without government involvement or regulation. European, Korean, and a few other nations' intransigent demands that the expansion be agreed to was the proximate cause of the Cancún Ministerial's implosion. The agriculture trade issues focused on by the press took a back seat at Cancún because the EU and others refused to deal with them unless the poor countries agreed to WTO expansion.

In a broader sense, the decision on the table at the Cancún WTO Ministerial was whether the WTO launched a massive expansion of its current model or was forced to reassess and transform its current rules. The Cancún Ministerial was an important crossroads. The WTO's corporate and government backers were desperate for a decision at Cancún to expand the WTO's scope—if only to show that WTO's momentum is restored. However, the many deep contradictions between countries and interests that were papered over at the Doha WTO Ministerial had meant a virtual standstill in many key WTO negotiations since Doha. Most simply, the divide was between Europe, the U.S., Canada and a few other developed nations who passionately defend the status quo WTO system of corporate globalization and seek to expand the model to cover more issues and the majority of the WTO member nations. These developing countries—joined by civil society groups—increasingly question the underlying model, strenuously oppose adding new subject matter to WTO governance and demand focus on changing the actual *trade* rules, which have failed most people during nine years of operation. The rejection of the "business-as-usual" agenda at Cancún provides an opportunity for civil society to win back ground and push its alternative agenda forward.

For instance, one global network of citizens' groups and social movements—the Our World Is Not For Sale Network—has a different WTO agenda. The "WTO—Shrink or Sink" plan calls for 11 transformational changes to the existing international commercial rules. This plan would scale back the WTO's scope to undo its inappropriate invasion of domestic policy making and remove some issues from WTO jurisdiction altogether. This proposal and more information on alternatives to the status quo system are included in the concluding chapter of this book. To learn more about what happened at the Cancún Ministerial, please visit our website at www.tradewatch.org.

We hope that after reading this book, you will be motivated to join others in a movement to halt the spread of the corporate globalization "trade" agenda and its totalitarian tendencies in favor of democratic and accountable governance and the more equitable, sustainable future it promises.

1

THE WTO'S ENVIRONMENTAL IMPACT: FIRST, GATTZILLA ATE FLIPPER

In 1994, when the legislation establishing the World Trade Organization was approved in the U.S. Congress, it was done without the support of a single environmental, conservation, or animal-welfare group.

While the year before several environmental groups had split away from the majority of U.S. nongovernmental organizations (NGOs) to support NAFTA, environmentalists were unified in opposition to the WTO. Then–U.S. Trade Representative Mickey Kantor claimed that U.S. law would not be undermined by the WTO: "The [WTO] clearly recognizes and acknowledges the sovereign right of each government to establish the level of protection of human, animal and plant life and health deemed appropriate by that government," he said.[1] But these assurances failed to persuade the environmental community.

Skepticism was not surprising. Some of the groups that had supported NAFTA in exchange for an environmental "side agreement" felt betrayed. First, early indications were that the side agreement would be ineffective.[2] Second, the groups had been promised by the Clinton administration that NAFTA would establish a "floor" for environmental protection that would be strengthened in subsequent trade pacts.[3] Instead, NAFTA's environmental side pact turned out to be the high-water mark. The next year it became clear that the Uruguay Round Agreements contained numerous provisions limiting the actions governments could take to protect the public and the environment, but included no environmental safeguards at all.

Environmentalists feared that the WTO's expansive new enforcement powers, combined with the antienvironmental bias in the substantive rules, would produce dire consequences for global environmental protection. They implored negotiators to refashion their approach to take into account environmental concerns.[4]

These entreaties were ignored by the negotiators. However, there was an effort to counter the growing political problems that environmental concerns were causing parliaments faced with voting on the Uruguay Round: negotiators made a last-minute decision at the Marrakech, Morocco, WTO signing ceremonies to establish a Committee on Trade and Environment (CTE). The committee was designated a study group, not a negotiating group, and has proven entirely ineffective as a mechanism for promoting environmental interests within the WTO.

Now, eight years of experience under the WTO have confirmed environmentalists' fears: the WTO is undermining existing local, national and international environmental and conservation policies.

Threats—often by industry, but with government support—are being used to chill environmental innovation. Several formal rulings by WTO tribunals on successful challenges to environmental laws have resulted in weakened domestic policies and new WTO jurisprudence, causing other nations to second-guess their environmental policies for fear of a future WTO attack. Japan's Kyoto Treaty implementation, a European toxics and recycling law, a European chemical safety testing and registration policy, European eco-labels, and an EU humane-trapping law have all been threatened. And prominent WTO panel decisions have ruled that regulations under the U.S. Endangered Species Act and the U.S. Clean Air Act violate WTO terms.

The WTO's terms also create antienvironmental incentives—for instance, "tariff escalation" (lower tariffs for raw materials and increasingly higher tariffs for value-added goods) promotes intensive "rip-and-ship" exploitation of natural resources. Increased trade flows are causing new threats to biodiversity by invasive species infestations. Multilateral environmental agreements (MEAs) are being undermined.

GATT AND THE ENVIRONMENT: PRE–URUGUAY ROUND AND WTO

When the General Agreement on Tariffs and Trade was established in 1947, policy makers were not focused on environmental or conservation concerns. Yet several GATT rules written then have been interpreted to undercut modern environmental principles and policies. Even prior to the 1994 approval of the Uruguay Round, two key U.S. environmental laws—the Marine Mammal Protection Act (MMPA) and the Corporate Average Fuel Efficiency (CAFE) standards for automobiles—were subject to successful GATT challenges.

In 1991, a GATT panel ruled that GATT Article III, which requires "national treatment" (treating domestic and foreign goods the same), prohibited governments from treating goods differently based on the way they are produced or harvested. (In technical terms, this ruling was that countries cannot condition access to their markets based on "Production and Processing Methods" [PPMs].) This interpretation arose from a challenge by Mexico to the MMPA, an effective, longstanding U.S. statute banning the U.S. sale of tuna caught by domestic or foreign fishers using purse seines—massive nets that are laid over schools of dolphins to catch tuna swimming below, a practice that has resulted in millions of dolphin deaths.[5]

Then, in 1994, a GATT panel ruled against U.S. CAFE regulations in a challenge brought by the European Community, concluding that although the CAFE rules were facially neutral—i.e., they treated domestic and foreign cars alike—they had a discriminatory *effect* on European cars. Under the CAFE regulations, a manufacturer's entire fleet of cars sold in the U.S. was required to meet a combined average fuel efficiency. European auto manufacturers had made the marketing decision to sell only their larger, high-end (and thus more profitable) models in the U.S., with the unintended consequence that to meet the CAFE standards such models had to be more fuel efficient than American or Japanese luxury cars, whose efficiency could be averaged against smaller, cleaner models that the American and Japanese makers also sold.

In both cases, the U.S. tried to invoke exceptions to the GATT that are contained in Article XX of the agreement. Article XX "exceptions" are supposed to allow countries to adopt or maintain some laws in vital areas such as national security and, theoretically, health or environmental protection that contradict GATT rules.[6] However, in both of these cases, the GATT exceptions were so narrowly interpreted as to render them moot.

Thus, before the Uruguay Round talks were complete, environmentalists had witnessed successful GATT attacks on environmental laws and had seen that the existing exceptions provided no protection.

WTO AND THE ENVIRONMENT: STRONG ENFORCEMENT OF ANTIENVIRONMENTAL RULES

Mindful of this disturbing pre-Uruguay track record, environmentalists urged Uruguay Round negotiators to strengthen Article XX exceptions so that they might be used effectively to safeguard environmental laws. They also sought to amend GATT provisions that had been, or could be, the basis for attacks on environmental policies.

Uruguay Round negotiators refused to remedy the existing problems, instead adding a vast array of new antienvironment, anticonservation provisions. These new rules subject a wider array of hard-won environmental laws to scrutiny as so-called "nontariff barriers" to trade. ("Nontariff barrier" is trade jargon for any law or policy that is not a tariff but affects trade. For instance, from the GATT/WTO perspective, a law that prohibits import of a product because it contains a toxic or ozone-depleting substance is considered a nontariff barrier to trade and may only be maintained if it meets WTO rules.) New market access terms for "tropical products" and other natural resources also created incentives for more intensive exploitation. Some of the new problems created by the WTO pacts include:

- *Incentives for Rip-and-Ship Exploitation of Natural Resources:* The Uruguay Round tariff schedules promote unsustainable rip-and-ship exploitation of forests, fisheries and minerals. The tariff escalation built into these schedules creates an incentive to ship unfinished materials. For example, rough tropical timber comes into the U.S. duty free, but plywood veneered with tropical wood has a tariff of 8%, and almost all furniture above a limiting quota receives a 40% tariff.[7]

- *Constraints on Environmental Standards on Toxics, Eco-labeling, and More:* The WTO Agreement on Sanitary and Phytosanitary Measures (SPS) explicitly restricts government actions relating to food and agriculture aimed at protecting the environment, human, plant and animal health, and the food supply. The WTO Agreement on Technical Barriers to Trade (TBT) requires that product standards be the least trade-restrictive version and, with limited exceptions, be based on WTO-recognized international standards,[8] many of which are set in industry-dominated fora, such as the International Organization for Standardization (ISO). Moreover, both of these agreements and the underlying GATT rules they amplify have been interpreted to forbid governments from creating or even maintaining policies that distinguish between physically similar goods according to the environmental or conservation conditions of their production or harvest.
- *Multilateral Environmental Agreements Undermined:* Countries seeking to implement their obligations under environmental treaties are facing increasing threats of WTO challenges against such actions.
- *Consideration of Environmental Factors in Government Purchasing Forbidden:* The WTO Agreement on Government Procurement (AGP) requires that governments' technical specifications for goods and services cannot have the effect of creating "unnecessary obstacles" to trade and that conditions regarding qualification of suppliers be limited to those essential to ensure a firm's capability to fulfill the contract, meaning requirements for recycled content or preferences for sustainably harvested timber or for "green" companies are exposed to challenge.
- *Biodiversity Threatened:* The increased volume of trade spurred by the WTO is contributing to an intensified spread of invasive species as plants, animals and insects are deposited on foreign shores in packing materials, bilge waters and forestry, fishery and agricultural goods. Invasive species are a leading cause of biodiversity loss. The WTO's SPS agreement has been interpreted to strictly limit government actions to counter invasive species infestations, as described in Chapter 2. As well, the WTO agreement on Trade Related Aspects of Intellectual Property (TRIPs) promotes biopiracy with large pharmaceutical and agribusiness firms collecting and patenting plant varieties and the processes for medicinal and other uses of wild flora and fauna in a manner that removes them from the public commons and designates them to be private property, as described in Chapter 7.

In addition to the WTO's many new rules, its enforcement power sets it apart from GATT. Under pre–Uruguay Round rules an enforcement ruling had to be adopted by consensus. (Requiring consensus for action is a typical sovereignty protection found in many international agreements.) Thus, a country whose domestic regulations were under fire could essentially block the enforcement of a ruling (although, in order to avoid undermining GATT when tables turned, countries rarely exercised this option).

International Organization for Standardization: Private-Sector Standards Given Key Role by WTO

The ISO is a private-sector body empowered by the WTO to set the presumptively WTO-legal standards for all nonfood products. When the ISO started in the 1950s, its goal was to standardize sizes for lightbulbs, screws, batteries and other consumer products to help industry expand markets. In the past six years, the ISO's areas of focus have expanded to include environmental products, eco-labels (labels identifying products as being manufactured in an environmentally friendly manner) and humane fur trapping. The ISO was given a powerful new role: the WTO's TBT Agreement requires member countries to base their non-food safety technical standards on international standards, even when those standards are not yet complete but their completion is imminent. Under WTO rules, only technical regulations that conform to international standards are *presumed* not to create unnecessary obstacles to trade. Standards providing more protection to consumers, public health, and the environment than do international standards are subject to WTO challenge. Indeed, the TBT Agreement lists as acceptable reasons for not using international standards only fundamental climactic or geographical factors or fundamental technical problems.[9]

In the past decade, the ISO has expanded its purview into "management" standards, which not only have social, environmental and public policy implications, but are also more likely to come into conflict with government-set regulatory standards.[10] The "ISO 14000 series" set standards on environmental-management practices, including providing a best "environmental practice" seal. Yet, a company is not actually required to meet any particular performance standards to obtain this ISO seal.

The ISO's recent expansion into these new issues concerns some environmental, animal welfare, and consumer groups who have tried to participate in the ISO process. Unfortunately, the ISO is designed in a manner that makes meaningful participation by nonprofit groups impossible. The ISO's standards-drafting committee is composed principally of executives from large international corporations, national standards-setting firms and consulting firms. The ISO has belatedly invited delegates from governments and citizens' groups, but the Environmental Benchmark Consulting group, which has researched ISO extensively, notes: "Decision-making in ISO is by member associations and firms. Other participants, while they may be invited and are recorded as 'participants' in a 'consensual' decision-making process, do not have voting rights."[11]

As described in more detail in Chapter 9, the WTO's Dispute Settlement Understanding turned the consensus safeguard on its head by requiring unanimous consensus to *stop* adoption of any WTO panel ruling, empowering three-person

WTO enforcement panels to make binding decisions, enforceable by trade sanctions. The intention of this change was to create a rule-based system in which all WTO member countries were equal; the former system was seen to give dramatically superior leverage to the financially stronger countries. Unfortunately, the new system has instead consolidated the dominant position of countries that can afford a large staff at the WTO and the considerable expense of initiating and prosecuting WTO challenges.[12] Indeed, now the mere threat of a WTO challenge leads some countries to concede because the plaintiff almost always wins and mounting a defense is costly. Worse still, the WTO's rulings are now being sold to the public as technical legal interpretations of commercial law and not recognized as what they are: political and policy decisions.

In a revealing attack of candor, in 1998 then–WTO Secretary General Renato Ruggiero stated that dealing with environmental concerns at the WTO was "doomed to fail and could only damage the global trading system."[13] Ironically, as the antienvironment bias of the WTO has been revealed through its record, the environmental community also has come to oppose the WTO having a role in environmental policy. The environmentalists' concern is that an organization that is so biased in favor of commerce at any cost can only wreak havoc on environmental policy, and thus they demand that the WTO stay out of environmental issues and give Multilateral Environmental Agreements precedence to the extent they conflict with WTO rules.

In contrast, the U.S. government systematically pushes for trade rules to trump environmental treaties. For instance, at the final Biosafety Protocol negotiations in 2000, the U.S. insisted that the pact explicitly contain a provision giving the WTO precedence over the new agreement. This would have destroyed the agreement's purpose, so other countries demanded the opposite language. The final deal contains both (conflicting) clauses. Similarly, at the 2002 Johannesburg Earth Summit, Australia—allegedly fronting for the U.S. and other G7 countries—sought to insert language into the final treaty that gave WTO rules priority over that pact's terms. Although this move was repelled, as described below, the whole Johannesburg Summit was hijacked from its ostensible focus on the environment to an agenda of trade, investment and privatization.

UN Environmental Negotiations Come Under WTO Siege: The Example of the 2002 Johannesburg World Summit on Sustainable Development (WSSD)

A new front has opened in the use of WTO terms to undermine environmental policies: U.S. and some other nations' trade ministers are on an offensive to graft the WTO mission and policies onto all other multilateral agreements. A recent and stunning example is the World Summit on Sustainable Development, which was held in Johannesburg from August 26 to September 4, 2002, ten years after the UN Conference on Environment and Development (UNCED) in Rio de Janeiro.

NGOs originally looked forward to the WSSD as an opportunity to address the failure of the Rio Summit to make tangible progress on sustainable development. However, it was clear from the beginning that other interests aimed to divert the summit. Frustration turned to exasperation as developed countries, particularly the U.S.-led "Juscanz group" (Japan, U.S., Canada, Australia and New Zealand), refused to include language in the summit declaration explicitly noting the often-contradictory relationship between globalization and sustainable development. The G77 (a bloc of developing nations with a common position) and China suggested language calling for a review of systemic flaws in globalization and argued that ecological issues had to be examined in light of international financial systems. The Juscanz countries refused, deadlocking and effectively ending the discussion,[14] and instead demanded language declaring economic growth through trade and globalization as the best hope for the environment.

The only "victory" at the WSSD was the defeat of some outrageous proposed language. The battle came over a clause describing the role of the WSSD as "Continu[ing] to enhance the mutual supportiveness of trade, environment and development in a manner consistent with WTO rights and obligations . . ."[15] NGOs objected to the phrase "consistent with WTO rights and obligations" because it gave the WTO and its dispute-settlement process a controlling role over the WSSD's decisions.[16] The NGOs turned to the G77 developing countries, as well as the EU, to fight against this wording. Negotiations were conducted in secret. In the end, the best the EU and G77 could do was kill the outrageous proposed language in favor of an ambiguous clause promoting "mutual supportiveness" between the UN and WTO systems.[17]

WTO'S NEW BINDING RULES USED TO UNDERMINE ENVIRONMENTAL SAFEGUARDS

Case 1: U.S. Weakens Clean Air Rule to Implement WTO Order

The WTO had only been in operation for a few months when the first attack on an important environmental law was launched. In response to a 1995 challenge initiated by Venezuela and Brazil, a WTO dispute panel in January 1996 ruled that U.S. Clean Air Act regulations violated trade rules.[18] The U.S. was instructed by the WTO to amend the gasoline cleanliness regulations adopted under 1990 amendments to the Clean Air Act.[19] The U.S. implemented the WTO ruling by replacing the regulations in question with a policy that the U.S. Environmental Protection Agency (EPA) had rejected years before as effectively unenforceable.[20]

This case generated significant press coverage as an example of how the WTO could be used to skirt a country's democratic policy-making and judicial systems. It was the first concrete evidence of the WTO's threat to environmental policy. As an early WTO ruling, it also brought credibility to critics' concerns that the WTO could threaten national sovereignty to set and effectively enforce important policies.

The sovereignty critique was especially relevant because the regulation struck down by the WTO had withstood all the challenges available through the U.S. legislative, regulatory and judicial systems. Opponents of the policy, including the Venezuelan government which retained the prominent U.S. law firm Arnold and Porter,[21] had lobbied Congress to change the underlying statute. Failing there, they intervened in the U.S. federal agency rule-making process.[22] When the EPA ultimately issued a regulation the Venezuelan industry opposed, its U.S. lobbyists went back to Congress to try to get the rule changed.[23] Lobbyists and lawyers representing U.S. oil refineries and related interests also tried to weaken both the law and regulation. The attempts by both the domestic and foreign interests failed. Meanwhile, U.S. environmental groups used similar tactics to get the policy strengthened because they believed the compromise regulation was too weak. These efforts also failed and the proposed rule became final.

At this point, with no further avenues for challenge remaining, U.S. domestic oil refineries began to comply. They claimed to have invested $37 billion to implement the policy.[24] The oil industries of Venezuela and Brazil, on the other hand, renewed their attack, with the governments of the two nations filing a WTO challenge on behalf of the oil industries. Only there, in a closed WTO tribunal, out of the public eye and before unaccountable, unelected trade bureaucrats, did opponents of the Clean Air Act regulations finally find success.

The Clean Air ruling confirmed environmentalists' gravest fears about the WTO. In typical WTO doublespeak, the panel rhetorically affirmed the right of sovereignty over environmental matters while acknowledging that, in practice, countries' environmental laws must conform to WTO rules: "WTO members were free to set their own environmental objectives, but they were bound to implement those objectives only through measures consistent with [WTO's] provisions."[25] This line is often quoted by WTO defenders to claim the U.S. "won" this case even though, in fact, the U.S. was ordered to weaken the regulations in question.

Clean Air Rules Attacked at the WTO

The Clean Air Act amendments were designed to regulate pollution attributed to motor vehicle fuels, which, with the exception of leaded gasoline, had been neglected in previous pollution programs. Gasoline contaminants produce emissions that result in ozone, smog and toxic air pollutants and are a principal cause of ground-level ozone.[26]

The reasons for the amendments were well documented. The adverse human health effects of ground-level ozone include respiratory irritation, breathing problems, aggravation of asthma, inflammation and damage to the lining of the lungs as well as a reduction in the immune system's ability to fight off bacterial respiratory infections.[27] A severe increase in the incidence of asthma in the U.S. corresponded to the increase in smog due to emissions from gasoline in the 1980s.[28]

In 1994, the EPA issued regulations implementing Congress's 1990 Clean Air Act amendments, which, among other things, required the cleanliness of gasoline sold in the most polluted U.S. cities to improve by 15% over 1990 levels, and all gasoline sold elsewhere in the U.S. to maintain levels of cleanliness at least equal to 1990 levels.

The difficulty in designing the regulation was finding an enforceable, trustworthy and economically feasible way to ensure that gasoline met the standards. The EPA could have simply set a single, absolute cleanliness target and required all refiners to comply immediately. However, given the varying levels of contaminants in gasoline produced at different refineries, that option would have resulted in a lowest-common-denominator approach because many believed that a uniform high standard would cause gasoline shortages and price hikes. On the other hand, a flexible approach—setting cleanliness standards based on each refinery's actual past performance—was also problematic. Some gas refiners (including U.S. refiners that had been in business less than six months and most foreign refiners over whom the EPA had no enforcement authority) lacked sufficiently reliable data to calculate an individual baseline standard.

In an attempt to minimize market disruptions and maximize health protection, the EPA settled on an interim solution: Those gasoline producers with EPA documentation of their 1990 gasoline cleanliness levels would have their improvement target set from that data. Gasoline from domestic refiners without documentation (new ones or those with filing violations) and from foreign refiners that sold less than 80% of their gasoline in the U.S. would have to match the average actual 1990 contaminant level of all gas refiners able to provide full documentation. This rule was set to expire in 1998, giving the EPA five years to obtain the additional data it felt were necessary to determine a single cleanliness target.

The WTO Challenge

Venezuela and Brazil claimed that the EPA regulation put their gasoline industries at an unfair disadvantage. The structure of the regulation created the unintended possibility that imported gasoline that failed to meet the average could be rejected while equally dirty gasoline from a U.S. refiner whose individual baseline was at the bottom end could be allowed.

The WTO panel sided with Venezuela's and Brazil's oil industries. The panel ruled that the EPA's mechanism to enforce the congressionally mandated air standards could result in discriminatory *effects* favoring U.S. refiners over foreign refiners.[29] A U.S. WTO appeal failed.[30] The final 1996 WTO Appellate Body ruling held that although air qualified under the Article XX GATT exception as an "exhaustible natural resource" worthy of protection, the U.S. policy to conserve the resource was not covered by the exception because the U.S. policy could result in a situation that discriminated against foreign gasoline.[31] The WTO instructed the U.S. to change the policy.

U.S. Implements WTO Ruling

In its submissions defending the Clean Air Act regulation, the U.S. claimed that if the regulation were changed it would be possible for annual nitrous oxide (N_2O)

emissions from imported gasoline to increase 5–7%.[32] The WTO's ruling forced the U.S. to make a "no-win" choice: repeal the regulation and permit imports of gasoline with higher contamination levels (and ironically put U.S. refiners at a competitive disadvantage for having made the investments to implement the regulations), or keep the policy and face $150 million in trade sanctions each year the U.S. failed to comply.

The decision had major implications: Venezuela was then the single largest exporter of oil products to the U.S., supplying 16% of the total U.S. crude oil product imports and 19% of all gasoline imports.[33] In August 1997, the EPA announced that it would implement the WTO order and replace the regulation with a new one that was "consistent with the obligations of the United States under the World Trade Organization."[34] The new WTO-consistent rules are identical to an industry proposal that the EPA had previously contended was unenforceable and too costly.[35] Environmental groups sued to stay the new regulation without success.[36]

The gasoline case inspired a run of successful challenges against hard-won environmental and public-health laws.

Case 2: Clinton and Bush Administrations Both Gut Dolphin Protections After Trade Rulings

Under amendments to the U.S. Marine Mammal Protection Act, the sale by domestic or foreign fishers of tuna caught with encirclement nets, known as purse seines, was banned in the U.S. in 1988. Over 30 years, seven million dolphins were drowned, crushed or otherwise killed as a result of purse-seine tuna fishing.[37] Two of four affected species of dolphin, the eastern spinner and the northeastern offshore spotted dolphin, have been designated "depleted" due to purse-seine fishing methods.[38]

In the 1980s, an environmentalist who slipped aboard a fishing boat as a cook captured the slaughter on videotape. The resulting furor—including millions of children writing to Congress to "Save the Dolphins"—led to the "dolphin-safe" tuna provisions of the MMPA.[39]

The GATT Dolphin Cases

In 1991, in a case initiated by Mexico, a GATT panel ruled against Section 101(a)(2) of the MMPA, which excluded from the U.S. market tuna caught by domestic or foreign fishers using purse seines.[40] Mexican environmental groups split over their views of the case. Some argued that the case was an example of the trade regime attacking environmental policy. Others joined with the government's claim that the U.S. should not be allowed to require standards of conduct outside its boarder even regarding a product destined for its domestic market. The panel interpreted language in GATT's Article III, which prohibits discrimination between "like products" on the basis of *where* they are produced to also forbid distinguishing between products based on *how* they are produced. The panel ruled that only the physical characteristics, not how a good was made or harvested, can be considered in determining if two products are "like products."

There is no basis in GATT rules for the panel to have determined that PPMs (distinctions in how a product is produced) cannot be considered in deciding if products are "like." However, in making this interpretation, this and later trade panels threatened the long list of environmental laws in countries around the world that focus on *how* seafood is harvested or *how* paper is manufactured. Thus, under GATT/WTO jurisprudence, unless there is literally dolphin meat in a can of tuna, making it physically different, a can of tuna caught with dolphin-deadly nets must be treated exactly the same as one caught by dolphin-safe methods.

The next year the European Community, which sought to export prepared tuna processed from fish caught by encirclement, launched its own challenge to the U.S. law. In 1994, GATT again ruled against the U.S. dolphin-protection law.[41]

In both cases, the U.S. argued that because dolphin protection is a legitimate environmental objective and the embargo was applied to both domestic and foreign tuna industries, the law would fall well within the protections of GATT Article XX(b), which provides an exemption for otherwise GATT-inconsistent laws which are necessary to protect human, plant or animal health or life. Both GATT panels rejected this argument. The first panel found that the law was not "necessary" to protect dolphin health because, in the panel's opinion, the U.S. could have attempted to protect dolphins through other GATT-consistent measures. It also found that the U.S. law targeted tuna fishing largely outside U.S. borders and ruled that exception applied only to actions taken inside a nation's borders.[42] This narrow interpretation of Article XX's reach was astounding, given that, inherently, many of the common natural resources such as fish or air, ostensibly covered by the exception, are not confined to any single country's territory.

GATT: Nations Cannot Regulate Imports Made Under Conditions that Violate International Human Rights or Labor Standards

The same rule that was used to undermine U.S. dolphin protection could also hamstring attempts to make corporations and governments accountable to universally recognized human and labor rights, such as bans of products made with slave or child labor. This principle also puts humane slaughter and other animal-welfare laws at risk of WTO challenge. Effectively, countries can enforce child labor, animal welfare and other PPM-based policies for domestic producers, but they must allow imported goods that do not comply with these rules. Under WTO rules, the U.S. federal law banning the sale of child-labor products can only be applied to products produced in the U.S., not to imports.

The WTO panel in the European challenge disagreed with the first panel's conclusion that a country can never, under GATT rules, protect resources outside of its territory if such protections limit trade. However, it agreed with the first panel that the "dolphin-safe" law was not "necessary."

In addition, the panel in the European challenge concluded that a nation cannot require another country to change domestic laws in exchange for market access.[43] The panel ruled that the U.S. could pressure individual tuna producers to change their behavior, but that one GATT country could not condition market access on producers' home country governments implementing certain policies. This line of reasoning would be recycled in a similar WTO case involving a U.S. embargo on shrimp caught without using devices to protect sea turtles (see below).

However, given that the rulings against the U.S. "dolphin-safe" law were issued by GATT (not WTO) panels, they were not automatically enforceable. Indeed, worried that implementation of the controversial 1991 GATT case—it had been dubbed GATTzilla vs. Flipper—could threaten NAFTA's 1993 congressional approval, the U.S. and Mexico originally used the GATT consensus process to block further action.

However, in 1995, with NAFTA implemented and the WTO enforcement mechanism now in effect, Mexico threatened a WTO enforcement case against the U.S. for failure to implement the 1991 dolphin ruling. To avoid the political embarrassment of having the WTO order the U.S. to weaken the dolphin protection (or face millions of dollars in trade sanctions), the Clinton administration obtained a reprieve from Mexico and launched a two-year campaign that ultimately resulted in the gutting of the MMPA.

Clinton Administration Guts Dolphin Law to Comply with GATT

President Clinton sent a letter to then–Mexican President Ernesto Zedillo declaring that changing the U.S. law to comply with the GATT ruling "is a top priority for my Administration and for me personally," promising to take action to satisfy Mexico's GATT claims within the first 30 days of his second term.[44] It would not prove easy to keep this promise.

The Clinton administration recruited several members of Congress with notoriously anti-environmental voting records, such as Representative Randy "Duke" Cunningham, a California Republican, and Senator John Breaux, a Louisiana Democrat, to introduce legislation to conform the MMPA to the GATT ruling, quickly nicknamed the "Dolphin Death Act" by many environmental groups.[45]

The MMPA's original champions, such as Senator Barbara Boxer and Representative George Miller, both California Democrats, and a coalition of environmental, consumer, and other public-interest groups were able to stall the progress of the Dolphin Death Act in 1996. However, after another yearlong battle, a slightly different version of the legislation, formally named the International Dolphin Conservation Program Act (IDCP), was passed in August 1997.[46]

The weakening of the MMPA required to implement the GATT ruling only passed Congress after a huge Clinton-administration push, led by then–Undersecretary of State Timothy Wirth and Vice President Al Gore.[47] The change meant two things: First, for the first time in decades tuna caught with the deadly purse seines could be sold in the U.S. Second, it also authorized imports caught with purse seines from countries that were members of the Inter-American Tropical Tuna Commission (IATTC) (including Costa Rica, Ecuador, El Salvador, France, Guatemala, Japan, Mexico, Nicaragua, Panama, Peru, the United States, Vanuatu and Venezuela) to carry the "dolphin-safe" label that consumers have come to know and trust if the tuna met certain criteria. An IATTC dolphin safety observer required on each tuna ship had to certify that he or she had not observed any dolphin deaths.

Effectively, the new law changed the definition of "dolphin-safe" to enable the tuna caught with encirclement nets to get the "dolphin-safe" label, and it based the "dolphin-safe" determination on each particular "set" (netting) in which the tuna were caught, not on the boat's overall record. However, the administration was forced to add a compromise provision: the change to the definition of "dolphin-safe" was to go into effect only if the National Marine Fisheries Service (NMFS) concluded that certain techniques (like using divers and other means to free dolphins) mitigated the effect of encirclement fishing.

On April 29, 1999, the Commerce Department announced that based on the results of the preliminary report by NMFS[48] it would implement the weakened labeling standard for dolphin-safe tuna.[49] The preliminary study concluded that dolphin mortality had declined in areas where monitors were aboard fishing boats using purse seines, but that dolphin populations were not recovering from decades of decline caused by encirclement netting, despite the use of monitors.[50]

Nevertheless, then–Commerce Secretary William Daley issued a determination declaring that there was insufficient evidence that encirclement fishing was having a significant adverse impact on depleted dolphin stocks. As a result, the "dolphin-safe" label standard was to be changed effective February 2, 2000, to permit the use of "dolphin-safe" labeling when purse seines were used.

The U.S. Commerce Department claimed that the new regulation would allow only tuna from catches during which no dolphin deaths were observed to bear the "dolphin-safe" label.[51] However, tuna trawlers are a football field in length, the nets are miles in circumference and there is only one observer required per ship, making it physically impossible to monitor thoroughly. Moreover, to enforce this policy, the U.S. would have had to track all tuna imports from the moment they were caught in the Eastern Tropical Pacific (the region the policy covered) to the time they entered the U.S. consumer market. This presented an impossible task for regulators, which is why the old law operated on a country-by-country basis (meaning a country was responsible for regulating the conduct of its tuna fleet and had to certify the entire fishery did not use encirclement techniques in order to import tuna to the U.S. from that country), not on a catch-by-catch basis. It remains unclear how the U.S. could, with any confidence, distinguish among tuna shipments that have involved the death of dolphins and those that have not. Instead, regulators would have to rely on the "dolphin-safe" reports of the producers themselves—those with the greatest incentive to downplay dolphin deaths. Consumer and environmental groups said that the new policy would degrade the "dolphin-safe" label to a cynical marketing ploy.[52]

Before the new rules actually went into effect, a group of environmentalists led by Earth Island Institute filed suit against Secretary Daley in federal court in August 1999.[53] The court temporarily stayed implementation of the policy change while the case went to trial. In April 2000, the U.S. District Court of Northern California ruled against the Commerce Department, deciding that tuna caught by dolphin encirclement could not bear the "dolphin-safe" label.[54] In July 2001, the Commerce Department lost an appeal at the 9th Circuit Federal Court of Appeals, which unanimously upheld the ruling.[55] This dealt with half the issue: while dolphin-unsafe tuna could still be imported, it could not be labeled "dolphin-safe."

Mexico remained adamant that the U.S. implement the change to the definition of "dolphin-safe" so that Mexican tuna could be marketed with the label. The U.S. had prohibited the import of tuna from Mexico altogether between 1990 and 2000 because the Mexican tuna fleet used purse seines.[56] In 2000, at the same time Secretary Daley issued his rules for certification of dolphin-safe tuna, he lifted the embargo on Mexican tuna.[57] In May 2000, NMFS had certified that Mexico was meeting obligations under the Inter-American Tropical Tuna Commission and the International Dolphin Conservation Program, meaning that Mexican tuna could bear the "dolphin-safe" label if the new definition was implemented.[58]

Meanwhile, in a separate federal court case in February 2000, several environmental and humane groups led by Defenders of Wildlife had filed a request for a Temporary Restraining Order at the Court of International Trade to prevent the lifting of the embargo on Mexican tuna.[59] While the lawsuit was proceeding, the 1999 Daley decision to lift the Mexican tuna embargo was implemented. The court ruled against Defenders of Wildlife on all issues in December 2001.[60]

Although Mexican tuna without "dolphin-safe" labels was permitted into the U.S. through 2002, Mexico has been unable to export dolphin-safe tuna because some fishers continued to chase and encircle dolphins, and because of other court rulings such tuna could not be labeled dolphin-safe. Recently, the Mexican government, which has invested millions in high-tech factory fishing fleets to sell fish in the U.S. market, has threatened to withdraw from the International Dolphin Conservation Program under the IATTC or to bring another WTO challenge if the U.S. does not implement the weaker "dolphin-safe" labeling rules.[61]

In 2002, the Bush administration's Commerce Secretary Don Evans attempted to introduce regulations substantively identical to the Daley rules.[62] In September 2002, NMFS released the final report on dolphin populations in the Eastern Tropical Pacific, required by the 1997 statute. The report found that dolphin stocks were depleted, that purse seines could exert stresses on dolphins (especially by separating mother and calf and in dolphin muscle injuries) and that the dolphin population growth was "not consistent with recovery from depletion," but the NMFS report concluded that it was impossible to determine whether population recovery would be hindered by purse-seine fishing.[63]

On the basis of the final NMFS report, the Commerce Department determined that there was "no significant impact" from purse-seine fishing and that the "dolphin-safe" label could be used on tuna if the injury or killing of dolphins was not observed during any particular fishing haul.[64] On New Year's Eve 2002, when Americans were not focused on public policy, the Bush administration announced it would allow "dolphin-safe" labels on tuna caught using dolphin encirclement.

Environmental and animal-welfare groups were outraged. The actual contents of the NMFS report had highlighted how dolphin populations were depleted. Northeastern offshore spotted dolphin stocks were at 20% of their former numbers and eastern spinner dolphins were at 35% of their former numbers.[65] The NMFS report noted that thousands of dolphins were dying in tuna nets—especially baby dolphins.[66] "A finding of no significant adverse impact is simply indefensible," said Humane Society Special Counsel Kitty Block.[67] Indeed, after the Commerce Department decision, the *New York Times* reported that two scientists who studied dolphin stress related to purse-seine fishery issues charged that their research grants had been terminated because they had not reaffirmed the Bush and Clinton administrations' claims.[68]

In January 2003 Earth Island Institute and eight other environmental and animal-welfare groups filed suit against Commerce Secretary Evans in federal court in San Francisco,[69] and on January 21, the U.S. District Court for the Northern District of California stayed the implementation of Secretary Evans's proposed changes.[70] On April 10, 2003, the U.S. District Court issued a temporary injunction to block the Commerce Department's regulation change while it proceeded to rule on the underlying claim (that the regulation violated U.S. law). On May 6, 2003, the same court denied the Mexican and Venezuelan tuna industries efforts to intervene in the lawsuit. Earth Island is confident that it will prevail in its suit on the basis of the scientific findings in the NMFS report.[71] Mexico has indicated that if the Bush administration loses the labeling case in domestic court, Mexico will bring a new challenge at the WTO.[72]

Case 3: WTO Rules Against U.S. Implementation of Environmental Treaty Protecting Endangered Sea Turtles

Provisions of the U.S. Endangered Species Act allowed sale of shrimp in the U.S. only if the shrimp was caught in nets equipped with turtle excluder devices (TEDs).[73] These devices, basically trapdoors within nets, are designed to allow sea turtles to escape from shrimp nets. The regulation implemented U.S. obligations under the Convention on International Trade in Endangered Species (CITES), a multilateral environmental treaty. In late 1998, a WTO panel ruled that the U.S. policy violated trade rules and ordered the U.S. to rewrite its sea turtle–protection policy.

Worldwide, the turtle population has plummeted, and all sea turtles that inhabit U.S. waters are listed as endangered or threatened.[74] Sea turtles are on the top list of species to be protected under CITES. Shrimp nets entangle, drown, dismember and kill as many as 150,000 endangered or threatened sea turtles each year. Indeed, industrial-scale shrimping kills more sea turtles than all other human threats to turtles combined.[75] Industrial-scale shrimp fishing, with huge boats employing massive drag nets, is also causing a depletion of stocks that is resulting in a crisis for small-scale coastal fisherfolk in many nations. Environmental activists in some developing countries argued that the case turned the issue into a North–South fight when the real issue was the devastation to turtles and shrimp being caused by industrial-scale over-fishing.

Under section 609 of the Endangered Species Act, all shrimp sold in the U.S. had to be caught using TEDs. Costing from $50 to $300, TEDs are a relatively inexpensive way to reduce sea turtle deaths by as much as 97%—without appreciably decreasing shrimp catches.[76]

The governments of India, Malaysia, Pakistan and Thailand joined forces to challenge the U.S. law. They repeated the argument that WTO rules forbid countries from distinguishing between products based on how they are produced.[77] Australia, El Salvador, the EU, Guatemala, Hong Kong, Japan, Nigeria, the Philippines, Singapore and Venezuela made third-party submissions to the WTO panel, also arguing that the U.S. law violated WTO rules.

Under the argument used by these nations—the same one used in the tuna-dolphin case—all shrimp are "like products" and therefore must be allowed into the U.S. market, regardless of whether or not the shrimp are caught using methods that kill sea turtles. These nations also argued that under WTO rules, the U.S. is not allowed to create or maintain policies that have a reach outside U.S. borders.

The U.S. argued that it was allowed to protect animal life, as long as the law applied equally to U.S. and foreign shrimp producers. Indeed, unlike the MMPA provisions challenged in the tuna-dolphin case, the turtle policy was *exactly* identical for foreign and domestic fishers. Thus, the U.S. argued that the shrimp law qualified for an exception under GATT Article XX.

The WTO panel disagreed. "We note that the issue in dispute was not the urgency of protection of sea turtles. . . . It was not our task to review generally the desirability or necessity of the environmental objectives of the U.S. policy on sea turtle conservation. In our opinion, Members are free to set their own environmental objectives. However, they are bound to implement these objectives in such a way that is consistent with their WTO obligations, not depriving the WTO Agreement of its object and purpose."[78]

The panel ruled that the U.S. law was *designed* to interfere with trade and thus the Article XX exceptions were inapplicable. This interpretation of the GATT and WTO rules totally eviscerated the entire exceptions clause of GATT. Remarkably, the panel went further and declared that because the regulations were unilaterally imposed on U.S. trading partners, the law deprived the WTO of its object and purpose of establishing a multilateral trade regime, regardless of the non–trade related objective that was being pursued and the lack of discrimination between domestic and foreign fisheries.

Major U.S. environmental organizations quickly denounced the decision and urged the Clinton administration to keep the sea turtle protections and to instead attempt to reform the WTO substantially—or to withdraw from it.[79] Even the pro-WTO *New York Times* editorialized about the "Sea Turtles Warning" (contradicting its past admonitions about WTO critics' unfounded concerns) by urging the WTO to reconsider and the U.S. not to change the law.[80] The U.S government appealed the ruling.[81]

In October 1998, the WTO Appellate Body reaffirmed the decision that the U.S. law was WTO-illegal. However, the Appellate Body ruling was also designed to calm the legal and political storm caused by the lower tribunal's ruling. First, the appellate ruling was packed with soothing (although not binding) rhetoric about the importance of environmental protection. Second, the Appellate Body reversed some of the most egregious and capricious elements of the lower panel's logic. For instance, the Appellate Body ruled that the Endangered Species Act *theoretically* could be covered by Article XX exceptions.[82] Reaching impressive heights of legal sophistry, the panel held that the law could have qualified for an environmental exception under Article XX but did not do so in this case. The office of the U.S. Trade Representative (USTR) issued a press release claiming the WTO had reversed its ruling on the U.S. turtle protections. Corporate and think-tank defenders of the WTO who have read only the news release and not the actual ruling will often claim the U.S. "won" this case. In fact, however, not only did the Appellate Body maintain the order for the U.S. to change the policy, but the U.S. has done so.

For those who have read the entire ruling, the Appellate Body's decision has been viewed as an attempt to defuse the criticism of environmentalists, while still maintaining the WTO's policy of giving trade primacy over all other goals. For instance, the Appellate Body acknowledged that sea turtles are endangered and that there is a legitimate interest in protecting and preserving them. It also acknowledged the appropriateness of the U.S. turtle excluder device policy. "We have not decided that the protection and preservation of the environment is of no significance to the Members of the WTO. Clearly, it is. We have not decided that the sovereign nations that are Members of the WTO cannot adopt effective measures to protect endangered species, such as sea turtles. Clearly, they can and should."[83] However, despite this positive-sounding political rhetoric, the WTO Appellate Body's bottom line was that the U.S. measure violated WTO rules because the law was implemented in a way that was unjustifiably and arbitrarily discriminatory.

The Appellate Body then recommended that the U.S. change its turtle protection law to comply with the ruling, leading one trade policy expert to quip, "Good dicta [legal rhetoric] for environmentalists, but I wouldn't want to be a sea turtle."[84]

Perversely, the ruling would put producers who had invested in TEDs at a competitive disadvantage. According to one shrimper, "We are the ones who have to pay the price to save the turtle. I thought we were going to have a level playing field to compete, but apparently not."[85]

As U.S. industries have observed that the WTO is hostile to strong environmental safeguards, these industries have begun to lobby against domestic environmental legislation on the basis that it disadvantages them vis-à-vis their foreign competitors, whose noncompliance is effectively sanctioned by the WTO. The combination of WTO environmental hostility and related industry pressure will make it increasingly difficult for any countries to assert environmental leadership in the absence of often slow or impossible international consensus.

The Clinton administration decided to comply by revising only the regulations, not the underlying statute. The U.S., India, Malaysia, Pakistan and Thailand had agreed that the U.S. could have 13 months to implement the WTO ruling.[86]

U.S. environmental groups unsuccessfully sued to halt implementation of the regulation. Although the Court of International Trade agreed with the environmentalists' claim that the regulations violated the Endangered Species Act, it refused to issue a stay halting the regulation's implementation.[87] On July 15, 1999, the U.S. informed the WTO that it would have a new regulatory structure in place by February 2000.[88]

The new policy was based on a "shipment-by-shipment" assessment of TEDs use, which allows certification of shrimp hauls catch-by-catch, rather than by looking at entire fleets. By deciding to allow the certification on a shipment-by-shipment basis, the new rules allow the certification of any shrimp catch that comes to port with turtle-protective technology, whether or not that ship caught the shrimp. Environmentalists argued that the new rules encourage the transshipment—effectively shrimp laundering—by shrimpers who may have significant turtle "by-catch."

In October 1999, the U.S. made its first approval of shrimp imports under the new rule, allowing in shrimp from the Spencer Gulf region of Australia under the new certification program.[89] Environmentalists immediately decried the decision to allow shrimp imports from a developed nation that refused to implement such cheap and effective technology as TEDs.[90]

Meanwhile, Malaysia brought a new WTO dispute in October 2000 against the U.S. for failing to fully implement the WTO ruling. Malaysia argued that the U.S. was required to amend the underlying statute (the Endangered Species Act) to remove import restrictions and to certify Malaysian shrimp for import even though Malaysia could not comply with the new shipment-by-shipment certification process.[91] A WTO panel ruled that the U.S. changes to the regulations satisfied the WTO ruling in the initial case. The panel also ruled that the U.S. decision under the new watered-down policy not to certify Malaysian shrimp although it was allowing imports from other developing nations was permitted under Article XX(g) of the GATT, which covers policies related to conservation of exhaustible natural resources.[92] In October, the Appellate Body upheld the panel's ruling.[93]

Meanwhile, in March 2002, the Department of Commerce prevailed in an appeal against the environmentalists' win at the Court of International Trade. The U.S. Court of Appeals for the Federal Circuit denied a request to rehear the case.[94] On November 6, 2002, the Turtle Island Restoration Network filed a formal petition with the U.S. Supreme Court requesting that it overturn the U.S. Court of Appeals for the Federal Circuit.[95] In April 2003, the Supreme Court refused to review the case, leaving in place the appellate court's approval of the weakened regulation.[96]

The State Department has certified 41 countries' shrimp imports as compliant with the Endangered Species Act under the new, less stringent but WTO-compliant rules.[97]

NOW MERE THREATS OF WTO ACTION ARE CHILLING ENVIRONMENTAL INITIATIVES

The WTO's systematic rulings against environmental policies are having a chilling effect on environmental innovation. Now, often the mere threat of WTO action can deter a government from following through on proposed public-interest rules and regulations. The formal cases may just be the tip of the iceberg relative to the threats of action that result in negative effects on environmental protection.

Many such threats have been made, linked to WTO provisions in the Agreement on Technical Barriers to Trade. The U.S. has threatened Japan to weaken its clean air laws and has attacked an EU prohibition on fur from animals trapped with cruel steel jaw leg-hold traps. The U.S. electronics industry got the trade office to threaten a European policy aimed at reducing the pollution caused by electronics equipment such as computers and TVs. U.S. and European toxics and health campaigners were dragged into expending significant time and resources to counter the WTO threat.[98] An enormous amount of U.S. environmental and consumer-group time and resources was similarly diverted to counter the 1996 WTO threat made by the U.S. on behalf of an industry coalition opposing European eco-labels.[99] Threats of WTO action are becoming a chillingly regular phenomenon after new environmental initiatives are unveiled. For instance, in May 2003, when the EU announced a new "Registration, Evaluation and Authorization of Chemicals" (REACH) program, the chemical industry and the U.S. government charged that the policy, which is widely supported by U.S. health and environmental advocates, would violate WTO rules.[100]

Sample Threat 1: Hong Kong Complains About U.S. Anti–Invasive Species Rule at WTO

On November 11, 1998, Hong Kong registered a complaint against the U.S. at a meeting of the WTO Sanitary and Phytosanitary Committee over a new U.S. regulation requiring solid-wood packing materials from China and Hong Kong to be heat-treated, fumigated or treated with preservatives before being exported to the U.S.[101] The U.S. Animal and Plant Health Inspection Service (APHIS) adopted the rule in response to infestations in the U.S. of the Asian Longhorned Beetle near ports and airports, which was traced to wooden packing materials from China and Hong Kong.[102] Many goods are shipped in wood crates and on wood pallets, and these packing materials and raw imported logs can carry a variety of damaging wood-eating insects that have no natural predators in the U.S. to keep them in check.

The Asian Longhorned Beetle lives off of tree tissue during the larvae stage and then burrows out of the tree, leaving one-half-inch holes. Since Asian Longhorned Beetles cannot be eradicated by pesticides once they have infested a tree, the only way to get rid of them is to uproot and burn the infected tree. The Asian Longhorned Beetle is anticipated to cost the U.S. approximately $138 billion if it continues to spread across the country.[103] In two U.S. states—New York and Illinois—the Asian Longhorned Beetle infestation has presented such a significant problem that the U.S. Department of Agriculture has implemented an Asian Longhorned Beetle Cooperative Eradication Program.[104] Through this program, agriculture officials have destroyed over 5,700 trees in and around New York City and over 1,500 trees in the Chicago area.[105] The eradication programs in New York and Illinois are expected to cost a total of $365 million between 2001 and 2009.[106]

The beetle has been detected at 30 other sites, including warehouses in Sauk County, Wisconsin, and Morton Grove, Illinois.[107] The USDA program anticipates inoculating 46,000 susceptible trees to prevent further infestation of the beetle.[108]

As international trade has brought an increasing number of exotic species to the U.S., from sea lampreys to kudzu to gypsy moths and zebra mussels, U.S. government agencies have stepped up efforts to catch infestations early to avoid irreversible environmental damage or monumentally expensive eradication programs. Invasive species that out-compete native species are the second leading cause of species extinction.[109]

However, being a member of the WTO may make it more difficult for the U.S. or other countries to create effective policies on invasive species. China, which was not in the WTO at the time the beetle rule was issued, criticized the U.S. policy regarding wood shipping materials but had no recourse to the WTO dispute body, and thus had to accept U.S. treatment guidelines or face an embargo of its goods packed in untreated wood.[110] On the other hand, Hong Kong, as a WTO member, was empowered to challenge the U.S. policy and threatened to do so. To date, Hong Kong has not filed a formal WTO challenge; nor has China, which is now a WTO member.

However, in an attempt to prevent a WTO challenge, a U.S. federal agency charged with the Asian Longhorned Beetle eradication effort is now considering replacing its current regulation with an international standard, as required by the WTO's standards harmonization provisions, which would provide less protection against this devastating insect infestation.[111] Among the reasons that the USDA has listed for reconsidering its policy is promulgation of a new international standard by the International Plant Protection Convention (IPPC) on mitigating pest risk from wood packing material. The IPPC is a multilateral convention adopted in 1952 to prevent the introduction and spread of pests and diseases of plants and plant products, and to promote measures for pest control.[112] The IPPC is recognized by the WTO as an international standard-setting institution whose standards are presumed to be WTO-legal. In the notice of Intent to Prepare an Environmental Impact Study on the proposed regulations, the USDA stated, "In addition to establishing the necessary framework for protecting U.S. agriculture and forests, we must give full consideration to harmonizing our regulations with the new international standards. . . ."

In its new standard, the IPPC requires that wood packing materials be heated to 133 degrees Fahrenheit for 30 minutes or fumigated with methyl bromide and marked when imported to all countries.[113] Under the present U.S. rule, wood packing material must be heat treated at a temperature of 160 degrees Fahrenheit for 75 minutes.[114] There is little information about the basic biology of the Asian Longhorned Beetle, so the temperature that will kill the larvae has only been estimated (between 95 and 104 degrees Fahrenheit).[115] It is possible that the shorter heat treatment at lower temperatures may not kill the larvae as effectively.

As an alternative to heat treatment, the IPPC presents fumigation with methyl bromide, a highly toxic chemical that poses significant environmental risks,[116] and human health risks such as weakness, vomiting, muscle spasms, coma and convulsions.[117] Exposure to high concentrations of methyl bromide can result in permanent central nervous system and respiratory system failure, as well as specific and severe damage to the lungs, eyes and skin.[118] In some instances, permanent disabilities and even death may occur.[119] In addition to the potential debilitating effects that this chemical can have upon humans, methyl bromide has an equally destructive impact upon the environment, as it is considered to be a significant ozone-depleting substance. Methyl bromide is so potent that the EPA has implemented a phaseout of the chemical, scheduled to reach 100% completion by 2005. The only exceptions to the phaseout are pre-shipment and quarantine uses and emergency uses.[120]

As of January 2003, the USDA had not issued a final rule regarding treatment of wood packaging materials and the Asian Longhorned Beetle. However, in October of 2002, it described the IPPC option as the preferred alternative. The USDA stated that, "APHIS must work within the framework of the international agreements to which the U.S. is a party."[121]

Yet, the harmonization of U.S. treatment of wood packing materials down to either the less potent or the more toxic WTO-recognized international standards potentially provides a greater opportunity for Asian Longhorned Beetles and other invasive pests to thrive in wood packing materials.

Sample Threat 2: Europeans Weaken Ban on Cruelly Trapped Fur

The European Union has long been concerned with animal-welfare issues and has enacted progressive anticruelty laws relating to farming, animal transport and slaughter practices. In 1991, the EU tried to extend this tradition to fur trapping, but encountered WTO-based threats by the U.S. and Canada that ultimately undermined the new proposal.

The EU prohibited the use of steel jaw leg-hold traps for hunting 13 fur-bearing animals as of 1995.[122] Importation of pelts from this list of animals would be banned starting in 1995 unless the exporting country forbid the use of steel jaw leg-hold traps or met other humane trapping standards.[123]

North American and Russian trappers and furriers contended that these laws and rules constituted unfair trade barriers. They focused on the fact that few of the species covered by the EU law were native to Europe.[124] Steel jaw leg-hold traps are allowed in many U.S. states, Canada and Russia. More than four million wild animals are trapped for the fashion industry every year in the U.S., the majority of them caught with steel jaw leg-hold traps.[125]

Those traps operate with a powerful spring that snaps a metal jaw shut, pinning an animal by its leg. This technique avoids damaging the animal's pelt, but unlike snare leg-hold traps, the steel jaw is painful, restraining the animals to await the trappers, who may not come for days, to bludgeon them to death. Some studies estimate that as many as one in four animals trapped in steel jaw leg-hold traps chew off their own limb to escape.[126]

Before the EU rule actually went into effect, the U.S. was already moving to protect U.S. trappers, and Canada had been expected to file a GATT challenge.[127] The EU granted a one-year delay of the regulations.[128] Negotiations continued between the trapping countries and the EU, but as a January 1996 extended deadline for the ban grew closer, the Clinton administration said that it would join Canada in a WTO challenge if negotiations broke down.[129]

Then–EU External Trade Minister Leon Brittan extended the waiver for yet another year, citing the threat of a WTO challenge and ongoing negotiations with the U.S., Canada and Russia.[130] The move triggered outrage in Europe, and the European Parliament reaffirmed support for the ban by vote. The EU Commission instructed customs officials to continue ignoring the ban, despite the European Parliamentary vote.[131] Only the Netherlands upheld, implemented and enforced the ban on time.[132]

Negotiations continued throughout 1996, but proceeded slowly, with Canada and Russia leaning toward a watered-down phaseout of leg-hold traps, which U.S. negotiators opposed as too tough.[133] By May 1997, Russia and Canada had signed off on a deal.[134] The European Parliament delayed a vote on the deal because parliamentarians felt that the proposal undermined the policy it had approved twice[135] and because the U.S. refused to join the pact.[136]

When the U.S. then offered to phase out steel jaw leg-hold traps over eight years, Europe initially rejected the proposal.[137] After more WTO saber rattling, a final weak deal was struck with the U.S. The proposal allowed a six-year phaseout of steel jaw leg-hold traps during which the U.S. could continue to export fur to Europe.[138] Although the U.S.-EU agreement contains similar substantive standards as Canada's and Russia's agreement on trap performance standards, the U.S. agreement does not bind the parties to adhere to the standards or have any provisions on dispute resolution.[139] The final agreement encouraged research into alternative models of trapping and monitoring to encourage U.S. state governments to implement the standards. However, the U.S. declared it had limited ability to force the states to meet the standards, and in an annex to the agreement, the U.S. threatened to challenge the EU rules at the WTO if the EU tried to enforce the ban on fur caught with leg-hold traps.[140]

The WTO threat effectively succeeded in halting the EU humane policy. The language in the U.S.-EU agreement is sufficiently vague as to make it unenforceable.[141] Carlos Pimenta, a Portuguese member of the European Parliament and an animal-welfare proponent, slammed the U.S. agreement, noting, "It is especially bad as regards to observation and enforcement." Said Anita Pollack, another member of European Parliament, "In reality it is a non-agreement. I would liken it to the Cheshire Cat, because all you can see is its smile."[142]

The outcome allows fur caught with steel jaw leg-hold traps to continue to be sold in Europe, providing no incentive for the U.S. fur industry to switch to less cruel techniques. As of 2002, only eight U.S. states had banned the use of leg-hold traps—Florida, New Jersey, Rhode Island, Arizona, Colorado, Massachusetts, California, and Washington.[143] In the future, threatened WTO action and subsequent weak agreement could have implications for other policies concerning humane treatment of animals, such as slaughter and transport rules, testing of consumer products on laboratory animals, and fur-farming standards.

The U.S.-EU agreement was signed in December 1997 and went into effect in early 1998. Thus, if the deal is implemented, the six-year phaseout of leg-hold traps should be complete by January 2004.[144] Meanwhile, in 2002, the United Kingdom animal-welfare organization Compassion in World Farming released a report that found that the EU has effectively abandoned its ban on imported fur caught in leg-hold traps.[145]

Sample Threat 3: U.S. and EU Auto Industries Attack Japanese Clean Air Rules Implementing Kyoto Treaty

The growing international concern over climate change led to a treaty signed in 1997 in Kyoto, Japan, formally committing countries to reduce emissions.[146] Called the Kyoto Protocol, this multilateral environmental agreement requires countries to implement measures to limit and reduce greenhouse gases.

The Japanese government committed itself in the Kyoto Protocol to cut greenhouse gases by 6% from its 1990 levels of emissions.[147] Japanese emissions have been on the rise and a major cause is increased use of cars.[148] Japan launched a comprehensive plan to cut CO_2 emissions, including revising its "Law Concerning Rational Use of Energy," which among other things set automobile fuel-efficiency standards. The new fuel-efficiency standards focused particularly on cars in the medium weight category, where standards had been less rigorous when compared to those applied to smaller and larger autos.[149] Japan set its standard using the best available technology, meaning that the law requires emissions levels equal to those achieved by the most nonpolluting engine existing in the middle-range weight class.[150] That engine was designed by Mitsubishi.

In 1999, the EU cried foul, shooting off a letter to the WTO Technical Barriers to Trade Secretariat complaining about the new rules.[151] The U.S. followed suit on behalf of Daimler-Chrysler and the Ford Motor Company.[152] In a March 8, 1999, letter to the Japanese ministry of foreign affairs, the U.S. claimed that Japan's new rules may be WTO-illegal.[153] Both the U.S. and the EU question Japan's basing of the new standard on the Mitsubishi engine; they argue that it discriminates against foreign manufacturers that do not use that engine. In its letter, the EU states: "[A]lthough the use of these technical criteria for the definition of the scheme does not appear to be *per se* discriminatory, the regime . . . puts a comparatively heavier burden on imported products." Japanese industry data indicated that most of Japan's domestic automakers would also have had to improve fuel efficiency to comply with the new standards.[154] Japanese officials also claimed that the new regulation had been written flexibly, allowing EU and U.S. automakers to meet the standards however they wish, and that it did not require them to use the Mitsubishi engine, just to meet a similar level of fuel efficiency.

The Japanese regulation is written to go into effect in 2008. Only time will tell if the U.S. and EU WTO threats—or a later formal WTO case—will affect the proposal. If the WTO is used to undermine the Kyoto Protocol—which itself doesn't contain any trade restrictions—then the WTO threat to human health and environmental protection is much broader than previously understood. Regardless of the outcome, this example demonstrates how mega-corporations like Daimler-Chrysler expect the WTO to be used: as a bogeyman to scare away environmental regulation. A developing country facing such a threat would not necessarily have the resources to fight to attempt to protect its environmental safeguards.

THE WTO'S IMPLICATIONS FOR NATURAL RESOURCE CONSERVATION: FORESTS AND FISHERIES

Concerns about the WTO's environmental implications have focused almost exclusively on environmental standards because these have come under attack in an array of WTO challenges. Less attention has been paid to the WTO rules' effects on sustainable resource management and the preservation of biodiversity. Yet, over the longer term, the WTO's impact on forests, fish, and other natural resources and biodiversity may be its most destructive legacy.

Rip-and-Ship Exploitation

WTO terms have substantially increased the global trade in raw natural resources with little or no concern for the impact this trade has on the environment or local economies. The WTO's reductions of tariffs and quotas on natural resources have increased the volume of global exchange of these items, creating new demand for the accelerated extraction of natural resources worldwide. This demand comes almost entirely from the wealthy industrialized countries. The majority of the world's natural resources (roughly 80%) is consumed by the 20% of the population that lives in developed countries.[155]

Nonrenewable resources, such as minerals, oil, and gas, are being extracted as quickly as possible. Theoretically renewable resources, such as fish and forests, are being harvested at unsustainable rates.

What does the WTO have to do with this situation? In the Uruguay Round negotiations, the wealthy countries sought access to cheap natural resources for their manufacturing industries. To accomplish this, they pushed for escalating tariff patterns for many commodities—especially for tropical products.[156] Tariff escalation imposes higher tariffs on manufactured goods than on the raw materials used to produce them. Thus, before the Uruguay Round, there were lower tariffs on semi-processed wood products than on raw wood, encouraging local economies to produce finished goods rather than to simply export their raw natural resources. In the Uruguay Round negotiations, the wealthy countries were able to reverse the tariff patterns.[157]

The tariff escalation built into the WTO encourages rip-and-ship use of natural resources. But by trading in raw products rather than in more valuable finished goods, a country must increase the *volume* of extraction and export to obtain the same earnings. The WTO's tariff escalation both encourages more intensive exploitation of resources and creates an economic incentive against developing countries establishing manufacturing industries to process raw resources—meaning less earnings for poor countries in addition to increased depletion of natural resources.

The increased harvesting of natural resources harms biodiversity and causes extinction of endangered plants and wildlife as well as jeopardizing the world's indigenous people and their cultures. Since the WTO has gone into effect, the trade in natural resources has grown tremendously. For example, U.S. imports of raw logs has more than doubled since the WTO went into effect, rising 133% from $92 million in 1995 to $214 million in 2002.[158] While imports of coniferous and nonconiferous logs were comparable to the average import increase, U.S. imports of tropical logs grew *astronomically* from a modest $12,438 in 1996 to $724,000 in 2002. During the same period, the value of global mining exports grew 55% between 1995 and 2001, even though most mining commodity prices declined.[159]

Preventing Natural-Resource Protection

WTO rules also hinder the ability of countries to act to preserve their natural resources, including forbidding the use of export limits designed to prevent depletion of resources. Import and export controls are fundamental parts of a larger strategy to conserve resources and foster local economic development. For resource-based communities, export controls create a more dynamic and diverse economy, and ultimately ensure sustainable resource management. For governments, the result can be greater tax revenue from the additional economic activities, in turn creating the fiscal resources needed for governments to invest in resource-enhancement and conservation measures, and providing a stronger rationale for doing so, as such expenditures would now benefit processing and manufacturing as well as the harvesting or extraction industries.

In 1990 after years of nasty political fighting, President George Bush signed a law restricting exports of raw logs harvested from U.S. federal lands.[160] The policy was part of a highly complicated political agreement hammered out as a condition for new limits on logging in the ancient forest habitats of the endangered northern spotted owl. The idea was to compensate for limits on cutting forests by creating new jobs in the timber-processing sector.

Japan immediately began to threaten GATT action on the export ban,[161] arguing that raw log bans—which other nations were also adopting in their forestry conservation programs—violated the GATT's Artcle XI prohibition on quantitative restrictions. While this GATT threat from Japan became ensnared in other U.S.-Japan trade fights, the U.S. proceeded to use a domestic trade law (called Section 301) to attack as an illegal trade practice a similar Canadian raw log export ban, for which Canada had negotiated a specific exception under NAFTA.[162]

Limiting Protection Against Invasive Species

The WTO Sanitary and Phytosanitary (SPS) Agreement's limits on quarantines (see Chapter 2) effectively restrict the ability of governments to keep out exotic pests, as we saw in the Asian Longhorned Beetle case. The current WTO jurisprudence requires that *before* a country can take action against an invasive species, it must conduct a detailed risk assessment showing not only a real risk but a risk that a WTO panel would deem serious! Given the costs and time involved in conducting such a risk assessment—which would then be left to the mercies of a subjective WTO panel without expertise in biodiversity or invasive species—the WTO throws a steep hurdle in front of countries interested in protecting against invasive species.

Undermining Sustainable Timber, Fishing Policies

The precedents set by the WTO disputes in the dolphin-tuna and shrimp-turtle cases curtail many national policies aimed at protecting natural resources by setting rules about *how* they may be harvested. Thus, rules on sustainable forestry or limiting use of certain nets with high by-catch of juvenile or nontarget species are exposed to WTO attack. Similar rules setting quantitative limits or processing regulations established in multilateral environmental agreements face the same threat.

Destroying Forests

The elimination of global commodity trade agreements (which used to set volume and price terms), as well as Uruguay Round tariff and quota cuts for many agricultural commodities such as coffee and cocoa, has increased the clearance of forests. Uruguay Round agriculture policy changes also have resulted in plummeting commodity prices, meaning that farmers have to produce more to make the same amount of money, pushing them to slash and burn more forests to expand their acreage. Meanwhile, in the face of falling commodity prices and continued pressure by the IMF and World Bank to pay back debts in hard currencies earned by exports, governments of developing countries are under pressure not to halt such forest destruction and indeed to intensify production of raw natural resources and cash crops that can generate export earnings.

As if the situation were not dire enough, prior to Seattle some WTO members had proposed a Global Free Logging Agreement to reduce tariffs on forest products.[163] This proposal drew a firestorm of criticism from environmentalists worldwide, but to what effect was never known because the failure of the Seattle Ministerial tabled all Seattle negotiations.

However, the Ministerial Declaration issued at the 2001 Doha WTO summit contains terms on market access for nonagricultural products including to "eliminate tariffs, including the reduction or elimination of tariff peaks, high tariffs, and tariff escalation, as well as non-tariff barriers."[164] This provision resuscitates the Global Free Logging Agreement by mandating the reduction of tariffs and quotas on nonagricultural goods (which includes forest products) without exclusion. Under this proposal, a country could not set tariff or quota restrictions to meet environmental policy goals. And the specific inclusion of nontariff barriers in the proposal would hinder the ability of countries to impose speedy quarantines to protect against invasive pests and to differentiate between sustainably and unsustainably harvested wood and other resources.

Endangering Marine Life

WTO terms applying to fish trade have helped empty the seas of life. Greatly increased volumes of trade in fish and seafood have had a huge impact on the stocks of not only food fish but also the marine life that lives around them. During the 1990s, fisheries' production grew by 20 million tons, or about 19%.[165] Since the WTO has gone into effect, U.S. imports of fish and fish products have grown by 23%, from $5.8 billion in 1995 to $7.9 billion in 2002.[166] During that same period, U.S. imports of fresh or chilled fish fillets have increased 281%—from $175 million in 1995 to $666 million in 2002.[167]

The WTO has not only increased commercial fishing but has made it more difficult to protect the oceans and wildlife. The WTO's lack of consideration for multilateral environmental agreements (discussed in the next section) has great significance for marine life.

Lastly, the WTO's prevention of export restraints would block countries from protecting fish stocks in their home waters. In order to establish sustainable management regimes for coastal fisheries, governments must be able to impose effective controls upon all those exploiting marine resources within these zones. For the domestic fishing industry serving local markets, the exercise is reasonably straightforward, and governments have created regulatory mechanisms to control what, when, where and how much is taken from coastal zones. While these regulatory regimes have failed dismally in some instances, authority did exist to establish sustainable management programs, had it been properly exercised.

The 2001 WTO Doha Ministerial Declaration proposed that negotiations begin on reducing domestic subsidies for fisheries. According to the OECD, nearly a fifth of the dockside cost of commercial fishing is provided through direct and indirect subsidies. In 2002 in Geneva, the United States, Argentina, Australia, Iceland, New Zealand, and Peru (which have no or low subsidies for their fishing industries) argued that eliminating fishing subsidies would also further the goal of promoting sustainability.[168] Korea countered that there was little evidence that fishing subsidies had a negative impact on fish stocks. Some environmental groups, notably the World Wildlife Fund, support WTO negotiations on the elimination of fishing subsidies.[169]

However, not all of the policies that the WTO might consider to be subsidies encourage stock-depleting overfishing. For example, countries have subsidies for conversion to less ecologically damaging fishing equipment, job retraining programs to reduce the numbers of commercial fishers and programs to purchase and put out of commission older, more polluting commercial trawlers.[170] If reducing fishing subsidies does become part of the WTO agenda, there is no way to determine which subsidies will be challenged. And by codifying the WTO's authority over this additional domestic policy, countries cede their democratic control of it.

ENVIRONMENTAL ISSUES NOW ON THE
WTO NEGOTIATING TABLE

Misguided WTO Committee on Trade and the Environment

Environmentalists had hoped that the WTO's Committee on Trade and Environment (CTE) would provide a forum for the development of changes to WTO rules to make them more compatible with environmental policy. One seemingly easy step would be to agree that in the case of conflicts between WTO rules and the terms of the multilateral environmental agreements, the MEAs trump.

The CTE was established in response to worldwide environmentalist opposition to the establishment of the WTO during a 1994 Marrakech WTO Ministerial where the Uruguay Round was signed. The body is to hold official meetings three times a year to identify issues arising between trade and environmental policies and to make recommendations, including to further the "avoidance of protectionist trade measures,"[171] meaning identification of environmental policies that interfere with trade. To date, the CTE has focused on MEAs, environmental dispute resolution (including within MEAs), market access (in fisheries, forest products, agriculture and nonferrous minerals), and eco-labeling.

CTE membership is open to all WTO member countries, but smaller WTO delegations frequently do not have Geneva-based environmental or natural-resource specialists.[172] Representatives from select international institutions such as the IMF, the Food and Agriculture Organization, the business-funded International Organization for Standardization and World Intellectual Property Organization and some select UN agencies are observers.[173] As of June 2003, no environmental or other NGOs have been permitted to be CTE observers.[174]

The European Union offered proposals at the CTE in 1996 for WTO recognition of the legitimacy and WTO-compatibility of MEAs, including MEAs that include use of trade sanctions. The U.S. neither supported the EU nor produced its own proposal.[175] As the CTE discussions dragged on but went nowhere, other countries grew bitter at the lack of leadership from the U.S., the country that had called for the creation of the CTE in the first place.[176] In the last few years, the CTE has continued to talk about the relationship between the WTO and MEAs, to no great end.

This ambiguity is problematic. There are several ways in which MEAs can run afoul of WTO rules and increasingly antienvironment interests are using the uncertainty about which rules take precedence to threaten WTO action against countries' proposals for implementing their MEA obligations.

First, some MEAs protect the environment by explicitly restricting trade. For instance, the Convention on International Trade in Endangered Species bans trade in endangered species; the Basel Convention on the Transboundary Movement of Hazardous Waste regulates the export of toxic waste from rich countries—which produce over 90% of the world's hazardous waste—to developing nations; and the Montreal Protocol bans trade in ozone-depleting chemicals.[177]

Second, these treaties and others sometimes employ the use of trade sanctions to enforce their objectives and to encourage full compliance with their rules, in the same way the WTO does.[178] Yet while WTO supporters consider trade sanctions to be a legitimate way to enforce intellectual property protections or to punish governments for not complying with other WTO rules, they oppose using the same means to enforce multilaterally agreed upon rules on environmental protection.

Third, some MEAs do not involve trade bans but may regulate trade through procedures requiring the "prior informed consent" of importing countries before trade takes place, or require countries to adopt policies that affect products of one country more than those of another. As discussed earlier in the chapter, the U.S. and the EU have used WTO obligations to attack the Japanese government for strengthening its fuel-efficiency laws, which was an element of Japan's implementation of its Kyoto Protocol obligations. Thus, MEAs of all stripes could have a significant chance of coming into conflict with WTO rules.

Finally, unlike the WTO, which has strong built-in dispute settlement, the MEAs provide internationally agreed-upon rules that countries commit to implement at the national level. For instance, CITES lists species for which its signatory countries have agreed that protection is needed—for instance sea turtles. Yet the main means for enforcement of CITES comes not through a central CITES tribunal but rather through the domestic laws of each signatory. Thus, many U.S. CITES obligations are enforced through the Endangered Species Act. That U.S. law bans import of CITES-listed species and products made from them, and endorses embargoes against countries that violate the rules.[179] Other countries have similar domestic laws implementing their CITES obligations. Yet, under WTO rules, such domestic laws can—and have been—challenged as illegal trade barriers as we saw in the case of the U.S. Endangered Species Act protections for the CITES-listed sea turtles.

The fact that a domestic law is based on an MEA is not considered a defense if the law is challenged at the WTO. While a very limited clause giving some precedence to three MEAs over conflicting rules was forced into NAFTA, it is conspicuously absent in the WTO or other Uruguay Round Agreements.[180]

In its somewhat beleaguered seven years of operation, the CTE has failed to agree to any recommendations for pro-environment changes to the WTO system. Indeed, some environmentalists criticize it as being used primarily to identify environmental measures that might conflict with WTO rules and to propose ways to get rid of such green policies.[181]

In 1999 the CTE officially shifted its approach. Dubbed the "win-win" strategy, the new approach abandons its purported goal of seeking compatibility between environmental regulations and existing WTO rules and instead focuses on identifying and eliminating trade distortions that are considered harmful for the environment.

At a March 1999 WTO meeting on the environment in Geneva, WTO officials sought out environmental groups to get their support for this strategy.[182] The so-called High-Level Symposium on Trade and the Environment and Sustainable Development included representatives from industry, academia, environmental organizations, and development and consumer groups.[183] A few groups such as World Wildlife International did issue positive statements on the idea of cutting fisheries' subsidies which was the initial "win-win" proposal.[184] However, the environmental community as a whole criticized the WTO's continuing failure to safeguard existing environmental policies coming under increasing WTO attack worldwide.[185] Instead at CTE meetings that year, the agenda covered market access for fisheries and agriculture products as well as trade in environmental services—a controversial proposal that has been criticized as promoting privatization and deregulation of water treatment and sewage systems.[186]

During the lead-up to Seattle, the Clinton administration shifted its WTO environmental strategy in the same direction, echoing the call for a "win-win" strategy.[187] However, simultaneously, the U.S. led the efforts to launch new cuts in tariffs and elimination of regulations in forest products (which was and remains vigorously opposed by environmentalists and was estimated by industry to increase depletion of forests by 3–4%[188]). Between the Seattle Ministerial and the Doha Ministerial, the CTE continues discussions, but with no effect on the WTO's rules or operations.

Doha Ministerial Further Rolls Back Environmental Consideration and Protection

As the Doha Ministerial drew nearer, the European Union began pushing strongly for what it dubbed new "environmental negotiations" at the WTO. Some interpreted this as a political maneuver to ameliorate growing domestic pressure in opposition to Europe's WTO service, investment, and procurement proposals. Others interpreted the proposal—which included new talks on environmental services and goods liberalization—as a backdoor push for Europe's huge water corporations to gain new concessions. The Bush administration and many developing nations opposed the proposal. However, ultimately to push Europe to make concessions on reducing its agricultural subsidies and thus avoid a total meltdown of the Ministerial, the Doha Ministerial Declaration adopted on November 14, 2001, authorizes negotiations on several environmental issues.

The two most important Doha elements are: proposed negotiations to determine the relationship between trade measures in MEAs and WTO rules and to liberalize trade in environmental services and goods. The text also calls for improved communications between MEAs' secretariats and the WTO, and for the development of official critera for observer status for MEA staff at the WTO. Finally, it sets out the future CTE work plan: identifying and debating environmental aspects of WTO negotiations. The CTE also was instructed to report to the Cancún Ministerial about the need for additional negotiations on environmental measures' impact on developing-country access to northern markets, the environmental aspects of intellectual property protections, and the use of eco-labels.[189]

WTO to Decide Relative Status of Multilateral Environmental Treaties vs. WTO

At issue in these talks is what takes priority when there are conflicts between existing WTO rules and the specific trade obligations set out in multilateral environmental agreements. Whatever the EU's intentions, empowering the WTO to determine this question of relative status frames these negotiations as a discussion about limiting the use of MEA trade provisions rather than on how the application of WTO rules would be limited by the MEAs' terms.

Much of the discussion has revolved around whether to take the EU approach, which is to discuss broad principles to guide the MEA-WTO relationship,[190] or to take the Australia approach, which first identifies specific MEA trade obligations, then looks at whether countries have experienced WTO problems in implementing the MEA-specific trade obligations.[191]

In any case, the results of the negotiations will be applicable only to WTO members who have signed the MEA in question. This provides a clear disincentive for WTO members who have not signed MEAs from doing so, or even from participating in the mandated negotiations on this subject. The corollary of this is that MEA signatories who are not WTO members will also not be bound by any new rules to which WTO members may agree.

Implications of New Negotiations on Liberalization of Environmental Goods and Services

The Doha Declaration also opened a new frontier for trade liberalization negotiations: environmental goods and services. And what are those, you ask? Well, even WTO trade officials are unsure about what is meant by environmental goods.[192] Obviously they include equipment, such as smokestack scrubbers and water systems, although some have proposed that incinerators and oil tankers be added to the list. Qatar, for example, has pushed for natural gas products to be considered environmental goods.[193] Negotiations on environmental goods and services were pushed as the next "win-win" WTO proposal for trade and environment, as well as a win-win prospect for both developed and developing countries. However, one thing is clear: right now, the principal producers and consumers of commercial environmental goods are developed countries. So trade liberalization in these goods naturally stands to benefit mainly developed countries, especially the corporations that produce such goods and seek to export them to developing countries. Unless WTO investment and patent rules that limit copying technology or requiring its transfer are changed, developing countries will not be assisted in developing such capacity themselves.

Unlike "environmental goods," the concept of "environmental services," at least in the context of the WTO's service-sector agreement (General Agreement on Trade in Services—GATS), is now fairly well defined. Environmental services in GATS include the following:

- Sewage and tank treatment services (but not collection, distribution or purification of water services)
- Refuse disposal services, focused on hazardous and nonhazardous waste collection, treatment, and disposal by dumping, incinerating, storing, landfill, composting, etc. (but not wholesale trade services of waste, scrap and other materials for recycling)

- Sanitation and similar services focused on outdoor sweeping, ice and snow removal, runway sweeping, beach cleaning and drain unblocking services
- Emission monitoring and control services of pollutants into the air, mostly caused by the burning of fossil fuels and concentration monitoring, control and reduction services of pollutants in ambient air, especially in urban areas
- Noise pollution monitoring, control and abatement services—i.e. traffic-related noise abatement services
- Nature and landscape protection services—including fauna, flora and habitat studies on the interrelationship between environment and climate
- Natural disaster assessment and abatement services; and other services such as acid-rain monitoring, control and damage-assessment services

The core services in this sector are end-of-pipe disposal services, meaning disposal of toxics and waste, versus services designed to prevent or remedy environmental damage. Environmental groups worry that the likely outcome of these talks will be expansion of multinational operations in such environmentally harmful activities as waste incineration. As described in Chapter 4, once a country commits to market access in a service sector, it must accept bids from foreign firms providing services in a committed category. New commitments on environmental services may also lessen the ability of host countries to develop their own technologies in ways that benefit the countries' environment. Furthermore, it could lead to developing countries committing themselves, inadvertently or not, to becoming recipients of waste for disposal from developed countries.

In addition, environmental and development specialists are concerned that new services, such as bulk water collection or sales, could be added to the definition of environmental service in the context of these new Doha negotiations, opening a back door for the water privatization agenda of many large European water multinationals. In Chapter 4, we explore the growing controversy over private ownership of commercial trade in bulk water, including lake, river and ground water.

CONCLUSION

What happens next regarding the European environmental proposals from the Doha agenda was to be discussed at the Cancún WTO Ministerial. However, unfortunately the WTO's many existing threats to the world's environment and its record of use to attack environmental policies was not on the agenda even before the summit collapsed. Despite the growing record of damaging evidence, neither the WTO Secretariat nor most WTO members (or at least the trade ministers representing nations at the WTO) view the WTO as causing environmental problems. Although as the threats of WTO action against green policies escalate, it appears some view environmental policies as causing trade problems.

2

THE WTO'S COMING TO DINNER, AND FOOD SAFETY IS NOT ON THE MENU

In 1986, animal disease control officers around the world began hearing of a new disease called bovine spongiform encephalopathy (BSE), or "mad cow disease." Scientists in the United Kingdom struggled to determine the cause of the ailment, marked by progressive degeneration of brain tissue. Some believed it was linked to cows eating other diseased animals that had been ground up and processed as feed, specifically sheep with a related brain disease called scrapie. Others believed that BSE originated as a genetic mutation in a single cow, which was rendered into animal feed and transmitted to other animals.[1] In 1988, the UK responded to the scientific uncertainty by banning the use of meat and bone meal in animal feed.

By 1993, the incidence of BSE was peaking in the UK cattle population, but the government was continuing to assure the public that meat was safe to eat.[2] The worst of the crisis seemed to be over. What went overlooked, however, was the fact that since the start of the crisis, the UK had continued to export potentially contaminated meat and bone meal for use in animal feed in other countries.

In 1996, UK health officials indicated that BSE had jumped the species barrier into humans, revealing a probable link between BSE and a new form of Creutzfeldt-Jakob disease (CJD) in humans. Given the name "new variant CJD" (vCJD) by scientists, it is a horrendous, fatal, brain-deteriorating disease for which there is no known cure. Even without absolute scientific certainty about how vCJD was spread and whether it had passed to humans from cows, other nations began to respond to the potential public health crisis by banning British beef. In 1996, Britain finally stopped exporting meat and bone meal.[3] However, other EU countries, who were found later to be harboring BSE in their own cattle, continued until 2001 to export live animals and other animal products that might transmit the disease. It was later determined that feed from the UK probably infected with BSE had been exported to 80 countries in the 1990s.[4]

In 2000, the World Health Organization (WHO) issued a global alert calling upon nations to begin surveillance and take other measures to be on the alert against BSE.[5] Today, 22 countries have confirmed cases.[6] As of September 2002, there have been 117 deaths in Great Britain attributed to vCJD, and other cases in

Italy, South Africa and Thailand.[7] Health care professionals worldwide are on the alert for the telltale Parkinson's-like tremors that are symptoms of vCJD.

The WTO's impact on countries' efforts to combat such preventable human and animal threats has been entirely negative. To the WTO, mad cow disease is a trade issue; its chief concern, to prevent a diversity of precautionary health and safety responses that limit agricultural trade by WTO member governments.[8] Yet health professionals have known for years that increased trade and globalization pose significant new hazards to the health and well-being of people around the world. The WHO recently reported that globalization of the world's food supply significantly contributed to the more than 2 million deaths a year from foodborne illness worldwide,[9] and many countries are documenting significant increases in foodborne diseases.[10] In 2000, 2.1 million people died worldwide from common illnesses such as diarrheal diseases attributed to contaminated food and drinking water.[11]

In the U.S., with its relatively well-developed food-safety system, 5,200 Americans die, 325,000 are hospitalized and 76 million become ill every year from foodborne illnesses.[12] Yet in countries with less developed food safety systems, the risks are far higher. In developed countries, it is estimated that thirty percent of the population suffers from foodborne disease annually, and as many as 20 per million die.[13]

Rather than encouraging countries to adopt a precautionary approach to unknown hazards, appropriate safeguards against known hazards and rigorous enforcement to protect the public health, WTO provisions serve to deter, threaten, and erode regulatory measures worldwide. Food industries in assorted WTO member countries have gotten their governments to threaten other countries to come into compliance with WTO guidelines by limiting domestic food safety policies—or face WTO challenges to domestic safeguards.

The rulings from the WTO's dispute-resolution tribunals in the food-safety area are especially galling. They have limited efforts by governments to prevent potentially risky food additives, chemicals and untested emerging technologies from entering the food supply, such as the EU's ban on artificial beef hormone residues in meat. Countries' efforts to combat known pests in their food and farms have been successfully challenged as well. In addition, WTO requirements to "harmonize" differing national regulatory requirements and standards to create global standards and to find different, often less protective, exporting country standards as "equivalent" to domestic standards has put significant downward pressure on countries' food safety standards.

GLOBALIZATION OF FOOD TRADE SPREADS FOODBORNE ILLNESSES

"With a global food supply, we worry less about the possibility that Grandmother's potato salad will affect 80 percent of the people attending a church picnic than about the prospect that hundreds of thousands of people in many countries will be exposed to a single contaminated product."
—*New England Journal of Medicine* editorial, April 27, 2000[14]

The WHO has identified the globalization of the food supply as a growing cause of illness worldwide.[15] A 1999 landmark report from the director-general of the WHO called attention to food safety as an "essential public health issue," and the increasing globalization of food as a major health risk.[16] A 2002 update noted that globalization of food trade puts increasing strains on food-safety regulators by allowing increasing transborder transmission of foodborne diseases,[17] and the rapid consolidation and concentration in the agriculture and food industries creates the potential for foodborne illnesses from a single high-volume facility to reach more consumers than ever, potentially generating "widespread outbreaks of foodborne illness."[18]

The advent of the WTO and other trade agreements has rapidly increased the international flow of both food and foodborne illnesses. During the 1990s, agriculture imports into the U.S. increased by 25%, rising from $582 billion in 1990 to $726 billion at the end of the decade.[19] Under NAFTA, agricultural imports into the U.S. from Canada and Mexico have increased by 89% between 1993 and 2000.[20] The respected Iowa State University Food and Agriculture Policy Research Institute's World Agricultural Outlook predicts that trade in beef and veal will grow 54% between 2001 and 2011,[21] trade in pork will rise 61%, and in broiler chickens 45%, amounting to an increase of 5 million metric tons of meat and poultry imports within eight years.

The rate of food inspection has not kept up with the growth in the volume of food imports. FDA inspections of imported food declined from 8% of total imports in 1993 to less than 2% in 1999, increasing the risk of contaminated produce reaching the public.[22] By 2000, the FDA inspected only 1% of the imported food it has jurisdiction to regulate (all imported foods except meat, poultry and processed eggs).[23]

Inspection of meat and poultry also has declined: in 1997 the 75 full-time USDA Food Safety and Inspection Service (FSIS) meat and poultry inspectors worked at 200 facilities inspecting 2.5 billion pounds of meat and poultry imports.[24] By 2001, the same number of full-time inspectors monitored the import of 3.7 billion pounds—increasing the per-inspector poundage from 91,000 to 135,000 a day.[25]

As a consequence, it is not surprising that dangerous food continues to enter the U.S. In 2002, the FDA halted imports of Mexican cantaloupes after they were linked to four salmonella outbreaks that hospitalized at least 18 people and caused two deaths.[26] FSIS recalled 2,300 pounds of cured ham imported into the U.S. from Italy because of listeria contamination.[27] In April 2000, a U.S. outbreak of salmonella was traced to sprouts from California-based Coast Sprout Farms grown from seeds imported from Australia or China.[28]

In addition, even as FDA inspection rates have declined, the FDA has found that the share of imported food with over-tolerance pesticide residues has increased significantly. In 1995, the year the WTO went into effect, about 1% of both domestic and imported food inspected by the FDA had pesticide residues higher than U.S. standards. In 2000, the FDA found that 3.8% of inspected imported food had pesticide levels that exceeded U.S. pesticide tolerance limits, or more than five times the 0.7% of the domestic food exceeding pesticide limits.[29]

Greater volumes of imported food, fewer border inspections, and increased concern about foodborne illness has led consumer and public-health groups as well as the U.S. General Accounting Office (GAO) to recommend that the U.S. adopt stricter food-safety inspection standards for foreign produce and provide the funding necessary to implement them.[30] But such a policy would violate the WTO's (and NAFTA's) rules requiring "national treatment," which guarantees that domestic and foreign goods will be treated the same.

The WTO's terms contribute to these food-safety problems not only by leading to substantially increasing food trade, but by constraining governments' ability to address problems posed by foodborne illnesses. Not only have nations' food-safety laws come under threat in the powerful dispute-resolution body of the WTO, but WTO rules embodied in the WTO Sanitary and Phytosanitary Agreement harm public well-being by encouraging an ongoing race to the bottom in food-safety standards.

Developing Nations Face Special Challenges Preventing Foodborne Illness

Under severe pressure from the IMF both to generate export earnings by selling food to wealthy nations and to cut domestic health and sanitation spending,[31] poorer nations cannot afford to police imports at the border, properly enforce their laws or inspect food produced domestically. Funding for such food-safety and public-health regulatory systems is often the first to be cut under IMF-required austerity plans.

For instance, in 1992, Mexico's spending on food-safety inspection was $25 million. Three years later, with food exports soaring under NAFTA but with Mexico reeling from the peso crash and obligated to implement "structural adjustment," Mexico's food inspection funding was slashed to $5 million.[32] By 2001, Mexico's food-safety and animal- and plant-health budgets had returned to the $25 million level—half a percent of Mexico's agriculture ministry budget and less than one dollar per Mexican citizen.[33] Yet during the interim decade, Mexican food exports and imports had risen substantially.

Developing countries catalogued the difficulty they had implementing and enforcing food-safety standards at a Food and Agriculture Organization (FAO)/WHO meeting in Marrakech, Morocco, in the summer of 2002. For instance, Indonesia reported that its food-safety regulatory implementation was unable to implement and enforce its own food-safety standards because of resource constraints on technology, funding, information and personnel.[34]

A tragic example of food-safety inspection failure in the developing world happened in 1998 in New Delhi, India. Tainted mustard seed oil, a staple cooking oil in India, reached consumers. Over 50 people died from dropsy, an excessive accumulation of serous fluid in tissue, which can lead to congestive heart failure.[35]

Least Developed Countries (LDCs) are in even more dire straits. Zimbabwe, for instance, reported that it had no documented procedures for inspecting imported food and that substandard imported food was therefore a common sight in Zimbabwean markets.[36] The country's food-safety program was undergoing an overhaul in 2002, but with limited funding.[37]

On average, developing countries spend $4 per person annually on all public health efforts, making dedicating resources to food safety a particularly important but difficult choice.[38] Although the WTO SPS Agreement calls for developing countries to receive technical assistance to implement food-safety regimes,[39] no source has provided necessary funds or technical assistance.[40]

World Bank economists note that to implement the WTO agreements on food standards and plant and animal health, intellectual property, and customs valuation, a typical developing country would need to spend $150 million— which is equal to the cost of all development programs in a year for many LDCs. For example, Sri Lanka would have to spend $1.95 million to train all of its 70,000 spice traders to meet WTO SPS guidelines, but it only has $24,000 dedicated for this effort.[41]

More recently, in September 2002, the World Bank announced a new fund to help developing countries implement international food-safety standards, as well as plant- and animal-health standards, but unfortunately only pledged $300,000, expressing "hope" that G8 nations would support the program.[42]

Increased financial assistance for poorer nations is a dire public-health necessity for residents of both poor countries and the rich countries that are increasingly importing food from them. Yet assistance for developing countries to improve food-safety systems has been a low priority for most developed nations that could provide resources.

THE WTO SPS AGREEMENT: TRADE TRUMPS PUBLIC HEALTH

"Under the SPS Agreement, WTO may force a nation to choose between weakening its health standards for humans, plants or animals or paying an international penalty."

—Bruce Silverglade, director of legal affairs,
Center for Science in the Public Interest, 2002[43]

The Sanitary and Phytosanitary Agreement (one of the Uruguay Round agreements enforced by the WTO) sets criteria that WTO member nations must follow regarding their domestic policies that affect trade regarding the protection of human life or health from risks arising from additives, contaminants, toxins, veterinary drug and pesticide residues or other disease-causing organisms in food or beverages.[44] It also sets parameters on member countries' domestic policies regarding livestock and fisheries, including quarantine, inspection and testing requirements. The primary goal of the SPS Agreement is to facilitate trade by eliminating differences in food, animal and plant regulations from country to country.[45] The agreement also sets strict limits on countries' permissible policy goals in these areas, and the means by which nations can pursue even the permitted goals. When challenges have arisen, WTO panels consistently have interpreted WTO member countries' SPS measures to be barriers to trade that must be weakened or eliminated, rather than as public-health safeguards or prudent measures aimed at avoiding the spread of pests or plant or animal disease.

The provisions of the SPS Agreement can be viewed as setting constraints in four areas: First, it limits the policy goals a country can seek using SPS measures. Second, the *level* of protection a country chooses for its citizens is also a matter for WTO review, even when the standard is applied equally to domestic and foreign goods.[46] Third, even for policies that meet the constraints regarding goals and level of protection, the *means* by which WTO-legal policy goals may be achieved is subject to another test. The agreement requires that a policy not be any more restrictive to trade than is necessary to obtain its WTO-allowed goal.[47] Fourth, the agreement contains affirmative obligations for WTO countries to harmonize their domestic standards to international ones, and to view other countries' differing (lower) standards to be "equivalent" to domestic standards.[48]

Since every WTO member country has agreed to conform to the SPS rules, it is worth reviewing a few of them more closely:

Article 2.1 defines WTO member nations' basic rights: "Members have the right to take sanitary and phytosanitary measures necessary for the protection of human, animal or plant life or health, provided that such measures are not inconsistent with the provisions of this Agreement."[49] This tautological provision is often cited by WTO defenders to misleadingly argue that countries may set any standard desired.

Article 2.2 defines WTO members' basic obligations, requiring SPS measures to be applied "only to the extent necessary to protect human, animal or plant life or health . . . based on scientific principles . . . and not maintained without sufficient scientific evidence. . . ."[50] This is a provision the U.S. argues forbids countries from food-safety policies which ban a pesticide or technology such as GMOs whose human health threat is not yet scientifically proved.

Article 3 requires WTO member countries to harmonize their domestic food-safety and animal- and plant-protection policies by basing them on international standards, such as the food-safety and pesticide-residue standards set by the Codex Alimentarius Commission. Policies based on such international standards are presumed to be WTO-legal. However, policies that achieve a higher level of human, animal or plant protection than relevant international standards must pass a series of tests in order to be proved *not* to be illegal trade barriers. One such test requires a "scientific justification."[51] A member has scientific justification only if it can analyze available scientific data to determine that the international standard is insufficient to attain the country's "appropriate level of sanitary or phytosanitary protection."[52]

A country's "appropriate level of protection" is defined as "the level of protection deemed appropriate by the Member establishing a sanitary or phytosanitary measure to protect human, animal or plant life or health within its territory,"[53] suggesting that WTO members have unfettered discretion to set their own level of protection. However, in setting this level of protection, countries must comply with SPS Article 3, which requires them to base their SPS measures on WTO-legal international standards and show "scientific justification" for more consumer-protective standards. Since the burden of proof falls on the country with the more protective standard, countries seeking higher standards must invest time and resources to prove a negative—that the international standard is unsafe.[54]

In addition, countries are required under Article 5 to base their level of protection on a "risk assessment," using techniques developed by relevant international organizations which means conducting extensive studies and developing scientific proof *before* taking any regulatory action. While this requirement is difficult enough for developed nations, it is an extraordinarily difficult task for poor nations.

The SPS elevates trade concerns in the food-safety risk assessment process, specifically requiring countries to "take into account the objective of minimizing negative trade effects."[55] Article 5.6 adds: "Members shall ensure that [SPS] measures are not more trade-restrictive than required. . . ."[56] Though zero-tolerance standards are theoretically permissible under the wording of the agreement, these two requirements place yet another burden on nations that want to ban dangerous products rather than trying to "regulate" the risk. Finally, Article 4 requires member countries to accept the SPS measures of other WTO countries as equivalent, even if they are different, if the exporting country can prove to the importing country that its measures reach the importing country's "appropriate level" of protection.

Combined, these provisions effectively eviscerate the Precautionary Principle, an internationally recognized theorem of public policy embedded in many local laws and international environmental treaties, such as the 1992 Rio Declaration on Biodiversity. The principle is generally understood to mean that in cases where there is scientific uncertainty, governments have an obligation to take action to avoid harm to public health or safety, or to the environment, by seeking out less harmful alternatives. Proponents of new products or technologies must demonstrate that their activity will not cause undue harm to human health or ecosystems. The Precautionary Principle is based on the premise that science does not always provide the information necessary to take protective action effectively or in a timely manner, and that undesirable and potentially irreversible effects may result if action is not taken until science does provide such insights.

Defenders of the SPS Agreement argue that Article 5.7 specifically allows nations to take precautionary measures in the face of scientific uncertainty, but this clause only covers "provisional" or time-limited emergency measures. Yet many scientific problems, such as the dangers of mad cow disease, the public-health ramifications of endocrine disruptors, and the threat of global warming have taken generations to understand. These and current matters, such as the possible health effects of genetically modified organisms (GMOs), do not lend themselves to easy cause-and-effect analysis or short time lines.

WTO SPS EQUIVALENCY RULES MEAN IT IS REALLY NOT "THE SAME" OLD HAMBURGER

"The very notion of equivalence allows for imprecise, subjective comparisons that are not appropriate when dealing with issues as important as public health and safety."

—Transatlantic Consumer Dialogue, February 2002[57]

Declaring "equivalency" as required by SPS rules is designed to allow goods produced under "equivalent," possibly less health-protective systems, free passage into the importing country's market, without reinspection at the border. Effectively, the importing nation is adopting the regulatory standards of the exporting nation for the purposes of trade facilitation. In the U.S., this is done without the notification, involvement or oversight of Congress. Significant laws and regulations have been abrogated or undermined through this process.

Countries in Europe have been engaging in equivalency determinations for years as part of the "common market" approach to integration. The U.S., however, only started engaging in equivalence decisions with the passage of the Uruguay Round Agreements Act which conformed existing U.S. law to the WTO's requirements, significantly modifying huge swaths of U.S. law and regulation.[58]

Before passage of the Act in 1994, the USDA required foreign countries to maintain meat and poultry inspection systems "equal to" the FSIS system in order to export meat and poultry to the U.S.[59] That meant those countries' laws, regulations and procedures for conducting inspections essentially had to mirror U.S. laws, regulations and procedures. After Congress passed the Uruguay Round Agreements Act, the USDA changed the language in its regulations from "equal to" to "equivalent."[60] As a result, countries that export meat and poultry products to the U.S. can have laws, regulations, and inspection procedures substantially different from FSIS's.

Equivalency rules have led the U.S. to declare beef inspected by employees paid by meatpacking companies in Brazil to be "equivalent" in safety to U.S. government-inspected meat as well as beef inspected under Canadian standards, which do not include tests for heavy metal contamination. These meat imports enter the U.S. and are packaged, labeled and sold as if they met the requirements of U.S. law. Meanwhile, consumers in countries with good inspection systems face similar problems regarding U.S. meat imports which are processed under a newly implemented and deeply flawed U.S. meat safety system.

EVIDENCE IS MOUNTING THAT NEW U.S. "HACCP" MEAT INSPECTION SYSTEM IS FAILING TO PROTECT THE PUBLIC

In the summer of 2002, ConAgra Beef Company of Greeley, Colorado, recalled 19 million pounds of ground beef from supermarket shelves as 41 people in 12 states were sickened with E. coli.[61] E. coli 0157:H7 is a virulent form of bacteria first reported in 1982 in the U.S., present in the feces of slaughtered cattle. In two decades outbreaks have spread to Australia, Canada, Japan, the U.S., Europe and southern Africa.[62] Although the USDA confirmed on June 11, 2002, that the Greeley plant had a problem with E. coli contamination, the USDA continued testing and delayed notifying the company about the initial results for two weeks.[63] Meanwhile, contaminated ground beef was distributed to retailers and was consumed by an untold number of Americans. ConAgra initiated a recall of 354,000 pounds of meat only on June 30, 2002 (19 days after the first positive test, and shortly before America's favorite barbecuing holiday, July 4) and expanded the recall to 19 million pounds on July 18, 2002.[64]

The ConAgra recall was the second largest in U.S. history, and the latest in a series of events that has convinced many observers that the U.S. meat-inspection system is in crisis.

The U.S. system for ensuring meat safety is based on a number of core statutes and regulations. The U.S. Federal Meat Inspection Act (FMIA),[65] which instituted sanitary standards for slaughter and processing plants, was passed in 1906 after the stunning exposé of the meat slaughter and packing industry by Upton Sinclair in his famous book *The Jungle*. In 1957, the Poultry Products Inspection Act implemented many of the same requirements for poultry.[66] In 1967, the FMIA was amended by the Wholesome Meat Act, which strengthened the enforcement authority of USDA and incorporated provisions against adulteration and misbranding.[67] After an E. coli outbreak linked to Jack-in-the-Box hamburgers in 1993 killed four people and sickened 700, the USDA implemented a zero-tolerance policy for fecal contamination on meat and poultry.[68]

In 1996, new regulations were passed, purportedly to address the need to test for microbial contaminants in meat and poultry. However, the core concept underlying the new regulation has begun to unravel the entire fabric of food-safety policy. This is relevant to discussion of the WTO because the U.S. exports this meat and because now the U.S. seeks to export this regulatory system using the WTO's harmonization and equivalence rules.

Called the Hazard Analysis and Critical Control Point (HACCP), the system was intended to identify hazards and establish procedures to eliminate them using scientific means.[69] The new risk-based inspection system requires that industry—slaughter, processing and packing plants—rather than government inspectors identify steps during production where the risk of food-safety hazards are highest and then establish plans and controls to prevent or reduce these risks.[70]

In 1999, Public Citizen's Critical Mass Energy and Environment Project (CMEEP) and the Government Accountability Project (GAP) surveyed government meat inspectors and published the following results in a report called *Jungle 2000*:

- Inspectors could not enforce the core requirements of the U.S. law as well under HACCP because they were limited to examining only the company-identified critical control points;
- Because the government is not required to approve companies' HACCP plans, the plans failed to identify obvious critical control points;

- Inspectors spent five times as much time checking company records under HACCP as they did before, and one-third less time inspecting meat and poultry products;
- Inspectors felt they had much less authority to require corrective action when they saw a problem. Instead they were instructed to "let the system work" (i.e., let the company's procedures and testing catch the problem).[71]

Not only were inspectors reporting that their hands were tied under HACCP, but the system's much-vaunted microbial testing program also proved to be seriously flawed. In 2002, Public Citizen's CMEEP and GAP published a report called *Hamburger Hell: The Flip Side of the Government's Salmonella Testing Program*. The report concluded that the government's microbial testing program was allowing large quantities of potentially contaminated ground beef to move through the system and land on supermarket shelves. The report also noted that the U.S. government's own data do not support the highly publicized assertion that the HACCP program has made the food supply safer for consumers of ground beef.[72]

By analyzing the raw USDA data, the Public Citizen/GAP study found that many of the largest ground beef plants in the United States repeatedly flunked salmonella tests, but were permitted to continue sending to market ground beef stamped as government-approved. Between January 26, 1998, and October 1, 2001, the USDA knowingly allowed an estimated 218 million pounds of potentially contaminated ground beef—enough for about a billion hamburgers—to enter the market bearing the USDA seal of approval before it informed plant managers of the need for corrective action.[73]

Concerns about the HACCP program further increased when, on July 10, 2002, a draft U.S. General Accounting Office study on the failure of HACCP to protect consumers from unsafe meat was leaked and made U.S. newspaper headlines. According to the *New York Times*, the leaked document described a system that was "poorly designed, badly supervised and riddled with problems."[74]

The leaked study reported that the GAO's in-depth review of a small portion of slaughter and processing plants indicated that 94% of the HACCP plans had failed to meet U.S. regulatory requirements, while 80% had inadequate verification of critical control points. The report also found that even when plants experienced multiple serious noncompliance violations, they were rarely closed down. At one plant, inspectors issued 155 noncompliance records for fecal contamination, an alleged zero-tolerance policy of the USDA, but no further action was taken.[75]

An even more extreme HACCP-based Inspection Models Project (HIMP) is being used in some poultry and hog processing plants, which has resulted in higher rates of contamination, a critical GAO report, a lawsuit, and media exposés, but not termination of the HIMP program.[76] The result of this flawed system is a skyrocketing rate of recalls of meat and poultry products.[77]

Finally, no discussion of the increasing concerns about unsafe meat in the U.S. is complete without mentioning irradiation. Until the 1990s, irradiation was promoted primarily to increase shelf life and thus plays a major role in promoting long-distance food trade and further globalization of the food supply. More recently, government officials and the food industry have been promoting the use of irradiation equivalent to tens of millions of X rays as the solution to microbial contamination in meat. Though no long-term studies have been done on the health effects of consuming irradiated foods,[78] a recent study has shown that chemical by-products of irradiation may aid the cancer-development process and cause genetic and cellular damage.[79] Instead of implementing rigorous farm-to-table safety systems to ensure that food is clean and wholesome, regulators would rather try an end-of-the-line cleanup using little-tested and potentially hazardous technology.

With each massive recall of meat products, industry's cry to implement irradiation grows stronger, even as consumer opposition builds. The USDA approved irradiated meat beginning in February 2000, and it is slowly starting to appear on supermarket shelves.[80] More recently, the USDA announced that by the end of 2002 it will develop guidelines for irradiating foods purchased for the school lunch program that feeds millions of underprivileged children annually.[81]

U.S. EXPORTS FLAWED MEAT-INSPECTION MODEL TO THE WORLD

When the USDA developed HACCP for domestic beef, it required trading partners to develop HACCP systems to be eligible for export to the U.S. thus forcing the export of this flawed system.[82] By 1999, FSIS reported that 32 of the 37 countries assessed had adopted HACCP requirements "equivalent" to FSIS. At the same time, FSIS published a paper describing the procedures it had used to determine whether foreign countries' regulatory systems were equivalent. A few months later, without providing the opportunity for public comment guaranteed under the U.S. Administrative Procedures Act (APA), the USDA made that paper the official U.S. regulatory policy on how to determine equivalence as required under WTO rules.[83]

A short time later, the USDA's Office of Inspector General (OIG) reviewed the USDA's performance with regard to these equivalency decisions. The resulting report, which noted systemic failures in the equivalence determination and enforcement processes for countries on every continent, was a scathing exposé on the threats posed when food-safety prerogatives and policies are trumped by trade goals. Numerous problems in foreign systems, extending far beyond the flaws inherent in the U.S. HACCP model, were identified, among them:

- FSIS granted equivalency status to six countries without even conducting on-site reviews;
- Procedures for determining equivalency were not adequately developed, and equivalency determinations had been based on insufficient documented analysis and support;

- Requirements for annual certifications and residue test plans were not enforced;
- There were no clear procedures for determining if other countries' alternative testing methods were equivalent;
- Seven foreign establishments that had lost their eligibility certification were found to have shipped 4,625,363 pounds of meat and poultry into the U.S.; and
- Nineteen plants that had not been recertified as meeting U.S. standards were allowed to continue to export meat to the U.S.[84]

The report concluded by stating that "FSIS cannot demonstrate that it judged the foreign food-safety systems of current trading partners according to U.S. standards. . . ." and that the agency had reduced its oversight to less than what is prudent and necessary for the protection of the consumer.[85]

What had the WTO served up? First, it required that countries declare meat from different, less protective systems to be equivalently safe. Second, U.S. officials implementing that policy subordinated safety goals to trade priorities and failed to set rigorous standards for determining equivalence. As a result, U.S. consumers were eating meat labeled with a U.S. government seal even though the agencies were not enforcing even the inadequate minimal domestic standards that the USDA had set. The U.S. continues to import meat and poultry and ship these products to their final destinations before the lab results on tested samples are returned.[86]

A more recent review reveals that significant problems continue:

- In Canada, the FSIS found that the Canadian Food Inspection Agency (CFIA) violated U.S. rules requiring monthly supervisory inspections, reducing those to four per year. One province, Manitoba, conducted no supervisory inspections for two years, despite U.S. concerns.[87] Regardless, the U.S. considers the Canadian system to be equivalent.
- Regarding Argentina, the USDA could not establish that the system met U.S. requirements; deficiencies in the Argentine system include contamination of meat with oil, hair, and feces in the rectum area of carcasses in the kill floor, and inadequate labeling of barrels for edible and inedible parts in the hamburger processing areas.[88] Regardless, the U.S. considers the Argentine meat safety system to be equivalent.
- Brazil had food-safety inspections conducted by plant employees rather than government inspectors. Eighteen of the 55 company-paid inspectors had administrative responsibilities as well as food-safety inspection. Fifteen of 16 establishments had one or more company-paid inspection employees.[89] Regardless, the U.S. considers the Brazilian meat safety system to be equivalent.

The failure of the U.S. government to uphold U.S. law raises serious concerns. Once a country's inspection system is deemed equivalent, meat imports from that country enter the U.S. and obtain a USDA grading sticker making them indistinguishable from domestic meat. Not only are U.S. consumers being put at greater risk because the U.S. government is failing to live up to the core standards of its own food-safety system, but developing countries are not being given the resources they need to ensure the soundness of their domestic regulatory policy and thus the safety of exports. Combined, these two policies are a recipe for disaster.

SPS HARMONIZATION REQUIREMENTS OUT OF TUNE WITH PUBLIC SAFETY

Harmonization is the term given to industry's effort to replace various national product standards and regulations with one global system, a movement that gained a significant boost with the establishment of the WTO, which explicitly requires harmonization of food and technical standards.[90]

Theoretically, international harmonization could occur at the lowest or highest levels of public health or environmental protection. Unfortunately, the actual WTO harmonization provisions promote lowering of the best existing domestic public-health, food-safety, plant- and animal-protection and environmental standards around the world. This is the case because, under the WTO, international standards serve as a ceiling which countries cannot exceed, rather than as a floor that all countries must meet. Thus, the provisions in the WTO promoting harmonization are likely to serve only as a one-way downward ratchet on domestic standards—the race-to-the-bottom effect.

To facilitate harmonization, the SPS Agreement names specific international standards that are presumed to be WTO-legal, such as those established by the Office of International Epizootics in Paris, the International Plant Protection Convention in Geneva, the Codex Alimentarius Commission (Codex) in Rome and International Organization on Standardization in Geneva.[91] International standards promulgated in industry-only organizations may have the same status at the WTO as governmental standards, promoting industry to create private standards drafted behind closed doors without with any role for health or consumer representatives.

Hundreds of committees in each of the WTO-specified institutions and dozens of other international standard-setting organizations and industry associations are working to implement the WTO harmonization mandate. These bodies have diverse processes for decision making, membership, transparency and public involvement. The most significant institution in the food arena is the Rome-based Codex Alimentarius Commission.[92]

Codex Now Sets WTO-Legal Global Food Standards

The Codex Alimentarius (Latin for "food law") was established in 1963 jointly by the World Health Organization and the U.N. Food and Agriculture Organization "to facilitate the world trade in foods [through] internationally accepted standards,"[93] and now establishes the food standards that the WTO's SPS Agreement recognizes as WTO-legal.[94] This means that when member countries' food-safety laws are challenged under the SPS Agreement, a WTO tribunal will evaluate their legitimacy by establishing whether they exceed standards set by the Codex.

At its inception, the Codex's focus was to assess the trade—not health—implications of varying pesticide tolerances.[95] Indeed the Codex describes its charge as:

> [T]o guide and promote the elaboration and establishment of definitions and requirements for foods, to assist in their harmonization and, in doing so, to facilitate international trade.[96]

At one point the World Health Organization almost terminated its support for the Codex on the grounds that its activities were not sufficiently related to the primary mission of the WHO: improved world health.[97] Although the Codex officially recognizes that its standards must protect public health, many observers have concluded that the Codex remains poorly suited to establish global food-safety standards because its primary mandate is to promote international trade. This contrasts sharply with the mandates in U.S. law, such as that found in the federal Food, Drug and Cosmetic Act, where health and safety are the priorities.[98]

The Codex standards, initially voluntary and consensus-based, were designed to help developing countries establish a sufficient level of sanitary protection to ensure their products would be accepted by trading partners. However, given Codex's new role as the developer of the world's trade-legal food standards, its standards are no longer strictly "voluntary" and the process is no longer truly "consensus-based." The WTO stands ready to enforce Codex standards as the presumptively trade-legal standards, imbuing Codex standards with tremendous weight. As a consequence, this little-known organization is now the focus of a great deal of governmental and industry attention. Debates within the Codex are becoming increasingly politicized. Instead of consensus discussions, some standards are passed through formal voting over stiff objections. Trade officials, not just food-safety or public-health officials, frequently show up at Codex meetings to represent their governments' points of view.

The Codex is officially a forum of member governments, but many government delegations also include scores of industry representatives. Other governments often cannot afford to participate in the process. Fewer than half the 170 Codex member nations sent delegations to the 2001 meeting, and at most meetings fewer than one quarter of the member countries participate—only 5% of member countries sent delegations to a 2001 working group meeting to develop international guidelines on risk analysis standards for GMO-related allergenic reactions.[99]

Codex meetings are closed to the public and press, and draft Codex standards are often not made public until well into the process,[100] in contrast to U.S. domestic laws which mandate public input throughout the rule-making process. To provide input at the Codex, members of the public must persuade a governmental participant to provide them with a draft proposal and then present their positions to other delegates. In contrast, industry representatives who can afford to fly all over the world can present their views directly by lobbying the delegates of many nations. Some global food corporations have representatives on so many different countries' delegations that the combined number from one company is larger than some countries' delegation size.

International Harmonization Undermines Open, Accountable U.S. Policy-making Process

Many international standard-setting bodies—some of which are literally industry trade associations—empowered by the WTO to set WTO-legal international standards provide few opportunities for citizen input or oversight, in sharp contrast to U.S. law, which requires that the public be notified and offered an opportunity to comment on regulatory proposals. With the international harmonization of health and safety standards, U.S. federal agency adherence to the domestic procedure for notification, balance, openness and public input has been at best ad hoc.

For instance, under the U.S. domestic process, all agency rule making must be conducted "on the record" under the U.S. Administrative Procedure Act. The APA requires advance notice about proposed regulations, opportunities for public comment and open review of draft regulations[101] as well as written explanation of how and why an agency came to its conclusion and on what basis it dismissed alternative proposals.[102] The APA also allows individuals to challenge a finished regulation in court.

Public access to information and decision making in the U.S. regulatory process is guaranteed by several laws, including the Freedom of Information Act (FOIA),[103] which guarantees access to most government documents; the Government in the Sunshine Act, which requires that government meetings be open to the public with notice given;[104] and the Federal Advisory Committee Act (FACA), which requires balanced representation and open operations of government advisory committees.[105] Public notices of policy-making initiatives are listed in the U.S. *Federal Register*, a widely available publication of official government business.

Open government laws are key aspects of U.S. policy-making procedures and guarantee that U.S. citizens have a voice in the development of rules and regulations that will impact their lives. However, in the U.S. government's conduct of WTO-linked international harmonization of environmental, health, safety and other regulatory standards, the principles of these four essential U.S. laws are being inadequately applied, when they are applied at all.[106] The result is an enormously reduced level of citizen and public-interest group involvement in the era of the WTO, and thus a dramatically scaled-back role for these interests in making the food-safety and other decisions that daily affect lives.

The Codex claims it "seeks the advice and assistance from international nongovernmental organizations" to "represent important sections of public opinion" and "play an appropriate role in ensuring the harmonizing of intersectoral interests of the various sectoral bodies concerned."[107] Internationally incorporated NGOs may participate in Codex meetings as observers. However, Public Citizen examined the Codex's list of official NGOs and found that more than four out of five of the NGOs were actually agribusiness or food trade associations.[108] Because of the prohibitive cost of airfare, only two internationally incorporated consumer organizations regularly participate in the Codex: the International Association of Consumer Food Organizations, based in Washington, D.C., and Consumers International, based in London.

Given the Codex's skewed mandate, its closed procedures, and the enormous role played by the food industry, it is not surprising that many Codex standards fall short. A systematic comparison of U.S. and Codex pesticide residue rules has not been done in years. When a comparative study was completed by the U.S. General Accounting Office in 1991, the GAO found that many Codex standards were weaker than public health–based food standards in the U.S. For example, some Codex standards allowed residues of pesticides that have been banned completely in the U.S.[109] Others allowed higher residues for pesticides such as heptachlor, aldrin, Diazinon, lindane, permethrin and benomyl.[110] In some cases, Codex standards allowed residue levels that were five times as high as U.S. standards."[111] The Codex has not undertaken major revisions of its pesticide standards, although a consumer campaign to highlight Codex's DDT tolerances resulted in the Codex changing its tolerance of DDT residues on fruits and vegetables. Still, Codex permits DDT residue levels in milk, meat and grain.[112]

The Codex continues to set international standards of the lowest common denominator variety. For instance:

- At its July 1999 meeting, the Codex approved maximum residue levels for the pesticide methyl parathion[113] that did not take into account the impact of the level on children, as is required under U.S. law.[114] Two months after Codex made this methyl parathion determination, the U.S. EPA banned the use of the chemical on fruits and vegetables because of the risk it posed to children.[115] As a result, the U.S. regulation is now exposed to challenge under the WTO's SPS Agreement because it provides greater protection than the WTO-recognized international standard.
- Codex standards allow for the use of cyclamates, which have been banned in the U.S. since 1970.[116] The FDA banned cyclamates after animal studies linked the artificial sweetener to birth defects, the impairment of testicular function, and the enhancement of the carcinogenic effect of some chemicals.[117]
- In July 2001, Codex adopted standards for maximum levels of lead in milk that are not consistent with U.S. FDA enforcement policy.[118] Some delegates "felt that lower levels were necessary to protect sensitive individuals, especially children, from a contaminant with severe public health implications."[119]
- Also in 2001, Codex adopted a maximum level of 0.5 micrograms per kilogram for the dangerous carcinogen aflatoxin M1 in milk, despite strenuous objections by the European Union, South Africa and other countries.[120] The EU standard was 0.05 micrograms per kilogram, while the U.S. standard was 1.0.[121] Evidently the Codex decided to split the difference and expose European consumers to ten times the level of danger.

In 2002, Codex chairperson and former USDA official Tom Billy proposed an aggressive harmonization agenda for the future, including moving the consideration and finalization of standards more quickly.[122] This accelerated schedule is sure to further marginalize developing countries, health specialists and civil society groups.

Codex Blows the Limits on Food Irradiation

Codex is currently considering a new proposal that could greatly expand the proliferation of irradiated foods throughout the world. The proposal would allow any food to be irradiated at any dose.[123] It also would eliminate virtually every assurance that irradiated foods will be of good quality, be handled by trained workers, and be processed under safe and clean conditions in government-inspected facilities.

In Geneva in September 2001, the Codex Executive Committee endorsed the Proposed Draft Revised General Standard for Irradiated Foods,[124] a proposal that would completely remove the maximum dose of radiation with which food can be "treated" and still be safe for human consumption.[125] The current dose cap in the U.S. varies from food to food, with poultry, for example, limited to the equivalent of 99 million chest X rays, while other foods, including spices, can be irradiated with the equivalent of one billion chest X rays.[126] The proposed Codex changes would remove even these limits.

Additionally, under the Codex irradiation proposal now pending:

- Irradiated foods would no longer have to be "of suitable quality," be in "acceptable hygienic condition" or be handled "according to good manufacturing practices";
- Food irradiation facilities would no longer have to be designed to "meet the requirements of safety efficacy and good hygiene practices of food processing," be staffed by "adequate, trained and competent personnel," be licensed or inspected by government officials or maintain records on radioactive activities; and
- Food irradiation would no longer have to be carried out "commensurate with . . . technological and public health purposes" or be conducted "in accordance with good radiation processing practice."[127]

The Codex Executive Commission endorsed the proposal despite a growing body of evidence suggesting that irradiated foods may not be safe for human consumption. In experiments dating back 50 years, animals fed irradiated foods have suffered dozens of health problems, including premature death, mutations, and other genetic abnormalities, fetal death and other reproductive problems, immune system disorders, fatal internal bleeding, organ damage, tumors, stunted growth and nutritional deficiencies.[128] Additionally, four consecutive experiments conducted since 1998 have found toxic properties in chemicals formed in irradiated foods that contain fat.[129] The chemicals—cyclobutanones—have not been found to occur naturally in any food.[130]

A new Codex standard could place additional U.S. regulations at risk of challenge by WTO member countries as being potential trade barriers and would
undermine the caps on irradiation that the FDA has placed on a number of food
products. The Codex proposal would also undercut the bans or strict limitations
on food irradiation that 11 EU nations have instituted: Austria, Belgium, Denmark,
Finland, Germany, Greece, Ireland, Luxembourg, Portugal, Spain and Sweden.
The proposal is very much alive, although Codex delayed further deliberation of
the proposal due to the controversy.[131]

WTO RECORD ON FOOD SAFETY
AND QUARANTINE LAWS

After nearly nine years, a WTO trend in the food arena has emerged: panels have
ruled against all food-safety regulations under review on the grounds that they
restrict trade more than necessary.

The WTO has also ruled repeatedly that the Precautionary Principle cannot be
implemented in a manner consistent with WTO rules, thus eviscerating the ability
of its member nations to safeguard against significant potential risks. For instance,
in the 1960s, U.S. regulators refused to approve the sale of the morning sickness
drug thalidomide because U.S. law uses a precautionary approach, putting the
burden on manufacturers to prove a drug is safe.[132] As a result, the U.S. averted a
disastrous epidemic of birth defects. In other countries, thalidomide is estimated
to have caused deformities in more than 10,000 babies. At the time of its approval
in Europe and Canada, tests in laboratory animals showed no negative effects.[133]
Thalidomide's damage was revealed only over time, not in the drug's users, but in
their children.

The WTO has turned the sensible Precautionary Principle on its head, yet
requiring governments to prove a product is dangerous is almost impossible for
new or emerging technologies. Cases in which the WTO has ruled against the
Precautionary Principle include the EU's consumer protection ban on artificial
hormone-treated beef, and Australia's quarantine on raw salmon imports (which
was designed to protect the health of the indigenous fish population). Now a
major fight is brewing over the emerging issue of consumers' and countries' rights
to regulate—or ban—genetically modified crops and foods made from them, with
the U.S. announcing in May 2003 that it was initiating WTO action against the
EU's halt on new GMO approvals while new EU rules on segregating and labeling
GMOs are being finalized. Already, mere threats of WTO action under the SPS
Agreement have resulted in Japan and South Korea lowering food standards. The
WTO also has set an unusually high standard which countries must meet to protect the integrity of their food and farms from nonindigenous and hazardous
pests and diseases in cases involving Japan's fruit pest testing requirements and
efforts to keep out an aggressive orchard-attacking bacteria and recent U.S. efforts
to keep Mediterranean fruit flies from entering the country via imported Spanish
Clementines.

Case 1: The WTO Rules Against European Ban of Artificial Hormone–Treated Beef

"As you recommended, we have initiated action against the EU ban under the dispute settlement procedures of the World Trade Organization."
—Letter from U.S. Trade Representative Mickey Kantor to the National Cattlemen's Association, February 18, 1996[134]

In 1988, the EU banned the sale of beef from cattle treated with any of six artificial hormones that are linked to cancer and premature pubescence in girls[135] and have been shown to have genotoxic (damaging to DNA) effects.[136] The ban was applied in a nondiscriminatory fashion to both domestic and imported beef products.[137] Although the risk to humans of artificial-hormone residues in the meat they consume is uncertain, the EU adopted a "zero risk" standard on the basis of the known risks from direct human consumption of the hormones in question and strong public demand for a ban on meat grown with artificial hormones.[138]

The U.S. beef and biotechnology industries long opposed this EU policy.[139] In early 1996, at the behest of the U.S.-based National Cattlemen's Association, the U.S. challenged the EU policy at the WTO.[140] In 1997, a WTO panel ruled that the policy was forbidden under SPS rules in large part because it was not based on the extremely controversial international standards developed at the Codex Alimentarius;[141] nor on a WTO-approved risk assessment[142] and in part because the hormones had not been scientifically proved to be dangerous to humans in the context of consumption of residues in beef.[143]

In January 1998, the WTO's Appellate Body narrowed the basis of the initial ruling but did not alter the outcome of the case.[144] The WTO Appellate Body stated that the WTO SPS rules would allow the EU to set standards different from the Codex standard but only if such an EU decision was based on a risk assessment that "sufficiently warranted" the difference.[145] Although the WTO SPS Agreement in Article 3.3 technically allows countries to set levels of protection that exceed Codex, Article 5.1 allows them to maintain that higher standard only if it is based on a risk assessment done pursuant to WTO-condoned risk-assessment rules. As the appellate ruling in the beef hormone case explicitly notes, the contradictory mandates in the WTO SPS Agreement operate to make it nearly impossible for a country to maintain a standard that provides more regulatory safeguards than the Codex standard.[146]

While the tone and logic of the Appellate Body ruling sounded more reasonable than the extreme lower-tribunal decision, it led to the same bottom line. The EU was ordered to begin imports of U.S. artificial hormone-treated beef by May 13, 1999, or to have conducted a WTO-legal risk assessment to justify not doing so.[147]

The EU began to implement the WTO ruling by initiating a risk-assessment analysis that could be used to justify the ban under WTO rules. The U.S. objected to the EU's move to do a risk assessment, arguing that the ruling meant that the EU's beef ban was prima facie incompatible with SPS rules because there was no scientific evidence that artificial hormone residues are unfit for human consumption.[148] Regardless of the U.S. contention, in 1998, the EU launched 17 studies into the risk of the hormones in question and asked the European Commission's Scientific Committee on Veterinary Measures Relating to Public Health (SCVPH) for an assessment of the risk to human health.

The EU's full risk assessment was not complete by the WTO deadline. Thus, the U.S. argued, the EU was required to lift the import prohibition.[149] When the EU failed to comply with the WTO panel ruling by the May 1999 deadline, the WTO on July 12, 1999, approved a U.S. request to impose retaliatory sanctions, but lowered the amount from the $200 million requested by the U.S. and authorized trade sanctions against $116.8 million worth of European-made products.[150] To avoid the U.S. being free to choose what EU goods would be hit with the sanctions, the EU offered to compensate the U.S. for maintaining the beef hormone ban until the assessment was done and the issue could be judged on the basis of more complete evidence.[151] Then–U.S. Trade Representative Charlene Barshefsky responded that the U.S. would accept a deal only if the EU pledged to open its beef market soon.[152] No deal was struck, and the U.S. levied 100% tariffs totaling $116.8 million annually on a variety of key EU exports the U.S. selected, including truffles, mustard, and cheeses.[153]

José Bové, the WTO Beef Case, Roquefort Cheese and McDonald's

Before the tariffs began, the United States was the third biggest foreign market for French Roquefort cheese. José Bové, a sheep farmer and co-founder of la Confédération Paysanne, the French small farmer's union,[154] was among thousands angered by the effect the WTO sanctions were having on farmers involved in producing Roquefort cheese. In 1999 Bové protested against the WTO with local farmers by dismantling a McDonald's under construction in the town of Millau, a county seat in the Roquefort-producing region in southern France.[155] The farmers dragged the disassembled parts of the McDonald's to Millau's town square and issued demands to local, regional and national officials to lift the tariffs. Bové was arrested and sentenced to three months in prison.[156]

Nicknamed "The Peasant Robin Hood,"[157] Bové's trial brought crowds of 100,000 to Millau.[158] WTO experts—including Ambassador Tran van Tihn, a former high-level GATT negotiator—and activists from around the world testified in his defense at his trial.[159] Bové, already a well-known activist and a leading figure among farm activists at the WTO Seattle Ministerial in 1999,[160] became a national hero, with whom French President Jacques Chirac and Prime Minister Lionel Jospin agreed to meet to discuss the tariffs.[161] Although the French prime minister and president opposed the WTO action, they informed Bové that they were powerless to do anything about it.

Meanwhile, the EU risk assessment established that the artificial hormone 17 beta oestradiol, one of the six artificial growth hormones at issue in the case, was a "complete" carcinogen, meaning that it had both tumor initiation and tumor promotion properties.[162] In the cases of the other five hormones, the committee found that, though there was insufficient evidence for a quantifiable risk assessment, there was identifiable risk to consumers of those products, especially pre-pubertal children.[163] Once the SCVPH report was presented, the European Commission recommended a permanent ban on 17 beta oestradiol and provisional prohibition of the other growth hormones. The European Parliament adopted those proposals on February 1, 2001.[164]

In the face of the new findings, the U.S. refused to address the scientific merits or faults of the risk assessment, sticking to the initial position that the WTO Appellate Body's ruling found the ban to be indefensible. Indeed, in the 2002 National Trade Estimates Report on Foreign Trade Barriers, the USTR noted the existence of the new studies, but commented that "none of these studies presented any *new* evidence to support the EU's hormone ban."[165] Thus, the $116.8 million per year trade sanctions and the EU ban remain in place. However, this is the only WTO ruling—with two wealthy nations, each of whom can afford continuing WTO litigation and bear sanctions—that has resulted in such an outcome rather than the losing country changing its policy.

Even Labeling Can Be Considered a Barrier to Trade

Even far less stringent regulatory approaches to food safety than a ban could run afoul of the WTO. A possible alternative to a ban on artificial hormone–treated beef sales in the EU and elsewhere is the labeling of meat raised with the artificial hormones. The U.S. argues that this relatively weak strategy may also be WTO-illegal.[166] In the beef hormone case, the WTO has already ruled that artificial hormone residues on food have not been shown to pose a danger to human health. Thus, mandatory labeling of beef hormones could be determined to serve no legitimate WTO human-health objective and not to be based on a scientific justification and thus could be ruled to be an unjustifiable discrimination against U.S. beef.[167] Presently the U.S. is making similar arguments about the labeling of GMO food products.

The Implications of the Beef Hormone Ruling

The WTO Appellate Body ruling toned down some of the more controversial aspects and antiregulatory findings of the initial WTO panel ruling.[168] In addition, it cut out an array of findings the lower panel had made on issues not directly raised in the case. However, it confirmed the basic findings: that even nondiscriminatory domestic regulations must either 1) be based on international standards;

or, 2) if they depart from international standards, be based on an extensive risk assessment.

Precautionary Principle Severely Undermined

The WTO Appellate Body clearly subjugated the Precautionary Principle to the WTO's SPS requirements, severely limiting the ability of nations to enact health regulation in advance of scientific certainty, by dismissing the EU's argument that it took action on the artificial hormones based on the Precautionary Principle and ruling that a government's reliance on the Precautionary Principle did not override the obligation of WTO members to base their measures on a risk assessment.[169]

Confirmed Opposition to Zero Tolerance

Even when scientific data are robust, value judgments and social priorities play the central role in policy making. People make judgments about whether exposure to a risk is avoidable (whether there are acceptable, affordable substitutes) and how much risk is reasonable in exchange for whatever rewards a new product promises. The WTO appellate ruling does not leave space for legislatures to decide to allow zero risk from a particular hazard rather than establishing an allowable level of risk.

The implications of this interpretation of WTO rules are far reaching. For example, Chile has a zero-tolerance level for salmonella in poultry, which applies to both foreign and domestic poultry, and which, when implemented, has successfully prevented contamination.[170] The U.S. considers the Chilean policy to be unnecessarily severe and thus listed the salmonella policy in the USTR's 2002 National Trade Estimate Report as a barrier to trade[171] and has raised it at the WTO.[172] Under the WTO SPS Agreement, the Chilean salmonella regulations could be challenged as illegitimate trade restrictions.

Case 2: Australian Salmon—WTO Adds Difficulty, Cost to Animal Health Protections

In 1998, the WTO Appellate Body ruled that an Australian quarantine on raw salmon imports, instituted in the 1960s[173] to protect the nation's indigenous fish population, was an illegal barrier to trade.[174] The policy required Australia's director of quarantine to ban raw salmon imports unless they have been subjected to treatment that would prevent the introduction into Australia of any infectious or contagious diseases affecting persons, animals or plants.

When Canada and the U.S. requested access to Australia's uncooked salmon market in 1994, Australia conducted a risk assessment as required by the WTO SPS Agreement. In 1996, on the basis of the risk assessment, the director of quarantine concluded that Australia should not permit uncooked salmon imports.[175]

In response, Canada filed a complaint with the WTO in 1997, arguing that the raw salmon ban violated the SPS Agreement.[176] The United States reserved its third-party rights to participate in Canada's complaint.

Among other findings, the Australian risk assessment revealed that some 20 bacteria not present in Australia were present in Canadian salmon. The Australian government concluded that the introduction of these contaminants into its salmon population could cause disease, and found that Canada had not developed a treatment to eliminate the bacteria. Moreover, the Australian risk assessment found that the bacteria can remain in animals after they have been killed, and that food prepared for human consumption has in a number of cases ended up in the animal food supply, thus creating a risk of exposure for Australian fish. The risk-assessment report confirmed that Canadian uncooked salmon could infect live Australian salmon.[177] Indeed, Australia noted in its WTO filings that Canada had not disagreed that there was a risk of disease spread through uncooked salmon, and further that Canada had refused to produce relevant scientific data pertaining to the diseases particular to Canadian salmon.[178]

Despite these findings, in June 1998, a WTO panel ruled that the Australian ban violated WTO requirements because it was not based on sound science; it exceeded international standards and therefore it was arbitrarily and unjustifiably discriminatory.[179]

Australia appealed, arguing that its risk assessment, which was conducted as required by the SPS Agreement and which established that there was a risk of disease from uncooked salmon, allowed it to determine for itself the *level* of risk to which it would expose its fish stocks in accordance with the SPS.[180] In its November 1998 ruling on Australia's appeal, the WTO Appellate Body concluded that Australia's risk assessment was unsatisfactory because it failed to calculate the *likelihood* of salmon disease entry and transmission.[181] "It is not sufficient that a risk assessment conclude there is a possibility of entry, establishment or spread. . . . A proper risk assessment . . . must evaluate the likelihood, i.e. the probability, of entry, establishment and spread."[182] Thus, the appellate decision expanded the WTO requirements by demanding that a risk be quantifiable and found significant, rather than "merely" present, thus subjugating a democratically elected government's policy judgment to the WTO's definition of what constitutes serious risk.

With this ruling, the WTO also established strict guidelines for conducting risk assessments relating to nonhuman disease, requiring that a risk assessment must be conducted *prior* to a WTO member's introduction or enforcement of a regulation relating to plant and animal pests and diseases.[183] This interpretation of the WTO rules imposes a significant financial burden on countries wishing to put into place such regulations, and thus discourages countries from doing so. Under WTO rules, a country cannot quickly act to avert an outbreak but rather must decide if it has the resources and/or expertise to perform a WTO-compliant risk assessment and then do so. According to an Australian government official, "There are not a lot of scientists around who are able to do these [types of risk assessments]. A thorough assessment requires a lot of time and resources."[184]

In light of the WTO's appellate ruling, in May of 1999 the U.S. exercised its third-party rights and requested a panel to rule on Australia's quarantine. Australia was given a deadline of July 1999 to lift the ban. In July 1999, the Australian Quarantine and Inspection Service issued a decision that lifted the import ban but increased the quarantine requirements for several species of fish, in line with risk assessments undertaken.[185] Australia contended that these changes met the requirements of the Appellate Body.

In late July 1999 Canada asked the WTO to authorize sanctions on the basis that the new quarantine measures were not compliant with the WTO panel ruling.[186] It requested that the original panel rule on the question of whether Australia's new measures were WTO-consistent. Australia made a counter-request that the WTO panel determine how much Canada was actually harmed by the Australian quarantine.[187] A Recourse Panel, which would determine whether the measures taken by Australia had brought them into compliance with the previous WTO rulings,[188] was established in June 1999.[189]

In February 2000, the Recourse Panel ruled on the Canadian challenge that, although Australia had performed a WTO-compliant Import Risk Assessment, the quarantine measures were nonetheless in violation of WTO SPS requirements because it was not the least trade restrictive way to achieve the goal of reducing the risk.[190] The Recourse Panel put the burden on Australia to prove that there was no other means than the one used that had a lesser trade impact (in other words, to prove a negative) or accept the judgment of a WTO tribunal of trade experts about the proper way to defend against the spread of salmon disease rather than the judgment of the Australian fisheries' scientists.

In light of the ruling by the Recourse Panel, Australia negotiated a settlement with Canada on May 17, 2000 and extended it to the U.S. on October 27, 2000. The settlement removed the provision that only consumer-ready salmon, as previously defined by Australia,[191] could be imported.[192]

The WTO Appellate Body ruling made clear that countries are strictly constrained in their policy options to protect against pests and animal disease and certainly have no latitude to err on the side of caution. The Appellate Body's ruling against the original guidelines, in concert with the Recourse Panel's ruling against the updated guidelines, set four precedents: The first requires WTO members to adopt SPS standards relating to plant and animal health only when precise risk to animals or plants can be quantified. Second, the actual likelihood of such risk of infection or infestation must be established with scientific certainty. Third, the risk must be judged serious by the WTO panel. Finally, the means used to counter the risk must be the least trade restrictive. Together, these requirements place countries in a straitjacket, with their wild flora and fauna and domesticated plants and animals at risk.

In its ruling against Australia's salmon measure, as in the beef hormone case, the WTO panel shifted the entire burden—financial and scientific—to the country whose law was being challenged, requiring it to show that prohibited products were unsafe. Exporting countries—or companies located therein—on the other hand, cannot under WTO rules be asked by importing countries to demonstrate that their products are disease-free before they are allowed into the country.

Case 3: A Blight on Japan's Diet: U.S. Moves to Limit Japan's Efforts to Protect Its Agriculture from Fire Blight

Japan has long sought to protect its farmland from new and dangerous pests. Japan's geographic isolation has provided a natural barrier to invasive species and agricultural diseases that cause considerable damage to crops in other parts of the world. In the U.S., for example, efforts to control invasive species and losses in the agriculture and timber industries cost $137 billion annually. More than half of these costs are associated with plants, animals and diseases that are subject to phytosanitary regulations.[193]

Japan's agricultural quarantine rules have successfully prevented the introduction of many hazards, such as rabies, and pests, such as codling moths and Mediterranean fruit flies, which are not indigenous to Japan. Japan imports 20 times more agricultural products from the U.S. than it exports, making it more susceptible to invasive-species introduction.[194] Typically, biological invasions are irreversible, and given the tremendous cost of combating invasions, it is easier, cheaper and more effective to focus on preventing their introduction.[195] In its annual report on agricultural trade in 2002, Japan noted its exposure to invasive pests was increasing every year as a result of the increases in and diversification of its agricultural imports.[196]

Japan's efforts to combat introduction of fire blight on apples and pears and other invasive species go back more than 50 years to the enactment of Japan's Plant Protection Law.[197] Japan imposed the fire blight quarantine rules in 1994, after it first opened its markets to imported apples.[198] The U.S. has been trying to fight them ever since.[199]

Fire blight, caused by the bacterium *Erwinia amylovora*, can be spread to fruit blossoms by wind, rain and insects.[200] It damages and kills trees in nurseries and young trees in the orchard, can delay fruit-bearing in young trees, and can kill older trees through girdling blight cankers.[201] Because diseases like fire blight are so difficult to treat, the best approach is prophylactic management to ensure the infestation never occurs.[202]

To date, Japan has not had a sustained fire blight outbreak.[203] And, if it had, weakening the fire blight quarantine would create additional risks, such as introducing the disease to new areas or presenting new genetic varieties which could be harder to control.[204]

Japan's quarantine requirements for fire blight have been targeted by the U.S. for removal, with USTR's 2001 and 2002 reports of trade barriers listing Japan's program as being overly burdensome because the quarantine rules "raise costs and reduce competitiveness of U.S. apples."[205]

On March 1, 2002, the USTR requested WTO consultations with Japan regarding import restrictions on U.S. apples to prevent the introduction of fire blight. The U.S. was unhappy with Japan's quarantine rules, which, among other things, prohibit importing apples from orchards where any fire blight is detected; require three annual inspections of orchards seeking to export to Japan for the presence of fire blight, disqualifying orchards within 500 meters of fire blight infestation; and require post-harvest treatment of apples with chlorine, which the U.S. contended is not supported by scientific evidence.[206] On May 7, 2002, the U.S. formally requested that a WTO dispute panel be convened to consider Japan's import restrictions on U.S. apples.

Japan argued that the U.S. WTO complaint lacked necessary scientific basis and that Japan's quarantine measures are consistent with its SPS obligations.[207] In July 2002, the WTO convened a dispute panel to rule on Japan's quarantine measures, and Australia (which also has a fire blight quarantine measure),[208] and Brazil, Taiwan, the EC and New Zealand (who all oppose the quarantine) reserved their right to participate as third parties.[209]

The USTR submissions to the WTO argued that billions of apples have been exported worldwide without a single documented case of fire blight transmission; that fire blight bacteria are "rarely" found on mature, symptomless apples; that cold storage, handling, and transport would make the bacteria's survival "unlikely"; and that there is no mechanism for the bacteria (should it exist and survive export) to be transmitted to orchards. Moreover, the U.S. argued that Japan has failed to present a risk assessment that meets the tests from the Australia salmon case: Japan's risk assessment focused on the possibility of entry but not the probability, according to USTR.[210]

Although opponents of fire blight quarantine barriers contend that fire blight transmission cannot occur from healthy fruit, there is no proof of this contention. USTR itself admits that some studies have found fire blight bacteria on mature fruit at harvest.[211] Researchers from the Horticultural and Food Research Institute of New Zealand (which favors eroding Japan's fire blight quarantine) could only show that it is *difficult*, though possible, to infect healthy apples with fire blight, and that healthy apples are *unlikely* to transmit fire blight across national borders through trade.[212] The difference highlights a significant problem with the WTO's risk-analysis rules: a country is not permitted to maintain a policy that makes the introduction of invasive pests impossible, only one which makes an infestation unlikely. The U.S. does not dispute that the Japanese fire blight restriction will prevent the introduction of fire blight, but contends that under WTO rules, Japan cannot maintain a policy that ensures that there will not be a fire blight introduction, but only a WTO-consistent policy that keeps the probability of an introduction low.[213]

Whatever one thinks about this particular situation, if the WTO again rules against a quarantine, it will have significant effects on the global capacity to prevent the spread of invasive plant, animal and disease species. To date, the WTO has ruled against every effort to prevent the entry of agricultural pests and invasive species. In each ruling, the WTO has progressively raised the bar for what policies are WTO-legal, making future efforts to keep out these agricultural pests, diseases and invasive species increasingly difficult.

Case 4: Genetically Modified Organisms in Food

As scientific innovation outpaces the ability of regulators to anticipate the adverse human health effects of new technologies, the potential threat WTO trade rules pose to cutting-edge domestic public health and safety policies will increase. For instance, barely discussed at the time the SPS Agreement went into effect, but of vital importance, were the potential human health and environmental threats posed by new biological technologies. (See Chapter 7 for a thorough discussion of GMOs.) More and more commodities for human consumption are being genetically altered to improve appearance or enhance resistance to agricultural chemicals. Agribusiness and biotechnology companies are pushing for the unregulated sale and trade of these genetically modified organisms without a full understanding of their impacts on human and environmental health.

Emerging data indicate that some GMOs cause allergic reactions in humans.[214] In addition, the environmental dangers of open-air crop trials, cross pollination, and on-the-ground and in-the-silo contamination of non-GMO crops with GMOs have been amply demonstrated on numerous occasions. For example, in November 2002, U.S. officials announced that an experimental plant that was genetically modified to make a pharmaceutical product had nearly slipped into the nation's food supply, even though it is not intended for human consumption,[215] and some GM crops not approved for human consumption have already made it onto the U.S. food market. In 2000, environmental and consumer groups detected "Starlink" corn, a strain only approved for use as animal feed, in taco shells for sale in grocery stores, prompting a voluntary recall by the U.S. Food and Drug Administration.[216] But the onerous burden of proof placed by the WTO on governments that try to establish or enforce regulations severely undermines their ability to protect the public from the possible dangers of GMOs, or to respond to public demand to ban, or at least label, such products.

While the EU has proceeded cautiously before exposing its public to GMOs, U.S. industry has been the leading advocate for GMOs and has successfully pressed the case with U.S. government and trade officials. U.S. industry considers GM foods to be "substantially equivalent" to non-GM foods and views requirements for process-based labeling and tracking or "traceability" of GM foods from farm to table as being without basis in any known health risk.[217] Industry also argues that the practical difficulties and huge costs involved in segregating and documenting GM foods would greatly hamper U.S. trade and could potentially encourage skeptical European consumers to avoid GM food products, effectively discriminating against U.S. exports.[218] Therefore, the industry view is that even labeling and traceability requirements constitute unnecessary restrictions on trade, claiming that labeling GMO products is unnecessary "in the absence of an identified and documented risk to safety or health."[219] In addition, industry complains that an EU hold on approvals of GMOs for sale in the EU is not based on scientific risk assessments, as required by the WTO's SPS Agreement, since all 13 of the GMO varieties have received clearance from EU scientific committees.[220]

U.S. government policy carefully follows the industry line and considers the EU's resistance to GMOs to be a trade barrier.[221] In November 2002, newspapers in the U.S. reported that the Bush administration was actively laying the groundwork for a cabinet-level decision on whether to bring a WTO suit against the EU.[222] Government officials were said to be focusing on solidifying their WTO case and "seeking the best way to frame the initiation of a WTO dispute in terms of public perception."[223]

Because the Bush administration sought European support for its war in Iraq, plans to initiate a WTO GMO challenge against the EU were postponed until May 2003. On May 13, USTR Robert Zoellick and USDA Secretry Anne Venneman held a news conference to announce they were filing the case.[224] In June, the EU completed its new regulations regarding the segregation and labeling of GMO products. However, the U.S.—which had claimed its WTO case was based on U.S. impatience that the EU GMO regulatory scheme was not in place, affecting a de facto moritorium on GMO approvals—proceeded in July to push its WTO case forward. The circumstances of the case are bizarre, as filing a case now after waiting years would seem to cast a pall over U.S.-EU cooperation on the WTO Ministerial in Cancún.

The USTR has spun its new WTO action as being based on the Bush administration's concerns about hunger in African nations that do not want to accept GM food aid for fear of later being banned from exporting to the EU, rather than on the demands of the administration's many agribusiness and biotech supporters for new market access rights. The claim that the case is based on concerns about hunger in Africa is remarkably cynical, even by Bush administration standards. As described in Chapter 7, African nations have played a leading role—based on their own judgment and determinations about GMOs' threat to their nations' long-term food sovereignty—in fighting for binding global rules to regulate spread of GM food and seeds. The U.S. was the African countries' leading opponent in these negotiations to establish a Biosafety Protocol.

What is sincere is the growing concern in agribusiness and thus the Bush administration about the number of nations that are following the EU's precautionary approach to biotechnology. Significant U.S. trading partners such as China and Brazil, and scores of countries in the developing and developed worlds, also have moved to restrict biotech imports, with many banning sale of GMO seeds to domestic farmers.[225] In the face of a looming famine, Zambia did refuse to accept U.S. genetically modified corn due to concerns that the corn could cross-pollinate with its own corn.[226] However, what the Bush administration fails to mention when it uses this case to defend its WTO GMO attack is that Zambia requested that the U.S. corn be milled so it could feed the hungry without risk that

---

U.S. Moves on GMO Labeling at Codex

The U.S. opposition to the regulation of GMOs has extended even to proposals that products containing GMOs be labeled. The latest U.S. proposal to the Codex listed conditions for a mandatory GMO food labeling program to be WTO-consistent. Under the U.S. proposal, the new food must have "undergone significant changes as regards composition, nutritional value or intended use," or the purpose of the labeling must be "to disclose the presence of new allergens."[227] That the seeds, plants and food that result from genetic engineering have undergone "significant change" relative to the seeds, plants and foods obtained through traditional methods is made clear by one simple fact: corporations that genetically engineer the seeds are able to patent them and to obtain a patent, an inventor must prove that the product is significantly different from all other products.[228] Thus, the continued U.S. opposition to broad mandatory GMO labeling seems logically flawed, or the U.S. proposed Codex conditions are not what they seem on their face.

The U.S. justifies its position, saying "[it] has seen no evidence to support that, as a class, foods obtained through bio-technology are inherently less safe or differ in quality or any other manner from foods obtained through conventional methods."[229] In fact, the U.S. Delegation to Codex compares genetic engineering to traditional crossbreeding.[230]

some of the corn would be used as seed. The U.S. refused. Zambia relied on food aid and purchase from non-GMO sources to get through the crisis without any hunger-caused deaths and this year is enjoying a bumper crop.

What Is the U.S. WTO GMO Case Against the EU?

The EU's precautionary approach to GMOs is reflected in a number of its laws and regulations. As early as 1990 the EU regulated the release of GMOs into the environment, such as by planting, ranching or marketing (sale).[231] A separate directive regulated "contained uses" of GMOs in laboratories.[232] Approximately a dozen GMOs were approved under the 1990 directive. However, in 1999, the EU halted new approvals of GMOs while a new policy on segregating and labeling GMOs was promulgated.

On February 14, 2001, the European Parliament voted to approve new rules governing the testing, planting and sale of domestic and imported GM crops and food products.[233] The directive regulates the "deliberate release" of genetically modified organisms into the environment, such as by cultivation or ranching, as well as the "marketing" of GMOs as food or food products.

However, the new regulation lacked some important provisions for labeling and traceability of GMOs and includes no framework for corporate liability in the event that a GMO causes injury to consumers or the environment. Therefore, six EU member states have indicated that they will oppose new approvals of GMOs until those issues are adequately addressed in additional legislation that was issued for comment in June 2003. It contains many but not all of the elements environmental and consumer advocates had sought.[234]

Even with certain key elements missing, the 2001 EU directive established the world's most comprehensive regulatory regime to date for GMOs, and includes a number of safety features demanded by consumer groups such as the Transatlantic Consumer Dialogue (TACD).[235] The new directive explicitly incorporates the Precautionary Principle, requiring such precautionary measures as an environmental risk assessment, a plan for monitoring the effects of the GMO on human health or the environment, and information on control, remediation methods, waste treatment and emergency response plans.[236] It also provides for public input to the approval process, and calls for the phase-out of the use of antibiotic resistance marker genes in GMOs.[237]

These are the types of precautionary measures that are needed in the face of scientific uncertainty, but they are just the type of measure that industry views as barriers to trade. The fundamental question in this case is democracy: will the people eating the food and living in the potentially affected environment be allowed to decide what they want? Polling shows that a vast majority of Europeans strongly oppose GM food and the demand for regulating it so they can choose to avoid it is intense. Interestingly, polls now show a growing number of Americans also seek labeling of GMO products.

Threat 1: Less Than Darling Clementine: Spain's Fury at U.S. Fruit Fly Restrictions

Ironically, while the U.S. has been challenging Japan's right to protect its domestic agriculture from foreign and destructive pests, it is facing an SPS challenge at the WTO for its own pest-avoiding import restrictions.

In December 2001, the U.S. Department of Agriculture halted the importation of Spanish clementine oranges, a Christmas holiday favorite, after Mediterranean fruit fly larvae were found in stores in North Carolina and Maryland.[238] Medfly infestations are extremely dangerous to U.S. agriculture. The Medfly is known to be one of the world's most destructive pests and threatens more than 250 varieties of fruits, nuts and vegetables.[239] A 1997 Medfly infestation in Central Florida cost state and federal authorities $22 million to eradicate.[240] Although the U.S. has had intermittent Medfly infestations since the first U.S. infestation in 1929, eradication programs have prevented an established Medfly population.[241] A University of California study estimated the cost of combating a Medfly infestation in that state could reach as much as $1.8 billion annually—including $100 million in higher food prices for consumers.[242]

Upon learning about the Medfly larvae, the USDA immediately banned all future imports of clementines from Spain, all clementine imports in transit and all distribution of clementines that had not left U.S. ports.[243] Ten million dollars worth of Spanish clementines were prevented entry by the Philadelphia Regional Port Authority, where 75% of Spanish clementines arrive.[244] Spanish clementine exporters had expected to sell $130 million worth of clementines that season, which meant a loss of $54 million—or 40%—because of the import ban.[245]

Spanish clementine industry representatives vowed to seek legal action immediately.[246] In August 2002, they sought an order to vacate the USDA's import ban in U.S. District Court for eastern Pennsylvania. In their U.S. court statements, they claimed that the USDA's action was arbitrary and capricious, violated the Administrative Procedures Act and that the USDA was in breach of contract when its inspectors left Spain without lifting the order. The U.S. court rejected this claim.[247]

The EU then raised concerns about the U.S. restrictions on Spanish clementines.[248] The EU noted that U.S action to resolve the clementine ban was urgent during the summer 2002 because the clementine October harvest season was rapidly approaching. The U.S. extended its Federal Register comment period regarding a proposed regulation on the matter to accommodate the EU's WTO demand that the U.S. lift the clementine ban.

In the summer of 2002, the USDA proposed new regulations aimed at preventing future live Medfly larvae from entering the U.S. and potentially threatening U.S. crops. The U.S. regulatory regime in place during the Clementine Medfly incident during 2001 had required that the clementines be cold treated for 10–16 days and that U.S. port inspections verify the documentation of the cold storage.[249] The proposed new rules would extend the cold-storage requirement and increase Medfly inspection before the fruit left Spain. The proposed rules called for improvements in Spain's Medfly management program to register growers, scientifically sample fruit, utilize pre-harvest traps, establish a pre-clearance program, and extend cold storage for two days.[250]

The new proposed U.S. Medfly rules for clementines failed to satisfy U.S. farmers. The director of the Arizona Department of Agriculture, Sheldon Jones, testified that efforts to rapidly normalize the clementine trading relationship between Spain and the U.S. put U.S. farmers at risk: the proposed plan provided inadequate oversight of Spanish Medfly eradication efforts, the USDA was providing insufficient personnel to clear Spanish crops, and the proposed rule would not protect U.S. citrus-producing states by limiting where clementines could be imported.[251] U.S. citrus farmers sought a total ban on Spanish clementines.

In October 2002, the USDA finalized the proposed rule, which the U.S. farmers opposed, with the exception that for the 2002–2003 season the sale of clementines would be prohibited totally in the citrus-producing states of California, Florida, Arizona, Louisiana and Texas.[252] Despite the exclusion of citrus-producing states, producers were still concerned. President of the California Citrus Mutual, Josh Nelson, which represents half the state's growers, stated that the move was a "rush to judgment" and that as growers, "We're not sure the protections are there."[253] But while U.S. farmers can fume, the EU retains the right to challenge even these protections much less stronger ones in the WTO.

CONCLUSION

Clearly, U.S. regulatory standards are not perfect; however, U.S. regulatory agencies have intervened in the market to save the lives of millions of Americans who otherwise would have been exposed to dangerous food, products and work environments. Sensible regulatory safeguards not only save lives but also generate savings—fewer injuries, fewer illnesses, fewer deaths and fewer hospitalizations. For instance, it is estimated that in 2000, the total U.S. regulatory system generated between $56 billion and $1.5 trillion a year in savings from cleaner air and water, safer cars, safer pharmaceuticals, safer workplaces and safer food.[254]

In 1989 the U.S. government responded to the outbreak of the BSE crisis in the UK by moving quickly to ban the importation of live ruminants (cattle, sheep, goats, deer, caribou and elk) and most ruminant products from the UK even though there was no risk assessment to support the move.[255] In 1997 they expanded the ban to all of Europe, and the FDA moved to ban the feeding of mammalian protein to cattle and other ruminants.[256] While more could have been done to close loopholes for potentially risky materials and testing for BSE in the U.S. could have been improved, quick U.S. action may have prevented the emergence of BSE in the U.S.

If precautionary measures applied by nations like the U.S. have succeeded in curtailing the potential for a global epidemic of vCJD due to mad cow disease, it will not have been with the assistance of the WTO. From the first revelations of tremors and loss of coordination in cows on a little farm in Sussex, the disease has been considered a trade issue by the WTO, and WTO officials continue to complain that nations were not following proper risk-assessment procedures or basing their BSE measures on international standards and sound science.[257]

Ironically given the beef hormone and GMO situations, this WTO line has even been echoed by the European Commission, which has listed the U.S. precautionary measures, which so far have successfully prevented BSE in the United States, as "barriers to trade." The EU complains that the U.S. has taken measures without a scientific basis and without due regard to international standards on the regionalization of animal disease.[258]

Outside the halls of the WTO in Geneva, most people believe that human health should take precedence over trade concerns, and most scientists understand that today, 14 years after the crisis began, science can still not fully explain with certainty either the original cause of the BSE crisis in England nor its likelihood to appear elsewhere.

What we face now is a race against time. Citizens must use their democratic institutions to reverse the race to the bottom incorporated in the core texts of the WTO or significant consequences for public health will start to be felt on an even more massive scale.

3

WARNING: THE WTO CAN BE HAZARDOUS TO PUBLIC HEALTH

"We are now approaching a new era. The WTO is used to dealing with only external issues and now it is time to deal with the domestic regulations that impede trade liberalization."

—incoming WTO Director-General
Supachai Panitchpakdi in a Bangkok speech[1]

For many doctors, government public health officials and others involved in protecting the health and safety of the American public, the WTO and globalization are off the radar screen. Unfortunately, this lack of awareness falls squarely into the category of "what you don't know can hurt you."

The core goal of the WTO and the agreements it enforces conflict with public health policy's primary goal: to promote health and safety, including through market regulation. The WTO's mandate is to limit government regulatory intervention into the market to the greatest extent possible by requiring elimination of certain policies and harmonization of remaining standards to one global norm, so as to increase the unencumbered international flow of goods, services and investment.

WTO supporters have long claimed that under WTO rules, countries may implement any policies they choose, as long as they do not treat domestic goods and companies differently from foreign ones. In fact, the WTO's rules go well beyond this objective standard to impose value-oriented policy priorities and require countries to adopt new policies to implement these values.

To a large degree, the lack of awareness of the looming conflicts between WTO rules and public health policies is a language problem. GATTese jargon does not lend itself to easy understanding, so we begin this chapter with a basic translation of which WTO provisions apply to significant public health issues.

Tobacco and Alcohol Control

The Technical Barriers to Trade Agreement sets constraints on national, state and federal policies regarding labeling of products and product standards, such as cigarette "plain packaging" rules and warning labels on alcohol and tobacco products. For instance, when the U.S. tobacco industry threatened a challenge under NAFTA provisions against a Canadian province's cigarette plain packaging proposal, the measure was never implemented.[2] The WTO's General Agreement on Trade in Services covers distribution, marketing and advertising services for tobacco and alcohol. The European Union and others have called for elimination of the alcohol distribution monopolies 18 U.S. states use to control access to that product.[3]

Bans or Controls on Toxic Substances

The U.S. has been threatening WTO action under the TBT agreement against other countries for bans or limits on phthalates, lead, and polyvinyl chloride (PVC). As described in Chapter 1, the U.S. is threatening trade action against the EU's new "REACH" Chemical Safety Policy. Later in this chapter we will discuss Canada's WTO challenge of France's ban on asbestos. Enormous political pressure regarding this case—given the political damage a ruling against banning asbestos would have caused to the WTO's already shaky reputation—resulted in the only WTO ruling preserving a challenged health or safety policy. A straight reading of the TBT agreement would have resulted in a ruling against the ban. In the legal sophistry used to avoid that result, the WTO tribunal established new jurisprudence making any successful invocation of the WTO's health exceptions even more difficult. In addition, harmonization negotiations now under way regarding chemical classification could implicate thousands of state and local community right-to-know rules. Meanwhile, attempts to require prior informed consent as a condition for importing products (such as asbestos or DDT), which are domestically prohibited in many exporting countries, have failed at the WTO.

Government Procurement Policies Promoting Public Health

The WTO Agreement on Government Procurement requires government purchasing decisions to be based only on commercial factors, meaning trouble for procurement policies aimed at creating public health incentives. For instance, governments cannot give preference to products produced by companies that provide workers health care benefits or products made using less-toxic processes.

Toxic Waste

Under the TBT requirement that government policies be "least trade restrictive," the U.S. is claiming that a European-wide directive requiring producers to safely dispose of computer, cell phone and other products containing toxic substances is more burdensome than necessary to U.S. companies.[4] (For more on this, see Chapter 1.)

Access to and Safety of Medicines

The Trade Related Aspects of Intellectual Property rules require adoption of the monopoly patenting favored by developed countries, meaning that all WTO countries must implement domestic intellectual property protection regimes that provide 20-year monopoly control over a wide array of patentable items, including medicine. At this agreement's core is a value-laden decision: creating a new category of property rights and protecting them is given priority over broad public access to new technologies.

In contrast, India specifically forbade patenting of medicine and seeds so as to ensure access to drugs and promote food security. However, a successful U.S. WTO challenge resulted in India changing its laws to accept applications for patents on these items so that when TRIPs' obligations come into full effect, India must issue such patents.[5] Yet, when the U.S. was a developing country, it lustily transferred technology from Europe. Only when U.S. industry became a powerful technological innovator did the U.S. adopt intellectual property protections.[6] Even so, entry into the WTO required the U.S. to extend its patent term from 17 years to the WTO's 20-year standard, resulting in higher prices for medications that otherwise would have been available as generics. The delay in a generic version of just one drug, ranitidine HCl, will increase U.S. consumer costs by $1 billion by 2009.[7] A 1995 study on the overall impact of the TRIPs Agreement on U.S. consumers "conservatively estimated" $6 billion in higher drug prices due to windfall patent extensions under WTO.[8]

The TRIPs Agreement is again at the center of controversy. At described below, developing countries battling the HIV/AIDS epidemic obtained a WTO interpretive note—the Doha Declaration on Public Health and TRIPs—affirming the compatibility of compulsory licensing with TRIPs' rules. At issue now is if and when, under WTO rules, developing countries and transition economies without domestic production capacity can import generic medicines produced under compulsory licenses.[9] The U.S. and Switzerland seek to limit the scope of compulsory licensing,[10] and a December 2002 deadline on this issue passed with the U.S. blocking any deal.

Access to Health Care

The definition of services covered under the rules of the WTO's GATS includes many public health issues, including access to and regulation of health care, health insurance, hospitals, nursing and homecare, and the qualifications of medical professionals. These health issues are discussed in Chapter 4.

Water and Sewage Infrastructure

GATS also covers an array of basic sanitation services from solid waste collection to sewage and water treatment and filtration. The GATS rules promote "progressively higher levels of liberalization," including pressure to privatize and deregulate public services. Issues of access to, and quality of, such essential services are included in Chapter 4.

Food Safety

The WTO Sanitary and Phytosanitary Agreement sets constraints on domestic food policy, including pesticide, additive, preservative, inspection and labeling standards.

This agreement also requires international harmonization of domestic standards and determinations that different foreign standards provide equivalent health protection. Under this WTO agreement, the U.S. successfully challenged the European ban on beef contaminated with artificial growth hormones. These rules, and their enormous implications for public health, are discussed in Chapter 2.

*   *   *

To date, only a few cases of open conflict between WTO rules and public health policy have risen to the surface. In this chapter, we describe WTO cases and threats, including: WTO intellectual property rules keeping affordable medicines from those dying from AIDS and other diseases in the developing world; trade challenges and threats against national and international tobacco control regimes and similar attacks on bans of toxic substances; the WTO challenge against France's asbestos ban; and threats of a trade challenge against Guatemala's implementation of the WHO-UNICEF breast milk substitute marketing law.

> "Private markets, unconstrained and inadequately regulated, are perhaps the most powerful globalizing force driving inequities in health."
> —Professor John H. Bryant, Council for International Organizations of Medical Sciences, March 2002[11]

In 2001, a World Health Organization background paper found that current globalization trends were damaging public health worldwide. Among the many deleterious effects noted were the global spread of strains of gonorrhea resistant to penicillin, due to increased international travel; worsening health indicators in many African countries, due to structural adjustment programs that impose increased debt burdens and austerity measures for health services; and increased incidence of certain diseases due to changes in food consumption practices related to globalization.[12]

In 2001, the *Bulletin of the World Health Organization* devoted an issue to looking

---

Health As a Tradable Good

The WTO's GATS rules presume that health care and other essential services can be most effectively delivered by the market, not governments. This push to commodify health services, leaving behind those who cannot afford to pay, parallels the conditions imposed by the international financial institutions. The austerity requirements of the IMF and the World Bank limit the ability of governments to implement and maintain basic public health services, such as immunizations, health clinics, schools, water treatment and sewage disposal. The loss of government revenue resulting from WTO-imposed trade tariff cuts further erodes the capacity of many developing countries to fund these services.

at the health effects of globalization. One article noted that, in most countries, the period of globalization has "been characterized by a . . . slowdown or stagnation in health gains despite the widespread expansion of highly efficient public health schemes, e.g. vaccination programs."[13] Another article claims that one consequence of globalization is "the unprecedented speed with which infectious diseases can now spread around the globe."[14]

The U.S. National Academy of Sciences also listed increased trade as one of the ten factors contributing to the emergence and reemergence of major infectious disease—but four of the other factors (access to health care, deteriorating public health infrastructure, urbanization and crowding, and modern travel) have worsened as a result of globalization.[15]

Trade has always facilitated the spread of infectious diseases, but now the transmission is faster. In the nineteenth century, increased trade flows transformed the rare disease of cholera, which was previously only known in a remote region of India, into a global pandemic.[16] However, the current globalization era allows the transmission of diseases as common as influenza, as rare as the ebola virus or as new as SARS to span the globe in the course of a day—increasing the risks of fast-spreading global outbreaks.[17]

Rising Income Inequality Resulting from Globalization Threatens Public Health

Health status correlates closely with income but is even more closely related to income inequality.[18] As we'll see in Chapter 6, trade liberalization is increasing income inequality between and within nations. The resulting disparities in health conditions and outcomes is one key effect.[19] Even in wealthy nations, the poorest are also the sickest. According to the WHO, the public infrastructure to care for children has been eroded in many countries that have undergone rapid trade liberalization, resulting in future long-term health inequalities.[20] A Center for Economic Policy and Research analysis of declining per capita income growth during the period of corporate globalization also found that there was a concomitant decline in health outcomes. Improvements in life expectancy declined for all but the wealthiest nations; infant and child mortality improvements slowed; and spending on education enrollment and literacy slowed for the poorest 40 nations.[21]

WTO THREATENS INTERNATIONAL PUBLIC HEALTH CONVENTIONS

The WTO has been used to attack several international conventions designed to protect public health. The U.S. tobacco industry has used trade threats to force countries to accept U.S. cigarette imports and discourage them from imposing restrictions on the labeling and packaging of cigarettes. The Bush administration argued fiercely that WTO and other trade rules should diminish the requirements of the recent Framework Convention on Tobacco Control. The Gerber company used a WTO threat to pressure Guatemala to exempt foreign baby formula makers from the WHO UNICEF formula marketing rules that ban using likenesses of healthy babies on packaging or advertising.

Global Tobacco Conspiracy: Trade Agreements Pry Open Markets, Undercut Public Health Regulations*

Over the last two decades, Big Tobacco—comprised of companies like Philip Morris, British American Tobacco, R.J. Reynolds and Japan Tobacco—has teamed up with U.S. officials to use trade pressures and trade agreements to open up markets for their products in developing countries. Already, tobacco-related illnesses kill four million people a year.[22] Now tobacco interests are trying to use the WTO and other trade deals to stop initiatives to curb smoking.

The U.S. Tobacco and Cigarette Export Offensive

In the 1980s, the office of the USTR, working hand-in-glove with U.S. cigarette companies, used the threat of trade sanctions to force Taiwan, South Korea, and Thailand to permit U.S. cigarette imports.[23] These countries subsequently opened their markets and the result was a rapid rise in smoking rates.[24] After South Korea opened its market to U.S. companies in 1988, smoking rates among male Korean teens rose from 18.4% to 29.8% in a single year.[25] The rate among female teens more than quintupled from 1.6% to 8.7%. Overall, according to World Bank estimates, the opening of Asian markets to U.S. cigarettes pushed Asian smoking rates 10% above what they would have been.[26] Price competition and advertising—the introduction of slick promotional strategies that linked foreign cigarettes with notions of sophistication, freedom and "hipness"—appear largely responsible for this rise.[27]

Having successfully forced Japan, South Korea and Taiwan to import U.S. cigarettes, the Bush administration turned its attention to Thailand. In 1989, the Cigarette Export Association (CEA), a Big Tobacco trade group, filed a petition with the USTR aimed at forcing Thailand to import cigarettes. They also sought to have a Thai ban on cigarette advertisements repealed. The CEA claimed that the ad ban discriminated against foreign tobacco companies, which need to advertise to gain market share from the government-affiliated Thailand Tobacco Monopoly.

Case 1: U.S. GATT Challenge to Thai Cigarette Regulations

Unlike the other Asian countries, Thailand refused to capitulate to U.S. pressure and the U.S. filed a GATT challenge. The U.S. argued that the ban was a GATT-illegal quantitative restriction on imports and that the advertising ban, not being the least trade restrictive means to combat smoking, was therefore an unfair barrier to trade.[28]

The WHO intervened on behalf of Thailand, emphasizing the public health

* This section on tobacco draws heavily from the work of Robert Wiessman, editor of *The Multinational Monitor*, with his permission.

benefits of restricting cigarette imports. Among other reasons, the WHO explained that the smoother international brands, and the multinationals' greater use of additives and flavorings, meant that these brands were more effective at addicting new, young and female smokers.[29]

The GATT panel ruled against Thailand on the issue of the import ban—ignoring exactly the area where the WHO had rested its claims. It concluded that there were other, less trade restrictive ways that Thailand could combat smoking than restricting imports, including limits on advertising.[30] The panel ruled that Thailand could maintain its advertising restrictions.

Upon taking office, the Clinton administration promised to cease using trade threats to force open tobacco markets, a promise it largely kept.[31] In 2001, as one of his last acts, President Clinton signed an executive order prohibiting the executive branch from "seek[ing] the reduction or removal of foreign government restrictions on the marketing and advertising of such products. . . ."[32] The Bush administration appears to have quietly continued the policy. However, in the course of negotiating the terms of China's admission to the WTO, the Clinton administration did negotiate an opening of the Chinese tobacco market. The U.S.-China bilateral agreement that preceded the grant of Permanent Normal Trade Relations (PNTR) to China included a provision requiring China to slash its tariffs on imported cigarettes by 61.5%.[33] Given the experience of other Asian countries, smoking rates in China, especially among women and children, are likely to rise as a result. Recently the second Bush administration has also reversed earlier pledges and pushed to include new markets for U.S. cigarettes in the 2002 U.S.-Chile Free Trade Agreement.

Trade Agreements vs. Tobacco Control Agreements

Trade agreements do more for Big Tobacco than secure market opening, however. A wide range of sound tobacco control policies might be found to violate existing WTO rules, as well as those included in NAFTA.

One area of concern relates to the relationship between trade rules and the recent Framework Convention on Tobacco Control (FCTC), a treaty sponsored by the WHO to regulate tobacco commerce. Negotiations were kicked off in 1999 and concluded in May 2003.[34] Many governments and a network of nongovernmental tobacco-control groups pushed for specific language specifying that the FCTC's public health rules should take priority over international trade agreements.[35] This is important because absent this specific provision, a country seeking to implement elements of the FCTC could be challenged as violating its WTO commitments. The United States and other powerful countries opposed this position and pushed for a provision specifying that implementation of the FCTC should not conflict with normal trade rules.[36] In the end, neither provision was included, meaning that if a country implemented FCTC policies in a way that conflicted with WTO rules, another WTO signatory could challenge the policy. While the U.S. government made positive comments about the Convention,[37] tobacco-control advocates charged the Bush administration with continually seeking to weaken it.[38] However, these attempts were largely rebuffed, and tobacco-control advocates triumphed.

U.S. negotiators objected to limits on cigarette advertising and efforts to limit or ban the words "light" or "mild."[39] However, the final pact included an advertising ban,[40] although it remains for signatories to adopt this policy domestically. Until the final moments, the Bush administration threatened not to sign the Convention, though it ultimately did. Now, tobacco-control advocates will work to get countries to implement the policies and hope that such domestic policies will not be challenged under WTO rules on trademarks, or on advertising or marketing services.

Threat 1: Trade Pact Intellectual Property Protections Used to Attack Tobacco Control

Tobacco companies already have made aggressive use of intellectual property rules to defend their interests. They have complained in the past that countries' large warnings and plain-paper packaging rules violate the intellectual property rights in trade agreements.[41] For instance, when Canada was considering a plain-packaging regulation for cigarettes, U.S. tobacco corporations hired former USTR Carla Hills to convince the Canadian government that the policy would violate the requirements of the trade pacts she helped negotiate. Hills wrote to the Canadian government that a plain-packaging proposal would violate Canada's NAFTA and WTO intellectual property obligations, and that, "under NAFTA, any such plain packaging requirement would constitute an expropriation of the investments of U.S. manufacturers of tobacco products and their subsidiaries in Canada, requiring substantial compensation, which you have told us would be in excess of hundreds of millions of dollars."[42]

Cigarette companies also argue that WTO and NAFTA intellectual property provisions prohibit countries from banning the use of the terms "light" and "mild" on tobacco packaging.[43]

Canada has proposed such a regulation in response to a consensus among public health experts that the "mild" and "light" descriptors are fundamentally misleading, citing data that suggest that more than a third of smokers of "light" or "mild" cigarettes choose these products for health reasons,[44] but these cigarettes are not less hazardous to smokers' health, in part because smokers compensate for reduced tar and nicotine by inhaling more deeply and by other means.[45]

In their response to the regulatory proposal, Philip Morris disclaims any health benefits for "light" or "ultra-light" cigarettes, and agrees that "consumers should not be given the message that descriptors mean that any brand of cigarettes has been shown to be less harmful than other brands,"[46] but insists it should still be able to use the terms, which it alleges communicate differences of taste.[47] Barring use of the terms, Philip Morris claims, would violate Canada's obligations under the WTO and under NAFTA's foreign investor protections "would be tantamount to an expropriation of tobacco trademarks."[48]

Under NAFTA's controversial Chapter 11, countries are barred from maintaining policies that could lower the value of investors' property (including intellectual property such as trademarks) without compensation.[49] NAFTA also confers on investors private standing before a trade tribunal to sue for compensation, meaning companies can bring enforcement claims directly against governments, whereas other international commercial agreements such as the WTO will only hear cases brought by governments. If Philip Morris were to bring and win a Chapter 11 NAFTA lawsuit, Canada would be obligated to pay the corporation the lost value to the trademark and associated goodwill.

Philip Morris also claims that the Canadian regulation violates WTO rules because it would "encumber the use and function of valuable, well known tobacco trademarks" in violation of TRIPs.[50] TRIPs includes a public health "exception," which tautologically only applies to countries' policies which are otherwise compatible with TRIPs.[51]

Finally, Philip Morris contends that the Canadian regulation would violate the Agreement on Technical Barriers to Trade, which requires countries to choose the least trade restrictive means to pursue legitimate regulatory objectives like protection of public health.[52] The company argues that a less trade restrictive means exists to ensure consumers are not misled into believing there is a health benefit to "light" and "mild" products—for example, labeling requirements that state that "light" products have not been shown to be safer than other cigarettes.

Philip Morris has not yet taken steps to bring a NAFTA Chapter 11 suit against Canada and is not likely to be able to get the U.S. government to file a WTO challenge on the matter. However even if Philip Morris takes no further action beyond its threat of a NAFTA Chapter 11 case, tobacco-control advocates say these trade threats will likely chill many other governments less resolute in pushing tobacco control measures and more vulnerable to legal threats from enacting Canadian-style tobacco-control regulations.

Once again we see this hidden threat of trade agreements: plausible threats of trade action against countries considering effective tobacco control measures. For developing countries—the market of the future for the cigarette giants—the ability to withstand such threats is orders of magnitude weaker.

Trade Conflicts over Alcohol Regulations

Alcohol's public health risks are well documented. The WHO reports that alcohol-related diseases worldwide are as pervasive as those associated with tobacco and illegal drugs. Many aspects of the alcohol industry—from brewing, distilling, marketing, distribution and sale down to pouring a pint of ale in a bar or restaurant—fall under the jurisdiction of WTO's General Agreement on Trade in Services. Governments use their ability to regulate the service sector for alcohol's public health threats, for instance requiring bars and liquor stores to be licensed, typically upon a condition of controlling sale to minors. Yet under GATS rules, which do not distinguish alcohol-related services from any other service, domestic licensing regulations must reflect the least trade restrictive option that meets the policy goal of promoting public health. In its 2001 GATS requests to the U.S., the EU demanded the elimination of the 18 existing state alcohol-distribution monopoly systems, which the U.S. has initially rejected.[53]

(continued)

Alcohol issues relating to tariff levels on alcohol products have already been the basis of several GATT disputes,[54] but many analysts suspect that the WTO may ultimately have its greatest impact on alcohol policy in advertising regulation.[55] Challenges to restrictions on alcohol advertising have not yet been brought to the WTO, but the European Court of Justice ruled against a Swedish advertising ban in a case brought by the European Commission.[56] The court found that the ban discriminates against imports because consumers are instantly more familiar with domestic producers.[57] This ruling suggests that similar WTO challenges could find success.

Threat 2: Trade Threats Pressure Guatemala to Weaken Infant Health Law

According to UNICEF's most recent figures, 1.5 million infants die each year because their mothers are induced to replace breast feeding with artificial breast-milk substitutes.[58] UNICEF reports that the major cause of death is fatal infant diarrhea caused by mothers in poor countries mixing infant formula with unclean water.[59] UNICEF attributes the fact that only 44% of infants in the developing world (even less in the industrialized countries) are breast-fed to the relentless promotion of breast-milk substitutes.[60] In the 1970s, a global citizens' movement, including a boycott against the infant formula giant Nestle, resulted in political pressure to establish public health rules on infant formula marketing.[61] A global WHO/UNICEF Code on Marketing of Breast-Milk Substitutes was signed by scores of nations.[62]

In an attempt to reduce its infant mortality rate, Guatemala passed a law to implement key elements of the WHO/UNICEF marketing code and issued regulations to implement it,[63] to encourage new mothers to breast feed their infants and to fully understand the health threats to their babies of using infant formula as a substitute for breast milk. Guatamala's policy included prohibitions on the use of words like "humanized breast milk" or "equivalent to breast milk."[64] To be accessible to illiterate people, the WHO/UNICEF code and Guatemala's regulations also included prohibitions against visual depictions of infants that "idealize the use of bottle feeding,"[65] including bans on pictures or drawings of fat, healthy babies or other symbols suggesting the products' outcomes. The Guatemalan law also prohibited both the free distribution of samples without approval of the Guatemalan Ministry of Health and the direct marketing of the product by sales personnel.[66]

With the prominent exception of U.S.-incorporated Gerber Products Company, all of Guatemala's domestic and foreign suppliers of infant formula and other breast-milk substitutes made the necessary changes to their packaging to comply with the Guatemalan law.[67] Guatemalan infant mortality rates dropped significantly after the law passed, and UNICEF held up Guatemala in its literature as a model of the code's success.[68]

Gerber was potentially in violation of the Guatemalan labeling law on many fronts, according to the Guatemala Ministry of Health. It allegedly marketed its formula directly to new mothers in hospitals, provided free samples to doctors and day-care centers, refused to remove the depiction of a pudgy infant—the "Gerber Baby"—from its label, and refused to state the superiority of breast-feeding over formula on its label.[69] The Guatemalan Ministry of Health made numerous attempts to negotiate with Gerber to seek compliance with the labeling law.[70] In autumn 1992, Gerber submitted its formula packaging to the Guatemalan Food and Drug Registration and Control Division (an agency similar to the FDA in the U.S.) for approval. The FDRC requested that Gerber remove the baby image and add the words "Breast milk is the best for baby."[71] According to the Guatemalan government, Gerber resisted these changes throughout the regulatory process.[72] In November of 1993, a Guatemalan Administrative Tribunal ruled in favor of the Minister of Health[73]—six years after the labeling regulations went into effect.

Instead of complying, Gerber continued to confront the Guatemalan government on trade-related fronts. It threatened the government with a challenge under the imminent WTO because of trademark infringement.[74] The letter from Gerber to the Guatemalan president includes an explicit threat: "Upon the favorable and permanent resolution of this matter, we will withdraw all complaints before . . . GATT."

According to Gerber, the "Gerber Baby" is an integral part of its trademark,[75] and as such, the Uruguay Round TRIPs Agreement would provide Gerber with new trademark protections. By 1995, Gerber's threats of WTO action, taken seriously by the Guatemalan government, succeeded: Guatemala changed its law so that imported baby food products would be exempt from the stringent infant food labeling policy.[76]

For a developing country like Guatemala, the mere threat of a WTO challenge poses a no-win decision: should millions be invested in a WTO legal defense which may or may not succeed when such funds are desperately needed for infant immunization and other basic public health needs?

Guatemala had no in-house expertise on the question of the WTO legality of its implementation of the WHO/UNICEF Code.[77] Indeed, it is possible that the Guatemalan law would have withstood an actual U.S. challenge at the WTO. First, although Guatemala prohibited the use of the "Gerber Baby" to sell infant formula, the government was prepared to respect and protect the trademark logo from potential competitors which is a key TRIPs requirement.[78]

Second, the TPIPs Agreement contains a public health exception.[79] Although the provision is weak and tautological, there could hardly be a better public health example, since a public health crisis had been identified and international efforts to address the crisis had been codified by the United Nations. Indeed, by concentrating on the marketing practices of formula manufacturers, the WHO/UNICEF code is tacitly operating on the assumption that the manufacturers are, in the language of the TRIPs public health exemption, "abusing their intellectual property rights" at the expense of babies' lives. However, Guatemala judged that the use of considerable public health funds on a WTO legal gamble was too risky. Because of its agreement with the Guatemalan government, Gerber remains able to promote its baby-milk substitute products in Guatemala in ways that violate the WHO/UNICEF guidelines. The International Baby Food Action Network, which monitors compliance with the international code of marketing breast-milk substitutes, found

Gerber's international promotions to the public in a variety of countries were in substantial violation of the Code in 2001.[80]

Pharmaceutical Giants Use WTO Patent Rules to Threaten Countries Seeking Access to Essential Medicines

One in five adult South Africans, one in seven Kenyans, and one in three Zimbabweans has HIV/AIDS.[81] Former U.S. Surgeon General David Satcher has likened the HIV/AIDS epidemic in Africa to the plague that decimated Europe in the fourteenth century.[82] In all, over 28.5 million people in sub-Saharan Africa have HIV/AIDS.[83]

Existing treatments enable many people with HIV/AIDS in the U.S. and other industrialized countries to live relatively healthy lives. However, these treatments are unavailable to all but a few people in Africa. Until recently, life-saving HIV/AIDS drug cocktails cost about $12,000 a year in many African countries—far out of reach of all but a small handful.[84] Over the past several years, brand-name drug companies have responded to negative publicity on drug pricing by announcing some concessionary deals on some of their AIDS products.[85] But these price reductions are insufficient, typically limited in scope, and have done little to make drugs available to HIV-positive people in poor countries.

Even in countries where pharmaceutical companies have made concessions, $500 annual medicine expenses are not possible when average income is $500. The negotiated price for a first-line treatment regime of antiretroviral drugs (ARVs) in Least Developed Countries (LDCs) varied between $2.27 and $3.17 a day.[86] Meanwhile, as we will discuss in Chapter 6, over 45% of sub-Saharan Africans live on less than a dollar per day.[87] Even in South Africa, a Developing Country but not an LDC, and after a settlement that reduced prices, the commonly recommended "triple cocktail" costs about 1,200 rand per month (approximately $114) in a country where 40% of workers earn under 1,000 rand per month and another 25% take home between 1,000 and 2,500 rand per month.[88] For all but a tiny few of those with HIV/AIDS in Africa, a diagnosis is a death sentence.

AIDS drug prices are high not because these medicines cost so much to produce, but because the drugs are protected by patent. A patent gives a drug manufacturer a legal monopoly—absolute control of the production, distribution and sale of the medicine and thus the right to charge whatever it pleases.

The WTO's Agreement on Trade-Related Aspects of Intellectual Property, which requires all member countries to adopt 20-year monopoly patent systems, was largely drafted by the multinational pharmaceutical industry.[89] At a 1995 speech to the U.S. Council for International Business, Pfizer Chairman Emeritus Edmund J. Pratt touted Pfizer's role in advancing the TRIPs agreement:

> The [Intellectual Property Committe, which Pfizer helped found] helped to convince U.S. officials that we should take a tough stance on intellectual property issues, and that led to trade-related intellectual property rights being included on the GATT agenda when negotiations began in Punta del Este, Uruguay, in 1986. . . .

The current GATT victory, which established provisions for intellectual property protection, resulted in part from the hard-fought efforts of the U.S. government and U.S. businesses, including Pfizer, over the past three decades. We've been in it from the beginning, taking a leadership role.[90]

The WTO's TRIPs obligations have compelled many developing countries to refashion their patent rules dramatically in favor of the multinational drug companies. These countries had followed the lead of virtually every industrialized country in enacting weak patent rules while they were still industrializing. Even Switzerland, now a pharmaceutical power, did not recognize pharmaceutical patents until the 1970s.[91] Yet under TRIPs, some developing countries were required to change their rules by 2001, while LDCs were given until 2006. (This deadline for LDCs was then extended to 2016 and others by 2006.[92]) Although most countries have already moved to adopt drug patents, with more and more countries coming into compliance with TRIPs, the problem of medicines priced out of reach of poor countries' patients is likely to get worse.

Unlike many other WTO agreements, within the TRIPs Agreement there is space to maneuver. However, as with all WTO issues, the ability to access this flexibility comes down to issues of power. Indeed, there are TRIPs-legal ways to promote affordable access to essential medicines. One crucial policy tool is compulsory licensing. Compulsory licensing enables any government to instruct a patent holder to license the right to use its patent to a company, government agency, or other party who could manufacture the drug for sale under a generic name and pay a reasonable royalty to the patent holder on each sale. Compulsory licensing lowers prices to consumers by creating competition in the market for the patented good, similar to how prices come tumbling down when generic competition occurs at the end of a drug's patent term. Compulsory licensing can lower the price of medicines by as much as 95%.[93] Compulsory licensing is permissible under the WTO's TRIP rules; indeed, it is regularly done in industrialized countries, including the United States, Japan, and the European Union, who issue compulsory licenses for pharmaceutical and nonpharmaceutical products and technologies.[94]

Yet, despite the WTO-legality of compulsory licensing, multinational pharmaceutical companies have objected passionately to the practice, which undermines their monopoly power and price-setting ability. Indeed, the Pharmaceutical Research and Manufacturers of America (PhRMA), the U.S.-based trade association of the pharmaceutical industry, claims, under the screaming headline, "Compulsory Licensing Violates Patent Protection," that "[l]ike other nonmarket interventions . . . compulsory licensing creates unanticipated negative outcomes and has not been shown to improve access to medicines."[95]

Threat 3: U.S. Attacks South African AIDS Treatment Law

The international pharmaceutical industry, with assistance from the Clinton administration, fought to reverse the effort by former South African President Nelson Mandela to make health care and medicines more accessible for South

Africans. The South African Medicines Law, enacted in 1997,[96] encourages the use of generic drugs, prohibits pharmaceutical companies from paying doctors bounties for prescribing their products (already illegal in the U.S. under antikickback laws) and institutes parallel importing as a means to control pharmaceutical costs. The Medicines Act also allows the government to require compulsory licensing. Under Article 31 of the TRIPs Agreement, such compulsory licensing is legal if royalties are paid to the patent holder.[97]

For many years, the U.S. government supported the Big Pharmaceutical claim that compulsory licensing was illegal or severely restricted under WTO rules. The Clinton administration's full efforts to force South Africa to "repeal, suspend, or terminate" its Medicines Law is detailed in a State Department report to the U.S. House Committee on International Relations.[98] After the representation of U.S. industry views by Ambassador James Joseph at a South African parliamentary hearing did not yield the desired results, then–Secretary of Commerce Richard Daley took up the matter with his South African counterpart. This led to a revision of South Africa's proposed legislation, addressing some of the U.S. industry's concerns. The U.S. was still not satisfied, and engaged in a "full court press" in late 1997 to persuade South Africa to suspend the law entirely.[99] In early 1998, Rosa Whitaker, U.S. Trade Representative for Africa, went to South Africa to make the case for U.S. industry,[100] and Daley met with the South African health minister.[101] Then, in August 1998, Vice President Gore spearheaded the "Vice President's Plan for a Negotiated Solution" between the two governments.[102] The U.S. would restore South Africa's suspended Generalized System of Preferences benefits "as progress was made in [the] negotiations."[103]

The U.S. position suddenly changed, however, beginning in June 1999. Although the growing evidence of the scale of the unfolding horror of the HIV/AIDS pandemic in Africa contributed to the shift, what more likely changed U.S. policy was protests by AIDS activists against Gore, whose formal announcement that he was running for president was interrupted by activists chanting, "Gore's Greed Kills."[104]

In response to continuing protests at Gore's presidential campaign stops in June 1999, a "senior Gore adviser" defended Gore's role in pressuring South Africa to eliminate the Medicines Law: "Obviously the Vice President's got to stick up for the commercial interests of U.S. companies."[105] After two of Gore's next three speeches were similarly disrupted, the White House began reaching out to activists, indicating it was looking at changing its position.

During the November–December WTO Ministerial in Seattle, the Clinton administration announced it would offer special treatment for health-related intellectual property disputes, taking into account health issues as well as commercial concerns. In May 2000, the Clinton administration issued an executive order stipulating that the United States would not challenge TRIPs-compliant policy measures to make AIDS medicines available anywhere in sub-Saharan Africa.[106]

Meanwhile, the brand-name pharmaceutical companies aggressively continued to defend their monopoly power in South Africa. The world's largest pharmaceutical companies filed a lawsuit against the South Africa law.[107] In the trial, industry lawyers alleged that the act violated WTO TRIPs rules (which it does not), as well as the South African constitution.[108] In the face of international pressure and castigation, however, the companies finally backed down and in April 2001 withdrew the lawsuit.[109]

In February 2001, with ever-heightening attention on the AIDS crisis, the Bush administration indicated it would continue the Clinton administration's executive order policy.[110] However, the executive order itself is limited by application only to sub-Saharan Africa and only to AIDS medicines, and the U.S. has interpreted it to permit some instances of direct pressure by the U.S government against countries seeking to advance compulsory licensing and related policies. Despite the 1999 policy shift, the U.S. treats compulsory licensing as an exceptional policy tool to be used only in emergencies, while the WTO TRIPs considers compulsory licensing a standard part of the intellectual property regime, and countries are free to use it routinely and under virtually any circumstances they choose.

However, the legacy of U.S. pressure and misinformation campaigns continues to deter developing countries from actually issuing compulsory licenses, the most important tool they have to counteract the multinational companies' pricing power. The mixed messages conveyed by U.S. action, along with confusion fostered by the pharmaceutical industry over what is permissible under WTO rules, has led most developing countries to remain fearful of the political consequences of exercising their rights to do compulsory licensing. The United States is also at work in regional trade agreement negotiations such as the Free Trade Area of the Americas (a proposed 31-country NAFTA expansion discussed in Chapter 10) and the U.S.-Chile and U.S.-Singapore Free Trade Agreements, seeking to restrict dramatically the legal scope of compulsory licensing.

Threat 4: U.S. Trade Attack on Thai Pharmaceutical Price Controls

After seven years of pressure and threats of WTO action by the U.S., Thailand finally amended its 1992 patent law governing medical access. Among other things, the amendments disbanded the Pharmaceutical Review Board (PRB)[111] which had the authority to control pharmaceutical prices in Thailand.[112] This PRB role was considered a critical public health tool since there are no Thai equivalents to the public health insurance programs, like Medicaid, that are available to some people in developed countries. The PRB had successfully lowered prices for such life-extending medications as fluconazole, which is used to treat a fatal form of meningitis contracted by one in five AIDS sufferers in Thailand. Fluconazole is marketed by Pfizer, which, until the PRB issued a compulsory license allowing three local companies to make the drug, charged $14 for a daily dose.[113] The price fell to $1 for a daily dose and the PRB forced down the monthly cost of the AIDS drug zidovudine from a prohibitive $324 in 1992 to just $87 in 1995.[114] Although compulsory licensing is allowed under the TRIPs Agreement, the U.S. justified its relentless campaign against the Thai law on the basis that it was not and, indeed, that the existence of the PRB itself was WTO-inconsistent.[115]

The Cipro Case: Good for the Goose but Not for the Gander

In September 2001, a series of anthrax letter attacks exposed thousands to inhalation anthrax in Florida, New York, New Jersey and Washington, D.C., and killed four.[116] Ciprofloxacin (known as Cipro), produced by German pharmaceutical company Bayer, was the first medication approved for inhalation anthrax.[117] The U.S. has a national stockpile of Cipro sufficient to treat 2 million Americans for the required 60-day treatment.[118] Department of Health and Human Services Secretary (HHS) Tommy Thompson sought to increase the stockpile to treat 10 million additional patients.[119] Cipro costs $4.67 per 500-milligram tablet at wholesalers, but the government has an agreement to purchase it from Bayer for $1.89.[120]

Bayer tripled production to meet the increased need, but Senator Charles Schumer (D-New York), an early skeptic about Bayer's capacity, urged the use of generic alternatives.[121]

In October, the U.S. threatened to override Bayer's patent on Cipro unless Bayer reduced the price of the medication,[122] and to issue a compulsory license, something the USTR had been pressuring South Africa and others not to do, even when faced with the public health scourge of HIV/AIDS, where millions are infected, compared to the relatively few people exposed to anthrax in a comparatively wealthier country. Paulo Teixeira, director of Brazil's national anti-AIDS program, lashed out at the duplicity of the U.S. seeking a generic Cipro alternative: "The situation with U.S. demands for cheaper Cipro is very similar to our demand for lower prices on AIDS drugs."[123]

Instead of overriding Bayer's patent, the U.S. negotiated with Bayer until October 24, when Bayer agreed to sell Cipro tablets for 95¢ each, with a total of $95 million in taxpayer dollars going to the company.[124] The Indian Drug Manufacturers Association noted that even the discounted Cipro from Bayer was more than five times more expensive than the Indian generic Cipro, which costs 17¢ a pill. As Asia Russell of the Health GAP Coalition remarked, "With the Cipro deal, [the U.S.] did not want to set a precedent that could be used against the U.S. administration at the upcoming WTO meeting, where the issue of affordable AIDS drugs and patent rights in poor countries will be a major controversy."[125]

Case 2: U.S. Files WTO Challenge Against Brazil's Compulsory Drug Licensing Law

The U.S. also filed—and then later, under political pressure, withdrew—a TRIPs challenge against a Brazilian compulsory licensing law.

In June 2000, the United States filed a WTO challenge to a Brazilian law that permitted local manufacturers to produce products if a patent holder does not produce them locally.[126] There were an estimated 597,000 Brazilians infected with HIV in 2001.[127] Brazil has, by far, the most successful developing-country program of delivering AIDS treatment drugs to people with HIV/AIDS. The Brazilian AIDS program, which grew out of a 1980s civil society campaign and coalesced into a national program by the mid-1990s, guarantees the entire population prevention and treatment for HIV/AIDS, the right to diagnosis, and the right for universal and free access to all resources to treat the disease.[128]

As of 2001, 98,000 HIV-positive patients were on antiretroviral drugs provided by the government at a total cost of $422 million.[129] These antiviral expenditures represented 2.9% of the Ministry of Health's total budget and only 0.06% of Brazil's GDP in 1999. Brazil's domestic production of the antiretrovirals indinavir and nevirapine generated savings of $80 million in 2000, about 30% of the cost of the program.[130] Between 1997 and 2001, the mean per-patient, per-year cost of one domestically produced triple therapy for HIV/AIDS declined 66%. Access to these therapies has drastically reduced the death rate from AIDS in Brazil. Between 1995 and 2000, deaths from AIDS declined by 54% in São Paulo and 73% in Rio de Janeiro and nationally, the death rate from AIDS has been almost cut in half from 12.2 deaths per 100,000 in 1995 to 6.3 deaths per 100,000 in 1999.[131]

The U.S. claim against Brazil involved a narrow technical detail that would not have inhibited Brazil's ability to issue compulsory licenses or continue its program. However, the very act of bringing the high-profile WTO case sent a powerful and dangerous message. The June 2000 complaint revolved around Brazil's "local working" requirement for patented medicines—the rule allowing local production under compulsory licenses if patent holders are sitting on a patent and not producing.[132] Weeks later, the EU filed a request to join in the WTO consultation between the U.S. and Brazil.[133]

The U.S. claimed that the TRIPs Agreement prohibits discriminating against products based on whether they are locally produced or imported, while Brazil's law allows the compulsory licensing of patents that are not manufactured in Brazil.[134]

In February 2001, Brazil announced that it might start producing nelfinavir and efavirenz, the two most expensive drugs used to treat HIV/AIDS.[135] New Jersey–based Merck & Co. sells efavirenz under the name Stocrin for $4,800 a year; nelfinavir is sold by Swiss-based Hoffman–La Roche and U.S.-based Pfizer for $7,100 a year.[136]

AIDS activists and consumer and health care advocates urged the U.S. to drop the WTO case. Critics of the TRIPs regime urged the WTO to reform its patent rules so that developing countries can unambiguously produce or import the cheapest possible drugs without fear of WTO challenges.[137] Bowing to the pressure from activist groups, USTR announced a consultative mechanism to promote cooperation with Brazil on HIV/AIDS issues in June 2001.[138] "Pressure from civil society seems to have helped compel the U.S. to back off this political case," concluded Maria Luisa Mendonca, director of the Global Justice Center in Brazil.[139] On June 25, 2001, the U.S. informed the WTO that it had come to a mutually satisfactory agreement with Brazil and was withdrawing its complaint.[140]

Forcing a WTO Declaration on TRIPs and Public Health

In June 2001, with the U.S. in retreat on its TRIPs threats in Africa and losing the public-relations battle over the Brazil TRIPs challenge, the African member states of the WTO forced a historic discussion at the TRIPs governing body (known as the TRIPs Council) on intellectual property and access to health technologies.[141] That meeting, where the issue of TRIPs as a threat to public health was forced to the forefront by several African delegates, created momentum for a declaration on TRIPs and public health, which eventually was issued at the November 2001 WTO Doha Ministerial.[142]

Three official documents resulted from the Doha Ministerial. One of these was the Doha Declaration on the TRIPs Agreement and Public Health, in which countries "affirmed that the [TRIPs] Agreement can and should be interpreted and implemented in a manner supportive of WTO members' right to protect public health and, in particular, to promote access to medicines for all," specifically mentioning countries' rights to do compulsory licensing.[143]

The battle to obtain the Declaration was a pitched one in which excellent strategy and the persistent efforts of developing country negotiators and health and AIDS activists around the world ultimately bested Big Pharma in forcing recognition of limits to the TRIPs rules. Although many corporate representatives and all but one U.S. congressman canceled their participation at the Doha Ministerial, representatives of the pharmaceutical industry were there in force.[144] In the weeks prior to the Doha summit, a working group on TRIPs and public health had prepared a draft text. African countries, with support from Brazil, Thailand and others, sought legally binding language stating that the TRIPs Agreement "shall" be interpreted and implemented to allow compulsory licensing and other public health measures. These countries also sought language making it clear that countries without the capacity or sufficient economies of scale to manufacture drugs under a compulsory license could import such drugs from a country with the capacity.

The pharmaceutical industry, with support from the U.S., Switzerland and other developed countries, sought nonbinding language and for that hortatory language to be as narrow as possible,[145] for instance stating that only in limited circumstances of extreme emergency and only for HIV/AIDS should compulsory licenses be considered, and blocking countries from importing compulsory licensed medicine.[146]

This deadlock remained until the last day of the Doha Ministerial.[147] With the TRIPs issue threatening to implode the entire ministerial, the WTO Secretariat obtained support from key countries to extend the summit for another day and maneuvering with the U.S. and EU to break Brazil and Thailand away from the African bloc in a divide-and-conquer move to weaken the TRIPs demands. A compromise proposal emerged that did not contain the desired mandatory language but did clearly state that countries could use compulsory licenses.

The TRIPs and Public Health Declaration deal infuriated the pharmaceutical industry, which attempted to spin the meaning of the text, suggesting that the

Declaration had no meaning. While the language is very broad, as demanded by health activists and developing countries, and very strong, it does not amend the TRIPs text. However, the context of the Declaration and its tone were an important political victory, and the Declaration provides a statement of WTO policy countries can raise to defend a compulsory licensing law in a WTO challenge—which is why industry was infuriated.

The final sticking point in Doha revolved around what rights countries that could not produce medicines—which is most of the developing countries—would have to import compulsory licensed medicines. The resolution was put off with the Declaration setting a December 31, 2002, deadline for an agreement on the terms under which such exports would be allowed.

After a year of negotiations on the issue, in December 2002, the U.S. scuttled a tentative agreement, complying with the demands of the U.S. pharmaceutical industry, which had returned from its Doha defeat to rage at the White House over USTR Robert Zoellick's role in brokering the Declaration.[148] Before the meeting, in a piece titled "The Assault on Drug Patents: The U.S. Ought to Stand Up for Intellectual Property Rights," the *Wall Street Journal* editorialized that the U.S. should tank the ongoing TRIPs and Public Health negotiations.[149] The U.S. stuck to its position that the new rules should only permit imports of compulsory licensed AIDS, tuberculosis, and malaria drugs.[150] The U.S. position differed only slightly from the pharmaceutical industry's position, in that USTR agreed that a few other diseases should be included besides HIV/AIDS.[151]

On December 20, 2002, discussions in Geneva imploded under continuing unilateral U.S. intransigence. The London *Guardian* laid the failure of the pact at the feet of U.S. Vice President Dick Cheney, who directed the USTR delegation in Geneva from Washington, D.C.[152]

The U.S. position on the export issue, incidentally, would inhibit the U.S. and rich countries' effective ability to assign compulsory licenses overseas; and, for example, would in the future make it much harder for Indian producers to export Cipro to the United States, an option HHS Secretary Tommy Thompson had considered during the anthrax attacks.

Days before the Cancún Summit, the WTO staff engineered another divide-and-conquer move on the issue, with a smaller group of countries signing off on the original text supplemented by a U.S.–demanded interpretive note adding yet more bureaucratic hurdles to countries' ability to import compulsorily licensed drugs. Other countries were pressured to sign off. The U.S. had backed down, but the deal reached was considered unacceptable by public health groups. And the real fight remains because the deal signed requires future negotiations to change the actual TRIPs rules.

While trying to hold its ground at the WTO, the United States is simultaneously working in diverse international trade negotiating fora to increase the monopoly protections afforded by patents, and to diminish the ability of countries to do compulsory licensing and parallel importing. The U.S.-Jordan Free Trade Agreement, completed in fall 2000, sharply limits the grounds for compulsory licensing.[153] Draft provisions of the proposed Free Trade Agreement of the Americas would:

- Limit compulsory licensing to the public sector and for emergencies.
- Prohibit the export of compulsorily licensed goods.
- Bar the use of compulsory licensing until four years after a patent was granted.
- Prohibit sublicensing of compulsory licenses.
- Require all countries to grant five years of exclusivity protections to marketing approval data, imposing an important bar to timely compulsory licensing.
- Extend the patent term, to offset regulatory delays and to match extended terms in other countries.
- Require harsh penalties, including criminal enforcement, for intellectual property violations—although, importantly, criminal enforcement would not be required for patent violations.

Generally, the inclusion of intellectual property provisions in multiple trade agreements makes it much harder to ratchet down international patent protection obligations. Even if changes were made so that the WTO TRIPs became less restrictive, for example, this would have little impact on countries that had separate intellectual property obligations—that were equivalent to or more severe than the WTO mandates—in the FTAA or other international trade agreements.

WTO THREATENS DOMESTIC BANS ON HAZARDOUS SUBSTANCES

Nations routinely impose regulatory restrictions on substances that are known to be dangerous to their citizens. The obvious public health need to prevent unnecessary exposures to dangerous chemicals or products has been the mainstay of the workplace safety, environmental, consumer and public-interest movements in the U.S. for decades. The U.S. Environmental Protection Agency regulates dangerous household pesticides and other poisons under the Federal Insecticide, Fungicide and Rodenticide Act (FIFRA); the U.S. Occupational Safety and Health Administration (OSHA) regulates workplace toxic exposures, safety training and disclosure rules; and the Food and Drug Administration monitors fruits and vegetables for dangerous pesticide residues. These sensible safeguards protect citizens and promote safety, and over the long term can be shown to save money.

Case 3: Canada Challenges French Asbestos Ban

As early as 1927, scientists have known that asbestos, a mineral which is currently used in industrial and consumer products such as seals, gaskets, brake and clutch linings, and cement products such as pipes and roofing materials,[154] causes lung cancer, mesothelioma (cancer of the tissues lining the chest and abdomen) and asbestosis (a deadly lung inflammation) in people who come into contact with it.[155] Often the diseases do not manifest themselves for 20 years after exposure. A study by the French

Institut National de la Santé et de la Recherche Médicale (INSERM) found that construction workers and people in the general public who incidentally came into contact with white asbestos products were most at risk for asbestos-related illness.[156]

Each year in France, at least 2,000 people die from asbestos-related cancer.[157] A British study concluded that asbestos exposure will lead to 500,000 deaths in the EU by 2020.[158] In 1996, France joined Germany, Austria, Denmark, the Netherlands, Finland, Italy, Sweden and Belgium to ban all forms of asbestos.[159] In 1999 the EU itself enacted a rule requiring that all EU nations ban asbestos, by 2005.[160]

The French law bans asbestos and any product containing it, unless the use of asbestos substitutes would pose a graver public health risk. Decree 96-1133, which applies to domestic production as well as the import of asbestos, made it illegal to import or sell varieties of asbestos, including chrysotile or white asbestos, subject to a few minor exceptions.[161]

Canada, the second-largest exporter of asbestos in the world,[162] challenged the French ban in the WTO in 1998 as a violation of the WTO TBT Agreement and of GATT Articles XI and III banning quantitative restrictions on imports and forbidding discriminatory trade measures.[163] Canada claimed that under WTO rules, countries can regulate but not ban asbestos. Canada has also claimed that even if the ban did not violate any specific WTO provisions, the French ban required Canada to be compensated because it impaired trade benefits Canada expected from the Uruguay Round for asbestos. Canada argued that asbestos use is safe when adequate safety measures are taken, and that France's ban was more trade restrictive than is necessary and therefore WTO-illegal. In addition, Canada began to threaten the EU with a WTO challenge over its July 1999 continent-wide ban of the substance.[164] The U.S. filed a third-party submission in support of the French ban.[165]

Least Trade Restrictive Rule

Canada noted that it was not challenging the right of WTO member countries to take necessary measures to protect the health and safety of their populations, but argued that the right must be exercised within the constraints of the WTO agreements. Canada claimed that less trade-restrictive measures were available to protect workers from the ill effects of asbestos; thus, France could not adopt a total ban on asbestos (with no distinction between fibers and products) without scientific proof of the health risk posed by modern products containing chrysotile. Indeed, Canada asserted that chrysotile asbestos is less harmful than other types of asbestos and that "it can be used without incurring any detectable risk."[166] Therefore, Canada argued, an alternative form of regulation—"controlled use"—exists that provided a less trade-restrictive means to satisfy the French objective to safeguard public health.[167]

International Standards Must Be Used

In its complaint to the WTO, Canada also pointed to international standards that support the "controlled use" asbestos regulation which involves setting standards for worker protection in all circumstances where workers may encounter asbestos, from manufacturing and handling to use.[168] Canada also cited as the presumptive legal standard for regulating asbestos the ISO guidelines for working with chrysotile asbestos.[169] The mandate of the ISO, formally an industry group, does not include the promotion of public health and safety. (See Chapter 1 for more information on the ISO.) In spite of the industry membership and funding and the narrow focus of the ISO, the WTO dispute panel consulted the organization to provide a list of experts to advise it on technical issues relating to asbestos regulation.[170]

Discrimination in Favor of Asbestos Substitutes

Canada also claimed that by banning asbestos, France was treating asbestos less favorably than the products that would be used as asbestos substitutes in France, violating the WTO rule forbidding discrimination between "like products."[171] Of course, there are always competing products that benefit from health bans of another product, but Canada argued that the incidental benefits that accrue to producers of competing products constitute a WTO violation. Such a definition of "like products" would be so general as to prevent countries from banning any products on health grounds, since all their substitutes would be "like products."

Canada additionally claimed that the health effects of substitute fibers and cement products are unknown,[172] and that France was discriminating against asbestos by replacing the use of chrysotile with these substitutes. Canada wanted the TBT Agreement to be read in a way that would compel any domestic regulatory action that would negatively affect commerce in a given product to be tested against the hypothetical risks engendered by the use of likely alternative products.

"Nullification and Impairment"

Finally, Canada alleged that the French asbestos ban "nullified and impaired" benefits accruing to it as a result of tariff concessions granted by the EU during the Uruguay Round and that the ban would have the effect of disrupting the conditions of competition between domestic substitute products and chrysotile asbestos.[173] Canada argued that it has a right to trade in dangerous substances if those substances were legal at the time it entered into a trade agreement with France. Obviously this line of argument would cover many products for which trade concessions were granted but whose adverse health impacts were unknown at the time of the concession.

*   *   *

The asbestos case raised many issues, including how much discretion each country will have to decide how to regulate hazardous substances, and many people viewed the filing of this case as an attack against the universally recognized right to a safe workplace.[174] According to the WHO, there are 160 million cases a year of occupational disease worldwide.[175]

According to the ILO, the majority of the 160 million victims of occupational disease reside in the developing world.[176] Seven of Canada's top ten asbestos markets are developing countries, which are the only growing markets for asbestos.[177] With a dwindling asbestos market in rich countries, Canada wanted to ensure it didn't lose markets in Africa, South America and Asia.[178] Indeed, there are reports that Canada targeted France among all EU members that have implemented asbestos bans because it feared the French ban would influence France's former colonies, particularly Morocco, Tunisia and Algeria—all of which are Canadian clients—to do the same.[179] Canada also hoped that a successful challenge of the French ban might force other WTO member states to revoke their bans, which had caused drops in asbestos sales in recent years.[180]

As the world's poorer nations industrialize, asbestos is often the most effective and cheapest way to make materials needed for water pipelines, power plants, factories, schools and prisons. Yet worker safeguards in these countries are often substandard or nonexistent.[181] Asbestos-related deaths in the developing world are expected to reach one million in the next 30 years.[182] Of the top ten countries to which Canada exports, only one has ratified the international resolution on the safe handling of asbestos first proposed in 1986.[183]

Canada's filing of the WTO challenge immediately caused an uproar. Many countries ban asbestos. The health threats associated with asbestos are well known. That the WTO provided a means for such a challenge spotlighted critics' concerns about how WTO rules might undermine domestic regulatory policies. A reasonable interpretation of the WTO rules invoked by Canada in the challenge would be to find the ban to be in violation of WTO requirements. Yet such a ruling would be enormously damaging to the WTO—which was already suffering from a crisis of legitimacy linked to the implosion of the Seattle WTO Ministerial and revelations about how members from developing countries had been treated during the Seattle summit.

Thus, insiders were not particularly surprised when on September 18, 2000, a WTO dispute settlement panel upheld the asbestos ban. Though public-interest groups were pleased that the WTO panel's decision preserved the ban, the contorted reasoning the panel had to use to obtain the result was frightening and illogical. The basic ruling was that France's asbestos standard was not covered by the WTO's standards rules, and thus, while the ban restricted trade, it was nevertheless permissible because it met a WTO exception for certain measures necessary to protect human health.[184] Canada appealed the decision.

On March 12, 2001, the WTO Appellate Body released its ruling.[185] It held that the asbestos ban was WTO-compliant, but it also refined the lower panel's interpretation of central norms and principles of WTO law.

The panel faced a major political problem. Given the weighty role the TBT Agreement gives to international standards and the existence of industry-influenced asbestos standards weaker than France's, the panel would be hard-pressed to achieve the result it needed—upholding the ban. The panel chose a bizarre legal maneuver—it declared that the asbestos ban was *not* a technical regulation and thus would not be covered under TBT rules. To do this the panel looked at France's asbestos decree as a whole and, using a stunning legal contortion, decided that the decree constituted a general prohibition on asbestos, not a regulation mandating or prohibiting any characteristics for any specific products.[186]

The panel then reverted to the national treatment provision of GATT Article III, which requires equal treatment of "like products" of domestic and foreign origin. The panel then set out to interpret this provision's application to the French policy. Ironically, the very purpose of the 22-page-long TBT Agreement was to set a negotiated understanding of how GATT Article III was to be interpreted as regards regulatory standards.

The worrisome precedent set by the panel's approach is that by analyzing the health protection aspects of the French ban under GATT instead of under the WTO TBT, the panel shifted the burden of proof from Canada to France, effectively making the French ban guilty until proven innocent. Under WTO TBT rules, France would have argued that its policy pursued a legitimate TBT objective. After raising that defense, Canada, as challenger, would then have had the difficult burden of showing that a controlled-use policy removed the health risks from asbestos use, and that a complete ban was therefore an unnecessary obstacle to trade. Reverting to GATT Article III, however, imposed that burden upon France. If a WTO panel found that the French ban violated the GATT national treatment requirement, then the EU would have to show controlled-use to be *ineffective* in order for the ban to qualify under the GATT exception for the protection of human health.

Because France was able to convince the panel of the practical impossibility of applying a controlled-use program to all people who might be exposed to asbestos, this shift of the burden of proof did not change the ultimate outcome of this particular case. But in the majority of nonasbestos cases in which the scientific evidence or facts are not as favorable to the defending party, such a shift of the burden of proof might make all the difference and could make an important health measure hard to sustain. Moreover, such a shift is inconsistent with the ostensible priority that the preambles of the WTO agreements give to the protection of the environment and human health,[187] and it is inconsistent with the panel's own statement that "each Member is free to adopt the health policies that it deems appropriate and to give each such policy the priority it deems necessary."[188]

Ironically, the Appellate Body concluded that the lower panel was incorrect in its decision not to apply the TBT Agreement but refused to analyze this case under the TBT Agreement itself. However, it did set out a number of considerations for determining whether or not a law is a "technical regulation" and thus comes under the TBT rules. First, the regulation must set down "product characteristics," which may include "any objectively definable 'features,' 'qualities,' 'attributes,' or other 'distinguishing mark' of a product." Second, compliance must be mandatory; a technical regulation must prescribe or impose one or more characteristics. Finally, the product involved must be identifiable, since otherwise enforcement would not be possible.[189] These criteria would seem to drag product labeling, including eco-labeling, under TBT restrictions.

The Appellate Body and Article XX

Article XX (b) of the GATT comprises a general exception for any law, "necessary to protect human, animal or plant life or health." The Appellate Body report ruled that the word "necessary" involved a certain "weighing and balancing" test.[190] The analysis undertaken in the asbestos case built on a previous interpretation of necessity, ruling that a country ". . . may, in appropriate cases, take into account the relative importance of the common interests or values that the law or regulation to be enforced is intended to protect."[191]

The Appellate Body went on to examine the balance between the French asbestos ban's public health goals and the restrictive effects of the ban. It stated:

> In this case, the objective pursued by the measure is the preservation of human life and health through the elimination, or reduction, of the well-known, and life-threatening, health risks posed by asbestos fibres. The value pursued is both vital and important in the highest degree. The remaining question, then, is whether there is an alternative measure that would achieve the same end and that is less restrictive of trade than a prohibition.[192]

While in the asbestos case, this "weighing and balancing" test *saved* the French import ban, there are concerns that this approach may prove detrimental in the future. In particular, it remains to be seen how important WTO tribunals will consider the importance of environmental or conservation goals as opposed to the importance of preserving human health. The very fact that the Appellate Body—a small group of unelected trade experts—weighed the *importance* of a nation's policy objective highlights the problem of WTO tribunals making value judgments about domestic policy goals.

DOWNWARD HARMONIZATION OF CARCINOGENICITY TESTING OF PHARMACEUTICALS AND TESTING ETHICS

The International Conference on Harmonization of Technical Requirements for Registration of Pharmaceuticals for Human Use (ICH) was created by industry and regulatory authorities to harmonize requirements for the production and registration of pharmaceuticals in the United States, EU and Japan. The ICH is comprised of three governmental bodies and three pharmaceutical industry trade associations—the European Federation of Pharmaceutical Industries Association, Japanese Pharmaceutical Manufacturers Association, and Pharmaceutical Research and Manufacturers of America. Again, consumer groups are excluded.[193]

In 1996, the FDA proposed changes to the guidelines for testing the potential carcinogenicity of pharmaceuticals.[194] The purpose of these proposed changes was to harmonize U.S. standards with those promoted by the ICH.

Previously, the United States required companies to test new drugs on two species, typically mice and rats. For sixty-five substances, tests in rats alone have failed to produce evidence of carcinogenicity, while additional tests on mice have yielded clear evidence. Yet the harmonized testing standard allows pharmaceutical companies to drop mice tests and substitute short-term tests for a second species test, even though short-term tests are less indicative than the longer-term animal studies.[195] In the end, the U.S. standard was weakened to harmonize with the ICH proposal.[196]

The United States has also had a role in lowering other nations' standards through international harmonization by pushing U.S. policy into international standards, for example trying to push the U.S. practice of using placebos in clinical trials onto other countries through the ICH.

On September 24, 1999, the FDA published a Draft Guidance on Choice of Control Group in Clinical Trials (the Guidance), which was prepared by the ICH. About ICH guidelines the FDA says: "Although [ICH] guideline[s do] not create or confer any rights for or on any person and [do] not operate to bind FDA, [they do] represent the agency's current thinking. . . ."[197]

The Guidance attacks active-controlled trials, in which a new drug's effects are compared to the effects of drugs that have already been approved and are on the market, and advocates the use of placebo-controlled trials, in which a new drug's effects are compared to the effects of a placebo. In an active-controlled trial the test group is given the new drug and the control group is given a drug that has been approved as safe and effective. In a placebo-controlled trial, the test group is given the new drug, but the control group is merely given a placebo.

Experts have criticized the FDA's reliance on placebo-controlled trials as uninformative and unethical. Patients and physicians do not need information about whether a new drug for a disease for which there already is an effective therapy is better than nothing; they need to know whether the new drug is better than the existing drug. Regarding ethics, the Declaration of Helsinki, an international medical ethics agreement, requires that patients in medical studies, including those in a control group, should be provided the best proven diagnostic and therapeutic method. The difference between the practices is clear: in an active-controlled trial all patients obtain treatment, while in placebo trials, many patients are left untreated.

CONCLUSION: WTO CAN BE HAZARDOUS TO OUR HEALTH

This chapter demonstrates the pervasive manner in which WTO rules implicate a broad array of vital public health issues. Yet, to date the WTO's public health ramifications have not been systematically investigated. In trying to research and monitor only the international standardization issues over the past five years, Public Citizen's Project on the Harmonization of Standards uncovered myriad fora where public health standards are currently being set in closed, industry-dominated bodies, often without any public health or consumer representatives. This chapter includes only a few of these cases. (For more, see Public Citizen's Global Trade Watch's "Harmonization Handbook—2002," available at www.tradewatch.org.) And the standards harmonization issues are only one aspect of the WTO's effect on core public health concerns. Absent greater focus on WTO and globalization issues by public health officials, scholars and advocates, we all may learn the hard way just how hazardous WTO can be to all our health.

4

THE WTO'S GENERAL AGREEMENT ON TRADE IN SERVICES: PERPETUAL SERVITUDE

When most people think about trade, they conjure up images of ships laden with goods—sacks of coffee beans, steel beams, shoes—ferrying products between nations. And indeed, before the advent of NAFTA and the establishment of the WTO, trade agreements were limited to setting the terms for such exchange, such as limits on tariffs and quotas.

Although proponents of NAFTA and the WTO refer to them as "trade agreements," in reality they are broad international commercial pacts in which terms covering trade are only a small element. WTO and NAFTA include expansive rules concerning what domestic policies countries are allowed to establish or even maintain on the federal, state and local levels, including government policy regarding the service sector which are contained in the General Agreement on Trade in Services. As with all WTO rules, member countries are required to conform all of their domestic service-sector laws and policies to the GATS rules.

Our daily lives intersect with the service sector constantly—from the store where we buy our food to the insurers that cover our homes and cars, the schools our children attend, the hospitals that treat our families, and the banks that cash our paychecks—meaning GATS has a much more direct impact on people's daily lives than traditional trade matters. One of the few things that supporters and critics of the WTO agree on is that imposing uniform rules over the entire realm of countries' domestic policies and political processes connected to the service sector was a revolutionary undertaking. And while the existing GATS rules pose a significant threat to governments' policy authority regarding services and people's access to essential services, a major push is now under way to broaden GATS further

These new negotiations, started in 2000 and thus dubbed GATS-2000, are aimed at dramatically expanding the WTO constraints on governments' right to regulate and at adding new service sectors to those already governed by GATS rules. However, before considering the implications of this push to expand GATS, it is important to understand how the rules came into existence and how they operate.

GATS Was a Controversial Experiment

GATS was one of the most controversial agreements proposed in the Uruguay Round. The very concept of including the service sectors in a "trade" agreement meant a stunningly broad swath of additional economic and social activity would be brought under the jurisdiction of global commercial disciplines. One easy definition of "services" is everything that you cannot drop on your foot—retail stores, banking, insurance, energy, telecommunications, maintenance and repair, construction, mining, toxic waste processing, tourism, museums, libraries, food preparation and restaurants and hotels, laundry and cleaning, and transport. Services also include what are often called "essential public services," such as education, hospitals, social security, mail delivery, police and prisons, and water and sewage systems. By subjecting the service sector to WTO disciplines, almost no human activity from birth (health care) to death (funeral services) remains outside WTO's purview.

Critics of GATS and similar service-sector negotiations now under way in the FTAA argue that certain elements of our lives, such as water, health care, and education, are simply too essential to commercialize for the purpose of enhancing business opportunities. Rather, these services should be considered a "global commons" fenced off from commercialization, basic rights of citizens which governments are responsible for organizing and delivering.[1]

GATS's Effects on Our Daily Lives

The provisions of the GATS can constrain governments from protecting the rights of citizens regarding the environment, health care, community development, and electricity. Among such rules are:

- prohibitions regarding government limits on the number of service providers or the range of services they provide in a particular sector, meaning that a state or community that has halted beach-front development for environmental purposes can be challenged by a foreign hotel or construction firm, even if the no-building policy applies to domestic firms also.
- limits on domestic regulation of services, even when domestic and foreign service firms are treated the same, threatening policies such as the U.S. Community Reinvestment Act (which requires banks to make loans in the communities where they take deposits to fight racial red-lining of loans) or hospital or insurance policies that require providers to offer certain coverage, or environmental requirements for bus companies or private electric utilities, or even rate mixing policies (cross-subsidization so that consumers in rural and other zones which are more expensive to serve can afford access).
- requirements that government regulations have the same impact on domestic and foreign service providers and do not undermine the "conditions of competitiveness." A similar provision in NAFTA is being used by the United Parcel Service to claim that Canada's postal service is obtaining privileged

treatment because its delivery of small parcels is effectively subsidized by the postal service's monopoly on first-class mail delivery.
* requirements that once a service sector comes under GATS, new government services or private not-for-profit monopolies can never again be established unless a country compensates other WTO countries for eliminating market opportunities, meaning that expanding government insurance-based social programs like social security or medicare or establishing a single-payer-style health care system becomes prohibitively expensive.

What's at Stake

In democratic societies, public services are the principal means for guaranteeing citizens' access to water, education, health care and security. GATS is designed to commodify these essential services into new private business opportunities by providing a set of tools to remove them from public control—for example, selling a city-owned or not-for-profit hospital to a for-profit company. GATS rules interfere deeply with the way such services, once privatized, will be provided, by constraining governments' rights to regulate in the service sector. To the extent that GATS rules threaten access to basic public services, the agreement becomes a set of tools used in the theft of people's most basic democratic rights.

Government provides universal access to many vital services that would be difficult for consumers to purchase individually on the open market. Health care advocate Dr. David Himmelstein put the balance of government services and taxes succinctly at a 1996 speech in Ontario: "In Cambridge, my city taxes come to about $1,300 per person, about what I pay for car insurance. For my taxes I receive police and fire protection, trash collection, schools for my two children, care at a public hospital whether or not I am insured, and snow-plowing of the streets. For my car insurance I get . . . car insurance. So where did I get the better deal?"[2]

GATS is an attack on the very notion that government has an important role to play in providing such "public goods." Originally an array of neoliberal think tanks and their allies in several rich governments joined with giant service-sector firms seeking new markets to push for the agreement in order to further their worldview. Government, they argued, had to be cut back and removed from people's lives as much as possible because the market is the wisest and best provides services, while government intervention creates subjectivity, inefficiencies and waste.

The Political Context of GATS

How was this ideological perspective to be transformed into a massive corporate expropriation of public property and an invasion of domestic governmental authority? How did it come to pass that the very elected officials whose authority GATS constrains approved of such a thing? One reason must be ignorance on the part of many countries' legislators and citizens about what "trade" negotiators were up to. As the implications of the GATS are becoming clearer, many people are saying: wait a minute, *that's* in a trade agreement? Many in the U.S. Congress and parliaments worldwide are only now realizing what they have gotten their nations into by approving the expansive Uruguay Round agreements. The proponents of this radical agenda used a Trojan horse strategy: By tucking items such as the GATS—which has little to do with trade—inside a package with what they were able to label "free trade," passage in parliaments around the world was assured.

Yet, even with this strategy, the GATS only came to fruition after intense lobbying by the U.S.,[3] the world's largest exporter of services by a factor of two.[4] The U.S. government promoted the industry view of services—as potentially rich new areas for business exploitation and profit. The U.S. sold this business agenda to the public by touting services as the fastest growing sector and the most promising for employment—a public-relations campaign that also prepared the ideological groundwork for service-sector companies to expand their business opportunities.

Indeed, the official U.S. private sector advisers on the GATS talks were massive service-sector corporations, such as American Express.[5] Companies serving on U.S. trade advisory committees not only were able to set the U.S. agenda, but also had exclusive access to negotiating texts and negotiators during the talks. These corporations, comprising the U.S Coalition of Service Industries (USCSI), include most of the top players in the recent U.S. corporate accountability scandals, including WorldCom and Arthur Andersen in 2002,[6] and several corporations that have been under investigation by the Securities and Exchange Commission— Citigroup, Halliburton and AOL Time Warner.[7]

At issue with the GATS is an attempt by for-profit corporations to vacuum up billions in government funds—our tax dollars. The global amount of money spent—much of it by our national, state and local governments—to provide services annually is mind boggling: $2.2 trillion in health care,[8] $1 trillion in education,[9] and $1 trillion in electricity.[10] Corporations want to transform a portion of this money into private profits. Basic math helps explain what has happened time and again when for-profit companies take over public services: with a chunk of the money skimmed off as profit, the private company seeks to provide the formerly government-run service, but with either less quality or at a higher cost to us.

Idealized markets operate in terms of supply and demand: consumer demand for goods and services is constrained by the market's willingness to provide them below a certain price. Under this model, consumers purchase as many widgets as they need based on their ability to pay, generating demand, and suppliers refuse to sell below a certain price, creating the supply-and-demand price equilibrium. However, this model fails to account for basic goods and services that every person needs in order to survive. It may be true that if the price of widgets were doubled consumers would purchase half as many, but we could not drink less water than we need to survive simply because the price was increased. It is unlikely that we would eat twice as much bread if the cost of loaves were halved. The same is true of health care services: the demand for appendectomies has little to do with pricing structures or market-based supply issues and more to do with appendicitis, which the market is poorly designed to measure and price.

Because the market cannot deliver things like sanitation, potable water, education, health care, social security, transportation infrastructure, or electricity to people on a universal or an equitable basis, one significant role of government has been to moderate the impact of the market on these basic services. Unfortunately, this reality has no role in U.S. negotiators' position regarding GATS even though the U.S. had had plenty of local experience with failed service privatization and deregulation. For example, Atlanta canceled a $20 million annual contract to run its municipal water system with private, for-profit provider United Water Services after operational failures including brown, rusty water and failure to repair broken lines that spilled water into the streets.[11] In California, ratepayers have been gouged for over $70 *billion* as a result of deregulation (an amount larger than even the WTO's most optimistic projection of trade-related growth for the entire United States through 2004!) and were even then subjected to days of "rolling blackouts," during which they intermittently lost power for six days in 2001,[12] leaving businesses closed, homes dark, and hospitals in crisis.

Disastrous service-sector privatization and deregulation experiments have also hurt people in Europe, yet the EU is now the most vociferous advocate of GATS expansion. In 1994, Britain started to privatize its rail system.[13] The integrated government rail network was broken up into more than 100 separate businesses, all held together by contracts.[14] Since then, the trains have gotten more hazardous, with major accidents bringing the system to a grinding halt in 2000.[15] The quality of service also has suffered greatly, with schedule cuts and daily delays. Trips between major cities now often take longer than they did at the turn of the century.

The threats to people created by the GATS agenda are particularly extreme in the developing world. One of the cynical "market opportunity" targets of the GATS (and now of the FTAA service-sector negotiations, which we'll discuss in Chapter 10) is the permanent locking in of the privatizations that developing countries were forced to conduct over the past two decades by the World Bank and the International Monetary Fund. Service-sector corporations including Citigroup, Shell, and AT&T have been big beneficiaries of the World Bank and IMF's enormous leverage over indebted countries and whose access to loans has been conditioned on privatizing government utilities, transport and telecommunications systems.[16]

In 1990, the Dominican Republic opened its energy production sector to private companies.[17] The World Bank approved a $132.3 million loan for a combined-cycle power facility at Puerto Plata in 1992,[18] and an additional $1.5 million currency swap in 1995 to support the project.[19] This was followed in 1998 by a $20 million World Bank infusion for the sole purpose of privatizing the country's power sector.[20] The Dominican Republic promptly privatized its distribution and generation of electricity, selling these assets on the open market to Enron and other companies.[21]

After privatization, electricity rates shot up between 51% and 100%.[22] Angry citizens refused to pay, and the government was forced to subsidize the price increases—costing Dominican taxpayers an additional $5 million each month.[23] By October 2001, the government owed $217 million, more than half of it to Enron and other private companies.[24] With the country in arrears, Independent Power Producers, whose electricity was generated by Enron, simply stopped providing power, leading to blackouts lasting as long as 20 hours, even in schools and hospitals.[25] Dominican protests over the imposed blackouts brought a police response, leaving at least eight dead.[26] Ironically, to raise additional funds to pay power producers, the Dominican government sold off even more of its power production assets—for almost $1 billion less than their actual value.[27]

In the context of the current GATS-2000 talks, for the many developing countries whose service sectors have been forced open by the IMF and World Bank, there is pressure to include these already opened service sectors. If a developing country was already required by the IMF to open its market by demanding services be privatized and such a privatization involved a foreign company, GATS MFN rules already require that country to provide access in that sector to all other countries' companies, unless as described below the country was able to schedule a time-limited MFN exception before 1993.

Canadian Health Care Vulnerable to GATS Attack

While, outrageously, 41.2 million Americans have no health insurance coverage[28] and an additional 31 million Americans are underinsured, many countries, and almost all other developed countries,[29] provide health services for their citizens. In some countries access to basic health care is a guaranteed constitutional right.[30]

The Canadian single-payer health care system, called Medicare, is among the most popular in the world; threatening to cut or dispose of it is widely considered political suicide for Canadian politicians.[31] The system is a national, coast-to-coast health insurance program that covers medically necessary hospital and physician services for all residents.[32]

Since the original GATS negotiations in the 1990s, Canadian citizens repeatedly have been told that government negotiators will make sure Medicare is immune from the effects of GATS.[33] However, this goal is quickly being shown to be elusive, given the numerous mechanisms GATS includes to extend its coverage over service sectors governments have not chosen to subject to GATS.[34]

Although Canadian Medicare is a federal system, the provinces administer the program and determine the covered benefits package and copayment schedules.[35] The federal and provincial governments finance the system jointly.[36] Each province offers a slightly different mix of benefits and copayment schedules. Individuals can only buy private coverage for services that are not covered by the provinces. Paying for services that are covered in the benefits package is prohibited.

This bifurcation between national and provincial responsibilities has opened up a possible GATS wedge that could gut the Canadian health care system. In 1999, the government of Alberta introduced legislation allowing private, for-profit facilities to offer overnight care.[37] This proposal poses a GATS threat for two reasons: First, it undermines Canada's efforts to shield health care completely from the GATS agreement because under GATS, only service sectors that are not explicitly *and exclusively* reserved for public action can qualify for GATS limited exception for some public services which does not cover services that are provided both by the government and privately.[38] A 1998 WTO background paper noted that, under GATS, countries that have a mix of public and private hospital ownership cannot argue for exemption for their public hospitals from GATS coverage.[39] Also under GATS rules, a signatory government is responsible for the policies and actions of all levels of its government. So if one Canadian province takes an action, the implications extend to all of Canada, as far as GATS treatment.[40] Thus, an experiment with partial privatization in one province would put Canada's entire public health care system at risk for becoming subject to GATS coverage.

Second, if Canadian health services were subjected to GATS disciplines, any future attempt to expand Canada's public health care system, or to return from partial privatization to an exclusively public system, would run afoul of GATS rules.[41] Canada would be required to negotiate compensation with all WTO member countries whose service providers are affected to make up for the withdrawn service-sector opportunity,[42] making attempts to reverse an experimental privatization prohibitively expensive. These GATS threats have implications for all health care systems that permit private coverage for services beyond the basic benefits packages. Although people may organize and pressure to include additional benefits in the basic benefits package, if the service already is partially or fully privatized, expanding the benefits of a national health system would be susceptible to a GATS challenge. This is why GATS is called a "one-way" agreement: It allows public systems to get more private and profit-driven, but prohibits them from getting more inclusive and public.

Understandably, developing countries were intensely opposed to service-sector liberalization,[43] because they feared that giant multinational service providers from industrialized countries would swoop in to take advantage of IMF and World Bank–ordered services privatization, overwhelming fledgling domestic operators.[44] (Indeed, when today's developed countries were developing, they themselves provided basic services through government monopolies or through highly regulated private sector providers protected from competition.)

Because of this resistance during the original GATS negotiations, not only from developing nations but from European countries and others who did not share the U.S. view that all services were commodities to be traded for profit, the U.S. industry goal of placing all services under the same WTO rules did not occur. As a result, GATS is a "hybrid" agreement—some GATS rules impose one-size-fits-all WTO requirements called "horizontal disciplines," and others allow countries to choose sectors to opt in for coverage by some of the GATS rules.

For instance, some requirements, such as national treatment, only apply to the service sectors designated in countries' lists of specific GATS commitments. At the time of original GATS negotiations, countries' negotiators listed their GATS commitments on a sector-by-sector basis. Because of this process, promoters of GATS insist that it is a flexible agreement, and that countries remain free to choose their pace of privatization.

In contrast, NAFTA's services rules apply top-down. This means that every service sector is covered and up for grabs unless a country negotiated an exception for a specific sector. The same top-down or "negative list" approach is reflected in the draft FTAA services chapter, as discussed in Chapter 10.

HOW GATS WORKS

GATS defenders insist that the agreement does not threaten essential public services or limit reasonable government regulation of service-sector corporations. We will see in this section that the very text of the GATS agreement belies these reassurances. This exposition of the GATS terms will also help put into context what is at stake with the ongoing GATS-2000 talks, which aim at both bringing more service sectors under GATS discipline and expanding on the scope of existing rules.

Scope of GATS Coverage

The first article of the GATS text states that the pact covers "any service in any sector," meaning no service is excluded from the agreement's scope. All levels of government—"central, regional, or local governments or authorities"[45]—must comply with GATS terms, meaning GATS covers local sewer systems, public hospitals, municipal trash collection, elementary education and water systems. Remarkably, GATS constraints also cover actions of "non-governmental bodies in the exercise of powers delegated by" any level of government.[46] This includes boards of universities, or hospital and private sector standard-setting or professional organizations, such as legal bar associations.

The GATS rules not only set constraints on government policies directly regulating services, but also extend to "measures by Members affecting trade in services."[47] This broad definition means that all government policies that affect services, including those not specific to services, such as general labor market policies or other broad regulations, are included under the GATS constraints.

The GATS agreement is explicit that no sector is excluded a priori,[48] meaning no sectors can be carved out altogether, and countries are bound to follow some of the GATS rules even if they do not explicitly agree to subject a service sector to GATS coverage. Claims by GATS defenders that GATS rules only apply to sectors that governments volunteer for coverage are demonstrably false. Some GATS rules, such as the important Most Favored Nation rules, apply unconditionally to all service sectors whether they are offered by a country to be covered by other GATS terms or not.[49] Practically, what the Most Favored Nation rule means is that if a government contracts out a public service activity or gives a tax break, special regulatory treatment or a subsidy to any single foreign service-sector company or investor, it must extend the same treatment immediately and unconditionally to every interested company from every WTO country.

While WTO dispute resolution tribunals have not yet ruled on many cases arising from the GATS rules, two of these cases have included broad interpretations of
the GATS Most Favored Nation rule. Defenders of GATS argue that countries were
able to list exceptions to the horizontal MFN rule when initial commitments were
made under the GATS, but what the GATS supporters rarely mention is that under
another GATS provision, countries are to phase out such exemptions within ten
years and that "[i]n any event, they shall be subject to negotiation in subsequent
trade liberalizing rounds."[50]

Another common line of GATS's defenders is that the rules explicitly exclude all
public services. This is also untrue. There is a provision in the GATS stating that certain government-provided services are excluded from GATS coverage, but the provision is written in such a way that it only applies to government services that are
provided neither on a "commercial basis" nor "in competition with one or more service suppliers."[51] It is hard to imagine a public service besides the national security
provided by the U.S. military that actually would qualify under this exclusion, given
the fact that if any U.S. state or city allows a private provider in a sector, the service is
no longer provided exclusively on a public basis in the U.S. and thus that sector is no
longer covered by the exception.

Most public services in the U.S., and increasingly in other countries, are provided by both government and private operators. Obvious examples are primary
education, medical and hospital services, retirement pensions and transportation.
For example, in the U.S. there are public hospitals (such as the world's largest hospital, the Cook County Hospital in Illinois), private not-for-profit hospitals (such
as religious-affiliated hospitals and charity hospitals such as the Shriners), and
for-profit operators (such as Columbia HCA and Humana).

Even for services provided exclusively by the government, only direct
government-to-people delivered services are exempt from the GATS. Yet, governments provide many public services through a "mixed system of delivery" that
includes both public and private components. Often, the private components are
not-for-profit private community organizations which obtain government grants
as well as other sources of funding to perform a service, such as elder care or soup
kitchens.

Indeed, as noted in a paper by the Organization for Economic Cooperation and
Development unearthed by the Canadian Centre for Policy Alternatives for their
excellent 2002 GATS booklet "Facing the Facts: A Guide to the GATS Debates,"
"This exception is . . . limited: where a Government acts on a commercial basis
and/or as competitor with other suppliers, its activities are treated like those of any
private supplier."[52]

Finally, confusion abounds about the relationship of GATS rules to government procurement. Defenders of GATS overstate a provision that now excludes
government procurement from GATS coverage. Under existing GATS rules, when
a government is procuring services "for government purposes and not with a view
to commercial resale or with a view to use in the supply of services for commercial
sale," (for instance electricity for use in its own buildings) most GATS rules do
not apply.[53] However, if the government is purchasing electricity from a private

generator for sale to the public—for instance through a public monopoly carrier—GATS rules can apply.

What GATS Rules Require

Given an understanding of how broadly the GATS rules apply, the next question is, what do those rules require, besides the Most Favored Nation treatment discussed above? One way to understand the substantive requirements is to view them as covering two overarching categories of provisions: First, market access; and second, regulation of service suppliers and the provision of services.

1. Who Controls What

The first category concerns who owns and controls services: are they public services or are they private, and if private companies are operating in a service sector—for instance telecommunications and banking—are there limits on how many such companies may be established and who can own them? Many countries that have privatized services that previously were operated by the government have done so by establishing private not-for-profit monopolies which are heavily regulated (in the U.S., for instance, Fannie Mae and Freddy Mac are government-sponsored enterprises which operate in the free market and guarantee demand for the secondary mortgage market, essentially generating a willingness to make home loans by banks who know they can sell the notes to Fannie and Freddy), or establishing several competing private for-profit firms, or regulating the percentage of foreign or absentee ownership allowed.

GATS covers all conceivable ways a service might be provided, enumerated as four "modes," only the first of which is what most people would consider "trade in services." In making their GATS commitments, countries can agree to provide access for all modes or only for one or some.

Mode 1: Cross-border trade in services.[54] This is the right to provide services from one country to another, such as international telephone calls, data processing and computer software engineering from remote centers, and "distance learning."

Mode 2: Use of service abroad.[55] This is the right to sell services in one nation to citizens of another nation—for example, through tourism and foreign exchange studies.

Mode 3: Establishment of a service business or investment in another country.[56] This is the right to establish a "commercial presence" or investment in the service sector, including setting up subsidiaries or acquiring or merging with local companies. The WTO calls the GATS Agreement the world's first multilateral agreement on investment, since it includes the right to set up a commercial presence in another country. This aspect of GATS is why some people consider it a backdoor means to revive the Multilateral Agreement on Investment a radical investment pact that was killed by public opposition in 1998.

Mode 4: Movement of natural persons.[57] This is the right to move people between countries to supply services. Currently this has mainly involved intra-company transfers of executives and short-term visits by professionals such as lawyers and consultants, with negotiations now under way to harmonize international professional qualification standards so as to facilitate this movement. In the GATS-2000 negotiations, some countries are requesting broader Mode 4 access, for instance, the right to provide workers from one country to work long-term in another country.

EU Claims Post-Enron Corporate Accountability Legislation Violates U.S. GATS Commitments

In August 2002, the Sarbanes-Oxley corporate accountability legislation was pushed through the U.S. Congress as a partial response to the corporate crime wave crested by Enron, WorldCom and other high-profile scandals. Within weeks of the legislation's passage, the European Union threatened that if it were implemented to apply to European accounting-service providers operating in the U.S., it would violate market access and other U.S. commitments on accounting services granted in GATS. The EU claims that under the law, accounting and legal firms would be subject to conflicting standards in the U.S. and Europe, for instance when one rule requires the submission of confidential documents and the other prohibits it.[58] The EU is particularly concerned about the creation of a regime that it argues would double compliance costs by requiring increased disclosure and CEO certification of financial numbers and accounting—with increased sentencing guidelines that include jail time. Don Cruikshank, chairman of the London Stock Exchange, noted that complying with these provisions would make the U.S. "far less attractive and welcoming to foreign issuers" of stock.[59] Other provisions require legal and accounting firms to be "whistleblowers" on clients they suspect are violating the law, which may potentially violate European confidentiality and attorney-client privilege.[60] An unnamed EU official told *The Times* of London that the accounting and corporate governance rules are "probably in contravention of international legal principals."[61] Unless the U.S. weakens the law by exempting EU firms from compliance with the regulations, this battle could become a GATS challenge.

Mode 4 raises numerous issues about labor standards and immigration policy. For instance, some Central American countries earn the majority of their hard-currency foreign exchange in the form of remittances, which is money sent home from emigrants working in the U.S. During 2001, $23 billion in remittances were sent from the U.S. by immigrants from Latin America and the Caribbean.[62] For El Salvador, remittances from the U.S. totaled $1.9 billion in 2001,[63] equivalent to the

$1.9 billion the El Salvador government holds in gold and foreign currency reserves.[64]

Yet, the notion of Mode 4 could mean that people would get paid at a rate according to where they were born, not where they are doing the work. For instance, one extreme scenario under Mode 4 would be for a U.S. construction company to subcontract for the provision of construction services with a company (perhaps even a subsidiary) in El Salvador for a set amount of money. The El Salvadoran company would then use Mode 4 rights to send construction service workers to the U.S. to perform the contract. The rate at which these workers would be paid would be determined by the El Salvadorian company (as opposed to the prevailing construction wages in the U.S.).

Another scenario currently being discussed in GATS talks relates to India's newest request for Mode 4 access for professional services contractors, such as independent computer professionals seeking to work within a service contract.[65] India is seeking to eliminate the numerical caps and the certifications (industry must demonstrate that there is a U.S. shortage of desired professionals, that guest workers will be paid the prevailing wage in their field and that the workers are not being brought in to break a strike) visa existing under the H1-B visa program through which a number of foreign service professionals now work in the U.S. Such a change essentially would allow software companies to import an infinite number of programmers to work at any salary above the minimum wage. Mode 4 provides a means to formalize a model of globalization that allows industry control over the rights of the movement of people while stripping away all regulations on the movement of goods and capital.

Race to the Bottom in High-Tech and Service Jobs

Amid the press coverage of massive U.S. manufacturing job losses and merger-related layoffs, the steady movement of high-tech and other service-sector jobs overseas has not received much notice until very recently. Yet a radical transformation of the traditional service-sector job—linked to the local economy and community and the result of secondary and higher education—is another significant aspect of the global economy. A major purpose of the WTO GATS, TRIMs and TRIPs agreements was to protect U.S. corporate investment overseas. However, instead of these rules promoting the shift to new U.S. jobs in the "clean" high-tech economy as promised by WTO promoters, evidence is mounting of even high-paying service-sector jobs being shifted overseas to seek cheaper labor. A recent report predicted that 3 million white-collar U.S. jobs and $140 billion in wages will shift overseas by 2015.[66]

Two types of service jobs are being moved away, or "outsourced": high-wage professional jobs relating to computer programming, medical diagnostics, architectural design, engineering and actuarial work, and low-wage jobs that can be separated from corporate centers, such as data processing, bookkeeping, telemarketing, directory assistance, reservation management and other "back office" operations.

The companies that created Silicon Valley, like Advanced Micro Devices and Hewlett-Packard, have been shifting employment to low-wage countries,[67] where high-tech sweatshops provide the services of highly educated, well-trained computer and other experts at prices at a fraction paid to similarly skilled U.S. workers. Many U.S. technology companies now contract with computer programmers in Bangalore, India, where workers holding Ph.D.s in computer science are paid $9,000 annually.[68] Meanwhile, GE Capital operates a center in India with more than 10,000 programmers that provide services not only for GE Capital's worldwide operations, but for all of GE.[69] Bangalore also is rapidly becoming the top location for "back office" operations from the U.S. and the UK, including GE, British Airways and Dell computer.[70] The Missouri government faced a barrage of press and political attention when it was revealed that its welfare hotline call center was operating out of India; however, given the widespread overseas outsourcing practices of the private call centers with whom many states contract, this phenomenon may be more widespread.[71]

The maquiladora region along the U.S.-Mexican border, originally intended to allow tariff-free manufacturing product assembly for reexport, now includes a fast-growing service industry, with supermarket chains cheaply employing the well educated and using the conveniently close Mexican labor market to enter computer data from coupons.[72] U-Haul, America West Airlines and the Gap all relocated their customer call centers to Mexico,[73] while NetLink Transaction Services LLC moved its accounting and human resources operations from Rochester, New York, to Reynosa, Mexico.[74] These examples only scrape the surface of this trend.

Countries negotiated an initial set of GATS commitments by sector and by mode before the 1993 signing of the Uruguay Round agreements. Countries are undergoing such negotiations anew in the GATS-2000 process. First, countries make "requests" of each other to have market access in specific service sectors and then countries submit "offers" in response. For GATS-2000, requests started in June 2002 and offers by March 31, 2003. This process occurs on many levels—bilaterally and by blocs of countries. However, in the end, because of the Most Favored Nation clause, all WTO member countries obtain access in the areas each country offers.[75] Each country's GATS market access coverage is listed in a "schedule" of commitments.

Two important sets of GATS rules apply only to the particular sectors that countries offered for coverage. Those rules are National Treatment and Market Access.

A. NO NUMERICAL LIMITS ON FOREIGN SERVICE FIRMS

GATS Article XVI bans countries from certain limits on market access for any sector that is offered for GATS coverage—unless a country listed them as exceptions in their GATS schedules in 1993. The following limits are forbidden:

- limits on the number of service suppliers, including through quotas, monopolies, economic needs tests or exclusive service supplier contracts;
- limits on the total value of service transactions or assets, including through quotas or economic needs tests;
- limits on the total number of service operations or the total quantity of a service;
- limits on the total number of natural persons that may be employed in a particular service sector;
- policies which restrict or require specific types of legal entity or joint venture through which service suppliers may provide a service; and
- limits on foreign ownership expressed as a maximum percentage or total value.

GATS Article XVI market-access rules are framed in absolute rather than relative terms, prejudging certain types of public policies and practices, whether they treat domestic and foreign providers the same or not.

What does this mean practically? Once a service sector is offered to be covered under GATS rules, countries are forbidden from limiting the number of service providers in that sector.[76] Thus, for instance, once a government offers GATS access for concessions in national parks, waste incinerators, oil drilling, or golf course construction it loses the right to limit the number of such businesses, even if the limit applies equally to domestic and foreign service providers. The same applies to anti-sprawl measures, which set limits on the construction of hotels, residences and resort facilities to minimize traffic problems, the development impact on the environment, and to protect open space. Economic needs tests—a market analysis to determine whether a market is saturated with a certain type of service—are also prohibited as a mechanism to judge whether there is demand for more service providers. Moreover, forbidding countries to have policies determining the type of specific legal entity required for providing a service means that some governments' requirements that elder care or childcare services be nonprofit entities are forbidden. For example, in the U.S., the state of Rhode Island prohibits for-profit hospital operators. Under GATS, a government's maintenance of any of these policies in a service sector covered by GATS would be subjected to a WTO challenge.

"Environmental Services"

There are significant environmental implications to service-sector rules in international commercial agreements. Consider tourism, transportation, waste management, and water and energy utilities and concessions in national and state parks: GATS rules forbid limits on the quantity of such activities and provide constraints on regulations seeking to shape how these activities are conducted. In addition, the processes of *obtaining* natural resources are considered services and, depending on governments' GATS commitments, may be covered by GATS rules. Thus, trade in logs is covered by WTO rules on trade in goods, but the cutting and milling of logs is a service, as is road-building. While minerals, oil or gas are goods covered under GATT rules, the GATS covers drilling, mining, processing and transportation of these goods. This has many implications, especially considering that the GATS general exceptions do not include conservation of exhaustible natural resources as an excuse for breaching GATS constraints. (GATT does include such a exception.) A domestic policy that might withstand a challenge under GATT rules may well fall under GATS rules. Finally, one subject matter that was approved at the 2001 Doha WTO Ministerial for future negotiations was called "Environmental Services."[77] Obtaining agreement on the environmental-services cluster was a major goal of the EU, which has several massive corporations, such as Suez Lyonnaise and Vivendi, that stand to benefit from privatizing control of bulk water and/or its collection. Growing fights against this has brought considerable attention to ensuring that countries do not commit to liberalizing specific services. Many analysts suspect the EU's zeal for environmental services negotiation is a backdoor push for water access. (For more on the environmental-services negotiations, see Chapter 1.)

B. FOREIGN SERVICE FIRMS ARE GUARANTEED FAVORABLE "CONDITIONS OF COMPETITIVENESS"

Under GATS, it is not sufficient for governments to treat foreign and domestic services and providers the same. The GATS National Treatment rule requires that when setting taxes and regulatory requirements, governments cannot promote domestic or local providers, but must give foreign service providers the best treatment available to domestic services or service providers.[78] The types of policy that could run afoul of these requirements include:

- restrictions on nonresident ownership of services;
- targeting government development or research funds to locals or nationals;
- special tax breaks or other benefits available to locals to start up day care or other "social" services;
- preferential tax treatment for women-owned, minority-owned or small businesses.

However, the actual National Treatment language in GATS goes further. It forbids not only domestic policies intended to treat foreign services or providers less favorably, but also laws that may unintentionally have such an effect. GATS Article XVII.3 states: "Formally identical or formally different treatment shall be considered to be less favorable if it modifies the conditions of competition in favor of services or service suppliers . . ."[79] This rule gives WTO dispute panels wide latitude in finding public policy measures to be GATS-illegal because if a policy can be shown to have a different impact on even one foreign service provider, it can be found to violate GATS. This language creates a de facto discrimination standard which means that even if a policy does not actually affect service trade flows, it is a violation of GATS if it limits an opportunity in the sector.

This problematic requirement could be used to attack neutral policies—for instance, requirements that retailers see to the recycling of the packaging of their goods, or that manufacturers deal with toxic waste on-site or at the nearest facility. These rules could be easier for local retailers or manufacturers to comply with than foreign companies, even though the legitimate goal of such laws is not to hinder foreign companies.[80] Almost any benefit that is provided to small businesses could also be called de facto discriminatory to the extent that more small businesses are local and larger ones are foreign-owned, requiring reverse discrimination against local businesses by favoring the interests of foreign-based, transnational corporations.

C. GOVERNMENT ACTIONS THAT DO NOT VIOLATE GATS RULES ALSO ARE SUBJECT TO CHALLENGE

As if these rules were not broad enough, the GATS also allows one country to take another to a WTO dispute resolution tribunal as having violated GATS even when no specific one of these extensive rules has actually been violated. Under GATS provisions called "nullification and impairment," a country can challenge another for failing to guarantee anticipated benefits of services liberalization. In the GATS, the actual provision is vast: "If any Member considers that any benefit it could reasonably have expected to accrue to it under a specific commitment of another Member . . . is being nullified or impaired as a result of the application of any measure which does not conflict with the provision of this Agreement, it may have recourse to a WTO tribunal."[81] A country whose expected benefit is judged to have been nullified or impaired "shall be entitled to a mutually satisfactory adjustment . . . which may include the modification or withdrawal of the measure." This vague and open-ended provision raises any number of serious problems. One country's notion of its "reasonable expectations" may not be another country's intended commitment—a matter over which a WTO tribunal meeting in secret would have total discretion. Not only does this open up opportunities for arbitrary and inconsistent rulings, but it promotes pro-liberalization rewrites of countries' actual GATS commitments by unaccountable WTO tribunals. This provision is based on the same logic as NAFTA's Chapter 11 rules requiring compensation for "regulatory takings," the draft MAI text and now the proposed FTAA: that the investor—in this case a foreign service sector corporation—is owed a standard of treatment by the government that goes beyond any explicit provision of the agreement.

D. COUNTRIES MUST PAY TO REVERSE ACCESS ONCE IT IS GRANTED

Remarkably, under GATS rules, once market access is granted, it cannot be reversed unless compensation is offered to all of the countries to whom access was ever granted for their lost future business, making reversals of even the most disastrous privatizations or deregulations excruciatingly difficult.[82] Countries were required at the time they made their initial GATS commitments to submit a list of all existing monopolies. Countries seeking to establish new monopolies—whether government or private sector, national or local—can only do so by paying for this "right" by compensating other countries.[83] Thus, a government had to have given notice by 1993 of all existing or future possible government services or be required to pay to maintain

or establish them. Obviously, even for governments that understood this requirement and sought to protect future policy flexibility, it was not possible to anticipate
all possible future needs. For instance, the Canadian province of Ontario decided
to establish a government system of no-fault auto insurance. This proposal was
killed after the U.S. insurance industry claimed that such an act would illegally
undercut Canadian commitments in insurance services made in the Canada-U.S.
Free Trade Agreement.[84] Before the GATS became so controversial, the WTO had on
its website a remarkably revealing online guide to what the GATS rules mean.
"[B]ecause unbinding is difficult, the commitments are virtually guaranteed conditions for foreign exporters and importers of services and investors in the sector. . . ."[85]

Thus, for instance, if California sought to remedy its disastrous electricity
deregulation by creating a new government service provider or allowing a regulated private monopoly services provider, it could only do so after the U.S. government offered compensation to other WTO countries because the U.S. has made
GATS commitments in electricity services.[86] This requirement is especially damn-
ing for developing countries, many of whom were forced to privatize services by
the IMF and World Bank's structural adjustment policies and lack the resources to
even contemplate compensating for the right to reverse such policies, no matter
how devastating their results have been on their populations.

Water Wars

In 1998, the IMF approved a loan of $138 million for Bolivia it described as
designed to help the country control inflation and stabilize its domestic economy.[87] The loan was contingent upon Bolivia's adoption of a series of "structural reforms," including privatization of "all remaining public enterprises,"
including water services.[88] Once these loans were approved, Bolivia was under
intense pressure from the World Bank to ensure that no public subsidies for
water existed and that all water projects would be run on a "cost recovery"
basis, meaning that citizens must pay the full construction, financing, operation
and maintenance costs of a water project.[89] Because water is an essential
human need and is crucial for agriculture, cost recovery pricing is unusual, even
in the developed world.[90]

In this context, Cochabamba, the third largest city in Bolivia, put its water
works up for sale in late 1999. Only one entity, a consortium led by Bechtel subsidiary Aguas del Tunari, offered a bid, and it was awarded a 40-year concession
to provide water.[91] The exact details of the negotiation were kept secret, as
Bechtel claimed that the numbers within the contract are "intellectual property."[92] But, it later came to light that the price included the financing by
Cochabamba's citizens of a part of a huge dam construction project being
undertaken by Bechtel, even though water from the Misicuni Dam Project would
be 600% more expensive than alternative water sources.[93] Cochabambans were

(continued)

also required to pay Bechtel a contractually guaranteed 15% profit,[94] meaning that the people of Cochabamba were asked to pay for investments while the private sector got the profits.

Immediately upon receiving the concession, the company raised water rates by as much as 400% in some instances.[95] These increases came in an area where the minimum wage is less than $100 a month.[96] After the price hike, self-employed men and women were estimated to pay one quarter of their monthly earnings for water.[97]

The city's residents were outraged. In January of 2000, a broad coalition called the Coordination for the Defense of Water and Life, or simply La Coordinadora, led by a local worker, Oscar Olivera, called for peaceful demonstrations. Cochabamba was shut down for four days by a general strike and transportation stoppage, but the demonstrations stopped once the government promised to intervene to lower water rates.[98] However, when there were no results in February, the demonstrations started again. This time, however, demonstrators were met with tear gas and police opposition, leaving 175 injured and two youths blinded.[99]

The threat that privatization of public services under GATS poses to democracy were demonstrated in March 2000. La Coordinadora held an unofficial referendum, counted nearly 50,000 votes, and announced that 96% of the respondents favored the cancellation of the contract with Aguas del Tunari. They were told by the water company that there was nothing to negotiate.[100]

On April 4, the residents of the city returned to the streets, shutting down the city. Again, they were met with police resistance, and on April 8, the government declared martial law.[101] The Bolivian military shot a 17-year-old protester in the face, killing him. However, protests continued, and, on April 10, the government relented, signing an accord that agreed to the demand of the protesters to reverse the water concession.[102] The people of Cochabamba took back their water.

Unfortunately, this inspiring story didn't simply end with the victory for the people of Cochabamba. On February 25, 2002, Bechtel filed a grievance using investor protections granted in a Bolivia-Netherlands Bilateral Investment Agreement at the World Bank, demanding a $25 million dollar payment as compensation for lost profits.[103] This case, which is pending, attempts to get blood from a stone. Bechtel is one of the world's richest companies, and had receipts in 2000 of $14.3 billion. It is attempting to extract millions from Bolivia, whose total national budget was a mere $2.7 billion.[104]

GATS one-way privatization rules highlight the WTO's deep conflict with democratic, accountable governance. Although the people can choose to change governments, they cannot choose to change policy. For instance, if a political party favoring privatization comes to government and implements such policies, a different party elected to government cannot reverse the policy decision in the future without compensating. Thus, a citizenry dissatisfied with one president's policies can change presidents, but not policies in their own nation absent paying other countries for the right. This calls into question the state of democracy and the future of meaningful democratic governance in the U.S. and around the world in the face of WTO rules such as those in GATS.

GATS and Privatization

GATS defenders note that there is no requirement under GATS that services be privatized. While in the narrowest sense this is technically true, it is not dispositive. For instance, the National Treatment rule creates enormous disincentives for public services to be able to survive once some private sector services are permitted in the same sector. For instance, right now U.S. law requires pharmaceutical companies to offer medicines at reduced rates to Veterans Administration facilities,[105] and for hospitalized Medicare recipients.[106] Similarly, the Medicare Disproportionate Share Hospital (DHS) program, which is the nation's primary program to support public "safety net" hospitals which provide care for the uninsured, requires higher reimbursement rates for DHS facilities. Yet by requiring equal access to such public funds and benefits for private sector, for-profit hospitals, the GATS would force the government to choose between continuing the program at a hugely increased cost, or ending the program, which would threaten the survival of the public facilities, leaving these populations without potentially life saving medicine. As well, GATS's Most Favored Nation rule in combination with its coverage of the actions of state and local governments makes it difficult for countries to avoid privatization by default because any local government can open an entire sector by merely providing access to any one foreign provider or private sector provision of a service otherwise exclusively performed by the government.

GATS Limits on Domestic Regulation of Services and Suppliers

The second broad element of GATS rules pertains to if, when, and how governments are permitted to regulate those services in which they allow private firms to participate. Defenders of the GATS often refer to a clause in the preamble that recognizes governments' rights to regulate in the service sector. However, preambular language is not binding in the same way that GATS actual rules are, and the rules that come after the preamble, which *are* binding, set clear restrictions on the ways countries may regulate.

> "Governments are free in principle to pursue any national policy objectives provided the relevant measures are compatible with the GATS."
> —WTO Secretariat, October 1999[107]

What does it mean for a domestic policy to be compatible with GATS? Under existing GATS rules are constraints on how governments may regulate service sectors they have already committed under GATS. Meanwhile, a central element of the GATS-2000 negotiations is the development of new "disciplines" on domestic regulation which are now envisioned to apply horizontally to all service sectors, whether committed or not. This proposal stands out as particularly outrageous.

The existing GATS rules (Article VI-4) on domestic regulation contain a commitment to undertake negotiations to develop "necessary disciplines" to ensure that "measures relating to qualification requirements and procedures, technical standards and licensing procedures do not constitute unnecessary barriers to trade in services."[108] These future disciplines are supposed to ensure that domestic regulatory policies are:

a) based on objective and transparent criteria, such as competence and the ability to supply the service;
b) are not more burdensome than necessary to ensure the quality of the service;
c) in the case of a licensing procedure, not in themselves a restriction on the supply of the service.

The scope of these proposed new disciplines is stunning. They would cover not only qualification requirements and procedures, technical standards and licensing procedures, but also "measures relating to" them. Qualifications cover not only professional standards and assorted consumer and quality assurances, but also accreditation of schools and hospitals. Licensing means obtaining not only permits and professional licensing, but liquor licenses, broadcast licenses, commercial drivers licenses and more. The realm of technical standards is endless—from safety, environmental and consumer standards to regulations about service quality and employment rules. It is hard to imagine a domestic regulatory policy that

---

Globalizing the Arthur Andersen Accounting Standards

To date, only one set of industry-specific detailed GATS "disciplines" setting global regulatory standards for a service sector has been completed: rules for accounting services. The U.S. pushed for the development of internationally harmonized regulations for the accounting industry to be negotiated first. A leading U.S. adviser in setting these rules was the U.S. accounting firm Arthur Andersen whose role in the Enron scandal led to tightening of U.S. accounting standards.[109] The GATS accountancy disciplines mandate that licensing, qualification and technical standards governing accounting and auditing may not be "more trade restrictive than necessary,"[110] raising the possibility that the post-scandal U.S. rules could run afoul of the GATS limits on domestic accounting regulation.

does not fall under the listed categories, making one wonder just what else is intended to be covered by the "relating to" clause.

The GATS-2000 talks now under way regarding Article VI-4 are aimed at establishing additional disciplines on a wide range of non-discriminatory domestic regulations, which would mean an absolute ban on certain government policies. Negotiators are considering listing what would be permissible goals for service-sector regulation. Another proposal would subject the means used to achieve

---

Enron Disaster Expanded Worldwide by GATS

In the U.S. the combination of unregulated state wholesale electricity markets and federal deregulation of commodity exchanges removed accountability and transparency from the energy sector. Government investigations concluded that companies like Enron intentionally withheld electricity supplies from the West Coast, creating a crisis of artificial shortages in order to increase prices. The electricity deregulation sham cost California consumers over $70 billion— and counting. Enron used the lack of regulation to "buy futures"—the right to purchase energy supplies for a set price on a set date—and then traded them on the open market. This meant Enron could control electricity that was available on a certain date—and then could sell the rights to control supply at higher prices caused by the shortage its withholding supply had caused. How was this manipulation possible?

Enron lobbied to significantly curtail U.S. government oversight of their operations—the same outcome GATS would deliver. Enron purchased this deregulation through aggressive financing of election campaigns. Between 1990 and 2001, Enron gave $6 million to federal politicians—75% going to Republicans.[111] Between 1997 and 2000, Enron gave an additional $2 million to state government politicians.[112] Over that same period, the company spent almost $9 million lobbying Congress.[113] George W. Bush directly received $737,000 during his political career from Ken Lay, Jeff Skilling, and Enron.[114]

Deregulation of energy markets and commodity trading allowed Enron to escape price regulations. This was the key factor to the company's meteoric 1,750%[115] increase in revenues between 1990 and 2000 rather than traditional business success models, such as incorporating innovations to improve the delivery of products at competitive prices.

Many people know about the Enron scandal and the California electricity debacle, but few are aware of how these two linked phenomena grew from the radical deregulation agenda GATS promotes. Enron's business model was built entirely on the premise that it could make more money speculating on electricity contracts than by actually producing electricity at a power plant. After obtaining removal of government oversight of energy services and commodity trading practices, Enron turned electricity services into a speculative commodity and

(continued)

exploited market deficiencies inherent to the electricity industry to manipulate prices and supply. When federal regulators finally reregulated California's market in June 2001[116] with price controls and reintroducing transparency, energy traders like Enron could no longer charge excessive prices and manipulate supply.

Enron's main "assets" were the futures it had traded in its unregulated power auctions. When caps were set on electricity prices, Enron quickly accumulated massive debts—the difference between the set-price and the ridiculously high-priced futures it had jacked up by trading between its own divisions and with other speculators. The curtailed revenue flow made it more difficult to conceal the firm's accounting gimmicks. Although the company declared bankruptcy in December 2001,[117] Enron's top executives walked away with billions of dollars stolen from California consumers, shareholders and employees. Instead of learning from this disaster, the U.S. and other governments are discussing making universal under GATS rules the very policies that caused this crisis.

even GATS-approved goals to a necessity test requiring countries to prove their policy is the least trade restrictive option. In the absence of such specific new disciplines, the GATS rules now allow countries to challenge another WTO country's domestic service regulations as GATS violations if they do not comply with the four criteria listed in Article VI-4 or if they nullify or impair a GATS commitment.[118]

Exceptions

GATS contains two "general" exceptions which set out grounds for countries to defend policies which otherwise violate GATS terms. Only one of these exceptions, for actions taken on national security grounds, is written in a manner that ensures it can actually be employed successfully.[119] In contrast, the other GATS general exception, which is what countries must rely on to defend actions taken for environmental, health and safety, and other non–national security reasons, is written in a manner that would make its effective use in a WTO dispute very difficult. "Subject to requirements that such measures are not applied in a manner which would constitute a means of arbitrary or unjustifiable discrimination between countries where like conditions prevail, or a disguised restriction on trade in services . . ." countries can have policies "necessary" to protect public morals, maintain public order, protect human, animal and plant life or health, or necessary to comply with regulations "which are not inconsistent with the provisions of GATS."

As described in Chapter 1, the chapeau language and the requirement that a measure be "necessary" as defined in GATT and WTO jurisprudence to fit this exception have meant that a similarly worded exception in GATT has only been accepted twice by WTO panels as grounds to save a challenged law even though the exceptions have been raised as a defense in scores of WTO cases. In addition, GATS does not contain the "related to conservation" of natural resources exception contained in GATT. Finally, the last clause in this GATS provision creates a tautology that provides an exception to the exception by limiting the provision's application only to domestic laws that comply with GATS rules.

The Current Push to Expand GATS—GATS-2000

At the conclusion of the Uruguay Round, the U.S. was able to insert provisions into the GATS text automatically restarting negotiations within five years on the matters it was unable to achieve up to that point.[120] These provisions commit countries to "progressively higher level[s] of liberalization." This means the obligation both to offer new sectors for privatization and to grant additional access rights for sectors already included.[121]

Also as part of the original GATS talks, countries committed to negotiate on establishing "disciplines" on service-sector subsidies and on government procurement in services,[122] a particularly sensitive issue in the U.S., where government services expenditures were $3.1 trillion in 2002, or nearly 30% of the U.S. GDP.[123]

Before the launch of the GATS-2000 talks, a coalition of developing countries called for an assessment of the outcomes of service-sector liberalization and GATS rules *prior* to undertaking further deepening of those rules under GATS-2000.[124] A global campaign of civil society groups called for a moratorium on the GATS-2000 talks until this assessment was conducted.[125] However, these demands have been steamrollered. The WTO Secretariat, the U.S. and the EU pushed tirelessly for the immediate launch of the built-in GATS expansion talks. Indeed, the December 2001 Doha WTO Ministerial Declaration not only dismisses the demand for a services assessment but sets a specific time line for the GATS-2000 talks to conclude by 2005.[126]

In part this renewed push toward the most extreme paradigm of service-sector deregulation and liberalization was made possible because the political context has shifted in the decade since the Uruguay Round talks, with the Reagan-Thatcher dream of radical deregulation becoming a reality in many nations. In the U.S., the promotion of market-driven industry self-regulation instead of government oversight brought economic disasters, such as the collapse of the savings and loan industry in the 1980s (costing taxpayers hundreds of billions of dollars[127]) and the

---

EU Demands Access to America's Municipal Water Systems in GATS-2000 Talks

While a large percentage of European drinking water and sewage systems have been privatized or turned over to for-profit corporations for operation and management, in the U.S. water is considered a public service. Only a very small percentage of water systems have been privatized or are operated by private firms. The EU demanded that the U.S. offer municipal water services for coverage in GATS-2000. If the Bush administration does so, the GATS Article XVI

(continued)

provisions would provide giant EU water companies such as Suez and Vivendi access to the "market" of our more than 60,000 existing publicly owned and locally operated municipal water-service providers and would restrain communities from establishing new public municipal water systems in the future.[128]

Privatization of government services is increasingly touted as the best way for cash-strapped governments to deal with expensive maintenance and repair needs of public utilities. However, in many instances, when this route has been selected the privatization of public utilities in the U.S. has not yielded positive results.[129] Water privatizations in countless U.S. cities including Jersey City, New Jersey, Charleston, West Virginia, and Chattanooga, Tennessee have led to charges of bad service and skyrocketing rates.

energy deregulation of the 1990s (which brought soaring energy costs for consumers and rolling blackouts in California). Yet the U.S. continues to push its model on other countries. Worse, the European position has shifted dramatically, and in the GATS-2000 talks, the European Union is perhaps even more vociferous in its service-sector demands than the U.S.

Examples of similar disasters in the developing world and Confederation of Independent States are myriad, including Russia's privatization, dubbed the "Looting of Russia,"[130] and the explosive fight in South Africa against electricity privatization.[131]

Unfortunately, these developments have not halted the push for more of the same. The request-and-offer process to deepen service-sector privatization and deregulation is now occurring again in the context of the GATS-2000 and the FTAA talks. In April 2002, details of the European GATS requests were leaked, and the public got a rare glimpse into what is on the table with GATS-2000. The EU requests included hundreds of pages, country-by-country, for new access to education, water, energy, insurance, transportation and entertainment services. The EU request to the U.S. contained a state-by-state list of zoning, land ownership, liquor distribution and other laws the EU seeks to have eliminated.

These demands for market access remain the most concrete illustration of the issues at stake in the current GATS negotiations. To access these documents and a glossary to guide the layperson through the jargon, as well as charts listing GATS-2000 demands to the U.S. and Canada, please visit www.tradewatch.org.

In the context of both the GATS-2000 and FTAA talks, Modes 3 and 4—the right of a foreign company to set up a presence in another country and the right to send people from one country to another to perform services—are the most controversial. This shift from a focus on trade across borders to establishment of a business within another country brings every *domestic* policy issue and priority under the scrutiny of GATS. For instance, local zoning and land-use rules are implicated in decisions about where big-box and other retailers open stores; the regulation of service providers—from toxic-waste processing plants to power plants—is endangered. Despite calm assurances that countries have flexibility in the GATS-2000 talks, in reality there is enormous pressure for countries to make significant new concessions during GATS negotiations.

GATS CASES: BANANAS, AUTOS AND MAGAZINES ARE SERVICES?

Nations often seek to regulate foreign control of cultural services such as of movies, television, radio and publishing to preserve cultural diversity, local heritage and national identity. Therefore, proposals to have the GATS agreement cover "cultural industries" was very controversial, especially pitting the U.S. against the French and Canadians, who wanted to protect their film and audiovisual industries from complete dominance by Hollywood.[132] In the end, a compromise was reached allowing some application of GATS rules to the cultural industries including MFN,[133] meaning that if a country allows *any* foreign company, for instance, to sell television programming it must allow firms from every WTO country to bid for the same access. While the French failed to obtain a GATS carve out for cultural industries, GATS allows countries to withhold specific commitments on audiovisual services,[134] meaning that when countries made their GATS commitments, they could exclude telecommunication, music and such totally. However, as a successful U.S. challenge to a Canadian magazine policy described below demonstrates, the WTO provides many avenues for attack. GATS implications for cultural homogenization have generated a growing global movement of activists, writers, and others. In 2001, UNESCO passed a resolution warning that "Globalization . . . presents the challenge of preserving and celebrating the rich intellectual and cultural diversity of humankind and civilization."[135]

Case 1: The WTO Says "No" to Cultural Diversity—Canadian Magazines

The WTO's 1997 ruling against Canada's ban on so-called split-run magazines sent the warning that under WTO rules, the interest in preserving domestic cultural forms has been eclipsed by new commercial rights bestowed on entertainment conglomerates to sell their products worldwide. Canada's market for foreign magazines was far from closed when the U.S. initiated its WTO challenge on behalf of Time Warner, Inc.[136] Half of the English-language magazines in Canada and four fifths of those sold on newsstands are from abroad.[137] However, in 1997, the WTO ruled that Canada could not maintain any nationality-based regulation of its magazine market.

Since 1965, Canada had levied a tariff on split-run magazines[138]—special editions that contain foreign editorial content but sell space to domestic advertisers or aim advertising at the domestic market. Canada enacted the tax to protect smaller Canadian-owned publications from losing advertising revenue to larger U.S. magazines[139] and thus being run out of business by U.S.-based publishing conglomerates.

In 1995, Canada amended the 1965 law to impose an 80% excise tax on split-run magazines[140]—in response to the evasion of the tariff by Time Warner's *Sports Illustrated,* which earlier that year had begun to beam its magazine into Canada via satellite to avoid the tariff.[141]

In 1996, the U.S. launched a WTO challenge against the 80% excise tax as well as the 1965 tariffs on split-run magazines and Canada's policy of subsidizing postal rates for domestic magazines.[142] (Through a program called Canadian Heritage, the government provided a financial subsidy to Canada Post enabling it to provide a preferential postal rate for Canadian magazines shipped within the country, in recognition of the challenges of distributing to a population that is widely dispersed geographically.)

The crux of the U.S. challenge was that GATT nondiscrimination rules forbid countries from treating domestic and foreign "like products" differently for regulatory and tax purposes. Canada maintained throughout that Canadian magazines were not "like goods," and thus the differential tax treatment did not constitute a National Treatment issue. The U.S. contended that Canadian content did not differentiate the products—and indeed argued before one panel in this case that measures to "ensure 'original content' in magazines sold in Canada . . . would be contrary to the object and purpose" of the WTO[143] and that Canada had no right to try to protect its culture or heritage and instead the market should be the sole determinant.[144] From the Canadian perspective, at issue was the disappearance of Canadian content and writing—a concern that is especially compelling given that Canada shares a language and a border with the U.S. Obviously, there is little demand in Canada for magazines that reflect the culture and sensibilities of Portuguese, Austrians, or Laotians.

Canada also defended the excise tax, arguing that *Sports Illustrated*'s advertising revenues from its U.S. edition more than covered the publication costs of the Canadian edition. The *New York Times* reported that *Sports Illustrated* was thus able to sell advertising in the local edition to Canadian companies at rock-bottom rates, threatening smaller Canadian publishers. To Canada, Time Warner's underpricing of advertising services amounted to a "dumping" offense (selling goods below the cost of their production in order to dominate the market).[145]

In March 1997, a WTO panel found the Canadian measures to be in violation of GATT rules forbidding discrimination and import restrictions.[146] It found that Canada's 80% excise tax on split-run magazines was a de facto discriminatory imposition in contradiction of the National Treatment provisions contained in GATT; that the provision of grants to Canada Post for Canadian magazine postal rates amounted to an illegitimate subsidy; and that provisions of the Canadian Tariff Code that limited the importation of certain periodicals violated WTO rules.[147] Canada appealed the ruling and the decision was upheld by the Appellate Body.[148]

Instead of allowing unrestricted import of magazines with American copy and Canadian ads, the Canadian government proceeded to implement the WTO ruling by proposing new legislation that focused on regulating sales of "advertising services," rather than regulating the magazines as products.[149] This strategy was aimed at implementing the cultural goal through policies that would be covered by GATS rules under which Canada had not made commitments covering this sector. This course of action would comply with the letter of the 1997 WTO ruling, yet maintain the goal of protecting domestic culture.[150]

The U.S. was infuriated by Canada's maneuver and threatened $4 billion worth of import sanctions, as well as the suspension of favorable tariffs accorded to Canada under NAFTA.[151] Washington then formally challenged Canada's new policy before the WTO Appellate Body.

Canada argued that the new policy concerned advertising services and thus should be allowed since Canada had made no GATS commitments respecting advertising services. However, the panel concluded that in this instance advertising was both a good and a service and therefore Canada's absence of GATS advertising commitments was irrelevant. The panel concluded that advertising was a service but because the ads appeared in magazines, also part of the contents of a good (the magazine).[152] The panel also ruled against all of the Canadian measures. In addition, the panel ruled that the financial subsidy from Canada Heritage, the subsidiary of Canada Post, was not a direct subsidy of cultural producers, permitted under WTO rules, but was rather a forbidden subsidy on the individual goods, magazines.

When Is a Banana a Service?

The definition of services in the WTO is so expansive and fluid that even nations with large trade negotiating teams have found themselves unaware of the implications of their GATS obligations. A glaring example was the 1997 U.S.-EU WTO banana war. As described in detail in Chapter 6, the U.S. challenged the EU's Lomé Treaty, which set aside a small amount of its banana market for imports from its former colonies in the Caribbean. Europe specifically had negotiated an exception to WTO rules on agricultural trade by giving concessions in other areas to safeguard the Lomé Treaty's special trade preferences. Understandably, the European negotiators had not thought to take measures to protect banana trade in GATS. However, U.S. trade officials recognized that GATS's expansive scope means sometimes a banana is a service. The U.S. challenged European GATS commitments regarding banana marketing and distribution services. The WTO ruled in favor of the U.S. Europe initially refused to change the policy, but after more than two years of $191.4 million in trade sanctions, it did comply,[153] with dire consequences for several Caribbean nations.

Finally, in May 1999, Canada was pressured into abandoning the new legislation. Canada cut a deal with the U.S. that allows U.S. publishers to sell 18% of their advertising space to Canadian clients if a "substantial" level of Canadian content is maintained in the publication.[154] "Substantial," however, is not defined in detail in the deal, which Maude Barlow, chairwoman of the Council of Canadians a national citizens group, has described as a "sell-out" of the Canadian publishing industry.[155]

The WTO made its decision in this case not on its merits but in the most effective manner capable of undermining Canada's domestic regulations by ruling that magazine advertising is not a service but a good. This case and the U.S. challenge of European banana trade policies as a GATS violation demonstrate how broadly the GATS's coverage can be interpreted.

Case 2: WTO Rules Against Canadian Auto Pact

Since 1965, Canada has had an agreement with U.S. automakers to encourage domestic Canadian production of automobiles and auto parts. In exchange for tariff-free treatment on qualifying imports, eligible manufacturers committed to selling as many Canadian-made cars in Canada as American-made cars, and making a significant portion of Canadian-made American cars with Canadian-made auto parts.[156] This agreement is known as the Canadian Auto Pact.

To be eligible, an auto manufacturer had to be producing cars in Canada when the pact was established in 1966, and meet certain sales and content requirements. Essentially to qualify for the special treatment U.S. manufacturers such as General Motors, Chrysler, and Ford were required to sell a greater value of Canadian-manufactured models of their cars than U.S.-made cars in Canada.[157] Additionally, to be eligible American-made cars exported to Canada had to have half their value derived from Canada (Canadian parts, labor, overhead, etc.) with that percentage scheduled to increase over time.[158]

The EU and Japan challenged this policy at the WTO as violating GATT antidiscrimination rules.[159] They contended not only that the Auto Pact favored American imports by offering duty-free access, but also that it was a WTO-illegitimate subsidy to these manufacturers based on export performance. To get the benefits, Canadian-made auto sales had to exceed sales of imports—so to achieve the benefit if imported sales were high, manufacturers would have to have increased their export sales of Canadian-made autos.

The EU and Japan also argued that the Auto Pact violated GATS because the Japanese and European manufacturers' auto dealerships were unfairly "affected," because the pact discriminated against dealerships of manufacturers ineligible to receive its benefits.

The WTO heard the dispute in early 1999, and in December of that year released its ruling,[160] finding that the domestic content provisions amounted to an export subsidy. The panel's rulings on the GATS provisions were highly controversial as the panel decided that the Auto Pact affected services because the differential tariff rates ultimately affected the service of "distribution of automobiles." The panel found that "GATS has a broad scope of application and accordingly no measures are *a priori* excluded from the scope and application of the GATS."[161] Although the Auto Pact is unquestionably a measure that affects the trade in goods, the panel ruled that because it indirectly had a potential impact on the distribution of these goods, it also affected the trade in services. Using this logic, there is no measure that would not fall under the rubric of GATS, because every good eventually must pass through the hands of a distribution or retail service operation.

Additionally, the panel ruled that the Auto Pact did not provide national treatment as required by GATS to all auto dealerships, because some manufacturers received favorable tariff treatment and others did not, based on where cars were produced.[162] Canada appealed the entirety of the panel's ruling, including the GATS determinations. Canada contended that the duty-free tariff exemption did not affect trade in services as defined by GATS Article I-1,[163] and that because of concentration in the industry, the National Treatment claim was weak (Ford owns Volvo while Mercedes and Chrysler had merged to form Daimler-Chrysler, etc.).[164] Moreover, Canada argued that dealerships do not purchase cars on the open market; they supply and distribute the cars their parent company manufactures, and therefore, because of the sole-source nature of manufacturers' dealerships, the tariff had little impact on dealerships' ability to provide services.[165]

In May 2000 the Appellate Body upheld the majority of the lower panel's GATT rulings but also determined that the lower panel had failed to demonstrate that the Auto Pact actually did have an impact on the distribution of services for auto dealerships, but rather had merely implied that there was a connection.[166] The WTO panel dismissed this claim. It curiously ruled that "no government measure prevents even a vertically integrated wholesale distributor from approaching different manufacturers for the procurement of motor vehicles" and that "vertical integration and exclusive distribution arrangements do not preclude potential competition among wholesalers for the procurement of vehicles from manufacturers."[167] In the WTO panel's world, there was no reason that Ford dealerships couldn't sell Hondas and Honda dealerships couldn't sell Toyotas.

Moreover, the Appellate Body determined that the lower panel had failed to demonstrate whether or how distributing dealerships which were affiliated with manufacturers ineligible for the auto pact's tariff benefits were damaged.[168] The Appellate Body concluded:

> In our view, the Panel has conducted a "goods" analysis of the measure, and has simply extrapolated its analysis of how the import duty exemption affects manufacturers to wholesale trade service suppliers of motor vehicles.[169]

This Appellate ruling narrowed the outlandishly broad interpretation by the lower panel that the Auto Pact's provisions on trade in goods somehow automatically affected the trade in services. However, by upholding the GATT elements of the ruling, the WTO panel gutted the Auto Pact, a successful industrial policy based on the principle that a company that wishes to sell vehicles in a country must make a commitment to invest, purchase parts, and create employment in that country.

WHAT IS AT STAKE FOR SERVICES AT CANCÚN

The GATS-2000 negotiations operate under their own internal timelines, so officially no major decisions on GATS were set for the Cancún Ministerial; however, the political reality is that the state of GATS-2000 talks helped set the tone for the Ministerial. And growing grassroots campaigns against GATS-2000 have slowed the talks. The critical decisions that were scheduled to be taken at the Cancún Ministerial are all connected and like a house of cards, if one piece slips the whole construct can collapse. For instance, the EU is under pressure from other WTO countries to make significant concessions in agriculture at Cancún; however, there also is major domestic political pressure within Europe not to do so. If the EU had obtained significant offers in response to its grandiose GATS-2000 demands, then EU Trade Minister Pascal Lamy could have leaned on the EU member states to agree to the major agriculture subsidy cuts so that the GATS offers can be "harvested" and turned into new opportunities for European service companies. Alternatively, because the EU has gotten few appealing offers and its extreme proposals on further restrictions on service-sector regulation are contested, then the only political cover for agreeing to steep agriculture concessions became progress on EU demands on other items such as starting new investment talks, which was passionately opposed by developing country WTO members. Yet, even though the Cancún Ministerial ended in a deadlock, the GATS-2000 talks will proceed back at the WTO's Geneva headquarters toward the 2005 deadline set for their completion.

However, whether that deadline is met and what will result is increasingly unclear. As the implications of the GATS and the new threats posed by the GATS-2000 agenda have become more publicly known thanks to major campaigns in numerous countries, negotiators are being subjected to a heightened level of scrutiny. Activists and increasingly parliamentarians and state and local officials are trying to subject their countries' trade officials to accountability. What happens next will rely on the level of domestic political pressure that can be generated regarding commitments at the GATS-2000 talks that would undermine the domestic public interest. So far, significant progress has been made in building public awareness in some key countries. However, it will take much more intense public sunshine to kill this Dracula-like proposal.

5

FOR RICHER OR POORER: FACTS AND FICTION ABOUT TRADE AND ECONOMIC GAINS IN THE DEVELOPED WORLD*

The opening up of markets for U.S. exporters is often touted as a means to create jobs and increase income in the United States. Economists heralding the benefits of WTO and NAFTA also have regularly emphasized the gains to the U.S. economy achieved by the import of cheaper goods from abroad. For instance, economist Gary Hufbauer of the business think tank Institute for International Economics predicted that new U.S. exports under NAFTA would generate $7 to $9 billion in U.S. trade surplus with Mexico and Canada as early as 1995,[1] and that this would lead to U.S. job gains under NAFTA. He used a formula projecting that for each $1 billion in new NAFTA trade surpluses, about 13,000 jobs would be created in the U.S.[2]

These sorts of arguments were central to securing congressional approval of NAFTA and the Uruguay Round and have been used in defense of the WTO since.

U.S. and European governments continually touted one finding of an Organization for Economic Cooperation and Development study, written with the World Bank, that concluded that world income would grow by $213 billion per year if the Uruguay Round were implemented.[3] Critical analysis of the report at the time revealed a small detail: The gains occurred only in the tenth year of WTO as measured against the implementation year. Given the background growth-rate forecast for the world over ten years, the seemingly huge Uruguay Round "boost" was actually less than 0.7% per year.[4] This revelation received no U.S. media coverage.

In order to press their case for new trade agreements, government officials also have made assertions about the benefits the WTO specifically and trade liberalization generally will have for the U.S. economy and for U.S. workers. For instance, at the time of the congressional debate about the Uruguay Round and WTO in 1994, the President's Council of Economic Advisors reported that the Uruguay Round would lead to an increase in annual U.S. Gross Domestic Product (GDP) of $100 to $200 billion by 2004, or 0.9–1.7% of the projected GDP.[5] Five years later, this figure had

* Parts of this chapter draw heavily from the work of Mark Weisbrot and Dean Baker, co-directors of the Washington-based think tank the Center for Economic Policy and Research, with their permission.

been revised down considerably. In a paper published in 1999, the Council of Economic Advisors estimated that the gains from the Uruguay Round were more likely to be 0.4–0.6% of the GDP, less than half the gains that it had projected just five years earlier.[6] This is a huge difference. For instance, the U.S. 2001 GDP was $10 trillion, making the modest gains from the Uruguay Round between $40 and $60 billion, a fraction of each year's U.S. trade deficit.[7]

Now, nearly nine years later, it is possible to begin to measure these predictions against the actual record provided by economic data during the period. There has been an expansion in the volume of trade but this has not necessarily meant more jobs or better wages. To the contrary, the 1999 UN Human Development Report found that in the wealthiest nations, job creation has lagged behind the growth in trade and investment volumes. For instance, in the U.S. from 1946–1973, there was an 80% gain in median wages, yet although trade now represents two times the share of U.S. economic activity that it did during that period, from 1972–2000, U.S. median wages were almost flat.[8]

FALSE PROMISES OF WTO: U.S. JOBS AND ECONOMIC BENEFITS

By inserting the actual data into Hufbauer's formula, the WTO has been a massive jobs destroyer in the U.S. Defenders of the WTO often argue that the sharp blow to U.S. exports caused by the 1995 Mexican peso crisis and the 1997 Asian financial crisis distort trade data trends. However, even if you consider the most recent three years and look only at U.S. exports, which have declined by $93 billion, 1.9 million U.S. jobs were eliminated.[9] But the real story is the trade *balance*, exports minus imports. Instead of the decline in the U.S. trade deficit promised by WTO supporters when the pact was being debated, the 2002 U.S goods trade deficit grew more than fourfold from before the WTO went into effect, to a record $436 billion.[10] Using the Hufbauer multiplier on a trade balance that is a deficit, the U.S. trade deficit would have eliminated nearly nine million jobs in 2002 alone.[11]

WTO and NAFTA boosters typically try to downplay the surging U.S. trade deficit by claiming that only the exports count. For instance, USTR Robert Zoellick stated that "between 1990 and 2000, exports of goods and services have accounted for one-fifth of U.S. economic growth."[12] Yet in making that statement Zoellick simply ignores the existence of imports or of a trade balance. Imports have actually grown far more rapidly than exports, such that the trade deficit today is five times larger than before the WTO was established.[13] USTR Zoellick's approach is equivalent to considering only deposits to one's bank account and ignoring withdrawals. Yet, given this dramatic increase in imports, and the fact that the value of imports is actually subtracted from GDP, if one considers the net data of both exports and imports, trade is shown actually to have been a serious drag on U.S. growth over the last decade.

As manufacturer after manufacturer relocated overseas to use NAFTA and WTO to send their production back to the U.S., and the U.S. trade deficit increased, the forecasters and economists with trade job growth models quickly backtracked. When it became clear that NAFTA would not generate a trade surplus but an enormous new deficit, Hufbauer recanted on his job gain predictions, saying in 1995 that "[t]he best figure for the jobs effect of NAFTA is approximately zero. The lesson for me is to stay away from job forecasting."[14]

Many WTO and NAFTA boosters shifted arguments, noting that while their predictions about declining trade deficits were wrong, the pacts were still benefiting the U.S. economy. They pointed to the exceptional growth in employment during the 1990s economic boom, challenging critics to show why WTO and NAFTA were economically damaging if so many jobs were being created.

The Economic Policy Institute (EPI), another Washington-based think tank, took up the challenge. Its analysis found that U.S. export growth between 1994 and 2000 created 2.7 million jobs, but faster import growth *eliminated* 5.8 million jobs, creating a net loss of 3 million jobs.[15] Thus, while impressive economic growth was creating jobs, many other U.S. jobs were being lost because of the trade flows. Attempts to focus congressional and media attention to these major losses was undermined by the cover provided by the background job growth. A key question, though, was what sorts of jobs were being lost and created? Many economists argue that trade does not so much affect the total number of jobs as the composition of job options.

Free-trade advocates contended that export jobs pay higher than average wages and thus the jobs lost to trade should not be emphasized. They paint a picture of the U.S. importing T-shirts and exporting computers and other high-end goods. The reality is quite different. Consider U.S. trade with China, whose $103 billion trade deficit with the U.S. makes it our largest, comprising about one fifth of the total U.S. trade deficit.[16] The U.S. has a trade deficit with China in stereo equipment ($4.4 billion), televisions ($4.2 billion), telecommunications equipment ($1.8 billion), and computers ($1.3 billion).[17] The entire U.S. manufacturing sector is under enormous trade-related duress, not only allegedly undesirable low-end jobs. The loss of manufacturing capacity and jobs is unprecedented in U.S. history and should be triggering an urgent review of this intensifying trend's implications for U.S. capacity to produce goods essential for its infrastructure and security needs and on what the hemorrhage means for the composition of U.S. jobs.

Indeed, a study commissioned by NAFTA and WTO supporter Representative Donald Manzullo (R-Ill.) found that the jobs lost to imports, primarily in the manufacturing sector, *also* paid higher than average U.S. wages, and worse yet, workers laid off from these jobs were finding new jobs in the lower-wage service sector.[18] With some notable exceptions in the professional-level information and finance sectors most susceptible to being outsourced overseas, such as computer programming, U.S. government data conclusively show that service-sector jobs on average are lower paying than those in the manufacturing sector.[19] They also do not typically include the permanence or the unionization rate and thus the benefits (health insurance, pensions) available in the manufacturing sector.[20]

Shifting Composition of U.S. Workforce

Recent figures from the U.S. Department of Labor demonstrate where this trend is taking American workers. During the 1990s, the U.S. shed 600,000 manufacturing jobs but gained 21 million service-sector jobs.[21] The trend is even more stark if you compare U.S. manufacturing employment in 1993, before NAFTA and the WTO went into effect, to 2003: 1.7 million U.S. manufacturing jobs have been lost.[22]

The composition of future employment, as predicted by the Labor Department, is equally bleak for the nearly three-quarters of American workers who do not have a college degree. The categories of employment predicted to have the fastest growth by 2010 are: computer application software engineers, computer systems software engineers, computer systems analysts and network systems administrators (high wage, requires bachelor's degree); computer support specialist (high wage, requires an associate degree); medical assistants (low wage, moderate on-the-job training); and home health aids, personal care aids, and security guards (very low wage, short-term on-the-job training).[23]

Burgeoning Trade Deficit

Gross Domestic Product is a measure of economic output for the entire economy, comprised of consumer spending, business and individual investment, government spending, and the trade balance. When the U.S. runs a trade deficit, imports exceed exports and the deficit is subtracted from GDP, creating a drag on the economic output. Indeed, Federal Reserve Chairman Alan Greenspan—a "free-trade" cheerleader—has testified to Congress that the huge U.S. trade deficit is causing an "unsustainable" drag on U.S. growth.[24] The U.S. trade deficit has had an increasingly negative effect on the GDP since NAFTA and the WTO went into effect. In 1993, the U.S. trade deficit was a 0.8% drag on GDP, but the negative impact on GDP rose every year except one since 1993 to a 5.6% drag on GDP in 2002.[25]

Moreover, returning to USTR Zoellick's fuzzy math relating to only counting exports: his logic would imply that the U.S. economy grows if General Motors exports car engines to Mexico so that they can be assembled in a car there instead of in the U.S. with the car then imported back for sale in the United States. This is an important point, because much of U.S. export growth in the last ten years was of this type: intermediate goods sent to manufacturing plants that had relocated, making products that were eventually imported back into the United States.

"Industrial Tourism" As a Significant Component of U.S. Export Growth

Although imports grew much faster, since NAFTA there has been growth in U.S. exports to Mexico, which is often cited as evidence of the economic gains to be achieved from trade liberalization.

However, a significant portion of U.S. "exports" to Mexico since NAFTA have been in parts and equipment—to build the factories and supply parts for assembly in automotive, electronics and other factories that relocated to Mexico from the U.S. Raw materials and parts for assembly into finished goods in Mexico's border maquiladoras assembly plants to be reimported to the U.S. consumer market are all tariff free.[26] In 1999, the most recent data available, more than 44% of U.S. "exports" to Mexico were industrial tourist products which would never reach the Mexican consumer market as assembled goods.[27] Even without considering this factor, NAFTA has resulted in a large new U.S. trade deficit with Mexico: the U.S. trade deficit with Mexico was $1.7 billion in 1993, and $37.2 billion in 2002, with U.S. imports of Mexican goods and services up 238% under NAFTA while exports grew 134%.[28]

NEW PREDICTIONS ON DOHA WTO TALKS

Showing no shame for wildly inaccurate past projections, the use of rosy predictions about economic gains to be gotten from trade liberalization continues now regarding the WTO Doha negotiations, despite the data showing the gap between past predictions and reality. For instance, a recent paper by Harvard economist Jeffrey Frankel suggested that the Doha Agenda for further WTO negotiations could generate $400 billion additional gains for the global economy (approximately 1.4% percent of world GDP[29]). Another model cited in the Frankel paper concludes that the increase in real world income would be $260 billion, with $130 billion coming from service-sector liberalization, $50 billion from agriculture liberalization and $80 billion from lowering manufacturing tariffs.[30]

Frankel's paper also cites studies indicating that Europe alone could increase its GDP by 7% if it carried through with the full liberalization of trade in agriculture and other sectors.[31] Since Europe's economy makes up approximately one quarter of the world economy, by Frankel's estimate, the gains estimated for Europe alone would be equal to one quarter of that approximate 7% gain, or 1.75% of world GDP. However, this 1.75% estimated world GDP gain, using his calculation of trade liberalization gains to Europe, is 75% larger than his 1% gain to world GDP estimate calculated separately in this study. These two numbers are inconsistent; if the figure for Europe is plausible, then the estimate of worldwide gains is far too low. Alternatively, if the estimate of worldwide gains is plausible, then the gains estimated for Europe are hugely exaggerated.

However, even if these specific predictions weren't dubious, given the record over the past 20 years of slowed economic growth in the developing countries that adopted the neoliberal model (see Chapter 6), general predictions of trade liberalization causing economic growth fly in the face of the empirical data.

New Zealand provides an example of the economic perils of this model on a developed country. Starting in 1984, New Zealand initiated the most comprehensive program of conforming its economic and social policies to the neoliberal orthodoxy ever seen in a developed country. Yet since the experiment in trade, investment, and finance liberalization; privatization; and the evisceration of labor law began, New Zealand's economic growth has been slower than the rest of the developed world. The standard of living has fallen from 1.25 times the average standard of living in high-income nations in 1965 to 0.62 in 1999.[32] As a *Financial Times* column concluded in 2000: "The past 15 years have completed New Zealand's transition into a very select group of states: those that were once rich, but are rich no longer."[33]

THE ECONOMIC THEORY OF ECONOMIC GAINS FROM TRADE*

Most economists who claim that trade liberalization will lead to economic gains do so on the basis of basic economic theory. The basic argument is relatively simple: consumers will benefit when the prices of goods imported into the U.S. drop due to the elimination or reduction of tariffs, quotas and other trade barriers. However, these imports can hurt producers in the industries affected—for example, some workers in the computer chip industry will lose their jobs if trade barriers are eliminated, since competing with goods from abroad will result in cost-cutting, including layoffs and plant closings, to make the U.S. industry more competitive. But with standard economic logic and analysis, it can generally be shown—given the important assumption of full employment—that the gains to consumers will exceed the losses to producers. Because of this result from economic theory, economists generally view the removal of trade barriers as desirable.

However, the fact that removing trade barriers can lead to increased economic output does not automatically imply that it is necessarily always a desirable policy. For instance, standard economic models used to show the benefits from trade liberalization also imply that such liberalization will lead to a redistribution of income, specifically from workers to capital, and from lower-wage workers to higher-wage workers. It is entirely possible that for most workers, the lost wages due to the upward redistribution caused by trade liberalization outweigh their share of the overall gains in the economy. This is especially true if trade liberalization results in long-term unemployment for workers in the affected industries. But even under the assumption of full employment which is an essential element of the standard model, it is very possible for trade liberalization to cause a net loss of income for the majority of the labor force that, for example, does not have a college degree. (That majority, by the way, would be 74% of U.S. adults.)[34]

If policy makers and the public at large are to have a reasonable basis for assessing the merits of future trade agreements, then it is essential that they have accurate data on the outcomes of past agreements and plausible estimates of the potential gains from liberalization, which can be balanced against the potential costs to the groups that are harmed. In this section we attempt to explain what an array of economists say about the range of these possible gains and losses.

---

* This discussion of trade theory and wage inequality is based on the paper "Will New Trade Gains Make Us Rich?" by economists Mark Weisbrot and Dean Baker, co-directors of the Center for Economic Policy and Research, with the authors' permission.

How Large Are the Economic Gains from Trade Liberalization?

In addition to the shameless political rhetoric about the economic benefits and losses of trade liberalization, there have been some serious efforts to document actual economic outcomes and to develop models to predict future economic effects.

For example, a 1999 study by the International Trade Commission (ITC) used standard economic methods to estimate the gains to the U.S. from eliminating the remaining tariffs and quotas on imported goods.[35] The study's findings are somewhat informative. It found that the net welfare gains to the economy from eliminating all tariffs and quotas, using 1996 prices and output, would be $14.9 billion annually.[36] This would be equivalent to approximately $19 billion annually when recalculated in 2001 dollars. While these gains are not trivial, they are less than 0.2% of U.S. GDP. It is important to consider, however, some of the factors that caused the ITC estimate of gains to be even this large.

Ignoring Losses Due to Import Quota Elimination

The ITC estimated that $3.6 billion of the gains from trade liberalization, or nearly 25% of their estimate of total gains, was attributable to the increases in economic efficiency due to the elimination of import quotas.[37] Estimates of gains in economic efficiency from quota elimination is standard in such modeling, as import quotas lead to large costs to the importing nations, while at the same time entailing large benefits to the producers in exporting nations. This is because decreased supply caused by quota-restrictions raises the price of imports—just as tariffs do—but unlike tariffs, quotas allow foreign producers to pocket the price increase in the form of higher profit margins rather than that money going to the government as a tariff. Thus, economists seek to calculate the benefits of eliminating these quota "rents."[38] In a 1990 study regarding the prospective gains from trade liberalization, Gary Hufbauer and Kimberly Elliott attributed almost 70% of the $70 billion in welfare gains from trade liberalization to the elimination of quotas.[39]

In standard trade models, such as the one used by the ITC, exporting nations will typically benefit when other nations apply quotas to their exports. This may seem initially counterintuitive, but in effect, quotas raise the profits of exporters much in the same way as a cartel, such as OPEC, can raise profits by restricting oil supply. In these models, the extraordinary profits associated with the higher prices due to quota restrictions more than offset whatever profit reduction results from selling fewer units of the good.

However, the hitch is that trade liberalization dictates that quotas must be eliminated multilaterally throughout the trading system. This means that if all quotas are removed throughout the world, the economic efficiency gains that come from eliminating quotas in the U.S.—which the ITC study calculates to be $3.6 billion, or a quarter of their total estimated gains from increased trade liberalization—will be offset by the *losses* to U.S. exporters from the elimination of these quotas in

The Textile and Apparel Quandary

Significant quotas remain in place on textiles and apparel under what is called the Multi-Fiber Arrangement (MFA), a multilateral pact allocating textile and apparel market share that was scheduled to be phased out by 2005 under Uruguay Round rules. The quotas now in place have been the target of considerable attention by developing countries and development organizations, which have pressured for rich countries to eliminate such quotas before 2005 to provide more access for developing countries in rich country markets. Yet the very fact that quota barriers are so important in the textile and apparel sector raises questions about the extent to which trade liberalization in these sectors will actually benefit developing countries. Under standard economic models, while the volume of poor countries' exports would increase if these barriers were eliminated, the economic benefits from increased sales would be largely offset by the reduction in profits per unit.

other countries simultaneously. Since import barriers—including quota-type barriers—are generally higher in other countries than in the United States, it is entirely possible that in a full model of multilateral trade liberalization, the loss of earnings abroad by U.S. exporters due to the elimination of quotas for U.S. goods in other countries will more than offset the gains that accrue to the U.S. by eliminating quota barriers here.

But even assuming that the loss of earnings to U.S. exporters from eliminating quotas abroad was just equal to the welfare gains from eliminating import quotas in the U.S., we would have to take this loss of earnings into account, which the ITC model does not. The ITC's estimate of the gains from trade liberalization would therefore be reduced by the $3.6 billion that the ITC estimates as the welfare gains of eliminating quotas in the U.S. Subtracting that $3.6 billion from the value of the ITC gains estimate, of $19 billion, means that the simultaneous elimination of quotas throughout the trading system would reduce the gains from trade liberalization in the U.S. to $15.4 billion annually.

Note that in standard trade models the vast majority of benefits from trade liberalization accrue to the nations that undertake liberalization, since they gain the consumer surplus that results from the opportunity to buy goods at lower prices. The only gain to exporting nations in these models are a result of having the opportunity to sell more goods at the world market price, which is assumed not to change as a result of trade liberalization. The ITC model assumes that the prices paid to importers do not increase as a result of the removal of tariff barriers in the U.S. Therefore, it is necessary to make the symmetric assumption that the price of U.S. exports does not increase as a result of other countries' removal of tariff barriers.

Ignoring Lost Tax Revenue

There is a second important reason for believing that the ITC estimate overstates the gains from trade liberalization given the assumptions of their model: the ITC's treatment of lost tax revenue. The elimination of all tariffs on imports and exports would result in a loss of tax revenue to the U.S. of approximately $20 billion a year. The ITC model assumes that this lost tax revenue is offset by a "lump-sum" tax of the same size. But lump-sum taxes are a purely hypothetical construction, which are not being advocated as part of any new trade agreements. In this way, lump-sum taxes just imply that the government pulls this revenue away from some other part of the economy—without affecting economic activity.

In reality, the government must impose specific new taxes—income taxes, payroll taxes, sales taxes, etc.—in order to obtain revenue. All taxes result in some economic distortions. Most economists put the range of these distortions at 10–20% of the revenue raised by the tax. This means that the tax increases needed to make up for the lost tariff revenue due to liberalization would reduce the ITC's estimate of welfare gains by the amount of the economic distortion due to the tax: 10–20 percent of $20 billion, or $2–4 billion. Even assuming that such a new tax were to be levied to make up for the lost tax revenue due to trade liberalization (which, given the Bush administration's passion for tax cuts, is unlikely), this would leave a net gain from liberalization of $15–17 billion annually. Combining this with the above loss of quota profits ($3.6 billion) would reduce the ITC's estimate of the gains from trade liberalization to $10.4–12.4 billion annually. This places the gains from trade liberalization, using the ITC model, at 0.10–0.12% of GDP. To put these numbers in perspective, the $12.4 billion figure is about one fourth of the *increase* in military spending proposed by the Bush administration for the 2003 U.S. federal budget.

Assuming Full Employment

As noted earlier, an explicit assumption of standard trade models like the ITC model is that there is no transitional unemployment due to trade liberalization.[40] Implicitly, then, this model assumes that workers who leave the industries that are losing jobs due to cost-cutting induced by an increase in cheap competing imports are immediately reemployed in the sectors where their skills can be best utilized. Alternatively, the ITC model can be seen as showing the gains from trade after a transition period in which all the displaced workers have either left the labor force due to retirement and/or found employment in other sectors. However, in reality, many of the workers presumed instantly into a new job will be unemployed for at least some period of time before they find another job.

The U.S. Bureau of Labor Statistics' most recent worker displacement survey found that over one quarter of manufacturing workers who had lost their jobs during the prior three years were still unemployed as of December 2001.[41] Since this was a period in which the U.S. unemployment rate was at a 30-year low, this particular record of reemployment should be considered significantly better than the norm. Therefore, making the assumption that those workers who become unemployed due to trade-related causes will automatically be able to find new work is not a credible one. Such spells of unemployment can significantly reduce the economic gains from trade liberalization, especially in the first years after barriers are reduced.

The ITC estimated that the job losses due to increased imports in 1996 would be equivalent to 175,000 full-time positions.[42] This job loss is equal to approximately 0.11% of the economy's total employment. If a significant percentage of these job losers take a long time to find new employment, or leave the labor force altogether without finding new jobs, then much of the gains from trade liberalization will disappear.

There is one final point worth noting about the effect of unemployment on the economic gains estimated in the ITC model. Insofar as there are government transfer payments associated with unemployment caused by trade liberalization, such as unemployment benefits, food stamps, or other means-tested benefits, they come with an economic cost. Tax revenue must be raised to cover the cost of the increase in such benefits due to higher unemployment, and those economic distortions caused by higher taxes must be subtracted from the estimated gains from trade. This cost can be especially large if the upward redistribution of income caused by trade liberalization leads to large increases in payments for programs such as Medicaid or the earned income tax credit. The cost of these programs may rise not only because of workers being displaced by imports, but also as a result of an upward redistribution of income toward more skilled and more educated workers due to trade. This issue will be considered more directly in the next section.

TRADE AND INCOME DISTRIBUTION

A point on which nearly all economists agree is that trade has been one of the factors that has increased income inequality in the U.S. in the last two decades. This is both a prediction of trade theory and an empirical finding in a large body of research. The prediction of trade theory—that in an industrialized country like the U.S., trade should increase corporate profits and the income of highly educated workers at the expense of less educated workers—has been accepted by economists for more than 50 years.[43]

Wage Inequality Linked to Trade

A large body of empirical work—studies looking at actual results of trade liberalization—supports this theoretical prediction. For instance, in a 1995 study, at the low end of estimates, Princeton Professor Paul Krugman attributed approximately 10% of the increase in wage inequality in the U.S. to trade.[44] It is important to note that Krugman, like other economists who have done research in this area, makes no effort to calculate any indirect impact of trade liberalization on wages, such as the effect that a threat to move jobs abroad can have on wage negotiations or a unionization effort. For this reason, Krugman's calculations almost certainly underestimate the impact of trade liberalization on wage inequality. At the high end, William Cline of the Institute for International Economics attributed 39% of the increase in wage inequality over the period from 1973–1993 to trade liberalization in a 1997 study. Cline calculated both a gross change and a net change in wage inequality. The gross change in wage inequality combines all the influences, including trade, that increased inequality over the 20-year period. The net increase in inequality is the result of both the equalizing influences (an increase in the pool of skilled relative to unskilled labor) and the unequalizing influences, and is therefore much smaller.[45] For purposes of this discussion it is appropriate to divide the inequality attributable to trade (7 percentage points) by the net increase in inequality (18 percentage points), since the latter corresponds to the actual increase in inequality that the nation has experienced. In other words, Cline's estimates indicate that 39% of the actually observed increased inequality (7 out of 18 percentage points) would not have occurred in the absence of trade liberalization. Cline's study also made no effort to incorporate any indirect effects of trade on wage inequality. If Cline's estimate of the direct effects is accurate, then it is plausible that the indirect effects could easily mean that trade is responsible for 50 percent, or more, of the increase in wage inequality in the U.S. over the last two decades.[46] These findings were similar to a 2002 Economic Policy Institute study, which found that between 1995, when the WTO went into effect, and 1999, the latest figures available, the income of the wealthiest 1% of Americans grew by 59%, but the income of the bottom half of earners grew by only 9%, and that the existence of that small growth in the bottom half was primarily as a result of full employment despite stagnant or declining wages for most production workers.[47]

The findings of the ITC report are consistent with other work on trade and inequality. The report found that eliminating the trade barriers it examined would benefit corporations more than workers. For example, it estimated that eliminating the barriers to textile and apparel imports, which account for almost 70% of the total welfare gains (i.e., by decreasing the cost to consumers by allowing more textile goods into the market, which would tend to drive prices down, and by reducing tax effect on consumers by lowering tariffs calculated in this study), would increase income to the capital side of production—i.e., corporate firms—by 0.14%, while increasing income to the labor side of production—i.e., workers—by just 0.06%.[48] It did not estimate the impact of trade liberalization on wage inequality, only the impact on total employment, because it did not distinguish between different occupations. But if just the top 20% of wage earners—who account for close to half of all wage income in the U.S.—experienced the same rate of income gain as corporations, then it would mean that the bulk of U.S. workers—not just textile and apparel workers who lost their jobs directly—were losers from trade liberalization in textiles and apparel.[49] This is exactly the sort of situation that could result from trade liberalization more generally.

Additional Indirect Effects on Income Distribution

It is important to recognize that the ITC study, like other research on this topic, does not attempt to measure *indirect* effects that trade liberalization could have on income distribution. Most obviously this indirect effect can take the form of threats to labor, where employers threaten to move their operations abroad unless workers make wage concessions. Professor Kate Bronfenbrenner of Cornell University has conducted a panel study on the question of threats of relocation affecting labor-organizing activities. She found that in more than half of all unionization drives, employers threatened to close down all or part of their operations.[50] The rate was much higher (68%) in mobile industries such as manufacturing, communications, and wholesale/distribution. The frequency of these threats increased after the establishment of NAFTA, which included provisions protecting foreign investors and cut tariffs and quotas on products shipped between the U.S., Mexico and Canada. Brofenbrenner found an increase in threats of relocation made during initial campaigns to form a union at a plant after NAFTA in comparison to before NAFTA went into effect.[51] Of the campaigns in which such threats were used, 18% of employers directly threatened to move to another country if the union were to win representation. This provides evidence of another negative impact on labor conditions and income inequality due to trade liberalization.

There is no easy way to measure the extent to which such threats might have lowered the wages of manufacturing workers, or less skilled workers more generally. Union-organizing campaigns where threats were used had a lower win rate (38%) than nonthreat campaigns (51%). For more mobile industries with threats, the success rate was 32%, versus 60% for less mobile industries such as health care or passenger transportation.[52] However, one piece of evidence on the effectiveness of such threats is the decline in the unionization rate among manufacturing workers. The unionization rate in the U.S. manufacturing sector fell by 46.8% from 1983 to 2000, the sharpest rate of decline in any industry.[53] By comparison, unionization rates in the construction industry fell by 33.5% over the same period, even though it started at an almost identical level as in the manufacturing sector.[54] Although other factors, including a less union-friendly National Labor Relations Board have also hurt unionization efforts, it is striking that the unionization rate has fallen so much more in manufacturing than elsewhere. Even the transportation and communications industries, which were deregulated during this period, have not seen as large a decline in their unionization rates as manufacturing has seen. It is reasonable to believe that trade has weakened workers' bargaining power in manufacturing, depressing unionization rates and leading to downward pressure on wages in ways that would not be picked up in standard economic models.

Trade Suppressing Wages, Opportunities for
High School Graduates

Real wages in the U.S. have been falling for workers with only a high school education for the majority of the last three decades. In 1973, the real hourly wage for high school graduates was $13.36—a wage level that was not attained again between 1973 and 2001.[55] Although wages for high school graduates grew every year between 1996 and 2001 because of the economic expansion of the late 1990s, the 2001 real wage for these workers was $12.81— still 4% below where it was nearly three decades earlier.[56]

One reason for these declining wages is the shift in the overall employment composition in the U.S. The growing trade deficit, especially during the 1990s expansion when the nation had nearly full employment, essentially shifted workers from production manufacturing jobs to service-sector jobs, where the impact of the trade deficit is relatively modest. Indeed, the very purpose of the GATS, TRIMs, and TRIPs agreements was to protect U.S. investment *overseas*, meaning many of the Uruguay Round agreements paved the way for the export of U.S. jobs to lower-wage countries. Corporations generally have made use of these new rights and protections: in 1994, U.S. companies' direct investment abroad was $613 billion. By 2001, it had more than doubled to $1.4 trillion.[57]

Without the economic growth over the past eight years, the trade deficit would have brought even larger waves of layoffs and plant shutdowns and would have resulted in high unemployment. With the economic expansion, job losses from surging imports were absorbed by the service sector. Although this change in the composition of U.S. employment maintained low levels of unemployment dislocation, the benefits and wages in the service industry are significantly less than in the manufacturing sector.

Between 2000 and 2010, many manufacturing occupations are expected to hemorrhage jobs, in no small part because of relocation to, or competition from, lower-wage countries. Of the 22 million new jobs expected to be created in the U.S. between 2000 and 2010, only 187,000 (0.1%) will be manufacturing jobs.[58] According to the Department of Labor, textile and apparel jobs are expected to take the hardest hit, with 103,000 apparel jobs and 34,000 weaving and thread mill jobs disappearing.[59] Blast furnace and steel product employment is projected to decline 49,000.[60]

In contrast, the expected employment growth for jobs that do not require any advanced training or degree (requiring short or moderate on-the-job training) and thus are available to the 74% of the American workforce without a college degree are primarily in the lower-paid, lower-benefit service sector. Employment in home health care and medical assistant fields, which have low rates of unionization, is projected to grow 47% between 2000 and 2010.[61] Other expected job increases are for guards (35%), receptionists (24%), landscapers (29%), cashiers (14%), waiters and waitresses (18%), and retail sales people (12%).[62]

GROWING INCOME INEQUALITY
WITHIN THE U.S.

As noted above, given the assumptions in standard trade models—most importantly that displaced workers are quickly reemployed—most economists conclude that trade liberalization will increase the overall output of the economy. However, these standard models also predict that trade will increase income inequality, shift income from wages to profits, and from low-wage to higher-wage employees. This means that even if trade leads to gains for the economy as a whole, the upward redistribution of income from wages to profits and from less skilled and less educated workers to more skilled and more educated workers that it causes means that most people will likely lose from expanded trade.

Not long ago, from 1967 to 1980, income inequality in the U.S. actually was declining. The poorest households had increased their share of the total income by 6.5% while the wealthiest fifth's share decreased by nearly 10%. The 1990s have brought even greater inequality, with the bottom fifth stagnating while the top fifth continued to increase its share of total income.[63] By 2000, the top 1% of U.S. households had 40% of the nation's wealth.[64]

A 2002 *New York Times Magazine* story compared the increasing wealth and income polarization in America to the Gilded Age, when the tycoons and dynastic families' fortunes of the 1920s lived in a world opulently foreign to the overwhelming majority of Americans.

> Paine Webber Inc. has advised investors to follow a 'Tiffany/Wal-Mart' strategy and avoid companies that serve the 'middle' of the consumer market . . . and for good reason. The middle class, who once seemed to include almost everyone, is no longer growing in terms of numbers or purchasing power. Indeed, it's the top and the bottom ends that are swelling. . . . The 90s have seen a greater polarization of income in the U.S. than at any point since the end of World War II.
>
> —David Lionhardt, *Business Week*, 1997[65]

The *New York Times* story, by Princeton economist Paul Krugman, focused on the undiscussed changes in the American economy.[66] For instance, between 1970 and 1998, real income for average workers in the U.S. increased by 10%. However, the top 100 corporate CEOs' income grew by 2,785%—from 39 times average workers' earnings to 1,000 times average salaries. Over the same period, real factory production wages have declined. In 1998, the wealthiest top 0.1% of U.S. families (about 1,300 households) had the same income as the poorest 20 *million* households—earning 300 times the incomes of average families. Despite America's stubborn belief that the nation's economic growth will benefit everyone (the cornerstone of the Reagan-era trickle-down economics), median family income only increased about 0.5% per year during the 1990s boom. This increase was primarily due to the increase in two-earner households.

Meanwhile, even with the global economic slowdown, U.S. corporate profits have increased by 88% since 1990 and corporate CEO pay rose by 463%. Incredibly, the CEOs from the companies mired in scandal during 2001–2002 made an average of $62 million between 1999–2001—70% higher than average CEOs from *Business Week*'s annual executive pay survey.[67]

This increase in wage inequality due to trade can be explained by the shift of income from labor to capital, and from non–college educated workers to college-educated workers. Between the late 1970s to the late 1990s, businesses managed to control an increasing share of the earnings gained during economic expansions, or peaks in the business cycle. The shift from labor to capital led to a 2.6% drop in workers' wages, as the capital share of corporate income increased from 17.7% in 1979 to 19.8% in 1999, where 1999 was the profit peak of the last business cycle.[68] Over the last two decades, the ratio of wages for college-educated workers to the wages of workers without college degrees rose from 1.36 in 1979 to 1.67 in 1997:[69] meaning that the wage value of having a college education increased a good deal. Wages for workers without college degrees fell by 4.2% from 1979 to 1999, during which time average hourly compensation for the entire labor force rose by 17.9%, again pointing to the growing discrepancy, due in part to trade, between less educated and more educated workers.[70] This means that wages for workers without college degrees would have been on average 23.1% higher in 1999, had there been no increase in wage inequality. If there also had been no shift from labor income to capital income this would have raised less-educated workers' wages by an additional 2.6%. Taking these numbers together,[71] this means that wages for workers with less education would have been 26.3% higher in 1999 if there had been no unfavorable shifts in income distribution over the prior two decades.

NET GAINS AND LOSSES

Many of the claims made about the gains from trade liberalization have little foundation. Even among those who have tried to seriously examine the issue, there is a wide range of estimates of the size of the positive impact of liberalization. At the low end, models such as those used by the ITC indicate that gains from past trade liberalization may have increased annual GDP roughly 0.1–0.2% over the last two decades[72]—about $12 billion each year, or about the amount that Medicaid funding increased in 2002. At the high end, some estimates—made by sources generally far less plausible, such as the Hufbauer estimate—have placed the gains as high as 1.0% of annual U.S. GDP.[73]

By comparison, looking at wage inequality caused by trade, at the low end, economists such as Paul Krugman have attributed approximately 10% of the increase in wage inequality in the U.S. to trade liberalization.[74] At the high end, Cline attributed 39% of the increase in wage inequality over the period from 1973–1993 to trade liberalization.[75] Neither of these studies made an effort to incorporate any indirect effects of trade on wage inequality. For the purposes of this discussion, Krugman's

10 percent estimate will be taken as a lower bound of the impact of trade on wage inequality, while the 50 percent figure, as the upward adjustment including indirect effects of Cline's estimate, will be taken to be the upper bound.

In analyzing this data, economists Dean Baker and Mark Weisbrot at the Center for Economic Policy and Research found that the net benefit from trade for the three quarters of the labor force who lack college degrees depends on the extent to which trade liberalization is responsible for growing inequality, compared with the extent to which trade has expanded the total amount of income by increasing growth. Weisbrot and Baker concluded that there is little doubt that most workers have been losers from trade liberalization over the last two decades. The high-end estimates of the gains from trade liberalization imply that it has increased GDP by 1.0% over the last two decades. Baker and Weisbrot found, by contrast, that even a low-end estimate of the impact of trade on inequality (10% of the total effect) would place the losses at 2.6% of wages for workers without college degrees. This means that the net loss due to trade liberalization for workers without college degrees has been 1.6% of their wages.[76]

Of course, less favorable assumptions imply larger losses due to trade liberalization. Taking the high-end estimate of the impact of trade on inequality—using Cline's estimate and adding to it the indirect impact of trade on workers' wages via the threat effects discussed above—trade is both directly and indirectly responsible for half of the increase in wage inequality over the last two decades. This implies that it has cost workers without college degrees an amount equal to 13.2% of their current wages (50% of the 26.3% loss suffered by less-educated workers). The net loss is then equal to 12.2% of their wages, assuming the high-end estimate of a 1.0% increase in U.S. GDP due to trade. For a worker earning $25,000 a year, this loss would be slightly over $3,000 per year.[77]

Will Gains from Trade Make Americans Rich?

Dean Baker and Mark Weisbrot

To help us answer this question, let's consider the claim raised by President Clinton: that the average American family would gain $1,700 annually from the trade liberalization of the Uruguay Round. In standard economic theory, countries gain from trade because the newly imported goods and services are produced more efficiently abroad than they could be at home. This is taught in the introductory economics courses as the "law of comparative advantage." Such gains accrue on the imports side of the ledger, rather than exports, since the importing country's consumers (and businesses) benefit from access to cheaper goods and services.

This theory also assumes full employment and that anyone who loses a job when we increase our opening to imports is immediately reemployed elsewhere, in jobs where their skills can best be utilized. The physical capital in the import-competing industry—e.g., plant and equipment—is also assumed to be reemployed for other types of production. Of course, this is not realistic. Nonetheless, it can generally be shown that the overall gains exceed the losses, and so most economists—usually relying on the argument that the winners could compensate the losers—support increased opening to trade.

In addition to the standard "static (comparative advantage) efficiency gains" that come from access to cheaper, more efficiently produced imports, economic models have come to incorporate what are called "dynamic gains." These are less well-understood than the old-style, comparative-advantage gains (which were discovered by David Ricardo more than 150 years ago). The dynamic gains are an attempt to capture some overall effect of trade on the growth rate of the economy. Because this relationship is not well-understood by economists, and because of the wide range of assumptions adopted, the gains from trade estimated by economists vary enormously.

The range of estimates for the gains from past trade liberalization that are considered seriously by economists is also very large. At the low end, those focusing on the more well-defined comparative-advantage gains, such as the ITC 1999 study on the benefits of decreasing trade barriers[78] find that the gains from trade liberalization over the past two decades may have increased GDP by about 0.1–0.2% annually. At the high end, some estimates—generally a lot less careful or plausible—have placed the gains as high as 1.0% of annual GDP.

But we must also consider how trade affects the distribution of income. There has been a massive shift in the distribution of income in the United States in the second half of the post–World War II era—perhaps the largest upward redistribution in our history. In the first half of this era (1946–73) it was roughly true that a rising tide lifted all boats: the median wage grew by about 80%. In the second half (1973–2001) it was a drastically different scenario: the median wage increased only about 7%.[79]

Looking at just the last two decades (1979–1999)[80] nearly all economists agree that trade has been one of the factors that has increased income inequality. The only real issue for most economists is the exact size of the impact of trade on inequality.

For the three quarters of the labor force that does not have a college degree, their wages would have been about 26.3% higher in 1999, if not for the unfavorable shifts in income distribution. There is no disagreement among economists about the size of this loss; the only question is how much is due to trade liberalization. It is easy to see that since this loss due to distribution is so large, even if only a relatively small part of it is due to trade, then most Americans will have suffered a net loss as a result of expanding trade. And this is indeed what we find: even if we use the smaller estimates of how much of the change in income distribution is due to trade, and the larger estimates of the overall gains from trade, the majority of the labor force has suffered a net loss. That loss ranges from 1.6% of wages to 12.9% over the 20-year period.[81] Yet

(continued)

there is good reason to believe that the losses are at the high end of the this range, since studies looking at the effects of trade liberalization on income inequality do not consider some very important factors such as increased ability of manufacturers to move production to poorer countries which has reduced U.S. workers' bargaining power.

It is also worth noting that conditions of new trade agreements, such as the Uruguay Round, could actually increase the costs of some goods in the United States. For example, the WTO TRIPs provisions require that the minimum patent length for prescription drugs be 20 years from the date of the patent application instead of the previous 17-year term. This extension could cost consumers billions of dollars annually due to higher prices for prescription drugs.

In sum, the claims put forward in the public debate over trade agreements such as the WTO or NAFTA, that these and similar agreements will bring economic gains to the majority of the American labor force, cannot be substantiated by the available economic research. Rather, the prevailing research indicates that at least three quarters of the labor force has suffered a significant net loss from trade liberalization under these conditions.

Given the size of the upward redistribution of income that has actually taken place over the last two decades, if trade is responsible for even a portion of this redistribution—even a portion so small as virtually all economists would acknowledge—Weisbrot and Baker concluded that the bulk of the workforce must have experienced a net loss of income from the trade liberalization that has taken place over this period. The potential gains from liberalized trade are far too small to offset the losses due to greater inequality.

Economists Baker and Weisbrot also point out that there are no obvious losses to delaying trade liberalization. In other words, standard models would not predict any smaller gains from liberalizing five years from now than at present. The fact that other nations may move ahead with trade liberalization in the meantime should not affect the potential gains to the United States or any other country, if it decides to liberalize at some future point. This is worth noting, since there continues to be a great deal of uncertainty around many economic issues related to trade. The range of estimates of the potential gains from trade is quite wide and the full extent of the impact of trade liberalization on inequality is still not well understood.

CONCLUSION

As for the United States, while it is theoretically possible for the vast majority of people here to gain from trade liberalization, the best available evidence—based on the most widely used standard economic models and research—indicates that the vast majority of people have not gained from trade liberalization as promised. Instead, it appears that a large majority of the labor force has actually suffered a net loss due to the liberalization of trade over the last two decades. There is no obvious reason to believe that further rounds of trade liberalization along the same lines, as proposed within the WTO (or FTAA), would yield better results. The remarkable slowdown in economic growth and the increase in inequality during the corporate globalization era were major factors in many countries' rejection of WTO expansion at Cancún even as the U.S. continues to push for more of what has already proved to be a failed model. Our purpose for this thorough review of the theory and findings on economic gains from trade is to demystify this confusing information so that the majority of us—who do not have Ph.D.s in economics— can force and then better participate in the desperately needed debate about future U.S. trade policy.

6

THE WTO AND THE DEVELOPING WORLD: DO AS WE SAY, NOT AS WE DID

The Poverty trap is international in scope and the current form of globalization is tending to reinforce it.

—UN Commission on Trade and Development, 2002[1]

During the Uruguay Round negotiations, developing countries raised concerns about the transformation of GATT into an expansive set of new international commercial agreements. Rich countries and the GATT Secretariat staff promised developing countries that they would experience major gains as industrialized countries lowered and eventually eliminated tariffs on such items as textiles and apparel and cut agricultural subsidies that had enabled large agribusinesses to dominate world commodity markets. Uruguay Round proponents also promised that the establishment of the WTO would level the playing field so that powerful economies, such as the U.S., could not threaten unilateral trade sanctions to obtain commercial benefits while refusing access to its own markets for products from developing countries.

Think tanks, public opinion makers and newspaper editorials have continued to relentlessly promote this notion of developing countries being the primary beneficiaries of WTO and globalization—despite a paucity of evidence to support such contentions and a growing record proving the opposite. During the 2001 WTO Doha Ministerial, the *Washington Post* repeated the same pitch it used to promote the Uruguay Round, editorializing that implementing the Ministerial Declaration "would greatly benefit workers in developing countries."[2] Critics of the WTO are caricatured by WTO defenders as greedy, ignorant northerners opposing the developing world's best route out of poverty.

*   *   *

Yet contrary to the rosy predictions, after nearly nine years of the WTO, few if any of the promised economic benefits have materialized for developing countries and for many, poverty has worsened. Economic growth in the developing world is lower than it was in the 1960s and 1970s. Workers in these nations who produce basic commodities such as cereals, timber and minerals are more impoverished than ever as a flood of commodities have crashed prices since the WTO's launch. Indeed, the number of people living on less than $1 a day (the World Bank's definition of extreme poverty) has risen since the WTO went into effect. For the poorest nations, trade liberalization has contributed significantly to a persistent and cyclical poverty, exactly the opposite of what the so-called "Washington Consensus" of business and opinion leaders had so confidently predicted.

This failure was predictable: imposing a one-size-fits-all model from the WTO's Geneva headquarters is destined to fail to meet the economic needs of people worldwide. In 2002, UNCTAD concurred: "The persistence of generalized poverty is less related to a low level of integration into the global economy, and to insufficient trade liberalization, than to the form of the trade integration."[3]

How has it come to pass that so many countries signed up for comprehensive, binding international commercial and other policies that are contrary to their interests? This question is raised by the frequent retort of WTO defenders: If the WTO is so damaging to developing countries, why did those countries agree, why don't they quit, and why are more countries seeking entry to the WTO now?

When reviewing the development of the WTO's rules and their outcome over the past years, one fact becomes obvious: developing countries—the Least Developed Countries (LDCs) in particular—did not and do not have the bargaining leverage or the technical staff to shape WTO rules in their favor. As a result, the developing countries involved in the Uruguay Round negotiations faced a Faustian choice which is now faced by countries outside the WTO: Agree to rules that are harmful, or remain altogether outside the global trading regime?

At the 1999 Seattle WTO Ministerial meeting, developing countries were routinely excluded from the process, which is discussed at length in the second half of this chapter. The major negotiations in Seattle were held in invitation-only "Green Rooms" where negotiators from the industrialized countries hammered out provisions with a select group of countries, while the overwhelming majority of the delegations were left in the dark over the terms of the negotiations. In the end, the developing countries faced the scenario they had faced at the end of the Uruguay Round—they were merely presented with what was produced in the Green Rooms on a *take-it-or-leave-it* basis. However, infuriated by their exclusion from the negotiating process in Seattle, developing countries refused to agree to the terms foisted upon them, and the talks broke down. At the 2001 Doha Ministerial, individual "Green Men" selected by the WTO staff and powerful countries were tasked with coming up with proposals by negotiating "privately" with key WTO member countries; the exclusivity remained in force. The result was predictable: Developing countries opposed a Ministerial Declaration not representing their positions and only "agreed" after unprecedented threats, pressure and an important modification. They remained highly dissatisfied with the outcome of the Doha Ministerial, which was an agreement to do more of the same.

What has this model wrought? The record shows increasingly frequent and severe economic crises: The Mexican peso crash in 1995, the Asian financial crises of 1997–1998, the shuddering economic collapses in Russia and Brazil in 1999. Most recently, Argentina's economic collapse in 2001–2002 and the spread of this economic influenza to the rest of Latin America have not dimmed the enthusiasm for the globalization model promoted by the WTO, the IMF and the World Bank.

In the nearly nine years since the WTO's launch, the developing countries which have most faithfully adopted the checklist of policies required under WTO rules have seen declining per capita growth rates, as detailed below. The destruction under WTO rules of small-scale agriculture in many developing countries has meant that hunger and malnutrition are now exploding. As described in Chapter 7, the terms of the WTO's Agreement on Agriculture have begun to transform nations' food systems from means to feed people into elements of a world food-trade market, with tragic results for poor consumers and farmers—often one and the same in the developing world where more than half of the population remains on the land.[4]

The Uruguay Round Agreements effectively transformed core components of the failed IMF economic development policy into new binding multilateral commitments. This means that for developing countries, the ability to gain market access for exports under global trade rules is now conditioned on implementing changes to domestic policy—such as new intellectual property protections and elimination of industrial policies—that undermine the ability of countries to develop. For instance, the rules in the WTO agreement called Trade Related Investment Measures specifically prohibit infant industry protection when it is linked to regulation of foreign investment.[5] Hence, a developing country cannot require that a foreign investor export products to generate foreign currency or to shield domestic producers from competition for the local market.

Yet the advocates of corporate-driven globalization have not swayed from a near-universal message that adopting their economic and other policies is the only path to wealth—despite the repeated failures of their model.

The WTO Agreement on Government Procurement requires that countries base decisions on how tax dollars are spent only on factors such as which bid is cheapest and who can perform. Countries are required to eliminate procurement policies, such as small-business set-asides or preferences for local products, meaning that the most basic mechanisms used for circulating citizens' tax dollars back into developing the economy are forbidden. Opposition to the WTO rules covering procurement at all resulted in these rules being a la carte and few developing countries signed on, triggering the current push to expand WTO procurement terms.

Likewise, the TRIPs Agreement inhibits flow of technology to developing countries, which used to be a benefit of foreign investment. The present industrial countries did not have patent and intellectual property protections as strict as those now in place while they were industrializing, which allowed them to import technology design from abroad. For instance, when the U.S. was a developing nation vis à vis European nations, the U.S. aggressively transferred technology from Europe.[6] Japan did the same regarding the U.S. and Europe as it developed.

The reality is that no country has ever developed under the conditions and terms required by WTO rules. Cambridge University Director of Development Studies Ha-Joon Chang noted in his landmark 2002 book *Kicking Away the Ladder* that until 1945, the U.S. maintained an array of industrial policies, such as protecting infant industries.[7] These same industrial policies were a key element of Japan's development strategy and were employed vis à vis the U.S., Europe and the rest of the world as Japan developed.[8]

POVERTY IS RISING IN DEVELOPING NATIONS

Ultimately, the IMF-WTO corporate globalization model has failed to deliver for developing countries, severely punishing those least capable of protecting themselves—the billions living on well under $400 annually. As Harvard University economist Jeffrey Sachs stated at a forum in February 2002, the first globalization issue to address was that "whatever you say about markets, pro or con, markets do not serve the poorest of the poor. . . . People are not just living at the edge; they are falling right over the edge by the millions."[9]

Defenders of the global economic status quo often toss around the notion that the number of people living on $1 per day has declined thanks to the IMF-WTO model.[10] In fact that claim relies solely on China's massive population combined with China's impressive record of per capita income growth. Of course, until 2001, China was not a WTO member and indeed has grown rapidly while employing mainly policies WTO forbids.

If one removes China, the world's largest economy and one that has operated outside the WTO-IMF model, the number of people living on $1 a day increased during the period of the WTO.[11] The number of people outside China living on less than $1 a day rose 2% from 916 million in 1990 to 936 million in 1999, and the number outside China living on less than $2 a day rose 16% from 1.9 billion in 1990 to 2.2 billion in 1999.[12] Despite the global economic growth in the 1990s, population growth increased the number of people living in abject poverty. However, the percentage of people living on $1 a day was steady in some regions. The percentage of people living on $1 a day in sub-Saharan Africa remained fairly steady in the 1990s and Latin America and the Caribbean.[13] The percentage of people living below the relative poverty line in Latin America and the Caribbean was slightly higher in 1998 than 1993 (51.35% and 51.08% respectively) before the WTO went into effect.[14]

Demonstrating the failure of this model, the LDCs who are strong participants in global trade suffer from higher rates of extreme poverty than the average. Between 1997 and 1999, 69% of the people in nations specializing in commodity exports lived in extreme poverty, significantly higher than the average extreme poverty rate in LDCs (50%).[15] Although extreme poverty is increased across the board in LDCs during the 1990s, UNCTAD reported that the LDCs that reduced their barriers the most had higher increases of extreme poverty than the LDCs that opened their markets the least.[16]

Deep trade liberalization often does not deserve the high priority it typically receives in development strategies.

—Harvard economist Dani Rodrick,
August 2002[17]

Unbelievably, the WTO's corporate and government boosters are now seeking to expand its control of countries' domestic polices even further by seeking to launch new negotiations on the so-called "Singapore" or "New Issues." These are issues—investment, procurement, competition policy and trade facilitation—on which the rich countries initially sought to launch negotiations at the 1996 Singapore WTO Ministerial. The developing countries refused and have continued to do so for reasons described at the end of this chapter, in a section written by Martin Khor, the executive director of Third World Network, a research and advocacy organization based in Malaysia, with branches in Africa and Latin America.

The WTO staff and developed-country WTO members are trying to shift developing-country WTO members away from focusing on the WTO's existing antidevelopment constraints by waving before developing countries the prospect of new, future "market access."

Yet, the siren song of new market access could lure developing countries up on the shoals of their own destruction: Market access is only useful to countries at a stage of development that allows for their engagement in world markets in a manner that promotes improved standards of living for their populations. But the negotiations on the "new issues" that rich countries also are promoting in exchange for new market access would establish new WTO rules that could devastate developing countries' economies. The promise of market access is at best a distraction and at worst a dangerous hoax.

WTO Encourages Sweatshops

The especially cruel irony of the WTO system is that elimination of the policy tools rich countries used themselves to develop is combined in the WTO with new mobility of capital. This means transnational corporations can exploit cheap labor and resources in developing countries in a manner that leads to neither improved standards of living nor broad-based development in the poor countries, while simultaneously causing downward pressure on the standard of living in rich countries. For instance, it is hard to obtain sympathy in the U.S. for "technology transfer" to developing nations. The reason why: the current reality is that a U.S. company such as Boeing would be "transferring" its technology between its division in the U.S. and its factories in China, where the government assures that workers have no right to organize independent unions to obtain a share of the wealth such transfer could generate.

Similar promises in the Uruguay Round negotiations foreshadow this latest plot: those market access promises were not fulfilled, and biases built in to the specific rules made the seeming access illusory.

For instance, developing countries were pressured to sign off during the Uruguay Round on rules regarding intellectual property and investment with promises of new access for so-called "tropical products" and agricultural goods. Yet, as described below, tariff escalation built into the Uruguay Round for tropical products meant that developing countries seeking to export high value-added products would face higher tariffs relative to the tariff levels for exports of low value-added raw commodities and natural resources. As well as environmental damage described in Chapter 1, the built-in bias to rip and ship natural resources has contributed to oversupply and an unprecedented crash in world commodity prices. This has meant lower returns on trade for developing countries while guaranteeing supplies of ever-cheaper raw commodities for rich countries' value-added industries.

Similarly, specific WTO agriculture rules allowed the countries that had subsidies in place at the time the WTO started to maintain many of them (including the huge export subsidies, which mainly benefit large agribusinesses and are opposed by small farmers in rich and poor countries alike). However, poorer countries did not have such subsidies to adopt new ones so as to compete with subsidized agricultural exports in the WTO world market.

However, most importantly, these hindrances on market access for exports play a relatively small role in a country's economic fate relative to the freedom of a country to choose from a full panoply of policies to develop their domestic economy. For instance, even in a major trading country such as the U.S., total trade flows made up under 21% of GNP in 2000, with 79% of GNP in the domestic economy.[18] Creating an obsession with new market access for exports is designed to shift developing countries' focus from what existing and proposed WTO rules mean for their domestic economies. Consider what has happened to developing countries that have adopted the policies the WTO requires.

DEVELOPING COUNTRIES WHO DID NOT ADOPT WASHINGTON CONSENSUS MODEL FARE BETTER THAN THE COMPLIANT

While the WTO has been in effect for almost nine years, the model on which the WTO is based and many of the specific policies required of WTO member countries have been under implementation in the context of IMF and World Bank Structural Adjustment Programs in an array of developing countries for 30 years. The data regarding these policies' outcomes and measuring their success using the IMF and World Bank's own standard—gains measured in per capita income growth—demonstrate that the WTO-IMF model has failed miserably. The per capita income growth rates of the developing regions before the period of structural adjustment are higher than the growth rates after the countries implemented the IMF-WTO model.[19] For low- and middle-income countries, per capita growth rates between 1980 and 2000 had fallen to half of where they were between 1960 and 1980.[20]

In sharp contrast, the nations that chose their own economic fortunes and policies, such as China, India, Malaysia and Vietnam, had more economic success. These countries had amongst the highest growth rates of the developing world over the past two decades—despite failing to follow the directives of the WTO, IMF or World Bank.[21]

China—whose government strictly controls investment and currency flows, has import controls on many industrial and agricultural products, and provides extensive protections to domestic industry—has grown an average of 10% per year in the 1990s (and an average of 9% per year during the past twenty years).[22] Even during the economic slowdown of 2001, China's economy grew by 7.3%.[23] China's economy is projected to continue to grow much faster than the rest of Asia in 2002–2003.[24] Unlike other Asian countries that have been pressured to eliminate trade, investment and finance (currency controls, banking regulations) policies as a condition of receiving IMF loans, China does not have a freely convertible currency and the government strictly controls the banks. As a result, China, as well as India, which also maintains currency controls, largely weathered the "Asian financial" crisis without significant damage.

In response to the Asian financial crisis in 1998, Malaysia temporarily all but eliminated trading in its currency bringing a torrent of criticism by the IMF and U.S. Treasury Department for this heresy against the neoliberal model. Yet the capital controls allowed Malaysia to stem the wild speculation that led to currency collapses in other nearby economies,[25] and to lower interest rates in 1999 and stabilize its economy, avoiding the crisis's worst ravages.[26] Unfortunately, China's, India's and Malaysia's relative successes are the exception in the region. Countries such as Korea, Thailand, Indonesia and the Philippines, which had adopted many elements of the IMF-WTO model, were devasted after decades of growth had earned several of the countries the label of "Asian Tiger economies."

Many proponents of the IMF-WTO model point to the economic successes of some East Asian economies as demonstrable proof that increasing exports are the key to increasing growth. Yet, this analysis attributed entirely too much to the role of exports. Indonesia, Thailand and South Korea all had export rates of more than 20% of GDP through the 1980s—but they also had comparable savings *and* investment rates at the same time, and exports were far from the entire picture of these countries' successes.[27]

Meanwhile, IMF policies requiring the deregulation of these countries' finance sectors—banks and currencies—directly contributed to the Asian financial crisis. South Korea, Indonesia, Malaysia, Thailand and the Philippines eliminated capital controls that had set requirements on short-term investments to insulate the economy from dramatic outflows of investment, and instituted significant financial deregulation.[28] This made possible the predatory speculation that collapsed currency after currency in the region. What had been a $93 billion net capital inflow in 1996 turned into a net capital outflow of $12 billion in 1997— erupting into an international crisis that hit the majority of working families and small farmers especially hard.[29]

The IMF policies fostering the conditions for the crisis are similar to the investment and financial services liberalization policies that the WTO promotes in the General Agreement on Trade in Services and its Financial Services Agreement (FSA). The President's Council of Economic Advisers, in its *1999 Economic Report of the President*, noted the role these policies had: "In most countries, significant liberalization of international capital transactions and the progressive elimination of capital controls preceded the crisis. . . . East Asian economies had embarked on financial liberalization, both domestic and international, over the course of the 1990s."[30]

Thailand, Korea and Indonesia, which year after year enjoyed annual growth rates of 8–10%, maintained full employment, and made progress in eradicating poverty, suffered severe economic contraction.[31] The financial press declared the crisis to be over the next year even though people in Asia experienced increased poverty and unemployment in some countries by as much as 200%,[32] and had effectively lost two decades of economic progress in a matter of weeks because of currency speculation made possible by policy changes ordered by the IMF and similar institutions.

Meanwhile, the increased integration of nations' economies, which the Uruguay Round is designed to intensify, meant that the Asian crisis spilled over into Latin America and Africa, since countries in these regions depend on trade with Southeast Asia. African countries depended on East Asia for 25–35% of their total export earnings.[33] African growth slowed to 1% in 1999.[34] And about 10% of Latin America's total merchandise exports went to Asia, where they had to compete with cheaper Asian goods for the OECD market, which comprises 60% of total Latin American exports. Latin America has been mired in its deepest economic slump since the debt crisis of the 1980s.[35]

However, before the "Asian flu" effect, and well after it, Latin America's economic experience with the neoliberal model is worth reviewing. As described in the next section, growth rates for the region have plummeted during the period of structural adjustment. Plus Mexico, touted as a poster child of the model after its 1994 accession to NAFTA, was the source of a financial crisis—the 1995 peso crash—that further chilled the region's growth, thanks to what was called the "tequila effect" of other Latin nations' currencies being devalued and investment declining.

In 1988, Mexico had liberalized its trade policies to meet the requirements to join GATT.[36] Under NAFTA rules (now also included in the draft FTAA), Mexico opened its financial services sector to foreign ownership, deregulated the sector and lifted investment and currency regulations as required by NAFTA's Chapter 11 rules forbidding restrictions on movement of investments and capital.[37] For a short while, Mexico was celebrated as an example of a developing country implementing the neoliberal economic policy model correctly as foreign investors rushed into Mexico and exports surged. But as investors focused on Mexico's limited hard currency reserves relative to the peso's value (which the government had been shoring up to avoid any devaluation during the contentious NAFTA debate), they became skittish there was a rapid $15 billion "net capital outflow"—otherwise known as a panicked herdlike flight from the Mexican market—in 1995. The peso collapsed, official unemployment rose to twice the level of 1993, and the proportion of the Mexican population living in extreme poverty rose 20%.[38]

Financial commentators declared the peso crisis over and a year later touted how Mexico's neoliberal policies had led to its recovery. Yet, real wages in Mexico have not caught up to pre-crisis levels,[39] and the Mexican rural economy has only grown more devastated, leading to rural unrest and demands to abrogate NAFTA's liberalization of agriculture.[40]

Argentina followed Mexico as the example touted by the IMF and World Bank as a success story, until it also imploded. Argentina's reliance on the free-market dogma from the IMF had encouraged it to rush toward broad privatization, deregulation and trade, finance and investment liberalization, which contributed to its economic devastation.[41] As with the Asian "rescues," international lenders then required that Argentina rigidly adhere to a fiscal austerity plan in the face of a significant recession, which further imperiled its economy.[42] This brutal budget tightening left many ordinary Argentines high and dry—by the end of August 2002, many teachers and doctors had not been paid in nearly two months.[43] Argentina's collapse was the worst economic crisis in Latin America in two decades, with its four-year recession putting one in five Argentine workers into unemployment and half the nation into poverty.[44]

The supporters of the IMF-WTO model are running out of countries to spotlight as success stories of their model. The most common refrain from these quarters now is that the countries that previously had been touted as examples of success actually had not fully implemented the model and only more of the same but faster will ultimately lead to economic growth.

Promise of Rising Living Standards Based on Non-existent Growth

To obtain the rising wages and living standards promised in the WTO's preamble, economies must grow. UNCTAD reports that growth in the developing world needs to reach 6% per year to close the income gap with industrialized nations.[45] Yet for most developing countries, similar liberalization and deregulation of their economies over the past two decades under the orders of the IMF has coincided with sharp declines in rates of growth.[46]

An examination by the Center for Economic and Policy Research of annual per capita economic growth rates worldwide between the period prior to broad structural adjustment (1960–1980) and after countries implemented the package of neoliberal policies also at the core of the WTO rules (1980–2000) shows a striking trend: Growth rates in the majority of the world have declined since the corporate globalization policies began to be pushed aggressively.[47]

Every region in the world was affected by this before-and-after phenomenon:

- Latin America's per capita GDP grew by 75% between 1960–1980, but between 1980–2000 it grew by only 6%.[48]

- Sub-Saharan Africa's per capita GDP grew by 36% between 1960–1980 but declined by 15% between 1980–2000.
- Arab states' per capita GDP declined between 1980–2000 after it grew 175% between 1960–1980.
- South Asia, Southeast Asia and the Pacific all had lower per capita GDP growth subsequent to 1980 than in the previous 20 years. (Only in East Asia was this trend not sustained, but this is because China's per capita GDP quadrupled during this period prior to China joining the WTO.)

The pattern of slower growth during the period when corporate globalization policies were adopted was also demonstrated across nearly every country. Of the 116 countries examined, the average economic growth between 1960–1980 was 83%, but between 1980–2000 was 33%.[49] The majority of the countries studied (89, or 77%) saw per capita growth rates that were significantly lower 1980–2000 than in the previous two decades. Only 14 countries (13%) had significantly higher growth subsequent to 1980 compared to 1960–1980.

Between 1997 and 2000, most LDCs had annual average growth rates of 4.5% (and averaged 2.1% per capita GDP growth), well below the level required to even start closing the income gap with the industrialized world.[50] Despite the enormous pressure on developing countries to liberalize trade, the causal relationship between increasing exports and increasing growth for developing nations has yet to be demonstrated. A survey by Harvard economist Dani Rodrick of the most cited studies that allegedly prove that trade liberalization generates economic growth came to the conclusion that "[T]here has been a tendency in academic and policy discussions to greatly overstate the systemic evidence in favor of trade openness."[51] The 2002 UNCTAD Trade and Development Report describes the failure of proponents to prove their assertion more bluntly: "The varying experiences suggest a complex relation between commercial policies and trade performance, and, more generally, between trade and growth, and they rule out an unequivocal causal link from the former to the latter."[52] Indeed, more than half (59%) of the 22 LDCs that had increases in their economic export orientation between 1987 and 1999 had annual economic growth rates below 1%.[53] Over the same period, two LDCs had declining exports as a share of its economies by 9% but still saw their economies grow.[54] Growing countries may increase exports, but increasing exports does not necessarily generate growth.

Logical jumps and conflicting cause and effect unfortunately have been a mainstay of studies that do allege a link between liberalization and growth. This has not stopped the WTO and IMF defenders from continually citing these studies. For instance, one study by World Bank economists David Dollar and Aart Kraay, which USTR Robert Zoellick includes in nearly every speech, concludes that "more open" countries have the highest growth rates.[55] First, the study makes several logical leaps that Evel Knievel would be scared to attempt: It reiterates a long-known fact that increased growth rates can lead to poverty reduction. However, it then proceeds to simply *assume* that liberalization *causes* growth. Yet, a growing body of empirical data shows the logical jump is unsupportable.[56] Thus, while growth may decrease poverty, the policies these studies tout do not necessarily lead to growth.

Second, the criteria used to judge a country's "openness" in the study are so arbitrary that it is impossible to draw any conclusion about what policies contributed to countries' growth. For example, China, which maintains broad restrictions on imports and foreign investment and has a nontradable currency but has significant exports, is labeled a "good" free-market globalizer in this study, despite being a communist state-driven economy. The study also weights countries by population. Thus, China's strong economic growth over the past two decades weighted by its population skews the entire data analysis to show "open" countries grow faster.[57]

Some commentators have suggested sarcastically that the Dollar and Kraay study and several similar ones were designed in reverse—a country was determined to be "open" if it had a high growth rate. In fact, the studies which rely on the high growth rates of countries such as China and Malaysia to show "openness leads to growth" serve as evidence of just the opposite. By using policies opposed by the IMF and WTO to protect their economies from the ravages suffered by countries adopting the full corporate globalization policy package, some developing countries have been able to promote growth and more easily integrate into the global economy through targeted use of trade combined with other policy tools.

Uruguay Round Agreements Include Provisions Especially Threatening to Developing Countries

Some development experts in the industrialized world admitted as early as 1993 that the trade and investment liberalization policies of the Uruguay Round Agreements would hurt many developing countries. In a report buried by WTO boosters in the developed world, the Organization for Economic Cooperation and Development reported that sub-Saharan Africa, in particular, had the most to lose under the Uruguay Round agreements.[58] The OECD was a supporter of the Uruguay Round, making this warning especially compelling. The OECD forecast was echoed by the U.S. Congressional Research Service (CRS), which predicted in 1995 that there would be both winners and losers from Uruguay Round implementation.[59] According to CRS, the Uruguay Round's big losers would be the LDCs and some other African, Caribbean and Pacific countries (ACP).[60] Indeed, prominent economists, including scholars from developing countries, where popular opposition to the Uruguay Round was often stronger than in industrialized countries, largely predicted what is now coming to pass.[61] These outcomes are being caused by several specific concepts and provisions in the Uruguay Round package.

A. Systematic Tariff Escalation Creates Barrier to Economic Diversification

Uruguay Round tariff schedules include an escalation of tariff rates as value is added to a product. Thus, the lowest tariff rate is for a raw commodity, increasing with processing and manufacturing.[62]

This Uruguay Round feature is one reason developing-country WTO critics say the Uruguay Round promotes economic "re-colonization" of developing countries that only recently gained political independence.[63] Tariff escalation creates an incentive for rip-and-ship natural resource exploitation in poor countries, as discussed in Chapter 1. In addition to its environmental threat, tariff escalation strongly favors countries with developed manufacturing sectors by increasing access to cheap raw natural resources. For instance, in Germany, companies import raw coffee beans to blend and process them and then export instant coffee back to the developed world.[64]

Tariff escalation also discourages developing countries from further industrialization because tariff rates increase and competitiveness decreases as value is added to products through manufacturing. So, for instance, a developing country that produces timber is forced into a no-win set of choices: to try to obtain export earnings it can flood the market and drive down prices by exporting a high volume of low-tariff raw logs, or slightly higher tariff but low-value-added processed wood, or it can export high-value-added furniture which would earn the highest return if it did not face the highest tariff.[65] This built-in design reduces poor countries' competitiveness in finished goods and thus poses a disincentive to invest in this processing capacity or in agricultural commodity processing.[66]

B. Falling Commodity Prices Destroy Developing Economies and Increase Poverty

In many LDCs, particularly those dependent on primary commodity exports, an interrelated complex of international trade and finance relationships is reinforcing the cycle of generalized poverty and economic stagnation which is, in turn, reinforcing the negative complex of external relationships.

—UNCTAD[67]

Nonpetroleum primary commodity prices fell by more than a quarter in the nearly nine years the WTO has been in effect and now are at historic lows.[68] Compounding the problem of lower export earnings caused by plunging commodity prices is the fact that LCDs have become net importers of food and therefore must have a steady stream of foreign exchange simply to finance the imports needed to feed the population.[69]

The decline in commodity prices has resulted from a variety of factors. The IMF and World Bank have pushed developing countries to increase commodity exports as a means to earn hard currency to service IMF and World Bank loans, and as supplies have increased, prices have declined. The WTO's tariff escalation also promotes oversupply of world markets with raw materials, driving down prices. The Uruguay Round also eliminated several commodity agreements which had regulated supply. "[Primary commodities] are important sources of foreign exchange, but they are risky because of the shift in world prices," notes a West African agriculture expert.[70]

Many of the declines in global commodity prices were in the products that were the backbone of many developing countries. Declines since the WTO's establishment—(between 1995–2001) include: cereal prices down by 31%; coffee prices down by 65%; cocoa prices down by 24%; food commodity prices down by 24%; timber prices down 18%; cotton prices down 51%; wool prices down 26%; and rubber prices down 62%.[71]

Workers from LDCs that produce and export these commodities have fared poorly. Because commodity prices declined so steeply, even though the export tonnage increased, the earnings from those exports declined.[72] Nearly seven in ten people (69%) from non-oil primary commodity exporting LDCs lived on less than $1 per day between 1997–1999.[73] Mineral prices also declined by 23% in the post-WTO environment,[74] and in nonpetroleum mineral exporting LDCs four out of five people lived on less than a $1 a day.[75]

Moreover, extreme dollar-a-day poverty for people living in these primary commodity-exporting countries is rising. The share of the population living in extreme poverty in nonpetroleum primary commodity exporting nations has risen since establishment of the WTO. The percentage of people earning under $1 a day in these countries grew 9.5% from 63% of the population in the 1981–1983 period to 69% in the 1997–1999 period.[76]

In contrast, total nonpetroleum commodity prices rose by 16% in the years immediately preceding the WTO (1992–1994) while mineral commodity prices declined slightly by less than half a percent over three years.[77] The WTO does not include any mechanisms to intervene in the global commodities markets, although its predecessor, GATT, explicitly permitted commodity-market interventions.[78] Oxfam launched a campaign in 2002 to get the WTO to readdress these issues including to create a commodities working group.[79] To date, this proposal has been rebuffed.

Share of Trade Declines for Most Developing Nations Since Launch of WTO

Although the complete impact of the Uruguay Round Agreements on developing countries can be gauged only after full implementation (because provisions within several key agreements phase in for some developing countries over extended periods), some general trends have already emerged during the nearly nine years since implementation began.

First, the developing world's share of trade has not increased as promised and in some instances—notably among least developed countries—has declined. The 1998 Least Developed Countries Report of UNCTAD measured developing countries' share of trade and found that the share of world exports and imports had fallen sharply in the LDCs since the Uruguay Round, and in the 2002 UNCTAD report, found that one in three LDCs saw their exports contract between 1997–2000, even as the global economy was expanding.[80] Second, an increasing share of trade in developing countries is controlled by multinational corporations, meaning investment decisions are designed to increase those companies' short-term profits, not the host country's development.

Despite the WTO proponents' promises to the contrary, global exports have actually grown more slowly since the WTO went into effect than in the years before, according to a Public Citizen analysis of the data provided in the WTO's own "World Trade Statistics" reports over the past decade.[81] The average annual growth in world merchandise exports between 1991–1994 was 7.0%, but between 1995–2001 the average annual growth of exports was 5.5–21.2% less than during the pre-WTO period.[82] While we do not argue that growth in exports is the crucial measure of a trade regime's success, it is worth considering the relative rate of export growth versus the raw export volume data that the WTO uses to tout its terms' "boost" to exports.

For the vast majority of countries in the developing world, the share of the world export market and total export growth remained stagnant or fell since the WTO went into effect. This was true across the globe.

- *Asia:* The value of Asia's merchandise exports grew more slowly after the WTO went into effect, and Asia's share of global exports declined significantly since the WTO began. Average Asian annual exports grew 12.0% a year between 1991–1994, but only grew by 5.0% between 1995–2001—a 58.1% decline. Asia's average annual share of global exports rose 4.7% a year between 1991–1994, but remained nearly flat between 1995–2001. The declines are even more marked without China. Non-Chinese average annual Asian merchandise exports grew 11.2% a year between 1991–1994, but only grew by 4.0% a year between 1995–2001—a 64.8% decline. The non-Chinese Asian average annual share of world merchandise trade grew by 4.1% per year between 1991–1994 but declined by 16% a year between 1995–2001. The most impressive export growth came from China. (Remember, China was not a WTO member until 2001.) China's tremendous export surge demonstrates that the implementation of the WTO's policy model is a poor predictor of exporting growth.
- *South Asia:* The average annual merchandise exports from South Asia increased 11.2% between 1991–1994, but only by 7.8% between 1995–2001—a 30.7% decline in merchandise trade export growth. South Asia's share of global merchandise exports grew an average of 4.1% between 1991–1994, but only grew 2.2% between 1995–2001—the increase in South Asia's share of global merchandise exports slowed by 46.4% during the WTO era.
- *South America, Central America and the Caribbean:* Merchandise exports from Latin America grew an average of 9.2% a year between 1991–1994 and 9.5% a year between 1995–2001. However, that small increase disappears if Mexico is not included. Latin America's merchandise exports, excluding Mexico, grew an average of 7.7% a year between 1991–1994, but only grew an average of 6.2% a year between 1995–2001—a 19.3% decline in export growth during the era of the WTO. A similar pattern emerges in Latin America's share of global merchandise exports. Latin America's share of global merchandise

exports increased an average of 2.1% a year between 1991–1994 and 3.7% between 1995–2001. Without including Mexico, Latin America's share of global merchandise exports increased an average of 0.7% a year between 1991–1994 but grew an average of 0.6% between 1995 and 2001—a 9.7% decline in the growth rate.

- *Mexico:* Mexico's share of world exports accounted for the only significant gain in Latin America. Mexico's merchandise exports increased an average of 12.6% a year between 1991–1994 and grew by 15.2% between 1995–2001. Mexico's share of global merchandise exports increased an average of 5.4% between 1991–1994 and increased an average of 9.0% a year between 1995–2001. However, nearly half (48.8%) of Mexico's total merchandise exports in 2000 were reexported goods to the U.S. from Mexico's maquiladora free-trade zones comprised almost entirely of intermediate goods and parts imported from the U.S.[83]

- *Non–Oil Exporting Africa:* Non–oil exporting African countries' merchandise exports grew an average of 4.7% a year between 1995–2001, but its share of global exports declined by 0.9% per year during that period.

- *Least Developed Countries:* The LDCs' total share of world trade flows, the total volume of exports plus imports, has been declining. In each year between 1995 and 1999, LDCs' share of world exports of goods and services was about 45% less than those countries' share of global trade in 1980. LDCs' share in nonfuel primary commodity exports was 2.8% in 1980, but fell to 1.5% in 1995, the WTO's first year, and never recovered to that level over the next four years. In 1995, nonpetroleum commodity exporting LDCs' share of global trade was 40% below where they were in 1980 and fell slowly but steadily after the WTO went into effect until 1999. LDCs' share of world manufacturing goods exports remained unchanged by the WTO, holding steady below 0.2% of global manufacturing exports between 1995 and 1999, meaning LDCs saw essentially no export gains at all from the WTO.[84]

Growing Share of Global Trade Benefits Go to Transnational Businesses

Although the developing world has not obtained the promised benefits under the WTO terms, international businesses have profited handsomely. Global corporations have increased dominance in the export sectors of the developing world. The UNCTAD 2002 Trade and Development Report described this trend: "a greater share of developing-country production and exports comes to depend on the decisions and performance of foreign firms and countries."[85] Although the proponents of the WTO model cite increases in some specific developing country exports as proof that developing countries are increasingly engaged in the global economy, it is more accurate to suggest that it is not the economies that are integrating but that global business networks are becoming more integrated. By the end of the 1990s, some estimate that transnational business exports account for 30% of all global exports, and that these integrated business exports have grown by 40% over the past 25 years.[86]

The expansion of exports from these internationally integrated businesses largely benefits the companies, not the nations where they are produced. First these companies rely on foreign rather than local suppliers; the basic assembly of high-technology goods prevents local economies from diversifying and expanding to new capacities.[87] Second, the value-added is concentrated in the foreign ownership's sales, not in productive ownership in the developing world.[88]

The mobility of many of the production facilities owned by companies from the developed world encourages the shift in production facilities to areas that can do the work with the cheapest labor and lowest regulatory or environmental costs. The increasing competition by developing countries to attract foreign direct investment encourages companies to seek out the lowest costs with the most favorable relocation benefits (taxes, infrastructure, etc.).[89] In the U.S., critics of the corporate managed–trade system have long contended that U.S. manufacturing plants were relocating to the developing world in a race to the bottom to pursue the cheapest labor and weakest environmental standards. The first step was the relocation to Mexico as a result of NAFTA. Now, companies are pitting developing countries against one another and are rapidly relocating between them. In 2002, Dutch-headquartered Royal Philips Electronics shuttered its Mexican computer monitor plant, laying off 900 workers, and relocated the production to an existing Philips Chinese factory.[90] Japan-based Canon closed a 13-year-old Tijuana ink-jet printer factory in the spring of 2002 and moved the production to facilities in Vietnam and Thailand, shedding 700 jobs in Mexico to pursue yet lower wages in Asia.[91]

The three products that have had the highest export growth over the past 20 years (electronics goods and parts, apparel, and high-tech finished goods) are also the ones that have been most impacted by the globalization of production through corporate international production sharing.[92] This trend is especially true in the high-technology electronics sector—the very sector that is touted as the savior of the East Asian economies. The high volatility of this sector and the declining global market for exports (even more so given the oversaturation of supply) suggest an elusive future for countries that rely on these high-tech exports.[93] Moreover, the reliance on transnational firms in East Asia for manufacturing export expansion has failed to generate the local capital improvements or broader integration of the local economy.[94]

Increasing Income Inequality Within and Between Countries

While the economic growth promised by WTO proponents has not materialized, an unwelcome economic development has been the intensified income inequality between and within countries. Instead of generating income convergence between rich and poor countries, as WTO proponents predicted, the corporate globalization era of the 1990s actually exacerbated the income inequality between industrial and developing countries as well as between rich and poor within countries

Even WTO Defenders Admit Promises Overstated Potential Gains

Even the most ardent WTO proponents, when pressed, have admitted that trade liberalization would have minor impacts on the economies of developing countries. The World Bank reported in 2002 that the effects of tariff reduction expected by the 2015 WTO tariff-reduction schedules by industrialized nations would only provide a 0.6% increase in the gross domestic product for developing countries and reducing their own barriers would only increase their GDP by 1.2%. One Washington-based think tank has calculated that the per capita income benefit for sub-Saharan Africans who earned on average $500 annually in 2002 would be an increase to a per capita income of $503 under the World Bank's estimate for eliminating industrialized trade barriers. Even using the most robust assumptions about full trade-barrier reduction, many developing countries would still benefit little, and these benefits would not come into effect until 2015.[95]

worldwide. This outcome has given credence to the warnings of WTO critics in developing countries. They had argued that under the Uruguay Round's "corporate managed trade" rules and new constraints on assorted development policies, the winners would be the giant multinational corporations that generally are incorporated in the developed countries.

According to the United Nations Development Program (UNDP), the differential in per capita incomes between the countries with the poorest 20% of the world's population and the richest 20% is widening as globalization picks up pace. The income gap between the fifth of the world's people living in the richest countries and the fifth in the poorest was 74 to 1 in 1997, up from 60 to 1 in 1990 and 30 to 1 in 1960.[96] By 1997, the richest 20% captured 86% of world income, with the poorest 20% capturing a mere 1%.[97]

In 1960, the 20 richest countries had per capita incomes 16 times greater than non–oil producing LDCs, and by 1999 the richest countries had incomes 35 times higher—doubling the income inequality.[98] The richest 10% of countries had median incomes 77 times greater than the poorest 10% in 1980, but by 1999 the richest earned 122 times the poorest countries.[99]

In almost all developing countries that have undertaken rapid trade liberalization, wage inequality has increased, most often in the context of declining industrial employment of unskilled workers and large absolute falls in their real wages, on the order of 20–30% in Latin American countries.[100]

—UNCTAD

UNCTAD also has noted that the growing polarization among countries has been accompanied by increasing income inequality within countries.[101] The National

Bureau of Economic Research conducted an in-depth analysis of the relationship between trade liberalization and rising wage inequality focusing on the 1985 Mexican trade reform required for Mexico's 1986 entry into GATT. The study concluded that wage inequality in Mexico rose after the reform, countering the "logic" that all members of society will benefit if a country opens its markets by deregulating its economy and relying on its comparative advantage—which in Mexico's case is low-wage labor—in world markets.[102] Even the World Bank has admitted that the push toward global economic integration has increased income inequality, noting that in Latin America, global integration increased the already high income inequalities by widening the wage gap,[103] and that China's income inequality increased during the 1990s as urban workers gained, while many rural poor were left behind during China's economic expansion over the past two decades.[104]

Vital WTO Decisions Still Made Without Developing Country Input at WTO

Many developing countries were virtually dragged into the Uruguay Round negotiations largely against their will and better judgment. The Uruguay Round was launched because of U.S. initiative with the support of most major industrial nations. "It really was about global production and production capacities" and not "technical issues like tariff and non-tariff measures . . . thus the main negotiations were a trilateral affair involving the U.S., the European Economic Community (EEC) and Japan," writes longtime GATT analyst Chakravarthi Raghavan in his book *Recolonialization: GATT, the Uruguay Round and the Third World.*[105]

As a result of many handicaps, ranging from lack of technical expertise to the limited financial and human resources available for the examination of the panoply of international commercial issues raised in the Uruguay Round, most of the developing countries' negotiators remained "uncertain" about the probable consequences and economic costs their countries would have to bear upon implementation of the Uruguay Round.[106] Because of this lack of information and the inherent power imbalance, it's little wonder that many negotiators from developing countries reacted to proposals during negotiations with a view to minimizing the negative effects and containing the damage, rather than negotiating to maximize their economic benefits.[107]

As the developing countries have begun to work together to overcome the technical and power imbalances, the WTO's Secretariat—allegedly a neutral staff to all WTO member nations—has instituted new procedural rules that freeze in or worsen the developing nations' weak bargaining power. Even after the Seattle Ministerial, in 2000, as many as 15 African countries had no representative at WTO's Geneva headquarters.[108] The predicament was expressed succinctly by the ambassador of Tanzania: "In a country like mine where so many people are starving, it is very hard to think about spending money for the GATT."[109] Yet the expansive Uruguay Round agreements can and are affecting LDCs' fate.

Developing countries do not always have the strength to oppose new initiatives even if they should come to the conclusion that the disadvantages outweigh the advantages. The problem lies in that the developing countries are dependent on developed countries in other areas and undue pressure occurs.

—Swedish International Development Agency, 2002[110]

The Doha WTO Ministerial

The Fourth Ministerial of the World Trade Organization took place at Doha in the Persian Gulf state of Qatar from November 9–13, 2001. The WTO's Ministerial meetings are where the organization's future direction and agenda are agreed. The U.S. and the EU plus Canada, Japan, Australia and a few other delegations sought to revive the so-called "Millennium Agenda" of massive WTO expansion which failed at the 1999 Seattle WTO Ministerial. The developing country members of the WTO plus the global NGO movement fought for a different agenda to come out of Doha, focused on the existing problems with many of the WTO's rules and agreements.

Selecting Qatar as the venue for the fourth WTO Ministerial limited broad civil society participation and rendered WTO deliberations inaccessible to all but a chosen few. The Qatari government agreed that only NGOs and other civil society representatives who were granted credentials from the WTO could obtain a visa, and only one representative per NGO was given accreditation. Ultimately, a small delegation of 70 civil society representatives overcame the enormous expense and WTO visa restrictions to attend. The official line from the WTO was that over 400 NGOs were present. However the other 330 were business organizations.

At the Doha Ministerial, the WTO continued its secret dealings and exclusionary practices. Negotiators had been unable to agree on many elements of a draft Ministerial Declaration–the summit's binding product. When trade ministers from the 160 WTO member nations gathered in Doha, they were met by a very determined and coordinated effort by the EU and the U.S. The WTO's Secretariat already had spent months lobbying around the world for the U.S. and EU agenda of WTO expansion. A Ministerial Declaration text was distributed containing terms developing countries had rejected. This text became the operating text. During the summit, unprecedented levels of pressure and coercion were exerted on developing countries to force them to accept the EU/U.S. agenda. Countries were threatened with revocation of foreign aid or trade benefits.[111] Plus, the post–September 11 political context allowed U.S. negotiators to play the "for us or against us" card with unsubtle insinuations that any country against the U.S. WTO position tacitly supported "terrorism."

The "Green Men" chosen by the WTO Secretariat, the U.S. and the EU circulated amongst the delegates, setting up bilateral discussions aimed at uncovering the weaknesses in each country's negotiation position. Then the Green Man for a particular topic would draft language on the subject. This strategy was designed to minimize the public-relations nightmare that arose in Seattle, with angry delegates literally pounding on closed doors after being excluded from multilateral negotiations wherein fellow WTO member delegates had full information and access.

Using the specter of the "shadow of Seattle," claims that the future of the world economy was contingent on the outcome of Doha, and jittery global politics post-9/11, trade negotiators from the EU and the U.S. were hell-bent on forcing a conclusion that they could label a victory. First and foremost, they intended to avoid another Seattle-style meeting collapse.

Despite this enormous bullying, several developing countries from the Caribbean and Africa, as well as India, held firm against the massive WTO expansion agenda. However, after the ministerial was extended by a full day, with round-the-clock arm twisting on the holdouts in an all-day and all-night closed-door session with the U.S. and EU, some of these countries finally agreed to sign a Ministerial Declaration that included the launch of some new negotiations and which excluded most of the developing world's demands relating to changing the existing WTO rules. However, after some countries still withheld consent, the deal ultimately was signed only after a "Chairman's note" was added, stating that at the next WTO Ministerial there would have to be an "explicit consensus" on whether negotiations of the new issues should begin.

The result was an ambiguous final document that leaves open the possibility for extending WTO rules over new issues, but forecloses the urgently needed changes to existing rules. To summarize briefly, the Doha Ministerial Declaration grants approval to continue the existing GATS service-sector and agricultural-sector talks. The Declaration included an agreement to start new negotiations on nonagricultural tariff and nontariff (i.e., regulatory standards) cuts, including those on forestry products; empowers the WTO to judge the relative status of Multilateral Environmental Agreements vis-á-vis the WTO; opens new negotiations on "environmental services," perhaps including water services; launched new negotiations to rewrite WTO anti-dumping rules (see Chapter 9); and calls for discussions of modalities for potential investment, government procurement, trade facilitation, competition and other negotiations. However, as columnists in many prominent developing countries' newspapers wrote, the forced Ministerial Declaration at Doha could be a Pyrrhic victory. The ambiguity in the text required to avoid a Seattle-style meltdown and the intensely bad feelings of most developing countries' negotiators mean the WTO's future course remains less than clear.

As the Doha agenda moves forward, developing countries remain excluded from the discussion. In the fall of 2002, the Australian government hosted an invite-only group of WTO members to discuss the future negotiations on the road to the Cancún Ministerial scheduled for September 2003. The Australia Mini-Ministerial hosted about 20 members of the WTO, leaving the majority of the 144 members out in the cold for the shaping of the Cancún meeting.[112] Similar invitation-only "Mini-Ministerials" have since been held in Egypt, Japan and Canada despite growing protest from the excluded countries.

> ### Uruguay Round Undermines Existing LDC Trade Preferences
>
> Under WTO rules, industrialized countries are permitted to maintain programs to benefit LDCs, such as the Generalized System of Preferences (GSP) programs used in the U.S. and the EU. These programs provide preferential tariffs to the poorest countries by granting waivers to countries that provide these benefits which would otherwise clash with Most Favored Nation obligations requiring the same treatment for all WTO countries.[113] Notwithstanding these waivers, Uruguay Round tariff reductions lowered the values of such programs as compared to regular post–Uruguay Round tariff levels. One example of this phenomenon is how WTO provisions on textile and apparel trade will wipe out all special preferences in these products provided by agreements such as the U.S. Caribbean Basin Initiative, African Growth and Opportunity Act and the Andean Trade Preferences Act. When the full WTO textile and apparel terms kick in in 2005, the global rules will be the same as the "preferential" rules.

CASE 1: U.S. ATTACKS CARIBBEAN BANANA TRADE POLICY ON BEHALF OF CHIQUITA

The "Washington Consensus" that underlies the WTO's trade policy includes a "Trade, Not Aid" bias.[114] Proponents argue that by establishing trade regimes with industrialized nations, LDCs expand the infrastructure that will allow them to grow out of poverty. Yet, when the EU took a step toward that stated goal, the U.S. complained to the WTO, called for a WTO panel, and succeeded in stopping the EU efforts.

The Lomé Convention—since replaced with the Cotonou Treaty—between the EU and its former colonies in Africa, the Caribbean and the Pacific established preferential tariffs and set aside some portion of the EU market for products from ACP countries.[115] This regime was considered indispensable for the economic and political stability of the ACP countries.[116] During the Uruguay Round, the EU negotiated a waiver for the Lomé Convention for GATT Most Favored Nation tariff requirements, but in 1996, the U.S. government, on behalf of the U.S. corporation Chiquita Brands International, challenged the EU, claiming that the Lomé banana regime violated other WTO obligations.

The U.S. itself does not produce a single banana for trade. Carl Lindner, Chiquita Brands International CEO, contributed $500,000 to the Democratic party two days after the Clinton administration filed a WTO challenge to the EU banana policy in 1996[117] and in 1998, before GOP leaders pushed legislation to punish the EU for not changing its ACP banana rules after the WTO ruling, he gave the Republican party $350,000.[118]

Chiquita had approximately 22% of the EU banana market.[119] All of the Caribbean Island producers combined had 8% of the EU market[120] and 3% of the world market.[121] Three giant multinational companies—Chiquita, Del Monte and Dole—control two-thirds of the global market.[122]

While most of the world's bananas are grown on large Latin and Central American plantations that rely on cheap farm labor,[123] eastern Caribbean banana producers, in contrast, tend to be small-scale farmers who own and work small plots of mountainous land and whose production costs are therefore higher. The ACP countries most dependent upon the Lomé Convention banana regimes include the Windward Island nations of St. Lucia, Dominica, St. Vincent and the Grenadines, where banana production accounts for between 63% and 91% of export earnings.[124] Also, 33% of Dominica's workforce and 70% of St. Vincent's population are involved in the production and marketing of bananas.[125] According to the prime minister of St. Lucia, "The trading arrangements of the Lomé Convention are not about diverting trade but providing opportunities [for countries] that otherwise would have little or no possibility of participating in the global trading system."[126]

The WTO Challenge

The U.S. claimed that the EU's policy of setting aside a specific small portion of its market for bananas exported by ACP countries was unjustifiably discriminatory under WTO rules.[127] The EU argued that paragraph 1 of its WTO Lomé waiver— stating that the MFN principle would be waived "to the extent necessary" for the EU to comply with its Lomé Convention obligations—implicitly included the market share guarantee, as any other interpretation essentially would render the Lomé Convention waiver meaningless. This argument however, was not accepted by the WTO panel.[128] The WTO panel also ruled that the EU's Lomé waiver failed to cover GATS rules relating to the allocation of import licenses for distributors and marketers of goods. The EU appealed.

In September 1997, the WTO Appellate Body handed down its ruling, affirming and clarifying the original panel's ruling that the Lomé waiver did not allow the EU to favor ACP bananas by providing them with a 7% guaranteed market access license at a guaranteed tariff rate that is lower than that imposed on other producers.[129] According to the panel, despite the EU's Lomé Convention waiver, the special tariff quotas enjoyed by ACP countries had to be eliminated or provided to all. This effectively eliminated the Lomé benefit and forced ACP countries to compete against multinational, large-plantation producers such as Chiquita.

In 1998, the EU issued a proposal to address the panel's ruling. It agreed to remedy other policies that the panel ruled against, but stood firm on the quota issue, proposing to maintain the two-tier tariff quota regime for ACP and non-ACP banana producers.[130] According to St. Lucia Trade Minister Earle Hunteley, "The simple tariff would leave us wide open to fruit from cheaper sources, thus making it even more difficult to compete."[131]

In response to the EU's proposals, the Republican leadership in the U.S. Senate introduced the Uruguay Round Agreements Compliance Act of 1998, which imposed retaliatory tariffs on the EU for not fully complying with the WTO's banana ruling.[132] At the last minute, the GOP leadership agreed to pull the bill after the Clinton administration promised to take action through the WTO mechanism to sanction the EU.[133]

In February 1999, the administration announced that it would impose tariffs against a wide range of European-made goods in retaliation for the EU's failure to comply with the WTO. Products subject to the sanctions included goat cheese, cashmere, biscuits, candles and chandeliers. The list added up to an annual value of $520 million, which is what the U.S. banana marketers claimed to lose because of the Lomé Convention.[134] A WTO panel rejected the U.S. tabulation of damages and reduced the amount to $190 million, but approved and legitimated imposition of sanctions, which took effect in March 1999.[135]

The EU argued that the U.S. could not impose retaliatory tariffs without a WTO panel ruling saying that the EU's new proposals did not comply with the previous WTO dispute body report.[136] In response to a complaint by Ecuador against the EU's proposed remedy, a WTO panel held in April of 1999 that the new EU regime did not comply with its earlier ruling.

The Settlement

On April 11, 2001, the U.S. and the EU agreed to a solution. In return for the U.S. dropping its tariffs and its opposition to the EU's Cotonou Treaty, which included temporary preferences for ACP countries, the EU agreed to change its tariff structure, transferring some of the quota from ACP countries to the U.S. and other Latin American countries. The EU pledged to move to a "tariff only" system, abandoning its ACP ties, by January 1, 2006.[137] Since then, a significant percentage of the small-scale banana producers, especially in the Windward Islands, have gone under.

The fallout from the WTO ruling could be seriously damaging to both the islands directly involved and the U.S. The end of the banana "middle class" in the Caribbean will destabilize the economic foundation of the region, leaving thousands of people with no means of independent livelihoods. Economic destabilization in the region in the past has led to social upheaval. Considering that this economic destabilization is permanent (unlike past weather- or blight-caused damage to the banana economies), it threatens to undermine the strong democratic traditions of these countries and their traditions of human and labor rights. Given the standard of living of these island nations—almost all of whom are democracies with voter turnout double U.S. rates—the potential threat to the well-being of the Caribbean people is enormous.

Indeed, from a purely economic perspective, the U.S. WTO attack undermines broad U.S. interests. First, the U.S. is the main beneficiary of the worldwide Caribbean tourism boom, which relies on the countries' safety and stability. Second, the Caribbean is one of the few regions in the world with whom the U.S. has a trade surplus.[138] The Caribbean sells bananas to Europe and uses the hard currency to buy U.S. exports.

Third, the U.S. has invested considerable public resources into trying to stop the flow of illegal drugs through the Caribbean from South America into the U.S., and there is widespread acknowledgment that a direct effect of the elimination of the Caribbean banana economy would be a surge in illegal drug cultivation and trafficking. Where bananas can grow, so can marijuana. Both St. Vincent and Jamaica have been producing marijuana for decades, and since 2000 have become points for transshipment of cocaine.[139] A 1996 article in the *Washington Post* quotes Marine General John Sheehan, commander of U.S. forces in the Atlantic and the Caribbean: Caribbean island nations "are dependent on a single crop—bananas. People need to provide for their families" and will resort to drug dealing or illegal migration if driven to it.[140] South American drug cartels, which have already worked their way into the Caribbean, encounter less resistance from displaced farmers who see no economic alternative to the drug trade. Indeed, Caribbean governments, outraged over the U.S.'s pursuit of the case against the banana regime, have withdrawn from cooperative narcotics efforts with the U.S.[141] Finally, another effect of the banana economy's demise will be a surge of unauthorized immigration to the U.S. because so many people in the Caribbean will be thrown out of work. This case politicized the WTO throughout the Caribbean, contributing to that region's concerns about proposals to further expand the WTO's scope being pushed at the WTO Cancún Ministerial, which is discussed in the next section.

THE DEVELOPING-COUNTRY PERSPECTIVE FROM SEATTLE TO CANCÚN: NEW WTO THREATS TO DEVELOPING COUNTRIES AND SUSTAINABILITY

by Martin Khor*

In the lead-up to the fourth WTO Ministerial in 2001 in Doha, the developing-country members of the WTO were united in a strong demand that, in the coming years, the WTO agenda should focus on resolving the problems arising from establishment of the WTO and the scores of new agreements it enforces. However, the major developed countries had a very different agenda: to expand the WTO's negotiating and rule-making mandate to incorporate new areas such as investment, competition policy, government procurement, trade facilitation, and trade and the environment. This attempt at expansion was strongly resisted by a majority of developing countries.

   The context for this push for WTO expansion is important: when the Uruguay Round was being negotiated, many developing countries were highly concerned about and some opposed to the broad scope of new issues that were to be covered. But, for the sake of finishing the Uruguay Round, compromises were ultimately struck on some of the most contentious issues. For instance, given developing-country opposition to including investment rules under the WTO, the WTO's Trade Related Investment Measures agreement is of a much narrower scope than,

* Martin Khor, a Ph.D. economist, is the director of Malaysia-based Third World Network, a leading research institute focused on an array of development issues.

say, the investment chapter in NAFTA. TRIMs rules only apply after an investment is made—meaning unlike NAFTA no right for foreigners to establish an investment is granted. And the definition of investment in TRIMs is limited to foreign direct investment—unlike NAFTA, which includes currency, land, contracts, stocks and more.

While developing countries were struggling just to implement their Uruguay Round obligations, developed countries again pushed to start negotiations on the items the developing countries had opposed during the Uruguay Round. This basket of issues is often called the "Singapore Issues" because it was at the WTO's second ministerial in 1996 in Singapore where the drumbeat to revive these proposals started in earnest. The developing countries rejected this call for new negotiations, and as a compromise, agreed to launch new WTO study groups on each of these issues. At every opportunity since, the developed countries—led most passionately by the European Union—have sought to transform these study groups into new formal negotiations. Meanwhile, developing-country opposition to expanding the WTO's mandate has only grown stronger as the full results—and problems—of the Uruguay Round have become more apparent.

Despite this opposition, in the lead-up to the Doha summit the major developed countries (along with the WTO Secretariat, which had abandoned its official role as impartial facilitator of the negotiations) undertook a series of manipulative tactics to overcome the unified developing-country position. As a result, the views and positions of many of the developing countries in key areas and topics were inadequately reflected—or not reflected at all—in the drafts of the Ministerial Declaration prepared prior to the summit in Geneva or in the backrooms of the Doha meeting itself. The result was sections in the Doha Declaration on the Singapore Issues (investment, competition, transparency in government procurement, and trade facilitation) as well as on the environment that were not acceptable to many developing countries. Most simply, the Doha Ministerial Declaration implies that the member countries have agreed to launch new negotiations (toward new agreements or new rules) on the Singapore Issues in 2003 following the fifth ministerial, on the basis of an explicit consensus on "modalities" of negotiations prior to the fifth ministerial.

This language caused outrage in the halls of the Doha Ministerial. The last hour of the last day of the ministerial came and went without an agreement. Developing-country negotiators were singled out by U.S. and European negotiators for extreme pressure. A chilling description of this outrageous process is provided in a 2002 report by the Bangkok-based organization Focus on the Global South called "Power Politics at the WTO."[142] After hours of this process had not broken the wills of the developing-country delegations, the WTO Secretariat, in consultation with the largest developed-country members, extended the ministerial for a day. Delegations from some developing countries began to leave—unlike the negotiators from the rich countries (some of whom came on military and other chartered flights), they did not have the resources to risk indefinite stays in Qatar and expensive new tickets on the packed commercial flights.

However, objections and requests for reformulation of this language were voiced at the last "informal" session at Doha—occurring late in the extra day of meetings. As a result, the declaration was tempered by a clarification by the Ministerial's chairman, the Qatari trade minister, at the final official session that an explicit consensus would be required for negotiations to begin (the implication being that the required consensus would not be only for modalities). The chairman also clarified that this would give each member the right to take a position on modalities that would prevent negotiations from proceeding until that member was prepared to join in an explicit consensus. This statement gave greater protection to developing countries that did not want to commit to negotiations on the new issues.

Developed countries have sought to dismiss the clear legal language of the chairman's note. In any case, the declaration did commit WTO member countries to discuss a list of elements and topics within each of the Singapore Issues before the Cancún Ministerial. These discussions were undertaken in Geneva throughout 2001 and 2002. Even as developing-country opposition to the Singapore Issues has intensified, the EU tabled an outrageous paper in February 2003 declaring that negotiations on the Singapore Issues *would* begin at Cancún and dismissing the need for agreement.[143] The paper served to harden developing countries' opposition.

Many developing countries and NGOs from around the world are adamant that these issues do not belong at the WTO, as they are not trade issues. They argue, for instance, that the application of national treatment to these new issues is inappropriate and would prevent or hinder governments from adopting policies and measures needed for development and other goals such as nation building and harmony among ethnic communities. The cynicism of these proposals cannot be ignored: The now-rich countries used the same nation-building tools and preferences during their own development that would now be forbidden to others in these new proposed pacts. The historical record of WTO operations—including, vividly, the run-up to and on the ground in Doha—demonstrates that during WTO negotiations, the developed countries have maximum leverage to shape the agenda, principles and provisions of an issue. If developing countries allow negotiations to be launched on subjects inherently against their interests, the final outcome can only be against the interests of developing countries.

The Developing Countries' Catch-22: Resolving the Imbalances First, or Paying Again at Cancún?

Developing countries are facing several problems in implementing their Uruguay Round commitments, many of which are described in the first half of this chapter. In a formal paper submitted in the fall of 2001 prior to the Doha Ministerial, a group of over 100 developing-country WTO members identified more than 100 necessary changes or clarifications to existing WTO rules. These problems raised the serious issue of whether developing countries can presently or in the future pursue development strategies and objectives on everything from industrialization and technology upgrading to the development of local industries and the attainment of food security and public health goals. The developing countries argued that the implementation issues be resolved as a matter of first priority in the sequencing of the WTO's future activities.

However, at Doha there was little progress on the implementation problems. Developed countries have maintained that developing countries must abide by their legally binding commitments; any changes would require new concessions on the part of the developing countries. Such an attitude does not augur well for the WTO, for it implies that the state of imbalance will remain. The developing-country members of the WTO consider that they already "paid" by making so many concessions, for example accepting agreements on intellectual property, services and investment during the Uruguay Round. If developing countries are being required to pay twice or pay three or four times with new concessions in order to obtain the changes to existing rules necessary to avoid those countries being devastated, then the imbalances and the burden will only intensify.

Developing countries are instead being told that their requests on implementation problems and on getting greater access in the rich countries' markets will be considered as a package deal in the post-Doha work program, but only in exchange for accepting negotiations on the Singapore Issues. But these proposed new agreements would not bring about reciprocal benefits, so developed countries stand to gain the most. Worse, the expansion of the WTO's scope to these issues would be detrimental to developing countries, which will find even more of their development options closed off.

Why Developing Countries Oppose WTO Expansion on the Singapore Issues

The common theme of the Singapore Issues is an attempt to maximize the rights of foreign enterprises to have market access for their products and investment; to reduce to a minimum the rights of the host government to regulate foreign investors; and to prohibit government from implementing measures that support or encourage local enterprises. Primarily, multinational corporations based in the developed countries stand to gain from these proposed WTO expansions. Below is a description of each of the four Singapore Issues and the implications for developing countries.

Investment

The main proponents of an investment agreement are seeking binding international rules that grant foreign investors a new right to enter countries without conditions and regulations, to operate in the host countries free from government regulations and to move funds without government regulation.

In technical terms, one of these demands is what is called "pre-establishment" national treatment and MFN status. This means that foreign investors would have the same right to buy land or a local company, or to privatize a service as a domestic interest—e.g., governments could not require foreign investors to apply to a national investment board for approval and could not give preference to local bidders on a privatization.

Another demand is the elimination of performance requirements, such as requiring domestic partners or technology transfer which are the tools governments use to shape investment to ensure benefits to the host country, not only to foreign investors. Requiring countries to eliminate restrictions on the movements of funds is also a demand. This has obvious implications on balance of payments and (if the definition of investment is as broad as is being sought so as to cover currency, stocks and bonds) would affect a country's currency value by forbidding capital controls. Even though currency controls have succeeded in safeguarding countries like Chile and Malaysia from the worst of regional currency crises, such a ban on capital controls was demanded by the U.S. in two recent bilateral free trade agreements with Chile and Singapore.

Also being proposed are strict new standards of protection for investors' rights. For example, under NAFTA's investment provisions, countries have demanded and obtained compensation from governments when health or environmental measures affect investors' expected future earnings, claiming these actions were "tantamount to expropriation."

An international agreement on investment rules of this type is ultimately designed to maximize foreign investors' rights while minimizing the authority, rights and policy space of governments and developing countries. This has serious consequences in terms of policy making in economic, social and political spheres, affecting a country's ability to plan in relation to local participation and ownership and the ability to build capacity of local firms and entrepreneurs. By eliminating governments' rights to make policies to protect the balance of payments or ensure certain levels of foreign reserves, this proposal could expose even more countries and people to the sort of crisis that wiped out a decade of income gains in Asia in the mid-1990s. These proposed rules also would weaken dramatically the already unbalanced bargaining position of government vis-à-vis foreign investors (including portfolio investors) and creditors.

Given the risks of such an agreement, it is hard to imagine any consensus on modalities of negotiations, nor even on the principle of whether there should be an investment agreement in WTO. Given the record of coercive tactics at the WTO, this reality will not stop developed countries from trying to force a false consensus on investment issues for Cancún.

Competition Policy

At present, there is hardly any common understanding let alone agreement among countries on what the competition concept and issue means in the WTO context. The whole set of issues of competition, competition law, and competition policy, and their relation to trade and to development, is extremely complex. The pre-Cancún proposal required all WTO member countries to establish national competition laws and policies which incorporate the "core principles of WTO." These include transparency, MFN and national treatment. An approach based on

WTO core principles would result in an agreement providing new and better market access and investor rights for large foreign commercial interests rather than rules to break up the mega-corporations whose takeovers and mergers have resulted in many multinational corporations with worth greater than the GNPs of many WTO member countries, and the disproportionate power to impose their commercial interests over small countries' public interests.

Competition law and policy, in appropriate forms, are beneficial, including to developing countries. However, having an appropriately flexible model tailored to local conditions is especially important in the context of globalization and liberalization, where local firms are already facing intense foreign competition. Developing countries need the flexibility to choose the competition policy/law that is deemed suitable to their level of development and their development interests.

From a development perspective, a competition and development framework requires that local industries, service firms and agricultural farms build up the capacity to compete locally and then, if possible, internationally. As the histories of the now-developed countries demonstrate, this requires a long time frame. Increasing local capacity to remain competitive also requires protection from the "free" and full force of the world market for the time it takes for local capacity to grow. Development strategy, therefore, has to be at the center of any competition policy.

There is not a convincing case for a multilateral set of binding rules to govern the competition policies and laws of countries. However, if a multilateral approach is needed, there are other, more suitable venues: UNCTAD, for example, has already established a Set of Principles on Restrictive Business Practices, and if the objective is cooperation among national competition authorities, then it is inappropriate for the WTO to be the venue.

Transparency in Government Procurement

The 1996 Singapore Ministerial Declaration included a clause committing WTO member countries only to set up a working group to study procurement transparency and, based on this study, to discuss what elements might be considered in an appropriate agreement. But, as with all of the so-called Singapore Issues, there was no commitment to start negotiations on any new agreement.

The working group was only mandated to cover the issue of transparency. This contrasts with the broader scope of the existing plurilateral WTO agreement on procurement, which seeks to bring the large worldwide government procurement market under the full WTO rules and system. At present, WTO members are allowed to exempt government procurement from WTO market-access rules if they choose. Since developing countries have opposed integrating government procurement and its market access aspect into the WTO, some developed countries have devised the tactic of a two-stage process: Draw all WTO member countries into an agreement on transparency, then extend the scope from transparency to other areas—for example, due process in bid appeals—and then ultimately to market access, MFN and national treatment for foreign firms.

If governments in the future will not be allowed to give preferences in recycling national tax and other revenue to local companies for the supply of goods and services and for the granting of concessions for implementing projects, the effects on developing countries would be severe. Government procurement and policies related to it have very important economic, social and even political roles:

- Controlling the level of expenditure, and directing the expenditures to locally produced materials, is a major macroeconomic instrument, especially during recessionary periods to counter economic downturn.
- National policies that give preference to local firms, suppliers and contractors boost the domestic economy and participation of locals in economic development and benefits.
- Specification that certain groups or communities, especially those that are under-represented in economic standing, be given preference is an important policy tool to avoid ethnic and regional conflict in developing countries.
- For procurement or concessions where foreign firms are invited to bid, being able to give preference to firms from particular countries (e.g., other developing countries, or particular developed countries, with which there is a special commercial or political relationship) is one of few commercially powerful international-relations policy tools a developing country with limited resources has.

Given the ambitions of the major countries, it is realistic to anticipate that if an agreement on transparency were established, there would be strong pressures to extend its scope to also cover market access, or the rights of foreign companies to compete on a national treatment basis for the procurement business. Thus, the discussions on transparency and on a transparency agreement should be seen in the light of the strategic objective of the majors to draw the developing countries into the real goal of market access and full integration of procurement practices under WTO disciplines. The existence of a transparency agreement would make an eventual market-access agreement very difficult to stop, as the transparency agreement would signify that all of the WTO member countries have agreed that procurement is a valid topic for a WTO agreement.

Trade Facilitation

Although the term "trade facilitation" may seem innocuous, the topics that would be covered if these negotiations were allowed to begin are anything but benign. The basic idea is to create binding international commitments that all WTO countries will provide certain customs, inspection and other trade facilitating services in a manner set out in a WTO agreement. Like any other WTO agreement, failure to meet the terms of this proposed agreement could result in a WTO enforcement tribunal ordering a country to comply or face trade sanctions.

The establishment of multilateral rules in this area poses an array of threats. For developing countries, the issues include difficulties in adhering to the envisaged one-size-fits-all standards and procedures, as well as being put in the situation of having a WTO agreement dictate how limited government resources should be allocated. One-size-fits-all trade-facilitation rules might also affect implementation of domestic trade policies. For example, a common demand of importing countries is that the physical examination of goods by the customs authorities be limited to a small number of cases selected on a random basis to improve the flow of goods through the customs barrier. But this increases the risk of avoidance of payment of adequate customs duties. Such a practice may be appropriate for the major developed countries where the chances of leakage is negligible, but it may not be appropriate for the developing countries where leakage is higher. Again, given the issues at stake, any agreement at Cancún for new negotiations on this issue would be a mistake.

CONCLUSION

Seeing the true nature of the WTO and its rules—undemocratic and unbalanced—becomes unavoidable when one considers the situation of the developing countries. Given the fact that the vast majority of WTO member countries are developing nations, how—absent a scandalous perversion of democratic process—could an international body ostensibly operating by one-country-one-vote or by consensus contain an entire body of rules which undermine an array of vital developing-country interests? And even as the damage from implementing the existing rules spurs demands for change on the part of developing-nation WTO members, the EU, with the energetic support of the U.S., Canada, Australia, Japan and other wealthy nations, came to the Cancún WTO Ministerial demanding an expansion of the failed "trade über alles" model to areas even more threatening to developing nations. The beautiful irony of the Cancún Ministerial was that the unyielding insistance on WTO expansion imploded the entire summit. Now attention must shift to addressing the severe failure of the existing rules.

7

THE WTO ON AGRICULTURE:
FOOD AS A COMMODITY,
NOT A RIGHT

The underlying premise of the WTO's agriculture rules is that food should be treated like any other good or commodity, subjected to global market forces and covered by the same sort of trade rules as tin ore, tires or automobiles. But food is not just like an automobile. Food—like water—is not an optional product that consumers may choose to purchase: food is the basis of life. People without food die while people without cars or tires walk and people without tin ore use local materials. Yet, the WTO's Agreement on Agriculture (AoA) and the patenting and monopoly control of seeds included in the TRIPs agreement seek to transform food and seeds into commercial units with profit—not sustenance—as the end goal. Food and agriculture policy has shifted from nation-states to global corporations and global markets, from food production to commodity trade. As a result real food security—and its necessary condition of food sovereignty—is declining.

However like many WTO rules, the terms on agriculture and food do not conform to the free trade principles employed to sell them. For instance, wealthy countries have increased their agriculture support since the advent of the WTO.[1] Within the rich countries, most of government support goes to the largest producers.[2] Simultaneously, more than 1,200 small farms throughout the U.S. are being eliminated each month.[3] The new U.S. farm bill increased U.S. subsidies not only to big farms but to commodity exporters by $82.8 billion over the next 10 years.[4] Perversely, only the largest farms and those commodity-trading companies who sell U.S.-subsidized agricultural products overseas are benefiting from this government largesse. Between 1996–2000, only 36% of U.S. farms received any farm subsidies,[5] 60% of farm-subsidy payments went to the largest 10% of producers,[6] and although only 30% of U.S. "residence" farms received any subsidies in 2001, 72% of U.S. large-scale commercial farms did.[7]

The EU and Japan provide direct income support for farmers. Stimulating overproduction and then subsidizing export of the surplus results in dramatic drops in the prices paid to farmers for their crops worldwide, destroying the livelihoods of millions of peasants in poor nations and small family farmers in rich countries.

In principle, importing countries are permitted under WTO rules to prohibit such "dumping"—exporting commodities at prices that are below the cost incurred in producing them. In practice, the dumping of agricultural products has increased in the era of the WTO. Stopping food dumping is the most vital priority for most developing countries because it destroys domestic markets, throws domestic farmers into ruin and causes growing dependency on imported food which developing countries do not have the hard currency to purchase. However, the WTO's agriculture rules explicitly allow the few rich countries who can afford it to continue dumping on other countries.[8] It is this dumping, not gains in efficiency, that is causing the crash in commodities prices that is devastating small-scale farming around the world.

The result is increasing hunger. Yet ironically, there is no shortage of food; in India and Brazil large stores of grains rot in silos. Hunger stems from lack of entitlements to food, as Nobel laureate Amartya Sen has described. And entitlements erode when farm incomes decline, due to rising costs of production or falling prices of agriculture produce, usually both. And in a mockery of free-trade theory, food prices worldwide generally have risen to match inflation. In the U.S., dramatically declining prices paid to farmers for agricultural goods have had little impact on the cost of food for consumers.[9] Farmers and consumers are losing; who is winning under the WTO's agriculture rules?

Facing growing criticism and attack, the EU, Japan and the U.S. agreed as part of the Uruguay Round to reduce subsidies, but carefully avoided making any commitments to reduce or eliminate dumping. Yet eight years later, it is evident the cuts have made little material difference. Some developing countries, such as Brazil, export large volumes of many crops, but most developing countries export a few cash crops—cocoa, coffee, etc., for which they seek market access and fair prices. An overwhelming focus on their food trade policy is ensuring their domestic markets—and domestic food security—are not crushed by dumped imports of food staple crops. Yet, the WTOs Agreement on Agriculture has relentlessly chipped away at developing nations' food security policies focused on helping small farmers or managing food supply. The implications for the livelihoods of billions, food safety and the environment are now only beginning to be felt. Consider one result if the AoA were fully implemented and all farming and food production around the world met the "efficiency" rates of western high-input farming: 2 billion of the 3.1 billion people now living on the land throughout the world would no longer be "needed" to participate in the rural sectors of their countries.[10]

Economic theory states that such "displaced" rural peoples will be more efficiently employed in other economic sectors. WTO defenders in wealthy nations celebrate how globalization liberates peasants from lives of grinding rural poverty. In country after country, where have the "liberated" gone? They will join an urban workforce whose constant oversupply continually suppresses wage levels and will exacerbate the existing crisis of chronic under- and unemployment in the cities of the developing world. In Mexico and China, the push to establish large-scale corporate agriculture has resulted in millions of peasants losing their rural livelihoods and being forced off the land.

An estimated 200 million of China's peasant farmers are expected to lose their livelihoods as their "surplus" labor is eliminated by China's agricultural "modernization."[11] At the time of China's WTO accession, even official Chinese government reports predicted that 10 million farmers would be displaced by China's implementation of AoA rules.[12]

Meanwhile, these same policies are wreaking the demise of small-scale agriculture in the rich countries. Corporate globalization has accelerated agribusiness consolidation and factory farming with alarming social, food safety and environmental consequences for family farmers in the U.S., Canada, Japan and Europe.

Implementing the high-input, large-scale corporate farming model on third-world food production also would have devastating environmental consequences as far as increased use of fuel, pesticides and water, and loss of biodiversity. Promoting mass-scale production of monocultures (one species of a crop or animal) means a reduction in agricultural biodiversity that is a potent threat to global food security and an obstacle to addressing global hunger concerns because of increased risk of losing large amounts of food to pests.[13] Increasingly horrific health problems are arising in the countries that have adopted the large-scale corporate agriculture model: mad cow disease, widespread food contamination from centralized high-speed slaughter and processing facilities, and obesity, malnutrition and childhood diabetes linked to consumption of overprocessed foods.

Perhaps the most remarkable fact is that between 1994–2001—during the period of NAFTA and WTO's supposed new benefits for U.S. agriculture—the total contribution of U.S. agriculture to the U.S. economy declined by $4 billion—a 5% decline.[14]

While the *volume* of food and agricultural trade has increased dramatically over the past decade, low prices paid on glutted commodity markets mean that increases in value have not kept up since the WTO went into effect. The U.S. volume of exports grew 16.4% between 1994–2002.[15] Over the same period, the value of U.S. agricultural exports grew by 14.8%.[16]

With exceptions described below, under WTO agriculture rules, countries are required to eliminate barriers—such as tariffs and quotas—on imported food. Indeed, one WTO agriculture rule aimed at increasing the flow of food trade requires every WTO member country to import at least 5% of every commodity, even if that country produces a surplus of the same food.[17] Just consider the absurdity of importing food that is produced locally in such abundance that the same commodity is also being exported.

While subsidized mass producers can survive the related drop in earned farm income, small, independent farmers in the U.S. and other industrialized countries are going under. The U.S. lost 38,310 small farms between 1995–2002.[18] U.S. net farm income was $36.2 billion in 2002—16% below the average net farm income of $43 billion between 1990–1995 before WTO went into effect.[19] In Canada, farm debt nearly doubled since Canada's first experiment with corporate managed trade—with the Canada-U.S. Free Trade Agreement in 1989—from C$22.5 billion to C$44.2 billion.[20] Between 1996–2001 Canada lost 11% of its farms.[21] The United Kingdom lost 60,000 farmers and farm workers between 1998–2001 and farm income declined 71% between 1995–2001.[22]

Obviously, something is seriously wrong with current WTO agriculture rules. The volume of food trade is up, but most farmers in rich and poor countries see their incomes decline, with many losing their farms and livelihoods while consumer food prices have not fallen. Perhaps the only beneficiaries are the global commodity-trading companies who were instrumental in writing the AoA rules. They can take advantage of their elimination of government price and supply management to manipulate supply and demand so that prices paid farmers in countries around the world can be pushed down but consumer prices for food increased or kept steady, creating profits for commodity trading firms and food processors.

WTO RULES ON AGRICULTURE AND FOOD

Before the WTO was established during the Uruguay Round negotiations, agricultural goods were theoretically covered by the same rules as other goods under the GATT. However, in practice, special exceptions in the rules applicable to agriculture as well as waivers granted to the U.S., EU and a few other countries protected agriculture from most GATT rules. GATT allowed export subsidies on agriculture goods, although it prohibited export subsidies on industrial goods.[23] Additionally, GATT allowed some limited import restrictions on agricultural products, including quotas under limited circumstances.[24] Countries used the limited quota exception to justify import bans, quotas that set maximum caps for agricultural imports and minimum import prices, and to maintain country- and product-specific import limitations they had protected at the time they signed GATT.[25]

The WTO Agreement on Agriculture was established during the Uruguay Round negotiations to establish specific terms for agricultural trade. The AoA chapeau (GATTese for preamble) states that the agreement's intent is to establish a more pure market-based agriculture system, including specific commitments to reduce domestic subsidies and export subsidies, to increase market access and to govern agriculture trade with more rigorous disciplines on domestic farm policies. The AoA text specifies that regarding agricultural goods to the extent of conflict, the AoA supercedes other WTO agreements, such as the Agreement on Subsidies, the Agreement on Safeguards and the Technical Barriers to Trade Agreement.[26]

Agricultural products covered by the AoA include commodities such as wheat and corn, veggies and fruit, live animals and milk (and products made from those things), tobacco and alcohol products, fiber products such as cotton and wool, and animal skins and hides for leather production, but fishery and forestry products are not covered. The agreement was to phase in over a six-year period for industrialized countries, going into full effect January 2001 with a 10-year phase in for developing countries.[27] The AoA also required WTO member countries to start in 2000 with new "built in" negotiations to further the AoA preamble's goals. These talks have been under way at the WTO's Geneva headquarters.

The role of agribusiness in establishing the AoA rules was not only as a possible beneficiary, but as a participant. Dan Amstutz, former vice president of the international grain trading company Cargill, literally drafted the AoA negotiating text while he was working at the Office of the U.S. Trade Representative; he later returned to the private sector in the grain trade industry.[28]

For many wealthy countries, the agriculture negotiations were among the most controversial elements of the Uruguay Round. The Uruguay Round negotiation ground to a halt over agricultural disputes between the countries: The U.S. was pressuring the EU and Japan to cut agriculture protections down to the level used by the U.S. Many other countries sought yet deeper reductions, and several delegations from the "Cairns Group" of food-exporting nations stalked out of the Uruguay Round talks over agriculture issues. The impasse put the Uruguay Round in peril, and critics held their breath hoping the threat of the WTO had been avoided. GATT representatives left Geneva as the 1993 Christmas season loomed, with many concluding that the Uruguay Round was dead. Meanwhile, the U.S. and EU opened secret bilateral talks held at Blair House, a diplomatic building in Washington, D.C., across the street from the White House. These sessions resulted in a bilateral rewrite of the draft agriculture text, transforming it into the current AoA. One prominent element of the Blair House deal was a change in the base year from which required cuts in domestic support would be calculated. By choosing 1986–1988 as the base year, the U.S. and EU were actually able to raise support levels from those then in effect while still conforming with WTO rules.

Ironically, the AoA was advertised to developing countries as the element of the WTO that was to benefit them. Many developing countries' economies were focused on agricultural production, particularly bulk commodities, with the majority of their populations living on the land. Poor countries were promised market access for agricultural exports in exchange for their acceptance of the more draconian WTO agreements to which they strongly objected—especially the provisions contained in the TRIPs (see Chapter 3 and below) and TRIMs (see Chapter 6) agreements.

The developing world's trade-off in accepting TRIPs and TRIMs for the AoA soon proved to be a double threat to food security and sovereignty in the developing world. International agribusinesses obtained more control over commodity prices and supplies, and gained the WTO-enforced monopoly patent protections on plant varieties, seeds and genetically modified crops.

At the 2001 Doha WTO Ministerial, the EU joined by the U.S. and most other wealthy countries again promised increased market access for poor countries' agricultural products into the industrialized world if the developing countries lifted their opposition to establishing new WTO agreements on vital issues such as investment and procurement policies (see Chapter 6 on "new" Doha issues). Yet the initial Uruguay Round promises to cut rich-country subsidies and to open developed-country markets to developing-country agricultural imports has failed to materialize. Instead, "market access"—the cutting of quotas and tariffs—allowed agribusinesses in the developed countries to dump subsidized imports on developing nations to gain control of those domestic markets by competing against domestically produced food grown by unsubsidized farmers.[29] A study by the UN's Food and Agriculture Organization found that for the 14 developing countries the FAO examined after reduction of agricultural tariffs, the growth in imports exceeded the commensurate growth in exports and that the value of food imports during 1995–1998 compared to 1990–1994 rose between 30–168%.[30] Although industrialized countries promised that reducing agriculture tariffs would open export opportunities and reduce poverty, the large rural populations in developing countries instead faced increased imports—much of it subsidized and thus sold at prices below local farmers' costs of production—that threaten their livelihoods.

The AoA includes rules to open access to countries' domestic markets by cutting tariffs and eliminating quotas, to reduce the subsidization of agricultural exports and to constrain farm policies that provide domestic support.

Market Access, Tariffication, Tariff and Quota Reductions

Prior to the AoA, the trade in many agricultural products was regulated not solely by tariffs, but also by product-specific quotas. The AoA prohibited countries from applying a range of quantitative restrictions on imports.[31] Quotas were frozen at 1986–1988 levels, unless a quota was below 5% of domestic production (which would mean almost no imports were allowed). In such instances, countries were required to raise their quotas, allowing imports up to at least 5% of the volume of domestic consumption in each commodity and food. Products entering under the quota were charged a WTO-bound tariff rate with a higher tariff applied to imports in excess of the quotas.[32] To conform with these rules, the U.S. eliminated the Section 22 Program, under which the U.S. president had set quotas on products such as sugar, dairy products, peanuts and cotton since the 1930s.[33]

These AoA rules also required developing countries to phase out quantitative restrictions, making their own agriculture sectors especially vulnerable given the fact that AoA tariff cuts would increase imports, including imports of subsidized food. The result for small farmers in the developing world is that they are literally drowning in imports as the glut created in domestic markets has crashed the prices paid farmers for their crops.

To phase out quotas, the AoA required countries to immediately replace their quotas with tariffs designed to provide the same level of protection through a process called "tariffication." (Practically, this might translate into a strict quota being converted into a 400% tariff.) Then, WTO countries were required to schedule reductions in these former quota tariff rates from the initial level bound for each product. Industrialized countries agreed to lower these bound tariffs by an average of 36% within six years on all agricultural products, with a minimum tariff cut of 15% on each product. Developing countries agreed to lower their tariffs by 24% on all agricultural products within 10 years, with a minimum 10% tariff cut on any specific goods.[34]

Export Subsidies, Export Finance Credits and Export Dumping

The proliferation of agricultural export subsidies was a primary motivation for establishing the Agreement on Agriculture. The AoA requires WTO countries to bind their level of export subsidies and then reduce these subsidies in equal amounts each year for six years by 21% of the volume of export subsidies and by 36% for budgetary outlays that fund these subsidies.[35] The approach means that countries that had the resources to have export subsidies in place when the AoA began will remain in an advantaged position relative to those who did not. Developing countries were permitted to maintain internal transportation subsidies and marketing subsidies.[36] Export subsidies include:

- direct subsidies tied to the product's export performance;
- below-cost sales overseas by governments of noncommercial agriculture stocks, such as government sales of surplus agriculture stocks;
- taxes on production used to subsidize some portion of the product for export, such as market promotional fees;
- government payment of export marketing costs, such as freight and handling costs;
- transportation subsidies for export goods; and
- subsidies on basic goods used in processed food exports.[37]

The AoA did not discipline a variety of "hidden" export subsidies such as below-market government financing of exports including the U.S. export credit programs. In the ongoing AoA negotiations these subsidies are now also on the table.

Reduction of Domestic Support

Under WTO rules, domestic agricultural policies are categorized by whether they have a significant effect on production and trade.

- Policies that have a substantial impact on the patterns and flow of trade are classified as "Amber Box";
- Policies that are not deemed to have a major effect on production and trade are classified as "Green Box"; and
- Policies that link government payments specifically to production-limiting programs are classified as "Blue Box."

Under AoA rules, Amber Box programs are frozen at pre-AoA levels and then must be reduced. The system for this reduction is based on an Aggregate Measurement of Support (AMS) which must be lowered by 20% over six years for developed countries or 13% over 10 years for developing countries. The AMS calculation includes all domestic support policies that are considered to have a significant effect on the volume of production, although countries are not required to reduce Amber Box programs of direct payments to producers if the total support does not exceed 5% of total agricultural production for that product or 10% for developing countries.[38]

Green Box programs are exempt from the required subsidies reductions. This includes warehousing food against famine, agricultural research, pest eradication, agricultural training programs, food and agriculture inspection programs, marketing and promotional programs, infrastructure, and direct payments not connected to agricultural production, such as income insurance and social safety-net programs and environmental programs.[39] Additionally, developing countries can provide some domestic support for development programs under the "special and differential treatment" provisions of the AoA. Blue Box programs that limit production to fixed areas or a set number of livestock are also exempt from AoA reduction requirements. Further, the U.S. and EU also can exclude Blue Box measures, such as direct payments to farmers and land set aside, from calculations of AMS. This concept of "decoupled income support" allows direct payments to support farmers' incomes, so that the overall cost of production will not be reflected in the commodities prices. Perversely, these exclusions mean that incomes of some farmers in countries wealthy enough to do so will be directly paid by governments and will thus be insulated from trade or market fluctuations. On the other hand, developing-world farmers cannot rely on direct income support from their governments and must survive on the basis of their actual production, leaving these farmers vulnerable to manipulated global trade patterns and artificially low international agricultural commodity prices caused in part by the subsidies of the rich countries. Direct payments also keep afloat a system that allows corporations to continually lower prices paid to farmers and engage in dumping without risking the total collapse of agricultural production.

Moreover, financial limitations meant that most developing countries had used tariffs and quotas as agriculture policy tools and had low or no subsidy regimes in place, and now, under the AoA, they are prohibited from establishing such programs or raising existing low levels to help their farmers compete against subsidized imports.[40]

ECONOMIC OUTCOMES
OF THE AOA

The independent farmers who criticized the WTO underestimated the devastating toll it would take on rural communities—both in rich countries and in the developing world. Newly empowered by the terms of the WTO and its domestic implementation, transnational agribusinesses were positioned to play farmers from different countries off of each other. Absent the domestic agricultural safety nets, small farms could not survive on the prices being paid by agribusinesses, which could manipulate prices by hoarding and then at harvest times releasing supplies of commodities. Independent farmers worldwide have seen agricultural prices plummet and farm incomes collapse after domestic agriculture safety-net programs were dismantled to comply with the AoA. Startling examples of this phenomenon can be seen in India and Mexico, where surges of cheap agricultural commodities first destabilized and then allowed agribusiness to capture local agricultural markets.[41] In the absence of small-farm safeguard programs, farm income has been slashed, and rural economies devastated.[42]

That the AoA—and its focus on increasing the volume of agriculture trade—has resulted in numerous countries rewriting their domestic farm policy to the detriment of domestic small farmers is particularly obscene because for farmers worldwide the domestic market is the most stable and reliable. Until recently, developing countries grew 90% of the food they consume domestically.[43] However, the AoA rules have moved more countries into reliance on an export-growth agriculture strategy that has developing-country farmers competing to cross-trade internationally at suppressed world prices the very crops that otherwise would be consumed at home.[44]

However, the crash in prices paid to farmers for their crops is not being passed on to consumers, most of whom saw prices rise at least at the rate of inflation during the same period that commodity prices collapsed. A UN Food and Agriculture Organization study of the post–Uruguay Round climate for farmers and food in 14 developing countries found that the cost of food imports rose in all the countries between 1995 and 1999.[45] Between the 1974–1979 period compared to 2000, consumer food prices in the U.S. have risen by 250%, while the prices that farmers receive have remained flat or even declined during that period.[46] According to U.S. Census Bureau figures, real prices for food eaten at home in the U.S. rose by 32.0% under the WTO (1994 and 2002).[47] A 2000 study of feedlot and retail prices for beef found that an East Texas feedlot sold a 1,000-pound choice steer for $620, but, by the time the meat was sold in the supermarket, it cost consumers the equivalent of $1,697 per steer—nearly three times the price the feedlot received which itself was greater than the price the rancher obtained from the feedlot.[48] Under NAFTA between 1994 and 1999, Canadian farmers received less than $C5 a bushel for wheat, but the prices for bread from the same bushel rose from about $C80 a bushel to $C90 a bushel over the same period.[49] As well in Mexico, the prices of the staple food corn tortillas have actually risen since NAFTA, despite a flood of cheap corn imports into Mexico which have collapsed Mexican corn commodity prices.[50]

While independent farmers and rural communities have struggled, transnational businesses have enjoyed a bonanza. Commodity trading, seed, chemical and processing agribusinesses have been liberated by the AoA-required deregulation to cross national borders in order to create new export platforms which play farmers in different countries against one another. Commodity export dumping has been steadily increasing since the WTO went into effect, according to a recent Institute for Agriculture and Trade Policy study. The U.S. export price of wheat in 1995 was 23% below the U.S. cost of production; by 2001 the export price was 44% below the cost of production, and the dumping margin for cotton rose from 17% below the cost of production in 1995 to 57% in 2001.[51]

This dumping is facilitated by the significant concentration in the agribusiness sector. Monopolies usually only imply high prices. But in the case of agriculture, they result in low prices for farmers and jacked-up consumer prices because the corporations are not producers but traders in agriculture commodities. By 2002, the largest six grain-handling facilities companies controlled three quarters of the world's cereal commodity market.[52] The top five food retailers controlled 42% of retail food sales in the U.S. in 2000, up from 24% in 1997.[53] By 2000, the top four U.S. cattle processors controlled 81% of the U.S. market—12% higher than in 1990. The top four pork packers in the U.S. controlled 59% of the market; and in 2002 the top four mills controlled 61% of the market.[54]

Meanwhile, even in very poor countries, costs of production are rising because transnational agribusiness companies have consolidated their control of seeds and other inputs. The top 10 seed companies controlled 31% of the $24.7 billion commercial seed market worldwide in 1999.[55] Although not one of the individual seed producers had a measurable share of the world seed market in 1980, 10 firms controlled one third of the world market in 2000.[56] Costly, nonrenewable, unreliable seeds and pesticidal and herbicidal chemicals needed to maintain genetically modified crops all have added to the costs of farming.

According to a landmark report on a recent epidemic of farmer suicides in India, the shift from open-pollinated farm-saved seeds to nonrenewable hybrids and genetically modified seeds has led to high levels of crop failure and farm indebtedness—leading factors in farmer suicides.[57]

The Food and Agriculture Policy and Research Institute 2001 survey of representative farms predicts that the next five years will be tough on most U.S. farmers. Contrary to the farm-economy boom promised at the time of WTO's passage, the study found that 76% of farms are expected to have a negative cash flow between 2000–2005.[58] Data from USDA's Economic Research Service show that farm debt in the U.S. also has risen steadily since the WTO went into effect, after falling during the late 1980s.[59]

In Canada, dropping prices meant that farmers' net income declined 19% between 1989–1999 although the volume of Canadian agricultural exports doubled during that period.[60] Yet in 1998 the return on equity for the cereal companies buying and using Canada's commodities such as Kellogg's, Quaker Oats and General Mills was 56%, 156% and 222% respectively.[61] However while the number of independent farmers has dropped under WTO, agribusiness giants such as ConAgra and Monsanto (now Pharmacia) had significant earnings gains. ConAgra's profits grew 45% from $437 in 1994 to $638 million in 2001, and Monsanto's profits more than doubled between 1994–2001, from $622 million to $1.5 billion.[62] Global commodity broker giants, not weather or sweat equity, were able to determine both supplies and prices of many commodities.

How Globalization Is Creating Hunger

While the volume of food now produced could feed the world, food and seed distribution and access problems leave many hungry.[63] The FAO estimates that 156 million children under five years old were malnourished in 2001 and more than half the deaths of children in that age group were attributable to malnutrition.[64] Although the percentage of malnourished people declined slightly (3%) during the 1990s, by 2000 there were still 799 million malnourished people in the developing world.[65] Between the 1990–1992 period and 1998–2000, several regions saw the number and percentage of malnourished people increase, including Central Africa, the Near East, Central America and Oceania.[66]

Hunger is not a result of lack of food but lack of access to food.[67] Thus, anti-hunger campaigns worldwide are calling for food sovereignty—control of food and farming by those who will eat the food—as the only guarantee of food security.

Case Study: U.S. Corn Dumping under NAFTA into Mexico Devastates Mexico's Rural Economy and Genetic Diversity of Corn

By guaranteeing new market access and eliminating Mexico's food security policies, NAFTA opened Mexico to imports of corn bought at rock-bottom prices from U.S. and Canadian farmers.[68] The import prices at which commodity-trading giants offered corn for sale in Mexico was well below the floor price Mexican farmers had received before NAFTA.[69] Some results were predictable: Mexican farmers who were unable to compete with U.S. and Canadian growers quit farming; and as a result Mexico has become increasingly dependent on corn imports. Mexico's increased dependency on staple food imported from the U.S. and Canada continues to threaten poor Mexican consumers' access to food: When foreign supplies of staple crops decline, the supply for Mexico dries up. A past U.S. corn shortage in 1996 resulted in the malnourishment of one out of five Mexican children.[70] According to the Mexican Institute of Social Security, since NAFTA, 158,000 Mexican children die each year before reaching five years of age from illnesses related to nutrition.[71] Post-NAFTA Mexico no longer has policies to ensure it can feed itself.

A result directly contradictory to free trade theory, however, is that corn prices for Mexican consumers rose despite the fact that corn growers received lower prices.[72] The price paid to farmers for corn in Mexico declined by 46.2% between 1993–1999.[73] At the end of 1998, Mexico ended the decades-old price controls over tortillas and ceased subsidizing tortilla mills.[74] Within one year of these price caps and subsidies being cut, consumer prices for tortilla dough in Mexico had risen 22%, tortilla prices in Mexico City rose by 50% and rural tortilla prices rose even higher.[75] Eliminating the tortilla protections meant that poor Mexican consumers, who receive half of their caloric intake in tortillas, were forced either to purchase the increasingly expensive tortillas made from imported U.S. corn or to go with less food.[76]

Other results were less widely predicted: the importation of the genetically identical monoculture corn from the U.S. and Canada is threatening the continued existence of the numerous traditional varieties of corn grown in Mexico where corn has been cultivated for about 5,000 years, in over 41 distinct racial complexes and thousands of recognized varieties. Approximately 60% of Mexican corn growers cultivate these locally bred, locally adopted corn varieties. As Mexican farmers who grow the indigenous varieties of corn are driven off the land, the genetic diversity of Mexico's corn is dwindling, which could lead to the destruction of the many wild corn varieties that are vital gene repositories for domesticated corn in Mexico.[77]

Mexican Corn Economics and Livelihoods

When NAFTA was being negotiated, corn produced in the U.S. cost $110 a ton at the U.S.-Mexico border, and farmers producing corn in Mexico received a guaranteed floor price of $240 a ton, the cost of production for farmers in Mexico.[78] The

Mexican government also set a price ceiling on tortillas. During this period, corn was Mexico's most important crop, accounting for 60% of cultivated land with 3 million producers.[79] NAFTA negotiators knew that cheap grain commodity imports would devastate Mexican peasant farmers.[80]

The Mexican government maintained a guaranteed floor price by managing the supply of corn, only allowing imports if domestic production failed to cover demand. NAFTA opened Mexico's corn market to U.S. imports, and ended its guaranteed floor-price subsidies for Mexican growers, reasoning that it would be able to import cheaper U.S. corn.[81] Moreover, although NAFTA originally permitted a 15-year phase-in of quota elimination for the corn sector, the government decided to eliminate corn quotas within 30 months.

The predictable result was that corn imports surged into Mexico, leading to reductions in prices paid to farmers 48% in 30 months of NAFTA.[82] Total U.S. corn shipments to Mexico grew 17-fold between 1993 and 2001 to 5.6 million tons and accounted for 25% of Mexican corn consumption compared to a pre-NAFTA figure of 2%.[83] Moreover, Mexican farmers receive very little in government support—typical farmers receive about $720 a year in government subsidies.[84]

Within a year, Mexican production of corn and other basic grains fell by half, and millions of peasants lost a significant source of income.[85] Mexican farmers could not compete with U.S. and Canadian imports, and millions migrated to urban areas in search of work.[86] Mexico's urban population has exploded, increasing by 44% over the course of NAFTA.[87] While the percentage of the Mexican population in rural areas declined by 4.2% between1995–2000, the population of Mexicans living in urban areas grew by 4.3%. By 2002, 600 Mexican farmers were being forced off the land every day.[88] Many more Mexican farmers and their families will be displaced in the coming years; some estimates run to as many as 15 million people, or about one in six Mexicans.[89]

When more NAFTA tariff cuts were phased in January 2003, public protest in Mexico over NAFTA's devastation of Mexico's rural economies exploded. The movement known as The Countryside Can't Take It Anymore (*El Campo No Aguanta Más*) demanded revocation of NAFTA's farm provisions.[90] In December 2002, angry Mexican farmers—including one on horseback—broke through a police cordon and forced their way into the Mexican Congress.[91] In early January 2003, hundreds of thousands of irate Mexican small farmers staged protests at seaports, airports, and two U.S. border crossings, and shut down power to demonstrate opposition to the flood of U.S. agricultural exports coming into Mexico.[92] Hundreds of farmers blocked the highway and prevented border crossings between Ciudad Juárez and El Paso.[93] In the second week of January 2003, farmers began a hunger strike at the Angel of Independence statue in Mexico City until Mexican President Vicente Fox agreed to negotiate with the farmers.[94] Although Fox did trigger emergency short-term safeguards slowing some imports, he also has responded to U.S. inquiries by reaffirming Mexico's commitment to complying with NAFTA rules. The majority of protesters at the Cancún WTO Ministerial were campesinos devastated by NAFTA.

THE WTO TRIPs RULES ENDANGER FOOD SECURITY*

Despite enormous growth in food trade, only 15% of the world's food supply is traded.[95] A large share of the world's population relies on subsistence farming for its food supply and harvesting and saving seeds is the only means by which subsistence farmers are able to grow crops year after year.

TRIPs Agreement rules regarding exactly what sort of intellectual property rights protections countries must provide for plant varieties are vague. However, what is clear is that WTO member countries must provide new property rights in this area. The TRIPs text technically allows countries to create their own sui generis regime (and thus does not exclusively require patent rules in this area),[96] but it is entirely unclear what alternative regime would pass WTO muster. For instance, countries that have attempted to take the measures necessary to protect against biopiracy's plundering and commodification of indigenous flora and fauna have been threatened with WTO challenges.

When corporations patent seeds, local farmers must pay annual fees they cannot afford to use the seed type, even if the seed was the product of breeding conducted over generations by the very ancestors of the farmers themselves. The same rules apply to genetically modified seeds. For instance, Monsanto requires farmers who purchase genetically modified seeds to agree not to save seeds for next year's crop, and it posts signs threatening investigations and legal actions against farmers breaking the contract.[97]

Patents on seeds and plant varieties have been rapidly increasing since the WTO went into effect. Between 1991–1993, an average of eight patents a year were awarded on corn and soybeans; by the 1999–2001 period, 281 patents were being awarded each year for these two crops.[98] In contrast, the TRIPs Agreement contains no protections for indigenous communities that have been planting and crossbreeding strains for centuries to develop that perfectly adapted variety that a bioprospector can collect and have patented to some distant corporation.

Seed Sovereignty = Food Sovereignty

It was not only pharmaceutical but also agribusiness companies that wanted new uniform global intellectual property rules to be established during the Uruguay Round negotiations. The TRIPs agreement was not so much negotiated by GATT members as it was imposed by aggressive U.S. government and corporate teams, both pushing an agenda handcrafted by some of the world's largest and most powerful corporations. The basic framework for the TRIPs patent system was conceived and shaped in a joint statement presented to the GATT Secretariat in June 1988 by the Intellectual Property Committee (IPC) of industry associations of the U.S., Japan and EU.[99]

---

* The section of this chapter covering the TRIPs Agreement, seeds and food sovereignty draws heavily from the work of Vandana Shiva, director of the Research Foundation for Science, Technology and Natural Resource Policy in India, with her permission.

James Enyart, director of international affairs of Monsanto, narrates how the corporate IPC coalition *drafted* the TRIPs Agreement.

> Industry has identified a major problem for international trade. It crafted a solution, reduced it to a concrete proposal and sold it to our own and other governments. The industries and traders of world commerce have played simultaneously the role of patients, the diagnosticians and the prescribing physicians.[100]

One of the most significant changes the TRIPs Agreement required WTO signatory countries to make to their domestic intellectual property rules was the expansion of what is patentable. Article 27.1 of the TRIPs Agreement on Patentable Subject Matter states that patents shall be available for any inventions, whether products or processes, in all fields of technology, provided that they are new, involve an inventive step and are capable of industrial application. Every country was required to implement these policies domestically. Yet, in many countries, food, plants, seeds and life-forms were excluded from patenting. For instance, the goal of India's pre-WTO law on intellectual property was to build up indigenous capacity, create self-reliance in medicine, and control prices for food and medicine to ensure these essential items are accessible to the poor. From a corporate perspective, such a policy meant lost profit potential.

The TRIPs Agreement also includes a weak definition of what qualifies as an "innovation." The TRIPs notion of innovation allows a distant company to slightly modify an existing process or "product" and then patent it as new. People everywhere innovate and create. Given the fact that the generations-old innovations of subsistence farmers and forest dwellers are not patented, a foreign bioprospecting firm can seize ownership over such knowledge by slightly modifying it and patenting it.

Since most innovation in the public domain is for domestic, local and public use, not for international trade, TRIPs' rules effectively enforce the rights of foreign corporations to monopolize production and distribution of seeds—and thus of food—to the detriment of citizens and small producers worldwide. However at the Doha Ministerial, a broad TRIPs review and reform agenda was blocked by wealthy countries with major pharmaceutical industries, and the Doha Ministerial Declaration reaffirms the TRIPs Agreement and includes only a promise to study the TRIPs Agreement's impact on the Convention on Biological Diversity and "protection of traditional knowledge."[101] The problems created by patents on seeds (a review of TRIPs Art. 27.3 [b]) was not addressed, nor is it on the agenda for Cancún. One of the first disputes in WTO was the challenge initiated by the U.S. against India's patent laws.

Case 1: Indian Parliament Coerced into WTO TRIPs Implementation

When the Uruguay Round Agreement came to the Indian Parliament for approval, the Parliament refused to approve the TRIPs Agreement and adopted only the other aspects of the Uruguay Round.[102] The prime minister of India then issued an executive decree that enacted the TRIPs rules on pharmaceutical and agricultural chemical patents in late 1994.[103] The executive decree had to be upheld by both houses of parliament, which twice refused to amend Indian patent law. Plants and methods of agriculture were excluded from patentability,[104] to ensure that the seed, the first link in the food chain, was held as a common-property resource in the public domain, and that farmers' inalienable right to save, exchange, and improve seed was protected.[105]

However, under enormous pressure from the U.S. and others, the Indian government developed an administrative procedure for keeping track of patent applications until the TRIPs Agreement was to go into effect.[106] The U.S. challenged India's policy at the WTO.[107] In September 1997, a WTO panel ruled that India was required to establish statutory procedures for receiving applications for patents on pharmaceutical and agricultural chemicals immediately, so that, upon its full implementation of the TRIPs Agreement, patents could be backdated to the date of filing.[108] The WTO panel ruled that India's administrative patent-tracking procedure does not trump Indian law, and thus does not give corporations a reasonable expectation that their patent applications—submitted while it was still illegal to patent—will be reviewed and accepted retroactively as required once the new rules go into effect in 2006.[109] In March 1999, the Indian Parliament satisfied the WTO's demand and approved the TRIPs Agreement implementing legislation amending the Patents Act.[110]

This first amendment introduced exclusive marketing rights and a "mailbox" arrangement to implement Articles 70.8 and 70.9 of the TRIPs Agreement, allowing companies to apply for patents prior to the agreement's effective date. However, pressure continued on India to change its patent law further. During a period of political crisis in late February 2002—genocidal reprisals against Muslims in Gujarat following the burning to death of a train of Hindu women and children; mounting terrorism inside Kashmir; and the impending threat of war between India and Pakistan—a second amendment of the Indian Patent Act was slipped through Parliament with little notice.[111]

The major change in the patent regime achieved through the second amendment was not in the area of medicines and drugs, but in seeds and plants, especially genetically engineered seeds, changing the definition of what can be patented and thus opening the floodgates of patenting genetically engineered seeds. The old Indian Patent Act of 1970 excluded the following from being patentable:

Any process for the medical, surgical, creative, prophylactic or other treatment of human beings or any process for a similar treatment of animals or plants or to render them free of disease or to increase their economic value or that of their products.

The amendments eliminated plants from the list, meaning that a method or process modification of a plant can now be counted as an invention and be patented.[112] Thus the method of genetic modification to produce Bt cotton, by introducing genes of a bacterium (*Bacillus thuringiensis*) in cotton to produce toxins to kill the bollworm, can now be patented. Many in India viewed this second amendment as satisfying extended efforts by Monsanto to change India's policy so that the company could profit in India from GM crops.[113]

Monsanto Charges Farmer Licensing Fee After His Field Is Contaminated with GM Plants

TRIPs rules mean that agribusiness giants can demand fees from farmers wherever the company's seed or variety appears. Yet often, modified plant genes reach non-GM crops through wind or pollinators. Drifting GM pollen is one of the most common forms of GM contamination.[114] One Canadian farmer, Percy Schmeiser, whose non-GM canola field was contaminated by Monsanto's Roundup Ready Canola, was successfully sued by Monsanto for $19,832 in damages for violating patent and $153,000 in court costs for "theft" of "intellectual property" when he saved seeds from his contaminated field for the next year's crop and planted them.[115] Other farmers have also been sued.

WTO TRIPs Agreement Facilitates Biopiracy of Developing Country Resources

Many WTO member countries in the developing world are turning to other arenas to write policy that protects communities and subsistence farmers from the trend toward agribusiness monopolization of the food supply. However, the WTO TRIPs Agreement threatens to undermine the principles and enforcement of these other international agreements, including two main ones. The 1992 Convention on Biological Diversity obligates parties to "respect, preserve and maintain knowledge, innovations and practices of indigenous and local communities" relevant to biodiversity.[116] The Convention acknowledges that communities and subsistence farmers have been responsible for the development of important agricultural crops, and that they have safeguarded the tremendous biodiversity that agribusiness now seeks to use as its source material. The second agreement, the "Principles of Farmer's Rights," was adopted under the United Nations' Food and Agriculture Organization in 1987 in order to devise legal and financial instruments to support farming communities in the ongoing development and conservation of the seeds and technologies their ancestors cultivated collectively over many generations.[117]

The TRIPs Agreement conflicts with these agreements' attempts to prevent "biopiracy"—when foreign corporations hunt out in developing countries indigenous seeds, herbs and traditional processes for obtaining medicinal or pesticidal benefits from local flora and fauna and seek to have them patented as the property of the company, even if indigenous communities have been cultivating the crop or processing a plant into medicinal use for hundreds or even thousands of years. To get the patent, companies claim that they have altered the plants, making them unique, even if that alteration does not change the plant in any meaningful way.[118] Since patent examiners often do not have access to facilities to test the alleged "new trait," the patent is often granted, and the only way to challenge the patent's validity is through civil litigation, which is too costly for indigenous communities to undertake.[119]

Once the TRIPs Agreement is fully implemented, developing-country WTO members will have the obligation to enforce seed companies' patent rights by either uprooting "illegal" crops or collecting the fees from subsistence farmers. Failure to do so would leave the country in violation of its TRIPs obligations and susceptible to trade sanctions.[120]

Indeed, patent rights for hundreds of indigenous species already may have been siphoned off into state or regional agricultural centers and even into the hands of private companies. A collaborative study by the Rural Advancement Foundation International and Heritage Seed Curators Australia found nearly 150 cases of research institutions and businesses applying for patents or licenses for naturally occurring plant varieties, some of which had been farmed for generations.[121]

Threat 1: U.S. Charges Thai Anti-Biopiracy Policy Violates WTO

In 1997, legislation was introduced in the Thai parliament that was designed to protect traditional medicines by granting them legal protections available to other forms of unique knowledge. The legislation would allow Thai traditional healers to register their traditional medicines so that, in the event that a biotechnology or pharmaceutical company sought a patent on the substance or process, the company would have to negotiate with the traditional healer.[122]

The impetus behind the legislation was a history of pharmaceutical raids on various Thai plants and insects. For instance, "Plao Noi," a Thai plant used to cure ulcers,[123] was patented by a Japanese company. Thais lost all rights to market it.[124] Thailand is also currently trying to protect its right to market its jasmine rice against a U.S. rice product called "Jasmati" that Thai officials say misleads consumers into thinking it was the same as Thai fragrant rice.[125] In December 1995, the International Rice Research Institute gave Jasmine germplasm to U.S. researchers without securing a Material Transfer Agreement to prevent the U.S. researchers from patenting the donated germplasm.[126] Rigorous defense of this patent by the U.S. patentholder, a company called Rice-Tec, could cost Thailand its $1 billion in annual Jasmine rice exports.[127] In November 2001, 1,500 farmers and activists demonstrated at the U.S. embassy in Bangkok over the Jasmine rice patent and other intellectual property issues.[128] In late 2002, Thailand continued to press for the revocation of the Rice-Tec patent on Jasmati, even though Thailand's efforts have failed, to date.[129]

In response to the Thai traditional-medicine registration legislation, the U.S. State Department sent a letter in April 1997 to the Royal Thai Government (RTG) warning that "Washington believes that such a registration system could constitute a possible violation of the TRIPs Agreement and hamper medical research into these compounds."[130] The State Department letter requested a copy of the draft legislation and official responses to eleven questions, beginning with the question: "What is the relationship of the proposal to the granting of patent protection in Thailand?" and ending: "Does the RTG envision a contractual system to handle relationships between Thai healers and foreign researchers in the future?"[131] Already Thailand was on a U.S. list of countries against whom trade action was threatened for failure to protect U.S. companies' copyrights and patents sufficiently.[132] The U.S. also had threatened Thailand over compulsory licensing of AIDS treatments. Attack on the traditional medicines law caused a firestorm—Thailand faced extreme U.S. pressure to pass new policies to implement the TRIPs agreement but was being threatened for designing a policy that covered its needs. On a parallel track, a "Plant and Plant Varieties Protection Act" also had been introduced, as well as other intellectual property policies the U.S. supported.

On June 30, 1997, more than 200 nongovernmental organizations and individuals from dozens of countries around the world signed a letter to U.S. Secretary of State Madeleine Albright expressing "concern at the manner in which the United States government is intervening in the domestic affairs of numerous other nations regarding their intellectual property laws."[133] The Thai law was seen as a test of the TRIPs Agreement's provision (Article 27-3-b), mentioned above, that allows countries to develop sui generis systems for the protection of plant varieties. Ultimately, the Thai government signed an "IPR Action Plan" with the U.S. and passed amendments the U.S. had pressured for to its Trademark Act and Patent Act.[134] A version of the traditional medicines act went into effect in May 2000. The law covers all types of plant species used for healing, and allows Thai healers to register traditional medicines. Companies or researchers seeking to use Thai traditional knowledge must obtain permission from the registered party. However, the law is only effective within Thailand. It is possible to use the registered knowledge or plant variety abroad without consent and the Thai government cannot force the payment as required for domestic use.[135]

U.S. Seed Company Raids Mexican Biodiversity

In the early 1990s, a Mexican-American businesswoman named Rebecca Gilliland started importing into the U.S. the yellow Mayacoba beans that she had eaten as a child.[136] The market took off immediately, among Latinos in the U.S. and among Anglos as well. In 1994, she imported half a million pounds of Mayacoba beans, and by 1999 she imported 6 million pounds—a 12-fold increase in five years.[137]

In 1999, a Colorado farmer named Larry M. Proctor applied for a patent in the U.S. for a common Mexican bean. According to Proctor's patent application on behalf of the U.S. seed company called Pod-Ners, the "enola" bean variety was cultivated by him over three years after starting with a package of dry beans purchased in Mexico in 1994 and brought to the U.S. Proctor defined the "new" enola bean variety as a bean that was derived from cultivation from the field bean *phaseolus vulgaris* of a certain yellow color.[138] The patent was approved in 1999, along with a plant-variety protection certificate which grants Pod-Ners the sole right to market the "new" bean commercially.[139]

In October 1999, Ms. Gilliland received a letter from Pod-Ners informing her that she was importing enola beans, and that they were patented.[140] The Pod-Ners letter said it would bring suit against the farmers and distributors for violating the Pod-Ners patent on the enola bean for selling Mayacoba beans, and asked for a 6¢-a-pound royalty fee from the Mexican farmers for the sale of beans the color of enola beans.[141] This would amount to a 23% surcharge on beans that sold for 27¢ a pound in Los Angeles, making them economically unviable for Mexican farmers and U.S. importers.[142] In October 2000, a bean-growers group representing 1,000 farmers in the Mexican state of Sinaloa was shocked when Pod-Ners brought a patent-infringement suit against its export of Mayacoba beans that Pod-Ners claimed was covered by the enola bean patent.[143] With the patent enforced, acreage of Mayacoba beans declined 76% between the 1999–2000 season and the 2000–2001 season.[144]

The rare and unusual twist to this case is that the affected bean farmers organization, the Asociación de Agricultores del Rio Fuerte Sur, the importer Tutuli Produce International and the Mexican government countersued Pod-Ners, charging that the U.S. patent was invalid because the enola bean is neither new nor nonobvious, qualities required by U.S. patent law; because it relied too heavily on color as a determinant; and because there was insufficient time for Pod-Ners to have bred a genetically different variety.[145]

In essence, the Mexican lawsuit argued that Proctor did not breed enola, but rather he stole it from Mexican genetic stocks. Archeologists have discovered yellow beans that predate the Incas in a cave in Peru.[146] The Mexican government claims the bean was identified by genetic fingerprinting and registered with the agricultural department in the state of Sinaloa in 1978, 16 years before Proctor and Pod-Ners filed for the "enola" patent in the U.S.[147] Moreover, plant and bean breeders and agricultural scientists believe that to breed a new variety of bean typically takes a decade and that a genetically distinct variety could not be bred in three seasons.[148] While the Mexican farmers had been growing the yellow Mayacoba bean for generations, the patent for the Colorado-bred "enola" bean (named after Proctor's wife) was awarded in 1999.

The Mexican government estimated it could cost at least $200,000 to overturn the enola patent, but determined that the expense was necessary since yellow beans, which constitute over 90% of bean consumption in northwestern Mexico, would require a 6¢-per-pound payment to a U.S. seed company unless the patent was overturned.[149] Meanwhile, one Mexican bean farmer, claiming that Pod-Ners had sent letters to bean importers throughout the U.S. discouraging them from buying yellow beans from Mexico, reports that already the patent-enforcement action has resulted in a wipeout of exports and a huge drop in farm income for Mexican farmers cultivating the beans.[150]

(continued)

In December 2000, the International Center for Tropical Agriculture (CIAT), one of 16 international research plant and agriculture gene bank groups that hold germplasm (genetic material) in the public commons instead of private hands, joined the opposition to the enola patent and filed a formal request with the U.S. Patent and Trademark Office to reconsider its awarding of the enola patent to Proctor.[151] CIAT's petition notes that it has the world's largest collection of beans in its gene bank, more than 28,000 varieties, and 260 of the varieties are yellow, with six of those being very similar to the patented enola.[152] In February 2001, the U.S. Patent and Trademark Office determined that there were sufficient merits to proceed with the challenge.[153]

While the patent case worked its way through the labyrinth of administrative procedures at the U.S. Patent and Trademark Office, Pod-Ners sued 16 Colorado bean processors and two bean marketers in December 2001.[154] The majority of the royalty fees Pod-Ners has collected for its enola beans have gone toward its legal fees.[155] In November 2002, Pod-Ners dropped its patent-infringement case against the bean distributors after they agreed to pay an undisclosed settlement and come to a royalty arrangement with Pod-Ners.[156] While this rare patent challenge moves slowly through the U.S. Patent and Trademark Office, farmers in the U.S. and bean marketers are paying royalties to Pod-Ners—and Mexican bean farmers are now unable to export their similar beans to the U.S.

Food Fight at the WTO: GMOs

The rapid development of new technologies in the area of biology, agriculture, medicine, and food production exceeds the speed with which we are able to assess their public health, social, environmental, and economic impacts, and thus hampers our ability to create adequate public policies to address their effects. In no case has this been more evident than in the development of genetically modified organisms. The inevitable collision between the primacy WTO's rules give unregulated global commerce and the public's concern over GMOs made the brewing WTO battle over GMOs foreseeable and guarantees to spotlight how the WTO conflicts with accountable public policy making.

GMOs are living organisms created through genetic engineering that permits scientists to transplant the genes of one species into those of another for the purpose of transferring desirable characteristics, for example, transplanting fish genes into tomatoes to improve their antifreezing characteristics or improving resistance to disease, pesticides and herbicides.[157]

GMO technology raises serious concerns in many areas where the WTO has proven most hostile: food security and safety, ecological sustainability and environmental protection. In the U.S., there is little regulation of GMOs. Numerous U.S. food products contain GMOs but there is no requirement for these foods be labeled. Even if GM foods were distinguished, consumers also have no way of knowing what threats GMOs pose to human health, given that neither the U.S. government nor the companies producing GMOs have dedicated resources to examining—much less explaining—their health and environmental impacts. For developing countries, GMO seeds raise several vital concerns. First, because GM seeds are patented, the TRIPs rules mean farmers must pay annual fees. Thus, GM crops—the seeds for which are often provided free to get farmers "hooked"— are a major threat to food sovereignty. Second, GM crops threaten to replace planting of diverse varieties with GM monocultures risking a single variety being devastated by one virulent pest and diminishing biodiversity.

Three existing WTO agreements may make it difficult for countries to maintain or strengthen their domestic safeguards regarding GMOs: the Agreement on Sanitary and Phytosanitary Measures, the Agreement on Technical Barriers to Trade and TRIPs. The first two agreements put heavy burdens on governments wishing to restrict the entry of GMOs into their countries. The SPS agreement set parameters for food-safety policy, but given the claim that GM foods raise no health or safety issues, countries might have to justify their GM policies under the TBT Agreement which covers non-food-safety standards. The TBT Agreement requires governments to minimize trade impacts when setting standards regulating products under the least trade-restrictive rule.[158] In addition, the mere labeling of a product to identify it as containing GMOs may fall under TBT rules, possibly undermining even this relatively modest form of product regulation.

The biotechnology industry claims that GMOs are "substantially equivalent" to their nonengineered counterparts. This has been the basis for refusing testing and labeling. The notion of "substantial equivalence" was introduced by President George Bush immediately after the Rio Earth Summit to blunt pressure for biosafety regulations. It was later formalized and introduced in 1993 by the OECD, and subsequently endorsed by the FAO and the WHO. The OECD document states, "The concept of substantial equivalence embodies the idea that existing organisms used as foods, or as a source of food, can be used as a basis for comparison when assessing the safety of human consumption of a food or food component that has been modified or is new."[159]

The assumption that GMOs are equivalent to their natural counterparts in terms of health and ecological impact is absurd—foods with Bt toxin genes are not the same as foods without. And there is increasing proof today that GMOs (and their health risks) are substantially different from their nonengineered parents, as the inserted gene can cause unpredictable reactions.

Despite Growing Evidence of Health and Environmental Impacts, U.S. Insists That GMO Restrictions and Labeling Are WTO-Illegal

Emerging data indicate that GMOs may have adverse consequences for human health, biological diversity and the environment. Ethicists and religious groups also have raised ethical questions about the genetic manipulation of living organisms.

We are not a nation of guinea pigs [but] the entry into the country of gene-
tically engineered crops and food products . . . may just as well make us one.
—Philippine Representative Prospero Pichay Jr.,
August 24, 2001[160]

First, crops engineered to resist pesticides and herbicides perpetuate reliance
on those chemicals, threatening the environment. In fact, increasing demand
for such products may be a goal of some corporations producing GMOs. For
example, Monsanto, manufacturer of the popular Roundup line of herbicides,
also genetically engineers Roundup Ready cotton seeds designed to resist its
herbicides.

Second, scientists believe that crops engineered to resist pesticides and herbicides
could pass those traits on to weeds, resulting in herbicide- and pesticide-tolerant
"superweeds."[161] Scientists in the U.S. and Denmark have shown that the herbicide-
tolerance gene can be readily passed from cultivated canola plants to closely related
wild plants, like wild mustard, in nearby fields.[162] The widespread use of Roundup
Ready crops and the herbicide Roundup for the last 30 years has engendered at least
two weeds that can survive being sprayed directly with Roundup—mare's tail and
water hemp.[163] If pesticide resistance were transmitted to pest plants, it would force
farmers to use more and more herbicides to control plant pests, with unknown
effects on the environment and added threat to public health.

Proponents of GM technology argue that it will lead to decreased pesticide use,
for instance, because some GM crops are engineered to produce their own pest
repellents such at Bt crops. However, researchers at North Carolina State have
found that the corn earworm (also known as the cotton bollworm) develops resistance to Bt corn—and that the moths that develop Bt resistance in the Midwest
cornfields fly south to U.S. Bt cotton fields.[164] The emergence of resistance in pests
like bollworm and creation of superpests is another consequence of genetically
engineered crops.

Third, GMOs may upset biological diversity. According to a report written for
the British government, if GMOs eradicate weeds and insects, species that depend
on them for food or habitat, including such birds as the corn bunting, partridge,
and skylark, will suffer.[165] Furthermore, crops engineered to resist insect pests also
may be toxic to harmless or beneficial insects, such as green lacewings and spring-
tails, thereby reducing insect diversity.[166]

Fourth, the creation of genetic uniformity and the erosion of genetic diversity
by monoculture agriculture also threatens food security. Aggressive marketing of
the products protected by intellectual property rights can lead to the displacement
of hundreds of local varieties of crops and breeds of livestock,[167] stamping out the
diverse crop and animal varieties that are useful to maintaining balanced ecosystems. The end product—the so-called "monoculture"—is a dangerously unstable
ecosystem that has lost its diversity and hence its resistance against pests, diseases
and environmental stresses. In 1970, a corn blight epidemic ravaged at least 15%
of the U.S. corn crop due to homogeneity and made the entire crop vulnerable to
the same fungus.[168] Monocropping—planting just one species of potato—was a

major factor in the deadly Irish potato famine after a crop blight wiped out nearly all of the uniform potato crop.

Fifth, genetically modified foods may run afoul of consumers with allergies and those who have specific dietary requirements because of ethical, religious or cultural beliefs. People allergic to fish could have a reaction to tomatoes with transplanted fish genes; vegetarians and persons of the Islamic and Jewish faiths may be averse to eating food containing pig genes. Already these issues have arisen with genetically engineered L-tryptophan and Brazil nut genes in soy beans.

Sixth, GMOs might pose human health risks. British scientist Dr. Arpad Pusztai first suggested this following a study on the effects of consumption of genetically modified potatoes on rats, in which subjects that ate the altered potatoes suffered stunted internal organ growth and weakened immune systems.[169] The Monsanto-funded[170] Rowett Research Institute suspended Dr. Pusztai, despite his stellar reputation, claiming the researcher went public without sufficient scientific evidence to substantiate his findings. A specially convened group of UK scientists later concluded that Dr. Pusztai's study, though possibly "flawed," underlined the uncertainty as to the safety of genetically modified foods. Indeed, the British Medical Association, representing Britain's doctors, promptly called for a moratorium on the planting of genetically modified crops in the UK.[171]

Cynical Claims of GMOs Solving World Hunger

Increasing food security and food availability is the main affirmative argument for promoting GMOs. Yet, ironically recent research is showing that there is no significant yield increase in transgenic crops, only increased safety risks.[172] Moreover, because the patenting of GM seeds undercuts the ability of poor farmers to replant such seed, even if the seeds produced larger yields those most susceptible to hunger would not be able to afford the use of such varieties. This is a significant basis for African countries' rejection of GM seeds. They also are concerned that countries worldwide now regulating GMOs will not accept their exports. Without labeling, neither importers nor consumers can discriminate between GM and non-GM foods, making it difficult to trace potential hazards to their source, which is why there is a call from citizens worldwide for strong biosafety regulations at national and international levels.

U.S. Trade Demands Jam Biosafety Protocol Talks; Result in Delay and Conflicting Provisions

Reflecting the growing international concern with the possible risks of GMOs, representatives of more than 140 nations met in Cartagena, Colombia, in February 1999 to complete a Biosafety Protocol which would include policies regarding the regulation of GMOs,[173] culminating almost seven years of international effort among countries to formulate a policy to safeguard the public from a technology whose long-term effects are essentially unstudied. From the adoption of the UN Convention on Biological Diversity in 1992, it had taken concerned countries more than three years to overcome U.S. and industry claims that a Biosafety Protocol was unnecessary. In December 1996, however, a formal negotiation group assigned to draft a protocol was finally inaugurated under the auspices of the UN Convention on Biological Diversity, and the final Biosafety Protocol was scheduled to be signed in February 1999.[174]

Throughout the drafting period, nongovernmental organizations and industry representatives tried to persuade governments, including the African countries that played a leadership role in the establishment of the negotiations, to adopt their respective positions.[175] The overwhelming majority of countries were seeking a treaty that would permit countries to prohibit imports of GMOs, require segregation of genetically modified grain from conventional grain and make producers of GMOs legally liable for any future environmental or economic damage.[176] The U.S.-led[177] "Miami Group," composed of major exporters of GMOs, including Canada, Argentina, Chile and Australia, however, wanted to protect industry interests by including a provision in the Biosafety Protocol that subjected its terms to the constraints of the WTO, meaning nations seeking to prohibit GMOs under the treaty first would have to justify their decisions on "sound science" and the other WTO rules.[178] Regulations based on unproven biosafety concerns, the U.S. argued, should be considered barriers to trade, and the protocol should underscore its subservience to WTO rules.[179]

In the end, the Miami Group blocked adoption of the Biosafety Protocol by refusing to include commodities (e.g., soy and corn) in the negotiations.[180] "This would in practice mean excluding 99, percent of the genetically modified organisms that the protocol is supposed to cover," reported a statement from the European Commission.[181] The Miami Group then proposed to extend the negotiations by a period of 18 months so that any adoption of the Biosafety Protocol would occur after the WTO Seattle Ministerial in November 1999.[182] The Miami Group proposed dealing with most biosafety issues by addressing trade rather than environmental aspects, thereby discussing health considerations tangentially rather than directly. The other countries rejected this proposal.[183]

At what were to be the final Biosafety Protocol negotiations in 2000, the U.S. insisted that the pact explicitly contain a provision giving the WTO precedence over the new agreement if there were a conflict. This would have destroyed the agreement's purpose, so other countries demanded the opposite language. The final deal contains both—conflicting—clauses, meaning countries are encouraged to regulate GMOs in ways that conflict with WTO rules, but such measures could be WTO challenged.

The USDA has interpreted the Biosafety Protocol to be a green light for exporting GM crops and a reaffirmation that the U.S. can use WTO trade-dispute mechanisms to open unwilling markets to U.S. GM exports, declaring that the Biosafety Protocol prohibits the "use of unfounded concerns about biotechnology as disguised trade barriers" and confers the right to make WTO challenges against any "unwarranted decision of an importing country not to accept a bioengineered product."[184]

The U.S. sought to then use the Earth Summit in Johannesburg in 2002, organized 10 years after the Rio Earth Summit, to further promote biotech, especially for

Africa—cynically, in the name of fighting hunger. Many southern African countries are facing famine under the structural adjustment policies required by the IMF and by WTO terms. Shortly before the summit, the Zambian and Zimbabwean governments had rejected GMO food offered as aid, and many African governments expressed outrage over U.S pressure on those countries and regarding Earth Summit agenda generally. One civil-society representative read to the assembly a statement endorsed by hundreds of African farm and other civil-society groups:

> We, African Civil Society groups, participants to the World Summit on Sustainable Development, composed of more than 45 African countries, join hands with the Zambian and Zimbabwean governments and their people in rejecting GE contaminated food for our starving brothers and sisters:
>
> - We refuse to be used as the dumping ground for contaminated food, rejected by the Northern countries; and we are enraged by the emotional blackmail of vulnerable people in need, being used in this way.
> - The starvation period is anticipated to begin early in 2003, so that there is enough time to source uncontaminated food.
> - There is enough food in the rest of Africa (already offered by Tanzania and Uganda) to provide food for the drought areas.
> - Our response is to strengthen solidarity and self-reliance within Africa, in the face of this next wave of colonization through GE technologies, which aim to control our agricultural systems through the manipulation of seed by corporations.
> - We will stand together in preventing our continent from being contaminated by genetically engineered crops, as a responsibility to our future generation.[185]

In the closing plenary of the Earth Summit, when U.S. Secretary of State Colin Powell kept insisting that African countries should import GM food, he was heckled by both African NGOs and governments. African farmers had come to Johannesburg with alternatives—small-scale, indigenous—based on farmers' rights to land, water and seed. In September 2002, Powell approached the Vatican foreign minister Jean-Louis Tauran to ask him to persuade the government of Zambia to accept U.S. genetically modified food aid.[186]

Southern Africa was facing a significant famine by the end of 2002, with nearly 15 million people facing starvation in Lesotho, Malawi, Mozambique, Swaziland, Zambia, and Zimbabwe.[187] In October 2002, Zambia refused U.S. food aid that came in the form of 18,000 tons of U.S. GM corn, asking the U.S. to mill the corn so none of it would be used as seed.[188] Malawi, Mozambique and other southern African countries joined Zambia's refusal to accept U.S. food aid if it was GM grain.[189] Other countries followed suit. In November 2002, India froze U.S. GM shipments of corn and soy food-aid shipments.[190] In January 2003, two U.S. relief agencies approached the Indian Genetic Engineering Approval Committee (GEAC) to gain permission to import U.S. GM corn and soy food aid that could not be certified as GM-free, but as of early 2003, GEAC has only approved the importation of GM cotton, disallowing GM food imports.[191] Instead of helping the African countries purchase food they sought fit or milling the corn, the U.S. used the situation as a PR tool in its GM trade war with Europe. In early 2003, an angry USTR Robert Zoellick lashed out at Europe for preventing GMO crops from entering their market and thus, Zoellick patronizingly claimed, leading developing countries to forbid GMO food imports. Zoellick called the European policy "Luddite" and "immoral."[192]

GMO Regulations Proliferate While U.S. Explicitly Threatens WTO Action

Despite the U.S. efforts to sabotage the African call for a Biosafety Protocol signing and years of threats of a WTO challenge, increasingly nations are taking steps to regulate GMOs. Between 1992 and 1998, the EU had approved a voluntary labeling scheme described in Chapter 2.[193] Now, the U.S.'s main target for GM food and seed sales, given the EU's current refusal to import GM crops, has been the developing world. In February 2002, USTR Robert Zoellick testified before the U.S. House of Representatives Ways and Means Committee, where he pushed the benefits of GM crops for the developing world, noting "biotechnology holds out tremendous potential for the developing world" but omitted references to benefits of GMO crops for other U.S. trading partners.[194]

Outside Europe, many countries have begun to regulate GM foods. In May 1999, Australia introduced a mandatory food-standard program prohibiting the sale of food produced using gene technology unless officially tested and included in a "safe-list."[195] China initiated a protracted skirmish with the U.S. over whether and how China would import GM soybeans during 2001–2002.[196] In early January 2003, Australian activists were outraged when 50,000 tons of U.S. GM corn to be used for chicken feed entered the country despite the fact that some GM products are not approved for use in Australia.[197] Even Japan, which has previously taken a hands-off approach similar to that of the U.S., was criticized by the U.S. trade representative for proposing mandatory labeling requirements on agricultural biotechnology products such as GMO corn, potatoes, cotton, tomatoes and soybeans.[198]

In the spring of 2003 the U.S. launched a GM trade war with the filing of a formal WTO challenge against Europe. A WTO ruling against countries' rights to regulate these foods could have a major boomerang effect: The notion that an unaccountable global commerce agency decides what is on everyone's plates—rather than the people eating the food—would dramatically clarify what is at stake with the WTO.

DOHA MINISTERIAL FAILS ON AGRICULTURE

As in Seattle, at the 2001 Doha WTO Ministerial, negotiations on agriculture proved to be the most acrimonious issue. France threatened to walk out of the Doha negotiations over the demand to cut export subsidies.[199] In South Korea, rice farmers protesting the summit clashed with riot police as they demonstrated their opposition to reductions in rice subsidies.[200]

The final Ministerial Declaration provisions on agriculture boiled down to four basic negotiating goals:

- A commitment to negotiate over:
  1) further lowering agricultural tariffs and raising quotas,
  2) reducing and ultimately phasing out export subsidies, and
  3) reducing domestic support;[201]

- A reaffirmation of the WTO's "special and differential treatment" policy for developing countries but without requiring specific WTO terms to deliver the policy. This policy to date has proved meaningless to farmers in the developing world because the policy has not been translated into operational policies in WTO rules;[202]

- A "nontrade concerns" clause, added for the EU, which raises issues such as employment, environment, land use, biodiversity, food security, animal welfare and other issues but does not commit to negotiations on these topics;[203] and

- A commitment that the WTO member countries would agree to "modalities" (the structure) for a future WTO agriculture negotiating agenda by March 31, 2003.[204]

However, as with most WTO texts, the text's meaning is a matter of dispute. For instance, the EU demanded that a clause be added that the negotiations would occur "without prejudging the outcomes," essentially contradicting the underlying "commitment" to reach agreement on reductions in tariffs, quotas, export subsidies and domestic support.[205]

Via Campesina, the international coalition of small farmers, railed against the Doha agriculture text, describing it as ensuring protections for agribusiness but doing nothing for small farmers in the developing world. In a post-Doha statement, Via Campesina noted: "The negotiations on agriculture still seem to be a fight between the 'corporate elephants of the agro-industry' represented by the European Union, the United States and the Cairns group instead of negotiation on how to come to fair, equitable trade relations that give protection to domestic food production and consumption and the world's environment."[206]

Absent from the Doha Ministerial Declaration is any "Development Box" provisions which would allow developing countries to design farm and food policies to increase development without fear of WTO reprisals—much as the developed countries use "Blue Box" programs to advance environmental agendas.[207] A coalition of developing countries had requested to add a "Development Box" to the AoA that would change WTO agriculture rules to allow policies—including quantative restrictions—designed to strengthen food security without incurring penalties for implementing trade-distorting policies in developing countries. The Development Box concept would have meant a significant departure and an overture to poor countries by protecting their rights to prioritize food security and development needs and inserting these rights directly into the negotiating objectives.[208]

Although the Doha Ministerial Declaration includes some soothing language on how food and farming needs of the developing world ought to be taken into account through special and differential treatment, it merely identified that there were real concerns but did not direct negotiators to address them. Indeed, the Filipino research foundation IBON characterized the Doha Ministerial's special and differential treatment language as "feeble."[209] The U.S. was instrumental in preventing this legitimate negotiating objective of the developing world from being included in the final Doha Declaration.[210] Additionally, the Doha Ministerial Declaration made no mention of the crucial agricultural issue of dumping agricultural products.

POST-DOHA AND THE ROAD TO THE CANCÚN MINISTERIAL

The schedule set for agriculture talks in the Doha Ministerial Declaration required countries to agree on "modalities" for negotiations by March 2003. This decision will predetermine much of the talks' outcomes. For instance, if an approach is taken to cut all subsidies by 25%, the countries with the highest subsidies remain highest. If the approach is a cap on subsidies of 10%, every country with subsidies becomes equal, while those without subsidies remain disadvantaged.

Over the course of 2002, countries met on the matter. At a July 2002 special session on market access, the Cairns group demanded steep declines in tariffs and increases in quotas in the U.S. and EU, as well as cutting export and domestic subsidies. Developing countries supported cuts in the industrialized world's tariffs, but were leery of implementing significant cuts in their own for fear of agricultural dumping from large-scale agriculture exporting countries, and sought a mechanism to use the special and differential application of safeguard measures to protect their domestic markets from surging, underpriced imports.[211]

Negotiations over domestic support had similarly broad divergence of positions. The Cairns group pushed an aggressive reduction in domestic support—the elimination of Amber Box direct support in five years for developed countries and nine years for developing countries, the elimination of Blue Box production-limiting policies, and capping the amount of Green Box so-called nontrade distorting programs. China proposed eliminating Amber Box and Blue Box programs within three years and a comprehensive review of Green Box programs. The U.S. proposed the elimination of Blue Box programs, limiting Green Box programs and maintaining *de minimis* 5% of production permissible agricultural supports programs.[212]

In December 2002, after continuing battles between European countries on the question, the EU unveiled its proposal for WTO agriculture negotiation: The EU would lower its agriculture tariffs, reduce its export subsidies and domestic farm support, and provide additional market access for developing countries. The EU's proposal includes another round of tariff reductions identical to the Uruguay Round AoA reductions—36% overall tariff reduction with a minimum reduction of 15% on each tariff line over six years.[213] It also proposed the reduction of the *de minimis* clause for developed countries.[214] The development proposals in the EU proposal were particularly modest, allowing some special safeguard from dumping provisions and codifying special and differential provisions.[215]

Members of the Cairns group claimed that the EU's reforms were too limited and "modest" to be the basis for negotiating at Cancún.[216] In the midst of the country-to-country frictions, the Agriculture Committee Chairman Stuart Harbinson released a text he sought to use as the basis of agreement on the modalities. The February 2003 text demanded extensive cuts in tariffs and the elimination of export subsidies for farmers within 10 years.[217] The so-called Harbinson proposal would cut the highest agricultural tariffs by 60% in five years, raise quotas and reduce domestic support.[218] It was attacked by all blocs.

The EU contended that it was unbalanced, and that it favored strong agricultural producers and exporters while sacrificing the aim of helping developing countries.[219] In particular, the EU noted that it kept its agreements in the AoA, reducing tariffs, export subsidies and domestic support, and that the EU is the world's largest importer of agricultural products from developing countries, importing 67% more that the U.S., the world's second largest importer of developing-country agricultural products.[220] The Harbinson proposal would eliminate not only the EU's export subsidies,[221] but Japan also felt the proposed tariff cuts would threaten Japanese rice farmers.[222]

The Cairns group criticized that the Harbinson proposal did not quickly expedite the phasing out of export subsidies.[223] Australia's trade minister, Mark Vaile, stated that "the level of ambition the [Harbinson] paper contains is disappointing" and that the proposal "simply won't do enough" to address subsidies in time for the March 2003 agricultural negotiations deadline.[224] The U.S. agreed with Australia.[225]

Developing nations and civil-society groups attacked the Harbinson proposal for failing to address the most pressing needs for developing-country farmers—preventing the dumping of agricultural products on developing farm sectors and allowing domestic policies for development and food security.[226] The Harbinson draft (and the EU proposal) ignored demands that developing countries delay reducing their barriers until the developed countries reduced their level of domestic support and export subsidies providing a rebalancing period.[227] Meanwhile, peasant farm organizations around the world, including the millions linked to Via Campesina, have demanded that agriculture be removed from the WTO entirely.[228] While multilateral talks continued at the WTO's Geneva headquarters, as the Cancún Ministerial approached, the U.S. and EU announced a bilateral deal suiting their needs which they proposed become the negotiating text for Cancún. The move—and the meager concessions offered—so infuriated other WTO nations that decades of differences among food exporting and importing developing countries were overcome to forge a new bloc of 21 nations including Brazil, South Africa, China, India, and many smaller countries united in offering a counterproposal. Another bloc of poor countries dissatisfied with the G-21's approach to safeguarding the food security of net food importing nations tabled another competing proposal. Days before the Ministerial's start, a draft Ministerial Declaration was issued in Geneva which relied heavily on the U.S.-EU text. It was resoundingly rejected and the G-21 demanded that its text be the basis for discussions in Cancún. As a result, the Ministerial opened with no ag text formally on the table. The EU and especially the U.S. ginned up a high-pressure campaign of threats and promises trying to break the G-21. Calls to presidents and prime ministers, threats of removing African and Latin American nations' trade preferences and more back-fired, as Egypt joined the group, which held its ground. On the summit's third day, a new draft text was tabled. The agricultural text was largely that rejected in Geneva, but new were clauses launching negotiations on three of the four Singapore Issues, including investment which the developing countries rejected. In contrast to past WTO talks, this time even countries with other geopolitical reasons to support the U.S. held their positions knowing that the political wrath of those injured by WTO at home was yet greater than the U.S. anger. Negotiations then moved into green room sessions—despite the promise that such tactics would not occur. Yet, while "movement" was being reported on some agriculture issues, the details were never revealed because, in a parallel session, European and Korean demands on the Singapore Issues ground the entire summit to a final halt.

CONCLUSION

Minutes after the Ministerial collapsed, the Brazilian minister Celso Amorin, who was a G-21 leader, held a news conference celebrating the unity of the new developed-country bloc—and reiterating that the WTO agriculture rules had to be altered. The rise of the new bloc was a seismic shift in WTO politics—effectively, the multilateral trade system suddenly got multilateral. This important power shift—if it can hold—may force more attention to other perspectives on agricultural trade. However, powerful interests support the existing rules which continue to ruin the livelihoods of farmers worldwide and increase hunger. And, even in the G-21 proposal, the focus remains on food trade rather than on how to ensure food sovereignty—and thus security—to the world's hungry.

8

HUMAN AND LABOR RIGHTS UNDER THE WTO

Ashwini Sukthankar and Scott Nova*

LABOR RIGHTS

The 1990s ushered in an era when the boundary between the domestic economic policies of nations, and their trade policies, was permanently blurred. Of course, there has always been a dynamic relationship between national economies and international trade, with countries imposing tariffs on imported goods to make indigenous industries more competitive, or devaluing their own currencies to encourage exports. However, domestic economies and trade were conflated in the 1990s by *discouraging* states from adopting domestic policies such as these, which had the impact of regulating international trade.

The establishment of the WTO intensified the trend toward blurring the lines. The WTO and the 23 agreements it enforces establish a comprehensive governance system, exemplified by the privileges and protections provided for corporations versus those offered to communities, individual workers or labor as a class.

For instance, new corporate property rights were created by TRIPs, TRIMs and GATS, but no countervailing rights for workers were established in the WTO. To the contrary, some policies promoting workers' rights are considered barriers to trade and therefore subject to challenge under WTO rules. Indeed, the 1996 WTO Singapore Ministerial Declaration invites challenges to laws that seek to enforce labor rights: "We reject the use of labour standards for protectionist purposes, and agree that the comparative advantage of countries, particularly low wage developing countries, must in no way be put into question."[1]

These requirements—and yet more explicit limits on domestic labor policies required of debtor nations by the IMF—have put labor policies under new pressure. Based on the logic that international trade and the profits of foreign

* The authors are, respectively, Director of Investigations and Research and Executive Director of the Workers Rights Consortium. The views expressed in this chapter are the authors' and do not necessarily reflect those of the organization.

investors are affected by national "aberrations," such as domestic labor laws permitting strikes, even domestic policies with a primarily domestic impact have been subjected to these disciplines, shrinking the sphere of state sovereignty and self-determination in policy and lawmaking. Given that the state is, by and large, the only source of labor-rights protection, the majority of workers around the world were suddenly left facing multinational capital directly.

WTO rules forbid treating countries differently because of their human-rights or labor records. First, as has been explained before, WTO rules generally prohibit distinguishing among products based on the way they are produced. Second, under the Most Favored Nation rule, one WTO country cannot treat other WTO countries differently, regardless of their labor or human-rights records. Third, the WTO Agreement on Government Procurement prohibits noncommercial considerations in governments' purchasing decisions, meaning for the nations that have signed the AGP, including the U.S., environmental or social bidding preferences or a ban on government purchase of goods produced in violation of ILO labor or UN human rights conventions violates WTO rules. Finally, the WTO dispute settlement body can be used to challenge worker safety regulations as technical barriers to trade, as described in Chapter 3 regarding Canada's WTO challenge of France's asbestos ban.

Taken together, these WTO rules set up formidable barriers to traditional methods of promoting labor and human rights. The sort of sanctions requested by South African leaders of the struggle against apartheid—which involved pushing countries, states and cities to refuse to do business with the apartheid regime and pressuring companies to divest their interests in South Africa—would have run afoul of the current WTO rules. In October 1998, the European Union and Japan challenged a Massachusetts law that effectively prohibited government agencies from purchasing goods or services from companies doing business in Burma (now known as Myanmar).[2] The EU and Japan only suspended their WTO case when a U.S. association of corporations sued Massachusetts and ultimately won their suit in the U.S. Supreme Court.[3]

And the WTO has widened the gap between the world's rich and poor. Primary among the "new trade disciplines" debated during the Uruguay Round was a demand by industrialized countries for greater openness to foreign direct investment. These countries insisted that their entrepreneurs should be allowed to compete with developing world firms free of handicaps to the former or state assistance to the latter. In exchange, the industrialized countries proposed, they would lift the trade barriers of tariffs and quotas they had imposed on imports of the labor-intensive, low-technology products in which developing countries had advantages, given the easy availability of cheap labor.

These two factors—providing new rights and protections for investors from the industrialized world to the developing world and to the movement of goods in the opposite direction—contributed to the phenomenon of the "wandering" transnational corporation. These corporations, willing to shift production locations repeatedly in a tireless search for ever-more-hospitable investment climates, in turn help produce what we call "the race to the bottom," where developing countries compete desperately with each other to offer the most lucrative deals to foreign investors, with cheaper labor and bigger financial incentives—meaning workers face the ultimate burden of producing more for less and less. When there are no ground rules for corporations concerning labor or human rights, the brutal race to the bottom in wages and working conditions rewards the country that can offer the cheapest production costs with production being moved there, but people working in that country—under horrific conditions and for starvation wages—lose, as do the people in the competing countries.[4]

Workers and labor unions in industrialized and developing countries opposed the Uruguay Round Agreements in 1994. They knew that absent a more balanced approach between the interests of industry and workers, the WTO would accelerate the process of corporate-dominated globalization that began in the late 1970s. And they knew that Uruguay Round agriculture rules would push millions of subsistence-farm families off their land and into cities, with the new migrants flooding labor markets and adding downward pressure on already unlivably low wage levels.

Now, after nearly nine years of the WTO, this scenario is coming to pass. Developing countries are pitted against each other in a race to the bottom spurred by the increasing security WTO rules provide for corporations to relocate. Since there is no floor of conduct to obtain WTO market access benefits, there is no market incentive for countries to meet even basic standards. Indeed, companies can punish countries trying to promote worker rights or environmental standards simply by relocating. The majority of savings in production costs are not passed on to consumers, but given the huge margin, prices can be lowered enough to push domestic producers meeting labor and environmental standards out of business. Meanwhile, wages and conditions in industrialized countries are being pushed downward as domestic industries cut costs to compete, until ultimately the companies simply cannot compete with $1-a-day average wages in China[5] or $5 a day in Mexico and they relocate or close.[6] At the same time, the living standards of workers in the developing world are not improving.

LABOR CONDITIONS IN THE DEVELOPING WORLD

The pressure wrought by the WTO on the developing world has only exacerbated the limits placed on developing countries' ability to regulate transnational corporations even *within* their own borders, implemented through policies like "conditionalities" attached to World Bank loans, or the structural-adjustment policies imposed by the IMF. These policies almost invariably require amendment of labor protections, such as minimum-wage laws and controls on hiring and firing, in an effort to create the "labor flexibility" sought by transnational corporations.

For developing-world manufacturing workers, the experience of globalization has been defined by harsh workplace conditions and inadequate compensation. Given the increased risks—habitual forced overtime, hazardous safety conditions and abusive treatment by supervisors—accompanying heavy production pressures, where should workers look for the protection of their basic rights, or for redress when those rights are violated?

The workers' own countries are not, for the most part, of much use in this respect. On the one hand, implementation of IMF and World Bank requirements has hollowed out domestic public law systems and shifted government spending away from social services such as unemployment benefits or food-provision programs (on the logic that such programs retard economic growth rather than stimulate it) leaving workers without even the prospect of a safety net. And on the other hand, there really are no private law remedies available either. The absence of meaningful "long arm" statutes that would give domestic courts jurisdiction over foreign entities, and the absence of the political will to enforce existing statutes, makes it largely futile for workers to file suit in their home countries against corporations that have shifted their operations across a border. Added to this is the problem of developing-country courts so overburdened and understaffed that plaintiffs might have to wait a decade, two decades, or even longer for judgments.

There have been some attempts by developing-world workers to use other jurisdictions using the Alien Tort Claims Act (ATCA), a 1789 statute allowing noncitizens of the U.S. to seek monetary damages in U.S. forums for violations of a U.S. treaty or of the law of nations.[7] For example, Burmese citizens have sued Unocal Corporation, alleging that when it participated in a joint venture with the Burmese military junta to build a gas pipeline, it did so with the full knowledge that military and police forces were marshaling forced labor to work on the project. The issue is still in the U.S. courts.[8] However, such litigation is expensive, time-consuming, and requires the claim of truly egregious harms. As cases like the Unocal suit go forward, we may see the ATCA provide remedies in some cases, but such suits do not constitute a broadly applicable strategy. Other attempts at litigation in the U.S. have included cases filed by advocacy groups citing the Generalized System of Preferences (GSP)—a U.S. statute that in theory makes trade between the U.S. and other countries dependent on the latter's compliance with "internationally recognized worker rights" among other requirements. But given the degree of discretion permitted to U.S. agencies by courts, such litigation has also been largely unsuccessful.

There are those who argue that the current state of affairs is a passing malaise. They view the unabated use of child labor—according to ILO figures, there are 44.6 million children under 14 working in Asia, 23.6 million in Africa and 5.1 million in Latin America[9]—as part of the "growing pains" of development. They assert that free markets will ultimately bring in their wake other freedoms—such as democracy, freedom of expression, and freedom of association—primarily through the operation of market forces, and insist that government regulation keeps down the developing world, while free markets will make it wealthy.[10]

THE MARKET ALONE WILL NOT PROVIDE WORKERS WITH FAIR TREATMENT

The challenge to this proposition that "fair trade is free trade's destiny"[11] has happened at all levels: empirical and theoretical, radical and mainstream. The harsh analysis of Joseph Stiglitz, former chief economist of the World Bank, is probably the best known, with its recognition that the "invisible hand" of the free market is, all too often, prone to severe "mishandling," in ways that leave the world's poorest paying for the mistakes.[12] Even Columbia University economist Jagdish Bhagwati, who continues to be a staunch champion of free trade, insists that arguments in favor of free trade cannot be extrapolated into a justification for the unregulated movement of capital.[13] For the most part, however, the distinction between trade in widgets and trade in dollars, to use Bhagwati's formulation, cannot be sustained at a practical level, since the two act in tandem, in terms of both the international financial institutions that promote them and their impact on labor. A critique of one inevitably bleeds into a critique of the system as a whole.

The "market" won't stop the problem of forced labor. In the absence of factors that are variable in *any* market—such as consumers willing to pay a premium for products made without bonded labor, prison labor or child labor—employers would find it expedient to engage in such practices. This certainly tends to be the case in the developing world, where the limitations of the domestic legal framework mean that employers need not take into account the possible expense of lawsuits brought either by individuals or by the state.

The reasons that companies in the industrialized world might decide that addressing these problems makes good business sense are not about the perfecting of pure market forces but about the power of federal agencies, courts, pressure groups, and public sentiment. And there is nothing inherent in the free market that makes such control mechanisms flourish. In fact, as economists tend to agree, there can be no such thing as a "pure" market. Nobel prize–winning economist Amartya Sen, for example, asserts that the ultimate social costs of inattention to basic education, primary health care, and access to justice are much higher than the cost of any initial investment. So the market economy's failure to commit resources to the poor is a symptom of the ways in which decisions *seeking* to be rational are routinely undermined by information deficits about long-term consequences.[14]

Besides, as University of Chicago law professor Cass Sunstein notes, even laissez-faire is a form of regulation, privileging certain interests over others. "Markets, free or otherwise, are not a product of nature. On the contrary, markets are legally constructed instruments, created by human beings hoping to produce a successful system of social ordering."[15] In developing countries today, new legal regimes, set up with the technical and monetary assistance of international financial institutions, regulate invisibly by tilting the balance of bargaining power toward employers. With their job security weakened by the amendment of laws that regulated the firing of workers and the closure of factories, and their capacity to bargain collectively pruned drastically through legal restrictions on the formation of unions, workers can do little more than sign on the dotted line.

Markets are equally ineffective at ending workplace discrimination on the basis of race, caste, gender, etc. Cass Sunstein attacks the popular theory that, in a free market system, pure meritocracies will operate in both hiring and promotion, since discrimination is equivalent to an overriding "taste" that the employer can't afford to indulge in.[16] Sunstein points out that the prejudices of third parties—whether other workers or customers—can make discrimination on the basis of race actually profitable. The employer may have even more direct incentives to discriminate against women, considering the costs of providing child care, or the inconvenience of accommodating conflicting domestic obligations. This is particularly the case in workplaces where turnover is high and workers are seen as interchangeable.

EMPIRICAL EVIDENCE THAT FREE TRADE DOES NOT LEAD TO FREEDOM OF ASSOCIATION

Most analysts agree that labor conditions tend to improve if workers have expansive associational rights, given the increased empowerment and bargaining power that accompany the combining of forces. Defenders of the current model of globalization claim that free trade and free markets enhance all freedoms and cause democracy and other political rights to flourish. However, it is simply not the case that freedom of association follows inevitably in the wake of free markets. In fact, the drive toward more export-oriented production and foreign investment has led to the proliferation of export promotion zones (EPZ). In EPZs global manufacturing firms import most of their components from overseas subsidiaries and pay workers starvation wages to assemble the products for export for sale in rich markets. For instance, a pair of Nike sneakers costing well in excess of $100 in the U.S. is made by Indonesian workers making pennies an hour.[17]

Restrictions on workers' associational rights range from Turkey's injunctions on strikes during the first 10 years of EPZ operation, to Bangladesh's total prohibitions on trade-union activity and collective bargaining in EPZs, to enforcement in El Salvador of labor law that is so lax as to render nominally protective laws meaningless. In El Salvador where freedom of association and the right to bargain collectively are enshrined in the constitution, 228 factories operate in free-trade zones and not one has signed a collective bargaining agreement with a union. The ILO has noted that the number of EPZs is likely to grow throughout the world, particularly in developing countries, and is urging governments to ensure labor protection and basic union rights, since these often are waived in the EPZs.[18] In the EPZs on the U.S.-Mexican border, the so-called maquiladora plants, workers are not paid nearly enough to live on.[19] A living wage for families including food, gas, rent, electricity, transportation, water and refrigerator totaled 193.86 pesos a day according to the most recent 2000 survey.[20] However, most maquiladora workers take home only 55.55 pesos each day (about $5).[21] Even with a special, if toothless, labor side agreement to NAFTA, labor-rights enforcement in Mexico has been abysmal in the nearly 10 years since NAFTA's implementation, and Mexico's wages have not kept up with productivity gains. Mexico's industrial production grew more than 30% between 1993–2001, but Mexico's manufacturing wages fell by 20% between 1993–1999.[22]

WORKERS IN DEVELOPED COUNTRIES ALSO SLAMMED

In the U.S., since the implementation of NAFTA and the WTO, the trade deficit in the U.S. manufacturing sector grew by 159% leading to 65% of the increase in job losses during those years.[23] But it is not only the labor-intensive, lower-skill manufacturing operations that are relocating overseas. In the first nine months of 2001, the U.S. had a trade deficit of $13.98 billion in high-technology products—up from $1.25 billion in the same period in 1996.[24] Commercial aerospace firms such as Honeywell and General Electric are increasingly outsourcing overseas.[25] As well, trade unions in the industrialized world are being weakened as employers use the threat of shifting production to defeat union organizing drives[26] and to convince unionized workers to moderate their demands during bargaining; and there's been growing pressure on states to pass antiunion "right to work" laws. From 1995–2001, the productivity of the U.S. workforce grew by 20.9%; average hourly compensation for the nonfarm workforce grew by 6.6%.[27] While a number of factors have combined to create this startling disconnect between productivity and earnings, the direct and indirect effects of trade liberalization are increasingly recognized, across ideological lines, as a central cause.

AGREEING ON SOLUTIONS: THE SEARCH FOR COMMON GROUND

It is clear that the issue of labor standards *could* be part of a common agenda for workers in the industrialized world and in the developing world. Activists, mainstream economists and labor analysts refer routinely to seven central conventions of the International Labor Organization grouped under four basic principles: the elimination of all forms of forced or compulsory labor (Conventions 29 and 105); the elimination of discrimination in respect of employment and occupation (Conventions 100 and 111); freedom of association and the effective recognition of the right to collective bargaining (Conventions 87 and 98); and the effective abolition of child labor (Convention 138). The centrality of these four principles, set forth in the ILO's constitution, were reaffirmed by the organization in 1998, in its Declaration on Fundamental Principles and Rights at Work.[28] While there is considerable international agreement on what constitutes "core" labor standards, there is little consensus on how they are to be achieved.[29]

From the perspective of workers in the developing world, some concerns of industrialized-world workers can conflict sharply with their own. The flow of capital and jobs to the global south has brought much-needed employment, even if the jobs have been of poor quality. Many developing-world governments, unions and workers have attacked the call for linking trade to labor standards as ill-disguised protectionism. It is worth disaggregating the opposition to enforceable labor standards, given some governments' motivations have not been particularly altruistic. Claims about how labor standards are a neocolonial encroachment on sovereignty, or culturally inappropriate, or protectionist, all too often mask a resistance to international scrutiny of outdated laws, unimplemented policies, or corrupt institutions. The fact that governments from rich countries with known antipathy toward labor rights have joined in decrying discussion of labor standards at the WTO adds to the notion that this line of argument can arise from assorted self-interests, not from concern about developing-world workers. For instance, USTR Robert Zoellick was quoted as claiming that, ". . . Republicans in Congress know [environmental and labor] provisions will be used for protectionism."[30]

The Bush administration has been openly hostile to labor interests at home. In March 2001, the administration supported the elimination of ergonomics standards;[31] in October 2002, they sided with West Coast port operators by imposing forced mediation on the West Coast International Longshore and Warehouse Union, making it the first federal intervention in a labor dispute in more than a quarter of a century,[32] and in November 2002, Bush unveiled a plan to outsource as many as 850,000 federal jobs to private companies, eliminating union benefits for many of the service-sector jobs within the federal government such as laundry services, lawn care and copying.[33]

For the most part, the argument that universal labor standards are equivalent to industrialized-world protectionism is simultaneously too sweeping and too narrow. In the first place, only the naïve in the industrialized world would support labor standards, and the dishonest in the developing world oppose them, purely on the grounds that competition for jobs pits the countries of the former against the countries of the latter. The theory underlying the race to the bottom is that developing-world countries will compete with *each other*, with investors who are primarily from the industrialized world telling them exactly how low to go. Meanwhile, the countries of the industrialized world already have mechanisms to link trade and labor standards including GSP and the 1999 Bilateral Textile Agreement with Cambodia,[34] though results, to date, have been mixed. The Bilateral treaty links quotas for textile imports from Cambodia to the level of enforcement of internationally recognized labor standards in Cambodian factories. The ILO monitors compliance, with inspectors conducting factory visits and producing public reports.

It is clear that the current piecemeal system is no solution to the race to the bottom. Perhaps a better catchphrase than "race to the bottom" as descriptor of the predicament for developing nations would be "prisoner's dilemma."[35] Developing-world countries, desperate for investment and creation of jobs and lacking information about each other's choices and motives, opt for bad bargains out of fear that their neighbors cannot be trusted to transact with common interests in mind. So, just as the early years of industrialization were accompanied by a heightened call for collective bargaining to ensure that workers were not pressed into that particular prisoner's dilemma, the task of ensuring that workers in today's global economy derive real benefit from it requires that there be solidarity *among* developing-world countries, and not just *between* the industrialized world and the developing world. Proposals for a successful link between trade and labor standards must enhance the bargaining power of governments and workers from the poorest regions of the world.

There have been several positive steps. In 1998, the main economic bloc within Latin America, Mercosur (composed of Argentina, Brazil, Paraguay and Uruguay), signed a Social and Labor Declaration that would govern trade principles among the four nations, and guarantee respect for certain social and economic rights.

Unions in Latin America have also been urging the development of a broader economic bloc in the region, beginning with an agreement between Mercosur and the Andean Community (Bolivia, Colombia, Ecuador, Peru and Venezuela) around labor standards.

WTO AND THE "SOCIAL CLAUSE"

Currently, the most tangible proposal for a system of universal labor standards is to be found within the very heart of the international trade framework: the WTO. The idea of connecting trade and labor standards within the WTO framework was raised even before the WTO's inception in 1995.

In 1994, during the Uruguay Round negotiations, the U.S. and France had suggested that a "social clause" should be included in the WTO.[36] (Different countries and organizations mean different things when they use the term "social clause," ranging from useless NAFTA-style side agreements to provisions included in the core text of agreements that would have authority equal to all other WTO rules.) The ILO had issued a report arguing that compliance with the most basic labor rights should be included among the obligations attached to membership in the WTO.[37] Such a linkage was included in the 1948 "Havana Charter," which would have established an International Trade Organization[38] (of which the GATT would have been the trade rules) had the proposal not been withdrawn from congressional consideration in 1950, after repeated failures to pass it.[39]

The Social Clause concept would allow importing countries to take trade measures against exporting countries that failed to enforce core labor standards with punitive actions ranging from reduced quotas or raised tariffs to complete embargoes on all imports from the country in question. This would deny the deluxe market-access privileges otherwise conferred by the Uruguay Round Agreements to goods and services produced in violation of internationally agreed basic rules concerning work conditions, the right to organize, and such. While such a policy would not inherently raise wages in poorer countries, it would eliminate corporate profit incentives to deny the labor rights necessary for workers to fight for improvements. The bottom line would be altered: If a product cannot be sold in the desired market, it does not matter how cheaply it can be produced.

At the very least, the U.S. had pledged in 1994 "not [to] approve the Marrakech Ministerial Declaration establishing the WTO unless it contains a reference to early consideration of the relationship of the trading system and internationally recognized labor standards,"[40] either through a WTO study on labor issues or through the creation of a WTO working group on labor. Working groups are the lowest level of formal WTO groupings which conduct studies and discussions but do not conduct negotiations or other activities that could lead to binding changes to WTO rules.

However, the U.S. approved the Marrakech Declaration in 1995 without a single reference to labor rights, much less the establishment of a labor working group.[41] At the Marrakech WTO Ministerial, the Clinton administration did successfully push for the establishment of a WTO working group on the environ-ment (see Chapter 1 for more on the WTO Committee on Trade and Environment).

The question of a labor rights–trade linkage reemerged at the first WTO Min-isterial Conference in Singapore, in 1996. The U.S. again made the modest pro-posal that the WTO study labor issues by creating a Labor Working Group.[42]

Most representatives from the developing world rejected the proposal, and the language in the Ministerial Declaration reflects an uneasy compromise. While the delegates affirmed their "commitment to the observance of internationally recog-nized core labor standards," they assert that "[t]he International Labor Organiz-ation (ILO) is the competent body to set and deal with these standards," effectively shifting the responsibility away from the WTO. While the Social Clause is not mentioned directly, the Singapore Ministerial Declaration also states that its sig-natories "reject the use of labor standards for protectionist purposes, and agree that the comparative advantage of countries, particularly low-wage developing countries, must in no way be put into question."[43]

Some international and national labor federations declared the Singapore Min-isterial Declaration to be progress on labor rights, arguing that merely getting the WTO to recognize labor was a positive development. In contrast, other analysts have interpreted this language as undermining the status quo ante by explicitly rel-egating labor issues to the ILO—a body with weak enforcement capacity (unlike the WTO). The ILO operates like the rules of Multilateral Environmental Agree-ments: Countries sign on to ILO conventions and are supposed to adopt and enforce the rules domestically. This is in sharp contrast to the WTO, where the fail-ure of one country to follow the mutually agreed-upon rules can be challenged by another member country in dispute panels empowered to authorize trade sanc-tions for violations. There is no similar enforcement at the ILO.

U.S. Presidents on Labor Rights and Trade: The Spectrum from an Insincere Clinton to an Openly Hostile Bush

The Clinton administration played a duplicitous game on trade and labor rights. It continually pledged to prioritize the modest goal of ensuring the formation of a WTO labor-rights working group but, time and again, prioritized obtaining controversial commercial demands—such as for a new WTO Information Tech-nology Agreement—rather than using its power at WTO on labor rights. U.S. trade officials admitted that the Clinton administration's motivation was to show the U.S. labor movement that it was trying hard to include workers' rights on the WTO agenda.[44] That way, when the U.S. ceded the labor issues in favor of higher-priority commercial goals, U.S. union leaders would be less likely to attack the outcome.[45] Clinton used his 1999 University of Chicago graduation speech to call for the signing of the new ILO agreement against the most exploitative forms of child labor.[46] Yet, under WTO rules, enforcement of the treaty by prohibiting U.S. sale of any goods—including imported goods—made with child labor would be WTO-illegal because countries are not allowed to make distinctions about what goods they allow in their markets based on how a good is *made*. Thus, while the U.S. could (and does) ban child labor, under WTO rules it could not ban sale in the U.S. of products made in other countries in violation of the new ILO treaty. Meanwhile the Bush administration has been outwardly hostile to establishment of such a working group or connecting trade and labor rights. USTR Zoellick joined developing nations to oppose European labor proposals at the Doha WTO Ministerial.

In 1999, as the Seattle WTO Ministerial loomed, the Clinton administration again called for future WTO talks to give high priority to "the relationship between trade and core labor standards."[47] However, the explicit U.S. goal in this regard was weak: to encourage ILO participation in the WTO as an observer. The second U.S. proposal was to seek to persuade more WTO members to commit to internationally recognized core labor standards, although how it would accomplish this was not described in the proposal. The U.S. itself has ratified only one of the ILO conventions defining core labor standards, and its credibility on this issue in the eyes of other countries is lacking. The third proposal was a call for the creation of a future work program to address trade issues relating to labor standards. This was by far the weakest attempt yet by the U.S. to pursue labor issues at the WTO, and it, along with the rest of the Seattle discussions, ended when the Seattle Ministerial collapsed. Ironically, while the formal U.S. proposal was its weakest yet, in a Seattle speech President Clinton said, "The WTO must make sure that open trade does indeed lift living standards, respects core labor standards that are essential not only to worker rights, but to human rights."[48] In perhaps the grandest irony, some developing-country delegates seized on Clinton's statement as a basis to walk out of the talks, contributing to their collapse.

The Fourth Ministerial Conference in Doha, in 2001, reaffirmed the Singapore declaration, and took note of "work under way in the International Labor Organization on the social dimension of globalization,"[49] thus rejecting once more the notion of locating labor standards *within* the framework of trade. And immediately after Doha, the now–Director General (then DG-elect) of the WTO, Supachai Panitchpakdi, told the *Bangkok Post* that the division of responsibility between the WTO and the ILO should be sustained, with the former "emphasizing job creation rather than core labor rights."[50]

It is noteworthy that the Doha Ministerial Declaration did, in contrast, proclaim that there *was* an overlap of responsibilities between the WTO and the Bretton Woods institutions, and the delegates made a pledge to work with the IMF and the World Bank "for greater coherence in global economic policy-making."[51]

The International Confederation of Free Trade Unions (ICFTU), the federation of central labor bodies from around the world, continued to push for the social clause at the Cancún Ministerial. The ICFTU seeks to address the imbalance of the WTO's powerful enforcement applying to intellectual property and

other advanced corporate protections but not even to basic labor-standards out-
rages by adding labor rights. Other civil-society forces oppose the proposal, noting that given its inherent anti–public interest bias and undemocratic operations,
the WTO's scope and power should be cut back significantly, including by elimination of the TRIPs Agreement, not expanded to any new issues. However, it is
also clear that all of the labor and public-interest advocates agree that the current
model of globalization is causing devastating consequences to the standards of
living of workers around the world and that something must be done to reverse
this situation. However, the prospects of a social clause ever coming to fruition
are very slim.

Developing-Country NGOs and Labor Unions Discuss Paths Toward Improved Labor Conditions

Governments of nearly all developing countries and many multinational corporations have loudly voiced opposition to any consideration of labor rights in
the WTO, arguing that it would harm developing-country workers' interests.
While these interests may not have workers' best interests at heart, many
developing-country NGOs that make the same point—but for very different
reasons—are sincerely interested in improving developing-country labor conditions. Recognizing that the global union movement and these southern NGOs
and social movements share the same goal of improved labor conditions, the
Bangkok-based organization Focus on the Global South has organized several
civil-society summits to discuss the WTO–labor rights questions. The summits
were aimed at exploring common ground on the substance of the issue and on
exploring how to limit the exploitation of the difference of opinion by common
corporate opponents.

Conclusions to the Bangkok Roundtable for Trade Unions, Social Movements and Nongovernment Organizations, July 18, 2002

1. On July 17–18, 2002, the second meeting of the Bangkok International
   Roundtable brought together a significant number of trade unions,
   social movements and NGOs from all regions to discuss the scope for
   agreement on common actions and approaches on a number of issues
   including the WTO, the IMF and World Bank, food sovereignty and people's rights, and privatization of water and power.
2. Since the first meeting in March 2001, the trends of declining wages,
   increasing unemployment, the spread of the informal economy, attacks
   on workers' rights, and worsening precariousness of employment in
   many countries had intensified.
3. The participants agreed that the world needs multilateral institutions

that are fundamentally different, with a much stronger role for the United Nations and its agencies, including the ILO. We need multilateral institutions that respond to the principles of subsidiarity, pluralism, inclusion, transparency and democracy, and that internationally recognized human rights, including fundamental workers' rights, environmental protection, food security, and in the opinion of many participants, food sovereignty, must have precedence over international trade and investment rules.

This discussion built on the initial summit's joint declaration that, among other things, noted: "The importance of promoting, respecting and realizing fundamental workers rights and other human rights by all relevant means, including action at the appropriate international institutions." These summits have helped clarify common support for the substance of the ILO standards, but there is deep disagreement on how they might be enforced effectively.

THE INTERNATIONAL LABOR ORGANIZATION IS TOOTHLESS

The WTO has declared that labor issues relating to trade belong to the ILO, yet, the ILO has no enforcement powers to speak of. The organization can marshal considerable moral and political pressure, and though such censure is not effective against the world's largest economies, it can have some impact on smaller economies. The resolution at the International Labor Conference (the ILO's annual assembly) in 1999 condemning Burma for the military leadership's systematic use of forced labor had a positive impact not only within the country, which scrambled to pass legislation banning forced labor, but also among other countries anxious to avoid comparison with Burma. However, the Burma case may well be the exception that proves the rule, since the ILO was able to bestir itself in a meaningful way only with respect to the most egregious practices in a nation already roundly condemned by the world as a gross violator of fundamental human rights. The ILO has demonstrated no inclination and no capacity to police worker-rights practices beyond such isolated and unusual cases.

The ILO has been attempting to adapt its agenda to address the impact of globalization. In 1999, it began to reorganize its priorities to address what it now terms the "Decent Work Deficit."[52] Along with the goal of full employment, the ILO emphasizes its three other "strategic objectives"—greater socioeconomic security, the strengthening of social dialogue, and the promotion of the Declaration on Fundamental Principles and Rights at Work. The Decent Work agenda adds to other pressure on the WTO to recognize that a program of economic growth is no adequate proxy for an agenda of fundamental rights. In March 2002, the Director-General of the ILO announced the formation of an 18-member World Commission on the Social Dimension of Globalization charged with preparing a report, to be discussed in 2003 by the Governing Body of the ILO, a tripartite structure representing governments, workers and employers.

THE ANTI-SWEATSHOP MOVEMENT
AND PRIVATE ENFORCEMENT

The cluster of advocacy groups and informal associations that make up the anti-sweatshop movement have cobbled together strategies that draw in many ways from the larger, more prominent frameworks outlined above. The movement, based on the principle espoused even by mainstream economists—that the responsibility for labor standards, in a global economy, does not lie in the region of production alone—puts pressure on the entire chain of production and consumption. It addresses developing-world factories and suppliers, certainly, but extends its analysis to the accountability of the multinational brands that invest in, and contract with, these production sites, as well as of the ultimate end users, who are, for the most part, consumers in the industrialized world.

In targeting consumers through publicity campaigns, the anti-sweatshop movement challenges the principle that customers automatically choose goods based on a simple formula of value-for-money; or rather, it redefines "value." Moral pressure on consumers, combined with economic pressure on multinational brands (fearing boycotts and damage to their brands' "goodwill") and political pressure on state machinery in countries of production, has proven itself to be an effective combination.

The Worker Rights Consortium, for example, is composed of over a hundred colleges and universities in North America, all of whom pledge that the goods that bear their names and logos will be produced under conditions that conform to their Codes of Conduct. The Codes create an obligation of compliance, both for the multinational brands that produce licensed apparel for the universities, and for the factories with which the brands contract. Workers at these factories have the right to complain to the WRC and ask for an investigation.

Following the initial verification of a worker complaint, the organization mobilizes member universities whose goods are being produced at the factory in question. The WRC does not urge product boycotts, which have often proven to be blunt weapons, but instead uses the economic and cultural power of universities to turn brands and retailers into allies of workers. This is designed to minimize workers being fired for making a complaint, factories closing as a result of the loss of contracts, or multinational brands moving production to other countries. The WRC model recognizes that Code of Conduct enforcement is not a substitute for worker self-empowerment, but instead, seeks to ensure that workers who are organizing themselves are able to exercise their right to do so without suffering retaliation. The Code of Conduct approach works best as a complement to civil-society interventions and a stimulus for legal solutions; it is not a substitute for either.

The WRC consults with civil-society and workers' representatives before making its recommendations in part to ensure that the agenda for change is determined, not by the purchasing power and the moral convictions of industrialized-world consumers, but by developing-world workers. Consultations with civil society and with state officials are part of a commitment to avoid the "two-tier" problem, meaning those situations where one set of standards is brought to bear on export-oriented production, while another, lower standard is in place in industries that produce purely for domestic consumption.

Of course, Code of Conduct processes—dependent as they are on the motives of the parties involved—can as easily serve negative goals. Many corporations have voluntary codes of conduct, which are monitored either internally or by for-profit consulting groups, an instance of the fox minding the chicken coop. Others question the wisdom of relying on notoriously fickle consumer preferences, or wonder about the ethics of marketing labor rights in the country of production as a "luxury good" in the country of consumption. Then there are the traditionalists, who fear the erosion of the ideal of universal labor rights through a system of private agreement and enforcement, and would like to return to the classic human-rights focus on state responsibility.

The most cogent critique, however, is simply that such private measures are necessarily limited in scope and are not (and should not be seen as) a comprehensive solution.

RESISTANCE TO FURTHER TRADE AND INVESTMENT LIBERALIZATION NOT LINKED TO WORKER-RIGHTS PROTECTIONS

The absence of affirmative steps to promote worker rights is the basis for some activists in the industrialized world, with some support from developing-world allies, to argue against further trade liberalization, through, for example, the completion of negotiations for a Free Trade Area of the Americas. Given the contribution of trade liberalization to the pressures felt by developing-world governments to reduce worker-rights protections—officially or through lax enforcement—it is logical to argue that the process of liberalization should be slowed until broadly acceptable solutions to the problem of labor standards are developed. Meaningful cooperation on this front between civil society and unions in the first and developing worlds has been achieved in recent years.

IDEAS AND PROSPECTS FOR IMPROVING WORKER-RIGHTS PROTECTIONS

Some proposals entail enhancing the ILO. This could include an expansion of its current advisory role and increasing its resources for its very useful provision of technical expertise to encourage the development of meaningful state-level institutions and stronger civil-society groups. It could also mean fortifying the organization's monitoring role. Many have suggested fleshing out the ILO's conceptualization of "decent work," perhaps through a new ILO convention. One specific plan, proposed by economists Ajit Singh and Ann Zammit, involves using the ILO's "decent work" agenda as the framework for what the authors call a global "social floor"—a set of labor standards below which no workplace should be permitted to go. They urge that the "social floor" operate, not through the connection of labor standards to trade sanctions, but through the recognition that the responsibility to pay for the costs of improved conditions is as universal as the standards themselves. This proposal is, of course, a direct challenge to the position from which advocates of a Social Clause in the WTO would have argued, that countries with lower labor standards have an "unfair advantage" for which they must be penalized through tariffs and quotas. On the contrary, Singh and Zammit urge that, given global structural inequities, developing countries deserve "special and differential treatment," for which industrialized countries must pay.[53] Perhaps the strongest argument against this proposal is its utopian improbability.

The sentiment against a Social Clause mechanism among developing-world states and, more importantly, developing-world workers, is very strong. The critique operates on multiple levels, ranging from the specific resistance to assigning responsibility for violated standards to the state (rather than to transnational corporations) to those who reject the very idea of placing the enforcement of labor rights in the hands of a body—the WTO—they blame for having produced the problem. At a minimum, it is unclear what real effect adding a Social Clause could have even if it was not abused, unless the many other antiworker core WTO provisions were eliminated as well.

A number of developing-world unions have suggested approaches involving the United Nations. This could mean advocating more strongly for existing human-rights norms, such as labor-rights guarantees within the Universal Declaration of Human Rights, to apply to the international trade regime.[54] Alternatively, a separate Convention on Labor Rights, passed through the General Assembly, could be lobbied for, with a specific emphasis on the accountability of transnational corporations in and to the country of their incorporation. While neither of these approaches would have the immediate impact of trade sanctions, it is positive that both place an emphasis on positive *results*, while a mechanism such as the Social Clause—emphasizing means rather than ends—often risks aggravating the problem. Most importantly, a human-rights approach is preferable to direct sanctions since it tends to alleviate suspicions that trade-related sanctions produce and aggravate, on both sides of the industrialized world–developing world divide. The industrialized world's concern that low labor standards provide some countries with an "unfair advantage," and the developing world's concern that sanctions serve only to promote some countries' protectionist agendas, are the inescapable confines of the debate as it stands.

Another set of proposals involves the unilateral implementation of trade policies in industrialized world countries that would condition market access on compliance with internationally recognized labor. Proponents of this approach point to the role of the U.S. Customs Service in enforcing intellectual property protections against pirated goods. This approach would be viewed by many in the developing world as a form of protectionism indistinguishable from the Social Clause except by method of application. However, there are ways of designing such policies that could place activists north and south on common ground. If import restrictions are applied against individual brands and retailers, rather than governments, and if these policies place the burden of proof on private complaining parties, then broad country boycotts are unlikely to result. Instead, activists in the industrialized world could work hand-in-hand with workers in specific developing-world factories, or in multiple factories that are part of the supply chain of particular brands and retailers, to use such trade laws as a lever to press brands and their suppliers to improve conditions.

BASIC HUMAN-RIGHTS TOOLS ELIMINATED BY WTO RULES

Lori Wallach and Patrick Woodall

The WTO's provisions also pose a significant threat to human rights and to existing human-rights treaties. Many WTO rules conflict with basic human rights enumerated in key United Nations treaties but this analysis is beyond the scope of this book. In this section we focus on how WTO rules have been used to undermine some human-rights policy tools. However, it is worth noting that, under the Vienna Convention on the Interpretation of Treaties, more recent treaties trump older treaties unless a specific "savings clause" has been added to the new treaty. Although the Uruguay Round Agreements were signed after most of the basic ILO Conventions and the major United Nations human-rights treaties, no such savings clause was included in the WTO.[55]

Regarding provisions in the WTO agreements that actively forbid consideration of human-rights conditions in developing certain commercial policies, important issues arise under the WTO Agreement on Government Procurement under which governments are not allowed to take into account a country's human-rights practices in awarding public contracts for government purchases.[56] The AGP also requires Most Favored Nation treatment, meaning that governments cannot distinguish their treatment of different WTO countries.

To date, two open instances of the conflict between human rights and WTO rules have come to light.

Case1: Massachusetts Burma Procurement Law Challenged at WTO

The serious human-rights violations and the deliberate suppression of democracy perpetrated by the military junta ruling Burma (which the junta has renamed Myanmar) since it came to power in 1988 are well known throughout the world. In 1998, the ILO issued a scathing report showing that the Burmese military dictatorship was systematically violating the basic human rights of Burmese citizens and non-Burmese minorities.[57] "There is abundant evidence before the Commission showing the pervasive use of forced labor imposed on the civilian population throughout Myanmar by the authorities and the military . . . , sometimes for the profit of private individuals. . . . Forced labor in Myanmar is widely performed by women, children, and elderly persons as well as persons otherwise unfit for work. . . . All of the information and evidence before the Commission shows utter disregard by the authorities for the safety and health as well as the basic needs of the people performing forced or compulsory labor."[58]

Burma's prodemocracy movement, led by Nobel Peace Prize holder Aung San Suu Kyi, has called for South Africa–style foreign divestment from Burma to financially starve the military dictatorship.[59] Some two dozen U.S. municipal and county governments, and the state government of Massachusetts,[60] acted on this request and terminated purchasing contracts with companies doing business in Burma.[61] The selective purchasing laws are based on the effective divestiture and selective purchasing initiatives that animated the antiapartheid movement in the U.S. in the 1980s and which are widely credited for helping to facilitate democracy in South Africa.

The attack on the Massachusetts selective purchasing law, passed in 1996, was two-pronged. Japan and the EU filed a case at the WTO. In parallel, the National Foreign Trade Council (NFTC), a coalition of corporations, challenged the measure in Massachusetts state court as a violation of the U.S. Constitution. NFTC's lawsuit was part of a larger campaign by a corporate front group called USA* Engage[62] to eliminate human-rights considerations from U.S. international commercial policy.

Vice President Cheney's Hand in the Burma Case

While current U.S. Vice President Dick Cheney was CEO of oil company Halliburton, the company actively opposed the Massachusetts Burma law and provided support and investment to the Yadana pipeline project in Burma.[63] Four oil companies (Total, Unocal, PTT, and MOGE) were involved in the pipeline project, which had a history of human-rights abuses at the hands of the Burmese military which provided security for the project.[64] Cheney himself inked a deal to build a pipeline between India and Burma in 1996.[65] Halliburton was a vital member of USA*Engage's campaign to eliminate the Massachusetts Burma law as well as other human-rights sanctions legislation such as legislation sponsored by Rep. Frank Wolf (R-VA) and Sen. Arlen Specter (R-PA) to impose sanctions on countries that persecute religious groups.[66] Halliburton submitted an amicus curiae brief against Massachusetts when the case went to the U.S. Supreme Court.[67]

The EU and Japan challenged the law at the WTO in the summer of 1997. The EU argued that Massachusetts' procurement policy had to conform to the WTO rules and that the Burma law contravened the WTO procurement agreement by imposed conditions that were not essential to fulfill the contract (Art. VIII[b]), imposed qualifications based on political instead of economic considerations (Art. X) and allowed contracts to be awarded based on political instead of economic considerations (Art. XIII).[68] Massachusetts officials were flummoxed to learn they were required to comply with WTO procurement rules that they had never approved. They later learned that a previous governor had sent a letter to the USTR during the Uruguay Round without legislative consultation, much less approval, which was the basis for the claim that the state was bound to the WTO procurement rules.

However, the EU and Japan suspended the WTO case pending the outcome of a federal lawsuit filed against that state by the National Foreign Trade Council (NFTC), an association of corporations engaging in foreign trade.[69] The NFTC argued that the Massachusetts law unconstitutionally infringed on the federal foreign-affairs power, violated the Foreign Commerce Clause, and was preempted by a U.S. federal law regarding Burma.[70] The District Court permanently enjoined enforcement of the state law, ruling that it "unconstitutionally impinge[d] on the federal government's exclusive authority to regulate foreign affairs."[71] Massachusetts appealed, but the U.S. Court of Appeals for the First Circuit affirmed the District Court's decision.[72]

Massachusetts appealed to the Supreme Court. Seventy-eight members of Congress, 38 state and local governments, all eight major state and local government associations, and 66 nonprofit organizations filed amicus curiae ("friend of the court") briefs supporting the Massachusetts law.[73] Nonetheless, the Supreme Court affirmed the lower courts' decisions, although on much narrower grounds, holding that a state or local selective-purchasing law sanctioning a nation is preempted only when Congress also has passed a corresponding law sanctioning that nation—as Congress had done in the case of Burma—and only then when the two laws differ.[74] This leaves the door open for state and local governments to pass several other types of laws.

For example, state and local governments could enact laws to avoid purchasing from companies that violate rights as long as the laws do not apply specifically to companies doing business in a country against which Congress has already enacted *different* sanctions.[75] Thus, state and local governments could divest their holdings in companies that do business in Burma or could require companies to disclose whether they do business in Burma as a condition of selling goods or services to the government because these actions do not conflict with the federal Burma law. Under the Supreme Court ruling, state and local governments also could use preferential purchasing policies regarding countries about which Congress has not passed conflicting legislation. Thus, the Supreme Court decision, in contrast to WTO AGP rules, does not rob state and local governments of all their options.

Since the EU and Japan suspended their WTO challenge pending the outcome of the domestic case, the provisions of the AGP were never interpreted. Given that the WTO has decreed that labor rights are solely in the jurisdiction of the ILO, it would have been revealing to see how a WTO tribunal treated the ILO's clear position on Burma's labor-rights violations.

Case 2: State Department Quashes Maryland Law on Human Rights in Nigeria to Avoid a WTO Challenge

The EU-Japan WTO challenge against Massachusetts' Burma policy did claim a casualty. The Clinton administration, concerned about another WTO suit and the bad press it would generate, launched a successful campaign against a similar Maryland human-rights proposal. The Clinton administration dispatched State Department Deputy Assistant Secretary David Marchick to testify before a Maryland legislative committee that was considering legislation targeting Nigeria's human- and labor-rights violations at the very time the Burma WTO case was coming to a head. Marchick informed the panel that the law would violate WTO rules, urging the state legislature to drop the propsal.[76] The law, which was expected to pass, was word-for-word the same as passed by Maryland regarding apartheid in South Africa, with the word "Nigeria" replacing "South Africa." The State Department launched an all-out offensive to kill the popular proposal before it could be passed into law. Ultimately, State Department lobbying convinced the Maryland legislature, which rejected the Nigeria legislation by a single vote.[77]

Migration for Service Workers, but Not Political Refugees

GATS contains an Annex on Movement of Natural Persons Supplying Services. The agreement was designed to let service providers move more freely from one country to another and prohibits signatories from implementing border-control regulations that will "nullify and impair" grants of market access under GATS mode 4, concerning movement of certain categories of professional workers across borders to perform services.[78] By contrast, human-rights concerns have never led to the same kind of border opening. Human-rights activists and lawyers working on behalf of people seeking political asylum and undocumented migrant workers often ask why managers have WTO-guaranteed rights to move freely across borders while political refugees and most workers do not.

9

THE WTO'S OPERATING PROCEDURES AND ENFORCEMENT SYSTEM: WORLD GOVERNMENT BY SLOW-MOTION COUP D'ÉTAT

THE DIFFERENCE BETWEEN GATT AND WTO ENFORCEMENT MECHANISMS

With the exception of the North American Free Trade Agreement, the WTO contains the most powerful enforcement procedures of any international agreement now in force. The remarkably broad reach of WTO rules and their implications, described in the previous chapters, for a wide array of domestic policies with only a passing connection to trade makes the WTO's powerful enforcement system a particular threat ensuring strong enforcement of inappropriately expansive, biased rules.

The WTO and NAFTA enforcement systems are different than those of the multilateral environmental agreements and the International Labor Organization conventions, in which signatories agree to substantive rules that are then enforced nationally by each signatory implementing the internationally agreed norms.[1] In contrast, the WTO is equipped with its own powerful enforcement system, including a binding dispute resolution process that empowers WTO tribunals to issue compliance rulings which are automatically binding unless there is unanimous consensus by all WTO members to reject the tribunal's enforcement order which is backed up with trade sanctions. One of the most dramatic changes made by the Uruguay Round was the establishment of the WTO's Dispute Resolution Understanding (DSU).

The WTO's binding enforcement system replaced the GATT contract (signatories to GATT were called "Contracting Parties") and its dispute resolution system, which relied more on diplomatic negotiation over disputes and which required consensus by all GATT countries for GATT dispute tribunal rulings to be adopted. In contrast, the WTO is a freestanding organization with "legal personality" which administers and enforces the 18 major Uruguay Round agreements, of which GATT is but one, and under which ongoing negotiations and the work of scores of harmonization and other technical committees operate continually.

The GATT contained the typical sovereignty safeguards found in almost every international agreement; consensus was required to bind any country to an obligation. Thus, while countries could challenge other GATT contracting party countries' laws before dispute panels, adoption of the ruling and approval of sanctions for noncompliance required a consensus decision of all GATT countries, including the losing country. In order to maintain the legitimacy of the GATT system, countries rarely objected to rulings against them, although the option existed as a sort of emergency brake. This was the mechanism the U.S. and Mexico used to stop final adoption of the 1991 GATT ruling against the U.S. dolphin law (see Chapter 1).

Unlike the GATT, WTO panel rulings are automatically binding and only the unanimous consent of all WTO nations can halt their adoption. Nor is any approval by WTO member countries required before the WTO authorizes trade sanctions against countries that are judged not to comply with WTO rules. Indeed, the WTO is unique among all other international agreements in that consensus is required to *stop* action. Once a WTO tribunal has declared a country's law WTO-illegal, the country must change its law or face trade sanctions. It is the official position of the U.S. government that such sanctions or negotiated compensation are only interim measures and that WTO rules require countries to amend their domestic laws to comply with WTO rulings.[2]

The enforcement system is not designed to be a neutral arbitrator of disagreements between countries; the WTO's stated purpose is "expanding . . . trade in goods and services" and its enforcement system is designed to implement that purpose.[3] WTO panelists consistently have issued interpretations that favor unrestricted commerce whenever that goal conflicts with other policy goals. The WTO rules listing criteria for the selection of panelists for the enforcement tribunals ensure that the "judges" consistently have a predetermined trade perspective and a stake in maintaining the primacy of WTO rules over national policies.

The operations of the WTO enforcement system additionally fail to provide safeguards for ensuring an open decision-making process or a full airing of all the issues involved, especially by those who will live with the results of the decisions—citizens of the countries involved in the dispute. Many national policies that can run afoul of WTO's expansive rules are aimed at noneconomic goals, such as environmental or public health protection or labor-rights guarantees. While such policy making on the domestic level takes into account economic considerations, once such laws are subject to a WTO panel's review their validity is judged exclusively according to their conformity with WTO rules aimed only at maximizing trade and investment flows.

The WTO's binding dispute resolution procedure and the Uruguay Round's expansive new rules encroaching into areas traditionally considered the realm of domestic policy effectively shift many decisions from democratically elected domestic bodies to secretive WTO tribunals. This systematic shift of decision making away from accountable, open fora, such as parliaments and city councils is inherently troubling to those committed to the future of accountable, democratic governance in the era of globalization. However, its implications are made worse by the abysmal lack of basic due process protection built into the powerful WTO dispute-resolution system. Although there has been ample criticism of the WTO's dispute-resolution mechanism and outcomes, little has been done to address the many demonstrated failures of the system.

When the WTO was first established, the signatory countries agreed to review, clarify and improve the DSU starting in 1997.[4] However, Geneva-based talks failed to generate an actual review and changes to the system were not on the agenda for the 1999 Seattle WTO Ministerial even before it collapsed. Revisiting the DSU was one of few concrete negotiating mandates that was agreed at the 2001 Doha WTO summit, but these talks were limited to "improvements and clarifications" rather than recognizing the crisis in the current system and calling for an overhaul.[5] Importantly, the DSU negotiations agreed at Doha are not part of the "single-undertaking" of negotiations launched in the Doha Ministerial. This means, as the WTO trumpets on its website, that the DSU negotiations "will not be tied to the overall success or failure of the other negotiations mandated by the declaration."[6]

Although the Clinton administration made statements about the need for greater transparency in WTO operations (particularly to allow access to the briefs and hearings in WTO disputes), WTO critics were dubious about the prospects for change because the administration seemed unwilling to put its political muscle to this effort and instead focused on commercial priorities at WTO. Since then, the WTO's enforcement system has earned it numerous new critics, ironically including some of the WTO's most enthusiastic congressional boosters. Senator Max Baucus (D-Mont.) wrote to USTR Robert Zoellick complaining about the system his boundless enthusiasm for WTO's establishment had unleashed and he urged the USTR to press to "make WTO documents and proceedings accessible to the general public and enhance the rights of non-government interested parties to participate meaningfully."[7]

Now, the Bush administration is using the opportunity of the Doha-mandated DSU talks to further pursue U.S. business interests—rather than transparency improvements—regarding WTO enforcement. For example, the U.S. has proposed that before rulings are shared with other WTO countries or become public, parties to disputes should be able to eliminate issues that they feel exceed the terms of the disputes, and has called for interim negotiated settlements by "consensus" where the wealthy nations' power disparity would allow yet greater leverage against opponents.[8]

PUBLIC INTEREST IS BIG LOSER UNDER WTO DISPUTE RESOLUTION

The WTO's powerful and enforceable dispute-resolution system was to be all things for all WTO member countries. U.S. WTO proponents promised that it would enable the U.S., which has among the most deregulated markets in the world, to enforce WTO obligations assumed by the rest of the world. By the same token, WTO proponents in other countries promised that it would protect the rest of the world from U.S. unilateralism and give nations at various stages of development equal access to remedies against powerful countries' violations of trade rules.

After nearly nine years of WTO panel rulings, however, the reality is quite different. First, when viewed outside the context of competition between countries, the real loser is the public interest. When the record of WTO cases is scrutinized by topic rather than by country, nearly every health, food safety or environmental law challenged at the WTO has been declared a barrier to trade. (The only exceptions are the challenge to France's ban on asbestos and a WTO panel's determination that the U.S. had weakened the Endangered Species Act turtle regulations sufficiently to comply with the WTO's ruling against them and thus the U.S. did not have to do more.)

It's OK when GATTzilla Eats Flipper, but Corporate Interests Suddenly Decry WTO Dispute Resolution When It's Their Tax Break That Is Zapped

When environmentalists screamed that "GATTzilla Ate Flipper" after the tuna-dolphin decision, the WTO's corporate boosters dismissed the criticism of the WTO as protectionist and misinformed. But when the WTO ruled against the U.S. Foreign Sales Corporation (FSC) tax break, American CEOs had a midlife conversion about the WTO—lamenting the democracy deficit in the WTO dispute-resolution process using language eerily similar to civil-society WTO critics.

- "This dispute cuts to the very heart of the domestic policy choices made by governments."—Stuart Eizenstat, deputy secretary of the U.S. Treasury Department, September 8, 2000[9]
- "Once tax policy is on the table, there's no end to what the WTO might meddle in."—*Wall Street Journal* editorial, January 17, 2002[10]
- "For the WTO to start commenting whether U.S. tax policy is acceptable is a huge expansion of its authority. You have to ask, where does it stop?"—Daniel Mitchell, senior fellow, Heritage Foundation, September 1, 2002[11]
- "The more the WTO tries to be a world supergovernment that trumps policies the less likely it will be to be able to do its real job of serving as an independent trade referee."—*Wall Street Journal* editorial, January 17, 2002[12]

The FSC provides a tax benefit to corporations by exempting exports made by subsidiaries overseas from corporate earnings for U.S. tax purposes. The FSC has long been the target of budget critics as corporate welfare—projected to provide $62 billion in tax breaks to eligible companies between 2001–2011.[13] However, FSC is not unique; the EU also limits taxation of profits earned overseas. Indeed, the U.S. and EU had an informal agreement not to challenge each other's export tax break policies. In what has become an epic WTO case, in 1997, the EU challenged the FSC claiming that it constituted a WTO-illegal export subsidy that violated both the WTO Subsidies Agreement and the Agreement on Agriculture.[14] Trade analysts surmise that the EU brought the

FSC challenge in part because of its frustration with the U.S. WTO victories in the banana (see Chapter 6) and beef hormone (see Chapter 2) disputes. In October 1999, the WTO ruled against the U.S., finding that FSC did constitute an illegitimate export subsidy under the Subsidies Agreement and ordered the U.S. to conform its law to WTO rules by October 2000.[15] The U.S. sought to negotiate the matter with the EU, but the EU, stinging from hundreds of millions of dollars in WTO-approved tariff sanctions in the beef and banana cases, would not back down.[16] The U.S. appealed and in February 2000 lost its appeal with the WTO Appellate Body again recommending that FSC be eliminated.[17] The U.S. declined to repeal the measure and U.S. corporations benefiting from the policy advanced a modified policy.[18] The "FSC-2000" coalition paid nearly $1 million to PricewaterhouseCoopers to write the new tax law, the "FSC Repeal and Extraterritorial Income Exclusion Act," which was supposed to be a WTO-legal version of the tax loophole.[19] The legislation was hurriedly passed to meet the WTO's October 1, 2000, deadline[20] and President Clinton signed it into law on November 15.[21]

The EU continued its criticism of the new FSC measure, although U.S. officials contended that it operated similarly to Dutch and French tax measures.[22] Two days after the president signed the bill into law, the EU requested to impose $4.043 billion in WTO retaliatory sanctions and asked the WTO to establish a compliance panel to determine the new law did not comply with the original WTO order.[23] The U.S. objected to the amount of sanctions, referring the dispute to arbitration.

In August 2001, the WTO ruled that new FSC measure still constituted an illegitimate export subsidy under WTO rules.[24] A coalition of 74 businesses urged the Bush administration to come to an agreement with the EU over the FSC dispute, writing: "Absent an appeal or suspension, the specter of massive EU retaliation would draw near and possibly take on a political life of its own."[25] In October 2001, the U.S. decided to appeal the latest WTO ruling, even though it had lost three previous times.[26] In January 2002, the WTO ruled against the FSC again.[27] Then in August 2002, the arbitration panel found the EU was entitled to impose the full amount in sanctions.[28] The dispute continues to simmer with the Bush administration now urging Congress to rewrite the tax code to come into compliance with the WTO.[29] As Senator Russ Feingold (D-Wisc) noted in a Senate floor debate on the issue: "While the FSC tax subsidy may be bad tax policy, it is our tax policy—a policy arrived at through the elected representatives of the people of this Nation. The ability of some international bureaucracy to effectively impose punitive taxes or tariffs on American goods should offend us all."[30] As of the summer of 2003, the EU has not imposed the massive $4 billion in sanctions the WTO authorized, perhaps to avoid further poisoning relations before the Cancún Ministerial. Two competing proposals have been introduced in the House of Representatives to again seek to conform U.S. law to the WTO order, however the bills are stuck in committee as different interests battle over what another tax rewrite would mean for U.S. jobs and which corporations will get what benefits.

Another trend is that in most cases the plaintiff wins, meaning that countries that can afford to launch challenges generally are winning. As a result, mere threats of WTO action now are causing many countries to change their policies. This is particularly damaging to developing countries that often lack the resources or expertise to defend their domestic laws before WTO tribunals in Geneva as described in Chapter 3 regarding Guatemala's weakening of its infant formula labeling policy after WTO threats.

To date, nearly one in four of the cases (66 of 279 or 23.7%) brought to the WTO were brought by developed countries against developing countries, according to a Public Citizen analysis of the WTO's DSU system results between January 1995 and January 2003.[31]

Despite the claims made to the developing countries that the WTO dispute system would level the playing field, developed countries have brought 177 of the 279 (63.4%) WTO challenges. The largest developing countries such as Brazil and India have also made use of system; however, to the extent smaller countries have been involved, it has been mainly as a defendant. As of January 2003, no least developed country (LDC) member brought a WTO challenge.[32]

Often the threat of litigation forces a settlement.
—USTR General Counsel Peter Davidson,
November 6, 2001[33]

We can only bring complaints if our industry is prepared to foot the bill. That makes it difficult to bring cases on matters of principle.
—anonymous ambassador from a
large developing country,
November 29, 1999[34]

To date, WTO tribunals have almost always sided with a challenging country and ruled against the targeted law. In only 13 out of 88 completed WTO cases did the respondents win—or 14.8%.[35] The success rates for plaintiffs—an astounding 85.2%—conceals significant disparities for developing nations. Of the 21 rulings in cases brought by developed countries against developing countries, 20 of them—94.4%—ruled against developing-country domestic laws challenged at the WTO. In contrast, the lowest success rate for plaintiffs at the WTO were in cases where developed countries challenged other developed countries whose domestic measures were upheld 25.6% of the time—twice the success of average defendants and five times more successful than developing countries challenged by developed countries.

Developed-country plaintiffs have won more than four out of five cases (81.7%) that have gone to completion between 1995 and 2002. Of the 60 completed cases brought against the developed countries (39 by other developed countries, 18 by developing countries, and four by a mix of plaintiffs) the defending country successfully defended their laws in 11 of them, or 18.3% of the time. In comparison, of 28 cases that have gone to completion against developing nations (21 brought by developed nations and seven by developing nations), the developing nations have only won two cases—or 7.1%, slightly less than a third the success of developed-country defendants.

The U.S.—which has brought more complaints than any other country—was a claimant or co-claimant in 74 of the 279 WTO challenges brought to the WTO between 1995 and 2002 that received a WTO case number. The U.S. prevailed as the plaintiff 78.4% of the time, slightly less than the average. Yet, cases the U.S. brought and "won" have not necessarily benefited the public interest. The U.S. has lost two important cases: the Kodak case and the EU computer case it brought. The U.S. has lost five out of six (83.3%) of the completed cases brought against it. In 25 cases, U.S. laws challenged at the WTO have been ruled against with the WTO labeling as illegal U.S. policies ranging from sea turtle protection and clean air regulations to antidumping policies. Complaints about the growing number of U.S. laws being ruled against by the WTO are increasingly ringing in the halls of Congress—most loudly by prominent WTO boosters. In five instances, the WTO upheld U.S. laws challenged at the WTO.[36] As lopsided as this record may be, the U.S. 25% defense rate exceeds the 15% aggregate of defendant wins at the WTO. Still, Europe has a better record of defending its domestic laws, prevailing 45.5% of the time with five laws defended successfully in 11 completed cases.

Top 5 WTO Plaintiffs

United States	74
EU	63
Canada	24
Brazil	22
India	15

WTO TRIBUNALS: SECRET PROCEEDINGS, LACK OF DUE PROCESS

WTO dispute panels operate in secret, documents are restricted to the countries in the dispute and the press and public are excluded.[37] The WTO's lower panels and Appellate Body meet in closed sessions and the proceedings are confidential.[38] All documents are also kept confidential unless a government voluntarily releases its own submissions to the public.[39] No outside appeal to a WTO ruling is available. These operational rules have remained in effect since the WTO and its powerful DSU were established.

The process begins when member countries file a complaint against another country's policy, usually at the behest of domestic business interests. In the U.S., which has numerous procedural rules aimed at providing opportunities for public input into other government decisions, there is no requirement that notice be given to the public—much less an opportunity to comment—before the U.S. instigates a

WTO challenge. The same applies to nearly all WTO member countries, meaning one set of interests—business—determines what cases will be brought to the WTO. At issue is not an unrequited desire by environmental or consumer interests to launch a WTO attack on another nation's laws, but rather the inability of non-commercial interests to *stop* U.S. WTO attacks that would undermine the public interest in other nations and/or boomerang in a later WTO case to destroy a related U.S. policy. For instance, the U.S. has systematically employed the WTO as a wrecking ball against the Precautionary Principle. Yet, many U.S. laws, such as our pharmaceutical approval process, rely on the same principle.

Furthermore, the closed nature of the process prevents domestic proponents of health, environmental or other policies under attack from obtaining sufficient information to provide input. This is in sharp contrast to domestic courts and even to other international arbitration systems, such as the International Court of Justice which deliberates in public and employs strict due process criteria.[40] The WTO's closed operations also stand in sharp contrast to the promises of the Clinton Administration officials who sold the WTO to Congress, such as then–U.S. Trade Representative Mickey Kantor, who stated "the Uruguay Round Agreements provide for increased transparency in the dispute settlement process."[41]

WTO disputes are heard by tribunals composed of three panelists.[42] These tribunals are comprised of an ever-changing cast of trade experts with the WTO Secretariat nominating panel members for each dispute from a roster. The disputing parties may oppose nominations only for "compelling reasons."[43] The only recourse after a WTO panel ruling is to appeal to the WTO Appellate Body which is a standing committee of seven trade experts with three selected to hear each appeal. To date, the Appellate Body has narrowed lower panels' jurisprudence in several cases but has reversed only two cases (in favor of the EU in a U.S. case against the European Union's computer tariff classifications and in favor of the EU in its case against U.S. countervailing duties against German carbon steel).[44]

1. Bureaucrats with Trade Expertise Judge Environmental, Public Health, Worker Rights and Economic Development Policies

WTO tribunalists are picked off a roster of people who meet qualifications enumerated in the DSU, including past service on GATT panels, past representation of a country before a trade institution or tribunal, past service as a senior trade policy official of a WTO member country, and teaching experience in or publishing on international trade law or policy.[45] These qualifications promote the selection of panelists with a stake in the existing system and rules, eliminating potential panelists who do not share an institutionally derived philosophy about international commerce and the primacy of the WTO system.

These qualifications also serve to narrowly limit the panelists' areas of expertise to international commerce, yet many disputes are about domestic policies to protect broad public interests such as the environment, animal and human health, and workplace health and safety. There are no mechanisms for ensuring that individuals serving as panelists have any expertise in the subject of the dispute before them and the DSU does not require panelists to consult with experts. A panel may, but is not required to, call on outside experts.[46] The record shows that WTO panelists have needed more than just trade law expertise, as the outcome of several cases has turned on the interpretation of environmental treaties or general rules of international law.[47] The outcomes have not always been consistent with conventional legal interpretations, and WTO panels have been criticized in international law journals for their excessively narrow interpretations of general rules of international law.[48] One very basic safeguard for minimally ensuring accurate legal analysis would be the selection of panelists with broader competencies. The International Court of Justice, for example, requires its judges to possess competence in international law and be of high moral standard.[49] In addition, the European Court of Justice employs a system of advocates general to represent the public interest.

2. Conflict of Interest Standards at the WTO: Don't Ask, Don't Tell

The WTO dispute resolution system lacks a mechanism guaranteeing that panelists do not have potential conflicts of interest in serving on a panel. In 1996, the WTO adopted the Rules of Conduct for the Understanding on Rules and Procedures Governing the Settlement of Disputes.[50] The document recognizes that confidence in the DSU panels is linked closely to the integrity and impartiality of its panelists.[51] The provisions designed to achieve this, however, are so weak that they are pointless. For instance, former director-general of the GATT Arthur Dunkel, a well-known figure in trade circles, served on a WTO dispute panel concerning an EU challenge of the U.S. Cuban Liberty and Democratic Solidarity Act (a law also known as Helms-Burton).[52] The law sanctions foreign companies benefiting from investment in assets illegally seized from U.S. nationals during the Cuban revolution and sets U.S. visa restrictions for the executives of such companies.[53] At the time, Dunkel chaired the International Chamber of Commerce's Commission on International Trade and Investment Policy, a body that has strongly opposed the very law he was appointed to judge.[54] He also served on the board of Nestle S.A., which operates a production company in Cuba,[55] and thus had an interest in the outcome of this case and in the status of U.S. commercial policy regarding Cuba.

Under the Rules of Conduct, discovery of the panelists' backgrounds is based on self-disclosure, leaving it up to the individual panelist to decide which aspects of his or her past should be known.[56] The rules stipulate that the disclosure "shall not extend to the identification of matters [of insignificant] relevance"; that it must "take into account the need to respect the personal privacy" of the panelists; and that it must not be "so administratively burdensome as to make it impracticable for otherwise qualified persons to serve on the panels."[57] In other words, if the person fulfills the criteria set out in the original DSU, it is up to him or her to disclose whether a conflict exists and if full disclosure is deemed burdensome by the panelist, it is waived, and the panelist still can qualify. The lack of meaningful WTO conflict-of-interest rules means that panelists with potential conflicts of interest are being empowered to judge countries' domestic policies.

Finally, contrary to the majority of court hearings, whether international or domestic, where the judges sign their opinions by name, opinions expressed in the final WTO panel reports by individual panelists remain anonymous.[58] This practice removes yet another important way for the public to monitor the relationship between the panelists' background and their work on the panels.

3. Adding Insult to Injury: WTO Limits Citizens' Ability to Rectify Panels' Shortcomings

The lack of competence on health, environment and other matters among WTO tribunal members could have been rectified to some extent by requiring the participation by ad hoc independent experts on panels or by requiring panels to consider third-party submissions from parties with a demonstrated interest in the case (*amici curiae* or *amicus* briefs). The WTO's dispute resolution system does not provide for any of these due process guarantees.

WTO panels are allowed, but not required, to seek information and technical advice from outside individuals and expert bodies. However, the names of such experts are kept secret until the panel issues its report on the case, making it impossible to prevent conflicts of interest among the technical experts. Also citizens of WTO member countries whose laws are challenged cannot serve on expert review groups, preventing participation by policy experts most knowledgeable about the reasons for and the operation of the domestic measures in question.[59]

The first effort to submit *amicus* briefs to the WTO was in the 1996 Venezuela gasoline case (see Chapter 1). These documents, which were submitted by environmental groups to demonstrate the technical necessity of the challenged U.S. regulatory approach, were returned by the WTO with a curt note stating that the WTO did not accept such materials and with directions to submit *amicus* briefs to the NGO's own government.[60] This approach is very limited, as demonstrated during the 1998 beef hormone case, when U.S. public-interest groups strenuously opposed the U.S. government's attack on a European health law and thus the groups' perspective was totally excluded from the U.S. brief. U.S consumer groups also attempted to submit an *amicus* brief to WTO supporting the European ban and an annex of medical research showing health risks associated with artificial hormone use but the WTO again rejected the submission, arguing that the WTO is a governments-only body.

The WTO lifted its absolute ban on *amicus* briefs in 1998, but allowed *amicus* briefs only if they constitute part of a government's formal submission in a case.[61]

However, governments always were able to include the contents of outside briefs or other materials in their submissions if they so chose.[62] However, if a sub-federal government or a public-interest or advocacy organization disagrees with the position of its government in a WTO case, it is unlikely that the government would submit it and thus such interests would be required to navigate the trade and litigation operations of another country involved in the dispute and somehow convince another country's officials to submit their *amicus* brief.

Many developing countries have been critical of *amicus* submissions. Under DSU rules, countries not involved in a particular dispute also are denied access to the documents and hearing. Some developing countries also have been denied meaningful third-party rights (the ability to observe or intervene) even when their interests are implicated directly. For instance, the Caribbean island nations whose bananas were contested in the U.S.-EU WTO banana case hired trade lawyers to represent them who were denied WTO access. Thus, some developing countries argue that *amicus* submissions would be accorded more flexibility than interested WTO country third-party filings and thus that NGOs and industry trade associations would have more preferential access to the dispute system than WTO members. Another approach to the real problem facing developing countries would be to improve their role rather than excluding other interested parties.

4. No Outside Appeal Allowed

WTO panels establish specific deadlines by which a losing country must implement the panel's decision. If this deadline is not met, the winning party may request negotiations to determine mutually acceptable compensation. If compensation is not sought or not agreed to, the winning party may request WTO authorization to impose trade sanctions. Once requested, sanctions are disallowed only if there is unanimous consensus against sanctions, requiring the winning country to also agree to drop its sanctions request.[63]

For a government that loses a case, there is no appeals process outside of the WTO's Appellate Body. Thus, the WTO's Appellate Body is the court of last resort.

The DSU merely provides that those persons serving on the Appellate Body are to be "persons of recognized authority with demonstrated expertise in law, international trade and the subject matter of the covered Agreements generally." Again, as with the lower panels, there are no provisions for environmental, consumer law or labor experts to serve on the Appellate Body. And unlike members of lower panels who are called to serve in particular cases, the appeal panelists are part of a seven-person standing WTO body, meaning that they are on the permanent WTO payroll.[64] This is a startling conflict in its own right, given that every case requires a determination of whether domestic law or the Appellate Body tribunalists' employer's rules take precedence.

Two of the Appellate Body's most dramatic actions have involved the U.S. The first one came after a lower panel ruling in the shrimp-turtle case that was so fanatical in its antienvironmental tone that it created a backlash among even WTO boosters—including the *New York Times* editorial entitled, "The Sea Turtles Warning."[65] The interpretation was based on nothing but the tautological whim of the WTO legal staff or perhaps the panelists on the case.[66]

In a dramatic display of politics—the politics of trying to save the WTO from itself—the Appellate Body wrote a remarkably soothing-toned opinion, which while spouting lots of nice, nonbinding, and green platitudes, upheld the lower panel's determination that the U.S. law violated the WTO and had to be changed. The Appellate Body ruling was such a sophisticated piece of political writing, as far as trying to appease enraged legislators and environmentalists, that the Clinton administration got away with using selected portions of it to spin the press into initially reporting that the U.S. won the appeal and the lower panel had been reversed.[67] Once the actual ruling was made public, it became clear that the bottom line was the same: the U.S. law had to be changed or eliminated.

The second unusual Appellate Body ruling involved only the second time the Appellate Body reversed a lower panel ruling. This case involved tariffs imposed by the EU on U.S.-manufactured computers. In February 1998, a WTO dispute panel ruled in favor of the U.S. in its complaint that the EU was violating the GATT by reclassifying computer equipment to impose higher tariffs.[68]

But in June 1998, the WTO Appellate Body reversed the earlier decision.[69] The USTR then reversed its initial proclamations that the earlier WTO win would affect "billions of dollars in U.S. exports,"[70] suddenly claiming that "this decision will have a limited economic impact."[71] In stark contrast, computer industry officials viewed the WTO Appellate Body ruling as a serious setback that would allow European competitors to establish market share in an industry where U.S. manufacturers have captured 50% of the market. "We thought the original decision was a significant victory for U.S. exporters and established an important precedent that switching classifications was a violation of world trade rules," one computer industry official said. "We are very upset that the decision has been overruled."[72]

5. WTO's Frivolous "Non-Violation" Clause: A Domestic Law Can Be Ruled WTO-Illegal Even if it Violates No WTO Rules

The WTO dispute-resolution rules also include very broad and vague provisions that can be used by any WTO member country to challenge another country's laws at WTO even if they violate no specific WTO rule. Called "Nullification and Impairment," these provisions allow challenges on the grounds that "any benefit accruing to it [a WTO member country] directly or indirectly" under WTO rules is "being nullified or impaired or the attainment of any objective of that Agreement is being impeded . . . whether or not it conflicts with the provisions of that Agreement."[73]

WTO Nullification and Impairment challenges do not require an actual breach of a legal obligation contained in any of the WTO's underlying agreements. All that must be alleged is that the actions of one country have impaired the benefits that another country had a reasonable expectation of attaining from the Uruguay Round Agreements overall. Allowing such a vague and subjective basis for a WTO challenge exposes even wider swaths of domestic policies to threats of WTO action.

WTO Rules Trump State and Local Laws

WTO rules trump state and local policy and national government signatories to WTO must take all constitutionally available steps to force subfederal compliance with WTO's rules or face trade sanctions. This principle was established in a 1992 GATT ruling in a case, dubbed "Beer II," which involved a successful

Canadian challenge to alcohol-related tax rules and distribution practices in 41 U.S. states and Puerto Rico.[74] In defending the various state laws, the U.S. argued that GATT rules only required an effort by federal governments to obtain subfederal GATT compliance, that the U.S. had taken all reasonable measures, and that this state activity was outside of its direct control. The GATT panel rejected that argument and ruled that a country has not satisfied its GATT obligations unless it exercises all powers against its subfederal entities that are constitutionally available to it. In the U.S. context, thus would include preemptive legislation, suing subfederal entities and/or pressuring them for changes by cutting off benefits, such as highway funds. Moreover, the GATT panel in Beer II ruled on the question of the relative legal effect of GATT versus U.S. state law: "GATT law is part of federal law in the United States and as such is superior to GATT-inconsistent state law."[75] This ruling was all the more difficult to fathom because the state tax breaks that the GATT had ruled against would have passed very onerous constitutional muster had they been challenged under the Commerce Clause of the U.S. Constitution as burdening interstate commerce.

TRADE SAFEGUARD RULES UNDER THE WTO DISPUTE SYSTEM

A large number of WTO cases and even a larger amount of controversy involve national trade safeguard laws that have been subject to repeated challenges at the WTO. Many formal disputes have involved such laws and now one of the most contentious issues in current WTO negotiations is about the rules regulating such policies. Trade safeguard regimes (including antidumping laws, countervailing duties, and import surge safeguard protections) are all designed to grease the global trade system by dealing with frictions caused by the increasingly rapid flows of goods across borders, for instance by setting temporary quotas against surging imports or raising tariffs to countervail against the price benefit of a subsidy. These mechanisms used to be seen primarily as a trade policy tool of wealthy countries—especially the U.S.—but increasingly developing countries that have dropped their tariff and quota regimes under the Uruguay Round are themselves facing surging imports and dumping of subsidized imports and thus also are relying on trade safeguard measures to maintain their domestic agricultural and industrial bases.

There was intense pressure on the U.S., especially by Japan, to eliminate its trade safeguard laws during the Uruguay Round and the U.S. threatened to walk unless key elements of U.S. trade law were maintained.[76] The Uruguay Round negotiations ended in a compromise: U.S. negotiators assured the U.S. Congress and industry that the most vital components of U.S. trade law mechanisms were maintained under the new WTO rules, which require that trade laws be fair, transparent and consistent with the WTO.[77] Yet to date, nearly half of the U.S. trade law orders that were reviewed under these WTO rules have been found in violation.

Among the elements of domestic anti-dumping and safeguard law that had to be consistent with WTO rules were the timelines for cases and the methodology used to determine if dumping was occurring when a surge of imports injured domestic producers.[78] One issue the U.S. successfully sought to be clarified in the Uruguay Round was that DSU panels would defer to national governments on the factual records in the investigations of trade law violations and remedies.

What Are Trade Safeguards?

- *Antidumping Measures* impose a tariff (called an antidumping duty) on imported goods sold below their cost of production, thereby raising the price of the good to fair value and allowing domestic products to compete fairly.
- *Countervailing Duty Measures* impose a duty on imports to counterbalance the effects of domestic subsidies or other benefits a product has enjoyed. Anti-dumping and countervailing duty mechanisms often operate in tandem and often are dubbed AD/CVD measures.
- *Surge Protection or Safeguards* are mechanisms under which import surges are investigated and tariffs are imposed to reduce the damage these imports can have on domestic producers. Key U.S. surge protection safeguards include Section 201 of the Trade Act of 1974.

These laws all require complex, extensive investigations and are based on complicated formulas and decades of trade law jurisprudence. All three mechanisms require proof that import trends and/or the pricing of imports are significantly hurting domestic producers. Antidumping investigations require that import prices be either below the cost of production or below the price in the exporting country's home market. Countervailing duty investigations require a demonstration that the exporting country's policies provide an unfair benefit to exporting businesses. Surge protection investigations require the demonstration of significant increases in imports and a demonstration of harm to domestic producers. These trade safeguard investigations and orders, when they are imposed, take months or even years to be put in place. In the U.S., before an order can be put in place, the case must be investigated by the U.S. International Trade Commission, only then can a recommendation be made to the president (who need not act on it).[79] Final recommendations to the president to impose anti-dumping, countervailing duty or import safeguards can take between nine and 14 months, depending on the outcomes of the stages of the investigation.[80]

Increasingly more developing countries are developing and using trade safeguard measures[81] as their domestic production faces increasingly volatile surges in imported goods—often sold at artificially low prices or with supportive subsidies unavailable to the domestic market. During 2000, developed countries initiated just under half the anti-dumping investigations reported to the WTO, initiating

45.5% of the 272 investigations: Argentina launched 45, India 41, South Africa 21 and Brazil 11.[82] In 2001, India reported more antidumping investigations to the WTO than the U.S.[83]

Trade Safeguards Targeted at WTO

Trade safeguard regimes frequently have been challenged at the WTO and they frequently have been ruled to violate WTO rules. Between 1995 and 2002, nearly one third (31.9%) of all WTO dispute-resolution cases and about the same share of completed cases (30.7%) were challenges of countries' trade safeguard measures.[84] Only three trade safeguard measures challenged at WTO have been upheld—slightly more than one in ten (11.1%).

The trade safeguard measures of developed countries were most often targeted at the WTO. Developed countries' trade safeguard measures were more likely to be ruled WTO-illegal than other types of measures challenged with only two such cases resulting in the safeguard measures being upheld— or 10.5% compared to an overall success rate of 18.3% for developed-country defendants.

Trade safeguard measures employed by developing countries also faced WTO challenge. Developing-country trade safeguard measures were challenged 28 times (nine challenges by developed countries and 29 by developing countries) at the WTO between 1995 and 2002. Developing countries were less likely to protect their trade safeguards than domestic measures generally. Only 12.5% of developing-country safeguard measures were upheld in completed cases, which is slightly less successful than the 14.8% of the total developing-country measures that were upheld.

The new use of safeguard measures by developing countries facing increased imports and import volatility is represented in the increasing number of WTO challenges to developing countries' use of such laws. More than three quarters (76%) of the challenges against developing-country safeguard measures are from other developing countries.

Challenges against U.S. trade safeguard law at the WTO already have been frequent and largely successful. Of the 11 completed cases against U.S. trade safeguard law the U.S. has only won two. More than half (59.2%) of the challenges brought against the U.S. at the WTO were against U.S. trade safeguard laws and their application. Developing countries' challenges to U.S. trade laws are one area in which developing countries have made regular use of the WTO and have never lost a completed case—the record is 7–0, including two cases filed with developed-country coplaintiffs.

The majority of WTO cases against trade safeguard regimes revolve around the interpretations of the factual record a government uses to justify its trade remedy. For instance the economic model to measure whether there was unfair pricing is challenged, but not the underlying trade law itself. For example, the U.S. lost a WTO case based on how the U.S. International Trade Commission calculated pricing differentials between Canada's softwood lumber subsidy and costs in the U.S.[85]

Some of the U.S. anti-dumping, countervailing duties and safeguard measures that have been challenged at the WTO have extensive domestic and international political histories. For example, the dispute between the U.S. and Canada over trade in lumber dates back to the 1800s. Since 1982, the U.S. has challenged Canada's lumber policies and practices as illegitimate subsidies that should be disciplined with countervailing duties under U.S. trade law.

This dispute has centered on the impact each country's timber policies have on the lumber industries in their respective countries. The U.S. ITC has contended that the Canadian government subsidizes lumber production by setting the price lumber companies pay for harvesting rights (known as "stumpage fees") from public land at artificially low levels.[86] Nearly all (94%) of Canadian forests are owned by the government.[87] In contrast, more than half (58%) of the timberland in the U.S. is privately owned, and timber is sold at public auctions, which are more sensitive to market forces.[88] Environmentalists also have argued that Canada's lumber policies create subsidies that promote intensive harvesting of Canada's forests and sales of lumber at a fraction of its real value.[89]

After years of battling, the U.S. and Canada entered into a Softwood Lumber Agreement (SLA) in 1996 to set bilateral trade terms for softwood lumber through March 31, 2001.[90] Under the terms of the agreement, the U.S. set a volume quota on the importation of Canadian softwood lumber at 14.7 billion board feet.[91] For every 1,000 board feet imported to the U.S. in excess of the quota, a $50 fee was imposed on the imports, up to the next 650 million board feet.[92] A $100 per thousand board feet fee was assessed on imports in excess of 15.25 billion board feet.[93] In exchange, Canada received commitments that the U.S. would not initiate anti-dumping or countervailing duty investigations or orders on Canadian softwood lumber trade.[94] While the agreement was in force, Canadian exports to the U.S. remained fairly stable at about $7 billion worth of softwood lumber each year, accounting for a third of the U.S. market.[95] As the expiration of the Softwood Lumber Agreement approached, the U.S. attempted to reach a compromise with Canada over a possible replacement for the agreement, but failed.

The day after the Softwood Lumber Agreement expired, the Coalition for Fair Lumber Imports, an organization of lumber mills, owners, and loggers representing 75% of U.S. production, asked the U.S. Commerce Department to begin an anti-dumping and countervailing duty investigation and to apply a 78% duty to future softwood lumber imported from Canada.[96] The coalition contended that cheap Canadian softwood lumber imports were responsible for 160 lumber mill closings and that further imports threaten the jobs of 700,000 U.S. workers in the timber industry.[97] U.S. initiation of trade action against the subsidized Canadian lumber imports led to Canada challenging the U.S.—successfully—at the WTO. Since Canada's first WTO challenge, the U.S. has tried to implement different safeguard measures. Each time the U.S. has acted, Canada has turned to the WTO for relief, resulting in five back-and-forths between the U.S. and Canada over trade law at the WTO as the U.S. attempts to counter Canada's lumber policies with countervailing duties or anti-dumping orders.[98] To date, the WTO has ruled in favor of Canada in two of the cases and the others are pending.

Another contentious trade law dispute is over U.S. efforts to minimize the impact of surging steel imports and steel dumping which put tremendous pressure on U.S. steel producers and workers. Nearly one in three U.S. steelmakers had filed for bankruptcy (29%) by January 2002; tens of thousands of steelworkers across the country were thrown out of work and retirees abruptly lost their health care and pension benefits.[99] Former U.S. Treasury Secretary Paul O'Neill estimated that there is a 35% global overcapacity in steel—meaning the world produces significantly more steel than it consumes, driving down prices when imports flood a domestic market.[100] The volume of steel imports into the U.S. has been higher since the WTO went into effect than any year before the WTO's launch, with volume increasing 12% each year between 1991 and 2000. If these trends continue, steel imports could increase to 66 million tons by 2005, which is an amount equal to about half of U.S. production.[101] The crisis was a perfect example of when safeguard measures would be appropriate, especially considering that the U.S. steel industry had undergone a painful restructuring in the 1980s and is one of the world's most efficient.

After enormous pressure from the United Steelworkers of America union and U.S. steel producers, President George W. Bush instructed the U.S. International Trade Commission to examine the impact imports had had on the U.S. steel industry *after* the Asian financial crisis, which had led to a sudden surge of steel imports. The investigation showed that even after the peak of the Asian crisis U.S. steel prices had continued to decline, below even 1998 prices. The composite price of steel in December 2001 was $285 a ton—12% below the low point of $325 during the 1998 peak of the Asian crisis.[102]

Given the ITC's findings Bush ultimately enacted steel safeguards on March 6, 2002.[103] The president took a first step in addressing the crisis by imposing an emergency import surge protection tariff of between 8% and 30% on certain categories of imported steel that would be phased out rapidly over three years.

This action drew an immediate response from steel producing countries worldwide. The Bush administration quickly began doling out exemptions to the tariffs—with nearly one thousand specific country-product exceptions granted by 2003. Despite this, the U.S. use of Section 201 safeguards for steel generated nine challenges at the WTO—from the EU, Korea, Japan, China, Switzerland, Norway, New Zealand, Brazil and Taiwan. The various challenges contested the U.S. action as inconsistent with the WTO's Safeguards Agreement, most-favored nation rules, tariff rate quota obligations under GATT, and the GATT safeguard provisions. The WTO established a Panel for the EU's challenge in June 2002, and four subsequent Panel requests from the other parties were all consolidated with the EU Panel. In July 2003, the panel ruled against the U.S. safeguards and the U.S. announced it would appeal even as the European Union reiterated that it would apply $2.2 billion in sanctions if the appeal failed and urge the U.S. to comply with the WTO and lift the tariffs given the string of similar cases it already had lost at WTO.[104] A final ruling will come in 2004.

Generally, although the U.S. has lost several antidumping, countervailing duty, and safeguard cases in addition to the Steel 201 case, including regarding hot rolled steel in a case by Japan[105] and circular welded pipe in a case by Korea,[106] it has done little to change the underlying trade safeguard laws and instead has lifted a handful of antidumping orders and let others expire. As a result of some of these actions, U.S. producers—including U.S. manufacturing workers and small farmers—have been wiped out by unfair trade surges.

In 1999, the EU and Japan had challenged the actual 1916 Anti-Dumping Act statute arguing that its allowance of private claims and criminal prosecutions of the companies that dump goods into the U.S. market violate WTO rules. The WTO panel ruled that the law's requirement of a specific intent to dump did not comply with the WTO rules and that the civil and criminal penalties of the law exceeded the WTO terms; in 2000, the U.S. unsuccessfully appealed.[107] USTR maintains that the ruling has no effect on U.S. antidumping law because current actions are initiated under a different statute, the Tariff Act of 1930, which is unaffected by the ruling on the earlier statute. The EU and Japan sought arbitration to implement the ruling. Legislation introduced in late 2001 to repeal the law failed to pass the U.S. Congress in 2002. The arbitration panel suspended its work in March 2002 while the U.S., EU, and Japan continue ongoing efforts to resolve the dispute.[108]

In 2003, the U.S. also lost a WTO challenge against another element of an actual trade law, itself, the so-called Byrd amendment. The Continued Dumping and Subsidy Offset Act of 2000, known as the Byrd amendment after its sponsor Senator Robert Byrd (D-W.V.), changed the U.S. Tariff Act of 1930 to transfer funds received under antidumping and countervailing orders to the injured U.S. companies (instead of the U.S. Treasury).[109] In December 2000, Australia, Brazil, Chile, the EU, India, Indonesia, Japan, Korea and Thailand, and later joined by Canada and Mexico, challenged the policy. The WTO ruled against the Byrd Amendment[110] and a U.S. appeal failed in January 2003.[111] USTR tried to minimize the political fallout by noting that the ruling upheld the underlying U.S. laws but found against the transfer of the funds to companies.[112] USTR has "stated its intention to implement the DSB recommendations and rulings."[113] The U.S. must change the laws to avoid trade sanctions, but to date, Congress has not been so inclined.

Doha Ministerial Launches New Trade Safeguards Negotiations

Prior to the 1999 Seattle WTO Ministerial, a variety of countries had begun a push for new negotiations aimed at *further* limiting countries' use of antidumping and countervailing duty laws. The U.S. was a special target of this effort, which was initiated by Japan, Korea, Brazil, and other countries but stalled by the collapse of the Seattle Ministerial.

Two years later at the Doha WTO Ministerial, Japan, Brazil, Chile and Korea, supported by all WTO members except Costa Rica, were demanding a renegotiation of WTO anti-dumping rules to further constrain U.S. domestic trade laws. Ironically, since the Uruguay Round, U.S. anti-dumping investigations have decreased by 42% and the number of CVD orders dropped by 34%.[114] Still other nations argued that the string of U.S. WTO losses on trade law cases proved that the U.S. laws must be changed and they sought new WTO rules to force such changes as a key element of Doha WTO talks.

The new Bush USTR Robert Zoellick was extremely eager to succeed in launching a new WTO "Round" of negotiations, a goal his predecessor had seen defeated by the implosion of the Seattle WTO Ministerial. Zoellick, known to be more focused on the art of the deal than on the substance of U.S. trade law, became the focus as the countdown to Doha began.

Thus, in mid-2001, 62 U.S. senators sent a letter to President Bush opposing the use of U.S. trade laws as "bargaining chips" during international trade negotiations.[115] Given the U.S. Constitution gives Congress exclusive control over the contents of trade policy, trade representatives generally heed such a bipartisan letter signed by a supermajority of senators—enough senators to reject a trade agreement. When USTR Zoellick remained unresponsive, a House resolution (H. Con. Res 262) was passed 410–4 on the first day of the Doha Summit instructing U.S. negotiators to keep U.S. trade laws off the WTO negotiating table.[116]

Regardless, in an act reported in the U.S. press as a flagrant insult to Congress, USTR Zoellick approved new negotiations that would "clarify" trade safeguard laws.[117] While the Doha Ministerial failed to launch negotiations on many of the new issues that had been proposed, new trade laws negotiations were launched.

The USTR also agreed in a special "Implementation-Related Issues and Concerns" Declaration to several specific changes to antidumping rules that went into effect immediately. These new policies undid some of the discretion the U.S. had fought to preserve in the Uruguay Round talks concerning how dumping margins are calculated and over what time periods such analysis is conducted.

Congress exploded in anger, as did many U.S. agriculture and manufacturing sector producers. Then–Department of Commerce Secretary Don Evans suggested that the U.S. had agreed to negotiate anti-dumping and countervailing duty issues because "all we want to do is strengthen them."[118] U.S. negotiators responded to Congress's outrage with claims that the specific wording of the Doha Declaration preserved the "concepts, principles and effectiveness" of U.S. "instruments" and that the new negotiations would not result in the U.S. having to weaken its current laws.[119]

However, given the demanders were countries seeking to limit U.S. anti-dumping and safeguard laws, this spin is implausible. Indeed, other countries described the U.S. agreement as a major concession. United Steelworkers of America President George Becker was the only U.S. union president who traveled to the Doha Ministerial. He reported to the press that USTR Zoellick had tried to avoid telling him that U.S. trade remedy laws were on the table, but that "as far as our trading partners are concerned, they're on the table."[120]

When he returned from Doha, Zoellick also tried to dodge the heat. For instance, he simply did not show up to a hearing of the Senate Finance Committee, the committee with jurisdiction over trade. Sen. Jay Rockefeller (D-WV) used that hearing to publicly chastise Zoellick for reneging on a commitment he made to protect U.S. antidumping or countervailing laws. Rockefeller charged "[Zoellick] promised me, facing me, looking directly in my eye, in my office that he would not in any way compromise anti-dumping laws, [and] he immediately did so within the first five minutes" on Doha.[121] Since then, negotiations have been under way in Geneva.

LACK OF TRANSPARENCY IN DISPUTES AND WTO SECRECY WAS A FOCAL POINT OF THE SEATTLE WTO MINISTERIAL

The 1999 WTO Ministerial in Seattle brought complaints about the secrecy of the WTO's dispute settlement process into high focus for much of the public for the first time. Critics of the WTO model outside the meeting noted the WTO dispute system's hearings and deliberations were closed to the public as well as to many member governments that are not parties to particular disputes. These inherently anti-democratic and elitist trade tribunals were one of the highlighted failures of the WTO by its thousands of critics in Seattle.[122]

Then–President Clinton urged the WTO ministers to address the issue. "I think it's imperative that the WTO become more open and accessible," Clinton said in a speech to the WTO during the Ministerial meeting. "If the WTO expects to have public support grow for our endeavors, the public must see and hear and, in a very real sense, actually join in the deliberations. That's the only way they can know their concerns were at least being considered."[123]

Charlene Barshefsky, U.S. Trade Representative in the Clinton adminstration, echoed this concern just before the Seattle Ministerial, although her words contradicted the priority her agency had actually given to the problem. "It's terribly important that the views of civil society not just be heard but incorporated into the work of the WTO. The openness of civil society is a stabilizing force and lends credibility to the system," she said.[124]

WTO critics were not duped by the Clinton administration platitudes on the need for transparency in the WTO dispute system. Although President Clinton stated that he felt that he should be out in the streets of Seattle during the Ministerial, he and his officials and corporate funders were actively pushing the meeting forward and little substantive change was expected to the dispute system even if the Ministerial had not collapsed. WTO officials snubbed the call for more participation by those who WTO rulings will affect: "The WTO is an intergovernmental organization, and the agreements of the WTO are made by governments," sniffed WTO spokesman Keith Rockwell repelling a press question about WTO's hostility to transparency.[125]

Despite the Seattle meltdown, in the two years before the next WTO Ministerial at Doha, nothing was done to remedy one of the WTO's most obvious failings. Instead, a steady increase in WTO challenges during the period added an additional set of concerns: was WTO litigation resulting in new trade frictions and barriers?

DOHA MINISTERIAL OFFERS LITTLE GUIDANCE OR ENCOURAGEMENT TO IMPROVE DSU

As the Doha Ministerial approached, several countries advanced proposals about improving the dispute resolution system. However, the biggest concern raised by most countries was over the timing of when countries could begin retaliation proceedings against WTO-illegal measures—the so-called "sequencing" issue. At question were how to ensure countries complied with WTO rulings promptly and how to quickly impose sanctions if they did not—including the order in which countries must take enforcement actions and the timing and the mechanism for compliance.[126] How the secrecy that was adding to the WTO's crisis of legitimacy was not addressed, nor were the WTO's other serious due-process flaws.

During 2002, WTO members began to submit their proposals to clarify and improve the DSU as directed by the Doha Declaration.[127] In October 2002, WTO Director General Supachai Panitchpakdi recommended that the DSU be modified to ensure countries do not use the dispute system to propagate trade wars through excessive litigation.[128] He also encouraged the creation of permanent, professional dispute panelists to handle the increasing number and complexity of these cases.

Several developing countries sought to improve the imbalance they face at WTO disputes. First, Haiti proposed that the DSU Agreement be amended to require the WTO Panels consider "any adverse impact that findings may have on social economic welfare" of LDCs, and that the WTO consider holding dispute consultations in the capitals of LDCs involved in WTO disputes.[129]

Haiti also had several substantial process-related reforms of the WTO dispute system including inclusion of more panelists from developing countries. Between 1995 and 2002, only 35% of DSU panelists have been from the developing world.[130] China recommended that the WTO provide technical assistance and capacity building for developing countries in disputes.[131] Haiti also noted that WTO Panel Reports should explicitly consider differential and more favorable treatment for developing and LDCs in disputes.[132] China proposed several specific special and differential considerations of developing countries at WTO disputes and that developed countries exercise restraint in bringing WTO challenges and not bring more than two cases against any given developing country per year.[133]

Some other issues being raised by WTO members during the DSU discussions launched at Doha included:

Monetary Concessions

Many developing nations noted that the dispute system discriminates against relatively poorer countries who may not be able to benefit from the imposition of trade sanctions against rich countries such as the U.S. or EU and thus would remain damaged by WTO-illegal measures. For example, sanctions as a remedy might have little impact, either because the developing country has few imports from the rich country to sanction or because sanctions might increase consumer costs in the "victorious" country for an irreplaceable good that cannot be acquired from another exporter. China noted that a developed country could refuse to comply with a WTO ruling and that developing countries could be "in an embarrassing situation of being short of necessary means for retaliation," and proposed voluntary compensation for small developing countries at the request of the developing country.[134] Ecuador proposed that a system of mandatory compensation be created where noncompliant parties would submit a compensation package to the Dispute Settlement Body that would be at least double the damages caused the country by the noncomplaint measure.[135] Australia opposed countries being allowed to make compensation arrangements that effectively buy their way out of WTO obligations and allow countries to keep the WTO-illegal measures in place. However, Australia's comments supported compensation agreements that are consistent with WTO agreements, including negotiated compensation for third parties that cannot apply retaliatory measures.[136]

Third-Party Submission Transparency and Access

Access for interested third-party members in the dispute system—submissions by WTO member countries with substantial interest in trade issues surrounding a dispute—has been severely limited, especially for the developing world. A variety of countries have raised concerns and proposals on these issues. The rights of WTO member countries not directly involved in a dispute are especially worrying to many countries because the WTO's past rulings in some cases have seemed to alter the rights and obligations of the countries involved and thus might have long-term implications on other WTO member countries.

Transparency in Disputes

In April 2002, ardently pro-WTO U.S. Senator Max Baucus sent a letter to USTR directing the U.S. to advocate earlier release of documents and proceedings from the DSU to the general public—including the release of written submissions of the parties and panel proceedings.[137] The U.S. has recommended that "all substantive panel, Appellate Body and arbitration meetings" be open to the public except for the portions that are confidential or proprietary, and that all submissions and transcripts that are not confidential should be made available to the public as well.[138] Many developing-country delegations do not consider transparency a priority for DSU negotiations, and indeed have registered concerns about how providing access to documents and information about proceedings could further favor participation of private interests from wealthy countries given their potential counterparts from poor countries could not afford to make use of such information.[139] Once again, the current U.S. administration has not made obtaining its stated goals for transparency a priority as far as its use of its bargaining power.

Strict Constructionism

The U.S. and Chile jointly proposed provisions that would prohibit WTO Panels or Appellate Bodies from ruling on issues beyond the scope of the disputed issues. This proposal arises from a series of rulings in which panelists are accused of "creating" new WTO obligations in their rulings or are accused of bringing in issues neither litigant raised. The joint proposal opposes rulings that exceed the scope of what plaintiffs and defendants believe is relevant to the dispute, rulings that add or diminish rights under the WTO or apply concepts beyond what are customary principles of international law, and further, recommends that parties could delete mutually agreed-upon provisions from the reports if they are "not necessary or helpful," before the rulings are shown to other WTO countries, much less the press or public.[140]

Time Frame for Disputes, Compensation and Sequencing

Many members commented that the length of time it takes to resolve disputes before the WTO is too long. Others have focused on whether the penalties for WTO violators are effective. Mexico noted that WTO-illegal measures can remain in place for more than three years and cost as much as $370 million from failing to meet WTO obligations and proposed that the damages determination be applied retroactively to prevent member countries from keeping WTO-illegal measures in place for free during the dispute process.[141] Mexico's proposal calls for the retroactivity to be calculated either to the imposition of the measure, to the request for consultations, or to the date when the panel was established and includes "loser pay" provisions for defendants whose measures are ruled WTO-illegal to pay legal fees and litigation expenses for plaintiffs.[142]

All of these proposals—and many more not discussed here—have yet to be sorted out in the DSU review process. In late May, the WTO committee working on the DSU review reported that it would miss its Doha-set deadline regarding a report on areas of agreement to be taken up by the Cancún Ministerial.[143]

CONCLUSION

Obviously, a highly politicized and arbitrary dispute resolution system relying on the personal whims of an ever-changing cast of characters is no way to operate the enforcement of the most powerful international agreement now in force, or for that matter to operate the enforcement system of any institution of lesser importance. When such an undemocratic enforcement system is paired with comprehensive one-size-fits-all rules for nearly all elements of our lives, the results are offensive to the principles and practice of democratic governance.

However, procedural reforms of the WTO dispute resolution system alone cannot deliver improvements in the organization's legitimacy, much less repair negative public perceptions of the WTO. Such change can only be achieved if there are also significant changes in the substantive rules of global commerce. Most simply, backward, anti-public-interest substantive WTO rules, even if implemented through an open and well-designed dispute resolution system, will still result in bad outcomes for the lives of many.

10

WTO AND FTAA: TWO PATHS TO THE SAME DISASTER

Pablo Solon, Roberto Bissio, and Timi Gerson*

With the specter of the implosion of the WTO Ministerial in Seattle still lurking fresh in everyone's mind, the Americas are emerging as the scene for several historic showdowns over corporate globalization—again. In 2003, the WTO held its sixth ministerial from September 9–14 in Cancún, Mexico. After a mixed outcome at its fifth Doha, Qatar, Ministerial, the WTO's crisis of legitimacy was brought center stage in Cancún. At issue was whether the major WTO expansion sought by the European Union would be launched. This proposal, with support from the U.S. and Japan, is aimed at adding several elements dubbed the "Singapore Issues" (see Chapter 6), now existing only in NAFTA, to the WTO. Most developing-country WTO members, as well as the overwhelming majority of global civil society, oppose this WTO expansion and instead seek transformative changes in the current rules of the global economy.

Meanwhile, a summit considered a make-or-break point for the proposed Free Trade Area of the Americas expansion of NAFTA's terms to 31 additional countries is planned for late November 2003 in Miami, Florida. Given that the underlying agenda of both globalization summits is to further expand and lock in the imposition of the neoliberal model of international commercial agreements, and that the gold standard of that model is NAFTA, the meetings' locations have added significance.

In 1994, high off of the "victory" of establishing NAFTA—the first of a new breed of international commercial agreements providing unprecedented new rights and privileges for corporate interests—the United States organized a "Miami Summit of the Americas," calling together trade ministers from all 34 nations of the Americas and Caribbean (except Cuba) to pitch the extension of NAFTA to the rest of the Western Hemisphere.

The proposal garnered a variety of responses from regional governments. Chile sought immediate accession to NAFTA. Brazil sought to first build a regional pact, MercoSur, in order to have a more leveraged position vis-à-vis the U.S. and argued

* The authors are, respectively, Director of Fundación Solon of Bolivia, Director of Social Watch, Uruguay, and FTAA Coordinator for Global Trade Watch.

for negotiations of new regional-integration terms, not accession to NAFTA rules. The small economies of the Caribbean and Central America worried about being steamrollered in competition with an array of larger hemispheric economies and feared losing the benefit of special trade preferences they enjoyed relative to other countries in the region under the Caribbean Basin Initiative (CBI), a package of special trade preferences which the U.S. had established during the Reagan administration.[1] Canada was in on pushing the NAFTA expansion idea. While Mexico publicly supported NAFTA expansion, it harbored significant concerns about losing the special status and trade benefits NAFTA provided Mexico relative to its non-NAFTA hemispheric neighbors. Meanwhile, civil society organizations throughout the Americas came out in opposition to the U.S. and Canadian governments' initiative as more of a bad thing. As the results of NAFTA began to prove NAFTA skeptics' fears, civil society groups redoubled their efforts against the NAFTA model—opposing its expansion and calling for its termination.

Despite an array of serious misgivings, in Miami the U.S.—with Canadian support—strong-armed all of the "invitees" into signing a declaration that committed them to negotiate a regional free-trade zone over the next decade.

This framework agreement became the proposed FTAA, dubbed "NAFTA on Steroids" by civil society groups. After several years of the many skeptical countries slowing the process, in 1998 the U.S. finally pushed an agreement to establish formal FTAA negotiating groups, and talks began to accelerate. The seventh FTAA ministerial meeting in November 2002 in Quito, Ecuador, passed the "Chair" for the final stage of the FTAA negotiating process to the biggest countries in the region—the U.S. and Brazil. While the Quito Summit was notable mainly for the lack of resolution to an array of issues clouding the FTAA's future, including the scope of FTAA agricultural, investment, intellectual property, services, and trade-law negotiations, the countries did reaffirm the mandate to finish the agreement by January 1, 2005.[2]

The convergence of FTAA and WTO ministerials in North America harkens back a decade. In the early 1990s, the U.S. had just signed NAFTA and was simultaneously completing the Uruguay Round of GATT that established the WTO. What was the U.S. strategy or goal then? The answer to this question is discernible by reviewing what corporate interests wanted in the multilateral GATT talks compared to what they ended up obtaining. The corporate goal was to eliminate the maximum number of government policies regulating trade, investment and finance, corporate conduct, food safety and other public-interest regulations while putting in place new property rights and protections. As well, the companies sought to commodify elements of the domestic economy not fully available to their exploitation, such as public services and government expenditures of tax revenues. In sum, the goal was to impose on all nations and lock in more permanently the full smorgasbord of the most extreme neoliberal policies the IMF imposed on debtor nations.

However, in the GATT context, U.S. corporate interests faced powerful countervailing forces. For instance, the EU—a major economic power in its own right, with an economy almost as large as the U.S.[3]—pushed back against U.S. demands on several issues, such as commodification of public services. Second, Japan was then viewed as the next emerging economic superpower and played a weighty role, for instance in opposing some U.S. agriculture, procurement and investment demands. Additionally, given the expansive membership of the GATT, groups of developing countries, such as the G77, also occasionally were able to band together to defy the most extreme elements of the U.S. corporate agenda, resulting in limited WTO investment and procurement agreements.[4]

In contrast, in NAFTA, Canada and especially Mexico had considerably less leverage. As a result, NAFTA contains many provisions that U.S. corporate interests—represented by U.S. trade negotiators—had sought in the multilateral context but failed to obtain fully. (For instance, the WTO includes broad new corporate intellectual property rights, but NAFTA's rules on the subject are considerably more extreme and are enforced even more strongly—including requiring signatories to change their domestic laws to create criminal penalties for violating some NAFTA intellectual-property rules.) NAFTA is considered the gold standard for commercial agreements by proponents of corporate globalization because it gave corporations hitherto unheard-of rights and powers.[5]

Both the so-called "Doha Agenda" negotiations to expand the WTO and the literal expansion of NAFTA to 31 additional countries via FTAA are about taking care of this leftover business by bringing more countries under the full NAFTA model. The final goal? To bind as many countries as possible to the kind of global trade, investment and domestic economic policies that corporate promoters such as Enron, WorldCom and Global Crossing have been dreaming of since the Uruguay Round. But what they view as unfinished business is the very model of extreme deregulation and cannibal capitalism that is finishing off their businesses and millions of people's jobs and pensions.

Both substantively and politically, then, the FTAA must be viewed as a regional manifestation of the WTO expansion the rich countries sought to launch at Cancún and vice versa: FTAA and the WTO Doha Agenda are just different sides of the same coin. For the promoters of the NAFTA model, the current scenario allows them to choose the best of both worlds. Often developing-country negotiating partners buy into their game. Absent a united developing-country position to safeguard core interests in all these venues, the promoters of corporate globalization can push for things in the FTAA that are more beneficial to multinational corporations than already exist in the WTO trade regime, while simultaneously sending the issues that might not accrue to their benefit in FTAA talks to the WTO venue.

Brazil Beware: Proposed WTO "New Issues" Also Are At the Core of the Proposed FTAA

Think of FTAA and the WTO Doha agenda as a two-front attack by the same forces—the same objective is being approached from two different directions simultaneously. For instance, the table of contents of the draft FTAA includes a "draft chapter on government procurement," a "draft chapter on investment" and a "draft of chapter on competition policies." The inclusion of the titles of these chapters or draft chapters followed by a wholly bracketed text (bracketed text denotes disagreement between the negotiating parties) is not of minor significance. It implies that the countries have already agreed to discuss issues like investment, government procurement and competition policy as part of the FTAA. These issues also are included in NAFTA. Brazil proposed wisely to remove these nontrade issues from FTAA, but did so by arguing such negotiations should occur at WTO.

Yet the biggest fight on the road to the Cancún WTO Ministerial is whether to discuss these issues at all. Politicians argue that "there is nothing wrong in discussing, in the end we will not include what we do not want to include." Diplomats know better. In a "single undertaking" (where nothing is agreed to until everything is agreed to) the very inclusion of a mention of the issue transforms it into a bargaining chip. Thus, while developing countries have opposed the new issues, the rich countries are trying to seduce them with offers for illusory market access in exchange for agreeing to allow the launch of WTO negotiations in the "new issues."—whether investment, procurement, competition and trade facilitation rules are in WTO or FTAA.

Additionally, what the U.S. is not able to achieve in either context it seeks via smaller regional agreements or bilateral agreements (again, such as a U.S.-Chile Free Trade Agreement or the proposed Central American Free Trade Agreement). The same interests use the FTAA, WTO and bilateral negotiations to gain momentum from each other and to provide a fallback venue for advancing the neoliberal economic agenda. For example, if one set of negotiations seems to have stalled, then negotiators push harder in the other seeking to create anxiety that the countries rejecting the demands against their interests will be "left behind." Or if the U.S. obtains major concessions from a trading partner in one set of negotiations (such as the NAFTA-plus patent-protection rules in the U.S.-Singapore bilateral), it can use this to pressure for the same concessions from other countries in the other talks.

This is precisely what the U.S. has just done by using the provisions Chile agreed to in its desperation to finish a bilateral agreement with the U.S., requiring compensation and providing investor-to-state enforcement if Chile puts capital controls into place—for instance to avoid a crash if speculators were to make a run on the currency.[6] (Chile's use of "speed bumps"—which penalize rapid withdrawal of certain kinds of short-term investments—was the reason Chile largely avoided the "Tequila" effect of currency crashes that spread throughout Latin America after Mexico's 1995 peso crash.) The U.S. then used Chile's concession on this issue to force similar terms on Singapore in its FTA after months of Singapore refusing such terms because Singapore sought the ability to use this policy tool without penalty if needed in the future.

The convergence of these two tracks now puts Brazil, with its considerable leverage by virtue of being the world's eighth largest economy and by far the most lucrative "prize" for U.S. corporate interests in the hemisphere, in a position of having to defend the rest of the hemisphere's interests, and indeed those of U.S. civil society and many in the U.S. Congress, in the FTAA context.

Meanwhile, the EU and Japan are now more vociferous in pushing investment and other "new" issues at the WTO than even the U.S. This means the developing countries as a group will need to act in unity in order not to have their interests vanquished in Cancún. Unfortunately, countries are instead lining up for FTAs with the U.S. In a sorry spectacle, countries are not only buying into the psychological game played by the U.S., but are fighting to be the first to give up everything. The only way to turn this domino effect of countries sacrificing their futures into fair negotiations is for them to stand their ground for their interests in all the negotiations—bilateral, regional and WTO talks.

Generally speaking, the relation between the WTO and the regional agreements in Latin America has always been a complicated one. The founding principle of a rule-based multilateral trade system is that of the Most Favored Nation treatment, which if it really became an "everybody is equal under the law" provision, would make impossible such regional trade areas as the one leading to the European Union or NAFTA, as every WTO member country could claim a right to join. As a result, the WTO has had to find a difficult peaceful coexistence with dozens of regional integration agreements, such as the EU; the MercoSur agreement between Brazil, Uruguay, Argentina and Paraguay; and others wherein groups of countries— usually neighbors with similar levels of development—make special deals among themselves in an attempt to share the benefits of larger-scale economies.

North-South arrangements where former imperial powers grant special treatment to their ex-colonies also abound, and they too conflict with WTO principles. Underlying the WTO banana dispute (see Chapter 6), where U.S. corporations and Latin American governments successfully challenged the EU preferences for fruit from certain ex-colonies, is an example of those gray areas. Separate from the U.S. WTO attack, the EU was pushing for renegotiation of the special deal between Europe and the Asian, Caribbean and Pacific nations in the name of conforming to WTO rules about MFN. (Or, seen from another angle, Europe used the WTO rules to tell those countries that "we still love you, but our special relation has to end eventually.") Indeed, the special trade preferences of the Lomé Treaty were replaced with a reciprocal free-trade agreement model by the new Cotonou Treaty. The proposed WTO expansion and FTAA are mechanisms to homogenize these different approaches to the extreme NAFTA model. Yet, too often, countries caught up in the intricate dance of these different negotiations lose sight of the bottom line: they all lead to countries being required to adopt an array of policies that have proven to be a failure in generating sustainable economic growth or satisfying the basic needs of most people in the countries adopting them.

Timeline of FTAA and WTO

The FTAA and the WTO are moving on parallel tracks, with a January 1, 2005, target date for completion of both negotiations. The nine FTAA negotiating groups meet monthly or more often originally in different countries and now in

FTAA: THE BASICS

FTAA (Free Trade Area of the Americas): Proposed NAFTA-style commercial agreement that includes all 34 countries of western hemisphere except for Cuba.

FTAA Country	GDP (in millions)[7]	FTAA Country	GDP (in millions)[7]
United States	$10,171,400	Bolivia	$7,960
Canada	$677,178	Jamaica	$7,784
Mexico	$617,817	Paraguay	$6,926
Brazil	$502,509	Honduras	$6,386
Argentina	$268,773	The Bahamas	$4,818*
Venezuela	$124,949	Haiti	$3,771
Colombia	$83,432	Barbados	$2,600*
Chile	$63,545	Nicaragua	$2,068‡
Peru	$54,047	Belize	$799
Dominican Republic	$21,211	Suriname	$758
Guatemala	$20,629	Guyana	$699
Uruguay	$18,429	St. Lucia	$689
Ecuador	$17,982	Antigua and Barbuda	$666
Costa Rica	$16,156	Grenada	$398
El Salvador	$13,963	St. Kitts and Nevis	$343
Panama	$10,170	St. Vincent and the Grenadines	$338
Trinidad and Tobago	$8,412	Dominica	$261

(Source: World Bank. Most recent data available: All data 2001, except * (2000) and ‡ (1998))

FTAA Nine Negotiating Groups: Agriculture; Competition Policy; Dispute Settlement; Government Procurement; Intellectual Property Rights (IPR); Investment; Market Access; Services; Subsidies, Anti-Dumping and Countervailing Duties.

Official FTAA Secretariat web address: www.ftaa-alca.org

Official FTAA Timeline:

December 1994	Miami Presidential FTAA Summit—Negotiations Launched
April 1998	Santiago Presidential FTAA Summit (negotiating groups agreed to)
April 2001	Buenos Aires, FTAA Summit
April 2001	Quebec City Presidential FTAA Summit
November 2002	Quito seventh FTAA Trade Ministerial
January 2003	U.S.–Central America (CAFTA) negotiations launched
February 15, 2003	FTAA market access phase request/offers deadline
November 2003	Miami eighth FTAA Trade Ministerial
December 2003	U.S.–Central America (CAFTA) negotiations conclusion deadline
January 1, 2005	FTAA negotiations conclusion deadline. (If a deal is completed before 2007, it would go to the U.S. Congress under Fast Track trade procedures established in 2002.)
December 31, 2005	FTAA implementation deadline

Puebla, Mexico, with ministerial meetings scheduled annually and presidential summits scheduled as needed. WTO negotiations are organized on three tiers. First, agriculture and service-sector WTO talks were part of a built-in agenda on which talks were launched in 2000 and have been ongoing at the WTO's Geneva headquarters. Second, at the December 2001 Doha Ministerial, countries agreed to start negotiations on several additional issues including antidumping and subsidies policy, industrial tariff cuts, cuts in barriers to "environmental" goods and services trade, and dispute resolution. A third tier of "new issues" was pushed at Cancùn by the EU for future negotiation, including investment, competition, procurement and trade facilitation. Developing-country opposition to negotiations on the new issues meant that a decision whether to launch talks on these issues had been put off until Cancún. The WTO conducts its continuous negotiating sessions on different topics at its Geneva headquarters with the work plan, priorities and political direction set at a ministerial summit every two years.

While the official summit meetings tend to be the events that garner large-scale media and civil society attention, such as the 1999 Seattle WTO Ministerial or the Summit of the Americas in Quebec City in 2001, the day-to-day negotiations in the WTO and FTAA venues are where most key decisions are being made. As a testament to the undemocratic nature of these talks, frequently the final deals and declarations of the high-profile meetings have been decided among small groups of more powerful countries in the closed-door sessions before the actual ministerial or summit meeting takes place. The pre-agreed provisions are presented to all the member countries for take-it-or-leave-it "approval."[8] A side-by-side comparison of some key elements of the WTO and proposed FTAA shows their synergy.

THE ISSUES
Investment (NAFTA's "Chapter 11" vs. WTO's TRIMs)

The promise of foreign direct investment (FDI) was one of the key items used to convince the Mexican government and public of the supposed benefits of NAFTA.[9] The sober reality almost ten years into NAFTA implementation is that the vast majority of new U.S. FDI has been along the border in the maquiladora sector (the "free-trade" sweatshop zones predominately located along the U.S.-Mexico border), instead of being distributed throughout the country. Since NAFTA began, the percentage of FDI that went to the maquiladoras increased from 6.0% in 1994 to 22.7% in 2000.[10]

The *maquila* industry has hardly been a boon for Mexican workers. A study of 15 cities in the *maquila* regions by the Center for Reflection, Education and Action revealed that the minimum wage paid at the maquiladoras was only between 17.4% and 25.6% of what was needed for a sustainable living wage.[11] Actual wages, which were higher than minimum wages, still provided, on average, less than half of what the workers needed to earn to cover the basics.[12]

Indeed, both unemployment and underemployment, including work in low-paying jobs, has grown rapidly in Mexico since NAFTA. While new investment in the maquiladora zone represented the creation of 458,000 jobs between 1994 and 2002,[13] the massive flood of imported subsidized U.S. corn and the demise of many small and medium-sized Mexican retail and manufacturing businesses under NAFTA resulted in net increased unemployment and underemployment.[14] Meanwhile, under NAFTA, Mexican wages have not kept up with productivity gains. Mexico's industrial productivity grew more than 30% between 1993 and 2001, but Mexico's manufacturing wages fell by 20% between 1993 and 1999.[15]

The NAFTA model of investment has shaped the Mexican economy increasingly to be dependent on assembly of foreign products. This contrasts with investment that would build a diversified industrial base.[16] And in the global race to the bottom, even the NAFTA-inspired FDI and the new *maquila* jobs it created are moving to China at an astonishing pace[17] with China's recent entry into the WTO in 2001[18] providing foreign investors more security to relocate for China's rock-bottom labor costs. Other investment in Mexico has been in the service sector, with retail giants such as Wal-Mart and COSTCO putting up stores, and telecommunications and financial service corporations buying up companies. Thousands of small Mexican retail and manufacturing businesses were crushed by NAFTA's red carpet welcome to the U.S. "big box" mega-retailers. The El Barzon movement, representing these exiles from the middle class, is made up of many who initially bought the NAFTA promises and now comprise some of the strongest FTAA critics in Mexico. The Mexican experience under NAFTA should serve as a warning for other countries, which can expect similar patterns under FTAA.

Indeed, both NAFTA and the WTO's existing investment agreement, the TRIMs Agreement, include provisions which actually prohibit governments from imposing "performance requirements"—such as a commitment to engage in technology transfer, commit to local investing and development, or environmental compliance—on investors.[19] For all the rhetoric that these trade agreements will lift all boats and help developing countries develop, the fact is today's rich countries and the so-called Asian Tiger nations have used policy tools these pacts forbid when they were developing countries to promote national and local development policies. Banning performance requirements is a rare thing the two pacts have in common. The WTO's TRIMs Agreement only covers foreign direct investment—for instance buying or setting up a new factory or service business. TRIMs rules apply only "post-establishment," which means once an investment has been made. This means that once an investment exists, TRIMs rules apply. These rules include national treatment (meaning local firms cannot be given preferential treatment) and the ban on performance requirements—regulation shaping investment that is described above. In contrast, NAFTA and the proposals for FTAA apply "pre-establishment," meaning foreign investors are given new rights to set up factories or buy land or service companies.

NAFTA and the proposed FTAA investment rules also cover not only FDI but additionally cover land, stocks and other financial instruments, contracts, intellectual property rights and currency, setting limits against capital controls that would normally prevent rapid outflows during economic panics. NAFTA prevented imposing controls that would have dulled the pain that rocked Mexico in 1995 when the peso collapsed and international investment fled Mexico. In contrast, as described in Chapter 6, in countries such as Malaysia and India, capital-control policies helped to prevent the total economic implosion that rocked Thailand during the Asian financial crisis.

Another proposed FTAA provision that exists in NAFTA but not in the WTO allows for private enforcement of the new expansive investor rights—with corporations suing governments directly in secret trade tribunals. This system, which circumvents domestic courts, can be employed when companies feel that municipal, state, or national legislation cuts into their profits. Successful suits under NAFTA have already included governments being forced to compensate corporations after a ban on a toxic chemical and a decision to shut down a toxic waste dump.

In the first case, U.S.-based Ethyl Corporation of Virginia filed a NAFTA claim against the Canadian government[20] over Canada's federal ban on import and interprovincial transport[21] of methylcyclopentadienyl manganese tricarbonyl (MMT),[22] a gasoline additive substance manufactured by Ethyl Corporation that included a known neurotoxin manganese.[23] The Canadian ban was to address environmental and public health concerns. The company's argument was that the MMT ban represented a NAFTA-forbidden expropriation of its assets in violation of NAFTA Article 1110. The Canadian government, instead of defending a case it knew it couldn't win under NAFTA rules, repealed its MMT ban, paid Ethyl $13 million as compensation for the money the company lost during the period the ban was in place, and even went so far as to write a public statement for Ethyl, advertising use declaring that "current scientific information" did not demonstrate MMT was unsafe.[24]

In the second case, the Mexican municipality of Guadalacazar in the state of San Luís Potosí refused to give the U.S. Metalclad Corporation a municipal construction permit to expand a hazardous waste transfer station into a toxic waste landfill[25] on land that has been designated by the local authorities as an ecological protected zone. Metalclad, which had secured the requisite Mexican state and federal permits, sued Mexico in a NAFTA tribunal.[26] The company claimed that the actions of the municipal government of Guadalacazar amounted to expropriation without compensation forbidden under NAFTA Article 1110, even though the city had also refused to issue the same permits to a previous Mexican owner of the site.[27] In August of 2000, a tribunal ruled against Mexico and awarded Metalclad compensation of $16,685,000.[28]

As was discussed in Chapter 9, investment rules in the WTO do not include an investor-to-state mechanism, which means that only governments can sue other governments. Although currently WTO investment rules only apply to government policy regarding FDI, the push for "new issues" is about launching negotiations of a new WTO investment agreement that would enlarge the rules to cover a much broader definition of investment as well as including the same "right" to establish an investment found in NAFTA. Meanwhile, the proposed FTAA would literally expand the NAFTA investment model to 31 more nations.

Agriculture

The FTAA would expand the NAFTA model of food commodification—treating agriculture as an industry, not life's sustenance. Under NAFTA, farmers in all three countries have suffered: U.S. farm income has been declining since NAFTA went into effect, Canadian farmers have seen farm income go down as farm debt rises, and millions of Mexican campesinos have been or will be pushed off their land.[29] The winners have been increasingly consolidated multinational agribusiness corporations. By encouraging increased global production both by eliminating farm price supports and promoting certain subsidies linked to production volume, the commodity trading companies have driven down global grain and other commodity prices paid to farmers to 30-year lows, pitting all the world's farmers against one another. The result is that no nation's agriculture producers can make a living.

NAFTA contained aggressive agricultural free-trade provisions, rapidly reducing tariffs on farm goods to zero. At the same time, using NAFTA both as a sales pitch and as the political instrument to force policy change, corporate and political elites in Washington, Mexico City and Ottawa set about eliminating domestic farm programs aimed at safeguarding growers. In the U.S., the same interests helped shape the 1996 Freedom to Farm Act, part and parcel of implementing the export-oriented NAFTA agriculture model. Mexico eliminated its state trading boards and price floors, including on corn, Mexico's key staple food. While assorted hidden U.S. export subsidies, useful to commodity traders, remained and support to the largest U.S. farms increased, domestic programs that had made family farming in the U.S. and Canada and peasant livelihoods in Mexico economically viable were cut. These domestic programs put protections into place to safeguard small farmers from the whims and dictates of the commodities' brokers and speculators, weather, and disease and to other buffers against wild market fluctuations.

The WTO Agreement on Agriculture was a less extreme undertaking than NAFTA although based on the same philosophy. It cut tariffs, required countries to eliminate quotas, and allegedly required countries to cut export subsidies and domestic farm support. At Doha, the Ministerial Declaration codified the plan in the WTO to increase market access (i.e., reducing tariffs and quotas) and cut export subsidies and domestic farm-support programs.[30] The FTAA negotiations on agriculture are designed to expand the NAFTA agriculture provisions to the entire hemisphere, meaning a relatively rapid elimination of all agriculture tariff quotas and domestic policies supporting small farmers—except perhaps on the crops the U.S. wants to protect such as sugar beef, soy and citrus products.[31]

However, exports cannot be increased unless the rich countries buy what the south has to sell. In the agriculture talks, "market access" is the issue around which all the Latin American presidents, from conservatives to revolutionaries, now rally.[32] This focus on more access to rich-country markets is based on the need to generate hard currency to service their debt. What price the developing countries are being asked in exchange and whether they will really get new market access are big questions.

Rich countries have pressured the developing world to make concessions on investment and services deregulation (both in the FTAA and the WTO). A few developing countries appear poised to condition these concessions on grants of real, significant access for their agricultural and manufactured products. Each side is waiting for the other to make the major concession that might make the other capitulate.

Yet, the reality is that developing countries are unlikely to get new real agricultural market access into the U.S. in either the FTAA or WTO agreement. The U.S. already has made clear that any agriculture agreement in FTAA depends on a similar agreement being reached in the WTO.[33] This allows the U.S. to take advantage of EU and Japanese unwillingness to make certain agricultural concessions at the WTO to limit U.S. concessions in the FTAA. The Europeans will not make sweeping concessions on agriculture (either on market access or reducing subsidies), since the French-German agreement that paved the way for enlargement of the EU to include Eastern European countries postponed until 2013 major change in their present agriculture policy.[34] And, as the 2004 U.S. presidential elections draw nearer, control over politically sensitive matters such as agriculture shift away from the U.S. trade office and into the control of the White House political operation headed by Karl Rove. There is a remarkable overlap between the agricultural products for which countries such as Brazil seek greater U.S. market access and the products grown domestically in the U.S. states Bush must win to be re-elected. Given America is rejecting developing-country demands for agricultural market access, Latin American governments should refuse to negotiate on investment, procurement, services and competition agreements in the WTO or FTAA.

Services

Currently, trade negotiators worldwide are in discussions to expand the deregulation and privatization of the service sector of national economies. Proposed new rules on services in trade pacts would lock in permanently the privatization and deregulation imposed on many poor countries by the IMF and the World Bank. This would occur by cross-linking countries' requirement to maintain such service-sector policies to countries' trade benefits. In the FTAA, the U.S. and Canada are pursuing NAFTA-style services rules. In the ongoing WTO talks on the GATS, the U.S. and Europe are seeking to expand the existing agreement to cover more sectors, decrease regulatory oversight and facilitate privatization or conversion of public assets into private enterprises.

The unequal balance of power in the NAFTA negotiations resulted in an expansive NAFTA Services Agreement that automatically covers all means of delivering a service—from opening a new company to buying a local service to cross-border provision of a service—for all sectors unless an exemption was negotiated, with the U.S. gaining considerable concessions that allowed U.S. service-sector firms, from giant retailers like Wal-Mart to U.S. banks, such as Citibank, to seize major chunks of the Mexican economy.[35] The U.S. is using the simultaneous negotiations on FTAA service and GATS-2000 to extract as many concessions as possible. The U.S.—on behalf of its powerful service industry—prefers a service liberalization regime that covers all service sectors. Many other countries—including many developing countries—seek a limited service deregulatory agenda because their services are either provided directly by the government or operate under government rules as private, regulated monopolies. The U.S. can advance its radical deregulatory agenda by aggressively pushing on both the FTAA and GATS-2000 track at the same time, a negotiating advantage Europe, whose service-sector demands at GATS-2000 are even broader than those of the U.S., and Japan do not have.

Under proposed FTAA rules, all services also would be covered automatically unless a country is able to negotiate a special "exemption." This is called a "top-down" or "negative list" agreement. For service sectors covered by the FTAA, countries would surrender the right to regulate who owns a service company (whether public or private), how many providers are established or how they operate. Basic public-interest regulations on private service companies could be challenged as illegal "trade barriers," even if they treat domestic and foreign service providers the same. Even if a country tries to exclude a particular sector, FTAA is likely to include loopholes like those in NAFTA, which companies can use to pry open "exempted" sectors. Essential public services would be threatened by the FTAA because a supposed "carve-out" for public services is being written to apply only to services that are exclusively provided by the government. Very few services are solely provided by the government, most are mixes of public, for-profit, and not-for-profit charity operations, making this exception effectively meaningless.

Under GATS, some rules apply to all service sectors, but several core requirements only apply to sectors governments agree to put on the table. This is called a "bottom-up" or "positive list" agreement. However, some GATS rules apply to all services and the GATS text commits countries to "progressive liberalization of services," meaning the continual privatization and deregulation of more and more service sectors. As noted above, the original GATS text automatically launched further negotiations starting in 2000. Countries are currently involved in what is known as "Request/Offer" phase in this GATS-2000 negotiation. For example, the U.S. has requested that Brazil make available for ownership by U.S. corporations some aspects of public higher education services and many energy services. On March 31, 2003, countries began responded to the "requests" they received with "offers" of what sectors they will open up under GATS. Once a sector is covered under GATS, foreign corporations have unlimited rights to establish businesses in the sector and government regulation is restricted. A country cannot withdraw a sector from GATS coverage unless it negotiates to pay compensation to every WTO country for this right.

Thus, the FTAA and GATS-2000 effectively are like two divisions of the same army, seeking to take over the same territory but using different strategies. Several examples of the type of privatization in the service sector that would be accelerated and made virtually irreversible by both FTAA service provisions and GATS-2000 already are occurring in Latin America. For instance, Bolivia was required to privatize some of its publicly owned service sectors as a condition for receiving support from international lending institutions such as the IMF and World Bank. This type of conditionality is common in international lending agreements and works hand-in-glove with the WTO and NAFTA regimes, which encourage public assets to be turned over to the private sector, resulting in situations like the water system controversy between the U.S.-based firm Bechtel and the citizens of Cochabamba, Bolivia, which is discussed in Chapter 4.[36]

Additionally, both GATS and the FTAA include proposals on immigration and temporary worker visas. Under GATS the movement of people across borders to perform services is covered. U.S. corporate interests are seeking to include special visa programs in which corporations would be able to import temporary, foreign workers, but only have to pay them according to minimum-wage laws, not according to the prevailing wage for that profession.[37] This would allow U.S. companies to employ an underclass of easily exploitable workers who might make more than they would at home, but make less than American workers with the same jobs. Additionally, these workers would be especially vulnerable to maltreatment because their continued legal status would entirely depend on keeping their employer happy. Efforts by workers to unionize or improve their working conditions would be severely undermined, even though they would be getting paid significantly less than their coworkers.

The outcome of the service negotiations in FTAA and GATS-2000 will hinge on the outcome of other issues all of which rely on countries' tenacity in defending their interests. Although developing countries see the risks and downsides of the U.S. services agenda, some are using concessions on services as a bargaining chip to advance their agenda on agricultural market access. The U.S. is in much the same boat: it wants to gain service concessions to please the service industries without having to make too many concessions on agriculture, particularly on farm subsidies. Many Latin American countries, most notably Brazil, had initially refused to even enter into negotiations over services, investment or procurement until the agriculture provisions are finalized, legitimately worried that concessions made before agriculture talks would go unreciprocated in the agriculture talks. Given the collapse of WTO talks where farm issues are to be decided, countries have even greater grounds to maintain this strategy.

TRIPs, Patenting and Access to Essential Medicines

After a huge struggle on the part of civil society, the WTO was forced, as an annex to its Doha Ministerial Declaration, to affirm in a Declaration on the TRIPs Agreement and Public Health that WTO rules "should not prevent Members from taking measures to protect public health."[38] However, pharmaceutical companies are angling to weaken and destroy this pro–public health interpretation in the lead up to the Cancún WTO Ministerial and by negotiating more pro-corporate terms in the FTAA. As described in Chapter 3, the Pharmaceutical Manufacturers and Research Association, a powerful pharmaceutical company lobby, has the Bush administration working in Geneva at WTO talks to undercut the modest progress in clarifying existing TRIPs rules' flexibility. At the same time, these interests have demanded "TRIPs-plus" in the FTAA negotiations, and both the Clinton and now Bush administrations have pushed this approach.[39] This could mean even more draconian corporate-monopoly control over seeds, medicine and technology than already provided in the WTO rules—which, as we saw in Chapters 3 and 7, are bad enough, as they include the strict enforcement of 20-year monopoly patents on essential medicines and seeds.

TRIPs-plus language in the FTAA draft text includes:

- *Compulsory licenses can only be issued to governments, not generic drug companies.* FTAA limits the granting of compulsory licenses to governments that would prohibit companies from manufacturing for a government-obtained license. Most developing-country governments do not have the capacity to start up pharmaceutical manufacturing and indeed have faced decades of pressure to privatize all government-owned industries.
- *Prohibits trade in drugs produced under compulsory licenses.* For most developing countries with little capacity—government or private—to begin manufacturing pharmaceuticals, it may be the only option to import generics from a country with capacity, such as Brazil, China and India. FTAA prohibition of the import of generics produced in other countries under compulsory license essentially dooms the sick in the developing world to death or a lifetime of illness.
- *Expanded patent protection.* The TRIPs-plus language codifies the WTO's 20-year patent protection, but also provides an extra five-year patent protection for undisclosed pharmaceutical test data, which would prohibit generic manufacturers from introducing the generic medicines promptly when patents expire unless they replicate the drug efficacy studies, a prohibitive burden to most.[40]
- *Increased patent penalties.* Under draft FTAA rules, violators of a company's patent could be required to pay compensation and suffer criminal sanctions. Moreover, the burden of proof would be reversed, requiring defendants essentially to prove that they are innocent instead of having to be proven guilty. This contrasts sharply with the more permissive language in the Doha Declaration and poses particular problems for Brazil, which could be hamstrung if the intellectual-property rules in the WTO and the FTAA were in conflict. This is another demonstration of the way the two distinct negotiations play off of each other.

An additional concern in both FTAA and TRIPs that has particular salience for Latin America is the patenting of life-forms, plant varieties and traditional medicines by corporations who then claim it as "their" intellectual property. In the Amazon basin, the plant and animal diversity is a tremendous value to the indigenous peoples culturally and potentially economically. Brazil alone is home to half of the world's biodiversity, with over 55,000 species of flowering plants, 30% of the world's plants, 300 species of mammals, 2,000 species of fish and 2.5 million arthropods (insects, arachnids, crustaceans and centipedes).[41] The extraction of this genetic diversity by pharmaceutical and agribusiness firms seeking traditional

---

FTAA Could Undermine Brazil's Success in Combating HIV/AIDS

HIV/AIDS is a public health epidemic throughout the world. At the XIV International AIDS Conference in Barcelona in July 2002, UNAIDS predicted that without access to necessary treatment, the five million that contracted HIV in 2001 would be dead by the end of the decade. The National Intelligence Council singled out Brazil's treatment program as a source of hope in the AIDS struggle, noting that "Brazil's successful emphasis on treatment and the expanded use of antiretroviral drugs has raised hopes for improving while costs are going down the length and quality of life for HIV/AIDS patients." Brazil's cutting-edge program, which provides universal, free treatment to all citizens infected with HIV efficiently and effectively, means that survival rates are improving while costs are going down (see Chapter 3). Brazil's successful public health program may be put in jeopardy at the FTAA negotiations by limiting Brazil's ability to import compulsorily licensed products and to export them to other nations who invoke their compulsory licenses. At the same time, even if Brazil rejects the FTAA TRIPs-plus, efforts to undermine the Doha Declaration on TRIPs and Public Health—for instance by cutting Brazil and other larger developing countries or poor countries with drug production capacity out of the deal's coverage—now under way at the WTO also must be defeated to avoid the same threat.

---

medicines and then patenting the result is known by the industry as bioprospecting and by indigenous groups and civil society as biopiracy.

As early as 1993, indigenous peoples claimed the genetic diversity of their homelands as their community property at the Mataatua Declaration on Cultural and Intellectual Property Rights of Indigenous Peoples.[42] Ecuador and Venezuela both grant indigenous peoples collective intellectual property rights in their constitutions.[43] In 1999, the council that represents 400 indigenous tribes in the Amazon basin challenged the U.S. Patent and Trademark Office on the legitimacy of a patent granted to the Plant Medicine Corporations on a sacred traditional plant called ayahuasca.[44] In 1998, Abbot Laboratory patented a toxin from the skin of an Amazon frog designed to be a painkiller that could replace opiates.[45] Because of the rich genetic diversity in the Amazon basin and the rain forests throughout Latin America, the threat of such corporate expropriations is especially great.

Procurement

In many developing nations, government spending through procurement is a larger share of GNP than private expenditures. Although there is now a WTO agreement on Government Procurement, it is known as a "plurilateral" agreement, which means it was not part of the "single undertaking" of the Uruguay

Round. Unlike any other WTO agreements, countries were able to decide if they would sign the AGP. Only 24 WTO members have done so. Rich nations seek to launch new procurement negotiations to expand this agreement and make it as binding on all members as the other elements of the WTO. However, there has been significant resistance from the developing world and civil society. After the Multilateral Agreement on Investment collapsed at OECD talks in 1998, proponents of more control over government purchases have been trying to insert much of the objectionable MAI language into the WTO by launching new negotiations on procurement and investment.

In countries that have signed the AGP, federal governments are forbidden from discriminating on the basis of national treatment. This means that when purchasing goods—from government vehicles to computers—and when contracting for services—from telephone services to National Park vending concessions—the government cannot give preferences to domestic producers or firms. As a result, many "Buy American" provisions and similar policies in other countries had to be scrapped. Developing countries oppose these rules because they constrain their ability to use the power of the state purse to promote economic development by recirculating tax dollars back into the domestic economy. As well, giving domestic preferences helps use government funds to build the local economy. If local suppliers had to compete with transnational businesses for every government contract, it would be difficult to develop local businesses, or for small business enterprises or women- or minority-owned businesses to survive. In the U.S., similar local business preferences were and in some limited cases still are used to promote local small businesses or environmental goals. Opponents of the new procurement negotiations that was pushed for Cancún note that these requirements would prohibit alternatives to the IFI model, promote foreign companies over local priorities, and encourage privatization of government industries and services.

In addition, the AGP forbids countries to require any conditions on bidders beyond proving the company has the capacity to fulfill the contract. Procurement policies—such as requiring a certain percentage of minorities be hired or that local materials be used—are forbidden. Also, the policies many countries adopted at the request of the African National Congress to boycott apartheid South Africa would violate AGP rules.

While developing-country participation in the current WTO procurement agreement is voluntary, in both NAFTA and the proposed FTAA, these procurement rules are included as part of the core text of the agreement without opt-out provisions. Moreover, the procurement language in the draft-FTAA negotiating text is all-encompassing, requiring all of the government purchases and expenditures throughout the hemisphere to be open on an equal basis for foreign firms. By using the same type of procurement language in the FTAA as NAFTA, the U.S. is trying to expand the NAFTA model of procurement. The U.S. supported the EU demand to launch new WTO procurement negotiations as one of the "new issues" at the WTO to accomplish one of its key overall trade negotiating efforts—imposing the most extreme NAFTA trade rules onto the rest of the world.

Shifting Politics in the Hemisphere

It is crucial to note that neither the proposed WTO expansion nor the FTAA negotiations happen in a vacuum. The first few years of the twenty-first century have seen significant changes in the continental landscape in terms of the globalization issue which are both the result of and have important consequences for the growing international civil society movement in the hemisphere against the FTAA and the WTO expansion that was defeated in Cancún specifically and the "Washington Consensus" of corporate globalization generally. The U.S. government imposition of steel tariffs and the passage of the 2002 U.S. farm bill (which raises the level of U.S. agricultural subsidies) enraged the governments, press and elite in many of the FTAA target nations[46] and were viewed as an interesting measure of the degree to which Washington plays "do as I say, not as I do." At the same time the hemisphere watched the U.S. electricity deregulation debacle and growing U.S. economic and unemployment woes, the crisis in Argentina delivered yet another body blow to the "Washington Consensus" model. Once the poster child of free-trade, market-based neoliberal "success," it now stands as an example to the rest of Latin America of what is wrong with the corporate globalization model reflected in the proposed FTAA and the WTO expansion that was pushed for Cancún.

The political shift caused by the painful results of these neoliberal policies throughout the hemisphere is demonstrated by the rise in power in a variety of Latin American countries of politicians and political parties critical of the "free" trade model. Luiz Ignacio "Lula" da Silva won a landslide 2002 presidential victory in Brazil after campaigning on a platform opposed to the neoliberal model, including opposing the current model of the FTAA as a "policy of annexation, not integration."[47] Venezuelan president Hugo Chavez has been the strongest FTAA opponent. While Lula moderated his tone concerning FTAA, Chavez remained unabashed, while facing a coup instigated is no small part because of Chavez's direct challenge to the entire neoliberal model, the temporary installment of Venezuela's Chamber of Commerce president as president, U.S. support for the coup and an economy-destroying rebellion by the management of Venezuela's national oil company. Meanwhile, in January 2003, the new president of Ecuador, Lucio Gutierrez, who campaigned on a platform that identified the FTAA as an economic threat to the people of Ecuador, was inaugurated.[48] In Bolivia, FTAA critic Evo Morales ran a close second in the 2002 presidential race.[49] These election results are coupled with increasingly frequent antiprivatization protests (and victories!). Indeed, the many failures of the corporate globalization "free trade" model in Latin America have created a tectonic shift in public and government opinion from "free trade" and privatization promoters to critics and opponents throughout Latin America.

Resistance by citizens from all over the Americas to both the substance of the FTAA proposal and to the undemocratic process in which it has been negotiated is widespread and growing. In September of 2002, 10 million Brazilian citizens voted against their country's participation in the FTAA process in an informal plebiscite organized by a multi-sectoral religious, labor, student and campesino coalition including the Brazilian National Conference of Bishops (CNOB), the Movimento dos Trabalhadores Rurais Sem Terra/Landless Farm Workers Movement (MST), the Central Union of Workers (CUT) and others.[50] In November of the same year, more than ten thousand protesters, led by the Ecuadorian indigenous peoples movement including the Confederation of Indigenous Nations of Ecuador and Front for the Defense of the Amazon,[51] took to the streets in Quito, Ecuador, to protest the seventh FTAA Trade Ministerial under the banner "Another America is Possible." A "Release the Text" campaign of inquiry to expose the hypocrisy of seven years of secret, closed-door FTAA negotiations forced the hemisphere's governments to begrudgingly release a "scrubbed" incomplete version of the FTAA draft text after the Quebec City FTAA Presidential Summit in 2001 and again after the Quito FTAA Trade Ministerial in 2002. The publication of the draft FTAA is proof of the growing civil society concern about the FTAA that has forced governments to at least pay lip service to the idea (albeit not the practice) of transparency.

The U.S. government response to this changed scenario has been to quickly finish negotiations with Chile on the U.S.-Chile bilateral agreement and to launch negotiations on a Central American Free Trade Agreement encompassing four additional FTAA target countries. The U.S. strategy has three goals. First, in grudging acknowledgment of the fragility of the FTAA's prospects and the increasingly consolidated and fierce developing-country opposition to the same agenda when it was pushed at Cancún, the U.S. seeks to lock in to the NAFTA/ FTAA model as many countries as possible via bilaterals and other smaller deals quickly before civil society movements can hold their governments accountable to their demands and needs. Second, the U.S. seeks to predetermine the terms of the FTAA by completing bilateral and regional pacts based on NAFTA so as to set a bar for the FTAA negotiations. ("But we have to include a ban on currency controls in FTAA or else it causes incoherence, given that is part of other pacts with the same nations!") Finally, USTR Zoellick thinks he will cause Brazil anxiety about being "left out" if Brazil does not submit to FTAA, given the fact that other countries in the region will have bilateral deals with the U.S. While the U.S. press has parroted this line, in Latin American, many laugh at the notion. Brazil is by far the largest economy in Latin America and the Caribbean, and, more importantly, is one of the few major world economies that has not been totally stripped of it industrial policies and control of its natural resources already by the IMF. This makes Brazil both an alluring target for U.S. corporations whose full ambitions—for instance in controlling Amazonia's riches—have to date been thwarted, and, to the extent Brazil provides a different model, an ideological threat to the hegemony of the neoliberal model. Brazil therefore is the biggest "prize" and the only *real* target for U.S. corporate interests in the FTAA negotiations. In Brazil, the notion of feeling threatened by U.S. trade with tiny Chile or the small Central American economies is bizarre. One joke circulating at the 2003 World Social Forum in Brazil was, "Everyone knows Brazil is the one the U.S. is really dying to 'marry,' so why do they think they will win over Brazil by flirting with the ones who throw themselves on the U.S.?"

Meanwhile, the push to expand the WTO by launching new negotiations on the "New Issues" at the Cancún Ministerial was another way to put pressure on Latin American countries and sneak in FTAA-type proposals through the back door—except that in the WTO the nations of the Western Hemisphere wouldn't just have the U.S. multinational corporations to contend with, but the European and Japanese ones as well. This is of particular concern regarding the privatization of essential public services given that in several key public-service sectors, it is European companies leading the privatization and deregulation charge. For example, two French water companies—Vivendi Universal and Suez-Lyonnaise des Eaux—dominate the push for global water privatization and deregulation[52] and would benefit greatly from increased market access into the Western Hemisphere via the GATS negotiations. These GATS talks continue even though the Cancún summit imploded.

LOCKDOWN OF IMF/WB MODEL

The final context for the two-front attack is what FTAA or expanded WTO rules would mean for the many Latin American and Caribbean nations that have already suffered under the Structural Adjustment Programs of International Financial Institutions (IFIs) such as the World Bank and the IMF[53] (along with the regional development banks; most notably the Inter-American Development Bank) which frequently "carries the water" for the imposition of pro-corporate trade and investment rules. The FTAA and WTO expansion would lock down these failed policies permanently by cross-linking compliance with these policies to a country's access to trade benefits.

The stranglehold that the IFIs have had over the developing world has been pointed to as one reason nations from the Global South were pushed into going along with the creation of the WTO in the first place, despite serious reservations about the process and the outcome. Filipino political theorist and activist Walden Bello writes: "With their economies dominated by the IMF and the World Bank, the vast majority of developing countries felt as if they had no choice but to sign on the dotted line."[54] The collusion between IFIs and corporate-managed trade deals is visible in several different ways. For example, the IFIs frequently require the privatization of state-run industries as conditions for loans, making it much easier for corporations to then demand access to these industries under the rules around trade in services. Another example is the investment of the IFIs in industrial "infrastructure projects" such as the Plan Puebla Panama (PPP). The PPP would be primarily financed with loans from the IDB, a regional arm of the World Bank (although there are also a number of corporate investors in the project).[55] These loans, in turn, would push the Central American countries further into debt. The PPP, which would cover the area from Mexico to Panama, would provide the physical infrastructure for the continuation of NAFTA and the implementation of the CAFTA and the FTAA by constructing hydroelectric dams and high-impact roadways throughout indigenous territories and intact rain forests, the dredging of deepwater ports in fragile ocean ecosystems and the creation of sweatshop factories in industrial development zones throughout the region.[56]

IFIs provide the hardware that allows the "software" of the trade and investment rules to function, whether that be the forced privatization of state-run industries (facilitating the entry of multinational service corporations in essential public-service sectors such as water, health care and social security), the construction of roads through the Amazon rain forest and its wealth of medicinal plants (at the expense of the environment and the indigenous communities that live there) to provide easy access for pharmaceutical companies bioprospecting for patents, or the investment in major hotel chains that can then use trade in services and government procurement rules to monopolize local tourist industries at the expense of small and medium-sized domestic businesses.

The FTAA and an expansion of the WTO would effectively exacerbate and, more importantly, would lock in the failed policies of these institutions. As one activist put it, the FTAA or a WTO expansion would be like pouring cement over every failed Washington Consensus policy. As the Washington Consensus crumbles and other countries throw out these policies, the Americas and the Caribbean would be frozen in failure.

CONCLUSION

At Cancún, the world witnessed the potential power of developing countries working together. The proposed WTO expansion opposed by civil society in rich and poor nations was defeated because of developing-country unity. This is an important lesson to bring to the FTAA struggle.

CONCLUSION

ANOTHER WORLD IS POSSIBLE

In 1994, when the WTO was being debated in the U.S. Congress, government, business and think-tank supporters of the Uruguay Round painted a glowing picture of the WTO's benefits—unprecedented economic growth, poverty reduction worldwide, increased U.S. income, and thriving consumer societies in poor countries, which would purchase U.S. goods, thus cutting the U.S. trade deficit. In countries around the world, parliaments and the public heard only promises of broad benefits from their trade negotiators, presidents and prime ministers.

Such promises were met with skepticism by the few observers without a direct economic stake in the WTO's establishment who were even aware that such a momentous decision loomed. Around the globe, individual citizens and a broad array of civil society organizations were awakening to the potential threats. The critics predicted not only that the WTO's promised benefits would not come to fruition, but that the WTO would do damage. These political struggles against approval of the Uruguay Round and establishment of the WTO had several common features. Most political decision makers had no understanding of the unprecedented breadth of the Uruguay Round's provisions, much less their implications. A powerful elite consensus in favor of anything characterized as "free trade" ensured that a long line of prominent figures worldwide would announce support for the Uruguay Round despite lacking awareness of its contents just as the label of free trade had generated a long list of ill-informed NAFTA boosters. When, prior to the WTO vote in Congress, Ralph Nader offered a reward to any U.S. senator who would sign an affidavit asserting that he or she had read the Uruguay Round text and publicly answer ten simple questions about it, not one senator accepted. Four months later, a senator finally stepped forward to meet the challenge—self-proclaimed free-trade advocate and NAFTA supporter Hank Brown, a Republican from Colorado—but, having finally read the Uruguay Round Agreement, he came out in opposition, decrying the threat the wide-ranging terms posed to democratic policy making.

Now, nearly nine years later, there is ample evidence that the rosy predictions have failed to materialize. Worse, the Uruguay Round and the WTO have failed

WASHINGTOON®

the most conservative of tests: do no harm. The real-life devastation being caused by the implementation of the WTO's terms—and the growing social and political backlash this pain is generating worldwide—is the reason the WTO is wracked by the severe crisis that burst into public view in Seattle and Cancún. This forced experiment has flopped and now we're living with the damage. What is truly alarming is that for many developing countries, fallout from the harshest of the WTO rules is yet to come, because the rules have multi-year phase-ins.

WTO FAILS THE "FIRST-DO-NO-HARM" TEST

In virtually every key area where the U.S. and other governments promised their citizens WTO benefits, there have been problems. But even if one narrows the review of WTO's record to simply its economic results, it is failing. This is an important point, because often the most ardent WTO defenders scoff at the very notion of considering the institution's record regarding the environment, health or democratic decision making: From their perspective, it is all about the economics.

Well, the facts have begun to come in, and as described in Chapters 5 and 6 so far the WTO has been an economic flop and worse. In the era of the WTO and corporate-led globalization, the world has been buffeted by unprecedented financial crises which have shattered the lives of millions and unraveled decades of development in Asian and Latin American countries. The promised spurt in worldwide economic growth failed to materialize. Instead, countries, such as Argentina, that have most closely followed the WTO model, have been devastated. Those who have resisted, such as Malaysia, or those who have been outside the rules, such as China, have fared better economically. But "better" is a relative term. In the U.S., we focus on the massive U.S. trade deficit with China that is getting working-class industrial jobs here, but under the corporate globalization model the results are lose-lose for many.

Millions of farmers in poor and rich countries alike have been squeezed beyond survival as global grain traders use the WTO rules to minipulate markets and increase the dumping of food. The desperation—of millions of peasant farmers in developing nations who have lost their livelihoods and now are packed into the slums multiplying around cities throughout the developing world—is leading to growing political and social instability. Despite efficiency and productivity gains, wages in numerous countries have failed to rise, while commodity prices are at an all-time low, causing a decrease in the standard of living for billions of people in the world. Hunger has increased during the era of the WTO, not from a lack of food but from a lack of purchasing power by the poor. Income inequality is increasing rapidly between and within countries. The small middle classes in countries like Mexico are disappearing as small and medium-sized independent retail and manufacturing operations fall prey to the Wal-Marts and Costcos. In the U.S. the unprecedented concentration of wealth prompted an alarming exposé in the venerable *New York Times Sunday Magazine.*

In the wealthy countries, the middle class is shrinking as increasingly consolidated multinational corporations play workers in different countries off of each other in a race to the bottom—seeking the lowest labor costs and laxest environmental and health regulations—that has no apparent end. Two million U.S. manufacturing jobs have been lost since the WTO's establishment. Middle-class U.S. union jobs went to countries such as Mexico, turning $40,000-a-year jobs with benefits into $5-per-day jobs—which is not, by the way, a living wage in Mexico. These manufacturing jobs then left Mexico for China and Vietnam, whose workers earn $1–2 per day. Back in the U.S., budget shortfalls in numerous states can be traced in part to revenue crises caused by workers—now in lower-wage jobs—contributing less, while corporate manufacturing taxes vanish.

And the profits of many large corporations playing this game skyrocketed.

This same syndrome has begun again, but now it is centered on the high-tech, computer and service-sector jobs that WTO boosters confidently promised us would be our future. The U.S. should expect to lose 3 million of these jobs in the coming years, according to a *New York Times* story reported in mid-2003. This phenomenon of outsourcing professional and other service jobs to low-wage countries is beginning to cause some of WTO and NATFA's boosters in Congress and the media to ask: wait a minute—so *what* jobs exactly will we have here in the U.S.?

"Free trade" ideologues celebrate this trend as "efficiency." But they have no answer for the other obvious economic question: Just who exactly is going to buy all of the goods and services global corporations can produce in this race to the bottom? Obviously, Mexican factory workers and their Chinese counterparts do not earn enough to purchase the consumer goods they produce. And their wages are likely to decline as more and more peasants, destroyed by the globalization rules regarding agriculture trade and seed patenting, come to cities to compete with the unemployed and underemployed.

For some companies, the answer has been to move into arenas where there is no "elasticity" in demand. People have no choice about whether they consume water, health care or food. Already many WTO rules treat food like tires, televisions, or any other commodity with WTO agriculture rules threatening starvation for millions in the developing world. Companies that specialized in oil are now opening divisions to trade in "blue gold," knowing that water is essential to life, and are pushing for new WTO rules to turn bulk water (otherwise known as our lakes, rivers, and groundwater) into another tradeable commodity.

The moral implications of this model have been left out of the equation altogether. Yet the poverty and economic instability being caused by the corporate globalization model is only part of the story. As critics cautioned, the WTO's built-in bias for markets, trade and commerce *über alles* has made the institution a perfect venue for industry and governments to pursue attacks on the public interest that would fail in democratic forums. With the WTO ruling that a growing list of public health, environmental, food-safety and development policies are illegal trade barriers, now mere threats of WTO action often result in governments weakening a policy or in chilling new initiatives established through democratic domestic policy making and supported by the public.

Meanwhile, the WTO has consistently insulated the worst corporate conduct from social responsibility. As we discussed in Chapter 6, the WTO enabled Chiquita Brands International to "rent" the U.S. government, undermining the economies of several tiny banana-producing nations in the Caribbean, and assisted the U.S. Cattlemen's Association in attacking a popular European law banning artificial hormone–treated beef. Now the Bush administration has launched an attack on behalf of biotech and agribusiness interests against European policies on GMO foods and seeds. This despite the fact that polling in the U.S. shows that a majority of consumers here also would prefer the labeling and segregation of GMO and non-GMO foods that is the core of the European policy.

Despite all of the compelling evidence of the WTO's failure, the European Union continues to lead a charge—strongly supported by the U.S., Canada, Japan, and other wealthy nations—for an ambitious expansion of the WTO's constraints on government action to a whole realm of new issues and areas. Although this agenda has failed spectacularly in Seattle and Cancún, the U.S., EU and a few other major countries continue to betray their own publics' interests and, in defense of special interests they represent, indict other nations' WTO positions to distract from the real cause of the crisis—the WTO's disastrous outcomes.

Yet, any prudent proposal concerning the WTO's future must be based on an honest assessment of its performance to date. This book establishes the urgent need for a 180-degree turnaround—effectively a replacement of the current international commercial rules.

ALTERNATIVES

Social movements all over the world are helping people connect the problems in their lives to the real causes within the current terms of globalization and are developing an array of alternatives. Unlike the proponents of the status quo, the critics are not for a one-size-fits-all approach.

Indeed, when defenders of the status quo say that we do not have "The Alternative Plan," they are missing a major element of the core critique: We do not believe that any one single plan should be imposed on all the people and governments of the world. A critique of totalitarianism was something we wrongly assumed we shared with the defenders of corporate globalization—a misimpression based on many of today's strongest corporate globalization defenders' oft-repeated declarations that Soviet-style centrally planned one-size-fits-all systems were doomed to fail. The fundamental ideology underlying the movement demanding the replacement of corporate-led globalization is democracy: We believe that the people living with the results must make the decisions important to their lives and families. Inherently, this means that there will be differences in priorities and choices and that diversity is a key element of our alternative models.

Opponents of corporate globalization are developing a range of alternatives, by learning about and sharing policies that have worked and by creating new answers. This work must occur on many levels: Creating the current model was a long-term project and replacing it will be too. Decades ago, as Holly Sklar's classic book *Trilateralism* recounted in 1980, the proponents of the current system described their vision of how the world should be organized. Once this vision was articulated, political and public-relations work was undertaken to shift policies and practices from there to here.

Now we must both articulate our long-term goals and develop the steps from here to there. Toward this end, the International Forum on Globalization (IFG), of which Public Citizen is a founding member, undertook a three-year process of compiling and considering alternatives. The IFG—an alliance of leading activists, scholars economists, researchers, and writers representing 60 organizations in 25 countries—was formed in 1994 to stimulate new thinking, joint activity, and public education in response to economic globalization. Because of its globally geographically diverse membership, IFG is uniquely poised to do effective work on alternatives.

In 2002, the IFG published the results of three years of analysis in a landmark book called *Alternatives to Economic Globalization: A Better World Is Possible.*[1] In the same way the IFG helped deepen many people's understanding of the parameters and implications of corporate-led globalization, this book is providing a framework for building common demands for alternative models. The book includes ten principles for sustainable societies, some of which are self-explanatory. All of these principles are vital:

New Democracy

"Living democracy" goes beyond the mere existence of an elected government. It means accountable governance—with those living with the results in control of the decisions.

Subsidiarity

Policy decisions and economic activity should occur at the most local level feasible, and only when goals cannot be satisfied locally should decision making or activity move to the next higher level—state, nation, region and globe. "Economic global-ization entails first and foremost the delocalization and disempowerment of local communities and economies. Yet a high percentage of people on earth still survive through local, community-based activities: small-scale farming, local markets, local production for local consumption. . . . It is necessary to create new rules and structure that consciously favor the local and follow the principle of subsidiarity."[2]

Ecological Sustainability

Some resources are a collective birthright of the whole species, a common heritage, to be shared equitably. The IFG book includes three categories of such resources: water, land, air, forests and fisheries on which everyone's life depends; culture and knowledge that are the collective creation of our species; and finally what is called the "modern commons" which include public services that governments perform on behalf of all people to address basic needs such as public health, safety and social security.

Diversity

Diversity is essential to the vitality, resilience and innovative capacity of any liv-ing system—cultural diversity means different communities thrive in different locations; biological diversity is the cornerstone of the planet's health. However, from a global corporate perspective, diversity is problematic because it means "market fragmentation" and a variety of different consumer demands. Thus, while globalization policies aim to homogenize the world into one unified mar-ket, diversity is essential for the planet, communities and people to survive.

Human Rights

In 1948, under the auspices of the United Nations, governments of the world agreed on a Universal Declaration of Human Rights, which included a "standard of living adequate for . . . health and well being . . . , including food, clothing, housing and medical care and necessary social services, and the right to security in the event of unemployment." In the years that followed, additional covenants—one on political and civil rights and one on economic, social, and cultural rights—fleshed out how the Universal Declaration would apply. Delivering on these basic rights must be at the core of all alternatives.

Jobs, Livelihoods and Employment

Food Security and Food Safety

Equity

The Precautionary Principle

When there is scientific uncertainty about a possible threat to the environment or human health by a policy or product, action must be taken to restrict exposure to such a risk. Instead of risking what may be irreversible damage, the presumption is with caution.

*   *   *

The book also sets forth proposals to curb corporate power and replace some of the "operating systems," such as the current dependency on oil and agribusiness food production, that have developed under the current rules. It includes proposals to transform existing international commercial rules and fill in missing international rules, such as the lack of a global bankruptcy system that could liberate developing countries from onorous debt and rules to limit the currency speculation that has caused such global financial turmoil.

Considerable thinking has also been done about what alternatives are needed to the commercial terms in the WTO. These specific demands for change, encapsulated in a worldwide campaign called "WTO: Shrink or Sink," are based on the same principles as those identified in the IFG book. Critics of the WTO believe we need trade rules, but that the current rules—which go far far beyond trade—are inappropriate and unacceptable.

The strategy for change is quite straightforward: The WTO is like a muscular pro-corporate, antienvironment, antiworker octopus with its many damaging arms prying into our domestic food safety, worker, environmental, and health safeguards. If the legitimate international trade rules—setting tariff levels, for instance—are to be saved from the WTO, then the WTO's excesses must be cut back. Groups such as Public Citizen support enforceable international trade rules to govern the trade in goods which countries determine suits their needs, but we have no tolerance for such rules being used to further undermine democratic, accountable governance or public-interest safeguards or access to essential services and to food, water and other necessities of life. The importance of narrowing the mandates and powers of global commercial rules and institutions is apparent. Some decisions, such as those regarding the *level* of *risk* a society is willing to bear regarding food or health or what economic or what policy priorities countries will select, are value-oriented decisions that must be taken by those who will live with the results—with subsidiarity (decisions taken at the most local level appropriate) being the rule.

And some elements of our lives and world should simply be kept outside of global commercial rules. The WTO commodifies and provides for trade in everything from our essential social services to our genetic material. If a country decides patenting life-forms is against its morals or religion, who is the WTO to override those values in the name of creating new commercial opportunities for large corporations?

For threats to the global environmental commons of air and seas, and other issues where multilateral approaches are needed for problems that span geographic boundaries, we believe international rules and institutions are needed. However, it is essential to create a system of checks and balances in international governance. Currently, the pro-corporate dictates of the so-called "Bretton Woods" institutions (the WTO, the IMF, and the World Bank) simply and literally trump the pro-people rules of existing international labor, environmental, human rights, health and other public-interest treaties. The fact is that there already is broad international agreement on the substance of many labor, environmental, health and human-rights rules. For instance, the International Labor Organization has set core labor standards. There are over 100 multilateral environmental agreements on issues from toxics to air and water pollution to biodiversity and waste dumping. The World Health Organization conventions and the UN Charter on Human Rights provide many guarantees regarding access to medicine and food security. Most WTO member nations are also signatories to these international agreements and rules.

Yet, a nation's choice to prioritize implementation of one of the international public-interest obligations would be subject to challenge at a WTO tribunal as an illegal trade barrier if it contradicted WTO rules. The WTO must be cut back dramatically—basically the current system must be replaced—so that countries can regain the right to give priority to these international rules over commercial rules, and a savings clause must be added to all commercial agreements ensuring this option in the case of conflict.

So, what sort of changes are we demanding to create checks and balances in global governance? The "WTO: Shrink or Sink" coalition demands that their governments agree to 11 fundamental changes:

- **No WTO Expansion** into new areas, like investment, competition, government procurement, biotechnology or tariff liberalization.
- **Protect Basic Social Rights and Needs** by eliminating existing WTO constraints on policies critical to human or planetary welfare, such as WTO rules on constraining even non-discriminatory government action concerning public access to food, water, social services, and regarding health and safety and animal protection.
- **Give Legal Priority to International Agreements on Labor and Social Rights and the Environment** over international commercial pacts.
- **Protect Basic Social Services** by excluding health, education, energy and other basic services from international commercial agreements.
- **Remove Special Interest Protections,** for instance by eliminating the TRIPs agreement and keeping IPR regimes out of "trade" agreements.

- **No Patents on Life**, meaning WTO rules allowing patents of human cells, seeds, and animal and plant varieties must be eliminated.
- **Food Is a Basic Human Right** and international commercial agreements must exempt measures to promote and protect food security and sovereignty, subsistence farming, humane farming and sustainable agriculture from international free trade rules.
- **No Forced Investment Liberalization or Speculation,** in other words, eliminate the Trade Related Investment Measures Agreement from the WTO, and thus ensure policy options such as local-content rules that allow increases in local capacity of productive sectors.
- **Fair Trade: Special and Differential Treatment** rights for developing countries must be recognized, expanded, and put into operation in the world trading system.
- **Democratize Decision Making** by requiring the decision-making process in international commercial bodies be democratic, transparent and inclusive.
- **Dispute the Dispute Settlement System** of WTO that enforces an illegitimate system of unfair rules using undemocratic procedures. However, the transformation of WTO requires more than transparency: The substantive rules and enforcement system both must be transformed if a new regime is to have outcomes that are broadly beneficial.

Those calling for the transformation of international "trade" rules recognize that other changes in the international commercial architecture are also vitally needed. For instance, the current system's damage to developing countries can only be effectively remedied by also dealing with the IMF and World Bank, which impose the same package of policies as the WTO.

THE PATH FROM A FAILED STATUS QUO TO ALTERNATIVES

The spectacular disintegration of the Cancún WTO Ministerial should have magnified the wake-up call sounded in Seattle. Yet, in the days following, instead of focusing on the cause of the crisis, which is the WTO and its failed corporate globalization model, major corporate interests and their client governments are scrambling to lay blame anywhere else—the majority of WTO member countries that defended their publics' interests at Cancún, the Mexican diplomat who chaired the summit, and global civil society groups and social movements.

This blame game is a wasteful distraction. Business as usual at the WTO is over. The devastating real-life results on people's lives of the WTO regime described in this book are leading to a new reality. When tens of millions of engineers, computer programmers, factory workers and farmers in developed countries *and* hundreds of millions of farmers, fisher people, industrial workers and indigenous people in developing countries are all losing, the issue is when change will occur, not if.

It will take concerted action by all of us who are demanding change to help the many government officials unable to accept this new reality to overcome their cognitive dissonance.

Often, after describing the alternatives to the WTO system, critics are asked: How could we possibly get from here to there? To start with, back at the WTO's Geneva headquarters, the vacuum created by repeated WTO ministerials' collapse must be filled with steps toward change before the defenders of the status quo squander more time with new attempts to revive their repeatedly rejected agenda of more-of-the-same. For instance:

- **Review, Not Expand WTO:** The attempt to expand WTO by adding the "Singapore" issues, such as investment, has been resoundingly rejected by the vast majority of WTO member countries and these issues belong in the dustbin of bad ideas. The immediate future agenda of the WTO should be the launch of a thorough review of the WTO's performance to date with an eye toward identifying which aspects should be scaled back, replaced or eliminated. The goal: an objective review, including an open process with access to documents and a meaningful opportunity for NGO and citizen input at the national and international levels to determining the scale and methodology.
- **Moratorium on GATS-2000 Negotiations:** Despite the Cancún Ministerial's demise, the "built-in" talks under way at the WTO's Geneva headquarters to further service-sector privatization and deregulation continue. A moratorium is essential if WTO member countries are to focus on reviewing the existing WTO rules rather than expending limited resources fending off the escalating pressure in the GATS-2000 talks to turn essential services and public services over to corporate control.
- **Cease-fire on WTO Challenges:** Until the existing WTO rules and their record have been thoroughly reviewed and decisions have been taken about what are the appropriate scope and content of international commercial terms, the WTO's increasing damage can be limited by a moratorium on challenges. This would stop the WTO tribunals' second-guessing of the value choices countries make, the level of public health or environmental protection they choose, the priorities they set regarding development or competing policies such as access to medicines and patent rights, and the many policies that the WTO forbids, even when countries apply them equally to domestic and foreign companies.
- **Open, Democratic Processes for the Public:** While the existing WTO rules are being reassessed, the WTO in all of its operations should adopt a presumption of openness—making all of its operations, including the review of its existing provisions and record, accessible to the public and press. All documents should be automatically de-restricted unless they meet clear confidentiality criteria.
- **Level the Official Playing Field:** During the process of review and reconsideration, the financial, human-resource and infrastructure constraints of developing-country delegations must be addressed in a manner chosen by the developing countries to ensure that all countries can participate effectively.

The movement demanding alternatives to the WTO is not going away—rather it is growing in diversity and in size.

Either those desperately defending the failed status quo will come to realize that their project is over and recognize that change is inevitable and must be planned, or their ideologically driven intransigence will be responsible for the autarchy caused by the current system's foreseeable erosion or implosion.

What is clear is that the status quo will not hold. The real-life results of the status quo corporate-led globalization are simply too dire for too many people worldwide. And the breadth of the ever-growing damage makes it impossible to dismiss those injured as a narrow special interest.

The corporate-led globalization of the WTO is not the way of the future.

A better world is possible. Join the fight—visit Public Citizen's Global Trade Watch at www.citizen.org/trade.

NOTES

INTRODUCTION: IT'S NOT ABOUT TRADE

1. Agreement Establishing the WTO, Article XVI-4

2. Steven Bates, "Billion Dollar Banana Split," *The Guardian* (London), Mar. 6, 1999; Thomas W. Lippman, "An Appeal for a Banana Peace: General Suggests U.S. Trade Fight May Undercut U.S. Drug Battle," *Washington Post*, June 6, 1996, at A27.

3. Frank T. Kelly, Gerber vice president for Latin America, Letter to the President of Guatemala, June 16, 1994, on file with Public Citizen; "Chronology of the Gerber Case in Guatemala," Ministry of Health Guatemala, Nov. 1993, on file with Public Citizen; "Gerber Uses Threat of GATT Sanctions to Gain Exemption from Guatemalan Infant Health Law," *Corporate Crime Reporter*, Vol. 10, No. 14, April 8, 1996.

4. Guy de Jonquieres, "Network Guerillas," *Financial Times*, April 30, 1998, at 12.

CHAPTER 1: THE WTO'S ENVIRONMENTAL IMPACT

1. U.S. Trade Representative Michael Kantor, Testimony to the House Ways and Means Committee, Jan. 26, 1994.

2. The North American Agreement on Environmental Cooperation (NAAEC) is ancillary to NAFTA, meaning its terms are not binding over NAFTA's core provisions. The NAAEC created the Commission for Environmental Cooperation (CEC), which can investigate citizens' complaints that a NAFTA member country is not enforcing its environmental laws, however it does not cover environmental problems caused by the absence of environmental law. The NAFTA environmental side agreement also specifically excludes from its coverage laws on natural resources, endangered species and other vital environmental issues. Seeking review for the limited areas covered is a long and tortuous process: For instance the report in its first case took CEC over two years to complete. While it found that Mexico was not enforcing its environmental laws in allowing the destruction of ecologically critical coral reefs to construct a pier in the port of Cozumel, the pier was built and the reefs destroyed for over a year before the report was even issued. (See "NAFTA Environmental Agreement: A Paper Tiger?," News-Journal Wire Services, Jul. 29, 1998.)

3. The Clinton Administration, "The NAFTA: Expanding U.S. Exports, Jobs and Growth," U.S. Government Printing Office, Nov. 1993, at 1.

4. Letter to President Clinton, Apr. 21, 1998, signed by the Center for International Environmental Law, Center for Marine Conservation, Community Nutrition Institute, Defenders of Wildlife, Earth Island Institute, Earthjustice Legal Defense Fund, Friends of the Earth, Humane Society of the United States, National Audubon Society, National Wildlife Federation, Natural Resources Defense Council, and Sierra Club; on file at Public Citizen.

5. Between 1958 and 1994, at least 6 million dolphins in the Eastern Tropical Pacific have been killed by purse seines. See Shannon Brownlee, "A Political Casserole of Tuna and Greens," *U.S. News & World Report,* Aug. 11, 1997, at 53.

6. For instance, Article XX allows countries to restrict trade in "national treasures" and products made with prison labor, as well as to "protect public morals." The Article XX terms considered relevant to the environment allow governments to take measures "necessary to protect human, animal or plant life or health" (Article XX[b]) and those "relating to the conservation of exhaustible natural resources" (Article XX[g]). However, to date, such departures from GATT restrictions have only been permitted twice when an actual case has been decided. Although they have been raised numerous times, most panels' refusal to apply the exceptions results in part from language in the chapeau (or introductory clause) to the Article XX exceptions, which significantly narrows their scope. The chapeau clause states: "Subject to the requirement that such measures are not applied in a manner which would constitute a means of arbitrary or unjustifiable discrimination between countries where the same conditions prevail, or a disguised restriction on international trade, nothing in this Agreement shall be construed to prevent the adoption or enforcement by any contracting party of measures . . ." (Article XX). In addition, Article XX(b), which covers measures "necessary to protect human, animal or plan life or health," has been interpreted to mean that to qualify for coverage, a law must use the least trade restrictive means available to meet a goal. This exception has only been allowed once by a WTO panel, in the Canadian challenge against France's asbestos ban. (For more on this, see Chapter 3.) Article XX(g) covers measures "related to the conservation of exhaustible natural resources." Note that this exception does not include the term "necessary," thus avoiding the "least trade restrictive" test. This exception was allowed by a WTO panel reviewing whether the U.S. weakening of its sea turtle regulation complied with a WTO order, even though the underlying law was not changed.

7. U.S. International Trade Commission, Harmonized Tariff Schedule of the United States (2003).

8. WTO, TBT Agreement at Article 2.4.

9. Ibid.

10. Jason Morrison et al., "Managing a Better Environment: Opportunities and Obstacles for ISO 14001," *Public Policy and Commerce* 97 (2000).

11. See Benchmark Environmental Consulting, ISO 14001: An Uncommon Perspective—Five Public Policy Questions for Proponents of the ISO 14000 Series 13 (1996) (noting that "the ISO process also effectively excluded small and medium-sized businesses").

12. See Chapter 9.

13. Robert Evans, "Green Push Could Damage Trade Body—WTO Chief," Reuters, May 15, 1998.

14. Goh Chien Yen and Celine Tan, "Deadlock at Summit on Trade, Finance and Debt," *Third World Resurgence,* Issue No. 145–146, September–October, 2002.

15. Martin Khor, "WSSD Survives WTO Takeover," *Third World Resurgence,* Issue No. 145–146, September–October 2002.

16. Alex Evans, "A Johannesburg Report Card," *IPPR Research Report,* September 2002.

17. Rosalie Gardiner, "Governance for Sustainable Development: Outcomes From Johannesburg," Presentation to Global Governance 2002: Redefining Global Democracy, Montreal, Canada, October 2002, at 3.

18. WTO, United States—Standards for Reformulated and Conventional Gasoline (WT/DS2/R), Report of the Panel, Jan. 29, 1996.

19. See WTO, United States—Standards for Reformulated and Conventional Gasoline (WT/DS2/AB/R), Report of the Appellate Body, May 20, 1996.

20. 62 Fed. Reg. 24776, May 6, 1997, at Appendix 19.

21. Foreign Agent Registration Unit data show Arnold and Porter representing Venezuela from Jun. 1992 through 2001. Data on file with Public Citizen.

22. Petroleos de Venezuela, S.A. (PDVSA), the state-owned oil company of Venezuela, submitted comments on the EPA's proposed gasoline rule on November 20, 1992, and May 17, 1993. Docket A-91-02.

23. 103rd Congress, H.R. 4953, Sponsored by Rep. Kim (R-CA), introduced Aug. 12, 1994.

24. The National Defense Council Foundation, Domestic Refining: Target of a WTO Power Grab, Feb. 21, 1996.

25. WTO, United States—Standards for Reformulated and Conventional Gasoline (WT/DS2/R), Report of the Panel, Jan. 29, 1996, at Para 7.1.

26. Jayne E. Mardock and Gina Porreco, Clean Air Network, "Smog Watch," May 1999.

27. See U.S. Environmental Protection Agency (EPA), Office of Air and Radiation, 1997 Air Quality Status and Trends, December 1998.

28. National Institutes of Health (NIH), National Asthma Education and Prevention Program data cited in "The Attack of Asthma," *Environmental Health Perspectives,* Vol. 104, No. 1, Jan. 1996. According to the NIH, between 1982 and 1993, the prevalence of asthma in the United States increased 46% overall and 80% among those under age 18. NIH estimates that more than 7% of American children now have the disease. A New Jersey study found that emergency room visits for asthma increased by 28% when ozone concentrations reached only half the federal limit. (Clifford P. Weissel, Ronald P. Cody, Paul J. Lioy, "Relationship between Summertime Ambient Ozone Levels and Emergency Department Visits for Asthma in Central New Jersey," *Environmental Health Perspectives,* supplement 2, Mar. 1995, on file at Public Citizen.)

29. WTO, United States—Standards for Reformulated and Conventional Gasoline (WT/DS2/R), Report of the Panel, Jan. 29, 1996, at Para. 6.10.

30. WTO, United States—Standards for Reformulated and Conventional Gasoline (WT/DS2/AB/R), Report of the Appellate Body, May 20, 1996, at 33.

31. WTO, United States—Standards for Reformulated and Conventional Gasoline (W/DS2/9), Consolidated Report of the Panel and the Appellate Body, May 20, 1996, at Part C (Conclusions).

32. WTO, United States—Standards for Reformulated and Conventional Gasoline, Second Submission of the United States, Aug. 17, 1995, at 3–5; see also Appendix at 387–89.

33. U.S. Department of Energy, Petroleum Supply Annual 1998, Vol. 1, Table 21, on file with Public Citizen.

34. 62 Fed. Reg. 24776, May 6, 1997.

35. WTO, United States—Standards for Reformulated and Conventional Gasoline, Second Submission of the United States, Aug. 17, 1995, at 22–24.

36. In early May 1998, Earthjustice Legal Defense Fund filed a federal lawsuit on behalf of Friends of the Earth, Defenders of Wildlife and the Center for International Environmental Law, charging that the EPA had exceeded its congressional mandate in the Clean Air Act by issuing a WTO-consistent regulation which weakened the U.S. gasoline cleanliness standards. (See *George E. Warren Corporation and the Independent Refiners Coalition vs. EPA,* D.C. Circuit No. 97-1651, as consolidated with 97-1656, Brief of Intervenor-Petitioners, Friends of the Earth, Inc., filed on May 1, 1998, on file with Public Citizen.) The groups argued: "[I]n relying on international trade rules and economic factors to justify the new rule, EPA violated the law and relied on factors that Congress did not intend the agency to consider." The groups also argued that WTO panel reports create no obligation for the U.S. to change its laws. In early 1999, the court ruled that the EPA was within its mandate to change the standard. The court also implied that the WTO panel ruling creates a treaty obligation for the U.S. that should not be contravened.

37. John Malek and Dr. Peter Bowler, "Dolphin Protection in the Tuna Fishery, Interdisciplinary Minor in Global Sustainability," Seminar (Irvine: University of California Press, 1997), at 1.

38. See Statement for the Inter-American Tropical Tuna Commission Meeting, Oct. 21–23, 1996.

39. The key provision that was the target of challenges under GATT is 16 U.S.C. Section 1371(a)(2), prohibiting the importation of tuna from countries that harvest tuna using purse seines.

40. GATT, United States—Restrictions on Imports of Tuna (DS21/R), Report of the Panel, Sep. 3, 1991.

41. See GATT, United States—Restrictions on Imports of Tuna (DS29/R), Report of the Panel, Jun. 1994.

42. See GATT, Findings on U.S. Tuna Ban, Report of Dispute Panel, Aug. 16, 1991, at Paras. 5.24–5.34.

43. GATT, United States—Restrictions on Imports of Tuna (DS29/R), Report of the Panel, Jun. 1994, at Para. 5.24.

44. "Clinton Pledges Early, Renewed Effort to Pass Tuna-Dolphin Bill," *Inside U.S. Trade,* Oct. 1996.

45. See 104th Congress, H.R. 2179, Sponsor: Rep. "Duke" Cunningham (R-CA); see also S.1420, Sponsors: Sen. Ted Stevens (R-AK), Co-sponsor: Sen. John Breaux (D-LA).

46. See 105th Congress, H.R. 408, Sponsor: Rep. Gilchrest (R-MO); see also S.39, Sponsor: Sen. Ted Stevens (R-AK).

47. International Dolphin Conservation Program Act, H.R. 408, became Public Law 105–42, Aug. 15, 1997.

48. 64 Fed. Reg. 24590, May 7, 1999. In its initial finding, NMFS concluded that there was insufficient evidence to show that catching tuna by encircling dolphins has a significant adverse impact on dolphin stocks.

49. U.S. Department of Commerce press release, "Commerce Department Issues Initial

Finding on Tuna/Dolphin Interactions—Will Adopt New 'Dolphin-Safe' Label Standard," Apr. 29, 1999.

50. 64 Fed. Reg. 24590, May 7, 1999.

51. U.S. Department of Commerce press release, "Commerce Department Issues Initial Finding on Tuna/Dolphin Interactions."

52. Scott Harper, "Rule Revised for Tuna Fishing, Encirclement Will be Allowed with Oversight to Help Protect Dolphins," *The Virginian Pilot*, May 18, 1999. A campaign by Earth Island Institute has resulted in commitments by some major tuna canners to use only tuna caught without purse seines.

53. *Earth Island Institute v. William Daley*, U.S. District Court of Northern California, Aug. 1999.

54. *Brower v. Daley*, 93 F. Supp. 1071 (No. Ca. 2000); see also U.S. Department of Commerce press release, "Commerce Secretary Disappointed at Federal Court Ruling: U.S. Also Lifts Tuna Import Embargo Against Mexico," Apr. 12, 2000.

55. *Brower v. Evans*, 257 F.3d 1058 (9th Cir. 2001); see also Earth Island Institute press release, "Lawsuit Victory in 'Dolphin-Safe' Tuna Label Case," Jul. 23, 2001.

56. Defenders of Wildlife press release, "Administration Overturns Environmental Keystone 'Dolphin-Safe' Tuna Standard to Fall," Dec. 31, 2002.

57. U.S. Department of Commerce press release, "Commerce Secretary Disappointed at Federal Court Ruling: U.S. Also Lifts Tuna Import Embargo Against Mexico," Apr. 12, 2000.

58. 65 Fed. Reg. 26585, May 8, 2000.

59. *Defenders of Wildlife v. Hogarth*, 177 F. Supp. 2d 1336 (Ct. Int'l Trade 2001).

60. Ibid.; see also U.S. Department of Commerce press release, "Court Decision Validates NOAA Fisheries Dolphin Protection in Eastern Tropical Pacific Tuna Fishery," Jan. 4, 2002.

61. "U.S. Eases 'Dolphin-Safe' Tuna Rules," Associated Press, Dec. 31, 2002.

62. 67 Fed. Reg. 54633, Aug 23, 2002.

63. Southwest Fisheries Science Center, NOAA Fisheries, *Report of the Scientific Research Program Under the International Dolphin Conservation Program Act*, Sep. 17, 2002.

64. Department of Commerce press release, "Commerce Department Determines No Significant Adverse Impact of Fishing on Dolphin Populations," Dec. 31, 2002.

65. Earth Island Institute press release, "Secret Dolphin Study Report Released!," Dec. 5, 2002.

66. Southwest Fisheries Science Center, NOAA Fisheries, *Report of the Scientific Research Program Under the International Dolphin Conservation Program Act*, Sep. 17, 2002.

67. Humane Society of the U.S. press release, "The Humane Society of the United States Blasts Bush Administration for Weakening 'Dolphin-Safe' Tuna Label," Dec. 31, 2002.

68. Christopher Marquis, "Two Scientists Contend U.S. Supressed Dolphin Studies," *New York Times*, Jan. 9, 2003.

69. *Earth Island v. Evans*, 256 F. Supp. 1064 (No. Ca. 2003). Earth Island Institute press release, "Environmentalists Sue to Save Dolphins," Jan. 2, 2003.

70. Ibid.

71. Interview with Earth Island Institute, Jan. 28, 2003.

72. "Financing to Support Mexican Tuna Fishing Sector," Atuna. Com, June 11, 2003, on file with Public Citizen. "Although the country's government has announced it would now involve the WTO to end the tuna/dolphin conflict that has been going on for the past 10 years, at the same time the tuna sector is advised to look for alternatives to maintain tuna fishing production in Mexico."

73. Public Law 93-205, 16 U.S.C. 1531 et seq.; see also 52 Fed. Reg. 24244, Jun. 29, 1987.

74. 52 Fed. Reg. 24244, Jun. 29, 1987. Five species of sea turtle fell under the Endangered Species Act regulations: loggerhead (*Caretta caretta*), Kemp's ridley (*Lepidochelys kempi*), green (*Chelonia mydas*), leatherback (*Dermochelys coriacea*) and hawksbill (*Eretmochelys imbricata*).

75. Sea Turtle Restoration Project press release, "Environmentalists Petition U.S. Supreme Court to Hear the Case of the Sea Turtles," Nov. 6, 2002.

76. Ibid.

77. WTO, United States—Import Prohibition of Certain Shrimp and Shrimp Products (WT/DS58), Complaint by India, Malaysia, Pakistan and Thailand.

78. WTO, United States Import Prohibition of Certain Shrimp and Shrimp Products (WT/DS58/R), Final Report, May 15, 1998, at Para. 9.1 (Concluding Remarks).

79. See Letter to President Clinton, Apr. 21, 1998, signed by the Center for International Environmental Law, Center for Marine Conservation, Community Nutrition Institute, Defenders of Wildlife, Earth Island Institute, Earthjustice Legal Defense Fund, Friends of the Earth, Humane Society of the United States, National Audubon Society, National Wildlife Federation, Natural Resources Defense Council, and the Sierra Club, on file at Public Citizen.

80. "The Sea Turtles' Warning," *New York Times,* Apr. 10, 1998.

81. WTO, United States—Import Prohibition of Certain Shrimp and Shrimp Products (WT/DS58), Appealed on Jul. 13, 1998.

82. WTO, United States—Import Prohibition of Certain Shrimp and Shrimp Products (WT/DS58/AB/R), Report of the Appellate Body, Oct. 12, 1998.

83. Ibid.

84. Jock Nash, trade analyst, written communication with Michelle Sforza, research director, Public Citizen's Global Trade Watch, Oct. 14, 1998.

85. "Louisiana Shrimpers Threatened By Ruling on Turtle Excluder," States News Service, Apr. 14, 1998.

86. WTO, United States—Import Prohibition of Certain Shrimp and Shrimp Products, Status Report by the United States, WT/DS58/15, Jul. 15, 1999.

87. The change allowed shipment-by-shipment certification of TEDs use, versus the country-by-country method that had been in effect. Environmental groups charged that the new boat-by-boat regulation violated the Endangered Species Act. In April 1999, the U.S. Court of International Trade sided with the environmental groups, but would not issue an injunction. (*Earth Island Institute vs. William Daley,* U.S. Court of International Trade, Case No. 98-09-02818, April 2, 1999, at 35.) While the Commerce Department appealed, the State Department issued new regulations on shrimp imports in early July 1999. The new regulations set the standard for certification of shrimp imports as not harming turtles, and thus being allowed into the U.S., based on whether the exporting nation had a comparable regulatory program, on whether the shrimp harvesting occurs in an environment unlikely to

harm turtles (cold oceans), and on whether the shrimping technique is unlikely to harm sea turtles (such as manual shrimping without mechanical winches) (64 Fed. Reg. 36946, Jul. 8, 1999).

88. WTO, United States—Import Prohibition of Certain Shrimp and Shrimp Products, Status Report by the United States, WT/DS58/15, Jul. 15, 1999.

89. WTO, United States—Import Prohibition of Certain Shrimp and Shrimp Products, WT/DS58/15/Add.2, Oct. 15, 1999.

90. Sea Turtle Restoration Project press release, "Australia Exploits Loophole in U.S. Turtle-Shrimp Law," Nov. 2, 1999.

91. WTO, United States—Import Prohibition of Certain Shrimp and Shrimp Products, WT/DS58/17, Oct. 13, 2000.

92. WTO, United States—Import Prohibition of Certain Shrimp and Shrimp Products, WT/DS58/RW, Jun. 15, 2001.

93. WTO, United States—Import Prohibition of Certain Shrimp and Shrimp Products, WT/DS58/AB/RW, Oct. 22, 2001.

94. *Turtle Island Restoration Network v. Evans,* U.S. Court of Appeals for the Federal Circuit, Aug. 15, 2002.

95. Sea Turtle Restoration Project press release, "Environmentalists Petition U.S. Supreme Court to Hear the Case of the Sea Turtles," Nov. 6, 2002.

96. *Turtle Island Restoration Network v. Evans,* 284 F. 3d 1282 (Fed. Cir. 2002) cert. denied, 123 S. Ct. 1748 (2003). See also Sea Turtle Restoration Project press release, "Supreme Court Refuses to Consider Fixing Loophole in Sea Turtle Law," Apr. 7, 2003, on file with Public Citizen.

97. U.S. Department of State media note, "Sea Turtle Conservation and Shrimp Imports," Apr. 30, 2002.

98. The EU proposal, the Directive on Waste Electrical and Electronic Equipment (WEEE), is designed to minimize pollution caused by electronic products and to shift the cost of subsequent environmental cleanup from the public to the electronics industry (see European Union, "Directive of the European Parliament and of the Council on Waste Electrical and Electronic Equipment," PE-CONS 3663/02, November 8, 2002) by making electronic companies responsible for their products from cradle to grave. The EU proposes to ban electronic products containing lead, mercury, cadmium, hexavalent chromium and halogenated flame retardants by the year 2006, and requires a 5% recycled-content rule for plastic electronic components. And electronics manufacturers would be made responsible for the recovery and disposal of electronic equipment. The American Electronics Association (AEA) has long attacked the EU proposal, which passed the European Parliament in 2002 and has been sent back to the member countries for ratification. The AEA claims the EU proposal is WTO-illegal because it restricts trade in certain heavy metals used to make electronics products. (American Electronics Association, Legality Under International Trade Law of Draft Directive on Waste from Electrical and Electronic Equipment, Mar. 1999, prepared by Rod Hunter and Marta Lopez of Hunton & Williams, Brussels, on file with Public Citizen.) After the industry began complaining, the U.S. State Department sent a "demarche" (a formal diplomatic communication that is not a formal WTO challenge) to the EU arguing that the proposed regulations are too trade restrictive and violate WTO rules. Specifically, the U.S. document claims that the recycled content and recovery/disposal requirements are "trade distorting," implying that these would violate the WTO

Agreement on Trade Related Investment Measures by forcing U.S. companies to purchase recycled materials and build collection facilities in Europe.

99. "TBT Committee Discusses Labeling, Standards," *BRIDGES Weekly Trade News Digest*, Vol. 3, No. 23, Jun. 14, 1999. The Coalition for Truth in Environmental Marketing Information included timber, plastics, chemical, electronics and packing industry associations in addition to the Grocery Manufacturers of America and the National Food Processors Association. In 1996, the coalition requested that USTR seek clarifications of the role of the WTO and TBT on eco-labeling. (Stephen Barlas, "U.S. Companies Say Eco-Labeling Hollow Echo," *Packaging World*, May 1996, at 26.) The corporate group's main focus was to push for a U.S. position at the WTO that would effectively end voluntary eco-labeling by bringing voluntary and mandatory eco-label systems under WTO disciplines. This would represent an enormous (and perhaps First Amendment–violating) expansion of WTO powers into the activities of the private sector, expanding WTO jurisdiction to include disciplining the Good Housekeeping Seal of Approval decisions and *Consumer Reports* ratings. In March 1996, the U.S. submitted a proposal with six criteria that would set the standard for WTO-legal eco-labels (WTO Committee on Trade and Environment Document WT/CTE/W/27, "U.S. Proposals Regarding Further Work on Transparency of Eco-Labeling," Mar. 25, 1996). The proposal was based on the presumption that the WTO's TBT Agreement covered eco-labels. Happily, a nearly identical six-point "Suggested Basis of U.S. Proposal Regarding Principles Applicable to Eco-labelling Programs" was accidentally released outside the U.S. government with the fax imprint of the corporate law firm that had drafted it still visible. The controversy that ensued about the Clinton administration forwarding as its own policy to the WTO a retrograde proposal literally written by industry helped fuel a quick campaign by environmental and consumer groups (working together as the "Save the Seals" coalition) and their allies in Congress. The Clinton administration USTR continued this aggressive posture on eco-labeling until the White House Council on Environmental Quality (CEQ) intervened in 1996. CEQ blew the whistle on USTR's efforts to undermine the EU's eco-labeling policy and informed USTR that the Clinton White House could not allow any further movement from USTR on EU's eco-labeling proposal.

100. Elizabeth Becker and Jennifer Lee, "European Plan on Chemicals Seen as Threat to U.S. Exports," *New York Times*, May 7, 2003.

101. Douglas P. Norlen, "Hong Kong Registers WTO Complaint Over U.S. Wood Crate Ban; Canada to Follow," Bureau of National Affairs, Nov. 18, 1998.

102. 63 Fed. Reg. 50099.

103. Cheryl Lyn Dybas, "Beetle From China Threatening U.S. Hardwood Trees," *Washington Post*, Jul. 9, 2001.

104. APHIS press release, "USDA to Continue Asian Longhorned Beetle Eradication Efforts," Feb. 22, 2002.

105. Ibid.

106. APHIS, "Strategic Plan for Eradication of Asian Longhorned Beetle," 2002 at 12.

107. APHIS press release, "Asian Longhorned Beetle: Questions and Answers," Dec. 2002; and "USDA Amends Asian Longhorned Beetle Quarantine and Regulations," May 16, 2003.

108. APHIS press release, "USDA to Continue Asian Longhorned Beetle Eradication Efforts."

109. Sierra Club, "Protect Our Neighborhood, Don't Trade Away Our Trees," Summer 1999.

110. P. T. Bangsberg, "China Criticizes 'Unfair' Beetle Ban," *Journal of Commerce*, Sep. 22, 1998.

111. 67 Fed. Reg. 52893, Aug. 14, 2002.

112. The Food and Agricultural Organization of the United Nations, International Plant Protection Convention, Rome, 1951.

113. International Plant Protection Convention, Report of the Fourth Session of the Interim Commission on Phytosanitary Measures, Appendix IV—International Standards for Guidelines for Regulating Wood Packaging in International Trade, March 15, 2002.

114. 7 CFR 319.40-7.

115. Melody A. Keena, Paul M. Moore and Steve M. Ulanecki, USDA Forest Service, "Effects of Temperature on the Life History Parameters of *Anoplophora glabripennis*"; M. A. Kenna, USDA Forest Service, "*Anoplophora glabripennis* Fecundity and Longevity Under Laboratory Conditions Comparisons of Populations from New York and Illinois on *Acer saccarum*," *Environmental Entomology*, Vol. 31, no. 3.

116. U.S. Environmental Protection Agency, Methyl Bromide Chemical Profile, CAS Registry No. 74-83-9, Nov. 30, 1987.

117. U.S. EPA, Emergency First Aid Treatment Guide for Methyl Bromide, CAS Registry No. 74-83-9.

118. U.S. Environmental Protection Agency, Methyl Bromide Chemical Profile.

119. Ibid.

120. 40 CFR 82 (2001).

121. APHIS, EIS No. 020464, "Importation of Solid Wood Packing Material Environmental Impact Statement," Oct. 2002.

122. European Economic Council (EEC) Regulation No. 3254/91, Nov. 4, 1991, at Articles 2 and 3, Annex I.

123. Ibid., at Article 3, Para. 1.

124. Willem Wijnstekers, "Implementation of Regulation 3254/91, Leg-hold Traps and Fur Imports," memo for European Parliament, Nov. 24, 1993. Only Sweden and Finland have wolves or ermines native to their countries; both have introduced muskrats, and Finland has introduced beavers.

125. U.S. Humane Society, "Trapping the Inside Story," 1998.

126. Ibid.

127. John Maggs, "U.S. to Protest EU Fur Ban involving Use of Leg-Hold Trap," *Journal of Commerce*, Jun. 22, 1994. In 1994, as the Clinton administration faced a tough fight in Congress over the proposed Uruguay Round, then–U.S. Trade Representative Mickey Kantor reassured members of Congress from trapping states who were withholding support for the WTO that the U.S. would ask for a one-year waiver to the EU import ban. See Letter from U.S. Trade Representative Michael Kantor to Senators Stevens (AK), Breaux (LA), Murkowski (AK), Danforth (MO), Baucus (MT), Burns (MT), Johnston (LA), Rockefeller (WV) and Wallop (WY) and Representatives Young (AK), Hayes (LA), Dingell (MI), Tauzin (LA) and Brewster (OK), cited in *Inside U.S. Trade*, Aug. 26, 1994, at 21.

128. EEC Regulation No. 1771/94, Jul. 19, 1994, at Article 1.

129. Letter from U.S. Trade Representative Michael Kantor to Canadian Minister of

International Trade Roy MacLaren, Aug. 10, 1995; see also "EU: Canada to Take Action if EU Bans Its Fur Exports," *European Report*, May 10, 1995.

130. Gillian Handyside, "MPES Want Brittan's Head Over Leghold Trap," Reuters, Dec. 11, 1995.

131. "EU Leghold Trap Ban Delayed Without Council, Parliament Approval," *Inside U.S. Trade*, Dec. 22, 1995.

132. Ronald van de Krol, "Dutch Ban Leg-Hold Fur Imports," *Financial Times*, Jan. 12, 1996.

133. "EU States Delay Fur Ban for Fourth Time," *Inside U.S. Trade*, Feb. 28, 1997.

134. Emma Tucker, "Brussels Reaches Pact on Leg-Hold Traps," *Financial Times*, May 30, 1997. The deal would prohibit leg-hold traps on land for more than half the specified species, phase out leg-hold traps on land for remaining species over three years, and permit padded leg-hold traps underwater.

135. "EU Blocking Minority Forces Delay of Vote on Fur Ban," *Inside U.S. Trade*, Jun. 27, 1997.

136. A letter from then–U.S. Trade Representative Charlene Barshefsky (who inherited the dispute from Kantor) to the EU's Leon Brittan stated that the U.S. would not participate in an arbitrary ban on certain traps, although this was not the EU proposal's requirement, "Barshefsky Letter on Leghold Traps," *Inside U.S. Trade*, Jul. 11, 1997.

137. Neil Buckly, "U.S. Fur-Trapping Offer Is Rejected," *Financial Times*, Nov. 28, 1997.

138. Neil Buckly, "New Offer by U.S. on Leg-Hold Traps," *Financial Times*, Dec. 1, 1997.

139. Nancy L. Perkins, Arnold and Porter, American Society of International Law, European Community–United States: Agreed Minutes and Side Letter Relating to Humane Trapping Standards, Introductory Note 37 I.L.M. 532, 1998. See www.asil.org/ilm/perkins.htm.

140. Ibid.

141. Animal Welfare Institute, "U.S. Evades Fur Import Ban, Leghold Trap Proponents Cheer," *American Welfare Institute Quarterly*, Fall 1997, at 4. For instance, the deal covers "conventional" leg-hold traps, but does not define "conventional." Also, the agreement explicitly provides for "Best Management Practices," allowing steel jaw leg-hold trapping to continue if the U.S. government determines that it is the best way to manage some American species.

142. Ibid.

143. Animal Protection Institute, "Exposing the Myths: The Truths About Trapping," Nov. 19, 2001.

144. European Commission, "Agreement Between the European Community and the United States on Humane Trapping Standards," OJ C 32, COM(97)726, Jan. 30, 1998.

145. "Welfare of Animals 'Wrecked by WTO,'" (Newcastle) *Journal*, Dec. 3, 2002.

146. 1997 Kyoto Protocol to the United Nations' Framework Convention on Climate Change, U.N. Document FCCC/CP/1997/L.7/Add.1.

147. Embassy of Japan Backgrounder on Amendments to its Law Concerning Rational Use of Energy Law 1999, on file with Public Citizen.

148. Ibid., citing OECD data.

149. Ibid.

150. Japan, Law Concerning Rational Use of Energy, Jun. 22, 1979, revised Jun. 5, 1998.

(The system employs lean-burn technology that reduces fuel used by means of air intake larger than the theoretical air-fuel mixture ratio, in order to achieve fuel economy.)

151. WTO, "TBT Notification 99.003," Letter from European Commission Industrial Secretariat, 1999, on file with Public Citizen.

152. According to Japanese government sources, the U.S. first weighed in against Japan's fuel-efficiency law on behalf of Daimler-Chrysler. At the U.S.-Japan summit in May 1999, Japanese officials reported that the president of Ford Motor Company also complained about the law to the prime minister of Japan. (Personal communication between Michelle Sforza, Research Director, Public Citizen's Global Trade Watch, and an official with Japanese Embassy in Washington, D.C., May 13, 1999.)

153. See letter from Ferial Ara Saeed, first secretary of the Economic Section of the U.S. Embassy, to Mr. Kazuyoshi Umemoto, director of the First International Organizations Division of the Economics Affairs Bureau of the Ministry of Foreign Affairs, Mar. 8, 1999.

154. Embassy of Japan Backgrounder on Amendments to its Law Concerning Rational Use of Energy Law 1999, on file with Public Citizen.

155. Walter R. Stahel, "The Functional Economy: Cultural and Organizational Change," in Deanna J. Richards, ed., *The Industrial Green Game: Implications for Environmental Design and Management* (National Academy of Engineering, Washington, DC, 1997), at 94.

156. Richard G. Tarasofsky and Stefanie Pfahl, Ecologic Institute for International and European Environmental Policy for Greenpeace International, "Trading Away the Last Ancient Forests," Dec. 2001.

157. Ibid.

158. U.S. International Trade Commission, Database Version 2.6, http://dataweb. usitc.gov. Results of query using Harmonized Tariff Schedule Codes 440320, 440399, 440391, 440349, 440392 run on Aug. 20, 2003. Results on file with Public Citizen.

159. WTO, International Trade Statistics 2002, at Table II.1: World Merchandise Exports, Production and Gross Domestic Product, 2002.

160. "Bush Signs Log Export Ban Aimed at Saving Owls," *Los Angeles Times,* Aug. 21, 1990.

161. "Japan Denounces Curb on U.S. Log Shipment," *Wall Street Journal,* Aug. 22, 1990.

162. Steve Scrybman, Canandian Environmental Law Association, "How a Log Export Ban Became an Unfair Trade Practice," 1993.

163. Tarasofsky and Pfahl, Ecologic Institute for International and European Environmental Policy for Greenpeace International, "Trading Away the Last Ancient Forests."

164. WTO, Ministerial Declaration, Ministerial Conference, Fourth Session, Doha, WT.MIN(01)/DEC/W/1, Nov. 14, 2001 at para 16.

165. Food and Agriculture Organization, "State of World Fisheries and Aquaculture 2000," 2000.

166. USDA, U.S. Department of Commerce, U.S. Census Bureau, Foreign Trade Statistics, harmonized tariff schedule 6-digit codes 030420, 030410, 030212, 030611, 030269, 030379, 030749, 030221, 030530, 030490, 030619, 030559, 051191, 030374, 030549, 030569, 030621, 030229, 030211, 030250, 030310, 030339, 030265, 030375, 030321.

167. U.S. Department of Commerce, U.S. Census Bureau, Foreign Trade Statistics, harmonized tariff schedule 6-digit code 030410.

168. "WTO Rules Negotiations: Deep Divides Prevail on Harmfulness of Fisheries Subsidies," *Bridges,* Vol. 6, No. 36, Oct. 24, 2002.

169. World Wildlife Fund, "Turning the Tide on Fishing Subsidies," 2002.

170. David R. Downes and Brennan Van Dyke, Center for International Environmental Law and Greenpeace, "Fisheries Conservation and Trade Rules," 1998.

171. WTO, Decision on Trade and Environment, Final Act Embodying the Results of the Uruguay Round of Multilateral Trade Negotiations, Marrakech, Morocco, Apr. 15, 1994.

172. WTO, Committee on Trade and Environment, List of Representatives, WT/CTE/INF/1, Jun. 10, 1998.

173. Ibid.

174. WTO, "International Intergovernmental Organizations, Observer Status in the Committee on Trade and Environment," WT/CTE/INF/6, WT/CTE/W/41/Rev. 10, Feb. 4, 2003.

175. Dan Seligman, "Broken Promises: How the Clinton Administration Is Trading Away Our Environment," Sierra Club Responsible Trade Campaign, May 13, 1998.

176. Ibid.

177. Especially Art. XIV(1) and (2) of the Convention on International Trade in Endangered Spieces, Arts. 4(5) and 5 to 10 of the Basel Convention on Trade in Hazardous Substances.

178. Some examples include Arts. 4 and 4A of the Montreal Protocol on Ozone-Depleting Substances, Art. 3(5) of the UN Framework Convention on Climate Change, Art. 2(3) of the Kyoto Protocol, Art. 3 of the Persistent Organic Pollutants Convention, and Art. 2(4) of the Cartegena Protocol on Biosafety.

179. 16 U.S.C. Chapter 35, Section 1538.

180. North American Free Trade Agreement (NAFTA) at Article 104.

181. See "U.S. Business, Environmental Groups Divided on Shrimp-Turtle Case," *BRIDGES Weekly Trade News Digest,* vol. 2, no. 15, Apr. 27, 1998.

182. "WTO Enviro Groups Getting Closer Together," *Washington Trade Daily,* Mar. 17, 1999.

183. WTO, Report (1999) of the Committee on Trade and Environment, WT/CTE/4, Oct. 14, 1999.

184. "Green Groups Challenge WTO," *Financial Times,* Mar. 17, 1999.

185. "Cuts Urged in Fishing and Farm Aid," *Financial Times,* Mar. 16, 1999.

186. WTO, Report (1999) of the Committee on Trade and Environment, WT/CTE/4, Oct. 14, 1999.

187. National Archives and Records Administration, "The Clinton Administration Agenda for Seattle WTO," Nov. 24, 1999.

188. The American Forest & Paper Association press release, "Forest Industry Leader Urges Worldwide Tariff Elimination," Apr. 28, 1999, citing study by the consulting firm of Jaakko Poyry.

189. WTO, Doha Ministerial Declaration, Nov. 20, 2001, WT/MIN(01)/DEC/1, at paras. 3; 32.

190. WTO, Multilateral Environmental Agreements (MEAs): Implementation of the

Doha Development Agenda, Submission by the European Communities, TN/TE/W/1, Mar. 21, 2002, at Section VIII.

191. WTO, Committee on Trade and Environment Special Session, Summary Report on the First Meeting of the Committee on Trade and Environment Special Session, Mar. 22, 2002, at paras 17–21.

192. Ibid., at paras 68–74.

193. WTO, Committee on Trade and Environment Special Session, Negotiations on Environmental Goods, Submission by the State of Qatar, TN/TE/W/14, Oct. 9, 2002, at paras 6–7.

CHAPTER 2: THE WTO'S COMING TO DINNER

1. "BSE: The End of a Mystery?" *The Independent* (London), Jul. 27, 2001.

2. "Timeline: The Rise and Rise of BSE," *New Scientist,* cited Nov. 23, 2002, available at www.newscientist.com/hottopics/bse/bsetimeline.jsp.

3. Ibid.

4. "Have Contaminated Feed Exports Spread BSE Across the Globe?"*New Scientist,* Feb. 10, 2001.

5. "Experts Back Global BSE Alert," BBC, Dec. 23, 2000.

6. Office of International Epizootics, "Number of Reported Cases of BSE Worldwide," Nov. 20, 2002, available at www.oie.int/eng/info/en_esbmonde.htm.

7. N. J. Andrews, "Incidents of Variant Cruetzfeld Disease, Onset of Deaths in the UK January 1994–September 2002," Quarterly Report of the Public Health Laboratories Service Statistics Unit, Oct. 14, 2002, on file with Public Citizen.

8. "SPS body looks at current epidemics, 'equivalence' and standard-setting," *WTO News,* Mar. 2001 at 7.

9. WHO,"Food Safety: Report by the Director-General," Report to the Executive Board, EB105/10, Dec. 2, 1999; WHO, "Emerging Foodborne Diseases," Factsheet No. 124, Jan. 2002.

10. Dr. Gro Harlem Brundtland, Director-General, World Health Organization, Video Message to the Opening of the Global Forum of Food Safety Regulators, Marrakech, Morroco, Jan. 28–30, 2002.

11. See WHO, "Food Safety and Foodborne Illness," Factsheet No. 237, Jan. 2002.

12. P. Mead, L. Slutsker, V. Dietz, L. McCaig, J. Bressee, C. Shapiro, P. Griffin and R. Tauxe, U.S. Centers for Disease Control (CDC), "Food Related Illness and Death in the United States," *Emerging Infectious Diseases,* Vol. 5, No. 5, Sep.–Oct. 1999, at 607–625; WTO, "Food Safety Report by the Director General," Report to the Executive Board, EB105/10, Dec. 2, 1999.

13. WHO and World Trade Organization (WTO), "WTO Agreements and Public Health: A Joint Study by the WHO and the WTO Secretariat," WHO ISBN 92 4 156214 5, 2002 at 63.

14. Michael T. Osterholm, Ph.D., M.P.H., "Emerging Infections—Another Warning," *New England Journal of Medicine* editorial, Vol. 342, No. 17, Apr. 27, 2000.

15. WHO, "Emerging Foodborne Diseases."

16. WHO, "Food Safety: Report by the Director-General," EB105/10, Dec. 2, 1999.

17. WHO, "Food Safety and Foodborne Illness."

18. WHO, "Food Safety: Report by the Director-General."

19. U.S. Department of Commerce, International Trade Administration, "U.S. Total Agricultural Imports from Individual Countries, 1993–2000," on file with Public Citizen and available on the Internet at www.ita.doc.gov/td/industry/otea/usfth/aggregate/HL00T19.html.

20. Ibid.

21. Food and Agricultural Policy Research Institute, Iowa State University, *FAPRI 2002 World Agricultural Outlook,* Staff Report 1-02, Jan. 2002, 243.

22. Joan Murphy, "Food Safety Import Bill Introduced by Dingell, Waxman," *World Food Chemical News,* Mar. 3, 1998, at 16.

23. General Accounting Office, Testimony Before the Subcommittee on Oversight of Government Management, Restructuring and the District of Columbia, Committee on Governmental Affairs, U.S. Senate, "Food Safety and Security: Fundamental Changes Needed to Ensure Safe Food," GAO-02-47T, Oct. 10, 2001, at 7.

24. Food Safety and Inspection Service, USDA, Annual Report to Committee on Agriculture of the U.S. House of Representatives and to the Committee on Agriculture, Nutrition, and Forestry of the U.S. Senate, Nov. 1999, at 38. The USDA FSIS regulates the safety of all meat from cattle, sheep, swine, goats and horses as well as poultry, Foreign Agriculture Service, USDA, "Food and Agricultural Import Regulations and Standards Reports," last updated Feb. 1999, available online at www.fas.usda.gov/itp/ofsts/us.html.

25. Food Safety and Inspection Service, USDA, Meat and Poultry Port-of-Entry Reinspection System, Jun. 8, 2001, at 515–516.

26. "FDA Halts Mexican Cantaloupe Imports," Associated Press, Oct. 28, 2002.

27. Food Safety Inspection Service, U.S. Department of Agriculture, press release, "New York Firm Recalls Imported Cured Ham for Possible *Listeria* Contamination," Jun. 21, 2002.

28. Greg Winter, "Contaminated Food Makes Millions Ill Despite Advances," *New York Times,* Mar. 18, 2001.

29. U.S. Food and Drug Administration, Center for Food Safety and Applied Nutrition, *Pesticide Program: Residue Monitoring 1995,* Apr. 2002.

30. U.S. General Accounting Office has repeatedly warned the U.S. Congress and American public that the state of the U.S. food safety standards and enforcement remains woefully inadequate. See U.S. General Accounting Office, "Food Safety: Federal Efforts to Ensure the Safety of Imported Foods Are Inconsistent and Unreliable," May 1998.

31. See Robert Naiman and Neil Watkins, "A Survey of the Impacts of Structural Adjustment in Africa: Growth, Social Spending, and Debt Relief," Preamble Center, Apr. 1999.

32. Organization for Economic Cooperation and Development (OECD), Examen de las Politicas Agricolas de Mexico, 1997.

33. Steve Suppan, Institute for Agriculture and Trade Policy, speech before the conference "Legal Platform for Consumer Concerns and International Trade in Food and Agriculture," Jul. 2002.

34. FAO/WHO, "FAO/WHO Global Forum of Food Safety Regulators," Marrakech, Morroco, Jan. 28–30, 2002, "Country Report Proposed by Indonesia," Agenda Item 4.2 a), GF/CRD Indonesia-2.

35. Dev Raj, "Adulterated Mustard Oil Kills," *IPS Inter-Press,* September 6, 1998. (Tests indicated that the mustard oil had been contaminated with argemone oil, outomotu oil, and polybromides.)

36. FAO/WHO, "FAO/WHO Global Forum of Food Safety Regulators," "Country Paper Proposed by Zimbabwe," Agenda Item 4.2 b), GF/CRD Zimbabwe-1.

37. Ibid.

38. Deepak Gupta, Ministry of Health and Family Welfare, Government of India, FAO/WHO Global Forum of Food Safety Regulators, "Capacity Building and Technical Assistance—New Approaches and Building Alliances," Marrakech, Morocco, Jan. 28–30, 2002, Agenda 4.3 b), GF 01/02.

39. WTO SPS Agreement Art. 9 (1).

40. Bruce Silverglade, Director of Legal Affairs, Center for Science in the Public Interest, "The WTO Agreement on Sanitary and Phytosanitary Measures: Weakening Food Safety Regulations to Facilitate Trade," *Food and Drug Law Journal,* Vol. 55, No. 4, 2000, at 517.

41. Steve Suppan, Ph.D., Director of Research, Institute for Agriculture and Trade Policy, and Rod Leonard, Executive Director, Community Food Institute, "Comments Submitted to the Independent Evaluation of the Codex Alimentarius and Other FAO-WHO Work on Food Standards," May 17, 2002, at 5.

42. WTO and World Bank press release, "World Bank Grant Kicks off Bank-WTO Assistance on Standards," Sept. 23, 2002.

43. Bruce Silverglade, "The WTO Agreement on Sanitary and Phytosanitary Measures: Weakening Food Safety Regulations to Facilitate Trade," *Food and Drug Law Journal,* Vol. 55, Nov. 4, 2000, at 517.

44. Agreement on the Application of Sanitary and Phytosanitary Measures, Annex A, para. 1. WHO and WTO, "WTO Agreements and Public Health: A Joint Study by the WHO and the WTO Secretariat," WHO ISBN 92 4 156214, at 63.

45. Ibid., at Preamble, Para. 6: "[T]o further the use of harmonized SPS measures"; see also Article 3 on harmonization of domestic standards.

46. Ibid. at Article 5.

47. Ibid. at Article 5.6.

48. Ibid. at Article 3.

49. Ibid. at Art. 2, para. 1.

50. Ibid. at Art. 2, para. 2.

51. Ibid. at Art. 3, para. 3.

52. Ibid. at Footnote 2.

53. Ibid. at Annex A, para. 5.

54. The agreement also refers to this as "acceptable level of risk." Yet, the word "acceptable" is unnecessary, except to subject a member's level of risk to a WTO challenge if it provides more consumer protection than the relevant international standard.

55. Ibid. at Art. 5, para. 4.

56. Ibid. at Art. 5, para. 6.

57. The Transatlantic Consumer Dialogue is made up of the largest consumer organizations in the U.S. and Europe. It was formed in 1998 to give consensus recommendations on

trade and consumer-related matters to the U.S. and European governments. Transatlantic Consumer Dialogue, *Principles of Harmonization,* at 3, available at www.tacd.org.

58. "The Uruguay Round Agreements Act," P.L. 103-465; Dec. 8, 1994, 108 Stat. 481.

59. 60 Fed. Reg. 38667, Jul. 28, 1995.

60. Ibid.

61. Allison Sherry and David Migoya, "Meat Recall Information Kept Hidden," *Denver Post,* Aug. 4, 2002.

62. WHO, "Emerging Foodborne Diseases," Factsheet No. 124, Jan 2002.

63. Allison Sherry, "USDA Inspectors Slow to Reveal Suspicions about Possibly Contaminated Beef," *Denver Post,* Jul. 7, 2002.

64. USDA, Food Safety and Inspection Service, "Colorado Firm Recalls Beef Trim and Ground Beef Products for Possible E. Coli 0157:H7," Recall Release FSIS-RC-055-2002, Jul. 19, 2002.

65. Federal Meat Inspection Act of 1906 Enacted Jun. 30, 1906, as chapter 3913, 34 Stat. 674, and substantially amended by the Wholesome Meat Act 1967 (P.L. 90-201).

66. Poultry Products Inspection Act, 21 U.S.C. 451.

67. The Wholesome Meat Act of 1967, as described in "The Origins and History of the FSIS Program," 60 Fed. Reg. 6775, Feb. 3, 1995.

68. 59 Fed. Reg. 35639 (Jul. 13, 1994) and 60 Fed. Reg. 6775 (Feb. 3, 1995.)

69. General Accounting Office, "Meat and Poultry: Better USDA Oversight and Enforcement of Safety Rules Needed to Reduce Risk of Foodborne Illness," GAO-02-902, Aug. 2002, at 1.

70. General Accounting Office, "Food Safety: Weaknesses in Meat and Poultry Inspection Pilot Should be Addressed Before Implementation," Dec. 2001, at 1.

71. Public Citizen's Critical Mass Energy and Environment Project and Government Accountability Project, *Jungle 2000: Is America's Meat Fit to Eat?,* Sep. 2000.

72. Public Citizen's Critical Mass Energy and Environment Project and Government Accountability Project, *Hamburger Hell: The Flip Side of the USDA's Salmonella Testing Program,* May 2002, at i.

73. Ibid.

74. Marian Burrows, "Federal Audit Departments Meat and Poultry Inspection System," *New York Times,* Jul. 10, 2002.

75. Government Accounting Office, Draft Report on HACCP, on file with Public Citizen, July 2002.

76. American Federation of Government Employees, *Community Nutrition Institute v. Glickman,* 215 Fed. 3rd. 7, D.C. Circuit Court, Jun. 30, 2000; Government Accounting Office, "Weaknesses in Meat and Poultry Inspection Pilot Should be Addressed Before Implementation," GAO-02-59, Dec. 2001, at 4, 26.

77. USDA, Food Safety and Inspection Service, food recall releases and databases from 1994 and 2001, available online at www.fsis.usda.gov/recalls/.

78. See Samuel S. Epstein and Wenonah Hauter, "Preventing Pathogenic Food Poisoning: Sanitation Not Irradiation," *International Journal of Health Services,* Vol. 31, No. 1, 2001, at 187–192.

79. M.H. Stevenson, "Identification of Irradiated Foods", *Food Technology,* 48: 141–144, 1994.

80. 64 Fed. Reg. 72149, Dec. 23, 1999.

81. Randi Fabi, "USDA Announces Irradiation for School Lunch Program," Reuters, Oct. 25, 2002.

82. 9 CFR 327.2 requires countries that export to the U.S. to have HACCP programs.

83. Food Safety and Inspection Service, FSIS Process for Evaluating the Equivalence of Foreign Meat and Poultry Food Regulatory Systems, March 1999, 64 Fed. Reg. 70690, Dec. 17, 1999.

84. USDA, OIG, *Food Safety and Inspection Service, Imported Meat and Poultry Inspection Process, Phase I,* Report No. 24099-3-Hy, Jun. 2000, Section III, available at http://www.usda.gov/oig/webdocs/imported.pdf and on file with Public Citizen.

85. Ibid. at Sec. III, pp. ii–iv.

86. USDA, FSIS, Office of Policy, Program Development and Evaluation, *Import Inspection Manual,* Aug. 1, 2002, at Part 4, Section 1, Subsection 4.3.1, www.fsis.usda.gov/OPPDE/op/IIM/P4S1.htm.

87. USDA, FSIS, Technical Service Center, "Audit Report for Canada, April 4 through April 20, 2000," at 10.

88. USDA, FSIS, Technical Service Center, "Review Report for Argentina, June 17 through July 21, 1997."

89. USDA, FSIS, Technical Service Center, "Audit Report for Brazil, February 24 through April 4, 1998."

90. For instance the U.S.-based National Association of Manufacturers 2002 Trade Agenda includes "regulatory harmonization efforts, including the acceptance of functional equivalence standards, mutual recognition of conformity assessment tests and greater efforts to develop international regulatory standards" in its goal to "Reduce the Trade Distorting Effect of Regulatory and Standards Process." See National Association of Manufacturers, "The NAM 2002 Trade Agenda," Mar. 2002. The WTO Harmonization requirements include Agreement on the Application of Sanitary and Phytosanitary Measures at Article 3, and WTO, Agreement on Technical Barriers to Trade at Article 2.4.

91. SPS Agreement at Annex A, para. 3.

92. Patti Goldman and Richard Wiles, Trading Away U.S. Food Safety, Public Citizen and the Environmental Working Group, Apr. 1994, at Ch. 6 detailing Codex standard-setting procedures.

93. FAO/WHO Food Standards Programme, Introducing Codex Alimentarius (1987).

94. SPS Agreement at Annex A, para. 3.

95. David Kay, *The International Regulation of Pesticide Residues in Food* (Washington, D.C.: American Society of International Law, 1976) at n. 18, and 33 and 46.

96. FAO/WHO, This is Codex Almentarius (1993) at 2.

97. Kay, *The International Regulation of Pesticide Residues in Food,* at 44.

98. 21 U.S.C. Sec. 301, et seq.

99. Steve Suppan, Ph.D., Director of Research, Institute for Agriculture and Trade Policy, and Rod Leonard, Executive Director, Community Food Institute, "Comments Submitted

to the Independent Evaluation of the Codex Alimentarius and Other FAO-WHO Work on Food Standards," May 17, 2002.

100. FAO/WHO, "Procedures for the Elaboration of Codex Standards and Related Texts," Procedural Manual of the CAC, 9th Ed. (1995).

101. 5 U.S.C. Sec. 551, et seq.

102. Ibid. Sec. 557.

103. 5 U.S.C. Sec. 552.

104. 5 U.S.C. Sec. 552b, Pub. L. 94-409, Sept. 13, 1976, 90 Stat. 1241.

105. 5 U.S.C. Sec. 562, et seq.

106. Public Citizen, *Harmonization Handbook*, 2002.

107. Codex Alimentarius, "NGO Participation: Principles Concerning the Participation of International Non-Governmental Organizations in the Work of the Codex Alimentarius Commission," on file with Public Citizen and available on the Codex website, www.codex-alimentarius.net/ngo_participation.htm.

108. Public Citizen analysis of the Codex Alimentarius accredited NGOs or NGOs with observer status as of October 2002. Codex list is on file with Public Citizen and available online at www.codexalimentarius.net/organizations_ngo.stm. Trade associations were determined by their own self-identification on their websites. In 2002, nearly a third of the U.S. delegation to the Codex Committee on Food Labeling in Halifax, Canada, were from the food industry or trade associations, including Nestle; the National Food Processors Association; the Corn, Soy, Cotton Coalition; and the National Association for the Specialty Food Trade. See Joint FAO/WHO Food Standards Programme, Codex Alimentarius Commission, 25th Session, Halifax, Canada, Jun. 30–Jul. 5, 2002, Appendix I, at 31–32.

109. See General Accounting Office, International Food Safety: Comparison of U.S. Codex Pesticide Standards (Aug. 1991).

110. Mark Ritchie, "GATT, Agriculture and the Environment: The Double Zero Plan," 20 *The Ecologist* 214, at 216–17 (Nov./Dec. 1990).

111. Ibid.; see also General Accounting Office, International Food Safety: Comparison of U.S. & Codex Pesticide Standards (Aug. 1991) at 4.

112. See Codex Alimentarius: Pesiticide Residues in Food, Maximum Residue Limits. Extraneous Maximum Residue Limits, Sept. 2, 1999. (MRLs last updated by Codex in 1999.)

113. Report of the Twenty-Fourth Session of the Codex Alimentarius Commission, Geneva, 2–7 July 2001. ALINORM 01/41, para. 144.

114. See Center for Science in the Public Interest press release, "Representatives Tell White House 'Modify Trade Agreement to Improve Food Safety,' " Jul. 26, 1999, on file with Public Citizen; see also U.S. law at Section 405 of the Food Quality Protection Act of 1996, amending section 408(b) of the Federal Food Drug and Cosmetic Act, 21 U.S.C. Sec. 346a(b).

115. Bruce Silverglade, Director of Legal Affairs, Center for Science in the Public Interest, "The WTO Agreement on Sanitary and Phytosanitary Measures: Weakening Food Safety Regulations to Facilitate Trade," *Food and Drug Law Journal*, Vol. 55, No. 4, 2000, at 517.

116. Codex Alimentarius Commission, General Standard for Food Additives at 58 (1998) ALINORM 99/12.

117. Bruce Silverglade, Director of Legal Affairs, Center for Science in the Public Interest, letter to Cathlene Woteki, Undersecretary for Food Safety, USDA, Jan. 22, 1999.

118. Bruce Silverglade, Director of Legal Affairs, Center for Science in the Public Interest, letter to USTR Zoellick, Aug. 23, 2001.

119. Report of the Twenty-Fourth Session of the Codex Alimentarius Commission, Geneva, 2–7 July 2001. ALINORM 01/41, para. 121.

120. "Aflatoxin M1 Standard Approved by Codex," *Food Chemical News,* Jul. 16, 2001.

121. Report of the Twenty-Fourth Session of the Codex Alimentarius Commission, Geneva, 2–7 July 2001. ALINORM 01/41, para. 127.

122. Steve Suppan, Ph.D., Director of Research, Institute for Agriculture and Trade Policy, and Rod Leonard, Executive Director, Community Food Institute, "Comments Submitted to the Independent Evaluation of the Codex Alimentarius and Other FAO-WHO Work on Food Standards," May 17, 2002.

123. Codex Alimentarius, "Proposed Draft Revised General Standard for Irradiated Foods," ALINORM 01/12A, Appendix VII. Thirty-third Codex Committee on Food Additives and Contaminants, The Hague, March 12–16, 2001.

124. Report of the Forty-Ninth (Extraordinary) Session of the Executive Committee of the Codex Alimentarius Commission. ALINORM 03/3. WHO Headquarters, Geneva, 26-27-2001.

125. "Proposed Draft Revised General Standard for Irradiated Foods," ALINORM 01/12A, Appendix VII. Thirty-Third Codex Committee on Food Additives and Contaminants, The Hague, March 2001.

126. See 29 CFR 179.26.

127. Public Citizen's Critical Mass Energy and Environment Program, Analysis of Proposed Draft Revised Codex Food Irradiation Standard, April 2001.

128. *Bad Taste: The Disturbing Truth About the World Health Organization's Endorsement of Food Irradiation* (Washington, D.C.: Public Citizen, 2001).

129. *Hidden Harm: How the FDA Is Ignoring the Potential Dangers of Unique Chemicals in Irradiated Food* (Washington, D.C.: Public Citizen and The Center for Food Safety, 2001).

130. M. H. Stevenson, "Identification of Irradiated Foods," *Food Technology* 48: 141–144, 1994.

131. Interview with Patricia Lovera, Public Citizen's Critical Mass Energy and Environment Program, March 2003.

132. 21 USC 355d.

133. Morton Mintz, "'Heroine' of FDA Keeps Bad Drug Off Market," *Washington Post,* Jul. 15, 1962.

134. Letter from U.S. Trade Representative Michael Kantor to Bob Drake, president of the National Cattlemen's Association, Feb. 8, 1996, on file at Public Citizen.

135. A. L. Fisher et al., "Estrogenic Action of Some DDT Analogues," 81 Proc. Soc.

Expt0'l Med. at 449–441; W. H. Bulger and D. Kupfer, "Estrogenic Activity of Pesticides and Other Xenobiotics on the Uterus and Male Reproductive Tract," in J. A. Thomas et al., eds., Endocrine Technology (1985), at 1–33; "Brie and Hormones," *The Economist,* Jan. 7, 1989, at 22; and Samuel S. Epstein, "The Chemical Jungle," *International Journal Health Services* (1990), at 278.

136. European Commission, Opinion of the Scientific Committee on Veterinary Measures Relating to Public Health, Assessment of Potential Risks to Human Health From Hormone Residues in Bovine Meat and Meat Products, April 30, 1999, at 24.

137. European Economic Council Directive Prohibiting the Use in Livestock Farming of Certain Substances Having a Hormonal Action, 88/146/EEC of Mar. 7, 1988, Official Journal L070, Mar. 16, 1988, at 16–18. 88/146/EEC, cited in European Community measures affecting meat and meat products (WT/D526/ABR), Report to the Appellate Body, Apr. 16, 1998, at 2.

138. Ibid.

139. Among the most vocal critics of the EU ban has been the National Cattlemen's Beef Association (NCBA). After the ban, NCBA President George Swan said, "Ten years of false accusations. Ten years of lost markets for U.S. cattlemen and lost opportunities for European consumers." (National Cattlemen's Beef Association press release, "Government Must Retaliate if EU Continues to Ban American Beef," May 10, 1999.)

140. WTO, European Communities—Measures Affecting Meat and Meat Products (Hormones) (WT/DS26), complaint by the United States, Apr. 25, 1996.

141. This Codex standard was issued only after a high-pressure, four-year campaign by the U.S. with the U.S. forcing two votes on the issue, even though second votes are almost unheard of at Codex (usually, the body sets standards by consensus). The U.S. lost the first vote, then forced a second vote and won by a slim majority.

142. WTO, European Communities—Measures Affecting Meat and Meat Products (Hormones) (WT/DS26R), Report of the Panel, Aug. 8, 1997, at para. 8.159. SPS Agreement Annex A para. 4 defines a Risk Assessment as, "The evaluation of the likelihood of entry, establishment or spread of a pest or disease within the territory of an importing Member according to the sanitary or phytosanitary measures which might be applied, and of the associated potential biological and economic consequences; or the evaluation of the potential for adverse effects on human or animal health arising from the presence of additives, contaminants, toxins or disease-causing organisms in food, beverages or feedstuffs."

143. WTO, European Communities—Measures Affecting Meat and Meat Products (Hormones) (WT/DS26/AB), Report of the Appellate Body, Apr. 16, 1998, at paragraph 254(1).

144. WTO, European Communities—Measures Affecting Meat and Meat Products. tWT/DS26R).

145. Ibid.

146. Ibid. at para. 176.

147. Ibid., at 12.

148. Elizabeth Olson, "253 Million Sanctions Sought in Beef Fight with Europe," *New York Times,* Jun. 4, 1999. The U.S. argues that the risk assessment merely recycles the same data rejected by the WTO panel as inconclusive.

149. USTR press release, "USTR Announces Final Product List in Beef Hormones Dispute," Jul. 19, 1999.

150. Elizabeth Olson, "$253 Million Sanctions Sought in Beef Fight with Europe," and "In Brief: EU Seeks End to Beef Row," *The Guardian,* May 12, 1999.

151. The WTO's Dispute Settlement Understanding, Article 22-2, allows a losing country to request negotiations with the victorious nation to agree upon compensation. Compensation means a mutually agreed arrangement through which the damages caused by the losing nation's WTO violation is "paid" in cash or by designated special trade concessions. However, if the winning nation refuses compensation, the winning nation can impose trade sanctions against the loser's trade.

152. USTR press release, "USTR Announces Final Product List in Beef Hormones Dispute," Jul. 19, 1999.

153. Ibid.

154. "José Bové, A Farmer's International?," *New Left Review* 12, Nov.–Dec. 2001, at 91.

155. Robert L. Jamieson, Jr., "French Farmer Bové Takes His Beef to McDonald's," *Seattle Post-Intelligencer,* Nov. 30, 1999.

156. Mark MacKinnon, "Canada Bars Famous Farm Activist," *Globe and Mail,* Mar. 31, 2001.

157. Richard Kuper, "D-day Near in French McJustice Campaign," *RedPepper,* Sep. 2000.

158. "Radical French Farmer Found Guilty," Associated Press, Sep. 13, 2000.

159. Ibid.

160. Robert L. Jamieson, Jr., "French Farmer Bové Takes His Beef to McDonald's."

161. Richard Kuper, "D-day Near in French McJustice Campaign."

162. EU, Opinion of the Scientific Committee on Veterinary Measures Relating to Public Health: Assesment of potential risks to human health from hormone residues in bovine meat and meat products, Apr. 30, 1999, at 42–43.

163. Ibid., at 48, 53, 54,71,72–73.

164. Official Journal of the European Communities, "Substances having a hormonal or thyrostatic action and beta-agonists," February 1, 2001, at C267/53–C267/56.

165. USTR, 2002 National Trade Estimates Report on Foreign Trade Barriers, at 113.

166. James O. Jackson, Nina Plank and Rhea Schoenthal, "Another Beef Over Beef," *Time International,* Apr. 15, 1996.

167. See Douglas Jake Caldwell, "Environmental Labeling in the Trade and Environment Context," Community Nutrition Institute, Oct. 1996.

168. The initial panel report in this case issued new WTO jurisprudence on issues that neither the U.S. nor EU had raised, including several extremely anti-health interpretations of WTO provisions which were fiercely attacked by consumer groups, but also by pro-WTO trade experts who criticized the panel for effectively writing new WTO rules to which signatory nations had not agreed.

169. WTO, European Communities—Measures Affecting Meat and Meat Products (Hormones) (WT/DS26/AB), Report of the Appellate Body, Apr. 16, 1998, at para. 253.

170. WTO, International Trade of Chile in Poultry Products, G/SPS/GN/3, at 1.

171. USTR, 2002 National Trade Estimates Report on Foreign Trade Barriers, at 38.

172. WTO, Committee on Sanitary and Phytosanitary Measures—Specific Trade Concerns—Submission by the United States Regarding G/SPS/GEN/204/Rev.1, G/SPS/GEN/265, Oct. 7, 2001, at 2.

173. WTO, Australia—Measures Affecting Importation of Salmon (WT/DS18/R), Report of the Panel, Jun. 12, 1998 at paras. 8.10–8.19.

174. WTO, Australia—Measures Affecting Importation of Salmon (WT/DS18/AB/R), Report of the Appellate Body, Oct. 20, 1998.

175. Ibid.

176. Ibid., at para. 4.52.

177. The Australian Final Report had concluded that there were extensive gaps in data relating to disease spread in fish. The Final Report therefore extrapolated data from studies demonstrating that other products for human consumption, such as meat and poultry, have been known to have spread diseases to live animals. Australia thus concluded that given both the difficulty of proving the spread of aquatic animal diseases through salmon meat and the very short history of aquatic animal medicine, it would be prudent to presume that it was only a matter of time and attention until there was definitive proof of the spread of aquatic animal disease via product for human consumption, rather than assume it was unlikely. WTO, Australia—Measures Affecting Importation of Salmon (WT/DS18/R), Report of the Panel, Jun. 12, 1998, at paras. 2.27–2.30.

178. Ibid., at para. 4.42–4.43.

179. Ibid., at para 9.1.

180. WTO, Australia—Measures Affecting Importation of Salmon (WT/DS18/AB/R), Report of the Appellate Body, Jun. 12, 1998, at para. 13.

181. Ibid., at para. 137.

182. Ibid., at para. 129.

183. Ibid., at para. 127. "WTO Salmon Ruling Clarifies Conditions for Banning Food Imports, Experts Say," BNA Daily Report for Executives, Oct. 28, 1998.

184. Ibid.

185. Australian Department of Agriculture, Fisheries and Forestry, "Revised Fish Import Policies Announced," Jul. 19, 1999.

186. WTO, Australia—Measures Affecting Importation of Salmon—Recourse to Article 21.5 by Canada (WT/DS18/RW), Report of the Panel, Feb. 18, 2000.

187. Ibid.

188. WTO Dispute Settlement Agreement at Article 21, Section 5.

189. WTO, Australia—Measures Affecting Importation of Salmon—Recourse to Article 21.5 by Canada (WT/DS18/RW), Report of the Panel, Feb. 18, 2000.

190. Ibid., at para. 7.42, 7.58, 7.71, 7.145. The panel established a three-pronged test for a risk assessment and found that Australia's 1999 risk assessment met each part.

191. Australian Department of Agriculture, Fisheries and Forestry, "Revised Fish Import Policies Announced."

192. Australia Department of Foreign Affairs and Trade, Text of Bilateral Settlement Between Australia and Canada, on file with Public Citizen.

193. Faith Thompson Campbell, "The Science of Risk Assessment for Phytosanitary Regulation and the Impact of Changing Trade Regulations," *BioScience,* Vol. 51, Issue 2, Feb. 1, 2001.

194. USDA Foreign Agriculture Service, U.S. Census Bureau, Foreign Trade Statistics.

195. Campbell, "The Science of Risk Assessment for Phytosanitary Regulation and the Impact of Changing Trade Regulations."

196. Japan's Ministry of Agriculture, Forestry and Fisheries, "Report on Agricultural, Forestry and Fisheries Trades in 2002," March 2002, at 20.

197. World Trade Organization, Request for the Establishment of a Panel by the United States, May 8, 2002, WT/DS245/2.

198. World Trade Organization, Request for Consultations by the United States, Mar. 6, 2002, WT/DS245/1.

199. USDA, "World Trade Situation and Policy Updates," *World Horticultural Trade and U.S. Export Opportunities,* Jun. 2002, at 19.

200. U.S. Department of Agriculture, "Fire Blight Control, Nature's Way," *Agricultural Research,* Jan. 1998, at 14.

201. Michael Ellis, Ohio State University Extension, "Fire Blight of Apples, Crabapples and Pears," *Extension Factsheet,* HYG-3002-94, 1994.

202. G. H. Lacy, "Control of Phytopathogenic Prokaryotes by Cultural Management and Chemicals," white paper, University of Vermont, Apr. 2000, at 1. According to the U.S. Department of Agriculture, the favored antibiotic treatment streptomycin to fight flaring fire blight introduced in the 1950s became significantly less reliable by the 1990s. (Fire blight, one of the class of diseases caused by bacteria called prokaryotes, which have rapidly reproducing outbreaks, is more likely to occur during wet weather when orchards are less likely or able to be tended, and strikes too far below the bark to be easily treated chemically.)

203. Daniel Pruzin, "U.S. Initiates WTO Case Against Japan Over Fire Blight Import Curbs on Apples," *BNA International Trade Reporter,* Vol. 19, No. 10, Mar. 7, 2002. There is some evidence that Japan may have had outbreaks of fire blight in the past, but no definitive evidence that there is a sustained fire blight presence in Japan.

204. Campbell, "The Science of Risk Assessment for Phytosanitary Regulation and the Impact of Changing Trade Regulations."

205. USTR, 2001 National Trade Estimate Report on Foreign Trade Barriers, at 253; 2002 National Trade Estimate Report on Foreign Trade Barriers, at 235.

206. USTR, "WTO Consultations Regarding Japanese Measures Affecting the Importation of Apples," Fed. Reg. vol. 67, no. 62, Apr. 1, 2002.

207. Japan Fair Trade Center, U.S. law firm of Willkie Farr and Gallagher, "Japan Blocks U.S. Request for WTO Panel Regarding Japan's Importation of Apples," *Washington Monitor: A Weekly Review of U.S. Trade Policy Developments Affecting Japan,* vol. 6, issue 21, May 24, 2002 at 6.

208. U.S. Department of Agriculture, "Fire Blight Control, Nature's Way," *Agricultural Research,* Jan. 1998, at 14. Australia has established a conservative Appropriate Level of Protection designed to keep the risk of dangerous invasive-species entry and establishment very low, contending that the only way to ensure that the risk of infestation from fire blight was "very low" instead of "low" was to set more reliable 500-meter buffers (like Japan's) around registered export block orchards.

209. World Trade Organization, Constitution of the Panel Established at the Request of the United States, Japan—Measures Affecting the Importation of Apples, Jul. 17, 2002, WT/DS245/3.

210. WTO, Japan—Measures Affecting the Importation of Apples (WT/DS245), Executive Summary of the First Written Submission of the United States of America, Sep. 11, 2002, at paras. 3, 12, 14, 16–28.

211. WTO, Japan—Measures Affecting the Importation of Apples (WT/DS245), Oral Statement of the United States at the First Panel Meeting, Oct. 21, 2002, at paras. 31–32.

212. Dr. C. N. Hale, "HortFact: Why Fireblight Shouldn't be a Market Access Problem," Horticulture and Food Research and Institute of New Zealand, 1996.

213. WTO, Japan—Measures Affecting the Importation of Apples (WT/DS245), Oral Statement of the United States at the First Panel Meeting, at para. 24.

214. Jose L. Doming, "Health Risks of GM Foods: Many Questions But Few Data," *Science,* Vol. 288, Jun. 9, 2000.

215. Scott Kilman, "ProdiGene-Modified Corn Plant Nearly Gets Into U.S. Food Supply," *Wall Street Journal,* Nov. 13, 2002.

216. Neil Franz, "Taco Recall Prompts Aventis to Halt Sales of Starlink Corn," *Chemical Week,* Oct. 4, 2000.

217. "Byrne Says U.S. Demands on Biotech Rules Could Be Accommodated," *Inside U.S. Trade,* Mar. 30, 2001.

218. "U.S. in Active Mode on WTO Case on EU GMO Moratorium, Decision Looms," *Inside U.S. Trade,* Nov. 8, 2002.

219. Bruce Silverglade, Director of Legal Affairs, Center for Science in the Public Interest, "The WTO Agreement on Sanitary and Phytosanitary Measures: Weakening Food Safety Regulations to Facilitate Trade," *Food and Drug Law Journal,* Vol. 55, No. 4, 2000, at 517.

220. "U.S. in Active Mode on WTO Case on EU GMO Moratorium, Decision Looms," *Inside U.S. Trade.*

221. USTR, National Trade Estimate Report on Foreign Trade Barriers, 2002, at 111–12.

222. "U.S. in Active Mode on WTO Case on EU GMO Moratorium, Decision Looms," *Inside U.S. Trade.*

223. Ibid.

224. Transcript of Press Conference with Agriculture Secretary Venneman and USTR Zoellick Regarding the EU Moratorium on Biotech Crops and Food, May 13, 2003.

225. "U.S. Conflict with China Over GMOs," Reuters, Feb. 6, 2002.

226. "U.S. in Active Mode on WTO Case on EU GMO Moratorium, Decision Looms," *Inside U.S. Trade.*

227. Proposed Draft Recommendations for the Labeling of Foods Obtained Through Biotechnology (Alinorm 99/22, Appendix VIII), CX/FL 99/6, Government Comments at Step 3 from the U.S., Codex Alimentarius Commission, Jun. 1999, on file with Public Citizen.

228. The requirement for originality as a basis for obtaining a patent is found at 35 U.S.C. Secs. 101–103.

229. Proposed Draft Recommendations for the Labeling of Foods Obtained Through Biotechnology (Alinorm 99/22, Appendix VIII), CX/FL 99/6, Government Comments at Step 3 from the U.S., Codex Alimentarius Commission, Jun. 1999.

230. Michael Wehr, Office of Constituent Operations, Center for Food Safety and Applied Nutrition, Personal Communication with Marianne Mollmann, Public Citizen, Aug. 10, 1999. Of course, the two methods are entirely different and result in different products. Genetic engineering allows the transfer of genes between totally unrelated organisms, even across natural species barriers, resulting in gene combinations that never would occur naturally. For example, soil bacterium genes have been introduced into soya plants to make them herbicide-resistant, and "anti-freezing" genes from arctic sea flounder have been transplanted into tomatoes, strawberries and potatoes to make them frost-resistant. Cross-breeding, by contrast, is the hybridization of two varieties or breeds within the same species. See Dr. Michael Antoniou, "Genetic Engineering and Traditional Breeding Methods: A Technical Perspective," *Living Earth,* Issue 197, Jan.–Mar. 1998, on file with Public Citizen.

231. Directive 90/220/EEC of 23 April 1990 on the Deliberate Release into the Environment of Genetically Modified Organisms, 1990 O. J. L 117 (May 8, 1990), at 15; "Revised GMO Directive Gets EU Parliament Nod," *Bridges Weekly Trade News Digest,* Feb. 20, 2001.

232. Directive 90/219/EEC of 23 April 1990 on the Contained Use of Genetically Modified Micro-organisms, 1990 O. J. L 117 (May 8, 1990), at 1.

233. Directive 2001/18/EC of the European Parliament and of the Council on the Deliberate Release into the Environment of Genetically Modified Organisms and Repealing Council Directive 90/220/EC, on file with Public Citizen. See also, "EU Assembly Approves Tough New GM Rules," Reuters, Feb. 15, 2001. One day later, on February 16, 2001, the EU Council of Ministers, which represents the governments of the member states of the EU, ratified the new directive. "EU Awaits Sign from United States on Trade Complaint over GMO Moratorium," *International Environmental Reporter,* Feb. 28, 2001, at 158. Legislative proposals generally come from the European Commission, which is the EU's executive and administrative body. They are then voted upon by the European Council after it receives a nonbinding consultative opinion from the European Parliament. In some policy areas, such as public health and the environment, the Parliament can also send legislative proposals to the Council. After going through legal review within the commission, the new directive will take effect as an EU-wide policy that must be enacted by the member states into their law. Ralph Folsom, *European Union Law in a Nutshell,* 2d ed., 1995, 34–48.

234. Michael Mann, "Six EU States Refuse to Back Modified Crops," *Financial Times,* Feb. 16, 2001.

235. TACD, Consumer Concerns About Biotechnology and Genetically Modified Organisms (GMOs), Feb. 2000, on file with Public Citizen.

236. Directive 2001/18/EC, Arts. 6, 13.

237. Ibid., Arts. 9, 24 and 25.

238. Caroline E. Mayer, "U.S. Blocks Imports of Clementine Oranges," *Washington Post,* Dec. 7, 2001.

239. U.S. Department of Agriculture press release, "USDA Suspends Spanish Clementine Imports," Dec. 5, 2001, Release No. 0251.01.

240. Florida Department of Agriculture and Consumer Services press release, "Medfly Eradicated from Central Florida," Apr. 17, 1998.

241. U.S. Department of Agriculture, "Medfly Cooperative Eradication Program, Southern Florida: Environmental Assessment," Apr. 1998, at 1.

242. Testimony of William J. Lyons, Jr., Secretary, California Department of Food and Agriculture before Public Hearing Regarding the Importation of Clementines from Spain, Aug. 20, 2002.

243. U.S. Department of Agriculture, Foreign Agriculture Service, "USDA/APHIS Bans Imports of Spanish Clementines," *World Horticultural Trade and U.S. Opportunities,* Jan. 2002, at 11.

244. Chris Gray, "A Bitter Turn for Clementines Holiday Tang," *Philadelphia Inquirer* Dec. 7, 2001.

245. Mayer, "U.S. Blocks Imports of Clementine Oranges."

246. Ibid.

247. Intercitrus, Ibertrade et al., V. USDA: No. 02-1061, U.S. District Court for the Eastern District of Pennsylvania, Aug. 13, 2002.

248. Pascal Lamy, "Steeling the EU/U.S. Relationship for the Challenges Ahead," Speech to European Magazine Luncheon, Washington, D.C., Jan. 25, 2002.

249. Testimony of Inder Gadh, Ph.D., USDA Animal and Plant Health Inspection Service before the USDA/APHIS Public Hearing on the Importation of Spanish Clementines, Aug. 20, 2002, at 9–10.

250. Ibid., at 15–19.

251. Testimony of Sheldon Jones, Director of the Arizona Department of Agriculture, before the USDA/APHIS Public Hearing on the Importation of Spanish Clementines, Aug. 20, 2002, at 35–36.

252. Caroline Mayer, "The Fruit Without the Flies; New USDA Rule Permits Spanish Citrus Shipping to Resume," *Washington Post,* Nov. 3, 2002.

253. Ibid.

254. U.S. Office of Management and Budget, Report to Congress on Costs and Benefits of Federal Regulations, 2000 Report, Jun. 2000, at 20, Table 1.

255. FDA, "BSE and Measures to Prevent its Introduction into the U.S.," Fact sheet, Feb. 2, 2001.

256. Ibid.

257. Ian Elliott, "BSE a Global Threat Says Scientists," *Feedstuffs,* Jun. 18. 2001.

258. European Commission, "Report on United States Barriers to Trade and Investment," Nov. 2002.

CHAPTER 3: WARNING: THE WTO CAN BE HAZARDOUS TO PUBLIC HEALTH

1. *Xinhua News Service* (China), Transcript of WTO DG Supachai Panitchpakdi, Bangkok Speech, Jul. 2, 2002.

2. See Neil Collins, Cynthia Callard, Michelle Swenarchuk, and Harley Stanton, "Briefing Paper Series: Trade and Investment," Canadian Centre for Policy Alternatives, Vol. 2, No. 7, Oct. 2001, at 4.

3. European Commission, "GATS 2000, Request from the EC and its Member States to the United States of America," MD 042/02, June 3, 2002, at 14.

4. See USTR, "2002 National Trade Estimate Report on Foreign Trade Barriers," at 115–16.

5. WTO, "India—Patent Protection for Pharmaceutical and Agricultural Chemical Products," WT/DS50, Complaint by the U.S.; "India's New Patent Law 'By Year-End,'" *Markletter* (London), Jul. 26, 1999.

6. Beth Burrows, "Conquest By Patents," *New Internationalist,* Sept. 1, 2002; Laudeline Auriol and Francois Pham, "What Pattern in Patents," *OECD Observer* 179, Dec. 1992/Jan. 1993, at 15.

7. Stephen W. Schondelmeyer, Economic Impact of GATT Patent Extension on Currently Marketed Drugs, PRIME Institute, College of Pharmacy, University of Minnesota, Mar. 1995, at Table I.

8. Ibid., at 6. The study also found that the TRIPs patent extension would have a negative effect on the U.S. health care cost-containment efforts with increased direct cost to federal and state government health programs such as Medicaid and Medicare totaling nearly $1.25 billion.

9. "New Chairman's Draft Moves Towards Developing Countries on TRIPs," *Inside U.S. Trade,* Nov. 15, 2002.

10. Statement of Jamie Love, Consumer Project on Technology, Dec. 20, 2002, on file with Public Citizen.

11. Professor John H. Bryant, "Globalization and Health—The Evolving Place of Equity in Developing Countries," The Seventh International Conference on the Impact of Globalization on Development and Health Care Services in Islamic Countries, Kuwait, Mar. 23–27, 2002.

12. Kelley Lee and Jeff Collin, "A Review of Existing Empirical Research on Globalization and Health," Draft Background Paper for Annual Meeting of WHO/HSD Scientific Resource Group on Globalization and Health, Mar. 2001, at 6–7.

13. Giovanni Andrea Cornia, "Globalization and Health: Results and Options," *Bulletin of the World Health Organization,* 2001, 79 (9), at 840.

14. "Globalization—How Health?," *Bulletin of the World Health Organization,* 2001, 79 (9), at 902.

15. Joshua Lederberg, Ph.D., Nobel Laureate and Sackler Foundation Scholar, the Rockefeller University, National Academy of Sciences, "Emerging Infectious Diseases from the Global to the Local Perspectives: Workshop Summary," 2001 at 1–2.

16. Ronald Labonte, Director, Saskatchewan Population Health and Evaluation Research Unit, Professor, Department of Community Health and Epidemiology, University of Saskatchewan, "Health, Globalization and Sustainable Development," Draft Discussion Paper Prepared for the World Health Organization Meeting, "Making Health Central to Sustainable Development," Oslo, Norway, Nov. 29–Dec. 1, 2001.

17. Natalie Angier, "Case Study: Globalization; Location: Everywhere," *New York Times Magazine,* May 6, 2001.

18. Labonte, "Health, Globalization and Sustainable Development."

19. Bryant, "Globalization and Health—The Evolving Place of Equity in Developing Countries."

20. Labonte, "Health, Globalization and Sustainable Development."

21. Mark Weisbrot, Dean Baker, Egor Kraev and Judy Chen, "The Scorecard on Globalization 1980–2000: Twenty Years of Diminished Progress," Center for Economic and Policy Research, July 11, 2001.

22. Prabhat Jha and Frank J. Chaloupka, "The Economics of Global Tobacco Control," *British Medical Journal*, BMJ 2000; 321 at 358.

23. See General Accounting Office, Testimony, Statement of Allan I. Mendelowitz, Director, Trade, Energy and Finance Issues, National Security and International Affairs Division before the Subcommittee on Health and the Environment, Committee on Energy and Congress, House of Representatives, *Dichotomy Between U.S. Tobacco Export Policy and Antismoking Initiatives*, GAO/NSIAD-90-42, May 17, 1990, at 2–4.

24. General Accounting Office, Report to Congressional Requestors, *Dichotomy Between U.S. Tobacco Export Policy and Antismoking Initiatives*, GAO/NSIAD-90-190, May, 1990 at 11.

25. Ibid.

26. Prabhat Jha, *Curbing the Epidemic: Governments and the Epidemic of Tobacco Control* (Washington, D.C.: World Bank, 1999).

27. Allyn Taylor, Frank J. Chaloupka, Emmanuel Guindon and Michaelyn Corbett, "The Impact of Trade Liberalization on Tobacco Consumption," in *Tobacco Control in Developing Countries*, at 346.

28. "Thailand—Restrictions on Importation of and Internal Taxes on Cigarettes," Geneva: General Agreement on Tariffs and Trade, 1990, para. 12–13, 62.

29. Ibid., paras. 52–54.

30. Ibid., para. 75.

31. Robert Weissman, "The Marlboro Man Rides to China," *Multinational Monitor*, May 2000, Vol. 21, No. 5.

32. President William J. Clinton, "Executive Order: Federal Leadership on Global Tobacco Control and Prevention," Jan. 18, 2001, at sec. 2.

33. Agreement on Market Access Between the People's Republic of China and the United States of America, People's Republic of China—Section 1-A Tariffs, Tariff item Number 24022000, Nov. 15, 1999, at 23.

34. WHO, Intergovernmental Negotiating Body on the WHO Framework Convention on Tobacco Control, Fifth Session, Provisional Agenda Item 3, Letter from Ambassador Luiz Felipe de Seixas Correa, Chair, Intergovernmental Negotiating Body, A/FCTC/IBN5/DIV/5, Jul. 16, 2002.

35. Statement of the Framework Convention Alliance, http://www.fctc.org/statement.shtml, on file with Public Citizen.

36. See Statement of Judith P. Wilkenfeld, Director, International Program, Campaign for Tobacco Free Kids Steering Committee, Framework Convention Alliance, Before the U.S. Department of Health and Human Services Public Hearing on the Framework Convention on Tobacco Control, Sep. 2002, on file with Public Citizen.

37. The Centers for Disease Control states, "The U.S. government currently is studying

the diverse and interrelated issues that may form the final FCTC." "Framework Convention on Tobacco Control," CDC's website Jan.13, 2002 at www.cdc.gov/tobacco/global/framework.htm, on file with Public Citizen.

38. Jessica Reaves, "U.S. Veto Can't Snuff Out UN Anti-Tobacco Campaign," *Time,* Nov. 29, 2001.

39. Ibid.

40. WHO Framework Convention on Tobacco Control, May 2003, Article 13.

41. Carla Hills, "Legal Opinion With Regard to Plain Packaging of Tobacco Products Requirement Under International Agreements," May 3, 1994. Hills, the former U.S. Trade Representative, wrote the memo for R.J. Reynolds and Philip Morris, as counsel at the law firm Mudge Rose Guthrie Alexander and Ferdon.

42. Ibid.

43. Philip Morris, "Submission by Philip Morris International Inc. in Response to the National Center for Standards and Certification Information Foreign Trade Notification, No. G/TBT/N/CAN/22," on file with Public Citizen.

44. Health Canada, Findings of the International Expert Panel on Cigarette Descriptors, http://www.hc-sc.gc.ca/english/pdf/media/cig_discrip_rep2.pdf, on file with Public Citizen.

45. Health Canada press release, "Health Minister Begins Regulatory Process on 'Light' and 'Mild' Tobacco Regulations," Number 2001-131, Nov. 28, 2001.

46. Philip Morris, "Submission by Philip Morris International Inc. in Response to the National Center for Standards and Certification Information Foreign Trade Notification No. G/TBT/N/CAN/22", at 4.

47. Ibid.

48. Ibid., at 2, 4 and 6.

49. North American Free Trade Agreement, Chapter 11: Article 1110: "Expropriation and Compensation."

50. "Submission by Philip Morris International Inc. in Response to the National Center for Standards and Certification Information Foreign Trade Notification, No. G/TBT/N/CAN/22," at 9.

51. WTO TRIPs Agreement, Art. 8. "WTO members may adopt measures necessary to protect public health, but only if those measures are 'consistent with the provisions of this [TRIPs] Agreement.'"

52. Philip Morris, "Submission by Philip Morris International Inc. in Response to the National Center for Standards and Certification Information Foreign Trade Notification, No. G/TBT/ N/CAN/22" at 10.

53. European Commission, "GATS 2000, Request from the EC and its Member States to the United States of America," MD 042/02, June 3, 2002. Alabama, Idaho, Iowa, Maine, Ohio, Oregon, Pennsylvania, Utah, Vermont, Michigan, Mississippi, Montana, New Hampshire, North Carolina, Virginia, Washington, West Virginia, and Wyoming have alcohol-distribution monopolies.

54. WTO, *Chile—Taxes on Alcoholic Beverages,* Appellate Body Report and Panel Report, Action by the Dispute Settlement Body, WT/DS87/12 & WT/DS110/11, Feb. 25, 2000; WTO, Japan Taxes on Alcoholic Beverages, Mutually Acceptable Solution on Modalities for Implementation, Addendum, WT/DS8/17/Add.1, WT/DS10/17/Add.1 & WT/DS11/15/

Add.1, Jan. 12, 1998; WTO, *Korea—Taxes on Alcoholic Beverages,* Status Report by Korea, WT/DS75/18, WT/DS84/16, Jan 17, 2000.

55. Ellen Gould, "Draft Trans Atlantic Consumer Dialogue Background Paper on Trade in Services," TACD, Oct. 2002, on file with Public Citizen.

56. Claire Cozens, "Court Rules Against Alcohol Advertising Ban," *Guardian,* Mar. 12, 2001.

57. Ibid.

58. UNICEF data, cited in the Right Reverend Simon Barrington-Ward, "Putting Babies Before Business," in *The Progress of Nations* (New York: UNICEF, 1997).

59. Ibid.

60. Ibid.

61. Edith Butler, "Nestle Practices Are Still Suspect, New Boycott Target, Taster's Choice Coffee," *WomenWise,* Mar. 31, 1983. The Infant Formula Action Committee (INFACT) was formed to combat Nestle's practices in 1977 and was instrumental in getting the WHO rules implemented. See Formula Promotion Hearing, Report U.S. Senate Sub-Committee on Health and Scientific Research, May 23, 1978. Nestle admitted that its product required "clean water, good sanitation, adequate family income and a literate parent" and could not be used safely "in areas where water is contaminated, sewage runs through the streets, poverty is severe and illiteracy is high."

62. International Code of Marketing of Breast-Milk Substitute, adopted by the World Health Assembly, 1981.

63. Law on the Marketing of Breast-Milk Substitutes, Guatemalan Presidential Decree 68-83, Jun. 7, 1983, and Rules for the Marketing of Breast-Milk Substitutes, Guatemalan Government Agreement No. 841-87, Sep. 30, 1987.

64. Guatemalan Presidential Decree 66-83, Jun. 7, 1983, Article 13: Labeling; Guatemala Government Agreement No. 841-87, Sep. 30, 1987, Art. 11a.

65. Guatemalan Government Agreement No. 841-87 at Art. 12.

66. Ibid. at Arts. 8a, 9.

67. Nutrition League Table, UNICEF, "Protecting Breast-Milk from Unethical Marketing," *The Progress of Nations.*

68. Ibid.

69. Guatemalan Ministry of Health, Memo Related to Gerber's Alleged Violations of Guatemalan Presidential Decree 68-83, Nov. 17, 1993.

70. Frank T. Kelly, Gerber's vice president for Latin America, Letter to the President of Guatemala, Jun. 16, 1994, on file with Public Citizen. The letter states, "We would like to thank you for all the efforts made in solving the commercial problem which originated from the misunderstanding among the Guatemalan Department of Health Services, the Office for Food Control," at 1.

71. "Chronology of the Gerber Case in Guatemala," Ministry of Health Guatemala, Nov. 1993, on file with Public Citizen.

72. Ibid.

73. Ibid.

74. Frank T. Kelly, Letter to the President of Guatemala.

75. Mario Permuth, Attorney Representing Guatemalan Ministry of Health, Letter to Dr. Gustavo Hernandez Polanco, Guatemalan Minister of Public Health, Feb. 16, 1994, on file with Public Citizen.

76. "Gerber Uses Threat of GATT Sanctions to Gain Exemption from Guatemalan Infant Health Law," Corporate Crime Reporter, Vol. 10, No. 14, Apr. 8, 1996.

77. Mario Permuth, Letter to President Bill Clinton, Dec. 12, 1993, on file with Public Citizen. (In the letter, Mario Permuth identifies himself as "the Attorney hired by UNICEF to help support the Guatemalan Ministry of Health.")

78. Mario Permuth, Letter to Dr. Gustavo Hernandez Polanco, Guatemalan Minister of Public Health.

79. WTO, TRIPs Agreement at Articles 8.1–8.2 (Principles).

80. International Baby Food Action Network, "Breaking the Rules, Stretching the Rules 2001," May 2001. Gerber's trademark baby face is on the label in Malaysia. In Mexico, Gerber products are given away for free at hospitals and shops. In Egypt, Gerber ran an advertisement stating that 3- to 5-month-old babies need Gerber complimentary food.

81. UNAIDS, "Report on the Global HIV/AIDS Epidemic 2002," Jul. 2002, at 190.

82. David Satcher, "The Global HIV/AIDS Epidemic," Journal of the American Medical Association, Apr. 28, 1999, Vol. 281, No. 16, at 1479.

83. UNAIDS, "Report on the Global HIV/AIDS Epidemic 2002," Jul. 2002, at 190.

84. See John Burgess, "Africa Gets AIDS Drug Exception," Washington Post, May 11, 2000.

85. "U.S. Firm Offers Cheap AIDS Drugs," BBC, Mar. 7, 2001; Medecins Sans Frontiers, Campaign for Access to Essential Medicines, "Untangling the Web of Price Reductions," Jun. 2002.

86. UNAIDS, "Accelerating Access to HIV/AIDS Commodities in Sub-Saharan Africa: Cost Estimates," UNAIDS/01.93E, Nov. 2001, at 7.

87. World Bank, "Poverty Reduction and the World Bank," Mar. 2002, at 13.

88. Darren Schettler, "South Africa AIDS Activists Attack 'Excessive' Drug Prices," Reuters, Sept. 19, 2002.

89. Beth Burrows, "Conquest By Patents," New Internationalist, Sep. 1, 2002.

90. Edmund J. Pratt, Pfizer Chairman Emeritus, "Intellectual Property," speech to U.S. Council for International Business, Washington, D.C., Mar. 1995, available at www.pfizer.com/are/about_public/mn_intellectualpropfrm.html, on file with Public Citizen.

91. F. M. Scherer, "The Pharmaceutical Industry and World Intellectual Property Standards," Vanderbilt Law Review, Vol. 53:6:2245, (2000), at 2247–48.

92. WTO, "Declaration on the TRIPs Agreement and Public Health," Ministerial Conference Fourth Session, WT/MIN (01)/DEC/W/2, Nov. 14, 2001, para. 7.

93. James Love, "Access to Medicines: Solving the Export Problem under TRIPs," Bridges, Year 6, No. 4, May 2002, at 3.

94. 42 U.S.C., Ch. 85, Sec. 7408. For instance, in the U.S., the Clean Air Act provides for compulsory licensing of patents related to air pollution control technology. U.S. antitrust authorities often seek compulsory licenses as remedies for problems of monopoly or

anticompetitive practices. National Public Radio (NPR) was granted compulsory licenses for noncommercial educational broadcasting use of the repertoires of the American Society of Composers, Authors and Publishers (ASCAP). See Consumer Project on Technology, frequently asked questions about compulsory licenses, Jan. 20, 1999.

95. Pharmaceutical Research and Manufacturers of America, 2002 Industry Profile, at 37.

96. South Africa (1997), Medicines and Related Substances Control Amendment Bill (B72-97).

97. WTO, TRIPs Agreement at Article 31: "Where the law of a Member allows for other use of the subject matter of a patent without the authorization of the right holder, including use by the government or third parties authorized by the government, the following provisions shall be respected . . . (h) the right holder shall be paid adequate remuneration in the circumstances of each case, taking into account the economic value of the authorization . . ."

98. Barbara Larkin, Legislative Assistant to the Secretary of State, Report to Rep. Sam Gejdenson (D-CT), House of Representatives Committee on International Relations, Feb. 5, 1999, at introduction.

99. Ibid. at 3.

100. Ibid. at 4.

101. Ibid. at 4–5.

102. Ibid. at 6.

103. Ibid. at 7.

104. Charles R. Babcock and Ceci Connolly, "AIDS Activists Badger Gore Again," *Washington Post,* Jun. 18, 1999, at 12.

105. Babcock and Connolly, "AIDS Activists Dog Gore a Second Day; Role in Drug Dispute with South Africa is Hit," *Washington Post,* Jun. 18, 1999.

106. Executive Order 13155, "Access to HIV/AIDS Pharmaceuticals and Medical Technologies," 65 FR 30521, signed May 10, 2000, published May 12, 2000.

107. Robert Block, "Big Drug Firms Defend Right to Patents on AIDS Drugs in South African Court," *Wall Street Journal,* Mar. 6, 2001.

108. Ibid.

109. Kurt Samson, "Drug Companies Withdraw AIDS Lawsuit," United Press International, Apr. 18, 2001.

110. Jim Lobe, "Bush Won't Fight Price Break for AIDS Treatment," *Inter Press Service,* Feb. 22, 2001.

111. USTR, 1999 National Trade Estimates Report (1999), at 403; see also U.S. Trade Representative National Trade Estimate Reports from 1995–1999. (These reports detail a campaign begun by the Pharmaceutical Manufacturers Association in 1991 to prevent Thailand from adopting a patents law that would increase patent protection for pharmaceuticals for 20 years but also create a Pharmaceutical Review Board that would ensure that the public had access to necessary medications.)

112. Aphaluck Bhatiasevi, "Patents Law: Groups Urge Review of Amendments," *Bangkok Post,* Aug. 17, 1999.

113. Sarah Boseley, "U.S. Attempts to Stop Developing Countries Producing Cheap AIDS Drugs Have Become a Political Time Bomb," *Guardian* (London), Aug. 11, 1999.

114. Ibid.

115. USTR, 1997 National Trade Estimates (1997), at 365. ("Thailand is in the process of amending its patent law to comply with the WTO Agreement on Trade-Related Aspects of Intellectual Property Rights. The Thai legislature is expected in 1997 to consider a bill abolishing the Pharmaceutical Review Board.")

116. John E. Calfee, "Bioterrorism and Pharmaceuticals: The Influence of Secretary Thompson's Cipro Negotiations," American Enterprise Institute, Nov. 1, 2001.

117. U.S. Food and Drug Administration Approval Letter to Bayer for Application NDA 19-537/s-038, Aug. 30, 2000; Sidney M. Wolfe, MD, Larry Sasich, Pharm. D, and Peter Lurie, MD, MPH, "Drugs for Possible Exposure to Anthrax: What Makes Sense," Public Citizen's Health Research Group Publication #1597, Oct. 18, 2001.

118. Calfee, "Bioterrorism and Pharmaceuticals."

119. Testimony of U.S. Department of Health and Human Services Secretary Tommy Thompson before the House Committee on Government Reform, Subcommittee on National Security, Veterans Affairs and International Relations, October 2001.

120. Sara Fritz, "Maker of Cipro Suspected of Blocking Generic," *St. Petersburg Times* (Florida), Oct. 17, 2001.

121. Chris Adams, "Bayer Sharply Boosts Production of Cipro," *Wall Street Journal,* Oct. 17, 2001. Until the 2001 anthrax attacks, Bayer was in an agreement with three generic drug manufacturers to keep generic Cipro off the market, by paying the three companies a total of $200 million. (Russell Mokhiber and Robert Weissman, "Corporations Behaving Badly: The Ten Worst Corporations of 2001," *Multinational Monitor,* Vol. 22, No. 12, Dec. 2001.) The Federal Trade Commission began an investigation into whether Bayer was using the agreement with the generic manufacturers to eliminate potential low-cost competition. (Fritz, "Maker of Cipro Suspected of Blocking Generic.")

122. Thersea Agovino, "Countries to Debate Over Drug Patents," Associated Press, Nov. 2, 2001.

123. Shasta Darlington, "Brazil Calls U.S. Stand on Drug Rules Inconsistent," Reuters, Oct. 30, 2001.

124. U.S. Department of Health and Human Services press release, "HHS, Bayer Agree to Cipro Purchase," Oct. 24, 2001.

125. Statement of Asia Russell, Health GAP Coalition, Oct. 25, 2001, on file with Public Citizen.

126. WTO, Brazil—Measures Affecting Patent Protection, WT/DS199/1, Jun. 8, 2000.

127. Brazilian Program of Sexually Transmissible Diseases and AIDS, "National AIDS Drug Policy," Jun. 2001.

128. National STD/AIDS Programme, Federative Republic of Brazil, 1997, at 7.

129. Brazilian Program of Sexually Transmissible Diseases and AIDS, "National AIDS Drug Policy," Oct. 19, 2001.

130. Ibid.

131. Ibid.

132. WTO, Brazil—Measures Affecting Patent Protection, WT/DS199/1, Jun. 8, 2000.

133. WTO, Brazil—Measures Affecting Patent Protection, WT/DS199/2, Jun. 20, 2000.

134. WTO, Brazil—Measures Affecting Patent Protection, WT/DS199/3, Jan. 9, 2001.

135. Kaiser Family Foundation, "Amid 'Increasingly Bitter' Dispute, WTO Reviews Legality of Brazil's Generic Drug Law," *Kaiser Daily HIV/AIDS Report,* Feb. 6, 2001.

136. Stephen Buckley, "U.S., Brazil Clash Over AIDS Drugs," *Washington Post,* Feb. 6, 2001.

137. Oxfam Great Britain, "WTO Patent Rules and Access to Medicines: The Pressure Mounts," Jun. 2001, at 1.

138. USTR press release, "U.S. and Brazil to Cooperate on HIV/AIDS and WTO Patent Dispute," Jun. 25, 2001.

139. Statement of Maria Luisa Mendonca, Director of the Global Justice Center in Brazil, Jun. 25, 2001.

140. WTO, Brazil—Measures Affecting Patent Protection, WT/DS199/4, Jul. 19, 2001.

141. WTO, Council for Trade Related Aspects of Intellectual Property Rights, "Special Discussion on Intellectual Property and Access to Medicines," IP/C/M/31, Jul. 10, 2001.

142. WTO, Doha Declaration on the TRIPs Agreement and Public Health, Ministerial Conference, Fourth Session, Doha, WT/MIN(01)/DEC/W72, Nov. 9–14, 2001.

143. Ibid.

144. Paul Blustein, "WTO Agreement Appears Near; Agenda for New Global Talks at Stake," *Washington Post,* Nov. 13, 2001.

145. Geoff Winesock and Helene Cooper, "Activists Outmaneuver Drug Makers at WTO," *Wall Street Journal,* Nov. 14, 2001.

146. Winesock and Cooper, "WTO Nears Broad Generic-Drug Accord; U.S. May Renegotiate Antidumping Rules," *Wall Street Journal,* Nov. 13, 2001.

147. Winesock and Cooper, "Activists Outmaneuver Drug Makers at WTO."

148. "Zoellick Faces Heat from Congress on Scope of TRIPS and Health Deal," *Inside US Trade,* Dec. 6, 2002.

149. "The Assault on Drug Patents: The U.S. Ought to Stand Up for Intellectual Property Rights," *Wall Street Journal,* Nov. 25, 2002.

150. "U.S. Holds Out on Scope of Diseases, as TRIPS and Health Deal in Doubt," *Inside US Trade,* Dec. 17, 2002.

151. Ibid. and "House Democrats Urge U.S. Change in WTO Drug Talks," Reuters, Dec. 20, 2002.

152. Larry Elliott and Charlotte Denny, "U.S. Wrecks Cheap Drugs Deal," *Guardian,* Dec. 21, 2002.

153. Letter from Robert Weissman, Co-director of Essential Action, and James Love, Director of Consumer Project on Technology, to USTR Trade Policy Staff Committee Executive Gloria Blue Concerning the U.S.-Chile Free Trade Agreement, Jan. 29, 2001.

154. Jim Young, "Cancer for Sale," *In These Times,* Sep. 5, 1999, at 2.

155. Debora MacKenzie, "In Safe Hands?," *New Scientist,* Apr. 3, 1999.

156. European Communities press release, "EU Backs French Asbestos Ban in Face of Canadian WTO Panel," Oct. 22, 1998.

157. MacKenzie, "In Safe Hands?"

158. Bill Schiller, "Why Canada Pushes Killer Asbestos," *Toronto Star,* Mar. 29, 1999.

159. French Decree 96-1133, Dec. 24, 1996, on prohibition of asbestos (J.O. dated Dec. 26, 1996), on file with Public Citizen.

160. Council Directive 1999/77/EC, 1999 O.J.

161. French Decree 96-1133, Dec. 24, 1996, at Articles 1 and 2. The exceptions were limited to those cases where there was no substitute which was proven to provide the same level of industrial performance as asbestos while posing a lesser occupational health risk. For more on this, see WTO, European Communities—Measures Affecting Asbestos and Asbestos-Containing Products, Report of the Panel, WT/DS135/R, at paras. 2.1–7.

162. Schiller, "Why Canada Pushes Killer Asbestos."

163. European Communities—Measures Affecting the Prohibition of Asbestos and Asbestos Products (WT/DS135), Complaint by Canada, May 28, 1998.

164. "EU Confirms White Asbestos Ban," *ENDS Daily,* Jul. 29, 1999.

165. United States, European Communities—Measures Affecting the Prohibition of Asbestos and Asbestos Products, Third Party Written Submission of the United States, May 28, 1999, available at the EPA Asbestos Ombudsman and EPA Public Information Center, and on file with Public Citizen.

166. WTO, European Communities—Measures Concerning Asbestos and Products Containing It, Canadian First Draft, Apr. 26, 1999. The Canadian government echoes the arguments of the Canadian asbestos industry that "white" or chrysotile asbestos is safe when managed properly, but the older "blue" and "brown" forms of asbestos are responsible for worker deaths. The U.S. Occupational Safety and Health Administration (OSHA) disputes this claim, finding that "chrysotile exposure should be treated the same as other forms of asbestos" and that it may be an even more potent carcinogen. See MacKenzie, "In Safe Hands?"

167. WTO, European Communities—Measures Concerning Asbestos and Products Containing It, Canadian First Draft, Apr. 26, 1999, at 3.

168. See International Labor Conference, Agreement Concerning Safety in the Use of Asbestos (Agreement 162), Jun. 24, 1986; see also International Labor Conference, Recommendation Concerning Safety in the Use of Asbestos (Recommendation 172), Jun. 24, 1986.

169. International Organization on Standardization, Standard ISO-7337, 1984.

170. Personal Communication, Aug. 21, 1999, between anonymous asbestos expert and Michelle Sforza, Research Director, Public Citizen.

171. WTO, European Communities—Measures Concerning Asbestos and Asbestos Products, Canadian First Draft, Apr. 26, 1999.

172. Ibid.

173. Ibid.

174. The right to safe working conditions is covered by the 1981 Occupational Safety and Health and the Working Environment Convention (C155, International Labor Organization); 1966 International Covenant on Economic Social and Cultural Rights, Article 7; 1988 Additional Protocol to the American Convention on Human Rights in the Area of Economic, Social, and Cultural Rights, Article 7; and 1961 European Social Charter, Article 3.

175. WHO, World Health Report 1997, Executive Summary, Geneva (1998).

176. Ibid.

177. Schiller, "Why Canada Pushes Killer Asbestos."

178. Young, "Cancer for Sale."

179. Schiller, "Why Canada Pushes Killer Asbestos"; see also Dennis Cauchon, "The Asbestos Epidemic—A Global Crisis," *USA Today,* Aug. 2, 1999.

180. Schiller, "Why Canada Pushes Killer Asbestos."

181. Andrew Schneider and Carol Smith, "Canada Fiercely Defends Industry," *Seattle Post-Intelligencer,* Feb. 11, 2000.

182. Cauchon, "The Asbestos Epidemic—A Global Crisis."

183. Schiller, "Why Canada Pushes Killer Asbestos."

184. WTO, European Communities—Measures Affecting Asbestos and Asbestos-containing Products, Dispute Settlement Panel Report WT/DS135/R, Sep. 18, 2000.

185. WTO, European Communities—Measures Affecting Asbestos and Asbestos-containing Products—Communication from the Appellate Body, WT/DS135/AB/R, Mar. 12, 2001.

186. WTO, TBT Agreement, at Annex 1:1. Canada argued that the French decree includes a ban on products based on their characteristic of containing asbestos, and that it therefore is a technical regulation and should be analyzed under the TBT Agreement.

187. GATT 1994, at Article XX(b); WTO TBT, at preamble para. 6 ("[r]ecognizing that no country should be prevented from taking measures necessary . . . for the protection of human, animal or plant life or health, [or] of the environment. . . ."); WTO SPS, at preamble para. 1 ("[r]eaffirming that no Member should be prevented from adopting or enforcing measures necessary to protect human, animal or plant life or health . . . [d]esiring to improve the human health, animal health and phytosanitary situation in all Members").

188. WTO, European Communities, Measures Concerning Asbestos and Asbestos Products, Report of the Panel, WT/DS135/R, Sep. 18, 2000 at para 8.302.

189. WTO, Report of the Appellate Body: European Communities—Measures Affecting Asbestos and Asbestos-containing Products, WT/DS135/AB/R, March 12, 2001, at paras. 67–70.

190. Ibid., at para. 172.

191. WTO, Korea—Measures Affecting Imports of Fresh, Chilled and Frozen Beef, AB report, WT/DS161/AB/R, Dec. 11, 2000, para. 162 ff.

192. WTO, Report of the Appellate Body: European Communities—Measures Affecting Asbestos and Asbestos-containing Products, WT/DS135/AB/R, Mar. 12, 2001, at para. 172.

193. International Conference on Harmonization; Draft Guideline on Testing for Carcinogenicity of Pharmaceuticals, 61 Fed. Reg. 43,297, Aug. 21, 1996. For more information on the ICH, see the ICH website at www.ifpma.org/ich1.html.

194. Comment letter from Sidney M. Wolfe, M.D., and Larry D. Sasich, Pharm.D., FASHP, to the U.S. Food and Drug Administration re: International Conference on Harmonization: Draft Guideline on Testing for Carcinogenicity of Pharmaceuticals, Nov. 1, 1996, on file with Public Citizen.

195. Ibid., 61 Fed. Reg. 43, 299.

196. International Conference on Harmonization Guidance on Testing for Carcino-genicity of Pharmaceuticals, 63 Fed. Reg. 8983, Feb. 23, 1998.

197. International Conference on Harmonization; Choice of Control Group in Clinical Trials, 64 Fed. Reg. 51,767, Sep. 24, 1999.

CHAPTER 4: THE WTO'S GENERAL AGREEMENT ON TRADE IN SERVICES

1. For more on the notion of the global commons see International Forum on Glob-alization, *Alternatives to Economic Globalization* (San Francisco: Berrett-Koehler Publish-ers, Inc., 2002).

2. Dr. Gordon Schiff and Dr. David Himmelstein, "Questions and Answers about Single-Payer National Health Insurance," Windsor, Ontario, May 19, 1996.

3. John Madeley, *Trade and the Poor: The Impact of International Trade on Developing Countries*, 2nd ed., (Intermediate Technology Publications, 1996), at 71–72. "At the GATT Ministerial meeting in 1982, the U.S government proposed that services be included in trade liberalization schemes, and vigorously campaigned on the issue throughout the 1980s. . . . The U.S. even proposed that the words 'and services' simply be added every time that the word 'goods' appeared in a GATT document. . . . Since 1985, the USA has refused to be involved in any trade negotiations that did not include services. Ironically, by 1992, when the USA realized that some developing countries stood to do very well by selling ser-vices to the American market, it argued in the UR negotiations that it should be exempt from around three-quarters of tradable services."

4. WTO, "International Trade Statistics 2002," at Table 1.7 Leading Exporters and Importers in World Trade in Commercial Services, Oct. 7, 2002.

5. William K. Tabb, "The World Trade Organization? Stop the World Takeover," *Monthly Review,* Jan. 1, 2000.

6. Membership list online from www.uscsi.org/members/current.htm, updated 7/31/02, on file with Public Citizen.

7. Marcy Gordon, "SEC to Investigate Cheney's Former Company," Associated Press, Jul. 14, 2002; Robert Schmidt, "SEC Probes Analysts' Supervision," *Los Angeles Times,* Jun. 3, 2003; David D. Kirkpatrick, "AOL Says S.E.C. Is Questioning Its Accounting of $400 Mil-lion," *New York Times,* Mar. 29, 2003; and James Doran, "US Watchdog Investigates Microsoft Shares Sell-off," *The Times* (London), May 31, 2003.

8. WTO, "Council for Trade in Services, Health And Social Services, Background Note by the Secretariat," S/C/W/50, Sep. 18, 1998, at para. 11.

9. See UNESCO, "World Teachers' Day 5 October 2001: 15 Million New Teachers Needed," Oct. 4, 2001.

10. Edson Luiz de Oliveira, "Restructuring of the Postal Section in Brazil in Response to the Changing World Economy," Institute of Brazilian Issues, George Washington University, Fall 2000, at 7.

11. Sarah Rubenstein, "City Blasts United Water," *Atlanta Business Chronicle,* Aug. 9, 2002.

12. "Hoax: How Deregulation Let the Power Industry Steal $71 Billion From California," *The Foundation for Taxpayer and Consumer Rights,* Jan. 17, 2002, at 2 and 15–16.

13. Bill Bradshaw, "A Radical Option—The Privatisation of Britain's Railways," *Japan Railway & Transport Review,* Jun. 1994, at 16.

14. Brendan Martin, "Derailed: The UK's Disastrous Experience With Railway Privatization," *Multinational Monitor,* Jan/Feb 2002, Vol. 23, Nos. 1 & 2, at 2.

15. Ibid., at 2–4.

16. "Bearing the Burden of IMF and World Bank Policies," *Multinational Monitor,* Sept. 2001, Vol. 22, No. 9 for a complete list.

17. Sustainable Energy and Environment Network, "Enron's Pawns: How Public Institutions Bankrolled Enron's Globalization Games," *Institute for Policy Studies,* Mar. 22, 2002, at 15.

18. Ibid. See also World Bank, IFC Project Number 4536, "Smith Enron Cogeneration Power Plant—Combined Cycle Power Plant."

19. Sustainable Energy and Environment Network, "Enron's Pawns: How Public Institutions Bankrolled Enron's Globalization Games." See also World Bank, IFC Project Number 7131, "Smith Enron Risk Management."

20. Sustainable Energy and Environment Network, "Enron's Pawns: How Public Institutions Bankrolled Enron's Globalization Games."

21. Ibid.

22. Ibid.

23. Brendan Martin, "Ripping Off the Public Purse," *Focus Magazine,* No.1, 2001.

24. Sustainable Energy and Environment Network, "Enron's Pawns: How Public Institutions Bankrolled Enron's Globalization Games."

25. Kate Bayliss and David Hall, "Independent Power Producers: A Review of the Issues," *Public Services International Research Unit (PSIRU),* Nov. 2000, at 6–7.

26. Sustainable Energy and Environment Network, "Enron's Pawns: How Public Institutions Bankrolled Enron's Globalization Games."

27. Daphne Wysham, "Enron's Final, Biggest Error . . . ," *Houston Chronicle,* Apr. 13, 2002.

28. U.S. Census Bureau, "Health Insurance Coverage: 2001," P60-220, Sep. 2002, at 1.

29. Bureau of Labor Education, "The U.S. Health Care System: Best in the World, or Just the Most Expensive?" University of Maine, Summer 2001, at 3.

30. For instance, the 1988 Brazilian Constitution (CF art. 196 Direito do Todos e dever do Estado) guarantees basic medical services and Brazil's remarkable record in providing anti-retroviral drugs to many of its citizens infected with HIV is an outgrowth of this public health right.

31. See, for example, Gillian Steward, "The Ghosts of Medicare Past," *Winnipeg Free Press,* Oct. 10, 2002.

32. Health Canada, "Canada Health Act Overview," available online at www.hc-sc.gc.ca/medicare/chaover.htm, on file with Public Citizen.

33. Jake Vellinga, International Affairs, Health Canada, "Canada: Health Services and GATS," Presentation to WHO Meeting, Jan. 9–11, 2002, available online at unstats.un.org/unsd/tradeserv/docs/who2002/vellinga-gats-rev.ppt, on file with Public Citizen.

34. Canadian Centre for Policy Alternatives, Consortium on Globalization and Health, "Putting Health First: Canadian Health Care Reform, Trade Treaties and Foreign Policy," Report for the Commission on the Future of Health Care in Canada, CP32-83/2002E-IN, 0-662-32996-1, Oct. 2002, at 1.

35. Health Canada, "Canada Health Act Overview."

36. Ibid.

37. Guatam Dutta, "NAFTA and GATS Undermine Canada's Health Care System," *Two Eyes Magazine,* Issue 3, Spring 2001.

38. GATS Article I, 3(b) and (c); See also Robert G. Evans, Morris L. Barer, Steven Lewis, Michael Rachlis and Greg L. Stoddart, "Private Highway, One-Way Street: The Decline and Fall of Canadian Medicare?" Centre for Health Services and Policy Research, Mar. 2000, at 31.

39. WTO, "Health and Social Services, Background Note by the Secretariat," S/C/W/50, Sep. 18, 1998, at para. 39.

40. Evans et al., "Private Highway, One-Way Street." See also GATS Article I-3-a-i.

41. Canadian Centre for Policy Alternatives, Consortium on Globalization and Health, "Putting Health First," at 28.

42. Ibid. See also GATS Article XXI.

43. Chakravarthi Raghavan, "Not So Fool-Proof: GATS Safeguards and Prudential Rights," *Third World Economics,* No. 175, Dec. 1997, at 3.

44. Years of participation in IMF structural adjustment programs had led to the mass privatization and selling off of domestic utilities, banks and telecommunications companies. See various "Letters of Intent" between the IMF and borrower countries available at www.imf.org/external/np/loi/mempub.htm, on file with Public Citizen.

45. GATS Article I-3-a-i.

46. GATS Article I-3-a-ii.

47. GATS Article I-1. (In one of the few WTO rulings on the GATS, what this provision means became a central question. The panel ruled that "Article I-1 refers to any measures in terms of their effect, which means that they could be of any type or relate to any domain of regulation." WTO, European Communities—Regime for the Importation, Sale and Distribution of Bananas, Panel Report May 22, 1997, at 7.280. WT-DS27-R-USA.)

48. GATS Article V. Section 1 (a), fn. 1, "This condition is understood in terms of number of sectors, volume of trade affected and modes of supply. In order to meet this condition, agreements should not provide for the *a priori* exclusion of any mode of supply."

49. GATS Article II. "With respect to any measure covered by this Agreement, each member shall accord immediately and unnconditionally to services and service suppliers of any other member treatment which is no less favorable than that it accords to like services and service suppliers of any other country."

50. GATS, Annex on Article II Exemptions, Article 6.

51. GATS Article I-3-b and c. ". . . (b) 'services' includes any serrvice in any sector except services supplied in the exercise of government authority; (c) 'a service supplied in the exercise of governmental authority' means any service which is supplied neither on a commercial basis, nor in competition with one or more service suppliers."

52. OECD. "The General Agreement on Trade and Services (GATS): An Analysis," Paris 1994, at. 7, cited in Canadian Centre for Policy Alternatives, Facing the Facts, at. 20.

53. GATS Article XIII explicitly excludes MFN, national treatment and Article XVII market access rules for this limited circumstance.

54. GATS Article I-2-a.

55. GATS Article I-2-b.

56. GATS Article I-2-c.

57. GATS Article I-2-d.

58. "Commissioner Pushes for Exemption from New U.S. Auditing Rules," *European Report,* Oct. 9, 2002.

59. "LSE Head Attacks U.S. Law," *The Times* (London), Dec. 10, 2002.

60. John Malpas, "Big Six Call for SEC Reprieve," *Legal Week,* Dec. 20, 2002.

61. Gary Duncan, "Europe Seeks Exemption on U.S. Act," *The Times* (London), Nov. 18, 2002.

62. Carlos Boyadjian, "Family Aid Boosts Latin American Economies," *Washington Times,* Oct. 22, 2002.

63. Inter-American Development Bank press release, "MIF Approves $1.5 Million Grant to Improve Financial Services and Remittances in El Salvador," May 31, 2002.

64. Bureau of Economic and Business Affairs, "2001 Country Reports on Economic Policy and Trade Practices, El Salvador," U.S. Department of State, Feb. 2002.

65. WTO, Communication from India, "Proposed Liberalisation of Movement of Professionals under General Agreement on Trade in Services (GATS)," S/CSS/W/12, Nov. 24, 2000, at IV, 1.

66. Peter S. Goodman, "White-Collar Work a Booming U.S. Export," *Washington Post,* Apr. 2, 2003.

67. "US Multinationals Take 'Brain Work' to Plants Overseas," *Wall Street Journal Europe,* Sep. 30, 1994.

68. Mike Mills, "In the Modem World, White Collar Jobs Go Overseas," *Washington Post,* Sep. 17, 1996, at 1.

69. Barbara Rose, "Tech Veterans Squeezed Out: Overseas Hiring, Ageism Blamed," *Seattle Times,* Mar. 14, 1998.

70. "Dialing for Dollars," *Newshour with Jim Lehrer,* Nov. 5, 2002.

71. "Missouri Welfare Hot Line Calls Go to India," Associated Press, Oct. 16, 2002.

72. Augusta Dwyer, "On the Line, Life on the U.S.-Mexican Border," (London) *Monthly Review Press,* 1995, at 6–7.

73. Joel Millman, "First Came Assembly, New Services Soar," *Wall Street Journal,* Feb. 28, 2000.

74. Millman, "The Outlook," *Wall Street Journal,* Dec. 4, 2000.

75. With the time-limited exception noted above which allowed countries to list exemptions from MFN.

76. GATS Article XV-12-a.

77. Doha WTO Ministerial Declaration at para. 31 iii.

78. GATS Article XVII.

79. GATS Article XVII-3.

80. Such a case already occurred in the context of the EU regarding Danish bottle reuse and recycling laws. German beer companies successfully claimed the policy was more costly

for them to comply with than Danish firms. European Commission, Judgement of the Court of Sep. 20, 1998, *Commission of the European Communities v. Kingdom of Denmark,* "Free Movement of Goods—Containers for Beer and Soft Drinks," Case 302/86, *European Courts Report,* 1998 at 04607.

81. GATS Article XXIII-3.

82. GATS Article XXI-2-a requires countries to negotiate compensation for withdrawing a GATS commitment. Article XXI-2-b requires that such compensation be available to all affected countries on a Most Favored Nation basis.

83. GATS Article VIII-4, GATS Article XXI-2(b–c).

84. Elaine Bernard, "What's the Matter With NAFTA?" *New Politics,* Vol. IV, No. 4, Winter 94, at 9.

85. WTO, "Trading Into the Future," descriptions of the WTO Agreements on WTO website printed in 1999, on file with Public Citizen.

86. The U.S. has no limitations to market access for energy services. The WTO database for all GATS commitments is at tsdb.wto.org/wto/wtohomepublic.htm.

87. IMF, "From the Executive Board: Bolivia ESAF," *IMF Survey,* Sep. 28, 1998, at 300.

88. IMF and IDA, "Bolivia: Initiative for the Heavily Indebted Poor Countries (HIPC) Completion Point Document," Sep. 4, 1998, at 6.

89. For example, in 1982, when the U.S. Congress was debating domestic water projects, it was noted that of the expected $3.8 billion to be spent for new construction over the succeeding five years, only $275 million in revenue could be expected to be repaid. Republican Policy Committee, Senate Vote Record Analysis, "Regulatory Reform Act of 1982 (S. 1867). Lugar-Proxmire Amendment No. 1935," 97th Congress, 2nd Session, Jul. 15, 1982, 2:47 P.M., Page S-8377 Temp. Record, Vote No. 215, 3rd.

90. Ibid.

91. Tim Johnson, "'Water War' A Test Case on Trade Transparency," *Miami Herald,* Oct. 13, 2002.

92. Jim Shultz, "Blame Bechtel, Not Narcotraffickers, for Bolivian Uprising," *Jinn Magazine,* Pacific News Service, Apr. 12, 2000.

93. Gregory Palast, "New British Empire of the Dammed," *The Observer,* Apr. 23, 2000.

94. Emanuele Lobina, "Cochabamba—Water War," *Focus,* Vol. 7, No. 2, Jun. 2000, at 2.

95. Mike Ceaser, "Water Rate Hikes Provoked Bolivia Protests," *Christian Science Monitor,* Apr. 13, 2000.

96. Lobina, "Cochabamba—Water War."

97. Ibid.

98. Jim Shultz, "Water Fallout: Bolivians Battle Globalization," *In These Times,* May 15, 2000.

99. Ibid.

100. Ibid.

101. Ibid.

102. Ibid.

103. World Bank, *Aguas del Tunari S.A. v. Republic of Bolivia,* Case No. ARB/02/3; Jimmy Langman, "Bechtel Battles Against Dirt-Poor Bolivia," *San Francisco Chronicle,* Feb. 2, 2002.

104. Langman, "Bechtel Battles Against Dirt-Poor Bolivia."

105. The Veterans Health Care Act of 1992, P.L. 105-585, Section 602–605.

106. Ibid. at Section 602; William J. Scanlon, "Testimony Before the Subcommittee on Health and the Subcommittee on Oversight and Investigations, Committee on Energy and Commerce, House of Representatives. Medicare Part B Drugs: Program Payments Should Reflect Market Prices," GAO-01-1142T, Sep. 21, 2001, at 6.

107. WTO, "A Training Package: Module 6 Services: GATS," Dec. 15, 1998 at 63, on file with Public Citizen.

108. GATS Article VI-4.

109. Charles P. Heeter, Jr., Associate Partner, Arthur Andersen & Co., S.C., "Testimony Before the Subcommittee on Trade, Committee on Ways and Means, U.S. House of Representatives," Feb. 1, 1994.

110. WTO, *Disciplines on Domestic Regulation in the Accountancy Sector,* Dec. 14, 1998, WTO document PRESS/118. The accountancy disciplines will become effective at the conclusion of the current GATS round in 2005. The WTO adopted a standstill provision that prevents WTO members from enacting new legislation in the interim that is inconsistent with the disciplines.

111. Data compiled by Public Citizen's Critical Mass Energy Program for Federal Election Committee information as on January 13, 2003, on file with Public Citizen.

112. National Institute on Money in State Politics, www.followthemoney.org., on file with Public Citizen.

113. Center for Responsive Politics, www.opensecrets.org., on file with Public Citizen.

114. Compiled by Public Citizen's Critical Mass Energy Program from Center for Responsive Politics data. Includes Enron contributions to the Republican National Committee during the 2000 election cycle, on file with Public Citizen.

115. Revenue as reported in Enron 10-k filings with the Securities and Exchange Commission, on file with Public Citizen.

116. "Order Addressing Price Mitigation in California and the Western United States," U.S. Federal Energy Regulatory Commission, June 18, 2001, www.ferc.gov, on file with Public Citizen.

117. From 8-k filed by Enron on December 17, 2001 with the Securities and Exchange Commission.

118. GATS Article VI-5.

119. GATS Article XIV *bis* provides that "Nothing in this Agreement shall be construed to . . ."

120. GATS Article XIX-1.

121. Ibid.

122. GATS Article XV; GATS Article XIII-2.

123. Bureau of Economic Analysis, National Income and Product Account Tables, Table 3.1 Government Current Receipts and Expenditures, last updated Apr. 25, 2003.

124. WTO, "Communication From Argentina, Brazil, Cuba, The Dominican Republic, El Salvador, Honduras, India, Indonesia, Malaysia, Mexico, Nicaragua, Pakistan, Panama, Paraguay, Philippines, Sri Lanka, Thailand, Uruguay, and the Members of the Andean Community (Bolivia, Colombia, Ecuador, Peru, Venezuela)," S/CSS/W/13, Nov. 24, 2000, at IV. (11).

125. Demand letter and list of signatories available at www.citizen.org/trade/wto/gats/ Sign_on/articles.cfm? ID=1584, on file with Public Citizen.

126. Doha WTO Ministerial Declaration, para. 15.

127. General Accounting Office, "Comptroller General's 1991 Annual Report," Dec. 18, 1991, at 6.

128. Letter from Water and Wastewater Equipment Manufacturers' Association, Inc., to Michael Smith, ISO Secretariat, "Re. AFNOR Proposal for New Field of Technical Activity ISO/TS/P194: Standardization of Service Activities Relating to Drinking Water Supply and Sewage-Quality Criteria of the Service and Performance Indicators," Jul. 20, 2001, on file with Public Citizen.

129. Public Citizen Critical Mass and Environment Program, "Water Privatization: A Broken Promise," Oct. 2001.

130. Paul Klebnikov (Interview), "Theft of the Century: Privatization and the Looting of Russia," *Multinational Monitor,* Vol. 23, No. 1 and 2, Jan. 2002.

131. Patrick Bond, "Power to the People in South Africa—Operation Khanyisa! and the Fight Against Electricity Privatization," *Multinational Monitor,* Vol. 23, No. 1 and 2, Jan. 2002.

132. Roger Cohen, "With Time Waning Europeans Reject U.S. Movie Compromise, Clinton May Shun Trade Pact Without Provision," *New York Times,* Dec. 14, 1993; David Gardner, "GATT Deal May Hinge on U.S. Demands in Audio-Visual Sector," *Financial Times,* Dec.14, 1993.

133. David Dodwell, "U.S. Opts to Bide Time on Audio-Visual Battle," *Financial Times,* Dec. 15, 1993; Sharon Waxman, "GATT-astrophe Averted," *Washington Post,* Dec. 15, 1993. See also, I. Bernier; "Cultural Goods and Services in International Trade Law," Seminar paper prepared for the Centre for Trade Policy and Law, Carleton University, Ottawa, Oct. 1997, at 2, 6.

134. Bernier, "Cultural Goods amd Services in International Trade Law," at 6, 7.

135. UNESCO, General Conference, Universal Declaration on Cultural Diversity, adopted Nov. 2, 2001, para. 9. of preamble.

136. John Urgquhart and Bhushan Bahree, "WTO Orders Canada to Drop Magazine Rule," *New York Times,* Jul. 1, 1997.

137. Drew Fagan and Laura Eggertson, "Canada Loses Magazine Case," *Globe and Mail,* Jan. 17, 1997.

138. Canadian Tariff Code 9958.

139. Fagan and Eggertson, "Canada Loses Magazine Case."

140. R.S.C. 1985, c. 41 (3rd Suppl.) as amended to 30 April 1996, s.114, Sch. VII, Item 9958 (1996 Customs Tariff: Departmental Consolidation) Ottawa: Minister of Supply & Services Canada, 1996.

141. Fagan and Eggertson, "Canada Loses Magazine Case."

142. WTO, Canada—Certain Measures Concerning Periodicals (WT/DS31), Complaint by the United States, Mar. 11, 1996.

143. WTO, Canada—Certain Measures Concerning Periodicals, Request for the Establishment of a Panel by the United States, WT/DS131/2, May 24, 1996.

144. WTO, Canada—Certain Measures Concerning Periodicals, WT/DS31/AB/R, Report of the Appellate Body, Jun. 30, 1997, at 14.

145. Anthony DePalma, "World Trade Body Opposes Canadian Magazine Tariffs," *New York Times*, Jan. 19, 1997.

146. WTO, Canada—Certain Measures Concerning Periodicals (WT/DS31/R), Report of the Panel, Mar. 4, 1999.

147. Ibid. at paras. 5.5, 5.11, 5.30 and 5.39.

148. WTO, Canada—Certain Measures Concerning Periodicals, WT/DS31/AB/R, Report of the Appellate Body, Jun. 30, 1997, at 1.

149. Edward Alden, "Canada Faces $4bn Sanctions Threat as U.S. Opens New Front in Fight to Make WTO Judgments Stick," *Financial Times*, Jan. 19, 1999.

150. Ibid.

151. Ibid.

152. WTO, Canada—Certain Measures Concerning Periodicals, WT/DS31/AB/R, Report of the Appellate Body, Jun. 30, 1997, at 18.

153. U.S. Federal Register, Vol. 66, No. 130, Jul. 6, 2001; Notices, at 35689.

154. Mark Bourrie, "Trade: Canada Backs Down on Periodicals Law," InterPress Service, May 31, 1999.

155. Ibid.

156. Raj Bhala and David Gantz, "WTO Case Review 2000," *Arizona Journal of International and Comparative Law*, Spring 2000.

157. Ibid.

158. Ibid.

159. WTO, Canada—Certain Measures Affecting the Automotive Industry, WT/DS139, Report of the Panel.

160. Ibid.

161. Ibid. at para 10.

162. Ibid., at 63.

163. WTO, Canada—Certain Measures Affecting the Automotive Industry, Report of the Appellate Body, AD-2000-2, WT/DS139/AB/R, May 31, 2000, at 52.

164. Ibid. at 64.

165. Ibid. at 52.

166. Ibid. at para. 54.

167. Ibid. at 234, 235.

168. Ibid. at para. 220.

169. Ibid. at 209–10.

CHAPTER 5: FOR RICHER OR POORER

1. Gary C. Hufbauer and Jeffrey J. Schott, *NAFTA: An Assessment*, Institute for International Economics, Oct. 1993, at 14.

2. Ibid. Bob Davis, "Free Trade Is Heading for More Hot Debate," *Wall Street Journal*, Apr. 17, 1995.

3. See Ian Goldin, Odin Knudsen and Dominique van der Mensbrugghe, *Trade Liberalization: Global Economic Implications* (Washington, D.C.: World Bank, 1993), at 13.

4. Samuel Brittan, "Where GATT's $200b really Comes From," *Financial Times*, Oct. 4, 1993.

5. *Economic Report of the President* (Washington, D.C.: U.S. Government Printing Office, 1994), at 234.

6. Council of Economic Advisors, "America's Interest in the World Trade Organization: An Economic Assessment," Washington D.C.: The President's Council of Economic Advisors, 1999, at 22.

7. U.S. Bureau of Economic Analysis, "Current-Dollar and 'Real' Gross Domestic Product (Seasonally Adjusted Annual Rates)," Nov. 26, 2002.

8. Mark Weisbrot, "Globalization for Dummies," *Harper's*, May 2000, at 15.

9. U.S. Census Bureau, Foreign Trade Division, "U.S. Trade in Goods and Services—Balance of Payments Basis," 1960–2002. Public Citizen calculations based on Hufbauer formula and U.S. Census Bureau figures.

10. U.S. Census Bureau, "U.S. Trade in Goods and Services—Balance of Payments Basis," 1960–2002.

11. Public Citizen calculations based on Hufbauer formula and U.S. Census Bureau figures.

12. United States Trade Representative, 2001, at 9. Undated USTR document prepared in response to 2001 Freedom of Information Request from Patrick Woodall, Public Citizen's Global Trade Watch, on file at Public Citizen.

13. U.S. Census Bureau, Foreign Trade Division, "U.S. Trade in Goods and Services 1960–2002," Mar. 12, 2003.

14. "Free Trade Is Headed for More Hot Debate," *Wall Street Journal*.

15. Robert E. Scott, Economic Policy Institute, "Phony Accounting and U.S. Trade Policy," Issue Brief #184, Oct. 23, 2002.

16. U.S. Census Bureau, Foreign Trade Division, FT 900—U.S. International Trade in Goods and Services, Exhibit 14, "Exports, Imports and Balance of Goods by Selected Countries and Areas, 2002," Dec. 2002.

17. U.S. Census Bureau, Foreign Trade Division, U.S. Imports and Exports from China from 1998 to 2002 by 5-Digit End-Use Code, 2003.

18. Trade in the Americas: Beyond the Santiago Summit, Hearing Before the Subcommittee on International Economic Policy and Trade of the U.S. House Committee on International Relations, Apr. 29, 1998, on file with Public Citizen.

19. Bureau of Labor Statistics, National Employment Hours and Earnings: Manufacturing and Services, Jul. 1999. Historically, manufacturing wages have driven wages in the rest of the economy.

20. "Contingent Worker Safety: A Full-Time Job in a Part-Time World," Occupational Hazards, Oct. 1997, at 2, citing Occupational Safety and Health Administration data.

21. U.S. Department of Labor, Bureau of Labor Statistics, 2000–2010 Employment Projections, Dec. 12, 2001, at Table 1.

22. MBG Information Services, "Manufacturing Share of U.S. Non-Farm Jobs," Apr. 2003.

23. U.S. Department of Labor, Bureau of Labor Statistics, 2000–2010 Employment Projections, at Table 4.

24. Patrice Hill, "'Strong Dollar' Policy Loses Its Grip—Challenge Awaits Treasury Chief," Washington Times, Jan. 27, 2003; Peronet Despeignes, "Messy Work for Volker, the Clean Up," Financial Times, Feb. 15, 2002.

25. MBG Information Services, "Components of the U.S. Economy," Mar. 27, 2003.

26. John R. MacArthur, The Selling of "Free Trade" (New York: Hill and Wang, 2000), at 36.

27. U.S. Department of Commerce, Bureau of the Census, "U.S. Goods Trade: Imports & Exports by Related Parties; 2000," Jun. 26, 2001.

28. U.S. Census Bureau, Foreign Trade Division, U.S. Trade Balance with Mexico, Mar. 2003.

29. J. Frankel, "Assessing the Efficiency Gains from Further Trade Liberalization," Harvard University, 2000, at 30.

30. Ibid. at 31.

31. Ibid. at 10.

32. John Kay, "Downfall of an Economic Experiment; New Zealand's Textbook Programme of Liberalization Has Left it Poorer than Before," Financial Times, Aug. 30, 2000.

33. Ibid.

34. U.S. Department of Commerce, Census Bureau, "The Big Payoff: Educational Attainment and Synthetic Estimates of Work-Life Earnings," Jul. 2002, at 2.

35. United States International Trade Commission, The Economic Effects of Significant U.S. Import Restraints, 1999, www.usitc.gov/wais/reports/arc/w3201.html, on file with Public Citizen.

36. Ibid. at 15.

37. Ibid. at 14.

38. For example, suppose the United States places a quota on the number of foreign-produced cars that can be sold in the United States. Since the supply of foreign cars is restricted, this move will raise the price, for example, from $20,000 to $22,000 per car. The foreign car producers can now make an additional $2,000 on every car they sell in the United States, and can keep this money as extra profit. By contrast, suppose the United States imposed a tariff of 10 percent on imported cars. While the tariff also raises the price of imported cars by 10 percent to $22,000, in this case the additional $2,000 goes to the United States government in the form of tariff revenue. Tariffs do not provide extra profits to foreign producers in the same way that quotas do.

39. G. Hufbauer and K. Elliot, Measuring the Costs of Protection in the United States (Washington, D.C.: Institute for International Economics, 1994), at 9.

40. ITC 1999, at 7.

41. U.S. Bureau of Labor Statistics, "Worker Displacements, 1999–2001," Aug. 21, 2002, at Table 8.

42. ITC 1999, at 178.

43. For instance, this implication of standard trade models can be found in Wolfgang Stolper and Paul A. Samuelson, "Protection and Real Wages," *Review of Economic Studies* 9, no. 1, Nov. 1941.

44. Paul Krugman, "Growing World Trade: Causes and Consequences," Brookings Papers on Economic Activity, 1995.

45. W. Cline, *Trade and Income Distribution* (Washington, D.C.: Institute for International Economics, 1997).

46. Ibid.

47. See Lawrence Mishel, Jared Bernstein and Heather Boushey, Economic Policy Institute, *The State of Working America 2002–3* (Ithaca, N.Y.: Cornell University Press, 2002).

48. ITC 1999, at 36.

49. If the top 20% of wage earners saw their incomes rise by 0.14%, the same as the increase for the capital side of production, this would give them an increase in wage earnings equal to approximately 0.07% of total wage income. Since the 1999 ITC report estimated that total wage income would rise by just 0.06%, this means that income for the bottom 80% of wage earners would have to fall.

50. K. Brofenbrenner, "Uneasy Terrain: The Impact of Capital Mobility on Workers, Wages, and Union Organizing." Paper submitted to the U.S. Trade Deficit Review Commission. Ithaca, N.Y.: Cornell University, School of Industrial and Labor Relations.

51. Ibid.

52. Ibid.

53. U.S. Bureau of Labor Statistics, "Union Members in 2002," Feb. 25, 2003.

54. Ibid.

55. Mishel, Bernstein and Boushey, *The State of Working America 2002–3*.

56. Ibid.

57. U.S. Department of Commerce, Bureau of Economic Analysis, "U.S. Direct Investment Abroad: Country Detail for Selected Items 1994–1998," found at www.bea.doc.gov/bea/di/dia-ctry.htm, on file with Public Citizen.

58. Donald Hecker, "Occupational Employment Projections to 2010," *Monthly Labor Review,* Nov. 2001.

59. U.S. Department of Labor, "Industry Employment," *Occupational Outlook Quarterly,* Winter 2001–2002, at 29.

60. Ibid. at 80.

61. Hecker, "Occupational Employment Projections to 2010," at 80.

62. Ibid.

63. International Forum on Globalization, "Does Globalization Help the Poor?" Aug. 2001, Annex 2, based on U.S. Census Bureau, Supplemental Income Inequality Table, 2001.

64. Mishel, Bernstein and Schmitt, Economic Policy Institute, *State of Working America,* (Ithaca, NY: Cornell University Press, 2000).

65. David Lionhardt, "Two-Tier Marketing," *Business Week*, Mar. 17, 1997.

66. Paul Krugman, "For Richer," *New York Times Magazine*, Oct. 20, 2002.

67. Scott Clinger and Chris Hartman, United for a Fair Economy, Sarah Anderson and John Cavanagh, Institute for Policy Studies, "Executive Excess 2002: CEOs Cook the Books, Skewer the Rest of U.S.," Aug. 26, 2002, at 14.

68. Bureau of Economic Analysis, National Income and Product Accounts, Table 1.16.

69. Mishel, Bernstein, and Schmitt, *The State of Working America, 2000–01*, at Table 2.42.

70. The fall in the wage for high school educated workers uses the data from Mishel et al., at table 2.18, with the CPI-U-RS as the deflator. The data on average hourly compensation can be found in the Economic Report of the President, 2001, table B. Calculation by Weisbrot and Baker, Center for Economic Policy and Research.

71. If the average hourly wage for workers without college degrees is set at an index level of 100 in 1979, it had fallen to 95.8 by 1999. By contrast, the overall average hourly wage had risen 17.9 percent over this period, which would place its index level at 117.9. This means that the wages of workers without college degrees would be 23.1% higher at present, if they had kept pace with the average wage (117.9/95.8 = 123.1). The average hourly wage, in turn, would have been 2.6% higher if there had been no shift from wages to profits over this period. This means that the average hourly wage for workers without college degrees would be 26.3% higher today, if there had been neither a shift in wage income from non–college educated to college educated workers, nor from wages to profits (123.1 × 1.026 = 1.263). Calculation by Weisbrot and Baker, Center for Economic Policy and Research.

72. ITC 1999.

73. Hufbauer and Scott, *NAFTA: An Assessment*.

74. P. Krugman, "Growing World Trade: Causes and Consequences."

75. Cline, *Trade and Income Distribution*.

76. Baker and Weisbrot, "Will Trade Gains Make Us Rich?" at 11.

77. Ibid., at 10.

78. ITC 1999.

79. Productivity grew less rapidly in the second period, but the difference was nowhere near the difference in median wage growth: productivity growth for 1974–2001 was about 75% of the productivity growth for 1946–73.

80. Although more recent data are available, 1999 is the profit peak of the most recent business cycle, and is therefore appropriate for looking at changes in income distribution.

81. An explanation of these calculations, as well as a more detailed discussion of most of the arguments raised here, is provided in Baker and Weisbrot, "Will Trade Gains Make Us Rich?"

CHAPTER 6: THE WTO AND THE DEVELOPING WORLD

1. UNCTAD, *The Least Developed Countries Report 2002: Escaping the Poverty Trap*, Geneva, Jun. 16, 2002, at 101.

2. "Democrats for Poverty," *Washington Post*, Nov. 18, 2001.

3. UNCTAD, *The Least Developed Countries Report 2002: Escaping the Poverty Trap*.

4. International Forum on Globalization, "Does Globalization Help the Poor?" Aug. 2001, at iv.

5. WTO, Agreement on Trade-Related Investment Measures, Article 2, read together with Article 5 and the Annex (illustrative list).

6. Laudeline Auriol and Francois Pham, "What Pattern in Patents," *OECD Observer* 179, Dec. 1992/Jan. 1993, at 15.

7. Ha-Joon Chang, University of Cambridge, "Institute Development in Developing Countries in a Historical Perspective—Lessons from Developed Countries in Earlier Times," Aug. 2001, at 2.

8. Michael Lind, Japan Policy Research Institute, "Do As We Say, Not As We Did," *JPRI Critique,* Vol. IX, No. 6., Dec. 2002.

9. Jeffrey Sachs, Director, Center for International Development, Harvard University, "Whither Globalization and Its Architects in a Post–Sept. 11, Post–90s-Bubble World," Roundtable discussion transcript, Dec. 4, 2002, available at www.cepr.net/globalization/2_04)02_debate_transcript.htm, on file with Public Citizen.

10. "UN Chief: World Not Meeting Goals," Associated Press, *New York Times,* Oct. 1, 2002.

11. UNCTAD, *1997 Trade and Development Report: Overview,* Geneva: United Nations Conference on Trade and Development (1997), at 6.

12. World Bank, "Poverty Reduction and the World Bank, Progress in Operationalizing the WDR 2000/2001," Mar. 2002, at 12.

13. United Nations Development Program, *Human Development Report 2002: Deepening Democracy in a Fragmented World* (New York: Oxford University Press, 2002), at 18.

14. Christian Weller, Robert Scott, and Adam Hersh, Economic Policy Institute, "The Unremarkable Record of Liberalized Trade," Oct. 2001, at 5.

15. UNCTAD, *Least Developed Countries Report 2002,* at 9.

16. Ibid., at 115, Chart 33 at 117.

17. Dani Rodrick, Harvard University, "Trade Policy Reform as Institutional Reform," Aug. 2000, at 17.

18. World Bank, *World Development Indicators 2002,* at table 6.1.

19. Mark Weisbrot, Robert Naiman and Joyce Kim, "The Emperor Has No Growth: Declining Economic Growth Rates in the Era of Globalization," Center for Economic and Policy Research Briefing Paper, Sep. 26, 2000.

20. Mark Weisbrot, "The Mirage of Progress," *American Prospect,* Jan. 1, 2002.

21. Ibid.

22. Mark Weisbrot, *Globalization: A Primer* (Washington, D.C.: Preamble Center, 1999), at 13.

23. World Bank, *Global Economic Prospects and the Developing Countries,* Washington, D.C., 2002, at Table A3.I, at 234.

24. Ibid.

25. Asian Development Bank, "Asian Development Outlook 2003," Apr. 28, 2003.

26. Mark Weisbrot, "Think Globally, Act Nationally: The Case for National Economic Sovereignty," *The Nation,* Jun. 21, 1999.

27. UNCTAD, *The Least Developed Countries Report 2002,* at 118.

28. Mark Weisbrot and Neil Watkins, "Recent Experiences with International Financial Markets: Lessons for the Free Trade Area of the Americas," Apr. 1999, at 10.

29. Ibid., at 7–9.

30. Council of Economic Advisors, *1999 Economic Report of the President* (Washington, D.C.: U.S. Government Printing Office, 1999), at 226. The WTO's Financial Services Agreement is designed to further deregulate the financial-services sectors of WTO member countries.

31. Steven Radelet and Jeffrey Sachs, *The East Asian Financial Crisis: Diagnosis, Remedies, Prospects* (Cambridge, Mass.: Harvard Institute for International Development, 1998), at 14–17.

32. See International Labor Organization press release, "Asian Labor Market Woes Deepening," ILO/98/42, Dec. 2, 1998.

33. UNCTAD, *Trade and Development Report, 1998: Overview* (Geneva: United Nations Conference on Trade and Development, 1998), at 4.

34. Christopher Wren, "Sub-Saharan Africa: Growth in Peril," *New York Times,* Oct. 20, 1998.

35. Anthony Faiola, "Deep Recession Envelops Latin America," *Washington Post,* Aug. 5, 1999, at 1.

36. Weisbrot and Watkins, "Recent Experiences with International Financial Markets," at 7.

37. Ibid.

38. Ibid., at 11.

39. Carlos Salas, La Red de Investigadores y Sindicalistas Para Estudios Laborales (RISEL), "The Impact of NAFTA on Wages and Incomes in Mexico," Apr. 2001, on file with Public Citizen.

40. Tessie Borden, "Mexican Farmers Say NAFTA Ruins Lives, Forces Migration," *Arizona Republic,* Jan. 14, 2003.

41. Jane Bussey, "Hard Lessons to be Learned from Argentina's Financial Problems," *Miami Herald,* Jan. 8, 2002.

42. Mark Weisbrot, Co-Director, Center for Economic and Policy Research, Testimony before the Subcommittee on International Monetary Policy and Trade Committee on Financial Services, U.S. House of Representatives, Mar. 5, 2002, at 3.

43. Nicholas Moss, "Ecuador Seeks IMF Cure for Economic Ills," *Financial Times,* Aug. 20, 2002.

44. Patrice Jones, "Latin American Economies Reeling," *Chicago Tribune,* Aug. 18, 2002.

45. UNCTAD, *Trade and Development Report, 1998: Overview,* at 2.

46. Mark Weisbrot, *Globalization: A Primer,* at 10.

47. Weisbrot, Naiman and Kim, "The Emperor Has No Growth."

48. Ibid., at 10.

49. Ibid.

50. UNCTAD, *The Least Developed Countries Report 2002,* at 3.

51. Francisco Rodríguez and Dani Rodrick, University of Maryland and Harvard University, "Trade Policy and Economic Growth: A Skeptic's Guide to the Cross-National Evidence," Dec. 1999, at 37.

52. UNCTAD, *Trade and Development Report, 2002: Part II Developing Countries in World Trade,* April 29, 2002, at 52.

53. UNCTAD, *The Least Developed Countries Report 2002,* at 119.

54. Ibid.

55. U.S. Trade Representative Robert Zoellick, Conference on Productivity and Competitiveness, Santa Marta, Colombia, "Competing in the Global Economy: Five Ingredients for Success," Mar. 14, 2002.

56. Weisbrot, Naiman and Kim, "The Emperor Has No Growth.

57. Branko Milanovic, "The Two Faces of Globalization: Against Globalization as We Know It," Second Draft, May 2002, at 18.

58. Ian Goldin, Odin Knudsen, and Dominique van der Mensbrugghe, *Trade Liberalization: Global Economic Implication* (Paris: OECD; and Washington, D.C.: World Bank, 1993); See also Mark Weisbrot, Center for Economic and Policy Research, "Whither Globalization and its Architects in a Post–Sept. 11, Post–90s Bubble World."

59. Susan B. Epstein, Congressional Research Service "GATT: The Uruguay Round Agreement and Developing Countries," 1995; and Wayne Sandiford, Eastern Caribbean Central Bank, "GATT and the Uruguay Round," 1994.

60. Epstein, "GATT: The Uruguay Round Agreement and Developing Countries."

61. Martin Khor, "The End of the Uruguay Round and Third World Interests," Third World Network Briefing Paper, Feb. 1994, on file with Public Citizen.

62. Chakravarthi Raghavan, "Third World Exports Still Face Major Tariff Barriers," *SUNS* 4087, at 4.

63. Chakravarthi Raghavan, "*Recolonization: GATT, The Uruguay Round and the Third World* (Penang: Third World Network, 1990). See also Raghavan, "WTO: North-South Differences Continue After Seattle," *Third World Resurgence* no. 114–115 February/March 2000.

64. Chakravarthi Raghavan, "Poverty Will Continue to Grow, But Can be Dramatically Reduced," *SUNS* 5142, Jun. 18, 2002.

65. Statement of Martin Kohr, Director, Third World Network, at the Panel on Synergies between Liberalization, Environment, and Sustainable Development, WTO Symposium on Trade and Environment, Geneva, Mar. 16, 1999.

66. Chakravarthi Raghavan, "Third World Exports Still Face Major Tariff Barriers," *SUNS* 4087, at 4.

67. UNCTAD, *Least Developed Countries Report 2002,* at 11.

68. World Trade Organization, *International Trade Statistics 2002,* Sep. 30, 2002, at Table A20.

69. Alison Matiland, "Agriculture Accord Could Leave Poor Worst Off," *Financial Times,* Apr. 14, 1994.

70. "West Africa: Focus on Indigenous Peoples, Crop Diversification," *BRIDGES Weekly Trade News Digest,* vol. 2, no. 34, Sep. 7, 1998.

71. *International Trade Statistics 2002,* Sep. 30, 2002, at Table A20.

72. UNCTAD, *Trade and Development Report, 2002: Part II Developing Countries in World Trade,* April 29, 2002, at 58.

73. UNCTAD, *Least Developed Countries Report 2002,* at 9.

74. World Trade Organization, *International Trade Statistics 2002,* Sep. 30, 2002, at Table A20.

75. UNCTAD, *Least Developed Countries Report 2002,* at 10.

76. Ibid.

77. WTO, "International Trade Statistics 2002," Sep. 30, 2002, at Table A20.

78. Oxfam, "Rigged Rules and Double Standards," 2002, at 173.

79. Ibid.

80. Ibid., at 3.

81. Calculation by Public Citizen based on data from WTO, "World Trade Statistics 2002," Sep. 1, 2002, at table 4A.

82. Ibid.

83. WTO, "World Trade Statistics 2002," Sep. 1, 2002, at Table 4A; Dr. Charles McMilllion, "NAFTA and the World," Jul. 2001, at 37.

84. UNCTAD, *Least Developed Countries Report 2002,* Chart 31A, at 113.

85. UNCTAD, *Trade and Development Report 2002,* at 76.

86. Ibid., at 63.

87. Ibid., at 75.

88. Ibid., at 53.

89. Ibid., at 74.

90. Elisabeth Malkin, "Manufacturing Jobs Are Exiting Mexico," *New York Times,* Nov. 5, 2002.

91. Ibid.

92. UNCTAD, *Trade and Development Report 2002,* at 62.

93. Ibid., at 75.

94. Ibid., at 52.

95. Mark Weisbrot and Dean Baker, "The Relative Impact of Trade Liberalization on Developing Countries," Center for Economic and Policy Research Briefing Paper, Jun. 11, 2002, at 12.

96. United Nations Development Program (UNDP), *Human Development Report 1999* (Geneva: UNDP, 1999), at 3.

97. Ibid.

98. UNCTAD, *Least Developed Countries Report 2002,* at 17.

99. Christian Weller, Robert Scott, and Adam Hersh, Economic Policy Institute, "The Unremarkable Record of Liberalized Trade," Oct. 2001 at 1.

100. UNCTAD, *Least Developed Countries 1998 Report: Overview,* Geneva: United Nations Conference on Trade and Development (1998), at 3.

101. UNCTAD, *Least Developed Countries Report, 1998* at 3.

102. Harrison and Hanson, "Who Gains from Trade Reform? Some Remaining Puzzles," National Bureau of Economic Research Working Paper W6915, Jan. 1999.

103. World Bank, *Globalization, Growth and Poverty* (New York: Oxford University Press, 2002), at 5.

104. Weller, Scott, and Hersh, "The Unremarkable Record of Liberalized Trade," at 6.

105. Chakravarthi Raghavan, *Recolonization: GATT, The Uruguay Round and the Third World,* at 32 and 36–37.

106. Vinod Rege, "Developing Countries and Negotiations in the WTO," *Third World Economics,* no. 191, Aug. 16–31, 1998, at 3.

107. Ibid., at 4; Chakravarthi Raghavan, "Poverty Will Continue to Grow, But Can Be Dramatically Reduced," *SUNS* 5142, Jun. 18, 2002.

108. United Nations Development Program, *Human Development Report 2002, Deepening Democracy in a Fragmented World* (New York: Oxford University Press, 2002), at 121.

109. See C. Christopher Parlin, "WTO Dispute Settlement: Are Sufficient Resources Being Devoted to Enable the System to Function Effectively?" 32 *The International Lawyer* 863, Fall 1998.

110. Cited in Shefali Sharma, Institute for Agriculture and Trade Policy, "Expansion of a Top-Loaded Agenda: Are We Ready for an MAI in the WTO," *Geneva Update,* Issue 7, Oct. 4, 2002.

111. Aileen Kwa, "Power Politics at the WTO," *Focus on the Global South,* Bangkok, Thailand, 2002.

112. Sharma, "Expansion of a Top-Loaded Agenda."

113. The waiver—contained in a 1979 Decision on Differential and More Favourable Treatment, Reciprocity and Fuller Participation of Developing Countries (BISD S/103), (known as the 1979 Enabling Clause)—allows countries to waive MFN obligations to provide preferential tariff treatment to products of LDCs "without being required to extend the same tariffs to the products of any other Member . . . provided [such treatment is] on a generalized, non-reciprocal and non-discriminatory basis . . . [provided it does] not raise barriers or create undue difficulties for the trade of any other Member." Under GATT Article I on MFN, WTO members must treat all other WTO members the same. The WTO waiver for development programs allows industrialized and larger developing countries to provide preferential access to their markets to goods produced in LDCs.

114. See, inter alia, Maria Livanos Cattaui, "Trade Not Aid Is the Way Forward," *Bangkok Post,* Jun. 25, 2002; John Vidal, "Trade not aid," *The Guardian,* May 27, 2002; Then–Vice President Al Gore, "The United States and Russia: A Vision for the Future," remarks at the U.S. Military Academy West Point, Oct. 17, 1995.

115. For example, bananas, coffee, cocoa, beef, veal, sugar and rum.

116. See "Vulnerable ACP States," Lomé 2000, no. 7, Feb. 1998, at 2. The Lomé Convention has been instrumental in boosting the growth of vulnerable states.

117. "How to Become a Top Banana," *Time,* Feb. 7, 2000, at 44. Steven Bates, "Billion Dollar Banana Split," *The Guardian* (London), Mar. 6, 1999.

118. Donations of Carl Lindner, CEO of Chiquita Brands International for Election

Cycle 1998, retrieved from the Center for Responsive Politics' contributor database at www.crp.org, on file with Public Citizen.

119. Nicholas Stein, "Chiquita: Yes We Have No Profits," *Fortune,* November 26, 2001.

120. Richard Bernal, "Banana Trade Vital to Caribbean," *Journal of Commerce,* Feb. 3, 1999.

121. Ibid.

122. Brook Larmer, "Brawl Over Bananas," *Newsweek,* Apr. 28, 1997, at 44.

123. Mike Gallagher and Cameron McWhirter, "Violence and Drugs: Armed Soldiers Evict Residents in Chiquita Plan to Eliminate Union," *Cincinnati Enquirer,* May 3, 1998.

124. John Tomlinson, MEP (Member of European Parliament), "Going Bananas?" *EU Development Issues,* Autumn 1997, at 1.

125. Claire Godfrey, "The Importance of Europe's Banana Market to the Caribbean," Oxford: Oxfam UK (Mar. 1998), at 2.

126. Prime Minister Kenny Anthony of St. Lucia, quoted in, "Go Easy on Us in Trade, Islands Plead, Give Us Time to Adapt, Decrease Dependence on Bananas, They Say," *Miami Herald,* Dec. 11, 1997.

127. WTO, European Communities—Regime for the Importation, Sale and Distribution of Bananas (WT/DS27/R), Report of the Panel, May 22, 1997, at para. 144.

128. WTO, European Communities—Regime for the Importation, Sale and Distribution of Bananas (WT/DS27/AB/R), Report of the Appellate Body, Sep. 9, 1997, at para. 183.

129. Ibid., at paras. 255(e) and 255(i).

130. RAPID (The Spokesman's Service of the European Commission) press release, "The Commission Proposes to Modify the EU's Banana Regime," Jan. 14, 1998.

131. James Canute, "Caribbean, U.S. Officials Go Bananas After Ruling," *Journal of Commerce,* Feb. 26, 1998.

132. 105th Congress H.R. 4761, Sponsor: Rep. Phil Crane (R-IL), introduced Oct. 9, 1998.

133. "Zoellick Shies Away from 'Carosel' Use," *Washington Trade Daily,* May 24, 2001.

134. Bates, "Billion Dollar Banana Split."

135. U.S. Mission to the EU press release, "WTO Authorizes U.S. to Retaliate in Banana Dispute," Apr. 20, 1999.

136. WTO, European Communities—Regime for the Importation, Sale and Distribution of Bananas, Recourse to Article 21.5 by the European Communities (WT/DS27/RW/ECU), Report of the Panel, Apr. 12, 1999, at para. 7.1.

137. USTR, "Joint U.S.-EU Release on Banana Agreement," April 11, 2001.

138. U. S. Department of Commerce, International Trade Administration, "U.S. Balance of Trade by Region and Country," 1998–2002, found on ITA database at www.ita.doc.gov, on file with Public Citizen. The U.S. had a trade surplus of $8.1 billion with the region between 1998–2002.

139. "Trouble in Paradise," *The Economist,* Nov. 23, 2002.

140. Thomas W. Lippman, "An Appeal for a Banana Peace—General Suggests U.S. Trade Fight May Undercut Caribbean Drug Battle," *Washington Post,* June 6, 1996, at A27.

141. "Caricom Fires Warning Shot Against U.S. in Banana War," *BRIDGES Weekly Trade News Digest,* vol. 3, no. 9, Mar. 8, 1999.

142. Aileen Kwa, "Power Politics at the WTO," Focus on the Global South, Bangkok, Thailand, 2002.

143. Submission of the European Union, WT/GC/W/491, Feb. 27, 2003.

CHAPTER 7: THE WTO ON AGRICULTURE

1. Sophia Murphy, "Managing the Invisible Hand: Markets, Farmers and International Trade," Institute for Agriculture and Trade Policy, Apr. 2002.

2. Environmental Working Group, Farm Subsidy Database, Concentration of Payments for Farms in California, available online at www.ewg.org.

3. USDA, National Agricultural Statistics Service, "Farms and Land in Farms 2001," Feb. 2002.

4. "Texas, Iowa Win With Farm Bill," Associated Press, May 7, 2002.

5. Environmental Working Group, Farm Subsidy Database, "Farms Getting Government Payments, by State," 2001.

6. Environmental Working Group, "Green Acre$," Apr. 2000, at 11.

7. Ibid.

8. Devinder Sharma, "Trading in Food Insecurity," *Hindu Business Line,* Oct. 1, 2001.

9. Bureau of Labor Statistics' Consumer Price Index for all Food at Home, U.S. city average, series ID CUSR0000SAFF11, extracted Jun. 7, 2001.

10. This arithmetic was first published by James Goldsmith in *The Trap* (New York: Carroll & Graf, 1994).

11. "Chinese Farmers Face Bleak Future," BBC, Dec. 14, 2000.

12. Shai Oster, "Rural China at Crossroads with Nation's Entry into WTO," *San Francisco Chronicle,* Nov. 28, 2000.

13. David Brough, "Saving Crop Diversity Key to Winning War on Hunger," Reuters, Jul. 3, 2001.

14. USDA, Economic Research Service, "Agricultural Outlook: Statistical Indicators 2003," Jan. 2003.

15. U.S. Department of Commerce, U.S. Census Bureau, Foreign Trade Statistics, www.census.gov/foreign-trade/www, retrieved May 2003, on file with Public Citizen.

16. Ibid.

17. Randy Green, "The Uruguay Round Agreement on Agriculture," Symposium on the First Five Years of the WTO, Georgetown University Law Center, Jan. 21, 2000.

18. USDA, National Agricultural Statistics Service, "Farms and Land in Farms 2002," Feb. 2003, at 1.

19. USDA, Economic Research Service, "Agricultural Income and Finance Outlook," Sep. 25, 2002; USDA, Economic Research Service, "Agricultural Income and Finance Outlook," Oct. 17, 1996.

20. National Farmers Union Canada, "' Free Trade': Is It Working for Farmers," Aug. 6, 2002.

21. Ibid.

22. National Farmers Union United Kingdom, "UK Agricultural Review—Farming in Crisis," 2002.

23. GATT 1947, Art. XVI-3.

24. GATT 1947, Art. XI-2-c.

25. WTO, "Agriculture: Explanation—The Uruguay Round Reform Programme for Trade in Agriculture," available online at www.wto.org/english/tratop_e/ag_intro01_intro_e .htm, on file with Public Citizen.

26. WTO, AoA, Art. 13.

27. WTO, AoA, Art. 1-f.

28. Sophia Murphy, Institute for Agriculture and Trade Policy, "Managing the Invisible Hand: Markets, Farmers and International Trade," Apr. 2002 at 24.

29. Food First, "Statement to Director General of the WTO on the Agreement on Agriculture," Nov. 13, 2002; and Third World Network, *The Multilateral Trading System: A Development Perspective,*" Dec. 2001, at 54.

30. Third World Network, *The Multilateral Trading System.*

31. WTO, AA, Art. 4 and note 1; see also, WTO, "Agriculture: Explanation—Market Access," available online at www.wto.org/ english/tratop_e/agric_e/agric_e.htm, on file with Public Citizen.

32. Ibid.

33. William D. Dobson and Robert A. Cropp, Univ. of Wisconsin–Madison, Department of Agricultural Economics, "Economic Impacts of the GATT Agreement on the U.S. Dairy Industry," Paper No. 50, Mar. 1995, at 2.

34. WTO, "Agriculture: Explanation—Market Access," on file with Public Citizen.

35. WTO, AoA Art. 9; see also WTO, "Agriculture: Explanation," on file with Public Citizen.

36. WTO, AoA, Art. 9-4.

37. WTO, AoA, Art. 9-1.

38. WTO, AoA, Art. 6 and Annex 3; see also WTO "Agriculture: Explanation."

39. WTO, AoA, Annex 2; see also WTO "Agriculture: Expalantion."

40. Third World Network, "The Multilateral Trading System: A Development Perspective," Dec. 2001, at 54.

41. "SURVEY–Mexico: Funds for Farmers Needed for Future: AGRICULTURE: After years of neglect and being starved of resources, peasants are now seen as engine for further economic growth," *Financial Times,* Dec. 14, 2000; Sharma, "Trading in Food Insecurity."

42. Alejandro Nadal, "The Environmental and Social Impacts of Economic Liberalization on Corn Production in Mexico," study commissioned by Oxfam Great Britain and WWF International, Sep. 2000.

43. Murphy, "Managing the Invisible Hand: Markets, Farmers and International Trade."

44. "Family Farmers Face Crisis; Global Forces Threaten to Plow Farms Under," *Orlando Sentinel,* Jul. 10, 1999.

45. Murphy, "Managing the Invisible Hand."

46. "ACGA President Dittrich Compared 250% Consumer Food Price Increase to Declining Farm Prices," *The Agribusiness Examiner,* Issue #71, Apr. 24, 2000.

47. Census Bureau Consumer Price Index for all Food at Home, U.S. city average, series ID CUSR0000SAFF11, extracted Jun. 7, 2001, on file with Public Citizen.

48. "Study Reveals Meat Consumers Pay More, Feedlots Continue to Receive Less While Processors Fatten Profits," *The Agribusiness Examiner,* Issue #92, Oct. 26, 2000.

49. Testimony of the Canadian National Farmers Union before the Senate Standing Committee on Agriculture and Forestry, "The Farm Crisis, EU Subsidies, and Agribusiness Market Power," Feb. 17, 2000, on file with Public Citizen.

50. Nadal, "The Environmental and Social Impacts of Economic Liberalization on Corn Production in Mexico."

51. Institute for Agriculture and Trade Policy, "United States Dumping on World Agricultural Markets," Cancún Series Paper No. 1, 2002.

52. Grain and Milling Annual Report, 2002; Mary Hendrickson and William Heffernan, Department of Rural Sociology, University of Missouri, "Concentration of Agriculture Markets," Feb. 2002.

53. "Consolidation in Food Retailing and Dairy: Implications for Farmers and Consumers in a Global Food System," Mary Hendrickson, Ph.D., William Heffernan, Ph.D., Philip Howard and Judith Heffernan, Department of Rural Sociology, University of Missouri, Jan. 8, 2001, at executive summary, on file with Public Citizen.

54. Hendrickson and Heffernan, "Concentration of Agriculture Markets."

55. "The Seed Giants: Who Owns Whom? Seed Industry Consolidation Update 2000," Rural Advancement Foundation International, Dec. 21, 2000.

56. "Erosion, Technological Transformation and Corporate Concentration in the 21st Century," Dag Hammarskjöld Foundation and Rural Advancement Foundation International, Apr. 11, 2001, at 74.

57. Vandana Shiva, *Stolen Harvest* (Cambridge, Mass.: South End Press, 2000), at 10.

58. "Representative Farms Economic Outlook for the January 2001 FAPRI/AFPC Baseline," Food and Agriculture Policy Center, Department of Agriculture Economics, Texas A&M University, AFPC Working Paper 01-1, Jan. 2001.

59. USDA Economic Research Service, "Agriculture Income and Finance Annual Lender Issue," AIS-78, Feb. 26, 2002, at 5.

60. Testimony of the Canadian National Farmers Union to the Canadian Standing Committee on Foreign Affairs and International Trade, "The Effects of the WTO and FTAA Negotiations on Farmers' Orderly Marketing Agencies, Safety Nets, and Agricultural Programs," Apr. 27, 1999, on file with Public Citizen.

61. Testimony of the Canadian National Farmers Union before the Senate Standing Committee on Agriculture and Forestry, "The Farm Crisis, EU Subsidies, and Agribusiness Market Power," Feb. 17, 2000.

62. "Business Week 1000: Alphabetical List of Companies," *Business Week,* Mar. 28, 1994, at 129; "Fortune 500 Largest U.S. Corporations," *Fortune,* Apr. 16, 2001, at F-52.

63. "The Economics of Famine," *Newshour with Jim Lehrer,* Oct. 15, 1998.

64. Food and Agriculture Organization, "Reducing Poverty and Hunger: The Critical Role of Financing for Food, Agriculture and Rural Development," Mar. 2002, at 1 and 11.

65. Ibid., at 8; FAO, "The State of Food Insecurity in the World 2002," 2002.

66. FAO, "The State of Food Insecurity in the World 2002," 2002.

67. Food and Agriculture Organization, "Reducing Poverty and Hunger: The Critical Role of Financing for Food, Agriculture and Rural Development," at 9–10.

68. Michael O'Boyle, "Growing Farm Crisis Will Shut Out Millions," *The News* (Mexico), Jul. 26, 2001.

69. Nadal, "The Environmental and Social Impacts of Economic Liberalization on Corn Production in Mexico."

70. Government of Mexico, National Nutrition Institute, 1997, cited in *Gene Wars.* Steven Stuppan and Karen Lehman, *Food Security and Agricultural Trade Under NAFTA* (Minneapolis: Institute for Agricultural and Trade Policy, Jul. 11, 1997), at 4.

71. Stuppan and Lehman, *Food Security and Agricultural Trade Under NAFTA,* at 4.

72. Nadal, "The Environmental and Social Impacts of Economic Liberalization on Corn Production in Mexico."

73. "Mexico: Senator Says U.S. Agriculture Subsidies Mean NAFTA Should Be Renegotiated," BBC, Nov. 4, 2000.

74. "Mexican Government Tries to Calm Discontent Over Tortilla Prices," Associated Press Worldstream, Jan. 7, 1999.

75. "Rise in Tortilla Prices," *National Public Radio–Morning Edition,* Jan. 20, 2000.

76. "Tortilla Price Hike Hits Mexico's Poorest," *Washington Post,* Jan. 12, 1999.

77. Nadal, "The Environmental and Social Impacts of Economic Liberalization on Corn Production in Mexico."

78. "Reform to New Trade Pact May Hurt Small Farmers," Interpress Service, Feb. 27, 2001.

79. Nadal, "The Environmental and Social Impacts of Economic Liberalization on Corn Production in Mexico."

80. "NAFTA, Mexican Agriculture Policy and U.S. Employment," Statement of Karen Lehman, Senior Fellow, Institute for Agriculture and Trade Policy before the Employment, Housing and Aviation Subcommittee, Oct. 28, 1993. (Mexican Undersecretary of Agriculture Luis Tellez predicted that NAFTA would push an annual average of one million farmers and their families off of their farms each year for ten years.)

81. "Mexico's Average Workers Left Behind Amid Recent Economic Gains," *Dallas Morning News,* May 26, 1999.

82. Nadal, "The Environmental and Social Impacts of Economic Liberalization on Corn Production in Mexico."

83. USDA, Foreign Agriculture Service, U.S. Maize Exports to Mexico 1993–2001; "Growing Troubles in Mexico," *Los Angeles Times,* Jan. 17, 2000.

84. Ginger Thompson, "NAFTA to Open Floodgates, Engulfing Rural Mexico," *New York Times,* Dec. 19, 2002.

85. Nadal, "The Environmental and Social Impacts of Economic Liberalization on Corn Production in Mexico."

86. "A New Sun Poverty; A People in Want; Poverty Stalks the Nation, But Nowhere Is it Worse than in the Countryside," *Houston Chronicle*, Nov. 26, 2000.

87. "Población y Número de Localidades," *Indicadores Sociodemografica de Mexico, 1930–2000,* Instituto Nacional de Estadistica, Geografia e Informática (INEGI). Urban areas are those with 500,000 or more inhabitants. Rural areas are those with fewer than 2,499 inhabitants.

88. Stephen Leahy, "Trade-Mexico: Farmers Take to Streets Over New NAFTA Rules," *Interpress Service,* Jan. 3, 2003.

99. "Reform to New Trade Pact May Hurt Small Farmers," Interpress Service, Feb. 27, 2001.

90. Leahy, "Trade-Mexico: Farmers Take to Streets Over New NAFTA Rules."

91. Tessie Borden, "Mexican Farmers Say NAFTA Ruins Lives, Forces Migration," *Arizona Republic,* Jan. 14, 2003.

92. Sara Silver and John Authers, "Mexico Divided Over Agricultural Agreements," *Financial Times,* Jan. 6, 2003; Thompson, "NAFTA to Open Floodgates, Engulfing Rural Mexico."

93. Leahy, "Trade-Mexico: Farmers Take to Streets Over New NAFTA Rules."

94. "Mexican Farmers Renew Protests Against NAFTA Tariff Openings," Associated Press, Jan. 20, 2003.

95. R. Gommes, "Climatic Risk Management," U.N. Food and Agriculture Organization, FAO Research Extension Division, May 28, 1999.

96. WTO TRIPs Agreement, Article 27-3-b.

97. Tom Bearden, "High-Tech Crops," *Newshour with Jim Lehrer,* Aug. 12, 1999.

98. GianCarlo Moschini, "Patented Agriculture," *Iowa Ag Review,* vol. 8, no. 2, Septemberr. 2002.

99. Michael P. Ryan, *Knowledge Diplomacy: Global Competition and the Politics of International Property* (Washington, D.C.: Brookings Institution Press, 1998), at 69. (Before the Uruguay Round, Pfizer and IBM established the IPC to advance their positions and to ensure the finalization of TRIPs in their favor and were joined by Monsanto, Merck, General Electric, DuPont, Warner Communications, Hewlett-Packard, Bristol-Meyers, FMC Corporation, General Motors, Johnson & Johnson, and Rockwell International.)

100. Mark Lynas, "The World Trade Organization and GMOs," *Consumer Policy Review,* Nov. 1, 1999.

101. WTO, Ministerial Declaration, Ministerial Conference Fourth Session, WT/MIN(01)/ DEC/W/1, Nov. 14, 2001, at para. 19.

102. Consumer Unity and Trust Society, "GATT, Patent Laws and Implications for India," Jun. 1995.

103. WTO, India—Patent Protection for Pharmaceutical and Agri Chemical Products, First Submission of the United States, Mar. 6, 1997, in 2–3.

104. The Patents Act (Act No. 39 of 1970), enacted Apr. 20, 1972.

105. India's Patent Act banned patents for substances "intended for use, or capable of being used, as food or as medicine or drug." Section 15(2) of the Patents Act states that the patent office "shall refuse" an application in respect to a substance that is not patentable.

106. All WTO countries were required to implement most aspects of the Uruguay Round as a "single understanding," however, certain agreements had phased-in application dates for developing countries including TRIPs.

107. WTO, India—Patent Protection for Pharmaceutical and Agricultural Chemical Products (WT/DS50), Complaint by the U.S.

108. WTO, India—Patent Protection for Pharmaceutical and Agricultural Chemical Products (WT/DS50/R), Report of the Panel, Sep. 5, 1997, at paras. 6.10–6.12.

109. Ibid., at paras. 7.26–7.28.

110. "India's New Patent Law 'By Year-End,'" *Marketletter* (London), Jul. 26, 1999.

111. Indian Patents Act (Amendment) 2002, Jun. 2002, on file with Public Citizen. Vandana Shiva, "Government Exploits Time of Political Crisis to Pass Second IPR Amendment," Memorandum to IFG Board and Associates, March 2002, on file with Public Citizen.

112. Ibid.

113. Interview with Vandana Shiva by Lori Wallach, Public Citizen, February 2003, on file with Public Citizen. Monsanto holds at least four separate patents on Bt technology. U.S. Patent and Trademark Office, U.S. Patent No. 6,153,814, Nov. 28, 2001; U.S. Patent No. 6,060,594, May 9, 2001; U.S. Patent No. 6,063,597, May 16, 2000; U.S. Patent No. 6,110,464, Aug. 29, 2000.

114. Ann Fitzgerald, "Researchers Seek Ways to Keep Crops Where They Belong," *Des Moines Register,* Nov. 24, 2002.

115. Craig Wong, "Trail Hears Sask Farmer Sprayed Roundup to Determine Resistance of Canola Crop," *Canadian Press,* Jun. 9, 2000.

116. "Convention on Biological Diversity," Jun. 5, 1992 at 8(j).

117. Resolution 5/89, "Farmers' Rights," Report of the Conference of FAO, Twenty-fifth Session, Rome, International Undertaking on Plant Genetic Resources, Nov. 11–29, 1989, at Annex to the FAO International Undertaking on Plant Genetic Resources.

118. Grain and Kalparriksh, "Traditional Knowledge of Biodiversity in Asia-Pacific: Problems of Piracy and Protection," Nov. 2002 at 7, on file with Public Citizen.

119. Rural Advancement Foundation International, "Basmati Rice Patent," *Geno-Type,* Apr. 1, 1998.

120. WTO, TRIPs Agreement at Article 64.1.

121. Rural Advancement Foundation International, "Plant Breeders Wrongs," Aug. 1998, at 19.

122. Thai Network on Biodiversity and Community Rights, "Rationale and Background to the Draft Thai Traditional Medicine and Local Knowledge Protection and Promotion Act as approved in principle by the cabinet on Jul. 15, 1997," on file with Public Citizen.

123. "Thailand: Tussle Over Fungi Strains Brings Painful Lessons," InterPress Service, Sep. 4, 1998.

124. Ibid.

125. Arindam Mukherjee, "Say No To Jasmati," *Outlook,* Jun. 25, 1997, and "Farmers Protest Copycat 'Jasmine' Rice," InterPress Service, May 13, 1998.

126. Action Group on Erosion, Technology and Concentration, press release, "U.S.

Acquisition of Aromatic Rice Breaks Trust, Tramples Farmers, Threatens Trade and Seed Treaty Talks," Oct. 30, 2001, on file with Public Citizen.

127. Action Group on Erosion, Technology and Concentration, "Biopiracy +10: Captain Hook Awards 2002," *Communique,* Issue 75, Mar./Apr. 2002, at 5.

128. Nicola Bullard, Focus on the Global South, "Thai Farmers, AIDS Activists March on U.S. Embassy," Nov. 9, 2001.

129. Phusadee Arunmas, "Thailand Won't Yield on Jasmati," *Bangkok Post,* Nov. 28, 2002.

130. Letter from the U.S. State Department to the Royal Thai Government, Apr. 21, 1997, on file with Public Citizen.

131. Ibid.

132. Thailand, 2000 Country Report on Economic Policy and Trade Practices, Bureau of Economic and Business Affairs, U.S. Department of State, March 2001.

133. Kristin Dawkins, "U.S. Unilateralism: a Threat to Global Sustainability," *Bridges Weekly Trade News Digest,* Vol. 1, No. 4, Oct. 1997.

134. Ibid.

135. Intellectual Property Research Institute of Australia, "Traditional Knowledge, Genetic Resources, Folklore and Biodiversity," University of Melbourne, May 2002, available at www.law.unimelb.edu.au/lpria/research/trad_know.html and on file at Public Citizen.

136. Scott Simon, "Profile: Controversy Over Patent Held by One American Farmer for a Yellow Bean with Origins to the Incas," *National Public Radio,* Jun. 9, 2001.

137. Ibid.

138. Patent application of Larry M. Proctor for field bean cultivar named enola, Nov. 15, 1996, Appl. No. 749449, contained in U.S. Patent to Proctor for field bean cultivar named enola, U.S. Patent 5,894,079, Apr. 13, 1999.

139. U.S. Patent to Proctor for field bean cultivar named enola, U.S. Patent 5,894,079, Apr. 13, 1999.

140. Scott Simon, "Profile: Controversy Over Patent Held by One American Farmer for a Yellow Bean with Origins to the Incas."

141. "Litigation Sprouts Up over Claim to Invent Bean," *Denver Post,* Mar. 21, 2000.

142. Ibid.

143. Ibid.

144. Laura Carlsen, "Little, Yellow . . . Different?" *Latin Trade Magazine,* Aug. 1, 2001.

145. Ibid.

146. Scott Simon, "Profile: Controversy Over Patent Held by One American Farmer for a Yellow Bean with Origins to the Incas."

147. "Patent on Small Yellow Beans Provokes Cry of Biopiracy," *New York Times,* Mar. 20, 2001.

148. "Litigation Sprouts Up over Claim to Invent Bean," *Denver Post.*

149. "U.S. Firm in Bean Patent Row; NGOs Accuse Firm of Biopiracy," *Mexico & NAFTA Report,* Latin American Newsletters, Ltd., Nov. 28, 2000.

150. Rural Advancement Foundation International, "Enola Bean Patent Challenged," press release, Jan. 5, 2001, on file with Public Citizen.

151. Ibid.

152. "Patent on Small Yellow Beans Provokes Cry of Biopiracy," *New York Times.*

153. Ibid.

154. John Accola, "No Small Beans: Inventor Sues Growers Over Seeds," *Rocky Mountain News,* Dec. 1, 2001.

155. Reed Fujii, "U.S. Dry Bean Production Business Gets Lucky," Knight-Ridder, Sep. 15, 2002.

156. John Accola, "Pod-Ners Drops Suit Stemming from Bean Patent," *Rocky Mountain News,* Nov. 21, 2002.

157. Matthew Stilwell and Brennan Van Dyke, An Activist's Handbook on Genetically Modified Organisms and the WTO, Center for International Environmental Law, Washington D.C., Mar. 1999, at 2–5.

158. WTO, Agreement on Technical Barriers to Trade, at Article 2.2.

159. OECD, "Safety Evaluation of Foods Derived by Modern Biotechnology," May 1993.

160. "Bill Proposes 5-year Ban on GMO," *Philippines Daily Inquirer,* Aug. 24, 2001.

161. U.S. Consumer's Choice Council, Letter to the Honorable Frank Loy, Undersecretary for Global Affairs, U.S. Department of State, Feb. 9, 1999.

162. R. Jorgensen and B. Andersen, "Spontaneous Hybridization Between Oilseed Rape and Weed: A Risk of Growing Genetically Engineered Modified Oilseed Rape," *American Journal of Botany* 81, 1995, at 1620–26; B. Hileman, "Views Differ Sharply Over Benefits, Risks of Agricultural Biotechnology," *Chemical and Engineering Microbiology,* Aug. 21, 1995.

163. "Roundup Unready," *New York Times,* Feb. 19, 2003.

164. Tom Clarke, "Corn Could Make Cotton Pests Bt. Resistant," *Nature,* Dec. 2, 2002.

165. Charles Clover and George Jones, "Government Stifled Report on GM Risks," *Daily Telegraph,* Feb. 17, 1999. See also report by the UK House of Commons Science and Technology Committee, May 12, 1999, published at www.parliament.the-stationery-office.co.uk/pa/cm199899/cmselect/cmsctech/286/28602.htm, on file with Public Citizen.

166. U.S. Consumer's Choice Council, Letter to the Honorable Frank Loy, Undersecretary for Global Affairs.

167. Vandana Shiva, *Biopiracy: The Plunder of Nature and Knowledge* (Boston: South End Press, 1997), at 88.

168. Ibid. at 89.

169. "Top Scientist Backs Calls for GM Safety Screen," *Guardian* (London), Mar. 9, 1999.

170. "Biotech: The Pendulum Swings Back," *Environment and Health Weekly,* No. 649, May 6, 1999.

171. "Royal Society Dismisses 'Flawed' GM Food Research," *Guardian* (London), May 18, 1999; "Hot Potato," *Guardian* (London), May 19, 1999.

172. Soil Association "Seeds of Doubt: North American Farmers' Experiences of GM Crops," press release, Sep. 2002.

173. "UN Talks on Genetically Modified Trade Protocol Collapse," *European Chemical News—CBNB,* Mar. 24, 1999.

174. Chee Yoke Ling, "U.S. Behind Collapse of Cartagena Biosafety Talks," *Third World Resurgence,* No. 104/105, Apr./May 1999. Chee Yoke Ling, "An International Biosafety Protocol: The Fight Is Still On," *Third World Resurgence,* No. 93, May 1998.

175. Lavanya Rajamani, "The Cartagena Protocol—A Battle Over Trade or Biosafety?" *Third World Resurgence,* No. 104/105, Apr./May 1999.

176. Ricardo Maldonado, "Biotech Industry Discusses Trade," Associated Press, Feb. 22, 1999.

177. The U.S. is not a party to the Convention on Biological Diversity, so had no vote at the negotiations. However, it was still entitled to participate in the negotiations, and essentially "voted" through the Miami Group initiative. Ling, "U.S. Behind Collapse of Cartagena Biosafety Talks."

178. Andrew Pollack, "U.S. and Allies Block Threat on Genetically Altered Goods," *New York Times,* Feb. 24, 1999.

179. Ling, "U.S. Behind Collapse of Cartagena Biosafety Talks."

180. "EU Accuses US, Others of 'Extreme' Positions That Will Block Biosafety Protocol," *International Environment Reporter,* Feb. 17, 1999, at 136.

181. Ibid.

182. Rajamani: "The Cartagena Protocol—A Battle Over Trade or Biosafety?"

183. Gurdial Singh Nijar, "Biosafety Protocol Talks to Resume in September," *South-North Development Monitor,* Jul. 4, 1999.

184. USDA, Foreign Agriculture Service, "International Protocol on Biosafety: What It Means for Agriculture," Feb. 2001.

185. African Civil Society Group, "Statement in Support of the Zambian and Zimbabwean Government Position to Reject Food Aid Contaminated by Genetic Engineering," Aug. 31, 2002, on file with Public Citizen.

186. Raj Patel with Alexa Delwiche, Food First, "The Profits of Famine," *Backgrounder,* Vol. 8, No. 4, Fall 2002, at 1.

187. Ibid.

188. Fred Guterl, "The Fear of Food," *Newsweek,* Jan. 27, 2003.

189. Geoffrey Lean, "U.S. Policy on Aid is 'Wicked'—Meacher," *The Independent* (UK), Dec. 1, 2002.

190. Guterl, "The Fear of Food."

191. Ashok B. Sharma, "GM Corn-Soya Import Issue Raised to Appellate Body," (India) *Financial Express,* Jan 13, 2003.

192. Elizabeth Becker, "U.S. Threatens to Act Against Europeans Over Modified Foods," *New York Times,* Jan. 10, 2003.

193. USTR, 2003 National Trade Estimate Report on Foreign Trade Barriers (2003) at 212–13.

194. USTR Robert Zoellick, Statement before the Committee on Ways and Means, U.S. House of Representatives, Feb. 7, 2002.

195. USTR, 1999 National Trade Estimate Report on Foreign Trade Barriers (1999), at 16.

196. USTR press release, "Veneman and Zoellick Pleased with Efforts to Keep American Biotech Farm Product Moving," Mar. 7, 2002.

197. GeneEthics press release, "Rejected Corn Dumped in Australia," Jan. 8, 2003.

198. Ibid.

199. Polly Stewart, "Rich Countries Urged to Further Cut Farm Subsidies to Reduce Global Poverty," Associated Press, Nov. 13, 2001.

200. Paul Geitner, "Pressure Mounts on European Union as Deadline Approaches for Trade Deal," Associated Press, Nov. 13, 2001.

201. WTO, Ministerial Declaration, Ministerial Conference Fourth Session, Doha, WT/MIN(01)/DEC/W/1, Nov. 14, 2001, at para. 13.

202. Ibid.

203. Ibid.

204. Ibid.

205. Ibid.

206. Via Campasina press release, "Via Campasina Strongly Condems Doha Declaration," Nov. 15, 2001.

207. Mark Ritchie, "Agriculture and Food Impacts of the Doha Declaration," Institute for Trade and Agriculture Policy, Nov. 2001.

208. IISD, "The Development Box: A Briefing for the SDC," 2002.

209. Jennifer del Rosario-Malonzo, "WTO Doha Meet in Retrospect: A Whole New Round," *IBON Features*, No. 44, Dec. 2001.

210. Daniel Pruzin, "Major Traders Throw Cold Water on Calls For 'Development Box' in Agriculture Talks," *International Trade Reporter*, Vol. 19 No. 7, Feb. 14, 2002 at 262.

211. Shefali Sharma, Institute for Agriculture and Trade Policy, "Reality Check: 12 Months to Mexico and the Fifth Ministerial," *Geneva Update*, No. 6, Aug. 8, 2002.

212. Aileen Kwa, Focus on the Global South, "WTO Agriculture Negotiations," Oct. 2002.

213. European Commission, "WTO and Agriculture: European Commission Proposes More Market Opening, Less Trade Distorting Support and a Radically Better Deal for Developing Countries," IP/02/1892, Dec. 16, 2002.

214. Ibid.

215. Duncan Green of CAFOD and Tim Rice of Action Aid, "Development and Agriculture in the WTO: A Comparison Between the Development Box, the EU's Food Security Box and the Harbinson Draft Modalities," Feb. 14, 2003.

216. Trade New Zealand, the New Zealand government's trade promotion agency press release, "EU Agriculture Proposal Falls Short: New Zealand Trade Minister," Dec. 19, 2002.

217. Charlotte Denny, "WTO Calls for Cuts in Farm Subsidies," *The Guardian* (London), Feb. 13, 2003.

218. Yuri Kageyama, "WTO Summit Ends with No Farm Tariff Deal," Associated Press, Feb. 15, 2003.

219. European Commission, press release, "WTO and Agriculture: 'Harbinson Draft Won't Bridge the Gaps,' EU Farm Commissioner Fischler Says," IP/03/231, Feb. 13, 2003.

220. EU press release, "Facts and Figures on EU Trade in Agricultural Products: Open to Trade, Open to Developing Countries," MEMO/02/296, Dec. 16, 2002.

221. Denny, "WTO Calls for Cuts in Farm Subsidies."

222. "WTO Ministers Meet in Tokyo on Farm Trade, Access to Cheap Drugs," Agence France Presse, Feb. 14, 2003.

223. Denny, "WTO Calls for Cuts in Farm Subsidies."

224. Australia Office of Trade Negotiations, Department of Foreign Affairs and Trade, "Overview Paper on Agriculture Modalities," *WTO Doha Round Bulleting*, Iss. 2003/05, Feb. 14, 2003.

225. U.S. Trade Representative Zoellick, transcript of press conference following WTO Informal Ministerial Meeting, Feb. 16, 2003.

226. Institute for Agriculture and Trade Policy press release, "New WTO Agriculture Text Ignores Export Dumping and Developing Country Proposals," Feb. 14, 2003.

227. Green and Rice, "Development and Agriculture in the WTO: A Comparison Between the Development Box, the EU's Food Security Box and the Harbinson Draft Modalities."

228. Via Campesina press release, "Via Campasina Prepares World Struggle Journey," Jan. 26, 2003.

CHAPTER 8: HUMAN AND LABOR RIGHTS UNDER THE WTO

1. WTO, Singapore Ministerial Declaration (WT/MIN(96)/DEC), Dec. 13, 1996, at 4, on file with Public Citizen.

2. "WTO to Decide Case Against Myanmar Curbs," *The Journal of Commerce*, Oct. 22, 1998.

3. *Crosby et al. v. National Foreign Trade Council*, U.S. Sup. Ct., No. 99-474, Jun. 19, 2000.

4. One prominent example of race-to-the-bottom employment is Nike, which first manufactured its sneakers in Taiwan and South Korea. When workers attempted to organize for better wages in the 1970s, Nike pulled out and began production in Indonesia, the People's Republic of China and Vietnam. See *Global Exchange*, "Nike Chronology," Nov. 1997. Other examples include the numerous U.S.-based manufacturing firms that have relocated to Mexico under NAFTA, or that have threatened to relocate to Mexico under NAFTA to discourage unionization and to depress wages. See Kate Bronfenbrenner, "Final Report: The Effects of Plant Closing or Threat of Plant Closing on the Right of Workers to Organize," Submitted to the Labor Secretariat of the North American Commission for Labor Cooperation, Sep. 30, 1996; see also Public Citizen's Global Trade Watch database containing U.S. Department of Labor data on companies that have used NAFTA to shift employment to Mexico, where the U.S. Bureau of Labor Statistics has determined that manufacturing wages are less than 10% of those in the U.S., at http://www.citizen.org/pctrade/taa97acs/KEYTAA.html.

5. Charles Kernaghan, *Made in China: Behind the Label*, Special Report (New York: National Labor Committee, 1998), cited in Robert E. Scott, "China Can Wait: WTO Accession Deal Must Include Enforceable Labor Rights, Real Commercial Benefits," Economic Policy Institute, Briefing Paper, May 1999, at 2, on file with Public Citizen.

6. George Kouros, "Workers' Health Is on the Line, Occupational Health and Safety in the Maquiladoras," *Borderlines* 47, vol. 6, no. 6, Aug. 1998.

7. Sarah H. Cleveland, "Global Labor Rights and the Alien Tort Claims Act," 76 *Texas Law Review* 1533 May 1998.

8. *John Doe I et al. v. UNOCAL Corp. et al.,* United States District Court for the Central District of California, Case No. CV 96-6959 and CV 96-6112. The most recent development in the saga is a positive one, with the Ninth Circuit Court of Appeals rejecting Unocal's motion to dismiss. The full text of the opinion is available at http://www.laborrights.org/projects/corporate/unocal/unocal091802.pdf, visited Dec. 5, 2002.

9. Dipak Basu, "Lost Childhood: WTO's Failure to Check Evils of Child Labor," *The Statesman* (India), Feb. 4, 2002.

10. See, e.g., David R. Henderson, *The Joy of Freedom: An Economist's Odyssey* (New York: Financial Times Prentice Hall, 2001). For somewhat more classic perspectives agreeing with the proposition, see the work of Simon Kuznets, winner of the Nobel Prize in Economics in 1971.

11. Brian Langille, "General Reflections on the Relationship of Trade and Labor (Or: Fair Trade Is Free Trade's Destiny)," in *Fair Trade and Harmonization: Volume 2, Legal Analysis,* Bhagwati, J. and R. Hudec, eds. (Cambridge, Mass.: M.I.T. Press, 1996).

12. See, e.g., Joseph E. Stiglitz, *Globalization and its Discontents* (New York: Norton, 2002).

13. Jagdish Bhagwati, "Why Free Capital Mobility May Be Hazardous to Your Health," Nov. 7, 1998, available at http://www.columbia.edu/~jb38/papers/NBER_comments.pdf, visited Dec. 3, 2002.

14. Amartya Sen, *Development as Freedom* (New York: Anchor Books, 2000).

15. Cass Sunstein, *Free Markets and Social Justice* (New York: Oxford University Press, 1997), at 384.

16. Ibid., at 151.

17. Nike's internal documents showed in November 1997 that Vietnamese workers were being paid nineteen cents or less per hour. See Global Exchange, Nike Chronology, Nov. 1997.

18. The ILO has gathered significant data on labor-rights abuses in EPZs worldwide and is urging governments to ensure the fulfillment of their international and domestic obligations with regard to labor rights. See International Labor Organization press release, "ILO Meeting Calls for Improved Social and Labour Conditions in Export Processing Zones and End to Restrictions On Trade Union Rights," ILO/98/35, Oct. 2, 1998.

19. Kouros, "Border Briefs: Study Finds Maquila Wages Insufficient," *Borderlines* 47, vol. 6, no. 6, Aug. 1998.

20. "Study Finds Maquila Wages Insufficient," *Borderlines 81,* Vol. 9, No. 8, Sep. 2001.

21. Ibid.

22. INEGI, "Manufacturing Industry Productivity Index, Selected Countries," Dec. 16, 2002; Carlos Salas, La Red de Investigadores y Sindicalistas Para Estudios Laborales (RISEL), *The Impact of NAFTA on Wages and Incomes in Mexico,* Apr. 2001.

23. Robert Scott, Economic Policy Institute, "Fast Track to Lost Jobs: Trade Deficits and Manufacturing Decline are the Legacies of NAFTA and the WTO," Oct. 2001.

24. U.S. Business Industry Council, "U.S. Trade Flows: Trade-Loser Industries Back Fast Track," *Globalization Factline,* Dec. 13, 2001.

25. "High-Paid Jobs the Latest U.S. Export," *Los Angeles Times,* Apr. 2, 2002.

26. Less than 10% of the U.S. private-sector workforce is now represented by a labor union, after a steady decline throughout the era of "free trade." Union representation began its decline in the 1950s, but the process accelerated sharply with the advent of the aggressive liberalization of trade and capital flows in the late 1970s and early 1980s. From 1953 to 1979, union representation declined by one third, from 36% of all workers (public and private sector) to 24%. From 1979 to 2001, union representation declined by 50%, to 12% of the workforce.

27. Productivity and median and average compensation, 1973–2001, Economic Policy Institute, Washington, D.C., www.epinet.org.

28. ILO, Declaration on Fundamental Principles and Rights at Work, Jun. 1998, available at http://www.ilo.org/public/english/standards/decl/declaration/text, visited Nov. 27, 2002.

29. Ibid.

30. Morton Kondracke, "Battles in Seattle Make Free Trade an Election Issue," *Roll Call,* Dec. 9, 1999.

31. Helen Dewar and Cindy Skrzycki, "House Scraps Ergonomics Regulation," *Washington Post,* Mar. 8, 2001.

32. Marla Dickerson, Joseph Menn, and Peter Gosselin, "West Coast Ports Ordered to Reopen," *Los Angeles Times,* Oct. 9, 2002.

33. Ron Hutcheson, "850,000 Federal Jobs Could Go Private," *Philadelphia Inquirer,* Nov. 15, 2002.

34. Because it is so toothless, the NAFTA labor side agreement does not merit discussion in this regard.

35. Robert Axelrod, "Effective Choice in the Prisoner's Dilemma," *Journal of Conflict Resolution,* vol. 24 (1980). In his now-famous article, Axelrod describes the predicament of two prisoners in isolation from each other, who know that if they cooperate, they will be able to escape penalties. However, each prisoner experiences strong temptation to betray the other and thus be punished only slightly, out of fear of *being* betrayed and suffering severe punishment.

36. George Graham, "Pressure for Social Clause in GATT Deal," *Financial Times,* Mar. 16, 1994.

37. John Zarocostas, "UN Agency Suggests WTO Social Standards," *Journal of Commerce,* Nov. 9, 1994.

38. ITO Charter, Art. 7:1. "The Members recognize that measures relating to employment must take into account the rights of workers under inter-governmental declarations, conventions, and agreements. They recognize that all countries have a common interest in the achievement and maintenance of fair labor standards related to productivity. . . . [T]he Members recognize that unfair labor conditions, particularly in production for export, create difficulties in international trade. . . ."

39. See, e.g., John Jackson, William Davey, and Alan Sykes, *Legal Problems of International Economic Relations* (St. Paul, Minn.: West Pub. Co., 1995), at 295.

40. "U.S. Waves Flag for Workers' Rights," *Financial Times,* Mar. 30, 1994.

41. Ibid.

42. Sandra Sugawara, "25 Nations Endorse Ending Many High-Tech Tariffs," *Washington Post,* Dec. 13, 1996; "World Trade Overload," *The Economist,* Aug. 3, 1996.

43. Singapore Ministerial Declaration (WT/MIN(96)/DEC), Dec. 13, 1996, available at http://www.wto.org/english/thewto_e/minist_e/min96_e/wtodec_e.htm.

44. Helene Cooper, "White House Seeks to Link Labor Rights, World Trade to Gain Union Support," *Wall Street Journal,* Dec. 10, 1996.

45. Ibid.

46. President William J. Clinton's remarks at the University of Chicago convocation ceremonies, Chicago, IL, Jun. 12, 1999, on file with Public Citizen.

47. Deputy U.S. Trade Representative Susan Esserman, Statement by the U.S. Delegation to the WTO General Council Session, Geneva, Switzerland, Jul. 29, 1999.

48. Robert Evans, "FOCUS—U.S. Backs Off Trade Labor Sanctions in WTO," Reuters, Dec. 1, 1999.

49. Doha Ministerial Declaration (WT/MIN(01)/DEC/1), Nov. 14, 2001, available at www.wto.org/english/thewto_e/minist_e/min01_e/mindecl_e.htm.

50. ILO, Washington Branch Office, "New Developments in Globalization Debate," available at us.ilo.org/news/focus/0201/FOCUS-3.HTML, visited Dec. 2, 2002.

51. Doha Ministerial Declaration.

52. For further details, see generally, International Labor Conference, 89th Session, *Report of the Director-General: Reducing the Decent Work Deficit, a Global Challenge.* Geneva: International Labor Office, Jun. 2001.

53. Ajit Singh and Ann Zammit, *The Global Labor Standards Controversy: Critical Issues for Developing Countries* (Geneva, Switzerland: The South Centre, 2000), at 79.

54. *Universal Declaration of Human Rights,* General Assembly resolution 217A (III), December 10, 1948. *Article 23:* "(1) Everyone has the right to work, to free choice of employment, to just and favorable conditions of work and to protection against unemployment. (2) Everyone, without any discrimination, has the right to equal pay for equal work. (3) Everyone who works has the right to just and favorable remuneration ensuring for himself and his family an existence worthy of human dignity, and supplemented, if necessary, by other means of social protection. (4) Everyone has the right to form and to join trade unions for the protection of his interests." *Article 24:* "Everyone has the right to rest and leisure, including reasonable limitation of working hours and periodic holidays with pay."

55. United Nations, the International Covenant on Economic, Social and Cultural Rights and the International Covenant on Civil and Political Rights.

56. Agreement on Government Procurement at Articles VIII-b and XIII-b.

57. International Labor Organization, "Forced Labour in Myanmar," Jul. 21, 1998.

58. Ibid.

59. "Burmese Leader in Exile Welcomes Limited U.S. Sanctions," Agence France Presse, Sep. 24, 1996.

60. Massachusetts Burma Law, June 25, 1996, codified at 7 M.G.L.A. §§ 22G-M.

61. Jim Lobe, "Government Opts Out of Court Case on Globalization," InterPress Service, Mar. 11, 1999. For instance, the Los Angeles City Council voted unanimously in Dec. 1997 to ban companies that do business in Burma from bidding for any city contracts.

62. Prominent USA*Engage members were: AT&T, Boeing, BP, Calix, Chase Manhattan Bank, Coca-Cola, Dow Chemical, Ericsson, GTE Corporation, IBM, Intel, Monsanto,

Siemens, and Union Carbide. For a full list, see http://usaengage.org/background/members.html, on file with Public Citizen.

63. See Kenny Bruno and Jim Vallette, Earthrights International, "Halliburton's Destructive Engagement," Oct. 2000.

64. Ibid.

65. Ibid.

66. Ibid.

67. Jim Vallette, "Cheney and Halliburton: Go Where the Oil Is," *Multinational Monitor,* Vol. 22, No. 5, May 2001.

68. World Trade Organization, "United States—Measure Affecting Government Procurement, Request for Consultation by the European Communities," WT/DS**/1, GPA/DS2/1, Jun. 26, 1997.

69. "EU suspends Massachusetts case," *Washington Times,* Feb. 9, 1999.

70. *National Foreign Trade Council v. Charles D. Baker* (Secretary of Administration and Finance of the Commonwealth of Massachusetts), Civil Action No. 97 12142(JLT), United States District Court, District of Massachusetts.

71. *National Foreign Trade Council v. Baker,* 26 F. Supp. 2d 287, 291 (Mass. 1998).

72. *National Foreign Trade Council v. Natsios,* 181 F.3d 38, 45 (CA1 1999).

73. Robert Stumberg, "No Business in Burma," *Legal Times,* Mar. 20, 2000.

74. *Crosby et al. v. National Foreign Trade Council,* U.S. Sup. Ct., No. 99-474, Jun. 19, 2000.

75. Robert Stumberg and Matthew Porterfield, "Preliminary Analysis of Supreme Court Decision: Impact on Options for Free-Burma Legislation," Harrison Institute for Public Law, Georgetown University Law Center, Jun. 20, 2000.

76. State Department Deputy Assistant Secretary David Marchick, testimony before the Maryland House of Delegates' Committee on Commerce and Government Matters, Annapolis, Mar. 25, 1998, on file with Public Citizen.

77. Maryland House Bill 1273 on Floor Mar. 25, 1998, Senate Bill 354 on Floor, Mar. 31, 1998 (emphasis added); see also, inter alia, Ken Silverstein, "Nigeria Deception," *Multinational Monitor,* Jan./Feb. 1998, vol. 19, nos. 1 and 2; and Human Rights Watch World Report 1999.

78. WTO, General Agreement on Trade in Services (GATS), Annex on Movement of National Persons Supplying Services Under the Agreement at Art. 3 and 4.

CHAPTER 9: THE WTO'S OPERATING PROCEDURES AND ENFORCEMENT SYSTEM: WORLD GOVERNMENT BY SLOW-MOTION COUP D'ÉTAT

1. For instance, as described in more detail in Chapter 1, the U.S. implements the Convention on International Trade in Endangered Species, a multilateral environmental agreement, through provisions of the U.S. Endangered Species Act which commit the U.S. not to allow into the U.S. markets products made from the species agreed in CITES to be endangered. However, unlike WTO, there is no CITES tribunal that has been empowered by CITES signatories to judge signatories' conduct and approve trade sanctions or other penalties against those in violation of CITES' terms.

2. DSU Articles 22-1 and 21-3-c; regarding the U.S. position, see, e.g., USTR press release, "USTR Barshefsky Committed to Resolving Beef Hormone Dispute," Apr. 19, 1999; "Thomas, Grassley Urge WTO Action Against EU's Food Stand," *Congress Daily,* Jan. 28, 2003.

3. Agreement Establishing the WTO, Preamble at para. 1.

4. U.S. General Accounting Office, "World Trade Organization: Early Decisions Are Vital to Progress in Ongoing Negotiations," GAO-02-879, Sep. 2002, at 46.

5. WTO Ministerial Declaration, WT/MIN(01)/DEC/W/1, Doha, Nov. 9–14, 2001 at para. 30.

6. WTO, "The Doha Declaration Explained," "unofficial explanation of what the declaration mandates" on the WTO website in 2002, available at www.wto.org/english/tratop_e/dda_e/dohaexplained_e.htm.

7. Letter from Senator Max Baucus (D-Mont.) to USTR Robert Zoellick, Apr. 15, 2002.

8. WTO, Dispute Settlement Body Special Session, "Negotiations on Improvements and Clarifications of the Dispute Settlement Understanding on Improving Flexibility and Member Control in WTO Dispute Settlement," Contribution by Chile and the United States, Dec. 23, 2002, TN/DS/W/28.

9. Stuart Eizenstat, "The Cloud Over Transatlantic Trade," *Financial Times,* Sep. 18, 2000.

10. "Pandora's Trade War," *Wall Street Journal,* Jan. 17, 2002.

11. Edmund L. Andrews, "U.S. Rebuked: Slapping the Hand that Fed Free Trade," *New York Times,* Sep. 1, 2002.

12. "Pandora's Trade War."

13. Institute for Taxation and Economic Policy, Citizens for Tax Justice and Public Campaign, *Buy Now, Save Later: Campaign Contributions & Corporate Taxation,* Nov. 2001, at 21.

14. WTO, United States—Tax Treatment for "Foreign Sales Corporations," Report of the Panel (WT/DS108), Nov. 1997.

15. Ibid. at (WT/DS/108/R), Oct. 1999.

16. Stephen Norton, ". . . As Baucus Chides EU Response Over Bananas, Beef," *Congress Daily,* Jul. 20, 2000.

17. WTO, United States—Tax Treatment for "Foreign Sales Corporations," Report of the Appellate Body (WT/DS108/AB/R), Feb. 2000.

18. Fowler W. Martin, "Summers Signals U.S. Won't Drop FSC Despite WTO Ruling," *Wall Street Journal,* Feb. 28, 2000.

19. *Buy Now, Save Later: Campaign Contributions & Corporate Taxation,* at 21.

20. Richard Lawrence, "A Month for all Trade Bills," *Journal of Commerce,* Aug. 24, 2000.

21. H.R. 4986, FSC Repeal and Extraterritorial Income Exclusion Act, Bill Summary and Status for the 106th Congress, Public Law 106-519, passed Nov. 14, 2000, signed Nov. 15, 2000.

22. "Administration Official Rejects EU Criticism of FSC," *Inside U.S. Trade,* Sep. 6, 2000.

23. "EU Requests WTO Compliance Panel and Authorization to Impose Sanctions

Against the U.S. in Foreign Sales Corporation Trade Dispute," European Union, news release, Nov. 17, 2000.

24. WTO, United States—Tax Treatment for "Foreign Sales Corporations," Report of the Compliance Panel (WT/DS108/RW), Aug. 20, 2001; "WTO Rules Against U.S. Tax Break Scheme," Reuters, Jul. 23, 2001.

25. Curt Anderson, "CEOs Urge Bush Over Taxes with EU," Associated Press, Aug. 9, 2001.

26. WTO, United States—Tax Treatment for "Foreign Sales Corporations," Recourse to Art. 21.5 of the DSU by the European Union, Notification of an Appeal by the United States (WT/DS108/21), Oct. 15, 2001; "U.S. to Appeal WTO Ruling on Foreign Sales Corporations," *Congress Daily,* Oct. 11, 2001.

27. WTO, United States—Tax Treatment for "Foreign Sales Corporations," Report of the Appellate Body on Compliance Panel (WT/DS108/AB/RW), Jan 14, 2002; Paul Geitner, "WTO Appeals Panel Rules Against U.S.," Associated Press, Jan 14, 2002.

28. WTO, United States—Tax Treatment for "Foreign Sales Corporation," Arbitrator's Report, (WT/DS108/ARB), Aug. 30, 2002.

29. U.S. Department of State, International Information Programs, "Treasury Urges Tax Code Reforms for WTO Compliance," Feb. 3, 2003.

30. Floor Statement of Senator Russell Feingold, Nov. 29, 2000.

31. Public Citizen analyzed the numbered DSU cases between Jan. 1995 and Jan. 2003 contained in WTO's Update of Dispute Settlement Cases as of Jan. 17, 2003. Completed cases mean cases that have gone through the entire WTO system culminating in a panel ruling; developing- and developed-country determinations were in accordance with WTO definitions.

32. WTO, Dispute Settlement Body, Special Session, "Negotiations on the Dispute Settlement Understanding, Proposal by the LDC Group," TN/DS/W/17, Oct. 9, 2002, at 1.

33. Jenna Greene, "U.S. Trade Laws in Cross Hairs of WTO Member Nations," *Legal Times,* Nov. 6, 2001.

34. Frances Williams, "Smooth Functioning Put to the Test," *Financial Times,* Nov. 29, 1999.

35. Public Citizen analysis of WTO disputes as of Jan. 17, 2003. See also, WTO, "Update of WTO Dispute Settlement Cases," WT/DS/OV/10, Jan. 22, 2003.

36. The U.S. successfully defended its policies in the following WTO disputes: DS165 Import Measures on Certain Products relating to U.S. imposition of penalties in the Banana case described in Chapter 7; DS194, Measures Treating Export Restraints as Subsidies; DS213, Countervailing on Corrosion-Resistant Carbon Steel-Germany, the WTO ruled against the sunset review of CVD, but it was overturned on appeal; and, DS221 regarding Section 129(c)(1) of the Uruguay Round Agreements Act.

37. WTO, Understanding on Rules and Procedures Governing the Settlement of Disputes (DSU) at Art. 14 and Appendix 3, paras. 2 and 3.

38. Ibid., at Appendix 3, para. 2, and Article 14.

39. Ibid., at Appendix 3, para. 3.

40. See Dinah Shelton, "Non-Governmental Organizations and Judicial Proceedings," 88 *American Journal of International Law* 611 (1993).

41. U.S. Trade Representative Michael Kantor, testimony to the Senate Commerce Committee, Jun. 16, 1994.

42. DSU at Article 8-5.

43. Ibid., at Art. 3-6.

44. WTO, European Communities—Customs Classification of Certain Computer Equipment (WI/DS62/AB/R), Jun. 5, 1998; WTO, United States—Countervailing Duties on Certain Corrosion-Resistant Carbon Steel Flat Products from Germany (WT/DS213/AB/R), Nov. 28, 2002.

45. DSU at Art. 8-1.

46. Ibid. at Art. 13.

47. See Palmeter and Mavroidis, "The WTO Legal System: Sources of Law," 92 *American Journal of International Law* 398 (1998), at 411.

48. Ibid.

49. International Court of Justice Statute at Article 2.

50. WTO Document WT/DSB/RC/1 (96-5267), Dec. 11, 1996.

51. Ibid. Preamble, para. 3.

52. WTO, United States—The Cuban Liberty and Democratic Solidarity Act (WT/DS38), Complaint by the European Communities, May 3, 1996.

53. P.L. 104-114, also known as the "Helms-Burton Act." Title III of Helms-Burton denies entry into the U.S. of corporate executives who have acquired property from the Cuban government that had been "expropriated" from U.S. citizens during the Cuban revolution. Title IV enables U.S. citizens whose property was expropriated to sue foreign investors who later acquire it from the Cuban government.

54. International Chamber of Commerce, "ICC Statement on the Helms-Burton Act," Jun. 19, 1996.

55. Annual report of Nestle, S.A., Nestle Management Report 1998, Directors and Officers (1999), Sep. 7, 1999, on file with Public Citizen. Members of the board serve five-year terms. Dunkel was up for reelection on Jun. 3, 1999.

56. WTO Document WT/DSB/RC/1 (96-5267) at Article VI.2.

57. Ibid. at Art. VI.3.

58. DSU at Art. 14-3.

59. Ibid. at Art. 13, Appendix 3, para. 3, and Art. 8-3.

60. Daniel Pruzin, "WTO Members Make Unfriendly Noises on Friends of the Court Dispute Briefs," *Bureau of National Affairs*, Vol. 17, No. 33, Aug. 17, 2000 at 1283.

61. WTO, United States—Import Prohibition of Certain Shrimp and Shrimp Products (WT/DS58/AB/R), Report of the Appellate Body, Oct. 12, 1998, at para. 100.

62. In 2000, the WTO accepted *amicus* briefs attached to the Australia brief from two fishermen in the Australia salmon case (see Chapter 3). In the May 2000 British Steel case two *amicus* briefs were submitted independently from steel industry trade associations, but the EU objected because the WTO Appellate Body rules made no provision for *amicus* submissions. In this case the WTO Appellate Body reaffirmed that *amicus* which did not inherently conflict with WTO rules, but that WTO tribunals were not *obligated* to accept submissions except from

parties of disputes that tribunals and did not need to review the non-governmental submissions before ruling, but ultimately did not consider the submissions. A WTO Panel also accepted a independent submission in 2000 from the U.S. music licensing company ASCAP which forwarded to the WTO a letter it had sent to USTR. ASCAP submitted the information in a WTO case considering music licensing ruling. The WTO did not reject the letter, but also did not consider it for its ruling. From Pruzin, "WTO Members Make Unfriendly Noises on Friends of the Court Dispute Briefs."

63. DSU at Arts. 21 and 22-2.

64. Ibid. at Art. 17.

65. "The Sea Turtle's Warning," *New York Times* (editorial), Apr. 10, 1998.

66. WTO, United States—Import Prohibition of Certain Shrimp and Shrimp Products (WT/DS58/R), Report of the Panel, May 15, 1998.

67. See, e.g., Marc Selinger, "WTO Fishing Decision Both Good, Bad for U.S.," *Washington Times,* Oct. 13, 1998, at B1, quoting USTR Charlene Barshefsky, "The ruling by the WTO's appellate body does not suggest that we weaken our environmental laws in any respect, and we do not intend to do so. The appellate body has rightly recognized that our shrimp-turtle law is an important and legitimate conservation measure, and not protectionist."

68. WTO, European Communities—Customs Classification of Certain Computer Equipment (WT/DS62, 67, 68), Report of the Panel, Feb. 5, 1998. European countries had reclassified the computers as telecommunications equipment, which carried tariffs that were nearly double what they would have been under the old classifications.

69. WTO, European Communities—Customs Classification of Certain Computer Equipment (WT/DS62, 67, 68), Report of the Appellate Body, Jun. 5, 1998; See also Martin Crutsinger, "U.S. Loses WTO Computer Trade Case," Associated Press, Jun. 5, 1998.

70. USTR press release, "USTR Barshefsky Announce U.S. Victory in WTO Dispute on U.S. High Tech Exports," Feb. 5, 1998.

71. USTR, "USTR Responds to WTO Report on U.S. High-Technology Exports," press release, Jun. 5,1998.

72. Crutsinger, "U.S. Loses WTO Computer Trade Case."

73. DSU at Art. 26-2.

74. GATT, United States—Measures Affecting Alcohol and Malt Beverages (DS23/R-39s/206), Report of the Panel, Feb. 7, 1992 (known as "Beer II").

75. Ibid., at para 5.80.

76. Greene, "U.S. Trade Laws in the Cross Hairs of WTO Member Nations."

77. Speech of Senator Max Baucus (D-Mont.), before Global Business Dialogue, Sep. 26, 2002, describing what U.S. negotiators had informed Congress.

78. See, e.g., WTO Agreement on Subsidies and Countervailing Measures, Art. 6, Art. 11, Art. 12, Art. 14, Art. 15, Art. 16, Art. 19, Art. 20, Art. 21, and Art. 27. "No specific action against a subsidy of another member can be taken except in accordance with the provision of GATT 1994, as interpreted by this Agreement" (Art. 32-1).

79. "Summary of Statutory Provisions Related to Import Relief," U.S. International Trade Commission, Aug. 1998.

80. Ibid. at 3.

81. Stefano Inama (Project Manager, Trade Negotiations and Commercial Diplomacy Branch, Division on International Trade in Goods, and Services, and Commodities), UNCTAD, "Negotiating Anti-Dumping and Setting Priorities Among Outstanding Implementation Issues in the Post-Doha Agenda: A First Examination in the Light of Recent Practice and Jurisprudence," UNCTAD White Paper, May 2002 at 6.

82. WTO, *Annual Report 2002,* Table AIII3., Initiations of Anti-Dumping Investigations by Reporting WTO Member and Affected Exporter, at 46.

83. U.S. General Accounting Office, "World Trade Organization: Early Decisions Are Vital to Progress in Ongoing Negotiations," at 33.

84. Public Citizen analyzed the numbered DSU cases between January 1995 and January 2003 contained in WTO's Update of Dispute Settlement Cases as of Jan. 17, 2003. Developing- and developed-country determinations were in accordance with WTO definitions. The anti-dumping, countervailing duty and safeguard cases were determined by the WTO's dispute classification from the WTO's "Dispute Settlement: The Disputes: Index of Disputes Issues," available at http://www.wto.org/english/tratop_e/dispu_e/dispu_subjects_index_e. htm.

85. U.S. Department of State, International Information Programs, "Senator Baucus Assails Record of WTO Dispute Panel Rulings," Sep. 26, 2002.

86. "Canada's Lumber a Knotty Problem," *Washington Times,* Mar. 2, 2001.

87. "A Border Battle on Lumber Imports," *Seattle Times,* Mar. 9, 2001.

88. "Timber Politics Puts U.S. and Canada at Loggerheads," *Financial Times,* Mar. 9, 2001.

89. "A Border Battle on Lumber Imports," *Seattle Times.* (U.S. environmentalists make identical charges against U.S. forest policies that provide subsidized logging roads on federal lands. The 2001 Green Scissors report, which highlights corporate giveaways in the U.S. budget that harm the environment, identified the U.S. timber sales program as costing taxpayers $330 million every year.)

90. "Canada Bristles at U.S. Tariffs on Lumber," *Washington Post,* Feb. 28, 2001; "Lumber Dispute Threatens U.S.-Canada Trade Ties," *New York Times,* Mar. 28, 2001.

91. Ibid.

92. *Softwood Lumber from Canada,* Investigations Nos. 701-TA-414 and 731-TA-928 (Preliminary), USITC Publication No. 3426, May 2001, at 13.

93. Ibid.

94. Ibid.

95. "Canada Bristles at U.S. Tariffs on Lumber."

96. "U.S. Lumber Industry Files Charges," Associated Press, Apr. 4, 2001; "Lumber Industry Wants Import Tariffs," Associated Press, Apr. 2, 2001.

97. "Big Buzz About Lumber; Mills Seek Tax on Canadian Wood," *Washington Times,* Apr. 3, 2001. In the past few years, softwood lumber mills have been shuttered in Bellingham, Washington; Kalamazoo, Michigan; Cascade and Emmett, Idaho; Lock Haven, Pennsylvania; Camden, Arkansas; Washington and Waycross, Georgia; Passadumkeag and Costigan, Maine; Moss Point and Louisville, Mississippi; Ruston and Bernice, Louisiana; and Mobile, Alabama. "Consolidation Squeezes Out Workers in Paper Industry," Gannett News Service, May 13, 2001.

98. In 2001, a WTO panel ruled that Canada's provincial sales agreement constituted

a subsidy, but ruled against the U.S. on the methodology used to calculate the subsidy amount and on the critical circumstances warranted CVD action. (WTO, United States—Measures Treating Export Restraints as Subsidies, Report of the Panel [WT/DS194/R], Aug. 23, 2001.) The U.S. withdrew the CVD order in November 2002. In March 2002, Canada challenged a preliminary U.S. anti-dumping order on softwood lumber arguing lack of necessary evidence. (WTO, United States—Preliminary Determinations with Respect to Certain Softwood Lumber from Canada, Report of the Panel [WT/DSU236/R].) The panel ruled that the U.S. finding of subsidy of Canadian lumber was inconsistent with U.S. WTO obligations. (See [WT/DS236/R], Sept. 27, 2001.) In May 2002, Canada challenged a CVD on Canadian softwood lumber disputing the evidence used to make the determination. (WTO, United States—Final Countervailing Duty Determination with Respect to Certain Softwood Lumber [WT/DS257].) A decision in this case is expected imminently. In September 2002, Canada again challenged an antidumping order contesting the evidence (WTO, United States—Final Determination of Sales at Less than Fair Value: Certain Softwood Lumber Products from Canada, [WT/DS264].) A ruling in the case is expected in late 2003. In December 2002, Canada challenged the final injury determination and CVD order. (WTO, United States—Investigation of the International Trade Commission in Softwood Lumber from Canada [WT/DS277].) A ruling in this case is expected in 2004.

99. "Steel Industry Retiree Health Care Benefits," United Steelworkers of America, Feb. 11, 2002 at 1.

100. "O'Neill: Overcapacity Root Cause of Steel Row," *Reuters*, Apr. 12, 2002.

101. "The Crisis in American Steel," United Steel Workers of America, Aug. 14, 2001, at 4 and 5.

102. "Steel Industry Retiree Health Care Benefits," at 6.

103. Paul Magnusson, "Bush's Steely Pragmatism," *Business Week*, Mar. 18, 2002.

104. WTO-United States—Definitive Safeguard Measures on Certain Steel Products (WT/DS248, 249, 250, 251, 252, 253), Report of the Panel, July 11, 2003; Statement of Richard Mills, USTR Spokesman, "WTO Panel Report on U.S. Section 201 Safeguard Measures on Steel Products," July 11, 2003; "WTO Formally Designates U.S. Steel Tariffs as Illegal," Paul Meller, *New York Times*, July 12, 2003, citing EU spokeswoman Arancha Gonzalez.

105. See, WTO-United States—Anti-Dumping Measures on Certain Hot-rolled Products from Japan (WT/DS184/R).

106. See, WTO, United States—Definitive Safeguard Measures on Imports of Circular Welded Carbon Quality Pipe from Korea, Report of the Panel (WT/DS202/R).

107. WTO-United States—Anti-dumping Act of 1916, Report of the Appellate Body (WT/DS136/AB/R).

108. USTR, Dispute Settlement Update, Jan. 30, 2003.

109. Ibid., at 15.

110. WTO-United States—Continued Dumping and Subsidy Offset Act of 2000, Report of the Panel (WT/DS217/R).

111. Ibid. at Report of the Appellate Body (WT/DS217/AB/R).

112. USTR Statement, "USTR in Response to the Report of the WTO Appellate Body Released Today in the Dispute Concerning the U.S. Continued Dumping and Subsidy Offset Act of 2000," Jan 16, 2003.

113. USTR, Dispute Settlement Update, Jan. 30, 2003, at 16.

114. U.S. International Trade Commission, "Five-Year Review Status," Dec. 9, 2002.

115. Letter from 62 U.S. Senators to President Bush, May 7, 2001, on file with Public Citizen.

116. 107th Congress, House Con. Res. 262, passed the U.S. House of Representatives, Nov. 14, 2001.

117. WTO Ministerial Declaration, WT/MIN(01)/DEC/W/1, Nov. 14, 2001, at 28, 6.

118. "Measuring Success: At Least the Talks Didn't Collapse," *New York Times,* Nov. 15, 2001.

119. USTR press release, "USTR Presents Views to Help Guide Ongoing Negotiations on Global Trade Rules," Oct. 17, 2002.

120. "Zoellick Stance on Trade Remedy in WTO Rules Provokes Criticism," *Inside US Trade,* Nov. 13, 2001.

121. Al Kamen, "No. Show on Trade Burns Up Finance Panel," *Washington Post,* Dec. 17, 2001.

122. Steven Greenhouse, "Trade Ministers Sidestep Issue of Secrecy," *New York Times,* December 4, 1999.

123. Remarks by President Clinton to the luncheon in honor of the Ministers attending the Meetings of the WTO, Dec. 1, 1999.

124. John Burgess, "WTO Listens to Critics on Eve of Meeting," *Washington Post,* Nov. 30, 1999.

125. Greenhouse, "Trade Ministers Sidestep Issue of Secrecy."

126. "WTO Convenes on Doha, Document De-Restriction, Dispute Settlement Review," *BRIDGES,* vol. 5, no. 18, May 2001.

127. WTO Ministerial Declaration, WT/MIN(01)/DEC/W/1, Doha, Nov. 9–14, 2001 at para. 30, at 6.

128. Scott Miller, "WTO Chief Says U.S., Europe Foster Other Trade Disputes," *Wall Street Journal,* Oct. 17, 2002.

129. WTO, "Text for LDC Proposal on Dispute Settlement Understanding Negotiations," Communication from Haiti, TN/DS/W/37, Jan. 22, 2003 at 1.

130. WTO, Dispute Settlement Body Special Session, "The European Communities' Replies India's Questions," Communication from the European Communities, TN/DS/W/7, May 30, 2002, at 4.

131. WTO, Dispute Settlement Body Special Session, "Improving the Special and Differential Provisions in the Dispute Settlement Understanding," Communication from China, TN/DS/W/29, Jan. 22, 2003 at 2.

132. WTO, "Text for LDC Proposal on Dispute Settlement Understanding Negotiations," Communication from Haiti, TN/DS/W/37, Jan. 22, 2003 at 2.

133. WTO, Dispute Settlement Body Special Session, "Improving the Special and Differential Provisions in the Dispute Settlement Understanding."

134. WTO, Dispute Settlement Body Special Session, "Improving the Special and Differential Provisions in the Dispute Settlement Understanding," Communication from China, TN/DS/W/29, Jan. 22, 2003 at 2.

135. WTO, Dispute Settlement Body Special Session, "Contribution of Ecuador to the Improvement of the Dispute Settlement Understanding of the WTO," Communication of Ecuador, TN/DS/W/9, Jul. 8, 2002 at 5.

136. WTO, Dispute Settlement Body Special Session, "Negotiations on Improvements and Clarifications of the Dispute Settlement Understanding," Proposal by Australia, Jan. 22, 2003, TN/DS/W/34, at 2–3.

137. Letter from Senator Max Baucus (D-Mont.) to USTR Robert Zoellick, Apr. 15, 2002.

138. WTO, Dispute Settlement Body Special Session, "Contribution of the United States to the Improvement of the Dispute Settlement Understanding of the WTO Related to Transparency," Communication from the United States, TN/DS/W/13, Aug. 22, 2002 at 2.

139. WTO, Dispute Settlement Body Special Session, "Negotiations on the Dispute Settlement Understanding," Proposal by the Africa Group, TN/DS/W/15, Sep. 25, 2002.

140. WTO, Dispute Settlement Body Special Session, "Negotiations on Improvements and Clarifications of the Dispute Settlement Understanding on Improving Flexibility and Member Control in WTO Dispute Settlement," Contribution by Chile and the United States, Dec. 23, 2002, TN/DS/W/28, at 2.

141. WTO, Dispute Settlement Body Special Session, "Negotiations on Improvements and Clarifications of the Dispute Settlement Understanding," Proposal by Mexico, Nov. 4, 2002, TN/DS/W/23, at 2.

142. Ibid., at 3–4.

143. "WTO Members Fail on DSU Deal, Further Negotiations After Cancún," *Inside U.S. Trade*, May 30, 2003.

CHAPTER 10: WTO AND FTAA

1. The *Caribbean Basin Initiative* was a Cold War "anti-communism" commercial program which was extended in 1999 through the "CBI NAFTA parity" Act. This program is not a full trade pact. It provides special access to the U.S. market for textile, apparel, and certain other goods made in the 26-country CBI region, which includes Central American countries from Guatemala to Venezuela and Caribbean island nations, including Haiti, but not Cuba. Then–President Reagan created the program as a perk for nations that sided with the U.S. in Cold War politics and demonstrated commitment to "free market" principles. Because NAFTA gave Mexico access to the U.S. market on terms yet more favorable than CBI, U.S. clothing manufacturers who relocated to Haiti and Guatemala to avoid unions and pay rock-bottom wages demanded parity to NAFTA for their imports from CBI countries. To qualify for the CBI program, countries are reviewed on several criteria, including a modest labor standard.

2. Ministerial Declaration of Quito, Seventh Meeting of Ministers of Trade of the Hemisphere in Quito, Ecuador, Nov. 1, 2002 at Article 1.

3. In the last year for which figures are publicly available for both, 2000, the U.S. had a gross domestic product of $9.8 trillion according to the Bureau of Economic Analysis, while the EU's GDP, published in Eurostat's Yearbook 2002, was $8.9 trillion.

4. Martin Khor, "G77, China Thwart EU Attempt to Reinterpret Doha," *Third World Network*, SUNS5052.

5. See Public Citizen report "NAFTA Chapter 11 Investor-to-State Cases: Bankrupting Democracy: Lessons for Fast Track and the Free Trade Area of the Americas," Aug. 2001, for a detailed discussion of the NAFTA Chapter 11 on investment which is one very extreme element of NAFTA that is replicated in the draft FTAA text.

6. Paul Blustein, "U.S., Chile Agree on Free Trade: Bilateral Pacts Are Special Focus of Bush Administration," *Washington Post,* Dec. 12, 2002.

7. World Bank, WDI Data Query, GDP (current US$) for FTAA Countries, downloaded on Jan. 23, 2003, on file with Public Citizen.

8. Shefali Sharma, Institute for Agriculture and Trade Policy, "Expansion of a Top-Loaded Agenda: Are We Ready for an MAI in the WTO," *Geneva Update,* Issue 7, Oct. 4, 2002.

9. "Mexico Set on NAFTA as is, Salinas Says," *Los Angeles Times,* Oct. 29, 1993.

10. Consejo Nacional De La Industria Maquiladora De Exportacion, A C, "Direct Foreign Investment in the Maquiladora Industry," *Boletín Informativo,* Nov. 28, 2002, Year 2, Vol. 28.

11. Ruth Rosenbaum, "Making the Invisible Visible: A Study of the Purchasing Power of Maquila Workers in Mexico 2000," Center for Reflection, Education and Action. Inc., 2000, at 68.

12. Ibid., at 68–70.

13. Embassy of Mexico, "Mexico: A Global Partner for Trade, Investment and Growth," 2000, at 4; Geri Smith, "The Decline of the Maquiladora," *Business Week,* Apr. 29, 2002.

14. Carlos Salas, La Red de Investigadores y Sindicalistas Para Estudios Laborales, *The Impact of NAFTA on Wages and Incomes in Mexico,* Apr. 2001.

15. INEGI, "Manufacturing Industry Productivity Index, Selected Countries," Dec. 16, 2002; Salas, *The Impact of NAFTA on Wages and Incomes in Mexico.*

16. Huberto Juárez Núñez, "Transferencia o adaptación del Know-How en las regiones receptoras de inversión extranjera directa," *Trabajadores,* Nov.–Dec. 1999, No. 15.

17. Elisabeth Malkin, "Manufacturing Jobs Are Exiting Mexico," *New York Times,* November 5, 2002.

18. China entered the WTO on December 11, 2001.

19. FTAA Draft Agreement, FTAA.TNC/w/133/Rev.1, Chapter on Investment, Article 7, Jul. 3, 2001; WTO, TRIMs Agreement, Art. 2, Art. 5, Annex: Illustrative list.

20. Notice of Arbitration, *Ethyl vs. Government of Canada,* United Nations Commission on International Trade Law, Apr. 14, 1997.

21. Canada argued that the transportation ban was necessary because given the constraints in the Canadian Constitution regarding what regulations the federal government can impose on the provinces, the fuel standards established in the federal Canadian Environmental Protection Act could not otherwise implement a ban on substances that may damage pollution control systems in cars, even if such damage leads to increased emissions that affect the entire country. Manganese-based Fuel Additives Act 1997, c 11.

22. "Methylcyclopentadienyl Manganese Tricarbonyl: Health Risk Uncertainties and Research Directions," *Environmental Health Perspectives,* Vol. 106, Supplement 1, Feb. 1998, at 191.

23. "MMT Déjà vu and National Security," *American Journal of Industrial Medicine,* Apr. 2001, 39 (4); 434–5.

24. Government of Canada, "Statement on MMT," Jul. 20, 1998, on file with Public Citizen.

25. Petitioner's Outline of Argument, in the Supreme Court of British Columbia, in the Matter of Arbitration Pursuant to Chapter 11 of NAFTA between Metalclad Corporation and the United Mexican States, ICSID Additional Facility, case number ARB(AF)/97/1, Jan. 22, 2001, at 3.

26. The notice of arbitration has not been made public. The date and amount claimed are known from the Final Award in the Matter of Arbitration under Chapter 11 of the North American Free Trade Agreement, *Metalclad Corporation v. the United Mexican States,* International Center for Settlement of Investment Disputes (ICSID), Aug. 25, 2000, at 4, 36.

27. Ibid., at 1.

28. Ibid., at 42.

29. Reform to New Trade Pact May Hurt Small Farmers, *Interpress Service,* Feb. 27, 2001.

30. WTO, Ministerial Declaration, Ministerial Conference, Fourth Session, Doha, Nov. 9–14, 2001, WT/MIN(01)/DEC/W/1, at para. 13.

31. Raymond Colitt, "Lula's Party Backs Free Trade Area Talks," *Financial Times,* Nov. 8, 2002.

32. Ibid.

33. See Anthony Faiola, "Pressing for a Trade Pact; Brazil Citrus Growers Seeks Concessions in Accord Covering Americas," *Washington Post,* Nov. 19, 2002.

34. Commission of the European Communities, "Explanatory Memorandum: A Long-Term Policy Perspective for Sustainable Agriculture," Final, Jan. 23, 2003.

35. "Mexico Probes Retail Competition as Walmex Dominates," Reuters, May 29, 2002; Citibank press release, "Banamex: Mexico Market Highlights," Jul. 2002.

36. Mike Ceaser, "Water Rate Hikes Provoked Bolivia Protests," *Christian Science Monitor,* Apr. 13, 2000.

37. WTO, Communication from India, "Proposed Liberalisation of Movement of Professionals under General Agreement on Trade in Services (GATS)," S/CSS/W/12, Nov. 24, 2000, at IV, 1.

38. WTO, Declaration of the TRIPS Agreement and Public Health, Ministerial Conference, Fourth Session, Doha, Nov. 9–14, 2001, WT/MIN(01)/DEC/W/2.

39. Oxfam International, "US Bullying on Drug Patents: One Year after Doha," Nov. 13, 2002, at 10.

40. At issue is "data exclusivity," which is a ban on making public—and thus available to generic manufacturers—the test data a company filed to get its patent. Exclusion from this data acts like an extension of the patent term because without it, a generic cannot be available when the patent expires.

41. Ana Paula Corazza, "Bio Plunderers," *Brazil,* Mar. 2001.

42. Laura Carlsen, Americas Program at IRC, "Indigenous Communities in Latin America: Fighting for Control of Natural Resources in a Globalized Age," Jul. 26, 2002.

43. Ibid.

44. Bill Lambrecht, "Amazon Tribe Protests at U.S. Patent Office in Washington Over 'Biopiracy' Theft of Traditional Sacred Drug," *St. Louis Post Dispatch,* Mar. 13, 1999.

45. Corazza, "Bio Plunderers."

46. The passage of Fast Track and the Farm Bill prompted the Brazilian House of Delegates to pass a resolution demanding Brazil leave the FTAA negotiations. Resolution of opposition to the FTAA from the Brazilian House of Delegates, December 12, 2001 (by Mr. Aloizio Mercadante).

47. Colitt, "Lula's Party Backs Free Trade Area Talks."

48. "Contra el FMI, el ALCAl y el Plan Colombia," BBC, Nov. 25, 2002.

49. Yvonne Zimmerman, "Interview with Evo Morales," *La Paz,* July 7, 2002.

50. Mario Osava "10 Million Brazilian Votes Against Hemisphere's FTAA," *InterPress Service,* Sep. 18, 2002.

51. Edmund L. Andrews, "Outside Halls of Power, Many Fear Free Trade," *New York Times,* Nov. 3, 2002.

52. Juilo Godoy, "French Firms Spearhead Water Privatization," *InterPress Service,* Mar. 22, 2002.

53. Mark Weisbrot, Dean Baker, Robert Naiman, and Gila Neta, Center for Economic Policy and Research, "Growth May Be Good for the Poor—But Are IMF and World Bank Policies Good for Growth? A Closer Look at the World Bank's Recent Defense of Its Policies," May 2001.

54. Walden Bello, "The WTO: Serving the Wealthy, Not the Poor," *Does Globalization Help the Poor? A Special Report by the International Forum on Globalization,* Aug. 2001, at 27.

55. No PPP Network, "Plan Puebla Panama: Battle Over the Future of Southern Mexico and Central America," 2002, at 8.

56. Brendan O'Neil, "Plan Puebla Panama: The Inter-American Development Bank Paves Latin America," Action for Community and Ecology in the Regions of Central America (ACERCA), Sep. 2002.

CONCLUSION

1. The book was a collaborative project of a drafting committee made up of 12 members of the IFG board of directors, along with seven other contributors. John Cavanaugh, director of the Institute for Policy Studies, and Jerry Mander, president of the IFG board of directors, coordinated the writing of the book and, along with IFG executive director Debi Barker, edited the book.

2. IFG, *Alternatives,* at 60.

INDEX